And whanJ had aduyfed me in this fayd bo
ke. J delybered and concluded to tranflate it in to englyſſhe
And forthwyth toke a penne & ynke and wrote a leef or
tweyne /Whyche J ouerfawe agayn to correcte it/And wha
J fawe the fayr & ſtraunge termes therin/J doubted that it
ſholde not pleafe fome gentylmen Whiche late blamed me
fayeng ẏ in my tranſlacyons J had ouer curyous termes
Whiche coude not be Vnderſtande of compn peple /and defired
me to Vſe olde and homely termes in my tranſlacyons. and
fayn wolde J fatyffye euery man/ and fo to doo toke an olde
boke and redde therin/ and certaynly the englyſſhe was fo ru
de and brood that J coude not wele Vnderſtande it. And alfo
my lorde abbot of Weſtmynſter ded do ſhewe to me late certa-
yn euydences Wryton in olde englyſſhe for to reduce it in to
our englyſſhe now Vſid/ And certaynly it was Wreton in
fuche Wyſe that it was more lyke to dutche than englyſſhe
J coude not reduce ne brynge it to be Vnderſtonden/ And certaynly our langage now Vſed Varyeth ferre from that. Whi
che was Vſed and fpoken Whan J was borne/ For we englyſſhe men/ ben borne Vnder the dompnacyon of the mone.
Whiche is neuer ſtedfaſte/ But euer wauerynge/Wexynge o -
ne feafon/ and waneth & dyſcreaſeth another feafon/ And
that compn englyſſhe that is fpoken in one ſhyre Varyeth
from a nother.

Facsimile of a portion of William Caxton's prologue to his translation of a French version of the Æneid, published in 1490. For a modernization of this passage see pages 144–145

CURRENT ENGLISH

A STUDY OF PRESENT-DAY USAGES AND TENDENCIES, INCLUDING PRONUNCIATION, SPELLING, GRAMMATICAL PRACTICE, WORD-COINING, AND THE SHIFTING OF MEANINGS

BY

ARTHUR G. KENNEDY

PROFESSOR OF ENGLISH PHILOLOGY
IN STANFORD UNIVERSITY

GREENWOOD PRESS, PUBLISHERS
WESTPORT, CONNECTICUT

*Copyright 1935 by Ginn and Company,
Boston and New York*

Reprinted by permission of Mrs. Frederic H. Webb, Jr.

First Greenwood Reprinting 1970

SBN 8371-3543-5

Printed in the United States of America

PREFACE

THIS book has been planned with a view to encouraging a more broadly comprehensive study of Current English by the college student and the general reader who may have had only the usual elementary training in pronunciation and spelling, grammar in its ordinary essential features, and practice in the composition of good literary English; it is for readers who have not had much opportunity to make a systematic and comprehensive survey of that subject which should be regarded as one of the most important in any curriculum — the English language.

No attempt has been made to introduce new and untried ideas on the subject; rather it has seemed that there is need of a more compact and concise presentation of a wealth of material gathered by various able scholars during the last few decades especially. But so rich is the material available, and so varied are the purposes and ideals of those who have provided it, that there is need to define carefully at the very outset the purpose and method of the book, in order that there may be a clear understanding, on the part of the reader, of the reasons for including some materials and excluding others.

In the first place, the purpose of the present study is chiefly scientific rather than artistic; the author has endeavored to present the facts of Current English usage for consideration by the thoughtful student of English, but he has not attempted to select the best usage in every instance. That is the business of those who are concerned with the art of speaking and writing good English, equally important but quite different in method of approach, since the scientific study of the English language examines all usages, good or bad, while the artistic study of the language is concerned chiefly with finding out the best in every instance. The one study is descriptive, the other prescriptive.

However, in spite of the author's desire to avoid prescriptive grammar, it has seemed his duty to set forth here and there throughout the book the preferences of those who use the best English; and in order that such matters may be readily available for teachers and students of English usage, a "Concise Index to Questions of Good Usage" has been compiled. This is offered as a concession to those readers who may come to the book seeking guidance in matters of usage; it is not a complete guide to good usage in English. Those who desire more guidance than can be found in the following discussions must rely upon the excellent handbooks and guides which have been especially prepared for the perplexed speaker and writer.

In the second place, the plan of this book is such as to provide for all the various phases of the study of present-day English as far as possible in a relatively brief treatment of the subject. English has been studied from various points of view, — phonological, etymological, inflectional, syntactical, semasiological, and so on, — and each is important for an understanding of our language. But it is difficult to do justice to any one phase of the study of English and at the same time take cognizance of all others, fully and adequately. Hence most of the studies of recent decades have been intensive and special and limited in scope. In this book all important branches of the scientific study of the language have been included, although the discussions have had to be restricted in many instances to mere statements of essential facts.

An attempt has been made to clear up some of the seeming inconsistencies in grammatical classification by examining certain linguistic usages from several different points of view. Methods of classification must vary according to the point of view of the surveyor of linguistic usage, and it should be emphasized that any scheme of classifying is largely a matter of convenience and by no means final. Despite the fact that an able committee has recommended a terminology for philological study, one is inclined to differ at times with the committee concerning some of its recommendations, and consequently most new grammars make some little offerings of new terminology, which usually encumber and make worse the present system. Even the carefully worked-out phonetic alphabet recommended by the International Phonetic Association does not fit every need of every language student; and almost every book on phonetics that has appeared during the past few decades has had slight differences of its own in phonetic symbols, which is not surprising if the further fact is recalled that no two people pronounce the sounds of English exactly alike or hear them alike when others pronounce them. It is hard to determine, for example, the length of some vowels or their distinctive qualities. Moreover, grammarians differ still as to the number of the parts of speech and as to their subdivisions. Sound changes are not consistently classified; some are named according to cause and some according to effect. Case and conjugation are controversial matters today because to some grammarians they mean form; to others, use. Even the reformers of English spelling have several quite different methods to offer for the improvement of our spelling.

And, finally, this is, for the most part, a study of the English of the present day, and historical considerations have been admitted only when they have seemed to be needed for the fundamental understanding of the language of today. It is hoped that a careful study of Current English will arouse an interest in the history of the language sufficient to induce the student to go on and make further philological studies. It is hardly conceivable that one should make a thoroughgoing study of the many and interesting aspects of Current English and not feel the need of more careful study of the English language of the past.

It has been the ambition of the compiler to make a book which might serve two somewhat different purposes. In spite of its size, it is hoped that it may be useful as an elementary introduction to English philology and may assist in promoting a more general study of the language from this point of view in colleges and universities than now prevails. It is apparent at this time that a college course of study is seriously needed which will of necessity be elementary in character because of the general abolition of "grammar" from the schools, and it seems desirable to make such a course so widely comprehensive that it will be more practical and at the same time more interesting than the older, more restricted grammar course, which has fallen into such desuetude. However, in attempting such an "omnium-gatherum", the author has greatly enlarged the book by including lists and examples which the general reader might wish to refer to from time to time. In thus combining the elementary textbook in English philology with the handbook for general reference, the author has, of course, sacrificed to some extent that consistency of attitude and treatment which would have been possible in the one type of book or the other, if either were taken by itself. So many students and teachers, however, are asking for one book which will satisfy a great variety of linguistic needs that the author has ventured to undertake a compilation which will be in some measure a response to that demand. Comprehensiveness cannot fairly be expected and at the same time such thoroughness as will be satisfying to all users of the book.

Hence a bibliography, subdivided according to the various chapters and sections, is offered to those students who may become interested in pursuing in more minute detail the study of the topics discussed in the chapters and sections. It contains not only the titles referred to in the text of the book but also a number of others likely to prove useful to persons desirous of reading more widely and thoroughly on the subject of Current English.

The sample list of words immediately following the bibliography can be utilized for further word studies. If each word in the list be analyzed according to the plan given at the head of the list, practically every topic in the book will receive further illustration, and the student will at the same time have greatly improved his understanding of his own vocabulary. Word studies can be started while the book is being read, if it seems desirable, although greater profit and satisfaction will probably be derived from the word studies if they be deferred until the reading of the entire book shall have been completed.

No provision has been made for other exercises bearing on the matter contained in the book. If the reader desires further practical application of the principles set forth in the various chapters, and also an examination of his own linguistic habits, he might select a passage of standard literary prose of some nineteenth-century essayist and rewrite it in colloquial English and also in current slang; rewrite in phonetic spelling any passage of English; list the words marked "Variables" in Chapter VI and seek to determine the best pronunciation in each instance; analyze the names in a page of the local telephone or college directory; experiment with eliminating as much inflection as possible from some passage of contemporary prose; and try out some scheme of spelling reform in still another prose selection. Such exercises would stress the arts of English speech and writing in a manner not otherwise provided for in this book.

As it is, the book has become somewhat larger than was originally intended. Such expansion, however, could not very well be avoided, since, in the course of a comprehensive survey of the various aspects of the English language of today, numerous important details have quite inexorably demanded a place in the discussion. The sixth chapter, on pronunciation, for instance, may seem too ponderously detailed; but inasmuch as the study of sounds lies at the very root of the study of any language such as English, apology need not be made for a careful and detailed laying of the foundation upon which the following word studies necessarily rest. It is likely that there will be more occasions to regret necessary omissions than to justify the inclusion of the many details that have found a place in the book.

It would be impossible to express adequately the obligation of the author and his indebtedness for the ideas and materials that have been incorporated in this book. A glance at the Bibliography will show that many contemporary scholars have been relied upon, as well as the older students of the English language. In view of the already expressed purpose of the author of this compilation to utilize the wealth of material that has been provided by many scholarly writers on the subject, it is hardly necessary to emphasize further his indebtedness for such help.

PREFACE

Special acknowledgment should be made, however, for aid and counsel received from various colleagues and students of English, particularly in the Department of English of Stanford University. The manuscript has been very carefully and helpfully criticized by Professor J. M. Steadman, Jr., of Emory University, and several readers and editors associated with the editorial department of Ginn and Company have contributed much scholarly and constructive criticism while the book has been in process of publication. The author is also indebted to Miss Evelyn C. Johnson for painstaking and thoughtful assistance in the planning and compilation of the indexes, and to members of his family for their interested collaboration in providing illustrative matter. The facsimile which serves as a frontispiece has been secured through the generosity of the Trustees of the British Museum.

And, finally, to various publishers gratitude should be expressed for permission to quote passages from their publications: to the G. & C. Merriam Co., publishers of the Webster dictionaries; to the Funk & Wagnalls Company and Dr. Frank H. Vizetelly, for passages from the Standard dictionaries and other books listed in the Bibliography; to the Columbia University Press and earlier publishers of *American Speech*, to which periodical this book is especially indebted for much illustrative matter which could hardly have been found elsewhere; to Little, Brown & Company, publishers of Lucy Furman's *The Quare Woman*; to the Director of Publication of the Bell Telephone Laboratories; and to the Secretary of the Simplified Spelling Board, for material pertaining to spelling reform. To many other publishers and authors indebtedness has been indicated by the listing of books and articles in the Bibliography at the end of the text.

THE AUTHOR

CONTENTS

	PAGE
CHAPTER I. PHILOSOPHICAL INTRODUCTION	1

The Purposes of Language, 2 · Physiology versus Psychology of Speech, 3 · Form versus Use, 5 · Terminology, 6 · Speech Units, 12 · Causes of Linguistic Change, 14 · Speech Levels, 15 · Linguistic Standards, 17

CHAPTER II. STANDARD ENGLISH AND ITS VARIANTS ... 22

Pure English? 22 · Colloquial Speech, 26 · Slang, 28 · Grotesque English, 34 · Archaic English versus Neologisms, 38 · Newspaper English, 41 · Children's English, 45 · Dialects of English, 49 · Jargons, 62

CHAPTER III. PHONETICS ... 70

The Organs of Speech, 70 · Vowels and Diphthongs, 72 · Consonants, 76 · A Phonetic Alphabet, 80 · Accentuation, 85 · The Interrelation of Sounds, 87

CHAPTER IV. THE RELATIONS OF ENGLISH TO OTHER LANGUAGES ... 90

Cognate Languages, 91 · English Borrowings, 96 · Foreigners' English, 102 · The Spread of English, 107 · Characteristics of English, 115

CHAPTER V. HISTORICAL BACKGROUNDS OF ENGLISH ... 122

Periods of English Linguistic History, 123 · The British Celts, 124 · The Romans in Britain, 125 · Anglo-Saxon England, 126 · The Scandinavians in England, 131 · The Anglo-Normans, 135 · The Age of Chaucer, 140 · The English Renaissance, 145 · Scientific and Scholarly Growth, 147 · Modern Trade and Conquests, 148 · The British Empire Today, 150 · American Speech, 154

CHAPTER VI. PRONUNCIATION OF ENGLISH ... 166

English Vowels and Diphthongs, 167 · Causes and Processes of Vowel Change, 192 · English Consonants, 199 · Combinations and Changes of Consonants, 215 · Accentuation in English, 221 · Rhythm and Pitch, 226

CHAPTER VII. ENGLISH SPELLING ... 230

Summaries of English Spellings, 231 · General Comments on English Spelling, 257

CONTENTS

CHAPTER VIII. THE CLASSIFICATION OF WORDS 263

The Parts of Speech, 265 · Nouns, 267 · Pronouns, 288 · Adjectives, 291 · Verbs, 295 · Adverbs, 305 · Prepositions, 308 Conjunctions, 309 · Interjections, 312 · Conversion and Confusion of the Parts of Speech, 316

CHAPTER IX. THE DERIVATION OF WORDS 329

Creation and Adaptation versus Borrowing, 330 · Original Creation, 332 · Word Composition: Suffixes and Prefixes, 335 · Word Composition: Free Compounding elements, 346 · Word Composition: Distinct Words, 348 · Amalgamated Compounds, 350 · Blends, 351 · Clipped Words and Back Formations, 354 · Conversion, or Functional Change, 357 · Semasiological Change, 359 · Confused Etymologies, 360 · Latin Borrowings, 368 · French Borrowings, 372 · Celtic Borrowings, 374 · Scandinavian Borrowings, 376 · Greek Borrowings, 378 Borrowings from Other Germanic Languages, 379 · Borrowings from Other Romanic Languages, 380 · Miscellaneous Borrowings, 382 · Hybrid Words and Phrases, 385

CHAPTER X. THE MODERN ENGLISH VOCABULARY . . . 389

Size and Nature of the Vocabulary, 389 · Cognate Words in English, 398 · Doublets and Triplets, 402 · Homonyms, 407 · Synonyms and Antonyms, 413 · Individual Vocabularies, 420 · Relative Frequency of Words, 425

CHAPTER XI. INFLECTION 434

The Breaking Down of English Inflection, 434 · Declension of Nouns, 436 · Declension of Pronouns, 447 · Comparison of Adjectives and Adverbs, 449 · Conjugation of Verbs, 451 · The Verbals, 464

CHAPTER XII. SYNTAX 467

The Sentence in General, 469 · The Subject, 472 · The Predicate, 475 · Modifiers, 483 · Independent and Introductory Elements, 485 · Phrases, 488 · Clauses, 492 · Concord, 495 · Word Order, 500 · Ellipsis, 508 · Irrational and Hybrid Constructions, 512 · The Noun, 515 · The Pronoun, 516 · The Adjective, 519 · The Verb, 520 · The Verbals, 529 · The Adverb, 534 · The Preposition, 535 · The Conjunction, 540

CHAPTER XIII. SEMASIOLOGICAL CHANGE 544

Figurative Change, 547 · Specialization in Meaning, 549 · Generalization in Meaning, 552 · Change from Concrete to Abstract, 555 · Change from Abstract to Concrete, 556 · Figurative Gender, 558 · The Weakening of Meanings, 559 · The Substitution of Meanings, 560 · The Pejorative Tendency, 562 · The Ameliorative Tendency, 564 · Popu-

CONTENTS

PAGE

larization of Learned Words, 566 · Extinction of Words and Meanings, 569 · Isolated Survivals, 571 · Ambiguous Words and Phrases, 572 · Idiomatic English, 577

CHAPTER XIV. IMPROVEMENT OF THE ENGLISH LANGUAGE 581

Movement for an Academy, 581 · Grammatical Methods and Nomenclature, 585 · Spelling Reform, 589 · Artificial Languages, 603 · The Future of English, 610

BIBLIOGRAPHY 619
LIST OF WORDS FOR FURTHER STUDY 649
CONCISE INDEX TO QUESTIONS OF GOOD USAGE 657
WORD INDEX 661
SUBJECT INDEX 725

CURRENT ENGLISH

CHAPTER I

PHILOSOPHICAL INTRODUCTION

A PHILOSOPHICAL introduction to the study of a language may lead to vague and endless discussion unless the term *philosophical* be defined at the very beginning in such a manner as to distinguish clearly and emphasize those general laws of cause and effect that are involved in the growth and use of language. The student of the English language must have a fairly systematic body of general conceptions or principles[35]* and must also know how to make a practical application of each one of them if he wishes to go somewhat farther in his understanding and appreciation of his language than do those uncritical and shortsighted users of English who are ordinarily content to rush off to "the dictionary" or to the nearest authoritative teacher of English whenever any linguistic problems arise. Of course a person cannot expect to go very far in acquiring a philosophy of language until he has collected an orderly array of facts with which to philosophize; but a few outstanding considerations and principles should be presented early in order that he may organize his thinking on the subject and try out the linguistic facts as he goes along. Most important, at the outset, are the considerations of the purpose of all language, the physiology and psychology of speech, the relation of form to use, linguistic terminology, the various speech units, causes of linguistic change, the varying levels assumed by language in different social classes, and the

* The superior figures scattered through the text refer to items in the Bibliography, pp. 619–648.

standards that should be set up for judging the quality of one's speech. Hence this first chapter must concern itself with these considerations before we can proceed to gather in orderly sequence the groups of facts that make up philological science.

1. *The Purposes of Language*

The chief purpose of language is the conveying of thought or emotion from one individual to another. There is no doubt that as a means of providing the necessities of life and the security and satisfaction of social intercourse, language is of the greatest value. But it is well to remember also that it is through language very largely that we make our impressions upon others for either good or bad. As we rise in the social scale, we watch more and more the effects that we produce in the use of language; and probably it is safe to assert that most of the instruction in English speech and composition in the high school and the college has for its purpose the making of favorable impressions almost as much as the conveying of thought. We preen and prune and polish linguistically in order to make a better showing — or shall we say, audition?

As a result, however, of an increasing recognition of this second purpose, not only is language, and more especially written language, used as an effective instrument for making a generally favorable impression upon hearers and readers, but journalistic and advertising writers have become much more aware of its usefulness in effecting sales of newspapers, magazines, books, and all the goods that may be offered for sale on a large scale. Indeed, more and more emphasis has been laid upon this journalistic and advertising style of using language; and because this purpose is largely mercenary and not much concerned with the more remote future, some very questionable linguistic practices have almost inevitably arisen, such as the exploiting of "headline English", the coining of freakish trade names, the exaggerated use of adjectives, and the flaunting of highly colorful idioms and phrases. For the purposes of publicity much writing is done which has only the ephemeral purpose of attracting the attention of the unthinking person and thereby selling goods, and not at all does the writer attempt to permanently establish ideas and induce thinking.

Indeed, as a result of this growing emphasis upon the immediate effects of language, there are nowadays two fairly distinct schools of writers — and speakers —, namely, those who employ the highly impressive style of the journalistic writer to produce immediate results, both good and bad, and those who prefer the more conservative style of the purveyor of sound and thorough thinking. And so the language that one uses should be judged both as to the effectiveness with which it expresses thoughts and emotions and also as to the impression that it makes upon other people.

2. *Physiology versus Psychology of Speech*

Language is not merely a matter of making use of the human organs of speech, on the one hand, or of thinking thoughts and shaping them into sentences, on the other. But the student of language must appreciate both the physiology and the psychology of speech if he is to understand the many changes that occur in his language even during a single decade, to say nothing of the changes that centuries bring to a language.

From the time of his first utterances, all through life, a man's speech is subject to the physical limitations imposed by the very nature of his vocal organs: he cannot round his lips and produce a vowel like the *a* in *father*; he cannot hope to pronounce well the nasals *m* and *n* if he has a bad cold in the head; he never keeps the vowel length in *the* and *you* in hurried and careless speech; and he is likely to drop out the *e* when he says *traveling* and *covering*. Probably the greatest difficulty that a child has in learning to speak the speech of his parents comes from the fact that he does not know how to place his tongue in order to produce a given sound. It is not strange, for example, that a certain child's earliest efforts to say *light* once resulted in the strange pronunciation *gite*, when the tongue positions for *l* and *g* are so relatively near to each other.

On the other hand, the psychological or mental influences that are at work constantly through life direct the growth of the language of the individual and modify little by little the speech of the entire race, often overcoming and even markedly counteracting the influence of the physical conditions of speech. Gradually, by a strong effort to imitate the sounds and words spoken by his parents, the child is able to speak very nearly as they do; and later he modifies the language that he learned by conscious imitation, introducing conscious innovations of his own, as when he shortens his mother's dignified *afternoon* to his own impatient *aft*; often, if he is not corrected by those who use the conventional but more irregular English, he will work according to the great principle of analogy and make the irregular individual word conform to the more usual group, pluralizing *man* as *mans* to conform to *pans*, *dogs*, *doors*, spelling *coming* as *comming* to conform to *humming*, *running*, forming the past tense of *blow* and *throw* as *blowed* and *throwed* through the influence of *rowed* and *snowed* and the hundreds of other regular verbs that take -*ed* in the past tense as a matter of course, and even saying *in regards to* because he has frequently heard *as regards* and *give my regards to your father*; confusion will cause him to etymologize *asparagus, chaise longue,* and *Welsh rabbit* as *sparrowgrass, chaise lounge,* and *Welsh rarebit,* and choose *audience, infer,* and *except* when he means *spectators, imply,* and *accept*; and, finally, as his mind becomes accustomed to working rapidly and without his conscious direction, by a peculiar kind of contamination or anticipation he may find himself hurriedly writing such strange expressions as 'a historical study would haved showed them', '*natury history*', '*Knoll all* men by these presents', involving a bank in a mad search for bookkeeping errors at the end of a busy day by writing *$216.16* instead of *$210.16*, or entertaining his hearers by such "Spoonerisms" as have recently been culled by the *Manchester Guardian*[64], notably from the man who interchanged his *b* and *r* so that he claimed to have traveled carrying 'two *rags* and a *bug*' and from that other person who hoped that the congregation would be 'filled with fresh *veal* and new *zigor*'.

To sum up the situation as regards the physiological and psychological elements in language, it may be said that the physiological is unchanging and permanent, determined from the very beginning of the life of the individual by the shape and relations of his various organs of speech; whereas the psychological, or mental, element varies and changes and grows according to the intellectual conditions of the individual, from day to day and year to year. The current of one's speech is very like that of some great river, which can never change the substantial facts of water and sand, but which nonetheless can overflow its banks or cut deeper its channel according to the general conditions of seasons and weather, throwing up sand bars here and there in very different places and times. The current of thought goes steadily on, but the details of the language change always and often. For thinking determines the language, but the language does not have an equally lasting or remarkable influence on the thinking. The general course remains through the centuries about the same; and while a sand bar of language may temporarily divert the current of thinking, sooner or later the current will eat away the sand bar and throw up a new one elsewhere in its course.

3. *Form versus Use*

An appreciation of the interrelation of form and use in language is also necessary for a proper understanding of the changes that are taking place in the English language of the twentieth century. But to gain the necessary perspective, in viewing some of the changing aspects of the present, it is helpful to glance at the language in some of its earlier stages of development. Anglo-Saxon, or Old English (before *c.* 1100), was a language of many inflectional forms; Modern English has almost none. Anglo-Saxon had, at a rough estimate, some thirty thousand words; Modern English dictionaries boast of more than five hundred thousand words and phrases. As the many inflectional endings disappeared, syntactical combinations and greater rigidity in word order were made use of more and more to accomplish what inflection had hitherto accomplished. In place of a genitive form of a noun, a phrase with *of* is frequently employed; instead of a dative form, either a phrase is composed with *to* or *for*, or else the indirect object is given such a fixed position in the sentence that it cannot well be misunderstood, as, for example, in 'He gave nis *friend* a book for Christmas', where we know that *friend* is the indirect object only because of its position; and instead of the older subjunctive forms of the verb, we now depend largely upon certain auxiliary verbs, particularly *would* and *should*, to aid in expressing those shades of meaning at one time indicated by the subjunctive forms of the verb.

But while the English language has gradually lost most of its earlier inflectional system during the past millennium, during this same period it has accumulated so many different words that the average speaker of English today seems inclined to unburden himself of some of this linguistic load. In two respects, especially, this tendency to eliminate forms or words is noticeable today, namely, in the making of one word serve as several parts of speech and in the giving of various different meanings to the same word. In *motor, to motor,* and *motor coach,* in *work, to work,* and *work days,* one form serves as noun, verb, and adjective; on the other hand, in the various meanings of the verb-adverb combination *make up,* some fourteen different words or phrases are represented, according to Webster's International Dictionary[26], of which the most important are *constitute, compile, invent* or *concoct, prepare, arrange for printing, compensate for, complete, dress, reconcile, decide, advance,* and *make love (to).* And so, varying the use of a word or phrase produces variations in general function or in meaning to such an extent as to greatly diminish the number of distinct forms that the speaker needs in order to express his thoughts.

4. *Terminology*

The terminology employed by students of the English language must be accepted and defined at the very outset if we are to deal with the subject in a scientific and reasonably satisfactory manner, since no fact can be discussed in a clear and intelligible way unless a term is available for naming that fact. The study of the English language has suffered greatly during recent years because on the one hand grammarians have coined a great variety of terms applicable to single facts and because on the other hand many teachers of English have become dissatisfied with the multiplicity and disagreement in terms and have gone to the other extreme by refusing altogether to name the facts of language.

It is not necessary to define here the many terms that will be needed for a broad and careful survey of present-day English; each term should be defined with the aid of a dictionary, however, as it appears, and made use of as a part of the equipment needed by the student of language. A few general terms must be considered early in the study of this subject, and perhaps the first to be defined should be *language*.

Language is, as already remarked, in the broadest sense of the word any vehicle that may be employed for the conveyance of thought from one individual to another or for the expression of emotion or feeling; but for the purposes of this study it is better to accept a narrower use of the word, one which connects it with its Latin original, *lingua*, meaning 'tongue', and define it as the expression of thoughts and emotions by means of articulate sounds or of the writing which represents those sounds. It is this articulation, or fitting together, of the sounds of speech by means of the tongue and the other speech organs which distinguishes human speech from the cruder intercourse of the lower classes of animals. Hilaire Belloc has even gone so far as to say, "The word is sacred because it is the bridge between one mind and another."*

The term *locution*, because it can be applied to almost any unit of speech, whether word, phrase, or clause, is a handy term and will be made use of frequently in this book. By locution is meant here that which is spoken, and usually only so much as may be comprised in a word, a phrase like *over the hill*, *having finished his work*, or *to tell the truth*, a clause, or

---

* *Commonweal*, Vol. 12 (1930), p. 669.

a sentence. Locution in the broader sense of 'speech or mode of speech' will not be used in this book, but only the narrower and more definite use of the word will be employed.

Philology, a word which has been used with marked difference in meaning by various scholars, may be applied in the narrower sense to the study of linguistics, pure and simple, or it may be broadened in its scope to fit more nearly the original meaning, "love of speech, both oral and written, and all the learning that language has made available down through the ages". Cook, in his *Higher Study of English*[4] (p. 21), argued for the broader meaning of the word and summed up the ideal philologist as "at once antiquary, palæographer, grammarian, lexicologist, expounder, critic, historian of literature, and above all, lover of humanity". And Pedersen has said, more recently, in his *Linguistic Science in the Nineteenth Century*[7] (p. 80):

> One may define philology briefly as a study whose task is the interpretation of the literary monuments in which the spiritual life of a given period has found expression. . . . It is impossible to define philology as foreign to linguistics; despite all theoretical definitions to the contrary, philology and pure linguistics are inseparable.

The linguist, that is to say, the student of language, may be, therefore, a philologist in the narrower sense of the word, concerning himself chiefly with language itself, or he may be a philologist of the broadest kind, interested in many phases of the life and thought and culture which language expresses.

Grammar, though at best a narrower and poorer term than philology or linguistics, is, nevertheless, a word susceptible of two widely different meanings. Down through the centuries the word has been employed to include, at one time or another, almost all branches of learning which could in any way be based on the study of language. Less than a century ago the usual grammar consisted of four parts: orthography, which dealt with both pronunciation and spelling; etymology, the study of isolated words; syntax, the study of sentence structure; and, finally, prosody, which treated of the art of versification. Recently a writer in attempting to sum up the trends in the study of grammar has said, "English grammar was considered an art up to about 1850, but since then it has been looked upon as a science."* Of late the most common application of the term has been, perhaps, to a rather narrow part of the field of linguistic study, namely, to the classification, inflection, and syntactical use of words as discussed in Chapters VIII, XI, and XII of this book. However, the meaning of the word *grammar* is frequently extended to cover the entire scientific study of a language, including pronunciation, spelling, classification and derivation of words, inflection, syntax, and even semasiology, which deals with the growth of meanings of words. In this broader sense of the term the word *grammar* will sometimes be used in this book, even though the danger of such broad and generous definition of the term has long been appreciated by the author.

It is obvious that a proper definition of a word not only characterizes that which it defines but also determines the boundaries or limits of it; hence the necessity for defining at times a thing in terms of that which it is not, as well as that which it is, justifies at this point a brief consideration of two terms which belong to the artistic study of language rather than to the grammatical or scientific, namely, *speech* and *composition*.

The term *speech* has been narrowed in its meaning and application of late, so that instead of signifying spoken language in general, with its use of sounds, words, and meanings, it is now commonly applied to the art of vocal expression, with special reference to pronunciation.

The term *composition*, which also pertains to rhetorical art, means in general the expression of thinking and feeling through the putting together of sentences into the larger units of prose and poetry. There is, it is true, another use of the term in connection with the making of word compounds, but this is a grammatical use of the word rather than rhetorical and will be discussed later in this book. Composition, in the sense of rhetorical putting together, deals with the larger units of thought expression and goes on from the point where

* Geo. H. Shankle, in *Education*, Vol. 51 (1930), p. 41.

grammar, or the grammatical putting together of words and sentences, leaves off.

The ground having been cleared by the definition of *grammar* and of those two terms (*speech* and *composition*) which pertain not to the scientific study of language but to the art of linguistic expression, it will be found helpful to define briefly those subdivisions of grammar which have been named above as constituting grammar in the broadest and most inclusive sense of the term.

Phonology is that phase of the study of language which treats of its system of sounds. Usually the word *phonology* is confined nowadays to the sound system of a single language or dialect or period or to a restricted group of languages, and *phonetics* is used in a somewhat broader sense as the science of all possible speech sounds. The dictionaries indicate that the two words have been employed in the past to express almost identical meanings; but at the present time one generally speaks of the phonology of English or German or uses the term in a similarly restricted sense, whereas the term *phonetics* is applied to a scientific study of the human organs of speech in general and the sounds that they are able to produce.

Orthography means spelling, usually, and unless one desires to flourish a high-sounding word when he names the process by which sounds are represented by letters, he might just as well call it *spelling*. Phonology and orthography are distinctive scientific terms quite generally agreed upon by philologists; but ordinarily the sounds and the representation of those sounds can be satisfactorily classed under the heads of "Pronunciation" and "Spelling".

In the classification of words according to their general speech functions, — for example, nouns if they name, adjectives if they modify nouns, conjunctions if they connect, and so on, — it is customary to name these general classes "the parts of speech". It should be noted that most words are used in a twofold manner at once — as parts of speech and as parts of sentences. A noun, for example, may be at the same time both a noun and also the subject of a verb. These two functions of the word will be discussed in detail in Chapters VIII and XII.

Etymology is generally defined as "that branch of philology which treats of the derivation of words". An etymology, then, would be a word history or word genealogy and should, to be convincing, take cognizance of both the changes in form that the word has undergone down through the years and also the changes in meaning that have accompanied its form changes. In the grammars of a century ago, as we have noted above, etymology was likely to embrace the entire study of a word, including its classification, its derivation, and even its inflection. But it is now customary to treat of the classification and inflection of a word separately.

By *inflection* is meant those changes in the form of a word by which the uses of the word in the sentence are indicated, as, for example, declension of a noun by means of a possessive ending to show that the noun modifies another, declension of a pronoun by change from nominative *he*, for example, to objective *him* to show that the pronoun is used as the object of a verb or preposition, comparison of an adjective to show degree of comparison, or conjugation of a verb to show time of action, manner of assertion, and so on. It should be noted, in contrasting derivation and inflection, that derivational changes in a word are relatively permanent, giving rise to new words which are entered separately in the dictionary (*horse-radish, newness, worker*), whereas inflectional changes serve the temporary need of the moment and do not get separate recognition in the dictionary but are usually noted under the most common form of the word (*horses, newer, worked*, listed under *horse, new,* and *work*, respectively).

Syntax, as the Greek original, σύνταξις, would indicate, means the putting together of words into phrases, clauses, and ultimately into sentences. It is concerned with the construction of the sentence, primarily. It is of great importance in the study of present-day English, because as inflectional endings have disappeared from English little by little, syntactical use has provided in their place prepositional phrases, phrasal verbs, greater rigidity in word order, and so on.

The latest, the most difficult for definite scientific treatment, but perhaps the most interesting and challenging of all the great phases of grammatical study is *semasiology*, or, as it is also named, *semantics*. Semasiology is the science or study of growth and change in the meanings of words. Because of the very gradual changes that word meanings undergo and the very erratic courses that some of them pursue, this is the phase of language study that is hardest to make positively scientific, and for that reason, possibly, it has been so slow in gaining scholarly recognition that even the terms *semasiology* and *semantics* are not more than a few decades old. But because the history of the meanings of words reflects clearly and interestingly the life and thought of the people who have used them and modified them to suit their special needs and tastes, the study of semasiology is receiving more and more attention.

5. *Speech Units*

The units of intelligible speech* are primarily two: the word that expresses the relatively simple idea and the sentence that expresses the complete thought. But in between these two extremes lie phrases, which combine several of the simpler ideas, as, for example, *under a white stone*, with the four ideas of relative position, oneness, whiteness, and stone, and the more complicated clauses, which so nearly express complete thoughts that they lack very little of being true sentences, as, for example, *because he went away*, which possesses subject and verb like any sentence but functions as an adverb, naming cause and taking the part in reality of a simple word idea rather than of a complete thought sentence.

When one is considering these speech units, however, it is not safe to depend always on the form of the locutions in attempting to classify them as word, phrase, clause, or sentence, since, again, use is likely to predominate over form, and

* Some linguists maintain that the simpler sound rather than the word is the essential unit of speech. But they overlook the fact that unless the sound is also a word (as *a*, *I*, *O*), it does not convey thinking and hence is not a unit of intelligible speech.

a phrase such as *out with you* may be used with all the value of a sentence, meaning 'Leave this room', while, on the other hand, a complete sentence, 'Look out', may be given with an emotional stress that makes it practically an interjection like *Oh!* Form is ever subordinate to use. Only the general function or meaning can be depended upon in classifying speech units. The very fixity and definiteness of a form make it often inadequate to express all the ideas that may become attached to it as the result of years of use; the simple noun *horse*, for example, undoubtedly carries with it for people familiar with the animal not only the general idea of 'animal' but also certain more or less definite ideas of size, shape, and color; or a word may be used with so restricted a setting that it carries with it the value of an entire sentence, as when one says to a player at cards, "Lead", meaning 'You play a card.' Often the teacher of grammar is forced to justify a diagram, or sentence-analysis, by supplying that which is "understood".

On the other hand, there are many idiomatic phrases or groups of words in English — as there are in most languages — which cannot be analyzed into several distinct ideas, as could the phrase *under a white stone* above, but which have gradually assumed quite simple meanings. These idioms vary in their make-up from relatively simple combinations like *right away, to put up with,* meaning 'tolerate', and *get over,* meaning 'to recover (from a sickness)', to more involved phrases much harder to analyze, such as *every once in a while, right off the bat, at sixes and sevens, had rather, at length, to go the whole hog, to blow hot and cold, to make no bones of.* Indeed, there are so many of these idioms in the English colloquial speech that a foreigner finds, even after he has learned well the grammar of English, that he still has a difficult task in familiarizing himself with all of them, and even the speaker of the language who has learned them gradually through many years of familiarity with them is often puzzled to explain them to a mature foreign student of English. Dixon, for example, has printed 372 pages of them[464], and Vizetelly and De Bekker have in their *Idioms and Idiomatic Phrases* 512 pages of idioms[468].

There are, moreover, some stereotyped phrases which do not fit into this definition of idioms and yet seem to have been used in a customary manner so long that speakers of English have come to feel that they are simple units and no longer the more complex kind of phrases that can be taken apart and changed at will. For example, one always says *rich and poor, good and bad, three by five cards, a two by four*, and never, or rarely, *poor and rich, bad and good, five by three cards, a four by two*.

6. *Causes of Linguistic Change*

The causes of linguistic change have been suggested in part; perhaps they might be summed up as of two kinds, chiefly: those on the one hand that result from the inability of speakers to perpetuate forms and usages unchanged, and on the other hand those that arise from a more or less conscious and deliberate effort to smooth out the irregularities and to improve the language. Each generation changes pronunciation a little just because it fails to imitate perfectly the speech of its elders; always, slovenliness is at work to break down forms, blur meanings, and introduce generally the elements of confusion; ignorance sometimes goes rather far in modifying forms and meanings. But, as has already been noted, the opposing principle of analogy is constantly at work to regularize and make for greater conformity; sometimes a conscious scholarly influence can be detected, as when the simple *dette* and *doute* of Chaucer's day were respelled as *debt* and *doubt* just because their distant ancestors, Latin *debitus* and *dubitare*, possessed *b's*, or as when a great flood of learned terms came pouring into England in the sixteenth and seventeenth centuries just because a group of active scholars and writers wanted to "embellish" the English language.

And yet, while the detrimental forces of deterioration are steadily at work, and the regularizing and constructive influences tend at times to offset them, the march of civilization goes inexorably on, and each generation discards many of the things and the habits of its predecessor and with them the language needed to fit them. Any person of advanced years could sit down and compile an interesting list of words and phrases that are today of little use to him but yesterday were a part of his active linguistic stock in trade. Such a list would probably contain *asafetida, butcher shop, coal oil, love apple, meetinghouse, Mother Hubbard* (a kind of loose full gown), *prairie schooner, saloon, spelling bee, spinning wheel, warming pan,* and *wigwam.*

And, finally, even though the older man might continue to use with propriety and satisfaction the words of his youth, a desire for novelty and a weariness caused by the monotonous repetition of the same locutions year after year would drive the young man to make deliberate changes in his linguistic inheritance, giving new meanings to old words, coining those new terms which are usually known as slang, exaggerating a word here and scorning one there, until the old man and the young would seem almost to be using different dialects in their discussion of matters of common interest.

7. *Speech Levels*

There are various speech levels which must be recognized and to a certain extent made use of if a well-educated speaker of the English language is to display a versatility in language equal to his versatility in other matters. There is the formal and dignified language of the scholarly or scientific address or paper, which must employ terms of such exactness and clarity that there will be a minimum of doubt and misunderstanding on the part of hearers, and on the part of readers if it be consigned to the printed page and read again long afterwards. The precision and stateliness of this uppermost level of linguistic usage is not merely a matter of pedantry but is a necessary accompaniment of thinking on a high plane. (For examples see Subject Index under "Formal (or literary) English".)

For the purposes of everyday life a less formal and more free and easy colloquial speech is to be preferred. It has certain shortcuts such as *can't* and *won't*; it abbreviates sentences because it is used between friends and acquaintances whose common understanding of circumstances makes it possible for them to fill in where strangers could not do so; it gives to certain locutions fine shades of meaning which may not be generally understood or even listed in the dictionary. And yet it is all good, respectable language for which one need not apologize. (For examples see Subject Index under "Colloquial speech".)

On a level somewhat below this is the speech of young people who like to pick up the latest slang, of workmen who indulge freely among themselves in technical slang and colloquialisms which other persons cannot comprehend, and of those careless speakers of English who admit into their speech little grammatical solecisms such as *ain't, It's me, Who did you see? growed,* and the like. While the speech of the second level can be regarded as generally acceptable to people of education and refinement, the speech of this third level can fairly be ranked as lower in the social scale because it indulges in locutions too new to be generally understood by all classes of English speakers, because it deals in expressions too technical and too limited in use to be generally comprehensible, and also because it shows a slovenliness as regards the grammatical proprieties which the user of better English would be ashamed of.

And, finally, at the bottom of the scale is the lingo, or cant, of criminals, hobos, and others of the lowest social levels, whose speech, if freely indulged in, would brand the user as alien to the life of the people ordinarily using the language of the other speech levels. For several centuries students of the English language have been interested in this criminal slang, or speech of "the canting crew", as B. E., Gentleman, called it in his New Dictionary, published in 1690 and dedicated to the usages of "the several tribes of gypsies, beggars, thieves, cheats, etc."

It would be as narrow-minded and foolish for one to insist upon living always upon the same speech level as it would be for a person of education and understanding of the practices of society to insist upon wearing the same garb upon all occasions; one does not wear his outing clothes to a formal reception, and he would be laughed at if he insisted upon going about his daily work in formal evening dress. An intelligent speaker who realizes fully, as we have insisted in our definition of the purposes of language, that language is both a vehicle for conveying his thoughts and emotions to others and a means of impressing his fellow men for good or bad will train himself to adapt his language to the needs of the situation in which he happens to find himself. As a self-respecting member of society he will carefully avoid letting his linguistic life deteriorate to the stupid and slovenly level of grammatical abuses and inane slang; he will not be so pedantic as to cling at all times to the cold and lonely heights of formal and highly specialized scientific and scholarly language. He will, in other words, let good common sense govern his speech, just as it should his dress and the other habits of his life.

8. *Linguistic Standards*

There are undoubtedly certain linguistic standards which every student of the English language can set up for himself and by which he can judge of the efficiency and suitability of the language that comes to his attention. Before we proceed further in the study of present-day English, it will be well to consider carefully those standards and attempt to formulate a code sufficiently definite so that the student can make for himself decisions and rulings, as every intelligent speaker of the English language ought to be able to do, and not merely fall back on the last resort of the helpless and ignorant person, who always rushes to some dictionary or grammar to see what it has to say. It should be remembered that even the makers of dictionaries and grammars are not omniscient and that their own definitions and decisions have been made by means of a code such as we offer here.

In considering standards for the evaluation of language it must be borne in mind that no one standard can be set up as of principal importance to the exclusion of all others. At one time one such standard may be employed; at another time some other standard will be needed, perhaps. But if a locution is tested by the entire code, usually it will not be difficult to come to a satisfactory decision.

a. Generality of usage does much to establish a locution as a useful and desirable part of a language. If it were possible to show that more than 99 per cent of English speakers understood a word and used it, there could be little question as to its status. Of course many words of highly specialized meaning occur in a complete dictionary and very seldom outside it. Such words live mainly on the highest linguistic level, and when they are needed by a speaker or writer, they are needed badly.

b. This leads logically to the setting up, as a second standard, of the proposition that any word that satisfies a real need, a need that would not be satisfied otherwise, is an acceptable and important member of linguistic society. Such words as *bluff* (verb), *cafeteria*, *gossip*, *kick-off*, *jitney*, and *radio*, while they differ very greatly as to their historical and social backgrounds, stand together today as acceptable and almost indispensable elements in our vocabulary.

c. It is true that the length of time that a word has been used by speakers of English is likely to determine in some cases whether the word shall be regarded as standard English or of that doubtful class of innovations which we term slang. Obviously, if a word is too new, it cannot be widely known and therefore will fail to reach the generality of English speakers as a good, useful word should. This is one of the most objectionable features of most slang, namely, that it is ephemeral and transient, coming and going so fast and so often that very few of its locutions gain a permanent foothold in English. Of course a word may be, on the other hand, so archaic that it is equally undesirable in the give and take of ordinary colloquial speech. But it is well for a careful speaker of English to assure himself that a word is old enough and mature enough to carry his idea effectively.

d. Of course one is influenced greatly by the knowledge that a locution is in good standing with the class of people who pride themselves upon using the best English. Occasionally a word appears in the upper levels of linguistic usage which at first reeked of the slums. While some persons would have scorned to indulge in the speech of the card gambler, for example, they have not hesitated to adopt *discard* in a broader sense, and *ace* was even promoted to a position of great honor during the World War. To a marked degree the slang that comes to the youth of the upper social classes has had its origin in the very lowest levels of linguistic usage. And it is probably a feeling that this is often true that prejudices many people against all slang or innovations of a popular nature. Just as a peculiar pronunciation may identify a speaker as of foreign extraction or a single unusual word place him as born to a certain dialect of English or a grammatical error rate him as of the untrained and illiterate, so a slang expression may drag him down to a lower social level in the estimation of one who hears it in his language. People of experience and understanding are likely to know something of the speech as well as the social habits of the various levels of society.

e. It is well to inquire whether or not the form or use of a word conforms to the generally accepted pattern of English usage. English has developed certain characteristic practices, such as the formation of noun plurals with *-s*, the formation of the past tense of new verbs with *-ed*, avoiding ending a word with *j* or *q* or *v* in spelling, placing the subject before the verb, and throwing the accent as near to the beginning of a word as possible. If a language is to maintain a separate personality among the tongues of earth, obviously its outstanding characteristics must be respected and preserved. Not every innovation conforms to these characteristic features of the language pattern; but one should have very good reason when he deliberately chooses to violate them. If the nominative case is still regularly employed after the verb *to be*, as many grammarians assert, then one cannot consistently say 'It is me'; if the pattern calls for the doubling of a consonant medially after a short vowel, then *pinning* should be spelled with two *n*'s; if the polysyllabic adjective is regularly compared with the help of *more* and *most*, then it would be unwise to insist on inflecting it with *-er* and *-est*.

f. The historical background of a word should carry some weight in any appraisal of the word. If the word has been in our native stock for a long time, it should have a greater claim to a place in good English than if it has but recently been introduced from some foreign tongue. To drop, for example, the good old English word *good-by* for the French *au revoir* is hardly commendable, to say the least; and to change the well-established *artist* to *artiste* is an affectation, likewise. Pedigree should carry weight in linguistic evaluations.

g. Undoubtedly there are times when the speaker is justified in choosing the locution that carries with it the more pleasing combination of sounds. Many attempts have been made to grade the various sounds of speech according to their effect on the ear of the listener, and most people have certain prejudices based upon their personal reactions to words and phrases. Euphony is frequently cited as one of the reasons why people prefer one foreign language rather than another or one dialect of English rather than another.

It is hardly necessary to add that the thoughtful study of good literature is always a great help in establishing linguistic standards. Beyond the obvious standards just discussed there lie various other critical tests which the connoisseur of good writing gradually learns to apply. He sees the forcefulness of the simpler words selected by one great master of style; he admires the beautifully fluent prose of another; he notes the effects of contrasting or balancing sentences in still another; and he senses the rugged irregularity of another. It is not hard to distinguish the author who has a vocabulary of thousands of good words from that impoverished writer who endeavors to get along with a few hundred well-worn ones. Nor is it difficult to pick out that prose expert who weighs every word and phrase that he builds into his linguistic structure.

Modern writers noted for their admirable prose style have often given the credit for their linguistic excellence to long and appreciative familiarity with great literary masterpieces, such as the Authorized Version of the Bible and the plays of Shakespeare; for the student of today there are numerous recent or contemporary writers whose excellent prose style is well worth studying.

Various suggestions will be made in the following chapters as to how a person can improve his choice and understanding of words, his emphasis of ideas, his sensitiveness to word values, and the clearness of his statements; but it is appropriate at this point to urge the careful and intelligent study of good literature as the one exercise most conducive to real literary success. For in the use of the English language, as in all the other arts, one goes to the great artists for guidance and inspiration, and does not adopt that easy policy of amiable acquiescence which is sometimes advocated by those who would make the common colloquial speech of the great illiterate their standard of literary excellence.

He who enters into the detailed study of his native tongue

will find his course greatly simplified if he has, at the very beginning, a well-defined terminology with which to work, a clear understanding of the purposes of language, a set of standards by which to judge the varying forms and details of his language, and a sane and sensible attitude toward innovation, on the one hand, and the elements of conservatism and stability, on the other. In this introductory chapter much more might have been said concerning all the subjects that have been discussed; but if the one outstanding fact has been clearly grasped, namely, that linguistic expression is as varied and as changing as the ideas and thoughts that it endeavors to express, then the thoughtful student of the English language will continue to ponder these subjects and will gradually enlarge upon this presentation of the matter for himself. Which is as it should be.

CHAPTER II

STANDARD ENGLISH AND ITS VARIANTS

9. *Pure English?*

THE terms *pure English, purist,* and *purism* have been bandied about for so long by people of such various tastes and opinions that they have largely ceased to have any real usefulness in English linguistics other than as they arouse to controversial discussion those students of language on the one hand who know the history of our mother tongue, with all its changes for good or bad, and on the other hand those critics who would unthinkingly fix the forms and usages of our language once and for all. If *pure* means "separate from all heterogeneous or extraneous matter", as the dictionary tells us, then *pure English* implies a fixity and finality utterly incompatible with our definition of language as a means of expressing thought and emotion. Unless thinking is to become absolutely fixed or else cease altogether, the language that expresses it must change and grow and be varied so as to keep pace with it. A speaker cannot take the stand, for example, that certain pronunciations are "pure" and those that differ are "impure", for he will find the very best of dictionaries showing uncertainty regarding them, as, for example, in the case of *advertisement, data, Elizabethan,* and *isolate*; he cannot well insist upon one set of spellings when another has almost equally good standing, as in the case of *analyse, grey, mould, plough,* and *traveller*; he certainly will find himself upon most debatable ground if he takes the stand that only the words of native, that is, Anglo-Saxon, stock are to be approved when new words are being coined. For at least four centuries the so-called purists have undertaken to discourage the importation of foreign words into the English language, and still the loan-words continue to trickle in. Krapp has remarked in his book *The Knowledge of English* [18] (p. 186): "The term 'purist' is an unlovely name for an unlovely kind of being. It applies broadly to any person who harasses himself or others by an unnecessary concern over the forms of speech."

But just because the purist is a nuisance and a bore in his insistence on "pure English", one must not go to the other extreme and assume that standards count for nothing and that language will take care of itself. It is not difficult to distinguish between good English and bad English. Good English is characterized by clear and pleasing pronunciation which conforms to that of the majority of thoughtful and well-educated people using the language; it is spelled according to the practice of the majority; it has a wide range of well-selected and carefully utilized words and phrases; it is observant of the rules of inflection and syntax that have been formulated in accordance with the general pattern of the language; and, finally, it is careful to maintain the word values or meanings that have come to be most generally accepted and most widely understood. The other, namely, bad English, is slovenly in pronunciation and indifferent to the practice of others, in many instances; it does not spell according to the orthography of the majority; it has few words, comparatively speaking, and those not always of the best; it does not conform to the rules of inflection and syntax; and, last of all and often most vicious in its effects, it twists and changes the meanings of words and phrases until they often seem entirely alien to the speaker of standard English.

With the introduction of the term *standard English*, an ideal is suggested which is reasonably attainable, even if pure English is not possible. Standard English is that English which is employed by the great majority of intelligent and self-respecting speakers of the language. But one immediately objects to the implication that there is a great majority, even of a given group, that agree at all times and everywhere in their use of the English language. And so at the very outset it becomes necessary to admit that certain parts of the English-speaking world, as, for example, Great Britain and the United States of America, differ quite materially in their use of the language, and, moreover, that the same person will modify his speech from time to time according as he wishes to be formal or informal. But these differences of place or of time have been greatly overemphasized by some critics and do not, after all, appear in a very great percentage of the English language. On the whole, the language has been largely standardized, and one may without great difficulty recognize standard English if one makes use of the criteria for judging it which have already been set up in Section 8, in the preceding chapter.

Before attempting further definition of standard English, it is necessary to make certain assertions regarding the people that use it: they are, as a rule, people of education and understanding; they use their language carefully and with some attention to the manner in which their words fit their thinking; they take pride in using speech well, just as a good workman prides himself upon a workmanlike use of his tools.

Standard English is, first of all, then, the language generally used by the most intelligent and careful English speakers. But sometimes a locution may be standard and yet known to only a very few persons, as in the case of numerous technical and scientific terms. Such terms are so necessary that, although they do not pass the first test, namely, generality of usage, by the second standard, that of satisfying a real need, they must be adjudged a place in standard speech. Time is usually needed for a locution to win a place of unquestioned usefulness in the language; hence many words and phrases will be considered a part of standard English just because they have been in use for a long time. The social status of the people who generally use a locution goes a long way toward establishing it as standard English or as poor English, as the case may be. These four tests are usually sufficient for the average student of English who may be endeavoring to determine what constitutes standard English.

But sometimes it becomes necessary to go somewhat more

deeply into the case of a verbal candidate for high linguistic rating. And then it becomes a question of whether the locution fits well into the traditional pattern of English, or whether it has a long and honorable history in the language. The verb form *motored* has been formed according to the Modern English practice of making all new verbs with the past tense and past participle in *-ed*, and in spite of the fact that it is not of long and honorable lineage, it has fallen into a place in standard English. On the other hand the reflexive pronoun *myself*, made with the possessive *my*, and *himself*, formed with the objective *him*, cannot both be said to fit logically into the pattern of English, and yet they are of such long standing that no one would venture to question their place in English. The use of *you* as a singular pronoun and subject of a verb instead of *thou* is not historical, and yet one would not think of questioning its use today.

What has just been said about pure English, good English, and standard English may be fairly summed up in the assertion that pure English is not only impossible of attainment but undesirable if it could be attained, standard English is an ever-changing and never-fully-attained ideal toward which the entire English-speaking race is steadily striving, but good English — or may we change the term to better English? — is the aim and goal of every intelligent speaker of the language, just as better thinking is always the desire of such a person. The more one improves his English, the nearer he is able to come to a realization of standard English, because he ultimately attains to a pronunciation that satisfies at least the ninety and nine, because he arrives at a stage of grammatical correctness so nearly perfect that it is no longer necessary for him to fear grammatical errors, and because with every year of thoughtful speaking and writing he acquires a more intimate and appreciative understanding of the values and possibilities of words and meanings.

The cumulative effect, moreover, of much striving by thoughtful individuals to thus improve their language is such that ultimately the language as a whole is bound to be improved and standardized by their efforts.

10. *Colloquial Speech*

The terms *colloquial speech* and *slang* have been employed until quite recently without much attempt at definition or distinction. But they should not be used as though they always meant the same thing. Colloquial English is, properly defined, the language of conversation and especially of familiar conversation. As such it may approximate the standard speech of the better class of English speakers, or it may drop to the level of the illiterate and careless speaker. In any event it is generally spoken rather than written English and consequently free from certain restrictions and intentions which the more formal standard English must acknowledge. The better type of this colloquial speech has already been defined and discussed in Section 7, but it may be helpful to discuss it more in detail here.

That colloquial speech which passes back and forth between two persons who thoroughly understand each other is characterized by little peculiarities of pronunciation which the more formal spoken language of the rostrum, lecture platform, or stage does not usually permit. The word *yes*, for example, may be spoken in such a manner that it becomes a question or an indication of skepticism rather than of acquiescence; little inflections of the voice often lend meanings to words or phrases which in formal standard English would require one or more complete sentences; and sounds occur which are not even recognized as words in formal English, such as the *uh-huh* and *unh-unh* of assent and dissent. In colloquial English numerous shortcuts of other kinds are also common. The contractions *I've* and *we're* and *you've*, as well as the negative contractions *don't*, *shan't*, and *mustn't*, are quite proper in informal spoken English. The very frequent ellipsis is possible, such as one finds in replies to questions or statements like 'Will you come?' — *Certainly*; 'Do I bother you?' — *Not at all*; 'I've lost my book.' — *Too bad*, and such as one finds in words and expressions like *thanks, good-by, look out*. And numerous other syntactical shortcuts are tolerated which in formal writing or speaking would be frowned upon, as, for example, when a lady says to her pet dog standing expectantly at the door 'Do you want in?' instead of 'Do you want to come in?' Most people in conversation with intimates make use of well-worn and general-utility words, such as *fine*, *nice*, *pretty good*, *get*, *thing*, *stuff*, even though they might choose much more exact words in more formal composition. And, finally, most people have favorite colloquial phrases that smack of the dialectal or the irregular which they employ commonly in informal speech, such as *quite a few*, *for quite some time*, *to tell the truth*, 'It's no go', 'How's yourself?' 'I bought me a coat', 'I must say'.

Judged by the standards set up for good English, few of these colloquialisms would be ruled out; they are not ungrammatical, they are in very general use, they satisfy a very real need, they have for the most part been long in use, and they are made use of by people of unquestioned social standing, very commonly. And yet they are not regarded as altogether acceptable in formal writing and speaking. A little consideration will make clear the reasons for this. They are undignified, very often, in that they presume an intimate understanding between speaker and hearer, or writer and reader, which is not warranted or desirable, usually, in formal speech. Moreover, they depend very often upon special circumstances to help out their meaning which do not accompany the printed language of a book, for example. And they also lack preciseness and clarity, which can be counteracted by further conversation and explanation if the speaker observes that he is not making himself perfectly clear to his hearer, whereas a speaker or writer who is attempting to reach the minds of many people and at different times, possibly over a period of many years, cannot run the risk of being misunderstood through the choice of words which are not exact or clear-cut in meaning. Formal standard English must stand the tests of time and of numerous hearers or readers; colloquial standard English need convey thinking and make favorable impressions only under the more intimate and limited circumstances of everyday conversation.

11. Slang

Slang has usually been regarded as of doubtful propriety, and most speakers of standard English have avoided it. Doubtless this is due largely to the fact that much of the slang that has come to the attention of people of education and refinement has been the so-called canting talk of the criminal world. Since the latter part of the sixteenth century, there has been an almost continuous stream of canting dictionaries, published, usually, for the edification of those young men of the world of fashion who liked to familiarize themselves with some of the talk of the sporting and underworld classes of England. But not all slang has been of this sort*, and it must be conceded that occasionally a slang locution has worked its way into standard English and is today accepted without question, as in the case of such words as *buncombe*, *bus*, *cab*, *cad*, *canter*, *chap*, *hoax*, *mob*, and *prig*. Moreover, it should be noted that slang is no longer so predominantly the language of the criminal world; but certain social and professional and trade groups in later times have developed to a much greater extent special slang expressions of their own. The college boy with his pet phrases such as *apple-polishing*, 'currying favor with a professor', *bawlout*, 'directory of officers and students', *to bone up*, 'to study up', *goofy*, 'infatuated, foolish', *pipe course*, 'easy course' [58]; the sports writer with his *attaboy*, favorite exclamation of encouragement, *homer*, 'run to home base', *lot*, 'baseball field', *socked*, 'hit', *twirler*, 'pitcher' [59]; the aviator with his *blimp*, 'nonrigid gas bag', *crack up*, 'to crash', *solo*, 'to fly alone', *zoom*, 'to climb suddenly and sharply' [60]; the soldier with his talk of *busting*, 'reducing in rank', *cooties*, 'lice', *doughboys*, 'infantrymen', *shavetails*, 'second lieutenants' [61]; the merchant with his *gas* for 'gasoline', *spuds* for 'potatoes', and *turps* for 'turpentine' — all these and many other speakers with special interests are making use of special vocabularies which have developed

---

* Hence the term *argot* [ärgō] is not used here as a synonym for 'slang' but is reserved for a later discussion (Sec. 16) where it is applied to the canting speech, or dialect, of criminals and hobos. (For an explanation of phonetic symbols, such as those just used for *argot*, see pages 82–83 and inside back cover.)

because of the fact that the speakers of each group are thrown together constantly and have a community of interests which expresses itself in a special and informal vocabulary.

But slang owes its continual and recurring existence to more than mere community of interests. Many lazy or uneducated speakers of English get hold of certain much-abused locutions which they use constantly to express a great range of ideas, especially approval and disapproval. Krapp has named these "counter words" in his *Modern English* [11] (p. 202), indicating such words as *awful*, *fierce*, and *nice*. When the favorite word of approval was *keen*, it might be applied to anything from a cake to an especially lovely sunset. On the other hand, any person of whom the speaker particularly disapproved might at one time be called a *pill*. To some impoverished speakers of English any social function would be a *blow-out*; anyone above the average of American intelligence, a *highbrow*; and any thing or person found especially bad, a *fright*. Of course the use of a counter word, such as *keen*, shows, when used by a small boy, that he is "a regular fellow" and can conform and can speak the language of his playmates; but when it is still in use by an adult, it may fairly be regarded as an admission of linguistic inefficiency and helplessness and poverty. A man or woman who has only a pair of hard-worked words to express all shades of approbation and disapproval is poor indeed.

It is not quite fair to assume that slang arises merely from a desire to conform slavishly to the familiar talk of a special group of people, such as aviators, sailors, or students; nor is it altogether fair to ascribe the use of slang to intellectual poverty. At the bottom of the tendency in younger speakers of English to break away from the standard, or conventional, use of the language, there lies, undoubtedly, a desire for change, an impatience with that which is old and long established, a striving to say things in a newer and a fresher way. While a gradually acquired sentimental love of old terms, a prudent and cautious respect for meanings well established, and a better understanding of the necessity of keeping language stable and relatively fixed, all make the older speaker of English suspicious of neologisms, and especially of those new slang locutions which do not come as a response to actual needs, the younger speaker, more especially the youth between the ages of ten and twenty years, takes liberties with his mother tongue, cultivates the newest slang, shifts the meanings of respectable and staid old words, and makes it quite evident generally that the world is moving merrily along. McKnight has very aptly remarked that "one of the most active forces in the creation of slang is youthful irreverence" (*English Words*,[298] p. 59). Those older students of language and life who realize the ephemeral nature of much that youth takes up with enthusiasm and soon drops again with loss of interest refuse to take too seriously most of the slang that comes in constantly recurring waves.

At times, it must be admitted, certain slang expressions have an appeal, a certain attractive quality, which is to be ascribed either to the picturesqueness of the idea or else to the euphonious nature of the word itself. There is a whimsical humor in extravagantly calling a young lady's new party gown a *knock-out*, a malicious suggestiveness in calling a waiter a *biscuit-shooter*, and a very satisfying condemnation in the expressions *flat tire*, *windbag*, and *gold-digger*; there is probably something pleasing about the sound of such words as *humdinger*, *flibbertigibbet*, and *lallapaloosa*, in the invitations to depart *skidoo* and *skedaddle*, in *bamboozle*, 'to deceive', and *spondulix*, 'money', since they tend to live on in some parts of the country after their generation of slang has passed away.

Perhaps the best method of dealing with the subject of slang is to present that gantlet of objections which the slang locution must run in order to arrive at a position of safety and general acceptation in standard English.

a. Slang is often to be avoided just because it is not widely enough known to be acceptable as a means of communicating thoughts. Not infrequently an older person will sit in the midst of children and hear slang words which carry little meaning for him, — words, moreover, which he cannot look up in any dictionary. One woman actually took offense when called a *whiz*, although the speaker was really trying to say that she was a most efficient and remarkable housekeeper; another innocently suggested warmer hose for a young person who was afflicted with *cold feet* when confronted with a difficult undertaking; and still another gazed with astonishment at the sleepy boy who expressed his intention of *hitting the hay*. She had never been compelled to sleep in a haymow, and consequently the figurative expression had no meaning for her. Sometimes a mother of growing children feels like the proverbial hen with ducklings as she listens to the slangy talk of her ultraprogressive offspring, and the dignified father is forced to turn intellectual handsprings to keep up with his boys and girls. Even though such intellectual gymnastics may be good for the elders, nevertheless, from the standpoint of linguistic efficiency, one must insist that such neologisms are not conducive to the most satisfactory social intercourse. A youth can generally look up learned and technical terms in the dictionary when he fails to understand them; but people of maturer years cannot be expected to compile slang dictionaries year after year in order to understand the flood of new slang that passes by their intellectual mill.

b. Moreover, slang is often superfluous. There is no real gain in calling a gun a *gat*, a woman a *skirt*, to steal *snitch*, and to be intoxicated *canned*, *orie-eyed*, *pickled*, or *soused*. The speaker of good English is usually able to find an acceptable and perfectly expressive term already established in the vocabulary of English if he is willing to take the trouble to search for one. Of course this objection applies not only to slang but also to the diction of not a few present-day writers who would scorn to indulge in the current slang and yet are too indolent to seek out just the right word for a given idea. Not long ago one wrote, for example, "It makes a man *uncontent* with half-truth" when he might just as well have said "dissatisfied", if one may judge from the sense that he succeeded in conveying by his remark. Philologists, it is true, are wont to insist that there are no true synonyms in our language, but that each so-called synonym has a slightly different shade of meaning which justifies its separate existence. So the user of apparently superfluous slang might always argue that he is enabled to give to his idea and its expression a fine shade of meaning such as no other word would express. But sound common sense should tell him that the book of English synonyms is already a very formidable and unwieldy instrument and that a limit must be set somewhere to the introduction of more such synonymous locutions.

Too often the slangy use of a word ruins a word already useful and long established in the language. That is the chief objection to the use of *keen* in the sense of 'excellent, desirable', of *all wet* in the sense of 'wrong, mistaken', of *boiled* for 'intoxicated', of *canned* for 'discharged', of *dumb* for 'stupid', and of *a frost* for 'a failure'. Meanings of good old words must be guarded and maintained with a certain degree of conscious effort if the integrity of the language is to be preserved.

c. We say that slang is too short-lived, too ephemeral, to be worthy of very serious consideration. If one could secure a list of slang expressions that have come to the fore, decade by decade, he would find few that survive more than a generation in general usage. A writer in the *New York Times* of April 10, 1922, discussing under the heading "Short-Lived Slang" the fears expressed by a famous English scholar for the future welfare of the English language, said: "Slang is of a day and for a day. The slang of Tom Brown of yesterday is a dead language to the Rugby boy of today." He went on to say, regarding lists of war slang published earlier in that year in the London *Times*:

> The lists published day by day by the London *Times* showed how quickly the language of the trench had become obsolete for the piping times of peace. Civilians turned into soldiers almost overnight found themselves faced by circumstances so strange and novel that nothing but a new language could express their reactions. Once the circumstances passed, the language they called into being passed with them. So complete has been the going of that vivid vocabulary that almost its only legacy to the speech of today is one word — camouflage.

This passing of slang might be illustrated very effectively if one could travel down through the generations and gather just the expressions utilized to show appreciation and admiration, such as *bang-up, corker, crackerjack, dandy, lulu, peach, pigsney, ripping,* and *scrumptious.*

d. We say that very often slang is suggestive of the life in the underworld of society, or at least of people who do not rank high in the esteem of their fellow men because they are slovenly and careless and ignorant. To term a policeman a *bull*, a pistol a *gat* or a *rod*, a drug addict a *hop-head*, would suggest either an aping of the criminal or a familiarity with underworld lingo not highly commendable, although it must be admitted that the earlier *copper* and its derivative *cop*, slang for 'policeman,' have risen to a place of common colloquial usage in the word *motorcop* for 'traffic officer.'

e. A slang expression is often too colorful. The very quality of picturesqueness which makes it appeal to many speakers of English, at the same time makes the word too forceful, lends to it more significance than the speaker may really desire at the moment. Of course all colorful metaphors are not necessarily slang. But when, for example, the term *baggage-smasher* is commonly applied to all handlers of baggage, good or bad, or *hash-slinger* to all waiters, however expert, a certain degree of resentment may well be felt by the person so characterized. When a small boy reported that 'he would have been *held up* for ten cents if he had bought his pencil at one shop and so he went to another store where he was only *held up* for a nickel', he was obviously making use of a verb somewhat stronger than he needed or intended. To say that one gets a *kick* out of attending symphony concerts is implying a slightly exaggerated pleasurable reaction to good music comparable to the exaggeration involved in the phrase *to die a-laughing*. It is this overemphasis of the colorful in slang that would make one smile to hear some gentle and refined old lady remark that she had been shocked to see her neighbor *badly soused* on some festive occasion. Highly colorful slang is likewise highly dangerous.

It would not be fair, of course, to use the objection that slang has no historical background, since by its very nature it is new and often ephemeral. Even though a slang word be an old one converted to a new use, there is probably nothing in the history of the word to justify its new slang meaning. But since the greatest portion of the speakers of English care little and know even less about the history of English words, historical background cannot in this connection well be insisted upon as one of the requisites for acceptance into good usage and polite society.

When it comes to a question of whether a slang locution is logical or not, whether it fits well into the pattern of the English language, probably it must be admitted that popular speech, of which slang is, of course, the latest manifestation, is usually more natural and less artificial than much of the older and well-established vocabulary which the learned employ. Such figurative locutions as *bonehead, cracked, fade away, good egg, hard-boiled*, are all very expressive of definite ideas, and their appeal is due mainly to their clearly figurative quality.

And, finally, one cannot argue that slang locutions are any less euphonious than standard English. Indeed, as has already been suggested, numerous slang expressions undoubtedly owe much of their appeal to the euphonious combination of sounds that enter into their make-up, particularly such locutions as *chief cockalorum, hullabaloo, humdinger, peacharino,* and *spondulix.*

In summing up, then, the whole matter of the use of slang, one is likely to arrive at the following general conclusions:

a. It must be admitted that one cannot safely or wisely brush aside all slang locutions with the categorical condemnation that they are "bad English" but must agree with Krapp that "intrinsically they are not bad, but rather good, in so far as they show activity of mind and a desire to be vigorously expressive on the part of the speaker". Hence certain tests must be applied to the slang locution as to all other questionable forms of speech.

b. Since slang is living speech, a slang locution often acquires for those persons who use it understandingly a significance much greater and far more varied than the lexicographer is able to give to the older standard English words, which have for a long period of years been trimmed and fitted into their snug and limited places in the dictionary. When one says, for example, that one's friend is *a good sport,* it would take a fairly large number of regular dictionary words to define adequately this expression of approval.

c. But while this is often true, on the other hand slang is too often an acknowledgment of intellectual laziness or linguistic poverty, the slang expression being too frequently employed because it is general and vague and undefined in meaning.

d. After all, it must be acknowledged that the term *slang* is essentially and through long usage one of disapproval, because it connotes language that is very new and seldom enduring, language that is understood by only a limited number of people, language that is often too highly colored on the one hand or too commonplace and shopworn on the other, and not infrequently with the stamp of the underworld still fresh upon it; and until slang locutions have run the gantlet and come out victorious, and hence ceased to be slang, they are not generally acceptable to the more conservative speakers of standard English.

12. *Grotesque English*

Occasionally, in the mouths of speakers who are either aware of the absurdity of their treatment of words or else are of that ambitious but ignorant class of speakers (typified by the notorious Mrs. Malaprop) who use big words in the most inappropriate ways, pronunciations, word forms, and often word meanings become so fantastic, so twisted and incongruous, that one may apply to them the term *grotesque English*. In her introduction to a collection of intentional mispronunciations, Louise Pound has said: "The current *grotesqueries* of language are worth noting, not only because of their linguistic interest but because they have a certain social significance. Mispronunciations are a permanent human phenomenon, and as such they deserve a passing record."[62] In listing such mispronunciations as she has observed, particularly among students, she has noted, among others, some showing vowel or consonant changes, such as *cleever* (for 'clever'), *camm* (for 'calm'), *ellum* (for 'elm'), *Henery* (for 'Henry'); blends such as *bumbersoll* (for 'parasol' and 'umbrella'), *stuffocate* (for 'stuffy' and 'suffocate'), *animule* ('animal' and 'mule'); those with syllable inversion like *ossifer* (for 'officer'), *hoppergrass* (for 'grasshopper'), *sin twisters* (for 'twin sisters'), *sideburns* (for 'burnsides'); and "stretch forms" like *be-youtiful* (for 'beautiful'), *k-nife* (with the *k* pronounced), *chee-ild* (for 'child'). Many of these will be recognized as unconscious pronunciations of careless or ignorant speakers, seized upon and popularized by students in a spirit of fun, although a few, such as *sideburns* and *teetotaler*, have been used so persistently as to be fairly standard English in some localities.

A number of mispronunciations may be ascribed to difficulty that speakers of English have had with foreign words, particularly French. During the World War, French phrases and place names were twisted into most grotesque forms by the British Tommy and the American doughboy, *Aix-les-Bains* becoming 'Aches-and-Pains', *Ypres*, 'Wipers', *très bien*, 'three beans', and *il n'y a plus* being changed to 'napoo'.

Differing somewhat from the deliberate twisting of words is that confused pronunciation met with at times, as in the case of the Somerset woman quoted in *Word-Lore* some years ago, who called a *tribunal* a 'dry-boonal', *espionage* 'es-spinach', and *concrete* 'consecrated'.[63] A particularly fine example of the confused blending of two words is also noticed in the same magazine; but this time it was a city business man who remarked of two friends who had recently quarreled that it was a pity "to see two men who were once such friends *at daggerlogs*". Doubtless *at daggers drawn* and *at loggerheads* had been confused by the gentleman.

That unintentional but most embarrassing form of mispronunciation which involves the interchange of the initial consonants or syllables of two neighboring words and to which the name of "Spoonerism" has long been applied, we have already illustrated in an earlier discussion of the psychological influences that produce changes in language (p. 4). Whether or not the Oxford professor W. A. Spooner was really guilty of the numerous funny slips of the tongue that have been credited to him, — he is said to have solemnly inquired of his audience, "Don't you ever feel a *half-warmed fish* in your heart?", to have explained that "it is *kistomary* to *cuss* the bride", to have entered the office of the dean with the question "Is the *bean dizzy* this morning?", and to have made various other amusing slips, — at any rate his name and fame will live on down through the years, and many a laughable slip of the tongue will be called by his name.[64]

When the dramatist Sheridan introduced into his play *The Rivals* the bombastic Mrs. Malaprop and made her, as Captain Absolute remarked, "deck her dull chat with hard words which she don't understand", putting into her mouth such remarks as the often-quoted "Sure if I *reprehend* anything in this world, it is the use of my *oracular* tongue, and a nice *derangement* of *epitaphs*", he was probably not offering to the world anything startlingly new but rather making sport of a type which has long existed and which has more recently flourished in the person of the notorious Andy of "Amos 'n' Andy" radio fame, and of others who make a similar misuse of words. Malapropisms are not, as a rule, so frequently heard in the conversation of one individual as was true of Sheridan's Mrs. Malaprop; but the occasional amusing misuse of a word is common enough, particularly among students, to have led to the making of some very edifying collections under the title of "Boners". Sometimes, as in the case of "an awful, *glutinous* bulldog", of the character who has "a *characteristic* face", or the drinker of red wine who "*looses* his *temperament* in a very bad degree", the very fact that the writer missed his mark by so narrow a margin adds humor to the malapropism. Sometimes, of course, the printer is to blame, and we will charitably assume that the respective writers wrote *deduce* and *congenital* in passages that appeared as "I am bold enough to *deduct* from this something of your taste in periodicals" and "in O'Malley's case it was his queer, *congenial* mistrust of women".

Of course the foreigner unfamiliar with English is likely to produce some very grotesque English because he has so many different things to confuse; pronunciation, inflectional forms, syntactical usage, and choice of words all cause him much worry. The American business man of foreign birth who remarked of certain business transactions that "there is nutting worser as when you don't got 'em in shape" covered practically the entire range of possibilities, since he mispronounced *nothing*, employed the wrong comparative form, *worser*, chose the wrong conjunction, *as*, and followed *don't* with a participle instead of an infinitive. Surprising effects are produced sometimes by a foreigner when he gets hold of the wrong idiom, as was illustrated by a writer in the *Bookman*, not many years ago, who told a school-teacher friend upon learning of her approaching resignation and withdrawal that he 'hoped she was going for good', meaning that he wished her well and hoped her going would be for her own good.[65]

Some incongruous word forms have gradually taken their places in the English vocabulary just because speakers have not clearly understood their original forms and so by a process of "folk etymology" have twisted them to make them appear in their origin and make-up something quite other than they really were. For example, an *acorn* is the fruit of the oak and related to *acre*, but it apparently did not require too great stretching of the popular imagination to associate it with *corn*; a *pickax* was not originally a form of *ax* at all; and the popular *sparrowgrass*, for 'asparagus', owes its form in dialectal usage to a very vague feeling that the plant resembles *grass*. However, not all folk etymologies are so badly twisted as to deserve a classification as grotesque English, and a fuller treatment of the subject will be found later in this book (see Sec. 69).

13. *Archaic English versus Neologisms*

An examination of any fairly complete dictionary of the English language will disclose a surprisingly large number of words, word forms, and meanings labeled "*Archaic*" or "*Obs.*" (or "*Obsolete*"). Of course the historian knows that some of these words have lost favor with the English-speaking public and have been gradually moved back onto an out-of-the-way shelf marked "For archaic English" because of a great variety of popular prejudices and dislikes, while others have ceased to be useful, having been discarded by an ever-changing civilization, and consequently have been carefully laid away by the lexicographers in little chests marked "Obsolete, but available when called for". On the other hand the general public will observe from day to day numerous newly made locutions, or neologisms, set out in the display windows of the dictionaries, that is to say, in the supplements that are added from time to time, and offered to linguistic shoppers as substitutes for or improvements on the old-fashioned words. It is our purpose here to consider some of the reasons for the marking down of so much of the lexicographer's stock in trade, and also to attempt a rough classification of these antiquated locutions.

The English people have been prone to take up many foreign linguistic fashions in speech, and the importations have often found favor to the exclusion of the older native stock. The French *alas*, for example, crowded out long ago the Anglo-Saxon *wellaway*; *thews* has yielded to *habits* or *customs*; *thou* has been replaced by the plural form *you* because in France and elsewhere the plural was regarded as a more formal and courteous form of address; *creature* or *person* has taken the place largely of the old general-utility word *wight*; and *wain* has gradually given way to its Continental cousin *wagon*. Even *airplane*, a word made up of thoroughly familiar materials, has in spite of its official adoption by the National Advisory Committee for Aeronautics, been replaced to some extent by a more exotic *aëroplane*.

Even in the case of long-established native words, meanings have come and gone with the passing of the centuries. Nearly every old and commonly used word in the dictionary has, listed among its meanings, a few marked "*Obs.*"; *come*, for example, no longer means 'to be seemly or becoming'; *do* no longer governs an infinitive in the sense of 'to cause, to make'; *fall* does not mean nowadays 'to move quickly, to rush'; and for *glee* more than half of the dictionary's definitions are labeled "*Obs.*".

Of course the march of the ages has been accompanied by the dropping out of well-defined words and word groups because the things that they named have been discarded and left strewn along the way: terms for chivalry and armor, such as *escutcheon*, *greaves*, *hauberk*, and *joust*; modes and means of travel, such as *Concord stage*, *galleon*, *postboy*, and *trireme*; forms of dress, like the *buskin*, *gipon*, *kerchief*, and *pantalets*; foods, like *galantine*, *paindemaine*, a *sufel*, and *wastelbread*. Even within the lifetime of people still living, certain words have almost dropped out of use which were once fairly common in American usage, notably *buffalo-wallow*, *calumet*, *muzzle-loader*, *scalp lock*, *sidesaddle*, *slaveholder*, *stagecoach*, and *stem-winder*.

But even though the ideas may still demand expression, the words used to express them do not always remain the same. Just now *undertaker* and *real-estate man* are seriously threatened by the newer *mortician* and *realtor*. And these newcomers are only samples of the mob of neologisms that clamor for admittance to the dictionary and seek opportunity to supplement or even replace some of the words already reposing there. In an article published a few years ago, on the making of dictionaries, the following assertion was made by one familiar with the work of keeping the Standard Dictionary up to date [68]:

If the new word is bona-fide, freshly minted, we take it into our care for five years, place it on file. We watch its use by the people and tally this against its record during the probationary period. . . .

At the end of the interval the record of the neophyte is computed, and if its score shows a popular demand, the new word is awarded a place in the dictionary.

The writer adds, however, this interesting and significant comment:

Incorporation in the dictionary, though, is no signal for a word to become indolent. It must work. We have a list of more than 50,000 words now in our word shop that have shown little or no activity in the language for a long time. We keep a tally on these words, too, that have been abandoned by the public, for possible ejection. It is a sort of waiting list — waiting for the ax. Infrequency of use means deletion from the dictionary.

Of course the lexicographer may be called upon at any time to bring out of its chest and mummy wrappings some old, old word and put it in a prominent place in his show window at the behest of changing fashion, of modern invention, or of some sudden need in another field. The fashions in ladies' dress, modern football, and modern warfare have all combined to resurrect the medieval *helmet*, and *tournament* has come back; one never knows when such words as *hoop skirt* and *mustache cup* may be widely needed; and authors like Rudyard Kipling have been busy resurrecting old words like *sib*, *carl*, and the participle *waxen*. Moreover, the antiquarian, the historian, and the student of earlier times, generally, are always in need of the older words to name the details of that earlier civilization with which they work. So the lexicographer is justified in including a great many obsolete and archaic words in his "complete" dictionary.

A few words have survived only in isolated phrases or uses. We speak of *widow's weeds*, although the word *weed* has long ago ceased to apply to clothing in general; the colloquial 'I would *just as lief* go with you' preserves the good old Anglo-Saxon word *leof*, which Shakespeare still used in such phrases as *my liefest liege*; *fro* persists in the phrase *to and fro*; while the form *wight* has been lost from standard English, we still like to say *not a whit*, using another form of the same word; and one can still *bandy about* ideas and truths, even though the verb alone would sound strange. The language of Shakespeare and the Authorized Version of the Bible persists in many instances just because the literature has been so generally read and memorized. And not merely because of love and respect for the literature of that early period, but also because the language has become a part of religious practices; many archaisms like *thou* and the verb forms in *-est* and *-eth*, as in *thou seest* and *man goeth*, tense forms like *spake* and *builded*, and inversions like 'Fill ye up then the measure' are still used in the restricted and exalted form of religious speech.

The poet, moreover, has always assumed the right to make use of archaic words like *anon, anent, meseems, ne'er, quoth, wot, yclept*, and others long banished from prose usage.

There is no better way to sum up and appraise that portion of the English vocabulary which we have characterized as obsolete and laid away or as archaic and relegated to the needs of the religious speaker or poetic writer, than to take a section of any large unabridged dictionary and examine the individual words in sequence. Beginning with C-words, for instance, one finds *cabal* with two definitions marked "*Obs.*" and one "*Archaic*", out of a total of six; for *cabin* four are "*Obs.*" out of seven; for *cabinet* three are plainly "*Obs.*", out of the total of ten definitions, while a fourth is "*Obs. or Archaic*"; *cabriole* has, out of three, one labeled "*Obs.*"; and even *cad* has lost two, out of five, to the enemy "*Obs.*".[26] Nearly half the meanings of these words are either obsolete or archaic.

14. *Newspaper English*

With the very rapid development of the newspaper during the last half-century, there have grown up also certain abuses in the use of the English language which have gradually aroused the criticism of scholars who have sought to maintain a high standard in writing, generally, and in journalistic writing, in particular. In 1880 Richard Grant White wrote[71]:

There is, first, the style which has rightly come to be called newspaper English, and in which we are told, for instance, of an attack upon a fortified position on the Potomac, that "the thousand-toned artillery duel progresses magnificently at this hour, the howling shell bursting in wild profusion in camp and battery, and among the trembling pines."

And a little farther along he added, "But not only are our journals and our speeches to Buncombe infested with this big-worded style." Only seven years later, however, another famous teacher of rhetoric and composition, Adams S. Hill, protested that "In newspaper English, the tendency is to sacrifice elegance and refinement to the 'forceful' or the funny." [72] Within two or three decades the criticism shifted again, and critics have been commenting most often upon the very much exaggerated and sometimes almost incomprehensible "journalistic jargon" affected by the sports writers and others, on the one hand, and on the other hand they have complained of the extreme condensation and vagueness of "headline English", as it has come to be called today.

As a matter of fact, it is only fair to say that there is a great variety of speech types to be found in the newspaper of today. Each department has its own special vocabulary and endeavors to appeal to a certain class of readers. The most extreme examples of unconventional or irregular English are, of course, to be met with in the department of the sports editor. When the sports writer really warms up to his task of reporting an exciting baseball or football game, one who is not fairly well versed in the sports slang of the moment may have difficulty in understanding just what the writer is saying. But the financial or automobile or fashion writer is sometimes too technical for the thorough understanding of one who is not well acquainted with the special vocabulary of the subject. The best literary efforts of the newspaper writer are usually expended in editorial-writing, and in the editorials of the better newspapers some very effective and pleasing English is encountered at times. When Talcott Williams insisted that "Taken as a whole, the newspaper was never better written and never did its work better in any of its fields" than when he wrote, in the year 1920, he was probably right, and his conclusion would be accepted today by those who view all the manifold purposes of the daily newspaper and are acquainted with the various phases of present-day life which the newspaper must serve.[74]

There is, however, a very marked influence, and a seriously detrimental one at that, in the condensed style of the large-type, front-page headline because of the manner in which word forms and word meanings have been subordinated to the mechanics of headline-printing, and also because of a strong tendency on the part of newspaper writers to imitate this condensation and radical abuse of words in other parts of the paper. In 1913 J. L. Lowes wrote, "In its striving for certain praiseworthy ends — brevity, conciseness, tellingness of phrase — the newspaper occasionally plays fantastic tricks before high heaven", and he cited "Grips Convict Toil Poser", explaining that this puzzling group of words meant "Tackles the Problem of Convict Labor".[73] In a leading San Francisco daily newspaper appeared, more recently, the very noncommittal heading "Chaplin Polls Fan as Guest of Selfridge", which the reader had to work out in puzzle fashion through the help of two clues, namely, the fact that the British public had been eagerly awaiting news from the polls concerning the election and a paragraph in smaller type to the effect that "Gordon Selfridge entertained 3000 persons at his store, one of his guests being Charlie Chaplin". In a similar heading appearing in the same newspaper, "Market Turn Held Break in Fear Complex", only the one word *in* is actually simple in use and meaning, since *market* and *fear* are just as often nouns or verbs but are used here as adjectives; *turn* and *break* are historically verbs but are used here as nouns; *held* is usually the simple past tense of the verb when it is used alone without the aid of an auxiliary, whereas it is employed here as a participle with auxiliary omitted; and *complex* has been more often used, until the psychologist seized upon it, as a general-utility adjective rather than a technical noun. Of the seven words four may be used in at least three different ways (as verb, noun, or adjective), two in two different ways (*held* as past tense and as participle and *complex* as noun and as adjective), and only one little preposition can be regarded as reasonably free from the suspicion of ambiguity. Hence, even though the reader might be aware that the stock market was receiving much attention at the time and likely to be the subject of the article following the heading, nonetheless he would probably be forced to go over the heading more than once, trying out the words as nouns, as adjectives, and perhaps even as verbs, before he could hit upon just the right combination and open the door of understanding.

Hicklin, in an article in *American Speech* which he entitled, in imitation of the slightly facetious journalist, "Scribes Seek Snappy Synonyms", has explained some of the difficulties encountered because of the mechanical limitations of headline-writing, showing how the writer resorts to old and unusual nouns and adjectives, such as *orb, quash, savant, sleuth,* abbreviates the longer and more dignified words into forms like *medico* and *prohi,* throws in an occasional slang or colloquial term, such as *booze, exams, gas* (for 'gasoline'), employs the compound nouns *comeback* and *hit-runner,* and converts to the use of a noun simple verbs like *cut, jump, spur,* and *upset,* and the interjection *okeh.*[75]

Much of the trouble with newspaper English arises, as several writers on the subject have made clear, from two causes inherent in newspaper work: the haste with which the daily newspaper must be made up and printed, and the youth and inexperience and often sheer incompetence of reporters and novitiates in newspaper work. Various striking but dangerous, because overcolorful and overworked, tricks are resorted to in an endeavor to attract public attention and interest. A favorite is the use of alliteration, that stringing together of words beginning with the same initial consonants, as in the introduction to Sandburg's *American Songbag,* where, in rapid succession, occur the expressions *strips, stripes,* and *streaks, characters* and *communities, layout* and *lingo,* and *student sing.* So pronounced, indeed, is this journalistic fondness for alliteration that it has become of late a part of the equipment of the satirical critic, and Stephen Leacock has made effective use of it in the titles of several satirical humorous books, such as his *Frenzied Fiction, Winsome Winnie,* and *Winnowed*

Wisdom. Occasionally one finds a renewal of that very flowery and big-worded style for which White criticized the newspaper writer a half-century ago, and not infrequently the journalist will dig up an archaic word or phrase with more courage than good judgment.

But aside from these more infrequently used tricks of the trade, two very important exigencies of the newspaper writer often get the young or mediocre journalist into trouble, namely, a need of varying his mode of saying things and an urge to be more "colorful" in his writing. A sports writer has been quoted who, in a single issue of a great newspaper and in a single article, expressed the idea of football defeat with eighteen different verbs, using *fell before, triumphing over, conquered, toppled, subdued, edged out, blanked, whitewashed,* and so on. One sometimes becomes so engrossed in watching the linguistic gymnastics of the writer that he loses sight of the thought content of the article that he is endeavoring to read. And what has just been said of the effect of exaggeration in word variation is equally true of the "color stuff", as a writer has termed it, which is to be met with in newspaper writing, especially in the sports columns of the newspaper. Perhaps the sports writer and likewise the sports reader have more justification for liking linguistic stunts than other departmental writers, since they are writing and reading pretty much the same tale of athletic accomplishment day after day and month after month.

The criticisms of newspaper English, as a whole, apply in equal measure to inefficient and commonplace writing in general; and it is chiefly in the realm of "headline English", with its accompanying mechanical restrictions, that the most serious threat to good English lies. Perhaps the only way to avoid that danger will be to avoid the greatly overemphasized headline itself.

15. *Children's English*

The study of children's English is both interesting and profitable to the student of language. It is interesting because the beginning and gradual development of the child are probably similar to those of the human race as a whole and also because any careful count of the vocabulary of the child at different ages will give a fairly accurate measure of the intellectual growth of the child. It is profitable in that it gives the philologist some useful examples of the working of those linguistic factors which we have already discussed (Sec. 6) as causes of linguistic change, particularly failure to imitate perfectly, ignorance, and analogy.*

It is not surprising that the child fails to imitate exactly the sounds spoken by a parent, since he cannot see the tongue position of the speaker or watch the placing of his own tongue. He must work by guess, for the most part. And so one hears the little child say *tan* and *tum* for 'can' and 'come', *div* for 'give', *muvver* for 'mother' and *bruvver* for 'brother', *es* and *ou* for 'yes' and 'you'; an older child sang, during the war, "It's a long, long way to *Dippaderry*, It's a long way to *doe*", substituting *d* for *t* and *d* for *r* in *Tipperary*, and *d* for *g* in *go*; the child frequently leaves one *r* out of *library*. As already noted (p. 3), a little child once strangely pronounced *light* as *gite*. If one will try out the pairs of consonants thus confused by the child, he will realize that the tongue-positions are not far apart, and hence the confusions in pronunciation are not so strange, after all, as one might think. The omission of bothersome sounds is the most natural thing in the world.

Of course the little child's total ignorance of the pattern of those forms and usages which make up the English language, and likewise of the many special words that are necessary to express the many special ideas which are constantly knocking at the door of his active little mind, causes him to do things that are very interesting to the student of language. Since he is slow about understanding the value of pronouns as shortcuts in speech, he is likely to say 'Baby wants the kitty' or 'Willie is a naughty boy', using *baby* instead of *I* and *Willie* instead of *you*. He has trouble in pronouncing longer words

---

* The other causes named in Section 6, namely, slovenliness, conscious scholarly influence, and the more deliberate changes of various kinds, cannot be discussed in connection with the speech of the very young child, but are characteristic of the more sophisticated age when the child has grown old enough to develop the habits of carelessness on the one hand or of intelligent constructiveness on the other.

like *stomach* and *grandmother* and *handkerchief*, and so he shortens them to *tummy* and *granny* and *hanky*. Even when he does acquire pronouns, he is likely to use *me* as subject and use *is* after *you*, and to coin a possessive form in such an expression as *him's book*, just because he does not comprehend all the little accepted irregularities of the English language.

On the other hand, the child has a strong tendency to make capital of his past experiences and to group forcefully together dissimilar words, by the principle of analogy making each linguistic newcomer conform as far as possible to the form of the words that he already knows and uses. Numerous examples of the addition of the diminutive suffix *-ie* or *-y* occur. Not only does the child add this suffix to hard words that he has simplified, like the three named above, but he takes such early acquisitions as *dada* and *mamma* and adds them to the class of diminutives as *daddie* and *mummie*. So one hears *horsie* and *bossie*, and *kitty* and *doggie*. Working according to this same principle of analogy, he forms the plural *mans* because he has learned to say *boys* and *girls* and *pans*, he pluralizes *foots* to conform to *hands* and *eyes*, and he regularizes the past tense of *blow, grow, know, throw,* and *draw* to *blowed, growed, knowed, throwed,* and *drawed* because he has heard *hoed, rowed, snowed, towed,* and *thawed*. One writer has listed no fewer than fifty-five instances of the regularization of irregular verbs by children, notably *creeped, flied away, I goed out, losed, rided,* and *stickt*.[77] The child even takes the adjectives of irregular comparison and forms *gooder, goodest,* and *badder, baddest,* to conform to the usual practice of English speakers.

But while the child is frequently failing to reach the standard of speech set for him by his elders, either because he is still incapable and ignorant or else because he applies the principle of analogy too drastically to the irregular forms and usages of English, nevertheless his intellectual growth is evidenced by a steadily increasing vocabulary. Those who have studied the speech of children have given various reports on the number of words used by children at the different stages of early childhood; Whipple found that one three-year-old boy had a vocabulary of 1771 words, and in the discussion of the fact summed up his studies of other reports as well with the assertion[78]:

> In the twenty-odd published vocabularies we find that children from 16 to 19 months are using from 60 to 232 words, that two-year-old children are using from 115 to 1227 words and that the vocabulary increases rapidly from that time on. It is perfectly safe to assert that the average three-year-old child makes use of 1000 words.

After making allowance for the two contradictory facts that, on the one hand, most of the children that have been thus carefully studied have lived in the very favorable atmosphere of homes of refinement and culture, and that, on the other hand, children probably have in reserve some words that they hesitate to make use of, the estimate given seems conservative, and it would probably be found that most students of language are inclined to underestimate the size of the vocabulary of the average alert child, as well as the rapidity of increase in the vocabulary of the young child.

This increase in vocabulary comes in various ways. One of the earliest is through the formation of onomatopœic (or onomatopoetic) words, that is to say, words that imitate sounds characteristic of the objects to be named, as *moo moo* for 'cow', *choo choo* for 'locomotive', *bowwow* for 'dog'. Of course the child cannot be given all the credit for this kind of word formation, since many a parent indulges in baby talk and helps along the process of word-coining. It is true also that at times the child fails to recognize new experiences and calls a haystack a *sand pile*, any old lady *grandma*, or any small animal *kitty* or *doggie*. But the parent gradually corrects these little misunderstandings by supplying the right names; and so, both by the process of correct observation and by the correction of mistakes, the child's vocabulary is definitely enlarged. As its mental horizon widens, its vocabulary increases.

The intellectual and linguistic development of the child has been interestingly and definitely measured by Margaret Nice through the measurement of the sentences of children of various ages. From the single-word stage, which she has found in the case of practically all very little children, the child progresses in sentence-building through a short-sentence stage in which many of the sentences are incomplete, with an excess of nouns and with relatively few of the connecting words of the more elaborate sentence, averaging at approximately three years of age from four to seven words to a sentence. The complete sentence of six to eight words apparently does not come commonly until after three years, after the inflectional forms have become familiar to the child and after a larger vocabulary has been acquired.[79]

It seems not unreasonable to suppose that the peculiar developments of a child's language as they have been briefly indicated above are similar to the phases and difficulties experienced by mankind in general during a long period of primitive language growth. The race doubtless made its discoveries just about as the child does and followed them up by coining more and more words after the patterns that had been slowly and laboriously evolved. In the older stages of the growth of various known languages — and not such primitive stages, at that — the philologist can find examples of confusion and lack of understanding, of inability to use the finer distinctions, and of failure to make the smoother connections and transitions in sentence structure. Primitive man had no more use for abstract nouns to name the learned concepts of philosophical and erudite thinking than the little child has; he was not much more capable of handling complex sentences than is the child; and when a primitive tribe failed to understand a word used by other peoples, the word was likely to assume quite different meanings.

16. *Dialects of English*

One of America's greatest philologists, William Dwight Whitney, for many years professor of comparative philology in Yale University and the editor in chief of the excellent Century Dictionary and Cyclopedia, discussed years ago the phases of language variation that we are now to consider. He gave to his chapter the caption "Dialectal Variation," introducing his discussion with this statement [80]:

Every item of difference between new speech and old, whether in the way of alteration or of addition, has its separate origin, beginning in the usage of individuals, and spreading and seeking that wider acceptance which alone makes language of it.

Whitney went on to discuss this tendency of the individual speaker to introduce variations in his language which might become dialectal variations when a group of people became associated together and set apart from the great body of speakers of the language because of special distinguishing conditions. He mentioned those speech variations which are characteristic of certain localities where people are separated from other localities, variations which are peculiar to certain classes, especially classes determined by occupation, "each trade, calling, profession, department of study" having its "technical vocabulary, its words and phrases unintelligible to outsiders", variations which are due to the differences in grade of education, and, finally, variations resulting from the differences of age. He might have added a fifth cause of variation, foreign influence, which is particularly noticeable in the United States in communities where foreigners have settled together who continue to use largely their native tongues, thereby modifying very noticeably the English language as they employ it along with their older foreign tongues. If, in the light of this very liberal interpretation of the term *dialect*, one examines the definitions of more recent writers on the subject, with their differing uses of the words *dialect* and *dialectal*, it will be apparent at once that the term *dialect* cannot be easily and definitely limited in meaning so as to satisfy every student of language. One will call it "the idiom of a district or class", while another will restrict it to "the speech of a certain community which has acquired characteristics peculiar to that community". Perhaps, for the purposes of this discussion, it will be most convenient to drop the idea of distinction due to differences in grade of education, which we have already discussed to some extent in Sections 9–11, and also of changes due to differences of age, as discussed briefly in Section 15. Those dialectal tendencies and variations which remain can then be more definitely defined under the two heads of "Local Dialects" and "Social Dialects". A local dialect is that form of a language which is peculiar to a locality or a section of the country where people are more or less isolated from the rest of the country or where, as is often true in America, people of a common foreign nativity have settled together. A social dialect is that form of the language employed by a group or body of speakers who are brought together by some common interest, such as a trade or profession, or even by a closely restricted habit of social intercourse.

a. For centuries people in isolated parts of England have made use of forms of speech which distinguished them both from people in other parts of the English-speaking world and also from the more educated and literate speakers of English who used the standard speech. These local dialects have persisted in England, and to a much less extent in America, through many centuries, and can still be found more or less distinct in certain communities. Poets and novelists have made use of them, in portraying special characters, with increasing frequency, and one has only to go to English literature to find numerous examples.

Tennyson's "Owd Roä" gives us a Yorkshire farmer who says of his dog, Old Rover:

"An' 'e kep his heäd hoop like a king, an' 'e 'd niver not down wi' 'is taäil, Fur 'e 'd niver done nowt to be shaämed on, when we was i' Howlaby Daäle.

"An' 'e sarved me sa well when 'e lived, that, Dick, when 'e cooms to be deäd, I thinks as I'd like fur to hev soom soort of a sarvice reäd."

Tennyson has illustrated certain peculiarities in the pronunciation of vowels, as in *heäd, niver, shaämed, sarved, soort,* and so on; he has introduced the Northern English use of *was* for 'were', *I thinks* for 'I think', and certain word-shortenings like *'e* for 'he' and *wi'* for 'with'.

More recently a story from Somerset in southwestern England appeared in the magazine *Word-Lore* which began [84]:

"Oh no! Ben wurden vrom theäze yer peärt o the country. I cooden tell ee vur zure wher a's one o, though zome d' zay as the neäme o'n d' mark en as one o Portland, wher the stwone d' come vrom, down Dosset waäy, an' Ben don't gainzaäy em."

Before one can get the full meaning of this passage, he must make allowance for an old Southern English tendency to voice certain initial consonants, speaking *vrom* for 'from', *vur* for 'for', *zure* for 'sure', *zay* for 'say', *gainzaäy* for 'gainsay', for the peculiar pronunciation of vowels which makes *theäze* from 'this', *peärt* from 'part', *neäme* from 'name', and *waäy* from 'way', for strange consonants in *stwone* ('stone') and *Dosset* ('Dorset'), for the two negative verbs *wurden* ('was not') and *cooden* ('could not'), for survivals of older pronominal forms in *ee* (for 'thee'), *a's* (for 'he is'), *en* (meaning 'him'), *em* (meaning 'them'), and also for the usual number of word-shortenings, such as *o* for 'of', *d'* for 'do', *an'* for 'and'.

Most people who have paid any attention at all to dialectal distinctions are familiar with Irish English as it has been presented in English and American literature for several centuries past. Indeed, the dialect of the Irishman is probably better known in America than any other dialect of the English language because of the outstanding position in American life assumed by the Irish immigrants from a very early time. As P. W. Joyce has presented the peculiar features of this English spoken in Ireland,[85] they may be classed as differences in pronunciation, to a less extent differences in the syntax of the sentence, and to a greater extent differences in the choice of words. A shift of vowels is to be seen in *sarvant* and *sartin* (for 'servant' and 'certain'), in *resave* and *lave* (for 'receive' and 'leave'), in *me* and *be* (for 'my' and 'by'), in *ould* and *could* (for 'old' and 'cold'), and in the change of *e* to *i* before nasals, a fairly common change in the earlier history of standard English itself, as in Irish *min* and *tin* (for 'men' and 'ten'). A tendency to roll the *r* in the combination *rm* gives such forms as *harum, warum,* and *wurrum* (for 'harm,' 'warm,' and 'worm') A curious interchange of diphthongs is observable in the pronunciations *bile* and *ile* (for 'boil' and 'oil'), on the one hand, and on the other of *foine* and *moind* (for 'fine' and 'mind'). The sound of *t* is also shifted to *th* in *arbithraather* and *gladiaather* (for 'arbitrator' and 'gladiator'). Of the peculiar syntactical usages mentioned by Joyce the use of *after* with some form of the verb *be* and the use of *do* in special ways are illustrated in the remark of a deserted Irish-American wife, "I am after looking for my man every day, but I don't know yet where Mike do be." The frequent use of *ye*, both as subject and as object, with the derived forms *yez* and *youse*, is of course familiar to many.

The vocabulary of Irish English is somewhat more striking than that of most other English dialects because the Irish speaker not only retains some archaic words like *adown* ('down'), *afeard* ('afraid'), *afore* ('before'), *anear* ('near'), and *gaffer* ('young chap'), but also utilizes numerous Celtic words like *banshee* ('female fairy'), *colleen* ('young girl'), *mavourneen* ('my love'), *shamrock* ('white trefoil'), *shillelagh* ('oaken cudgel'), and *spalpeen* ('low rascal'). The use of *blarney* (from Blarney Castle) and *wake*, a peculiarly Irish custom associated with the burial of the dead, needs no explanation for most Americans who have lived near Irish-American communities. It should be noted that the Irish English shows the influence of a non-English language (the Gaelic) more strongly than any of the other older dialects of Great Britain, and for that reason has a much more varied vocabulary, resembling in that respect certain other foreign-English dialects to be discussed a little later in this section, notably the English of India, of the so-called Pennsylvania Dutch, and of the Mexicans of the southwestern portion of the United States.

Perhaps equally familiar to many readers of English literature will be the Lowland Scots dialect, such as is employed by the minister's aunt in Ian Maclaren's *Beside the Bonnie Brier Bush*, who consolingly remarked to the minister:

> "Dinna be cast doon, laddie, nor be unbelievin'. Yir mither has heard every word, and is satisfied, for ye did it in remembrance o' her, and yon was yir mither's sermon."

Here, again, appear certain dialectal pronunciations of vowels as in *dinna* for 'do not', *doon* for 'down', *yir* for 'your', and *mither* for 'mother'; the rather common British practice of modifying the end of a word ending with *-ing*, as in *unbelievin'*; and the use of *yon*, which would hardly occur in American speech at all.

However, to turn to American dialectal usage, James Russell Lowell has immortalized Yankee speech in the characters of the *Biglow Papers*, and almost any passage will illustrate certain peculiarities of speech, as, for example:

> "Ez we're a sort o' privateerin',
>   O' course, you know, it's sheer and sheer,
> An' there is sutthin' wuth your hearin'
>   I'll mention in *your* privit ear;
> Ef you git *me* inside the White House,
>   Your head with ile I'll kin' o' 'nint
> By gittin' *you* inside the Light-house
>   Down to the eend o' Jaalam Pint."

A somewhat different kind of vowel pronunciation appears in *ez* for 'as', *sheer* for 'share', *wuth* for 'worth', *ile* for 'oil', *gittin'* for 'getting', *'nint* for 'anoint', *eend* for 'end', and *Pint* for 'Point'. The British change in the *-ing* ending appears here also in *privateerin'*, *sutthin'*, and *gittin'*, and the form of word-shortening already illustrated in all the other passages taken from dialect literature is seen here in *o'* for 'of', *an'* for 'and', *kin' o' 'nint* for 'kind of anoint'.

The dialect of the Southern mountaineer of the United States can be illustrated in some detail by means of a passage selected from Lucy Furman's *Quare Women* as spoken by the aged Uncle Ephraim:

> "Then last summer, about the time the crap was laid by, I heared how some strange women had come in and sot up tents over in Perry, and was a-doing all manner of things for young-uns. And one day I tuck my foot in my hand, — though I be eighty-two, twenty mile still hain't no walk for me, — and went acrost to see 'em. Two days I sot and watched them and their doings. Then I said to 'em, 'Women, my prayers is answered. You air the ones I have looked for for seventy year — the ones sont in to help us. Come next summer to the Forks of Troublesome and do what the sperrit moves you for my grands and greats and t'other young-uns that needs hit.' And here they be, doing not only for the young, but for every age."

Again one observes peculiar changes in vowels, as in *crap* (for 'crop'), *sot* (for 'set'), *tuck* (for 'took'), *air* (for 'are'), *sont* (for 'sent'), *sperrit* (for 'spirit'); again one finds plural subjects followed by singular forms of verbs, as in *my prayers is*; and here in the isolated speech of the Kentucky mountaineers are surviving earlier English expressions like *a-doing*, the uninflected noun plurals *twenty mile* and *seventy year*, the contraction *t'other*, and the earlier pronominal form *hit*; and, finally, there are certain colloquialisms more typically American than British, particularly *young-uns*, *hain't* (for 'aren't', 'isn't', etc.), and the two shortened words, *grands* (for 'grandchildren') and *greats* (for 'great-grandchildren'). It is worthy of note, moreover, that *acrost* has been increased by a final *t*, just as *lest*, *against*, *amidst*, and others were long ago.

These samples and analyses of six outstanding dialects of the English language show, as a group, four general differences from standard English. Of these four, pronunciation, as one might expect, is most noticeable. And if one could hear phonographic reproductions of the speech of each of these six dialects, he would realize that there are numerous little peculiarities of pronunciation which the authors are unable to indicate with the ordinary system of English spelling. A second difference lies in the older forms and usages, such as *yon*, *gaffer*, and *a-doing*, which are more likely, of course, to linger in the out-of-the-way corners of the English-speaking lands. Then, again, shortcuts like *i* (for 'in') and *grands* are to be expected in the colloquial speech of comparatively uneducated speakers of dialect. And, naturally, peculiar words and phrases develop in isolated communities which are not met with in standard English.

A similar examination of the characteristic features of Canadian English [86] or Australian English [87] or Welsh English would bring to light similar dialectal peculiarities. But in general the differences could be grouped as stated above, and the causes of such differentiations would be found to be those inherent in the circumstances, namely, isolation of a group or body of people for a long time, persistence of older linguistic features of English, development of peculiar forms because of special geographic conditions, and, finally, the working of some colloquial tendencies in language unhampered by those general conditions which have gradually shaped and fixed the standard literary language of England.

b. There are, however, some sections of America and also some other countries using the English language largely, such as India, where the language shows certain marked peculiarities which are not due so much to the causes just named as to the influence of foreign languages. In the United States of America are located communities populated largely by peoples from various foreign lands who have clung at first to their native tongues and then later have yielded to the encroachments of English, retaining, however, certain words and phrases and idioms peculiar to their mother tongues. Most famous of these dialects, perhaps, is that of the so-called Pennsylvania Dutch, who were in reality Germans, a dialect used by such American writers as Brooke Hanlon, Oma Alomona Davies, and Elsie Singmaster in stories published in the *Saturday Evening Post*, and by Helen R. Martin in her novels dealing with Mennonite characters, such as *Tillie, a Mennonite Maid* (New York, 1904). While the accuracy of such "literary dialect" is sometimes seriously questioned by the dialect student because of the tendency of the creative artist to invent little phrases and idioms in order to enhance further the dialect effect, nevertheless in such expressions as *och* (German '*ach*'), 'Leave him go' ('Let him go'), 'It don't give such a good market', meaning 'There isn't such a good market', 'It makes nothing to me', meaning 'It makes no difference to me' or 'I don't care', and in a peculiar use of *dare* in the sense of 'may', as in the sentence 'You dare take this book if you wish', one who is at all acquainted with the German language can readily detect the influence of the corresponding German idioms. A few words have shown a slight tendency to spread over the country from this Pennsylvania dialect; but for the most part the dialectal influence seems to have been through the spread of the grammatical idioms of Pennsylvania Dutch speech. One would doubtless find queer pronunciations of English words as well if he were to go among these people, but the writers who have used the dialect have not made much effort to show differing pronunciations.

The influence of Swedish and Norwegian settlers in Minnesota, Wisconsin, and other North Central states, especially, is reflected in the English of the region in numerous ways. Robert Beckman has summarized the transition from Swedish to American English as follows [88]:

There are two categories of speech among the Swedish-Americans who have not yet mastered the unbroken tongue of the land. Some of them speak mostly Swedish, interpolating a few telling American words, others, having been in this country longer and still cherishing certain native phrases, will *reverse* the process, so that the balance is in favor of American.

He goes on to speak of the difficulties in pronunciation, which have led the writers of character sketches to stress such Swedish-American words as *yoost* ('just'), an illustration of the difficulty with initial *j*, *yah* ('yes'), and the supposedly characteristic *bane* for 'am', 'be', etc. In the vernacular speech of Wisconsin, Minnesota, and the Dakotas, moreover, the Swedish idiom has been reproduced in such expressions as 'He wants to go with' ('to go along') and 'It is to be ready till Christmas' ('ready at Christmas').

States bordering on Mexico retain numerous Spanish or Mexican words like *chili*, *cholla*, *frijole*, *rodeo*, and the more familiar Anglicized *tamales*; Spanish place-names are numerous and often embarrassing to the Easterner crossing the Mississippi westward for the first time. At *La Junta*, Colorado, he will probably meet his first *j* which is locally pronounced as *h*, and as he moves on to *La Jolla*, *San Jose*, *Paso Robles*, and *Los Angeles*, he will appreciate more and more the lingering influence of Old Mexico.[90] While these words of Spanish and Mexican origin do not, of course, constitute a distinct Southwestern dialect, they do, nonetheless, set off noticeably the language of that section of the United States.

In some of the larger cities of the United States, particularly in the East Side of New York City, a strong Yiddish-English dialect has sprung up which has been utilized very effectively by Milt Gross in his book entitled *Nize Baby*. Here, again, there is a marked difference in the pronunciation of vowels, but a difference due largely to the external influence of the native Yiddish, and not the result merely of centuries of isolation, as in the case of the dialects of England already discussed. Menner, in analyzing the dialect, has called attention to the interchanging of the short vowel in *bit* and the longer one in *beet*, giving as examples of this confusion *seex* and *deesh* for 'six' and 'dish', and *quin* and *spitch* for 'queen' and 'speech', explaining this seemingly haphazard confusion of the two sounds as due to the fact that the speaker is accustomed to a Yiddish vowel "loosely described as midway between short *i* and long *e*"[91]. Other changes of vowels peculiar to this dialect are illustrated in the pronunciations of *pens* and *esk* for 'pants' and 'ask', and *nasts* and *kags* for 'nests' and 'kegs', in which the interchange of the two short vowels of *ask* and *nest* is likewise to be explained by the fact that the Yiddish speaker pronounces these two slightly different short vowels with approximately the same sound, namely, one that lies somewhere between the two. A similar process is shown by the spellings *dunt* and *dug* for 'don't' and 'dog', and *bot*, *ronning*, and *ponch* for 'but', 'running', and 'punch'. The pronunciation *kink* and *rink* for 'king' and 'ring' is characteristic of the Yiddish-English dialect, but it will be noticed also in the pronunciation of some other German-Americans who are not of Yiddish (that is, German-Jew) extraction. Of late there has been a tendency on the part of etymologists to explain a few recent words in American speech as derived from the Yiddish, notably *flivver*, *guy*, and *kibitzer*.

Sometimes the Englishman has attempted to foist his language upon a conquered people, and the result has been a dialectal form of English, such as that spoken in India, South Africa, or the West Indies. In India, with its numerous languages and peoples, so many foreign terms have been employed along with the English tongue that a large volume has been compiled for the enlightenment of those who enter the English-speaking circles of India.[93] These words are often quite troublesome to the foreigner because of his having to modify their forms to make them fit the English language, and the term *Hobson-Jobson* has been used to cover this entire process of popular etymology, or popular adaptation of unfamiliar Indian terms to the uses of the English people in India. (In the first place the term was merely the British soldier's translation of the wailing cry of the Mohammedans in religious procession, "Ya Hasan! Ya Hosain!") In the English of India the problem is one of assimilating numerous foreign words rather than of resistance to strange changes in pronunciation.

c. As has already been stated, scholars are not yet agreed upon a definition of dialect which will include the strongly differentiated language of a great number of special arts, trades, professions, and even of social groups. Attention has been called to the slang of the college boy, the sports writer, the aviator, the soldier, and the merchant (Sec. 11); but it is well to call attention also to the fact that these forms of slang do not in themselves constitute dialects. There is no such difference in pronunciation in the speech of these groups as we have observed in local dialects of Yorkshire, New England, and so on. However, there is, often, a highly selective vocabulary, made up of terms necessary to the art, trade, or profession, or acquired through the social segregation of a group of people, and for that reason these special forms of language are frequently called social dialects [94]. There is, for example, the language of anatomy [96], the vocabulary of the automobile business, which has so strongly colored our Modern English language generally with its talk of *carburetor, chassis, clutch, flivver, magneto, roadster, sedan* [97]; there is that great postwar development and popular use of aviation terms like *air pocket, dirigible, monoplane, strut, volplane* [98]; the beet-sugar industry has its own special expressions, such as *beet-puller, crystallization, sucrose, thin juice, weeding-knife*, not to mention the technical slang that goes with the sugar business [99]; library work carries with it a body of professional terms like *circulation, shelf-list, stacks, title-entry* [100]; the *cow-puncher* talks of *corrals, dogies, drives, rodeos, round-ups*, and *wranglers* [101]. A man even has to get up a little on the language of the insurance business nowadays if he wants to understand what it all means when he goes to *take out* life or fire insurance and hears much talk about *beneficiary, disability, nonforfeiture, premium, straight-life*, and so on [102]. The law has, of course, a great and mysterious vocabulary of its own, some of which has gradually oozed out into popular use, particularly such words as *appeal, contract, judgment, mortgage, habeas corpus*, and *re* [103]; medical terms are bandied about by the unscientific speaker with a certain degree of familiarity but with a maximum of inaccuracy, for the most part, even such words as *eczema, flu, infection, rheumatism*, and *tumor* being often misapplied (the great majority of terms pertaining to medicine never come into the experience of the average person, except as an individual here and there learns a few terms exactly, through unhappy personal experience) [106]; the language of the miner has come and almost gone again in many an American community, just as the *mill* and *placer* and *shaft* have been abandoned with the failure of *lode* and *nuggets* and *pay dirt* [107]. On the other hand, the coming of the *movie* to every American town and hamlet is gradually introducing a new body of professional terms such as *fade-*

out, long shot, on location, scenario, silver screen, talkie [108]; nautical life still requires a special vocabulary, though the good old words of the seagoing life which penetrated the speech of the landsman as well, long years ago, have to a large extent lost their nautical flavor because of the many changes that have taken place in the mariner's calling [109]. And, finally, in any list of special class dialects, one must not overlook the vocabulary of the politician, with his talk of *dark horse, favorite son, filibustering, lobby, logrolling, pork barrel, slush fund, straight ticket, wets and drys* [110].

d. In addition to these special vocabularies, or so-called dialects, of the arts, trades, and professions, there are several other languages within the English language — they might almost be called "little languages" — which are employed in several different strata of society. Benjamin Musser has summed up what he calls "the Catholic language," asserting that the many technical terms in constant Catholic usage, such as *decretal, matins, monsignor, scholastic,* constitute "what can be broadly called a lingual entity," a language so highly specialized that the non-Catholic will sometimes quite fail to understand what is said in an official utterance of the Church [111].

The "plain language" of the Society of Friends, or Quakers, is in a very different way a social dialect. While the language of the Catholic Church is built largely on the Latin of the medieval period, the Quaker speech eschews learned or high-sounding terms and goes quite to the opposite extreme with its talk of *first days* and *second days* for Sundays and Mondays, its *meetinghouse,* and so on [112]. One who has made a study of the Quaker speech says: "Even modern Friends still speak a language of their own, a language more distinct than most local dialects, in that it varies, not in enunciation only, but in vocabulary and in the specialized use of whole classes of words." Outstanding among the peculiarities of this dialect of the Friends is the use of *thee,* not only as object of a verb but also quite commonly as subject. Their doctrinal and theological terms to a large extent retain the meanings and flavor of that earlier period of English history when the society had its beginnings.

Quite at the other end of the social scale is the argot, or language of criminals and hobos, often so involved and incomprehensible as to seem a foreign language altogether. The framework is English, the pronunciation is not very different from that of standard colloquial speech as used by the illiterate and slovenly speaker; but the words are so different often that the dialect of the criminal or hobo serves to disguise the expression of thinking in much the same way that the schoolboy makes use of pig Latin to converse secretly with his close friends. Only as they have emerged into the speech of newspaper writers, novelists, and others interested in the speech of the underworld have speakers of standard English become aware of *bughouse* ('crazy'), *cooler* ('jail'), *dicks* ('detectives'), *framed* ('plotted against'), *frisk* ('to search'), *hoosegow* ('jail'), *hop-head* ('drug addict'), *jungle* ('hobo camping place'), *kale* ('money'), *mug* ('face'), *ride the blind* ('to ride on the front platform of the baggage car'), *in stir* ('in jail'), and many similar expressions [113]. For several centuries the "canting crew" have been coining these strange words and phrases. The vocabulary of the underworld is by no means fixed and well defined, but new expressions are constantly being introduced and old ones changed, as, for example, *in hock*, generally defined as 'pawned' but recently used to mean 'in prison', and *wop*, usually 'an Italian' but more recently 'serving less than a month in prison'. Moreover, different classes and groups of the underworld have varying vocabularies, bums, crooks, hobos, lags, yeggs, and so on, speaking slightly different dialects, if one may so use the term. Glossaries have even been compiled for the argot of automobile thieves [114], the language of the speak-easy [115], and convicts' lingo [116]. It is the language of the lawless, drifting, unsettled world, and it would be vain to expect of such a language either uniformity or permanence.

The language of the American negro has received much attention from both the philologist and the writer of fiction, the novelist and the dramatist in particular [117]. Everyone is familiar with the use of it in the writings of such authors as Harriet Beecher Stowe, Mark Twain, and Joel Chandler Harris. But it is not easy to classify it as a dialect, or to account for its development satisfactorily. It is, of course, largely the speech learned by negro slaves from their masters and is, therefore, Southern English of the United States. But it was also early modified by the illiteracy and ignorance of most of the negroes who used it and so cannot fairly be regarded as typically Southern dialect. Moreover, it varies, ranging from the almost unintelligible Gullah dialect as isolated in the coastal region of South Carolina and Georgia and the upland negro English of Harris's Uncle Remus to the more westerly speech of the negroes of the Mississippi Valley. Finally, it should be noted that with the spread of the negro people over the United States in recent years the more notable features of the dialect, or patois, have been gradually disappearing. The portrayer of negro characters in recent fiction still puts into the mouths of his characters a distinctive speech, but to a certain extent this literary negro dialect is forced and artificial, and some of its outstanding peculiarities are probably due to the creative genius of the author, largely. If one wishes to find a markedly differentiated form of negro dialect, the Gullah will illustrate the workings of illiterate and slovenly pronunciation, of inflectional leveling resulting from ignorance of grammatical rules, and the survival of primitive word forms, as they appear in the speech of an isolated people. In *The Black Border* of A. E. Gonzales, for example, when Joe says of his wife [118]:

> "Da 'ooman keep on fuh onrabble 'e mout' 'tell uh w'ary fuh yedy 'um. 'E stan' sukkuh briah patch w'en blackberry ripe. 'E gi' you bittle fuh eat, but 'e 'cratch you w'ile you duh eat 'um!"

he means:

> "That woman keeps on unraveling her mouth until I weary of hearing her. She stands like a brier patch when the blackberries are ripe. She gives you victuals to eat, but she scratches you while you eat them!"

With this excellent illustration of the degeneration of the English language under the combined influences of ignorance and isolation, our discussion of dialectal variation may well close. It would be futile to attempt too detailed and exact a classification of dialects, either local or social. There are available dialect studies for almost every county of England, and, in the case of Yorkshire and some other counties, students of language have gone so far as to localize dialects in single valleys or districts, even. As for social dialects, one can, if he wishes to insist upon very minute details, list a very great number of them under the different arts, trades, professions, and so on. Furthermore, it is not wise to trust too implicitly to the literary dialects of writers of fiction, as we have already remarked. Dialect is, after all, largely a matter of individual peculiarity, and the person who uses it and the writer who attempts to reproduce its salient features may introduce elements which illustrate general tendencies and characteristics and yet owe their particular existence to the personality of the individual speaker or writer. Dialect, broadly defined, is everywhere, and it plays a very important part in linguistic history.

Moreover, the thoughtful student of language will not only observe a great amount of dialectal variation, but will also find it difficult to classify some of these variants of standard English, as is evidenced by the number of different names that have been applied to them. The study of the peculiarities of the local dialects of England has fairly well established their dialectal standing; but because of the lack of strict isolation in America, some philologists insist that American English has no true dialects. Even James Russell Lowell remarked in the introduction to his *Biglow Papers*, "I should be half inclined to name the Yankee a *lingo* rather than a dialect." Most of the so-called social dialects discussed are in reality little more than highly specialized vocabularies; writers on the strange speech of criminals and hobos have termed it variously "argot", "cant", "lingo", and even "jargon", while the speech of the negro has sometimes been called a "patois."

17. *Jargons*

The term *jargon* has been very loosely used as the equivalent of cant, of lingo, of artificial languages in general, even of dialects of a certain kind; it is often applied to any irregular, formless speech or gibberish. But it has also been given a more limited meaning by the exact student of language, and for the sake of convenience and clarity this limited meaning will be employed throughout this discussion. A jargon is, then, any crude form of speech arising from the confused and haphazard mixture of two or more existing languages. The Century Dictionary calls it "A barbarous mixed speech, without literary monuments; a rude language resulting from the mixture of two or more discordant languages, especially of a cultivated language with a barbarous one; as, the Chinook *jargon*; the *jargon* called Pidgin-English." [21] Since we are interested chiefly in matters pertaining to the English language, only those few jargons will be considered here that make free use of English words or phrases.

In view of the very general confusion in the use of the word *jargon*, it might be helpful in promoting clear thinking on the subjects of dialects and jargons to pause for a moment and set forth the reasons for including certain dialects in the foregoing section rather than in this one. Dialects as a group are variants within the English language, whereas a jargon arises among peoples outside the English-speaking race. The canting talk of criminals and hobos has sometimes been called a jargon; but since it merely coins its own peculiar words and phrases, preserving the inflectional and syntactical framework of the English language and in general the pronunciation also, it is to be regarded as a class dialect and not a jargon. Because of its almost incomprehensible mispronunciations and grammatical solecisms, the Gullah dialect has sometimes been termed a jargon; but in view of the fact that it preserves the body of the English vocabulary for the most part and the inflectional and syntactical framework of English (in a badly mutilated form, it is true), it is rather a dialect within the English language than a jargon. For the jargon possesses almost none of the inflectional and syntactical framework of English, and only a meager portion of the vocabulary of English.

At least as early as 1800, travelers brought back from the American Northwest samples of a lingua franca, or popular speech, which they called "Chinook jargon", and from time to time down through the years small glossaries of Chinook-jargon words have been published, mostly on the Pacific coast, for the use of traders and missionaries going among the Indians of the Pacific Northwest. In 1888 Franz Boas wrote [119]:

> The needs of the trade were such that a means of readily conversing with the natives of all parts of the country was necessary, and out of the clumsy attempts of the Indians and of the French and English traders to make themselves understood sprang a *lingua franca*, which is known as the Chinook jargon, and which has rapidly spread northward. At present it is spoken from Washington Territory to Lynn Channel, in Alaska; the older Indians only do not understand it. It is used as well in the intercourse between the Indians and whites as between members of tribes speaking different languages. The jargon consists principally of English, French, Chinook (proper), Nutka, and Sahaptin words. . . . In course of time the number of English words

contained in the jargon has increased, while the other elements have become proportionately less prevalent. The structure of the jargon, so far as it has any structure, shows certain characteristics of the Chinook.

Although the Century Dictionary defines a jargon as a speech without literary monuments, a small body of songs in this jargon can be found, and samples from them will give an idea of the character of the jargon [119]:

> Good-bye, barkeeper! naika tlatowa alta okok *sun.*
> Dja! Potlatch patlem *cocktail* naika.

Translated into English:

> Good-bye, barkeeper! I am going now today.
> Come! Give me a full cocktail.

> Ya kanowe *sun* naika *sick* tumtum.
> Kopa naika *man* kopa Caliponia

Translated into English:

> Ya, always I long
> For my husband in California.

Even a superficial analysis of this language will make manifest its bareness and poverty. The total vocabulary in common use about 1889 was estimated at not more than six hundred words. In 1894 Eells had collected about fourteen hundred words altogether [121]. In the thirty-nine short songs from which the foregoing samples have been taken, only about seventy-four native Chinook words occur, the others being English words like those italicized in the samples above. Verbs are omitted whenever possible, and frequently a word serves as both verb and noun, as in the case of *muckamuck*, either 'food' or 'eating', and *potlatch*, a word sometimes met with in American literature dealing with the Indians of the Northwest, meaning 'gift' or 'give'. Onomatopoetic words like *kah-kah* ('crow'), *moos moos* ('cow'), *tumtum* ('heart'), are common in the Chinook jargon. But for abstract concepts the speaker must often use one poor word in a variety of ways: the word *tumtum* (said to have been coined in imitation of the beating of the heart) is used with *sick* to express 'longing', in other combinations it means 'glad spirits', 'to forget', 'humble', and in the Chinook version of the Lord's Prayer it translates 'will'. As a language for the expression of concrete ideas, this jargon has flexibility; by means of compounds a great variety of ideas can be expressed. But, like all undeveloped tongues of primitive peoples, it lacks the words necessary for the expression of the more abstruse and erudite thinking; and apparently with increased teaching of English in the schools of the Pacific Northwest, the Chinook jargon is gradually disappearing, though it has been estimated that at one time at least a hundred thousand people used it [123].

Another jargon, known as "Beach-la-Mar", from the name of the once common *bêche-de-mer*, or edible trepang, became very popular in the southern and western Pacific islands during the latter part of the nineteenth century. In 1911 Churchill wrote [124]:

> It was the labor trade [in Polynesian natives] which made Beach-la-Mar a jargon and extended its currency. It gathered material from every source, it fused them all and created a language which yet remains the only means of intercommunication in the Western Pacific.

But it should be noted that while the Chinook jargon has as a base Indian and English words, in this jargon of the South Seas the base is predominantly English, with Polynesian and other words added; and the English is a very poor and ungrammatical speech at that, for it was brought to the Polynesians by sailors and beach-combers and illiterate drifters of all sorts. If one examines a paragraph of the "Eden Sermon", printed by Churchill, — literature of this jargon is scarce, — one will find a minimum of grammatical framework, but one will have little difficulty in understanding the language as a whole. In relating God's conviction of Adam's sin of disobedience, the preacher says:

> "And God he come walk about along garden, and he sing out 'Adam!' Adam he no speak. He too much fright. My word. And God he sing out 'Adam!' And Adam he speak, 'You call'm me?' God he speak, 'Me call'm you too much.' Adam he speak, 'Me sleep

strong fella too much.' And God he speak, 'You been eat'm this fella apple.' Adam he speak, 'No, me no been eat'm.' God he speak: 'What name you gammon along me. You been eat'm.' And Adam he speak, 'Yes, me been eat'm.'"

Variation of the verb form is almost altogether lacking, only the phrase *been eat'm* expressing completed action and possibly some emphasis. The word *fella* (from *fellow*) is a general-utility word used to lend definiteness to adjectives, pronouns, and even numerals, as, for example, *strong fella* ('strong') and *this fella* ('this'). The objective-case form of the pronoun *me* is regularly used as subject, and the redundant *he* is added to noun subjects. There are no gender forms of pronouns, *he* or *him* being used for man or woman. Some peculiar pronunciations occur in the sermon, such as *marster* (for 'master'), and *fennis* (for 'fence'). Such words as *kaikai* ('food') and *tabu* or *tambo* ('taboo, forbidden') will illustrate the intrusion of the Polynesian element into the jargon. *Mary*, meaning 'woman' in general, *nusipepa*, 'any written document', and *gammon*, 'to deceive, joke, lie', testify to the peculiar effect on meanings which such a mongrel growth can have. The words *pickaninny* ('child') and *savvee* or *savvy* ('know, understand') show Romance influence, while *tomiok* ('tomahawk, hatchet') has come from North America.

Perhaps the most interesting of these foreign-English jargons, however, is the pidgin English, spoken along the Asiatic shores of the Pacific, in the Philippines, in Hawaii, and even in California to some extent. This jargon is the result of the linguistic needs of English and Chinese traders trying to do business together, and the word *pidgin* is explained as a Chinese distortion of the English word *business*. The Chinese have taken the words of the Englishman and treated them in the simplest manner possible, with a minimum of grammatical apparatus and with only such non-English words as the occasion might demand. Pidgin English is both older than the Chinook jargon and Beach-la-Mar and of more immediate interest to Americans today because of its close approach to American life in Hawaii, especially, where American teachers in the schools have to reckon with it to a certain extent in their teaching of the mixed races now inhabiting the islands. Very little literature is available in pidgin English, but a few songs and poems have been translated into the jargon, and perhaps a stanza from a version of Longfellow's "Excelsior" will suffice to illustrate some of its more striking features [126]:

> That nightee teem he come chop chop,
> One young man walkee, no can stop;
> Colo maskee, icee maskee;
> He got flag; chop b'long welly culio, see —
> Topside Galah!

In certain respects the pronunciation differs from that of standard English: *teem* is, of course, 'time'; regularly the Chinese substitute *l* for *r*, hence such forms as *culio* for 'curious', *welly* for 'very', *Melican* for 'American', and *lain* for 'rain'. An unaccented syllable is often added, variously spelled *-ee* or *-ey*, as in *nightee, walkee, maskee, icee*. In this respect pidgin English is like Beach-la-Mar, as also in the use of the adverb *no* instead of *not*. *B'long* or *belong* is also commonly employed in this jargon, but in a somewhat different manner from that of Beach-la-Mar, sometimes almost as the equivalent of *to be*, as in *chop b'long welly culio*, 'the design is very curious', *my belongy Consoo boy*, 'I am the Consul's servant.' Certain expressions occur often which are not recognizable as English words, notably *chow chow* ('food'), *Joss* ('God'), *chin chin* ('compliments, salutation'), *bamboo* ('bamboo'). A certain fondness is noticeable for words that repeat, that is, reduplicated words, such as *chin chin, chow chow, chop chop* ('quickly, hastily'). And, finally, the almost complete lack of inflectional and syntactical apparatus is to be remarked again, just as in the other jargons already described; there is very little attempt to distinguish tense in verbs, or case in nouns or even in pronouns. Grammatically pidgin English is stripped to the merest essentials.

In his book entitled *Language* [127] (pp. 233–234) Jespersen has, in commenting upon the lack of inflectional or morphological practice, summed up the situation most excellently:

The morphology of all these languages is practically identical, because in all of them it has reached the vanishing-point. This shows conclusively that the reason of this simplicity is not the Chinese substratum or the influence of Chinese grammar, as is so often believed. Pidgin-English cannot be described, as is often done, as English with Chinese pronunciation and Chinese grammar, because in that case we should expect Beach-la-Mar to be quite different from it, as the substratum there would be Melanesian, which in many ways differs from Chinese, and further we should expect the Mauritius Creole to be French with Malagasy pronunciation and Malagasy grammar, and on the other hand the Oregon trade language to be Chinook with English pronunciation and English grammar — but in none of these cases would this description tally with the obvious facts ... the truth on the contrary is that in all these seemingly so different cases the same mental factor is at work, namely, imperfect mastery of a language, which in its initial stage, in the child with its first language and in the grown-up with a second language learnt by imperfect methods, leads to a superficial knowledge of the most indispensable words, with total disregard of grammar.

Perhaps no better matter could be hit upon for the conclusion of this discussion of standard English and its variants than these comments of Jespersen's concerning the kind of jargon that develops under the very primitive conditions of ignorance and disregard of the rules of grammar. From the ideal of "pure English", with its overmeticulous insistence upon minute details, we have come quite to the other extreme in considering these jargons of the edges of civilization. Between these two extremes we have noted a great variety of unconventional forms of English, and in most of them we have found things to commend, because they were constructive and manifested the presence of intellectual activity; but we have also come upon evidence of superficiality and linguistic laziness and slovenliness, here and there. Only on the higher level of standard literary English can one find an undivided adherence to that form of English which is clear and forceful and pleasing. Colloquial English as it is employed by people of education and intelligence is entirely commendable and desirable; but in the mouths of careless and incompetent persons it may be restricted and impoverished until it constitutes a form of language little better than the jargons just discussed. Slang is often due to a linguistic exuberance which enriches and refreshes the language; but it is invented by the very few who have imagination and ingenuity, and it is spoken for the most part by a great body of illiterate and unthinking folk capable only of using it over and over in a very limited and superficial manner. The grotesqueries of speech are often the unintentional products of stupid, ignorant persons and are spread abroad and imitated by clever people for the fun of it. Archaisms and neologisms represent two other extremes which wise speakers endeavor to avoid; and while they are deliberately employed at times by poets and other courageous people, at least they are not likely to come within the ken of the impoverished speaker of English, since he is incapable of using language other than the most ordinary. Newspaper English shows, like the language in general, varying degrees of excellence; but it is peculiarly liable to the evil effects of superficial and hasty speech because of the conditions under which the newspaper man must work. Unfortunately it caters too often to the tastes of people of the lower social levels. In the speech of the child there is usually observable intellectual alertness and a linguistic growth which very soon lifts his English far above the level of mere jargon if it is not adversely affected by social deterioration or handicap. And the dialects of English, in so far as they are the result of the long isolation of a self-respecting and intellectual people or of the more immediate needs of an art, a trade, or a profession, are in no respect to be criticized or scorned. It is only when a dialect in its development takes the lines of least resistance, with an accompanying loss of all that linguistic apparatus which we have come to value as characteristic of the English language at its best, and is pronounced and spoken after the manner of Gullah negro dialect, that it is avoided by the speakers of good English and, like the jargons last considered, serves its purpose for the period of need and then gradually passes out of use as better social conditions prevail and higher intellectual ideals are established in the community.

CHAPTER III

PHONETICS

THE subject of this chapter, phonetics, has already been defined as the science or study of all possible speech sounds, and in Section 2 the permanent and ever-present physical influence of the vocal organs has been contrasted with those unstable and fluctuating mental, or psychological, influences that bring about growth and change in the speech of both the individual and the race. Because the physiological influence is so fundamental, it is desirable to understand it well before going on to a consideration in later chapters of the various manifestations of mental activity in the shaping of our language.

If one takes too seriously the definition of phonetics as the study of "all possible speech sounds", he will find himself very soon involved in so exact a study of human speech sounds, with the numerous little variations both among individuals and among races as a whole, that he will need a laboratory with very nicely adjusted recording instruments and more time for experimentation than the ordinary student of the English language cares to afford. But if one is willing to make allowance for a certain amount of inexactness, both in the description of the ordinary sounds of his language and in the representation of them in writing, it is possible to present the subject very briefly and usefully. In the following discussion of the organs of speech and the sounds that may be produced by means of them, only the most general and fundamental facts will be presented.

18. *The Organs of Speech*

Since all discussion of the formation of speech sounds will have much to say about the manner in which the stream of breath passing to and from the lungs is utilized, it is necessary

THE ORGANS OF SPEECH

to remark at the very outset that this stream varies from the full, strong current necessary in singing words clearly in a large concert hall to the very faint breathing that produces some such sound as the elusive *h*, and from the continuous use of it in the making of sounds like *z, s, f, th*, to the stopping and starting of it in such sounds as *t, b, k*. But all speech depends upon this stream of breath and is conditioned upon the varying use of it.

The vocal cords, or membranes, lying at the top of the windpipe and stretched across a sort of cartilaginous box called the larynx, can be drawn tight so as to vibrate and produce sounds like *a, o, u,* or they can be allowed to lie slack while the breath is directed against other parts of the oral passage higher up.

These other organs which are employed in shaping the sounds of speech consist of the lips, the teeth, the hard palate, which forms the front portion of the roof of the mouth, the soft palate, or velum, forming the posterior portion of the roof of the mouth, and the nasal passage, which is not ordinarily left open in speaking but which can be employed for the formation of nasal sounds.

The diverting of the stream of breath to these various organs of speech is done largely by means of the one freely movable organ, the tongue, which is necessary for almost all shaping of speech sounds and without which speech is impossible. When the tongue is tied, that is to say, hindered in its activity by some unnatural physical bond, the making of speech sounds is so restricted that one is said to be "tongue-tied"; and when the tongue is cut out, — a favorite expedient of tyrants in days of old, — then speech becomes impossible. Of course other accidents to the speech organs may greatly handicap the speaker, such as loss of front teeth, a bad cold which partially closes the nasal passage, adenoidal growths tending to hinder the free passage of breath through the throat, and so on. Even the ability that one possesses of making the tongue thick or thin determines to a great extent the quality of the sounds that are produced, and a clear understanding of the difficulties that a learner has in shaping the tongue and in forcing the stream of breath against various parts of the oral passage will aid greatly in understanding why speech sounds cannot be too exactly classified and imitated. There is no exact line between the front palate and the back, between the tongue high in the mouth and low, between teeth and palate; everything is relative and approximate, and one learns to place the tongue in much the same way that one learns to use the slide of the slide trombone, by listening and experimenting intelligently. As has already been noted (Sec. 2), the difficulty which a child experiences in learning to speak is explained by the fact that there are no definite rules for the placing of the tongue, and the learner can judge of his success only by the results of his experimentation.

19. *Vowels and Diphthongs*

If one will think of the continuous flow of speech, for a moment, rather than of the individual sounds and words and phrases that compose it, one will realize that it is made up of a succession of fully voiced sounds made with the vibration of the vocal cords, accompanied by a succession of partially voiced or voiceless sounds, which go to make up what is known as articulate speech. The fully voiced sounds are known as vowels, and may be prolonged somewhat (long vowels) or cut short by the consonants that intervene every so often (short vowels). Of course this length is largely relative, and it is not always easy to determine whether one is dealing with a long vowel or a short one. If a word is pronounced alone and no final consonant checks the flow of the breath passing through the vibrant vocal cords, there will usually be little question as to the length of the vowel; but if a stoppage is effected by a consonant like *d* or *k* immediately following the vowel, whether the consonant belongs at the end of the word or at the beginning of a following word spoken immediately after, the vowel is likely to be shortened. So the vowel in *the* is fairly long when the word is being pronounced by itself or emphasized; but the moment it is incorporated in a phrase or a sentence, it is almost sure to be shortened, as in *the top of the hill,* for example; and this unconscious variation in the length — as well as the quality — of the vowel in *the* has caused perplexity to many a little child learning our language.

If one starts a study of long vowels by relaxing the tongue so that it lies low in the mouth, and then allowing the vocal cords to vibrate freely, the sound of *a* as in *far* is the result. A slight raising of the tongue in a forward direction will produce the long vowel heard in *fair,* although the sound in *fair* varies somewhat in English from a longer form of the short vowel in *fat* to the long form of the vowel in *fell,* according to the dialect or speech habit of the speaker. If the tongue is moved a little farther still in the same upward-forward direction, the vowel in *fail* is produced; and the last stage in this forward raising of the tongue will give the vowel in *feel.*

But one can start again with the low vowel *a* and run the scale in the opposite direction by keeping the tongue farther back and rounding the lips a little more each time, thus producing a series of three vowels, as in *fall, foal, fool,* the greatest rounding of the lips being observable in the highest back tongue position in *fool.*

In some words, more particularly as they are pronounced outside of Great Britain, New England, and the southern part of the United States, there is a vowel sound which is made with the tongue held in a higher central position, as in *fur, her, bird, further,* and *worry.* In the pronunciation of words containing this vowel, the English language varies greatly; the tongue can be forced up in the pronunciation of *burst, curse, worst,* for example, until it almost rubs the palate, or it can be relaxed and allowed to drop until the words become *bust, cuss, wust,* as sometimes occurs. Since the sound is always accompanied by *r,* sometimes actually pronounced but often merely spelled but not spoken, it is difficult to classify it as either long or short. Usually it is fairly long in a monosyllable, and certainly it is when followed by a prolonged *r*; in a dissyllabic word like *hurry* it is shorter, especially if allowed to drop to the tongue position of *cuss.* So it may not be amiss to include it in the diagrams of both the long and the short vowels.

This series of long vowels can be roughly indicated, as regards tongue positions, as follows*:

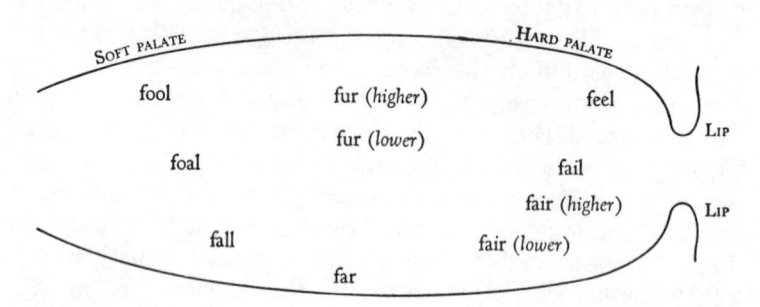

```
    SOFT PALATE                HARD PALATE
       fool          fur (higher)        feel
                                                    ⌒ LIP
                     fur (lower)
         foal                             fail
                                      fair (higher)
                                                    ⌒ LIP
             fall                  fair (lower)
                         far
```

While the short vowels correspond in general to these long vowels, the muscular relaxing that is likely to accompany shorter sounds produces some variations in the short group. One can start with the vowel in *folly* (American pronunciation) as the lowest medial short vowel and, by pushing the tongue in the upward-forward direction toward the upper teeth, secure the series *folly, fat, fell, fit*. Likewise the backward-upward movement of the tongue with increased rounding of the lips will be illustrated in the series *fortune, foment, full*. But it should be noted that the tongue is a trifle lower for the high front vowel in *fit* than for the corresponding high front long vowel in *feel*; the same is true of the high back short vowel in *full* as compared with the long vowel in *fool*. Moreover, the relaxation in the pronunciation of short vowels opens up the way for the laziest vowel in all language, the vowel in *fuss*. It is the vowel produced in moments of most careless and slovenly speech, as well as in the standard pronunciation of a large group of words like *mother, cut, us, other, ugly*, and is not high enough to cause effort in upholding the tongue, nor low enough to allow of a full stream of breath, nor forward enough to force one to move the tongue much, nor far enough back to cause one to round the lips; but it is an indifferent, easily made, middle, short vowel.

* If one will make a set of nonsense syllables in place of these words by substituting *k* for the initial *f*, he can easily observe the various tongue positions by standing before a mirror while he pronounces them in order, *kar, kair, kail,* and so on.

Sec. 19]   VOWELS AND DIPHTHONGS   75

If a shorter form of the vowel with *r* be included, as in *further*, the diagram of the short vowels will be as follows:

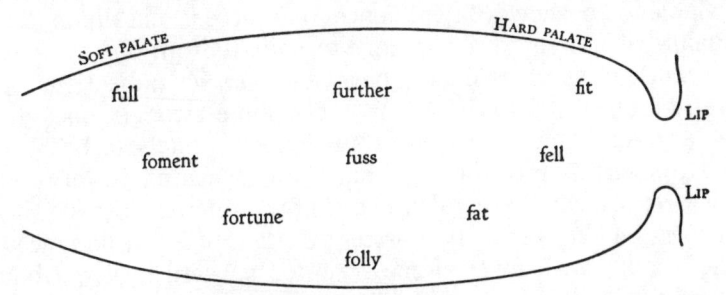

```
   SOFT PALATE              HARD PALATE
       full         further          fit      ⟩ LIP
         foment      fuss       fell
           fortune         fat         ⟩ LIP
                   folly
```

When two vowels are run together in pronunciation, they become a diphthong. When the low *a* is merged with the high front *i*, becoming *a* + *i*, rapid pronunciation will result in the sound heard in *fine, my*. When the *a* is merged with the high back vowel *u*, producing *a* + *u*, the resultant sound is that of *foul, brow*. So *i* + *u* gives the diphthong heard in *feud, mule*, and the lower *o* + *i* gives the diphthong in *foil, boy*. These are the common diphthongs of Modern English, although several others may be detected if one listens to the speech of the average person and analyzes his sounds carefully. It should be noted that a diphthong is not necessarily a digraph in Current English spelling; a diphthong is composed of two vowel sounds, whereas a digraph is merely two letters utilized in Modern English spelling to represent almost any kind of sound, either simple or complex. The sound in *fine*, for example, is a diphthong represented by the simple letter *i*; and the vowel in *fool* is a simple sound but represented by the digraph *oo*. The student of Current English sounds must forget, for the time, the many and various spellings and direct his attention to the sounds themselves.

In all the examples of vowels discussed, the vowels occur in accented syllables and are easily classified. But when the vowel is embedded in an unaccented syllable, as, for example, *a* in *abóve*, *e* in *mónetary*, *i* in *decápitate*, *o* in *colláteral*, and *u* in the noun *mínute*, the sound is so hurried and indistinct that it is not easy to find any difference in pronunciation.

Consequently it is customary to speak of "the unaccented vowel", by which is meant any vowel in an unaccented syllable. To show the influence that accent has upon the quality of vowels, one has only to shift it from one syllable to another, as in *mínute* (noun) and *minúte* (adjective) or *désert* (noun) and *desért* (verb). The more strongly one syllable is accented, the weaker its neighbor is likely to be.

However, despite the fact that the unaccented vowel is so obscure, one can distinguish two slightly different forms of it: in *abóve* and *colláteral* the unstressed *a* and *o* are pronounced like a very weak form of the accented *u* heard in *fuss*; but in *mónetary, decápitate,* and *mínute* the sound of *e, i,* and *u* is more nearly like a very weak form of the accented *i* as heard in *fit*. This is, of course, to be expected, since some weak vowels would be pronounced with the tongue toward the back of the mouth, while others would be made farther front. In many instances there is likely to be difference of opinion as to the exact quality, or sound, of the unaccented vowel, for it is never very definite or positive in its nature.

20. *Consonants*

Those sounds which accompany the vowels but which have no voicing or only partial voicing, forming by their frequent and noticeable occurrence in the flow of speech a succession of hindrances and modifications of speech, are called consonants. In the following sentences they are printed in boldfaced type; and although the vowels may be varied in value, the consonants remain fairly steadfast and constant, as may be seen if the sentences are read aloud several times:

These sounds of speech are heard in full if each is read with great care. The consonants that accompany the vowels are required to give coherence to the succession of vowels, interfering, however, in some measure with the smoothness of the stream of sound whenever they occur.

After these sentences have been read aloud several times, with careful enunciation of the consonants, certain peculiarities will become apparent. The sounds of *b* and *p*, of *d* and *t*, of *g* and *k* (sometimes spelled *c*), can be distinctly enunciated only when the breath is stopped and then released with a little explosion. Hence these six are called stop consonants, or explosives. But the breath is not thus checked for the pronunciation of *v* and *f*, of *th* as in *these* and *th* as in *thin*, of *z* (often written *s*) and *s*, of *s* in *measure* and *ss* in *succession*. They can be prolonged indefinitely and so are known as continuants, or spirant consonants.*

It will be observed that in both of these groups (the explosives and the continuants) the sounds have been paired. The first of each pair can be pronounced only with a certain amount of voicing, or vibration of the vocal cords; hence *b*, *d*, *g*, and *v*, *th* as in *these*, *z*, and *s* as in *measure* are known as voiced consonants, that is to say, voiced explosives and voiced continuants, respectively. The second of each pair has no voicing, only the sound of the breath as it is exploded or continued; hence *p*, *t*, *k*, and *f*, *th* as in *thin*, *s* as in *sound*, and *ss* as in *succession* are known as voiceless consonants, that is to say, voiceless explosives and voiceless continuants.

If, however, one gives attention during the pronunciation of the two illustrative sentences to the activities of the tongue rather than to the way the breath is exploded or continued, or to the way the consonant receives voicing or no voicing, if he attempts to note the various positions of the front movable portion of the tongue, he will observe that sometimes it touches the teeth lightly, as for *d*, *t*, sometimes the tip is between the teeth, as for *th* (both voiced and voiceless), then it is pushed up behind the teeth a trifle higher for *z* and *s*, it is kept up near the teeth but shaped differently for *s* in *measure* and *ss* in *succession*, it approaches the front, or hard, palate for *g* in *give* and *k* in *kill*, and the back, or soft, palate for *g* in *go* and *k* in *kodak*, and, finally, it drops back out of the way when *h* is to be spoken. Moreover, the two lips will be called into action for *b* and *p*, and the teeth and lower lip will be used for the labiodentals *v* and *f*. These consonants may be roughly summarized according to the plac-

---

* For *w* and *y* see page 78.

ing of the tongue as labials (made with the lips), labiodentals (made with teeth and lip), dentals (made with the teeth), palatals (made with the front, or hard, palate), and velars, sometimes called gutturals (made with the back, or soft, palate). They can be conveniently tabulated as follows:

| | Explosives || Continuants ||
	Voiced	Voiceless	Voiced	Voiceless
Labials	b	p		
Labiodentals			v	f
Dentals	d	t	th, z, zh	th, s, sh
Palatals	g	k		
Velars	g	k		

Since the sound of *h* varies greatly, from a strong breath sound to one so weak that it can scarcely be heard, and since it is spoken with the mouth open and with the tongue in various positions, as may be observed in *hart, hole, heat, hat, hill,* or lost entirely, as in *honor,* it can be classed somewhat vaguely only as "the breath sound *h*".

Two other consonants that vary as regards tongue position according as they are used with front vowels or back ones are the so-called liquids *l* and *r*. They are both made with the tongue up near the roof of the mouth; but while the tongue is pressed up in the formation of *l*, it is relaxed in *r*. This accounts for the difficulty experienced by Chinese speakers in pronouncing *r*; it is easy to confuse the two tongue positions.

Sometimes the nasal passage is not entirely shut off when the breath is being directed against certain vocal organs, and so a nasal consonant arises. With the use of the two lips, nasal labial *m* is produced; with the teeth, the dental *n*; with the hard palate, the palatal *ng*, as in *sing*; and with the soft palate, the velar *ng*, as in *sung*.

Two consonants, *w* and *y*, are known as semivowels and call for special attention because they are of an elusive and slippery nature, sometimes occurring as consonants (when they accompany vowels) and at other times lapsing or merging into vowels (when other consonants are next to them). They represent the two extremes of vowel formation, so to speak, the labial *w* being often due to or accompanying the rounding of the lips for the higher back vowels *o* and *u*, while the palatal *y* sometimes grows out of too much forcing of the tongue up against the roots of the teeth in pronouncing the long vowel heard in *eat*. In *go* and *do* only a rounding of the lips is observable; but when another syllable is added, as in *going* and *doer*, while the medial *w* is not spelled out, it is spoken just as plainly as in *knowing* or *fewer*. Likewise the vowel *y* (= *i*) of *pity* becomes consonantal in *onion* and *menial* (pronounced as two syllables), and in the prolonged cry of *Fire* one often hears a medial consonantal *y*, just as though the word were spelled *fiyer*. Hence *w* and *y* become vowels when used with consonants, and consonants when used with vowels; but since they are transition, or glide, consonants, they have practically no sound and are little more than shaping of tongue to palate (for *y*) or rounding of lips (for *w*).

For a different reason the liquids *l* and *r* and the two nasals *m* and *n* may be used as vowels and constitute entire syllables by themselves, and so are often called vocalic consonants. They are always pronounced with some vibration of the vocal cords, that is to say, with voicing; and when they form the unstressed second syllable of such words as *table*, *river*, *chasm*, and *heaven*, they may be regarded as short, light vowels. Indeed, in the speech of Great Britain, New England, and the Southern states, the final *r* in such words as *river* loses its consonantal character entirely and is pronounced very much like the vowel in *cut*, only more obscurely. When used as vowels, *l*, *m*, *n*, and *r* are always unaccented syllables.

To a certain extent consonants are combined, just as vowels are made into diphthongs. But while the two vowels of a diphthong merge their identities to such an extent that it is difficult to distinguish the two, consonants remain fairly distinct. So *g*, *k*, and *h* may be labialized by the rounding of the lips so that a consonantal *w* is added, giving the combination sound of *gw* in *anguish*, of *kw* in *queer*, and of *hw* in *when*. Likewise explosives may be followed by continuants, producing the sound of *gz* in *exert*, of *ks* in *box* and *socks*, of *dzh* in *jill*, *gin*, *ridge*, and of *tsh* in *rich* and *chill*. Of course these combinations of consonants are not different from others that might be cited, such as *ts* in *lots* and *ps* in *lips*. But in the case of those named first, peculiar spellings disguise their complex character, such as *qu* for *kw*, *x* for *ks*, and *j* or *g* for *dzh*.

21. *A Phonetic Alphabet*

While an attempt has been made in the two foregoing sections to describe the vowels and consonants as clearly and concisely as possible, certain difficulties have been encountered which have necessitated a very cautious selection of illustrative words and some awkward and roundabout explanations. In the discussion of long vowels, for instance, the highest front vowel has been illustrated by the choice of *feel*; but instead one might have chosen, to illustrate this sound, *meter*, *meat*, *machine*, *deceive*, *field*, *key*, *anæmic*, *subpœna*, *quay*, or *people*. For each one of the long vowels has numerous spellings which could be used in the tabulation of the long vowels, and the same is true of the short vowels. As for 'the unaccented vowel', there is no generally accepted spelling for it; it appears, for example, in different forms in the unaccented syllables of *apostrophe*, *city*, *journey*, *pivot*, *gracious*, and *conduit*, and has many other spellings. On the other hand, one letter must often represent several sounds, as, for example, *a* in *hate*, *hall*, *care*, *car*, or *o* in *hot*, *note*, *mother*, *do*. In the case of consonants it was necessary to distinguish the two dental continuants as "*th* as in *these*" and "*th* as in *thin*", and another pair of continuants as "*s* in *measure*" and "*ss* in *succession*". This is awkward and unsatisfactory, and it becomes obvious at once that each sound should have a letter by which it can be represented in writing and printing, exactly and clearly and always in the same manner.

In order to do this, it becomes necessary for students of language in general, not merely the students of English, to agree upon the use of certain existing letters to represent certain sounds, to cast out a few that overlap unnecessarily,

A PHONETIC ALPHABET

as, for example, *c* (for *k* and *s*), and to adopt a few new characters or letters to indicate sounds that cannot be properly spelled by the existing alphabet. Such an alphabet has been gradually agreed upon by students of language, has been recommended by the International Phonetic Association, and is usually known as the phonetic or scientific alphabet.

Before further attention is given to this phonetic alphabet, however, it should be noted that many lexicographers and writers on English pronunciation still use that older and more familiar system which indicates the various vowel and consonant sounds by employing the letters used most commonly today to represent those sounds; for example, $\bar{a}$ as in $\bar{a}le$, $\bar{e}$ as in $\bar{e}ve$, $\overline{oo}$ as in $f\overline{oo}d$, *ch* as in *chair*. For the generality of users of an English dictionary this system has been found easier to understand and to use than the more exact but less familiar scientific phonetic alphabet. Obviously neither system can lay claim to finality and to absolute authority, since the one is based upon Current English representation of our speech sounds as understood and agreed upon by all the users of present-day English but is subject to the limitations and imperfections characteristic of a system that has, like Topsy of story fame, just naturally "growed", whereas the other depends upon the agreement of the phonetic specialists of all lands upon a set of symbols which have been gradually selected from the spellings of various languages or else deliberately coined to satisfy deficiencies in our present system. Neither system of phonetic respelling can be arbitrarily condemned and brushed aside: the one is practicable for people who have only the usual elementary knowledge of English sounds and spellings; the other is almost indispensable for the careful, scientific study of English pronunciation and has, therefore, been adopted for this book.

Part of the phonetic alphabet, which is presented in the following table and which will also be found inside the back cover, will be familiar to speakers and writers of present-day English; but nearly a third of the symbols will seem strange, and a few misleading at first because they are employed in an arbitrary and unusual manner.

PHONETIC ALPHABET

I. *Long Vowels*

[ū] as in *far*
[ǣ] as in *fair* (lower)
[ɛ̄] as in *fair* (higher)
[ē] as in *fail*
[ī] as in *feel*

[ɔ̄] as in *fall*
[ō] as in *foal*
[ū] as in *fool*
[ɜ̄] as in *fur* (higher)
[Λ̄] as in *fur* (lower)

II. *Short Vowels*

[ɑ] as in *folly* (American)
[æ] as in *fat*
[ɛ] as in *fell*
[ɪ] as in *fit*

[ɔ] as in *fortune*
[o] as in *foment*
[ʊ] as in *full*
[ɜ] as in *further*
[Λ] as in *fuss*

The roman letter [a] can be used when a short vowel is heard intermediate between [ɑ] and [æ], as in *flask*. And the symbols [i] and [u] must be employed when short high front and back vowels are heard in syllables of secondary or weakened accentuation. These are more tense and slightly higher than [ɪ] and [ʊ], occurring in such words as *magazine* and *lunatic*.

III. *Unaccented Vowels*

[ə] as in *abóve, jéalous*
[ɪ] as in *mínute, píty*

IV. *Diphthongs*

[ɑɪ] as in *ride, my*
[ɑʊ] as in *house, now*

[ɔɪ] as in *foil, boy*
[ɪu] as in *feud, mule*

PHONETIC ALPHABET (*Continued*)

V. *Consonants*

[b] as in *bold, cob*	[r] as in *run, or*
[d] as in *do, add*	[s] as in *sit, pass*
[f] as in *full, off*	[ʃ] as in *show, cash*
[g] as in *give, go, cog*	[t] as in *top, at*
[h] as in *heard, hold*	[θ] as in *thin, ether*
[k] as in *kill, cold*	[ð] as in *then, either*
[l] as in *light, lone*	[v] as in *vowel, over*
[m] as in *may, come*	[w] as in *waste, away*
[n] as in *no, pin*	[j] as in *yet, onion*
[ŋ] as in *sing, long*	[z] as in *zero, as*
[p] as in *pale, up*	[ʒ] as in *azure*

VI. *Some Consonant Combinations*

[hw] as in *when*	[ks] as in *box, socks*
[gw] as in *Guinevere*	[dʒ] as in *judge, gin, lodge*
[kw] as in *queer, acquit*	[tʃ] as in *chill, rich, catch*
[gz] as in *eggs, exact*	

VII. *Vocalic (or Syllabic) Consonants*

When the vocalic consonants, *l, m, n, r*, are used as unaccented vowels in words like *table, chasm, heaven, father*, a small circle can be placed below each to indicate the fact that it functions as a vowel, as [l̥], [m̥], [n̥], [r̥].

Some symbols (like [ā] in *far*, [b] in *bed*) are English; some will be recognized as conforming to the practice of most Continental European languages (for example, [ē] for the vowel in *fail*, [j] for the initial consonant in *yet*); but some will prove utterly unfamiliar and new to the ordinary writer of any modern language (for example, [ɔ] for the *o* in *fortune*, [ʃ] for the *sh* in *show*). The alphabet, as presented here, has thirty-five distinct letters, thirteen for vowels and twenty-two for consonants, besides an [a] for those who wish to make finer distinctions. Each symbol is presented in brackets and will be so used throughout this book in order to distinguish a phonetic respelling of a sound from the ordinary English spelling.

It will be noted that the letters *c*, *q*, *x*, and *y* have been dropped altogether, and, on the other hand, the six entirely new vowel symbols [æ], [ɛ], [ɔ], [ʌ], [ɜ], [ə], have been added, and also the five new consonant symbols [ʃ] and [ʒ], [θ] and [ð], and [ŋ].

Moreover, the differences in tongue positions of long [ī] and short [ɪ], of long [ū] and short [ʊ], have been emphasized by the use of slightly different types of letters, and the letter *j* has been utilized (in the symbol [j]), as in most Continental languages, to indicate the value of English consonantal *y*.

In contrast to these attempts at careful differentiation of vowels, the possible differences in the pronunciation of front (or palatal) and back (or velar) consonants, especially *g* and *k*, have been ignored in this phonetic alphabet, since speakers of English unconsciously vary these consonants according as they use them with front or with back vowels. Hence the one *g* and the one *k* serve for all tongue positions, forward and back.

The older method of indicating vowel length by the use of the macron, or bar, over the letter, as, for example, *ā*, *ō*, *ū*, has been used in this book; but one can also follow the practice of numerous present-day phoneticians, if he desires, and use a colon (:) after the long vowel, as in [mo:tr] for *motor*.

It should be noted that no silent letters are employed in phonetic writing. Consequently the great number of silent *e's*, as in *rapped, bide, due, type,* must be entirely ignored in changing from the ordinary English spelling to scientific phonetic spelling.

For the purpose of indicating the accentuation of a word, as explained in the following section, two different accent marks have been used. The acute accent (´) is used ordinarily and for the primary accent in words having both primary and secondary accentuation; the grave accent (`) is used for the secondary accent. When two or more letters compose a vowel digraph or vowel trigraph, the accent mark is placed on the first letter of the group. For example, *táble, exàminátion, béautiful.* Inasmuch as the contemporary dictionaries generally follow the different practice of placing the accent after the entire syllable (*gra'di-ent*), and inasmuch as some phoneticians have attempted to introduce the confusing practice of putting the accent before the syllable that is accented (*a'bout*), the practice of putting it exactly above the vowel has been adopted for this book on the ground that the vowel is the heart, or core, of every accented syllable, and if it be marked exactly, there can be no misunderstanding in the matter.

22. *Accentuation*

The influence of accentuation, or stress, on the quantity of a vowel has already been touched upon (Sec. 19). Doubtless, in the reading aloud of the practice sentences on page 76, the tendency of the speaker to stress syllables or words at frequent intervals will have been observed. The amount of stress used in accentuation varies noticeably, the strongest being used when the speaker wishes to give special prominence to a word; it is the succession of accents, or stresses, that gives rhythm to speech, such as would otherwise be lacking. Nouns, verbs, and adjectives are likely to receive more stress, while the little connectives like *and, or, if,* pronouns like *he, it, them,* prepositions like *in, by, from, up,* are usually passed over hurriedly with very little accentuation.

In words of several syllables there are usually two accents, a stronger, primary accent and a weaker, secondary accent.

as in *exàminátion, sùperflúity,* and *pròbabílity.* If the word be shortened to some other derivative form so as to do away with the need of a secondary accent, the stress shifts and the quality and the quantity of the vowels are likely to be changed, as can be seen in the shorter *supérfluous* and *próbable.* Sometimes even the consonants are changed by the shift of accent; a voiceless explosive or continuant is likely to be voiced if it is passed over in the sentence without receiving any stress, and the voiced consonant may become voiceless if it be given unusual stress. While *have* is usually pronounced as little more than [v] in such a sentence as 'I fear I've lost my book', the child, in emphasizing the need of finding the book, would be likely to say 'I just háff to find my book'. The Old English preposition and adverb *of* appears in Modern English with the [v] sound because as a preposition it is seldom stressed; but it has retained the earlier voiceless [f] sound in the adverb *off* because the adverb usually receives a stronger accentuation, especially if it comes near the end of a sentence, as in 'Where should we leave off?'

The sentence has its own accentuation, as well as the word. The beginning and the end of the sentence are likely to receive more stress than other parts; and so, as will be noted again later in the discussion of word order (Sec. 100), words are sometimes moved to the front or relegated to the very end of a sentence in order that they may receive special emphasis.

But aside from the influence that change in sentence stress may have on the form of a word or the emphasis it may receive, variation in the accent of two-syllable words is frequently resorted to in order to distinguish between a verb, on the one hand, and a noun or adjective, on the other, as, for example, in the verb *colléct* and the noun *cóllect,* the verb *contráct* and the noun *cóntract,* the verb *absént* and the adjective *ábsent.* Sometimes, in word pairs of this kind, the removal of the accent from the second syllable to the first also causes unvoicing of a consonant in the last syllable, as in the verb *refúse* and the noun *réfuse.* This change in voicing, however, is due in part to historical developments in the word and not merely to a shift of accent.

23. The Interrelation of Sounds

While it is customary for linguists to speak of the influence of one sound upon another, they mean, of course, the relation of one speech organ to another in the making of speech sounds. If the student of language will keep in mind the physiological aspect of this matter of the interrelation of sounds to one another, he will more easily understand why one combination of sounds, for example, is popular while another is unpopular, and why the bringing together of several sounds as a group may produce marked changes in some members of the group. A vowel, as has already been remarked (Sec. 19), cannot become a long vowel if a consonant stops it too abruptly. Consequently, when two consonants occur in a dissyllabic word, such as *donkey*, *banter*, *chilblain*, or *plaster*, the word is ordinarily so divided that one consonant ends the first syllable, making it a "closed syllable", with a short vowel, and the other consonant introduces the following syllable (for example, *don-key*). Likewise, in a monosyllabic word ending in a consonant, such as *bit*, *at*, *not*, the vowel is likely to be short, since the word is a closed syllable. But when there is only one consonant in the middle of a dissyllabic word, such as *donor*, *later*, *paling*, *notion*, it is taken with the following syllable in the syllabic division of the word, and the first syllable is an "open syllable" and its vowel is usually long (for example, *do-nor*). Also, in a monosyllabic word not ending in a consonant, as, for example, *go*, *no*, *see*, or *by*, the vowel is generally long, because it is in an open syllable.

Some few consonants, however, especially [r], tend to prolong, or draw out, a preceding vowel and at the same time to give it a lower tongue position or quality, as in *far*, *heart*, and *Clark*. On the other hand, a back vowel makes an accompanying [g] or [k] a velar consonant, as in *go*, *call*, whereas the same consonants are palatals when used with front vowels, as in *give* and *kill*. An understanding of this interference of vowels and consonants with each other is very necessary for the historian of language and will help, often, in the study of present-day phonetic tendencies.

In the pronunciation of certain consonant groups, or combinations, also, the tongue does not readily respond, and so one finds difficulty sometimes in speaking a labial and a dental together, as in *fifth, chimney,* and *naphtha,* and in running together a voiced and a voiceless consonant, as in *cupboard, blackguard,* and *cold storage*; and difficulty with a continuant and explosive combination is probably responsible for the silencing of the explosive consonant in *listen, fasten, soften,* and *often*. In the change of the old word *godsib* to *gossip*, the explosive [d] has been assimilated to the continuant [s], and the final voiced [b] has been unvoiced so that it will go better with the voiceless [s].

Sometimes, however, the addition of a prefix or suffix will bring together two distinct vowels or diphthongs in contiguous syllables, producing that "concurrence of two separate vowels without an intervening consonant"[25] which is known as hiatus. The word *hiatus* itself is a good example, and in various others like *egoist, trio, Boethius, coördinate, zoölogy,* and *readjust* some effort is required to keep the two vowels distinct. And in a sentence the same effect is produced at times by the bringing together of two words, as in 'The fire will *go out*' or 'He got *extra ice*.' Pure hiatus is not very common, on the whole, since, as already explained in the discussion of the semivowels (Sec. 20), transition from a front vowel to a back one will usually produce at least a faint palatal "glide" [j], and from a back vowel to a front one, the labial [w], generally. Unless a speaker is very careful, he is likely to say *ego-wist* and *tri-yo* instead of *ego-ist* and *tri-o*. The reason hiatus is not more common in language is that it interrupts the flow of speech.

An intelligent study of the articulate sounds of human speech must be based, then, upon an understanding of the nature and limitations of the organs of speech; and one must expect that these physical limitations will be the same always, generation after generation and century after century, so that the stream of human speech will always have certain permanent characteristics in spite of the ever-changing influence of the psychological factors in language.

Sec. 23]   THE INTERRELATION OF SOUNDS   89

PHONETIC TRANSCRIPTION OF LAST TWO PARAGRAPHS

[General, or Western, American Dialect]

sʌmtɑ́ɪmz, hɑʊévr̥*, ði ədíʃn̥ əv ɑ prífɪks ɔr sʌ́fɪks wɪl bríŋ tugéðr̥* tū́ dɪstíŋkt vɑ́ʊəlz ɔr dífθɔŋz ɪn kəntígɪʊəs síləbl̥z, prodū́sɪŋ ðǽt kɑnkɚ́rəns əv tū́ sépərɪt vɑ́ʊəlz wɪðáʊt æn ɪntrvínɪŋ kɑ́nsənənt hwɪtʃ ɪz nṓn ǽz hɑɪétəs. ðə wɝ́rd hɑɪétəs ɪtsélf ɪz ə gū́d ɛgzǽmpl̥, ænd ɪn vérɪəs ʌ́ðrz* lɑɪk ígoɪst, trío, boíθɪəs, koɔ́rdɪnet, zoɑ́lədʒɪ, ænd rɪədʒʌ́st sʌm éfərt ɪz rɪkwɑ́ɪrd* tu kíp ðə tū́ vɑ́ʊəlz dɪstíŋkt. ænd ɪn ə séntəns ðə sḗm əfékt ɪz prodū́st æt tɑ́ɪmz bɑɪ ðə bríŋɪŋ təgéðr̥* əv tū́ wɝ́rdz, ǽz ɪn ðə fɑ́ɪr* wɪl gō ɑ́ʊt ɔr hi gɑ́t ékstrə ɑ́ɪs. píur* hɑɪétəs ɪz nɑ́t vérɪ kɑ́mən, ɑn ðə hṓl, sɪns, ǽz ɔlrédɪ ɛksplénd ɪn ðə dɪskʌ́ʃən əv ðə sémɑɪvɑ́ʊəlz, trænzíʃən frɑm ə frʌ́nt vɑ́ʊəl tu ə bǽk wʌn wɪl jū́ʒʊəlɪ prodū́s æt líst ə fént pǽlətəl glɑ́ɪd [j], ænd frɑm ə bǽk vɑ́ʊəl tu ə frʌ́nt wʌn, ðə lébɪəl [w], dʒénr̥əlɪ. ʌnlés ə spíkr̥* ɪz vérɪ kérfʊl, hi ɪz lɑ́ɪklɪ tu sḗ ígo-wɪst ænd trí-jo ɪnstéd əv ígo-ɪst ænd trí-o. ðə rízən hɑɪétəs ɪz nɑ́t mṓr* kɑ́mən ɪn lǽŋgwɪdʒ ɪz ðæt ɪt ɪntərʌ́pts ðə flṓ əv spítʃ.

æn ɪntélɪdʒənt stʌ́dɪ əv ði ɑrtíkɪʊlɪt sɑ́ʊndz əv hɪúmən spítʃ mʌst bī́ bḗst, ðén, əpɑ́n æn ʌndr̥stǽndɪŋ əv ðə nétʃɪur* ænd lɪmɪtéʃənz əv ði ɔ́rgənz əv spítʃ ; ænd wʌn mʌst ɛkspékt ðæt ðɪz fízɪkl̥ lɪmɪtéʃəns wɪl bī́ ðə sḗm ɔ́lwez, dʒɛnr̥éʃən ǽftr̥* dʒɛnr̥éʃən ænd séntʃʊrɪ ǽftr̥* séntʃʊrɪ, sō ðæt ðə strím əv hɪúmən spítʃ wɪl ɔ́lwez hæv sɝ́tən pɝ́mənənt kærɪktrístɪks ɪn spɑ́ɪt əv ði ɛvr̥*- tʃɛ́ndʒɪŋ ínflʊəns əv ðə sɑɪkəlɑ́dʒɪkl̥ fǽktr̥z* ɪn lǽŋgwɪdʒ.

* In British, New England, and Southern speech, the final *r* is vocalized and should be transcribed by the symbol [ə].

CHAPTER IV

THE RELATIONS OF ENGLISH TO OTHER LANGUAGES

THE student of English who has made a study of one or more foreign languages, particularly the classical Greek and Latin and the modern German, Swedish, French, Spanish, or Italian, will undoubtedly have observed that in certain respects there exist similarities between the English and the foreign tongues which suggest a relationship both in general and in numerous details. The more thoughtful student will have noted that even in the general plan, or make-up, of these languages, especially in the methods of inflecting words and in the arrangement of sentences, the languages correspond; and even the superficial observer cannot fail to see that in numerous instances words look somewhat alike in spite of minor differences. The resemblance of words may, of course, be due to the fact that many words have been borrowed from these languages and adopted into the English vocabulary. But after one has traced back many good old English words and found them in constant use even in the very earliest Anglo-Saxon, such words as *man, father, bring, bear* (verb), *fish, can* (auxiliary verb), and *mouse,* one is forced to the conclusion that a relationship exists and has long existed which cannot be explained merely on the ground of borrowing from one language to another. The words are too numerous and the correspondences in both form and meaning are too striking to be accounted for by any other explanation than that of relationship due to a common origin of the languages involved. So the question gradually forces itself upon the student of languages: How many of these modern languages are related through common descent from a more primitive ancestor, and just how close is the relationship?

A satisfying answer to this question can come only after a careful comparison of the modern languages and a following back of each to its earliest forms. Since it is not the purpose of this discussion to enter into the history of languages, either English or foreign, the proofs will not be examined in detail; the relationships which many philological students have carefully worked out will be taken for granted, and the genealogy or relationship presented as briefly as possible, with some of the evidence to illustrate the relationship.

24. *Cognate Languages*

Philologists have adopted the term *cognate languages* as meaning "related through descent from a common linguistic ancestor", just as in general the term *cognate* is applied to persons descended from the same ancestor. If one is willing to forego for the moment any consideration of the more striking resemblances of certain languages of the great linguistic family to which English belongs, and also to bear in mind two difficulties that lie in the way of establishing definitely linguistic family relationships, — namely, the fact that linguistic genealogists have been at work proving these relationships and tracing them less than two centuries, and, secondly, that the only factual evidence which the philologist has for establishing proof consists of the relatively recent written literature of the languages involved, including, of course, the earliest inscriptions, — then it is possible to begin this discussion by accepting the conclusion of philological historians that long before the dawn of history, in some portion of the world earlier thought to be the Mesopotamian country of the Tigris and Euphrates, but more recently regarded as probably farther west in the region of southeastern Europe rather than in Asia, a race of people sometimes called the Aryan or Indo-Germanic, but most commonly named by philologists the Indo-European, used a language which was different from a hundred or more employed by other races scattered over the earth.[135] This language was distinctive in that it gradually developed a system of inflection for nouns, pronouns, adjectives, and verbs, whereas some others, like the Chinese, have no such inflection at all; it employed a set of vowel and consonant sounds which in many instances can be definitely traced down into modern tongues if one applies certain laws of sound change; and it gave to us many words whose descent can be satisfactorily traced by the understanding of the common inflectional forms and the application of the laws of sound change cited above. Sounds, inflectional forms, and word forms and word meanings must, of course, be reconstructed very cautiously by the method of deduction, since no literature is extant in this primitive Indo-European language, since the language would naturally not be a well-developed and highly polished one but rather one serving the needs of a crude and very primitive culture, and since, moreover, the growth of the language in its descendent racial branches would not be an unmixed and continuous growth but would be liable to foreign interminglings and contaminations, as can be seen in the case of the English language. But there are some nine great branches of this linguistic family which possess so many distinctive features in common that their unique ancestry seems pretty well established.*

These groups, or branches, of the Indo-European family are: the Indian, which in the course of many centuries has included various tongues of India, notably the older religious and scholarly Sanskrit, Prakrit, and Pali, and the modern Hindustani, Bengali, Hindi, etc.; secondly, the Persian (or Iranian), comprising the Old Persian and the sacred Zend, or Avestan, as well as the Modern Persian; thirdly, the Armenian of Asia Minor; fourthly, the Hellenic, embracing the various Greek dialects of Attica, Ionia, Doris, Sparta, the Æolian group, etc.; fifthly, the Albanian, employed by the relatively small race of Albanians; sixthly, the Italic, including Oscan, Umbrian, Latin, and others; seventhly, the great Balto-Slavic branch, with the Old Prussian, Lithuanian, and Lettic of the Baltic region, and the neighboring Russian,

* A tenth branch, known as Tocharian, has been assumed recently because of the discovery of certain fragmentary texts in East Turkestan; but its characteristics are too vaguely known to warrant its inclusion here.

Bulgarian, Czech (or Bohemian), Polish, etc.; eighthly, the Germanic, or so-called Teutonic, with which the student of English is primarily concerned; and, ninthly, the Celtic of Gaul, Ireland, Wales, the Scottish Highlands, etc.

Since the Germanic branch had become definitely separated from the rest of the Indo-European family only a few centuries before Christ, it is possible to bring together some fragmentary evidence bearing upon the history and development of this branch, particularly upon the social and political conditions that caused it in turn to break up into a great number of dialects and subdialects. When Cæsar took charge of the Roman armies in Gaul in 58 B.C., one of his chief tasks was to overcome a centrifugal force in Germany which was impelling various overgrown tribes to burst out across the Rhine and seek more spacious and richer homes. From that time on, the pages of history have been filled with accounts of various Germanic peoples that made excursions in search of better homes; the Goths went into the Danube valley and thence into Italy and southern France; the Franks seized what was later called France; the Vandals went down into Spain, and via Africa they "vandalized" Rome; the Angles, part of the Saxons, and the Jutes moved over into England; and the Burgundians and the Lombards worked south into France and Italy.

Probably very early during these centuries of migration the three outstanding groups of the Germanic peoples — the North Germanic people of Scandinavia, the East Germanic branch, comprising the Goths chiefly, and the West Germanic group, comprising the remaining Germanic tribes — developed their notable group traits. Then, while the East Germanic tribes (that is, the Goths) passed gradually out of the pages of history and disappeared completely, the North Germanic, or Scandinavian, or Norse, peoples, as they are variously called, became a distinctive people, more and more unlike the West Germanic folk who inhabited Germany itself and, ultimately, Holland and Belgium and England. While that great migration of nations which the Germans have named the *Völkerwanderung* was going on, the Scandinavian division of the Germanic peoples had kept their habitation well to the north of the others and had been splitting up into the four subdivisions now known as the Swedes, Norwegians, Danes, and Icelanders. Long after the West Germanic and East Germanic peoples had made history farther south in Europe, the North Germanic tribes of Scandinavia began a series of expeditions which, during the eighth and ninth centuries, in the so-called Viking Age especially, led them to settle Iceland, to overrun England and even annex it to Denmark temporarily, and, most important of all, to settle in northern France and merge with the French to such an extent that *Northmen* became *Normans*, and later these Normans became the conquerors of England.

During these centuries following Cæsar's attempts to stem the tide of Germanic expansion and scattering, the Germans of the highlands of southern Germany and the upper Rhine region developed a new set of consonant sounds which have more or less persisted down to the present day, separating their so-called High German from the Low German of the numerous tribes that remained in the lowland country of northern Germany and also the few lowland tribes that migrated to England. While the shift of consonants did not remain quite as clear-cut as it was at first, nevertheless the literary German of today, the Austrian German, and the Swiss German stand apart from the Dutch of Holland, the Frisian of North Holland, the Flemish Dutch of Belgium, the Plattdeutsch, or Low German, of northern Germany, and, finally, the English. Whereas the English has *tide* and the Dutch *tijd*, the High German has *zeit*; whereas the English has *word* and the Dutch *woord*, the High German has *wort*; for English *to give* and Dutch *te geven*, the High German has *zu geben*.

But there are some words that show little or no change in the consonants, such as English *land*, which has the same spelling, though not quite the same pronunciation, in High German, in Dutch, and even in Swedish, Danish, and Icelandic. So also English *winter* and *summer* appear in Danish as *winter* and *sommer*, in High German as *winter* and *sommer*,

The Genealogy of the English Language

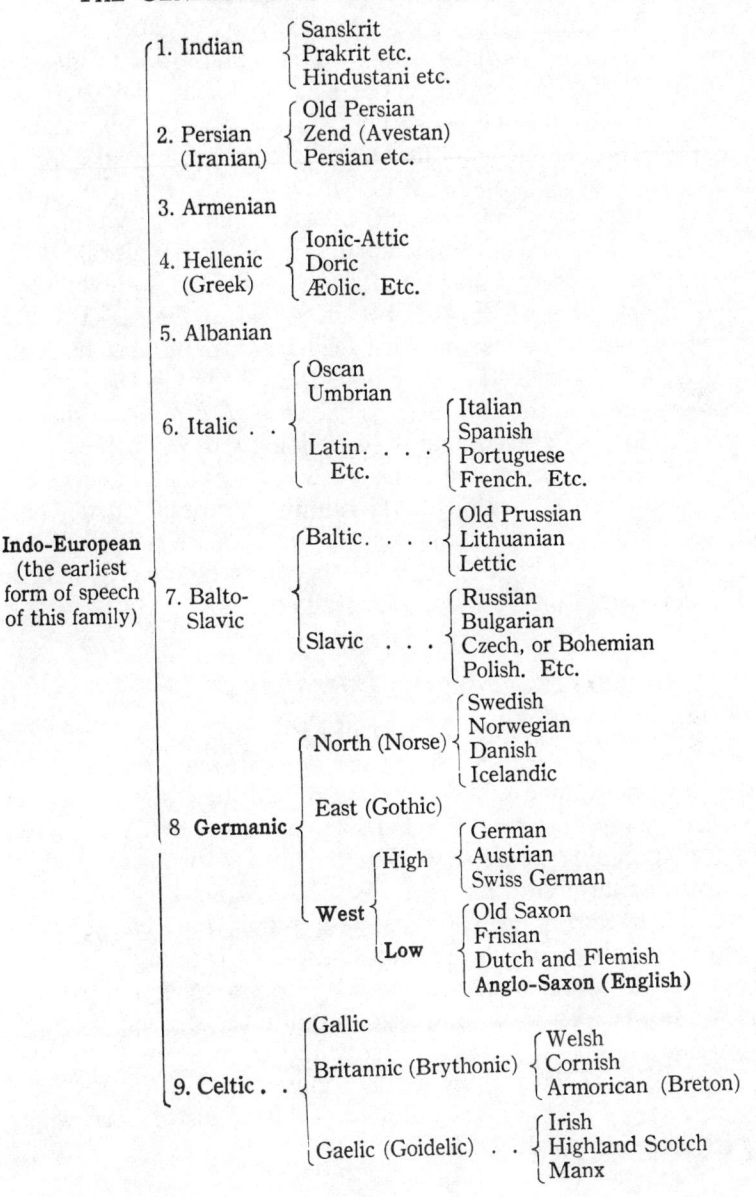

Indo-European (the earliest form of speech of this family)

1. Indian
   - Sanskrit
   - Prakrit etc.
   - Hindustani etc.

2. Persian (Iranian)
   - Old Persian
   - Zend (Avestan)
   - Persian etc.

3. Armenian

4. Hellenic (Greek)
   - Ionic-Attic
   - Doric
   - Æolic. Etc.

5. Albanian

6. Italic
   - Oscan
   - Umbrian
   - Latin. Etc.
     - Italian
     - Spanish
     - Portuguese
     - French. Etc.

7. Balto-Slavic
   - Baltic
     - Old Prussian
     - Lithuanian
     - Lettic
   - Slavic
     - Russian
     - Bulgarian
     - Czech, or Bohemian
     - Polish. Etc.

8. Germanic
   - North (Norse)
     - Swedish
     - Norwegian
     - Danish
     - Icelandic
   - East (Gothic)
   - West
     - High
       - German
       - Austrian
       - Swiss German
     - Low
       - Old Saxon
       - Frisian
       - Dutch and Flemish
       - **Anglo-Saxon (English)**

9. Celtic
   - Gallic
   - Britannic (Brythonic)
     - Welsh
     - Cornish
     - Armorican (Breton)
   - Gaelic (Goidelic)
     - Irish
     - Highland Scotch
     - Manx

and in Dutch as *winter* and *zomer*. The English verb *mean* is in Danish *mene* and in High German *meinen*.

In inflectional forms numerous correspondences will be noted, although the dialects of the Germanic branch differ in the forms that they prefer; the English forms the plural of nouns with *-s*, as in *clocks*, but it has a few plurals in *-en*, such as *oxen*, it changes the vowel in a few nouns like *teeth*, and it has even a dialectal plural *childer* in *-er*; the High German uses *-e*, *-r*, and *-en* and internal change of vowel, for the most part, and does not normally use the *-s* plural; the Danish has usually a plural ending in *-e* or *-r*, as, for example, *heste*, plural of *hest*, 'horse', *kroner*, plural of *krone*, 'crown'. If one looks in the Latin third declension of nouns, he will find several plurals that resemble the Germanic *-n* plurals, represented by the *-in* nouns like *homo*, *homines*, 'man', 'men'. And so the comparative philologist goes farther and farther afield, finding the same word in various languages of the Indo-European family, and running across frequent correspondences in inflectional forms, until, as we remarked at the beginning of this chapter, he becomes convinced of the common origin of the languages studied.

25. *English Borrowings*

Though a fairly large number of Modern English words, as well as most of the inflectional and derivational apparatus of the language, have come down to us through direct line of descent, as indicated by the names printed in bold-faced type in the foregoing genealogy (that is, from a primitive Indo-European, through Germanic, West Germanic, Low German, into Anglo-Saxon, or Old English), more than half of the words contained in the English dictionary cannot be traced back as far as Old English at all. So the question arises, How did the English language acquire these alien words? And the answer is, By later borrowings from a great variety of sources, especially from cognate languages. Since the circumstances which led to various notable spells of borrowing need some detailed explanation, they will be enlarged upon in Chapter V, which will deal in a general way with the linguistic history of the English people; and since the borrowings themselves need much careful study, they will be taken up more in detail in Chapter IX, which will attempt to classify the borrowings and trace some of them to their various sources. But in order that the truly remarkable indebtedness of the English language may be appreciated from the very start, a superficial analysis of the vocabulary of the present day will prove suggestive and helpful.

In estimating the proportion of loan-words to native words, philologists have employed various methods of calculation and consequently have gained quite different results. Numerous loan-words will be found in the English dictionary which are rarely met with in either written or spoken English, such as *discalceate, quadrillion,* and *pandiculated.* Some of these are probably "hothouse words" and never have seen much use,[139] while others are brought out only on the rare occasions when a learned man wishes to express an idea very exactly and carefully. A very much smaller number of loan-words will be found in the printed pages of the best contemporary novelists, — such words as *simile, prowess, contemplate, habiliments,* and *unappeasable,* — while the loan-words used by the ordinary speaker of standard colloquial English are so few compared with the number of good old Anglo-Saxon terms that the vocabulary of the dictionary appears almost neglected in comparison with the spoken vocabulary.

Moreover, in estimating the importance of the borrowed element in English, some philologists count each word only once, no matter how often it is used, whereas others count all occurrences of all words. These two methods give, of course, very different results; and when they are applied to two different levels of speech, the differences are astonishing. In his *History of the English Language*[10] (p. 126), Emerson has shown the proportion of native and foreign words used by various English authors, the percentages being gained by counting every occurrence of each word. Some of his figures, which have been quoted many times since they were first compiled by an earlier scholar, are as follows:

	NATIVE	FOREIGN
Shakespeare	90 per cent	10 per cent
Bible (three Gospels)	94 per cent	6 per cent
Addison	82 per cent	18 per cent
Gibbon	70 per cent	30 per cent
Tennyson	88 per cent	12 per cent

A study was made recently for the Bell Telephone System of some five hundred telephone conversations and the words listed in order according to the frequency of their occurrence. Of the first hundred listed in order of frequency, 83 per cent were of native origin and 17 per cent foreign, and of the 17 per cent most were borrowings from the Scandinavian language as used at one time in England.[376]

In marked contrast to these results, an examination of the first page of the preface to Krapp's *Knowledge of English* [18] (p. iii) reveals only sixty-five different words of native origin (scarcely 43 per cent), eighty-six words borrowed from other languages (over 56 per cent), and one hybrid constructed with a native prefix and a borrowed stem.

In a study of some twenty thousand words made by Vizetelly, the editor of the Standard Dictionary, in 1915 [140], some of the more important elements of the English vocabulary appear as follows:

Anglo-Saxon and English	3681 words	= about 19 per cent
French, from Latin	5671 words	= about 29 per cent
Latin, direct	2880 words	= about 15 per cent
Greek, direct or indirect	2493 words	= about 13 per cent

Since this study is based upon not more than one twentieth of the words contained in a complete Modern English dictionary, one cannot, of course, take these percentages too seriously. But a count of the lists of native and borrowed words arranged in the back of Skeat's Etymological Dictionary (Fourth Edition, pp. 761–776) gives very similar results, as can be seen from the following table of distribution. While the figures in this table may need slight revision because some of Skeat's etymologies have been questioned by later students, on the whole the picture that is given of the make-up of the English vocabulary is a trustworthy one.

English	3339 words = about 22.6 per cent
French, from Latin	3895 words = about 26.4 per cent
Latin, direct	2339 words = about 15.8 per cent
Greek, direct or indirect	1646 words = about 11.2 per cent
Scandinavian	669 words = about 4.5 per cent
Other Germanic words	792 words = about 5.4 per cent
Celtic	166 words = about 1.1 per cent
Other Romanic words	655 words = about 4.4 per cent
Slavonic	32 words
Persian and Indian	162 words
Non-Indo-European of Europe	20 words
Non-Indo-European of Asia	400 words
Non-Indo-European of Africa	32 words
Non-Indo-European of America	101 words
Hybrids	488 words
Etymology unknown	14 words
	14,750 words

In attempting to reconcile the very different results gained from the last four studies of the component elements of the English vocabulary, it is necessary to bear in mind that the first and second deal with the *used* vocabulary of the present day, the one that of many individual telephone conversations and the other that of a scholar writing a technical book, whereas the third and fourth are concerned with the *recorded* vocabulary and comprise many words which the ordinary speaker of English may never have encountered, such as *crake, rantipole, pompelmoose*, in Skeat's list. Moreover, the third and fourth studies are based upon only a portion of the contents of a complete Modern English dictionary. Since it is probable that many of the words not considered by Skeat and Vizetelly are words of highly specialized meaning, it is likely that a majority of them are of Latin or Greek origin, which would increase the percentages of those two sources of borrowing. This would seem to corroborate the statements of Grinstead, who concluded in a recent report on the Latin-English word count of the American Classical League that "(1) By any system of counting other than unweighted frequency, Latin comprises fully half of the English vocabulary, (2) about one fourth of the English vocabulary is native, and (3) Greek furnishes about one tenth of the English vocabulary." [144]

Of course the influence of foreign languages upon English has not been confined entirely to that of introducing a great part of the vocabulary, although that is by far the most important phase of foreign influence. English spelling has numerous earmarks of foreign influence, such as the *u* in *guess* and *guest* (a French method of indicating the so-called hard sound of the *g*), the *b* inserted by overzealous scholars in *debt* and *doubt* because they happened to know that the original Latin forms had been *debitus* and *dubitare*, the French endings *-re* and *-ue* in *metre* and *catalogue*.* It would not be surprising if some day the English ending *-ive* of such words as *adjective* and *native* should lose the *-e* through the foreign influence of German and other languages which spell the ending without the *-e* (cf. German *adjektiv*, French *adjectif*, and so on).

A few noticeably foreign constructions remain in English usage, as, for example, the use of the adjective after its noun in *knights errant*, *letters patent*, and *sum total*. In the use of late borrowings from the Latin there is still much trouble over the formation of the plural of such nouns as *gladiolus*, *cactus*, *index*, *phenomenon*, and *memorandum*. In America, especially, foreign speakers have introduced quite widely certain idiomatic uses of English based upon their own ancestral idioms, and one frequently hears 'Leave it go' (for 'Let it go') and 'He was waiting on the station' (for 'at the station'), both German-American usages.

For four centuries, ever since the Englishman became actively interested in developing a more elaborate and sophisticated vocabulary, there has been an almost continuous debate between those persons who would improve the language by introducing foreign words and phrases and those other writers and scholars who would keep the language "pure" by restricting it to native words. One ardent "purifier", William Barnes, even went so far as to publish, in 1878, *An Outline of English Speech-Craft*, from which he rigidly excluded all the old borrowed terms of English grammar, substituting *word-strain* for 'accent', *thing-names* for 'nouns', *outreaching* for

---

* Simplification of English spelling has led some lexicographers to give precedence to *meter* and *catalog*.

transitive', *time-taking word* for 'verb', and so on.[141] The chief trouble with his grammar is that his words coined from "our own strong old Anglo-Saxon speech" carry little meaning for the reader, as a rule. Barnes is more concerned about the elements entering into the make-up of his words than he is about the way they function in conveying ideas and thoughts. A similar misunderstanding of the nature of a live and functioning language is displayed by a writer who said in *The Library* [142] in 1891 (p. 294):

> Leave out all that is not Saxon in our tongue, and we have still left us a speech, of itself enough for all the great needs of our outer and of our inner life; a speech, too, that has in it a strength and a power of growth from its own inborn sources which, if it only got free play, would fit it for all the new uprising wants of our growing enlightenment.

It is but fair to those writers who protest so vehemently against the use of polysyllabic borrowed words and learned phrases to confess that many half-educated users of English have employed these borrowed words with no exact comprehension of their real meaning; but it should be urged also that many good old native words are being constantly given quite new and unfamiliar meanings which only the specialist in up-to-date slang can hope to comprehend. The sensible student of English will apply to the matter of borrowing those same tests which we have suggested in a preliminary discussion of linguistic standards (Sec. 8).

This controversy between the conservative purists and the enrichers, or borrowers, owes its vitality in more recent times largely to the fact that the controvertists have failed to recognize that for different speech levels and different attendant circumstances, different vocabularies are required. The more learned and less shopworn words of classical origin, for example, are necessary for the discussion of abstruse scientific or philosophical matters; for the conversations of everyday life, often more emotional than intellectual, the simpler native words are likely to serve better. Some words are like the instruments of the skillful surgeon; they must be kept carefully segregated and rarely used because their fine edges are needed for very special operations. These are very largely words that have been borrowed. The blunter but more powerful native words are in constant use by all kinds of careless speakers, and some of them have become so worn and changed as to be no longer recognizable as tools intended for special kinds of work. Some of them are now merely "counter words", as Krapp has called them. Lounsbury summed up the need of both native and foreign elements in the English of today when he said, in his article "The French Element in English" [143] (p. 700):

All poetry which gives utterance to deep emotion contains comparatively few terms of Latin origin; of recent Latin origin, hardly any at all. But the moment we leave the domain of common life, the moment we come to the consideration of matters which appeal to the intellect rather than to the heart, the inadequacy of the native element to express what we have to say forces itself upon the attention. In abstract discussion, philosophical disquisition, historic investigation, not merely the extensive but the preponderating use of the Romanic element becomes a necessity.

It is not true, however, that all words of colloquial and commonplace English are of native origin and that the literary and scientific terms are all borrowed from other languages. While we have taken over the German *Weltgeist* and *kindergarten*, and the French *amateur, flair*, and *connoisseur*, we have also adopted the German *sauerkraut* and *wienerwurst* and the French *beef, sausage*, and *marmalade*. It is true that the English have borrowed more learnedly from the Greeks and Romans, and have received more of the words pertaining to everyday life from those peoples with whom they have had closer contacts, such as the Danes, Normans, and Dutch.

26. *Foreigners' English*

While the use of the term *borrowing* in the study of the English language is a convenient one, it must be admitted that the word may prove somewhat misleading unless it is carefully defined and its meaning, in two important respects, modified.

For one thing, borrowing implies returning or repaying that which has been borrowed, and it is obvious from the foregoing discussion that a great many foreign words have become the permanent property of English, while, on the other hand, the English language has repaid this great "loan" by contributing comparatively few words to other languages, although, as we shall see in surveying the spread of English (Sec. 27), the other languages have been showing increasingly the influence of English during the last few generations. Still, though more than half of the English vocabulary has been borrowed, no such proportion of English words can be found in any foreign language.

Then, again, one is apt to think of a borrower as going out and asking for a loan, whereas a very large part of our loan-words have been brought into England or, more recently, into America by the foreigners themselves. After the Angles, Saxons, and Jutes had established the English language in England, the Danes spent more than two centuries in over-running and conquering Anglo-Saxon England, and then for two centuries more the Normans were busy ruling England and living there. It is true that since the Norman period of English history Englishmen have gone abroad and brought back into the language a very great number of words from all parts of the earth. But in America at the present time, as we have already noted in discussing certain foreign-English dialects (Sec. 16, *b*), as the result of peaceful invasions by immigrants speaking German, the Scandinavian tongues, Yiddish, Mexican Spanish, and other languages, American speech has been acquiring a miscellaneous collection of words, idioms, meanings, and even some noticeable changes in pronunciation in some communities. Indeed, it is surprising that the influence of foreigners' speech in the United States is not greater when one considers that in 1910, out of a total of 64,000,000 whites ten years old and over, almost 13,000,000 were foreign-born and nearly 3,000,000 were unable to speak English.[149] In a few decades the linguistic influence of so large a proportion of foreign-born speakers of English might well be very great.

A second important influence has been exerted upon the English language when speakers of English have carried it into large areas of the earth where they have secured political or economic dominion over foreign peoples. In India, for example, the English language has taken unto itself a great number of native terms; in the English language as spoken in Australia and Canada, and in Hawaii and the Philippines, foreign words are numerous; Jamaican English differs from these; and in South Africa the Boer tongue has left its stamp on the English. If the world continues to grow smaller and to be more closely knit together with improvements in transportation and communication, these imperial or colonial forms of English will contribute more and more to the general body of the English language (see Sec. 16, *b*).

But while foreigners have acquired the English language through immigration into England and the United States of America, and while the language has been carried to great masses of foreign peoples scattered over the earth, an increasing number of foreigners have been studying it in their own countries, voluntarily, for cultural or business purposes. Indeed, since the end of the Middle Ages and the beginning of printing, textbooks, dictionaries, and the like have been produced in great quantities for the use of those foreigners who would learn to speak and read the English language (see Sec. 27, p. 109).

Foreigners find certain difficulties in learning to speak the English language; and it is important for the student of English to understand these difficulties as they have been encountered by foreigners settling in England and America, by whole races forced to learn the language as it has been introduced into their midst, and by other millions scattered over the earth who have voluntarily sought to learn to speak it, because the cumulative effect of the use of English by so great a number and variety of foreigners has been very marked in the course of the centuries of English history.

One of their chief difficulties lies, of course, in the pronunciation of English sounds and especially in pronouncing the dental continuants [θ] and [ð], as in *three* and *then*; they often simplify [hw], as in *where*, to [w], pronouncing it as in *wear*; the [r] causes trouble for the Chinese speaker because he confuses it with [l]; the vowel [ɜ], as in *her, worry, hurt*, is unfamiliar and hard to reproduce. Of course the spelling of English causes the foreigner much trouble because it is not consistent or logical, and moreover is much farther removed from the Continental European spellings than any other modern spelling system, for the reason that it has not been materially changed and brought up to date since the end of the Middle Ages. A foreigner is likely to pronounce such words as *conduit, corps, massacre*, and *often* just as they are spelled, and he is quite sure to pronounce as a separate syllable the ending *-ed* of such verb forms as *walked, reached*, and *preached* until he becomes accustomed to the silent *e*. Nearly a century ago the great German philologist Jacob Grimm remarked that the "whimsical, antiquated orthography" of the English language stood in the way of its universality, and more recently the Swedish scholar Zachrisson, in recommending English as an auxiliary world tongue, has added [152]:

Not only Jacob Grimm but everybody who has had the time and the opportunity of seriously considering these matters, will have to admit that of all languages of culture English has the most antiquated, inconsistent and illogical spelling.

The second obstacle which the foreigner has to overcome in learning to use the English language accurately consists in the unusual number of synonyms and in the wide range of meanings possessed by certain words and phrases. If he happens to look into *Putnam's Word Book*, for example, under the heading "Stiff", he will find offered him some thirty-five words, more or less synonymous, among which are *inflexible, rigid, firm, unbending, inelastic, stark, impliable, rigorous, unyielding, inductile; strong, violent, forcible, inopposable; pertinacious, obstinate, tenacious*. If it puzzles an English or American writer to select from this list just the right word, how much more will it defy the ingenuity of a foreigner? On the other hand, the trouble that the foreigner has with certain words in English has long been a matter of comment. "One of the most perplexing features of the English tongue", wrote one foreigner some years ago, " is the fact that, as a rule, the same word has different significations. My dictionary attributes to the verbs *see, lead, hold,* and *draw* 14, 18, 19, and 32 meanings, respectively. Now, for a foreigner to be able to distinguish all their various meanings is a herculean task. The words which have only one or two meanings are comparatively very few. Is it surprising that a foreigner is often puzzled by the numerous and sometimes opposite meanings of many an English word? Just for an illustration consider the perplexity of a persevering Frenchman arising from the word *fast,* as is shown from the following dialogue:

'Zis horse, sair, he go queek, what you say?'

'Yes, he is a *fast* horse.'

'Ah, pardon, monsieur, but your friend say he make *fast* his horse, and he tie him to a post so he no go at all.'

'Very true: he is made fast by being tied.'

'Ah, zat cannot be: he cannot go fast. But what you call a man that keeps *fast*?'

'O, he is a good man that does not eat on *fast* days.'

'But I have seen one bon vivant, who eat and drink and ride, and do everything. Ze people say he is a bad man — he is very *fast.*'

'True, that is called living a *fast* life.'

'Ah, certainement; zen all ze days of his life must be *fast* days.'

'Certainly they are.'

'Eh, bien. Does he eat every day?'

'Certainly he does.'

'Zen how can he keep *fast*?'

'Why, he keeps going, to be sure.'

'Vy, you tell me to stand *fast* when you want me to keep still, and go *fast* when you want me to run — how can I understand?'" [65]

Beyond these difficulties, however, there await the foreigner a vast number of grammatical niceties, peculiar idioms, and modern slang locutions with which he must familiarize himself if he is to speak the English language like a native. A very nice feeling for word order would impel an American to say 'to send *them to us*', whereas a foreign scholar recently wrote, "You believed you would be able to send *us them*", not realizing that one can place a simple dative pronoun before a noun object but ordinarily not before a pronoun object in English. In any language a foreigner finds native idioms (see Sec. 5) which perplex him, because an idiom cannot be analyzed word by word through the use of the ordinary dictionary. Hence a foreign student of English might well inquire, "How could a man *be beside himself with anxiety?*" Such a sentence as 'He set about winding up his affairs', with the idiomatic use of *set about* and the colloquial phrase *winding up* (for 'finishing'), might well puzzle the most astute foreigner.

27. *The Spread of English*

Yet in spite of difficulties experienced by foreigners in learning it, the English language has spread amazingly during the nineteenth century and the early decades of the twentieth. Just how extensive the use of English has become one cannot easily say. Varying statistics have been given as to the number of people employing the English language as their native tongue: Brander Matthews estimated nearly 130,000,000 about 1900 [153]; Vizetelly placed the number at 150,000,000 in 1915 [156]; and Zachrisson raised the figure to 200,000,000 in 1930 [177]. Schinz has quoted a certain Englishman's calculations regarding the probable relative growth of English, Russian, and German during the twentieth century, with his conclusion that "if the probable increase is calculated at the average rate of the last four centuries, the end of the twentieth century will show the following figures: English spoken by 640 million; Russian by 233; German by 210" [154]. Since, however, the future growth of languages may not go according to their past developments, these figures must be accepted with some reservation.

In addition to these figures, showing the number of persons using the English language as their native tongue, an effort has been made to compile others to show the number of foreigners familiar with the language or likely to come into contact with it: one writer stated in 1929 that "it is the native tongue of 160,000,000 and is understood by 60,000,000 more" [160]; another maintains that it "is spoken by more than two hundred million people, and is the administrative language of five hundred millions, i.e. one third part of the world's population" [177].

Lest these estimates seem utterly preposterous, it will be well to pause a moment and consider the spread of the English-speaking peoples geographically and politically. In England, Scotland, Ireland, and Wales, some 50,000,000 users of English represent the core of this great world body, the speakers of English. Greatly overshadowing this parent, the one-time colony the United States of America now numbers 120,000,000 more speakers of the same tongue. Scattered over the earth, but a part still of the great British Empire, lie Canada, Australia, New Zealand, certain of the West Indies, and the Union of South Africa, totaling half as many people as the British Isles themselves. Then, in addition to these more or less closely affiliated groups of English-speaking peoples, at least 400,000,000 more people are at present dominated by Great Britain in India, Palestine, Malaya, Northwest Africa, Egypt, Central Africa, and numerous islands of Oceania. Likewise the language of the United States is the official tongue in Hawaii, the Philippines, and the Canal Zone. These English-speaking groups are so placed, moreover, that almost every large section of the earth has its English-speaking country. All of North America is English-speaking except Mexico and Central America. Little of South America is politically English, but nonetheless English has penetrated to almost every part of the continent, largely through the channels of business and travel. More than a quarter of Africa is under British control or protection, notably a great strip running from Cairo to Cape Town. All of Australia is English. The great part of Asia comprised in India is under English influence, and the English have traded so long with China and Japan that a special jargon, pidgin English, has developed. Only the continent of Europe is free from English political control, but on this continent, more than any other with the exception of North America and

Australia, the English language has been studied in schools and learned for purposes of travel and trade by many foreigners. And, finally, in every one of the great seas numerous islands are inhabited by people speaking English as their native or else as their official tongue, in the West Indies, in Oceania, in the Philippines, and so on.

But not only have the numbers of inhabitants of English-speaking lands and of peoples under English and American dominion greatly increased during the past century, but a most remarkable interest has been manifested in English by people of other lands who have learned to read and speak it for commercial or cultural reasons. The English-speaking traveler can go almost anywhere in the larger cities of the world today and find people who can speak his own tongue. The hotels, tourist bureaus, clerks in stores and offices, professors in universities, clergymen, statesmen, and the educated people in general, provide English for the traveler who knows no foreign tongue. The manager of a European office of one of the great travel companies remarked recently that if he wished to send a communication to any part of the world and be reasonably certain that it would find someone who could understand it, he wrote it in English.

It is also interesting to note the swing to English since the World War by those scholars of Holland, the Scandinavian countries, and elsewhere who are writing learned articles and books for an international public. Writing for journals which welcome articles written in German, French, or English, especially, many scholars choose English as a medium of communication who at one time would doubtless have written in German or French. Diplomacy has become largely bilingual at Geneva and elsewhere, employing both French and English, whereas not many years ago French would have been employed exclusively.[160]

Perhaps the best way of gauging the increase in the study of English in foreign countries is to investigate the teaching of the subject in the schools abroad. There has been much discussion lately by Continental educators as to whether French or English should be the "first foreign language" in

Continental schools. Indeed, when one considers that until a few decades ago French was "*the* foreign language" in all such schools, the very fact that there is a debate between advocates of the two languages is significant. "English", says Karpf, the Austrian scholar, "is at present the first language in a slowly but steadily increasing number of secondary schools (for boys and girls) in Germany" [158]. Another writer has stated that "Latvia (Lettland) has decided to adopt English as its second language, there is a marked increase in the study of English in Lithuania, and English is obligatory in the modern section in the Gymnasia of Rumania" [177]. Professor Carnoy of the University of Louvain is quoted as saying: "The hold England has now on the Near East will be a decisive factor. French and Italian will gradually be replaced in the Mohammedan world by English" [177]. Speaking of the use of English in Italian schools, Emilio Re said in 1919 [165]:

Ten chairs for the teaching of the English language and literature have this year been founded at the various universities. And this, we may say, has placed the crowning arch on the teaching of English in the State Schools of Italy — which began, as we saw, sixty years ago, in 1859.

From Sweden comes interesting testimony to the widespread use of English in the fact that when a leading Stockholm newspaper made a survey of representative business and professional men and of people in various walks of life, it was found that every fourth person addressed in Stockholm was able to understand or speak English. In 1926 Ichikawa, Japanese student of English philology, wrote [166]:

To-day English is taught as a compulsory subject in all secondary schools (age 12–15), five to seven hours a week being devoted to it, and it is continued in High Schools, or, more properly, Colleges (age 16–18), i.e. preparatory to Universities. In recent years English has been taken up in a few primary schools (age 6–11), but the results still remain to be seen.

Similar evidence of the growth of interest in the English language comes from Mexico [169], Holland [34], the Philippines [170], Russia [171], and many other countries.

Partly because of the increased study of English abroad and partly because of the more intimate contacts between these foreign countries and the English-speaking peoples, there has been an increasing influx of English words and phrases into foreign languages. Naturally one of the countries earliest invaded by English locutions was France. Words pertaining to sport, daily life, business and governmental customs, have been trickling into the French language since about 1660, and one notes, for instance, *bifteck* ('beefsteak'), *blackbouler* ('to blackball'), *boulingrin* ('bowling green'), *plaid, poudingue* ('pudding'), *redingote* ('riding coat'), *rosbif* ('roast beef'), *sport*.[163] Modern German has adopted, likewise, words pertaining to sports, clothing, English and American inventions and customs, and the like, such as *Caddy, Elevatoren* ('elevators'), *flirten* ('to flirt'), *Jazzmusik, Knickers, Outsiders, Poker, Tea-room,* and *Trade-union*.[164] But even more interesting, because they illustrate the very rapid and striking penetration of English and American words and customs, are the examples of influence on the Japanese. Ichikawa has gathered a large number which are current in Japan, classifying them under the heads "Food and Drink", "Clothing and Toilet", "Sports and Games", "Political and Social", "Science", and so on. Many of them show changes in form which have been brought about by the Japanese pronunciation, such as *bisuketto* ('biscuit'), *chikki* ('check'), *donatsu* ('doughnut'), *kon bifu* ('corned beef'), *sakkā* ('soccer'), *storaiki* ('strike').[167] Probably there is no important language in the world today that does not have in some modified form the English *roast beef* and the American *beefsteak*.

Another phase of the spread of the English language may be seen in several "Anglo-foreign" dialects. We have already discussed foreign-English dialects (Sec. 16, *b*), which have gradually developed through the attempts of foreigners to learn the English language, especially in the United States. But though these foreigners ultimately learn to use English, at the same time they continue to employ their native tongues, which become modified by the influence of English reacting upon them and producing what may be termed Anglo-foreign dialects. The Pennsylvania Dutch form of English speech has been discussed; but for generations a form of German has been spoken by these same inhabitants of Pennsylvania which has diverged so far from their original tongue that it may now be regarded as a distinct form of German. Likewise Canadian French, which has persisted alongside English in eastern Canada, making such communities as Quebec and Montreal practically bilingual, shows various modifications which must be ascribed to the influence of the English co-language. And the Acadian French of Louisiana has been so strongly modified that it can no longer be regarded as like the Canadian French.[173] American Italians have adopted various English words, as Vaughan has shown, and not infrequently these are carried back to Italy by returning Italians.[174] Norwegian settlers in Wisconsin use many words borrowed from English;[175] and elsewhere, scattered over the United States, are numerous settlements of foreigners still employing largely their native tongues, but with numerous instances of increasing use of borrowed words and phrases. The frequent return of members of these communities to the Old World helps, to a very marked degree, to increase the influence of the English language, and so constitutes one more factor in the spread of English.

And, finally, in our survey of the ways and means by which the English language has been scattered abroad over the earth, we should note the important part played by the development of English jargons (see Sec. 17). Many Indians of the Northwest have learned English words through the agency of the Chinook jargon; countless Chinese and other people of the Far East have likewise acquired English words and phrases through pidgin English; and to the inhabitants of the islands of Polynesia and Melanesia English words in somewhat different form have become familiar as the basis of Beach-la-Mar. In all these jargons, as Jespersen has insisted, English has been employed with its grammar almost entirely discarded. It is a poor form of English, it is true, reduced to the very lowest terms of linguistic usage, but it is still a form of English, and a very widespread one at that.

So, through the rapid increase in the number of people in English-speaking lands, the expansion of English and American political influence over the world, the greatly extended study of English by foreigners, the incorporation of English words into foreign languages, the development of numerous Anglo-foreign dialects with their reaction on the mother tongues, and, finally, through the spread of English jargons among the illiterate folk of the Pacific lands, the English language has spread most amazingly in the past few decades.

Considering this spread of English, it is not surprising that there has been an increasing discussion of English as a possible world tongue, during the last few decades. Back in the early nineteenth century scholars began to talk seriously of the need of a universal language. At that time they had a vision of a language which would ultimately supersede the various tongues then in use. But because no one existing language was altogether acceptable to people not born to it, they concluded that it would be necessary to manufacture a brand-new language which would be economical and efficient and free from national prejudices. One after another these artificial languages have been launched (see Sec. 129) and have run their short-lived courses, while the older, better-established national tongues have lived steadily on, refusing to yield to the new, artificial creations. People have come to appreciate the desirability of encouraging a varied world culture through the preservation of the various racial tongues and their literatures, and so the enthusiasm of those persons who would wipe out all linguistic differences and universalize the use of one tongue has cooled or else has been overcome by the calmer judgment of wiser heads. Gradually the proponents of international speech have shifted their stand in the matter and have more and more advocated an auxiliary or supplementary language which would serve for international communication but which would not replace the national tongues.

During this period of growing need of better intercommunication and of experimenting with artificial languages, the English language has grown steadily in scope and in influence over the world. As we have observed, the numbers of speakers of English have increased amazingly. The political dominion of the English-speaking people has likewise expanded very greatly. The commercial influence of England and the United States has become felt in every country of the earth. And, finally, with the sudden promotion of sound pictures and the radio, largely by England and America, problems have arisen which can be completely solved only through some sort of international linguistic agreement.

In the past it has usually been the English-speaking people themselves who have somewhat arrogantly suggested the possibility of making English the auxiliary international speech, but more recently the suggestions have been coming from foreigners. A South American writer has said [161]:

> It would be foolish to suppose that the babel of languages which now stands in the way of easy intercommunication between the peoples of this tiny world will continue for very many years. More than three thousand languages, used by small or large groups of people, still exist. They serve as a means of communication within various groups — local, regional, or national — but at the same time they offer a serious obstacle to communication between members of different groups.... Any one who has given serious study to the problem has felt the need of a change, either through the creation of an artificial international language, or through the universalization of the use of one of the existing languages. To put either of these steps into effect, an international accord has been envisaged.... Everything points to the ultimate predominance of English.

With a recognition of the great spread of English and the acceptance of the idea of an auxiliary language, two philologists have offered two quite different plans for the international use of the English language. At Cambridge, England, Ogden, after experimenting for some years to determine which are the fundamental words of the present English vocabulary, has recommended a list of eight hundred and fifty words as the foundation for a new, simple, international language which he calls Basic English. Under the heads of "Operators", "Necessary Terms", "Qualifiers", "Common Things", "Opposites", and the like, he recommends such words as *come*, *get, give*; *account, act, adaptation*; *able, acid, bitter*; *angle, ant, ape*; *awake, bad, bent*. He calls his language "a scientific attempt to select the most fundamental words in the current language to form a practical auxiliary language for all nations".[176] The grammar of Basic English is to be of the most simple and elementary kind, and presumably it is expected that the new language will expand somewhat and develop its vocabulary as it becomes increasingly used. The difficulty seems to be to keep any linguistic project of this sort alive long enough for it to manifest a convincing growth.

In contrast to this, Zachrisson, of the University of Uppsala, in Sweden, has noted the rapid spread of English and, after a careful examination of its outstanding characteristics, has recommended to the world at large that it adopt the English language as its auxiliary tongue. He has, however, found the very illogical and muddled spelling of English a great obstacle to the learning of English pronunciation and has, therefore, undertaken to improve the spelling. This English with simplified spelling he calls Anglic. It does not present a radical departure from Current English spelling except that for the voiced spirant [ð], as in *then*, it offers *dh* (*dhen, dho*, etc.), and to show vowel length in certain instances, it would put *e* immediately after the simple vowel letter, as in *raes* ('race'), *oever* ('over'), *niet* ('night'), *pleez*. Whether or not the English-speaking lands adopt Zachrisson's mode of spelling the language, its author hopes that it will greatly facilitate the learning of English by foreigners.[177]

28. *Characteristics of English*

The English language possesses certain outstanding characteristics which have helped to popularize it over the world, although at least one feature already mentioned has undoubtedly retarded its spread. "For simplicity of grammar", says Zachrisson, "and a cosmopolitan vocabulary, English has no rival." But he goes on to say that it is "handicapped by its antiquated spelling, which is rather a disguise than a guide to pronunciation". [177] An examination in some detail of the three points made by Zachrisson will aid greatly in any attempt at appraising the characteristic features of the English language as they differ from or are similar to those of other well-known tongues of today.

Simplicity of grammar seems to mean relative lack of inflectional endings. English has very few. The noun usually has only one change, namely, the addition of -s, as in *halls*, although an appearance of greater inflectional variety is produced by the insertion of an apostrophe to show the genitive singular, as in *hall's*, and the addition of the same sign to mark the genitive plural, as in *halls'*. The verb has one change in the present tense, namely, the addition of -s to indicate the third person singular, as in *walks*, and there is usually a change of form to show the past tense, as in *walked* or *sang*. The pronouns have only a few inflectional changes, and the adjectives none, except those employed in showing degree of comparison, as in *taller, tallest*. Compared with the elaborate inflectional systems of most other languages of the Indo-European family, the English system of inflection is very simple indeed.

Two phases of this simplicity of inflection in English cause an English-speaking person to be exceedingly thankful for his native tongue when he attempts to learn various other contemporary or ancient tongues. One is the lack of grammatical gender. It is not necessary to remember, as in German, for example, that one noun is masculine and that adjectives used with it must be given a set of masculine endings, whereas with other nouns the endings must be changed to feminine or neuter according as the gender of the nouns may require. And the speaker of English may be even more thankful that he does not have the additional burden of keeping in mind that bothersome distinction in the use of weak and strong adjectives, namely, that weak endings must be used with the adjective when it follows the definite article and certain other forms, and strong endings when no such form precedes the adjective. The complete absence of all declension of adjectives in English is one of the most important phases of the grammatical simplicity of the language.

Sec. 28]   CHARACTERISTICS OF ENGLISH   117

With the loss of most inflectional endings from English, many words have become monosyllables. This is true especially of the more commonly used words, the native words, the more forceful words, of the language, very often. In Thorndyke's list of the most commonly used words, out of the first five hundred nearly four hundred are monosyllabic.[373] Of course the proportion of monosyllabic and polysyllabic words differs according to the writer, the style of writing, and the level of speech involved, just as we have observed this to be true in the case of native and borrowed words (see Sec. 25); in Van Doren's *Swift*, for example, a five-hundred-word passage of text shows 346 monosyllabic words and 154 polysyllabic words, every occurrence of every word being counted; in a passage of equal length taken from Neihardt's *Song of the Indian Wars* there are 391 monosyllabic words and 109 polysyllabic words. In his recent study of monosyllabism in English, the Danish philologist Jespersen has estimated that there are some eight thousand monosyllables in actual use in English.[182]

Not only have numerous monosyllabic words resulted from the wearing away of the Anglo-Saxon inflectional endings, but the longer words have experienced also a certain amount of contraction or abbreviation, so that the English language of today is more nearly like the monosyllabic Chinese than any other tongue of the Indo-European family. A count of the syllables required to render the Gospel of Matthew in forty of the Indo-European languages brings out very clearly the brevity, or, as the author of the study has termed it, the "laconicism", of the English language.[181] Some of his findings are as follows:

English	29,000	Average of Germanic group	32,650
Norwegian	30,000	Average of Greek group	39,000
Greek	39,000	Average of Latin group	40,200
Persian	40,000	Average of Indo-European	43,100
Bengali	48,000		

This strongly laconic characteristic of English is, moreover, being accentuated by a tendency on the part of certain writers to favor the shorter, largely native Anglo-Saxon words and also to shorten syntactically, omitting connectives, auxiliaries, pronouns, especially. Indeed, it is badly overdone in many instances, so that the music and rhythm of the language is sacrificed to produce a style comparable only to that of a very terse and business-like telegram. Some of the writing of today suggests strongly that the author has endeavored to save money here and there by omitting words.

If, for the moment, the broad definition of grammar given in Section 4 be set aside and the narrower meaning of the word be employed, even then it cannot be said — as some writers have said — that English is a "grammarless tongue". For grammar means at least two things, namely, inflection and syntactical usage. As fast as the inflectional forms of English have been discarded, syntactical practices have replaced them. In the past English was what the philologists call a synthetic language, putting together stems and inflectional endings to express variations in meaning (for example, *act-ed*), whereas in the present it is strongly analytic, expressing the same variations in meaning by the use of prepositional phrases, phrasal verbs, and the like (for example, *did act*). English now has a grammar of syntactical usage, while it once had a grammar of inflectional forms, to a greater degree.

If one has any doubts about this, he can see how far the English language still goes in the emphasis it lays upon "grammar" by studying the English of certain very illiterate foreigners who have acquired a knowledge of words but very little understanding of the grammar. When one of them says, "He no come", he may mean, "He has not come", "He will not come", "He is not coming", "He did not come", and so on. He even manages to give his simple statement a subjunctive effect of doubt or uncertainty by the way he uses it, as, for example, "I 'fraid he no come" for "I'm afraid he may not come". The manifold use of the phrasal verb is one of the outstanding features of Modern English (see Sec. 106), and the complete ignoring of it is one of the most noticeable features, on the other hand, of such illiterate jargons of English as pidgin English and Beach-la-Mar. Not only does the phrasal verb play a very important part in Modern

English, but prepositional phrases are also employed as substitutes for older genitive and dative forms, for adverbs, and so on. Moreover, word order has assumed a greater fixity, or rigidity, since the use of words is less often indicated by inflectional endings; and so the subject and the object can usually be determined by their positions before or after the verb, certain positions are assigned to the indirect object, and in various other respects the order in the sentence is important. Indeed, the verb itself is less likely to be moved about in the sentence, since subject and verb are not inverted as much as in Old English, and the verb is no longer transposed to the end of a relative clause, as formerly.

Two other interesting results of grammatical simplification may also be said to characterize English today, namely, conversion and the use of verb-adverb combinations. Conversion is a change in function, a shift from one part of speech to another, as in the case of *go*, which becomes a noun in 'He made a go of it', or of *book*, which is a verb in 'He wishes to book passage on the boat' (see Sec. 58). The verb-adverb combination is merely the combining of a simple verb with a prepositional adverb, such as *in, out, over, up*; and while it appears, on the face of it, to be tending toward greater simplicity in language, as a matter of fact the foreigner is likely to experience difficulty in making proper use of these combinations because they are developing such a variety or range of meanings (see Sec. 53). The words *hold up*, for example, are simpler in form than *sustain* or *discontinue*; but when one stops to think that this innocent-looking combination may mean *raise, support, display, rein in* or *check, rob, yield, wait* or *stop, remain unbent, cease, keep up*, and so on, he begins to realize that a language may grow simpler in form while it becomes much more elaborate as regards niceties in meaning.

As to whether the English language has gained or lost by this shift from synthesis to analysis, the Czech scholar Trnka has observed [183]:

> In conclusion, we may revert to the interesting question already stated, whether an analytical language is more perfect from the technical point of view as an instrument for the expression of human

thought and feeling. The simplicity of English morphology [inflection] suggests the idea that English is more perfect than synthetic languages, as the same grammatical relations are expressed by the same simple means, e.g. the preposition *of* corresponds to many endings, e.g. *-a, -e, -u, -i, -y* in Modern Czech.

The second feature of Current English for which it has been often commended of late, namely, its cosmopolitan vocabulary, hardly needs further comment, since it has been examined in some detail already (see Sec. 25). A foreigner familiar with almost any language of the Indo-European family is likely to meet cognate words in English, such as *land* and *mouse*, which still retain enough resemblance to his own forms of the words to make them seem familiar. But even more numerous are the borrowed words, which render much of the English vocabulary familiar to a speaker of almost any of the more important languages of the earth, borrowings from Latin doing this service for the Romance linguist, from Norse for the Scandinavian, from Germanic for the German, and so on. Except for a slight difference in form, such words as *adjective, renaissance,* and *culture* might easily belong to any one of several languages.[184]

As a consequence of the widespread borrowing of words, the English language possesses a wealth of synonyms such as no other existing tongue has (see Sec. 83). For no other language is it necessary to compile word books or books of synonyms even for the use of the natives themselves to such an extent as it is done for English. But this very embarrassment of synonymous riches gives to the writer of English opportunity for greater versatility and exactness in the expression of thoughts and feelings. Some philologists have even gone so far as to insist that English literature would not have attained its high level of artistic beauty and strength if the vocabulary had not been so richly endowed through borrowing from the languages of the entire world.

In spite of all the borrowings, however, it must be insisted that English still preserves certain outstanding Germanic features. Its consonants are still, after many centuries, essentially those of the Low German group of languages, notably Dutch, Frisian, and Low German (Plattdeutsch). The method of accentuation is Germanic rather than Romanic, the tendency being to place the accent as near as possible to the beginning of the word. This can be seen in the present-day tendency to pronounce *résearch* and *ínvite* (colloquial noun). Then, again, the most commonly used words of English are largely of Germanic origin, particularly prepositions, conjunctions, auxiliary verbs, and pronouns.

The spelling of English, while it may be said to be strongly characteristic in that it represents many sounds in a very different manner from that of most European languages, must be regarded as the one most serious weakness in the language. It is unsystematic, so that it cannot be learned by the use of a set of clear-cut rules, many words having to be memorized individually. It is inadequate in that there are no separate characters to represent the sound of *aw* in *law*, of *er* in *her*, of *a* in *hat*, of *th* in *then*, and others. It is wasteful in that one sound can often be spelled in almost a dozen different ways, as, for example, the sound [ē] in *aye, fete, gaol, gauge, hate, maelstrom, main, pay, steak, they, weigh*; and it is wasteful in the use of so many silent letters. It is illogical in the use of a letter at one time for one sound and at another for a quite different sound, as, for example, *c* in *cat* and *nice*, or *a* in *hall, at, far, fare*, and so on. And sometimes it is utterly absurd, as in *choir, colonel, once, phthisic, quay* (see Sec. 48).

There is, finally, a richness and colorfulness in the English language which cannot be ascribed to the influence of foreign languages but which goes back as far as the literature can be traced and which is due to the love of the English for figurative usage. From the 'kenning' of earliest Anglo-Saxon poetry down to the latest American slang, figurative use of words and phrases has played an important part in the development of the language. Period by period this figurative usage has been influenced by the life and thinking and chief interests of the people, in earliest times by the sea and warfare, later by chivalric and feudal interests, in American colonial life by the frontiersman's interests and experiences; but always it has been a colorful and ready characteristic of English.

CHAPTER V

HISTORICAL BACKGROUNDS OF ENGLISH

IT IS impossible to make an intelligent survey of the English language of today without paying some attention to the history of those conditions of life and thought which have been responsible in a large measure for the distinguishing and outstanding characteristics of English just discussed. It is true that some of its most peculiar features were inherited from the Germanic group as a primitive ancestor, and if there had not been a succession of national experiences to change and enlarge the language, it would still be essentially a Low German dialect. It is true, as already observed, that the relationship of English to other languages of the Indo-European family can still be seen in certain cognate words here and there. But it is also true that so preponderatingly large a part of the present-day vocabulary has been "borrowed" during the past twelve or fifteen centuries that it is not easy to decide today whether the language is more strongly Germanic or Romanic. And yet, notwithstanding all its Germanic inheritance and its Romanic borrowings along the way, the English language has departed so radically from both groups that it has no strong resemblance to any language in these groups. A brief study of the conditions into which it originally migrated when it came to England, and the many vicissitudes that it has experienced in the centuries since, will assist very greatly in understanding some of the present-day features of Current English which will be considered in the following chapters. For the history of the English language is essentially a record of the development of English national life and culture, and consequently the language of today must be regarded as an epitome of all that has persisted in English intellectual life.

29. Periods of English Linguistic History

For the sake of convenience it is customary to divide the history of the English language into three general periods. The first period is called the Anglo-Saxon, or Old English, period and is roughly dated from the coming of the Angles, Saxons, and Jutes to England, about 450 A.D., to about 1100. The second period is called the Middle English period and dates from about 1100 to about 1500. The third, or Modern English, period extends from about 1500 to the present time. In the Old English period some four great dialects prevailed in England, owing to the tribal differences and scattering location of the Angles, Saxons, and Jutes; in the Middle English period these dialects persisted for some time, but toward the end of the period they tended to yield to the dominance of the language spoken in London, which even in the late fourteenth century was the literary tongue of the leading writers, such as Chaucer, Wyclif, Gower, and Langland; in the Modern English period the literary English became so well established that it was quite uniformly used by writers, compilers of dictionaries and grammars, and other educated folk, although many local dialects continued in use. In the first period the language was quite highly inflected; in the second period most of the inflectional endings had worn down to final *e's*; in the third period they were almost completely lost. In the period before 1100 the vocabulary was almost altogether Germanic, with only a few Latin borrowings; in the following period there was a great influx of Romanic words, particularly French; after about 1500 the continued and almost world-wide borrowing added a still greater load and variety of loan-words. In the earliest period, moreover, Latin was the tongue of scholars and writers, and the vernacular writings that have been preserved represent a relatively small proportion of the literary output of the time. In the Middle English period Latin was still used largely by scholars, and French was for a time the tongue of the upper classes, of the law, of the schools, etc.; it was only very slowly that the vernacular English fought its way to general acceptance as a tongue suitable for scholars and writers. But after 1500, foreign tongues were discarded, on the whole; and with a great display of patriotic zeal the learned persons of England set to work in earnest to embellish and improve their native tongue, even increasing their study of other languages for the help they might gain thereby in improving their own.

A few additional comments may help to a better appreciation of the dates that have been given for the three periods. Before about 450 A.D. there was no English language in England. Though the Anglo-Saxons began to trickle into England from the Continent about 450, even so no vernacular literature seems to have been produced much before 700. The year 1100 is a convenient date for the end of the Anglo-Saxon period, because the coming of the Normans in 1066 gradually subordinated the native tongue, but not immediately. By 1100 the use of Anglo-Saxon by people of the upper classes seems to have yielded to Norman French almost altogether. The year 1500 is approximately the beginning of the English Renaissance movement, not long after the introduction of printing into England, and about the time when English exploration and national and commercial expansion got under way.

30. *The British Celts*

Before the coming of the Anglo-Saxons to England a branch of the great Celtic group known as the Britons occupied the island. When Cæsar led his troops into England in the summer of 55 B.C., he fought with these Britons and defeated them. When, later, the Romans returned and subjugated the island, they seem to have enslaved the Britons and made them very dependent and helpless. For after the last Roman soldiers withdrew in the fifth century and left the Britons to their own resources, they were so beaten and terrified by the Picts and Scots, who constantly attacked them from the north, that (tradition says) they finally called in some of the Anglo-Saxon wanderers to help them. Unfortunately for them, their helpers soon turned upon them and enslaved them, and ultimately drove most of them into the highlands of Wales, into Cornwall, and elsewhere, so that England knew them no more. That is probably the explanation of the almost entire lack of British Celtic words in the English vocabulary. A few common nouns, it is true, survive, such as *bin, brat, down* ('hill'), *mattock,* and numerous place names like *Abercrombie, Caerleon, Dumbarton*; but on the whole it may be said that the British Celts withdrew and left almost no impression on the English language. Most of the Celtic element in present-day English came later from the Gaelic Celts of Ireland and of the Scottish Highlands rather than from the indigenous Britons. In English literature some of the Celtic leaders have lived on, such as King Arthur and King Lear; but in the language few survivals can be found.

31. The Romans in Britain

Nearly a century after Cæsar had invaded Britain, the Romans returned during the reign of the emperor Claudius and in the year 43 A.D. began in earnest the conquest of Celtic Britain. The steps in this progress of conquest and accompanying Romanization of the Britons are set forth somewhat sketchily in two old historical compilations, — that earlier one known as *The Ecclesiastical History of the English People*, by the scholar Bede, and the later *Anglo-Saxon Chronicle*. Gradually the Britons were beaten down by the Roman armies. In the year 61 A.D. the Roman governor Suetonius went farther northwest to the sacred island of Mona (Anglesey) and subdued the Druids, the powerful priests of the Celtic religion known as Druidism, clearing the way for their own pagan gods and religious beliefs. Under later governors they built up great colonial centers like York, Chester, and Caerleon-on-Usk. About 122 the emperor Hadrian began the construction of a great wall on the northern frontier between the river Tyne and the Solway. Later, in about the year 142, a shorter wall was built across the island farther north between the Forth and the Clyde. Gradually a system of military roads was developed, of which the most famous was the long Watling Street, which ran northwest from London to the military outpost at Chester. Little by little the Britons seem to have accepted the Roman tongue, at least those in the towns and the more educated country folk, and Roman customs and buildings and furnishings were everywhere prevalent. Indeed, the Romanization of the town-dwelling Britons must have been so complete and permanent that when the Romans withdrew about 400 A. D., because of political pressure at home, the Britons no longer possessed enough of their own old Celtic culture to have any strong Celtic influence upon the Teutonic barbarians who succeeded the Romans in Britain. Christianity slowly worked north into Britain; and when it was officially recognized as the Roman state religion in 325, under the emperor Constantine, it was already well established in the island.

It is not easy to determine which Latin words appearing in the language of the Anglo-Saxons were brought along from their earlier Continental homes and which may have been adopted by them after they invaded and conquered the Romanized Britons in the middle of the fifth century. But it seems likely that such words as *street, port, wall,* and the name *Chester,* which appears also in the town names ending in *-chester* and *-caster* (*Colchester, Lancaster*), and possibly words pertaining to domestic life, such as *butter, cheese, chest,* and *kitchen,* may have lingered on in Romanized British speech and been taken over by the Germanic Anglo-Saxons when they came to England.

At any rate, the amount of Latin that came into the English language as the result of the four centuries of Roman occupation of Britain was not very great in comparison with the amount of Latin borrowing that began when Christianity came back to England a little later.

32. *Anglo-Saxon England*

To those who may be impatient to begin an intensive study of that great hybrid, the English language, it may seem unnecessary to spend as much time as many historians do on the five-hundred-year period just considered, during which Britain was successively Celtic and Roman but not in the least Germanic or English. But such study of preliminary conditions may be justified on two grounds, at least. In the first place, it is sometimes necessary, in attempting to define a term such as *English*, to draw a clear line between that which it is and that which it is not, as we have already insisted in Section 4, and obviously there was no English language and no England until the Angles (English) arrived in the island. Secondly, to understand the reasons why these Germanic peoples came to England and so readily took possession of a long-inhabited and well-governed land, it is desirable to know something of the changing circumstances that opened up the way for their coming.

Of the various tribes constituting the Low German section of the great Germanic group of peoples, three tribes migrated, in whole or in part, to England and fused into the English of later days. The Jutes apparently held the mainland of Denmark, still known as Jutland; the Angles lived south of them in the present district of Schleswig; and, spread out south of the Angles and along the north-German shore, was a third tribe called the Saxons. These people were restless, as all the other Germanic tribes were, during the period of the so-called *Völkerwanderung*, or wandering of the peoples, and were going out in increasingly numerous bands or boatloads to plunder, and to seek more spacious homes. Even while the Roman provincial government was still fairly strong in Britain, it had been necessary to take steps to protect the north coast against their incursions. When, later, the Romans withdrew and left the weak and helpless Britons to fight off the Picts and Scots of the north, these Germanic peoples apparently saw an opportunity to enter Britain under more favorable terms. For the old historian Bede relates that one British king, Vortigern, actually decided after consultation with his people "to invite and call in to their aid the people of the Saxons from the parts beyond the sea". Bede's account, which appears in the twelfth chapter of Book I of the West Saxon version of the *Ecclesiastical History*, is as follows:

It was 449 years after our Lord's incarnation, when the emperor Martianus succeeded to the throne. . . . At that time the Angles and Saxons were called in by the aforesaid king [Vortigern] and arrived in Britain with three great ships. They received settlements on the east side of the island by order of the same king, who had invited them here, to fight as for their country. They at once took the field against the foe, who had often before overrun the land from the north; and the Saxons won the victory. Then they sent home messengers, whom they bade to report the fertility of this land, and the cowardice of the Britons. Immediately a larger fleet was despatched here, with a stronger force of warriors; and the host when united overpowered resistance. The Britons gave and assigned to them settlements among themselves, on condition of fighting for the peace and safety of their country and resisting their enemies, while the Britons also provided them with a maintenance and estates in return for their labours. The new-comers were of the three strongest races of Germany, namely, Saxons, Angles, and Jutes. Of Jutish origin are the men of Kent, and the Wihtsætan; that is the tribe dwelling in the Isle of Wight. From the Saxons, that is the people called Old Saxons, came the East Saxons, the South Saxons, and the West Saxons; and from Angle came the East Angles and the Middle Angles, Mercians, and the whole race of the Northumbrians. This is the land which is named Angulus, between the Jutes and Saxons, and it is said to have lain waste, from the time they left it, up to this day. Their leaders then and their commanders were at first two brothers, Hengist and Horsa, sons of Wihtgils, whose father was called Witta, whose father was Wihta, and the father of Wihta was called Woden. From his race the royal families of many tribes derived their origin. Then without delay they came in crowds, larger hosts from the tribes previously mentioned. And the people, who came here, began to increase and multiply to such an extent, that they were a great terror to the inhabitants themselves, who originally invited and called them in.

Bede, in his little cell in the old monastery at Jarrow, up in Northumbria, wrote this history of England a few years before his death in the year 735 A.D.; and probably it is as dependable an account of the coming of the Anglo-Saxons to England as any that can be found, for at best the history of these early times must remain largely traditional or conjectural.

During the period of almost three centuries that had elapsed from the time the first three boatloads were said to have come to Vortigern's assistance until the Christian monk compiled his careful story of the growth of ecclesiastical England, many things had happened to the Anglo-Saxons, and others were to occur, which, taken as a whole, went far toward creating that Old English civilization and language which stand in the civilization and language of the English people of today as the one most important formative element, in spite of all the invasions and excursions and borrowings that have made so marked a change in later centuries.

At first, during the period of increasing invasions and conquest, Christianity seems to have been almost entirely driven out of England. But slowly the Irish monks brought it back through Scotland into Northumbria; and in 597 the great missionary Augustine was sent direct from Rome into Kent, with some forty companions, to convert the Kentish king. The Christian movement crept north, setting up churches and monasteries, and the Northumbrian kings gradually accepted it. By the time that Bede wrote his chronicle, Northumbria had assumed a cultural and political leadership which flowered in literature, practically the first manifestation of literary art that has come down to us from Anglo-Saxon times. But that other great branch of the Angles who had settled in the middle of England and were known as the Mercians also grew in power and culture until, in the time of their famous king, Offa (reigned 757-796), they too were producing literature of some importance. Unfortunately, as that other early history, *The Anglo-Saxon Chronicle*, relates, three ships came to the coast in the year 787, "the first ships of Danish men who sought the land of the Anglian race", and these marked the beginning of a rapidly growing series of raids by the pagan vikings, coming this time from the North Germanic, or Scandinavian branch, which played havoc with the civilization of the whole of Anglian England and very nearly submerged English Christian civilization.

Fortunately the West Saxons had been expanding and growing in power south of the Thames, and by the time all the northern part of England had been overrun by the Danish invaders, a truly great West Saxon leader, King Alfred, came to the throne and fought his way up from almost complete loss of his country in the gloomy winter of 878 to a sweeping victory which compelled the Danes to remain for some time in the strip of country known as the Danelaw, from London north. It was Alfred who took time in the midst of wars and invasions to translate what he considered the best of Latin literature into his West Saxon tongue; and about this time, fortunately for English literary history, much of the literature of the earlier Northumbrian and Mercian periods was rewritten in this same West Saxon dialect. So, before the year 900, enough literature was produced at Alfred's court at Winchester and elsewhere in his southern realm to give us a fairly satisfactory idea of the nature of this Early West Saxon language, even though we have very little to show in the dialects of Northumbria, Mercia, and Kent.

After Alfred's death, in the year 901, the kings of the West Saxons fought off the Danes with varying degrees of success. However, several baptizings which Alfred had been enabled through his victories to force upon Danish kings and great numbers of their followers had led to the gradual Christianization of these newly arrived neighbors; and periods of relative peacefulness in southern England gave opportunity for increased literary activity, which may be said to have culminated in a Late West Saxon period, just a century after Alfred's time. A fairly large mass of West Saxon writing of this later period survives, notably the sermons, textbooks, and other compositions of Ælfric, who had been trained in the schools of the West Saxon capital, Winchester. So, while the Danes were only waiting for the time to arrive when they should actually sweep England politically and seize the English throne for a short period, they did not sweep the slow-growing and hard-gained civilization of the Anglo-Saxons from the land as the Angles, Saxons, and Jutes had overrun and crushed the Christian and Roman culture of the miserable Britons in the early years of their invasions. For numerous centers of learning had come to stay, and from them emanated writings of all sorts — legal, scientific, poetical, ecclesiastical, educational — in both the Latin and the Anglo-Saxon tongue.

The extant vernacular literature of this period before the Norman Conquest in 1066 would fill at least twenty good volumes of prose and poetry, including that splendid old epic *Beowulf*. The vocabulary of this literature has been reckoned at no less than thirty thousand words, and the language is of a more highly inflected, though far less polished, character than the English of the present day. Several poets are slightly known to us and a few great prose-writers like Bede, Alcuin, Alfred, and Ælfric; scholars abounded in the centers of learning, such as Durham, York, Canterbury, Winchester, Worcester, and London. Although it is necessary to talk of the literature and dialects according as they flourished in Northumbria, Mercia, Kent, or the West Saxon south, nevertheless these sections gradually came to feel themselves one people to the extent that they adopted the term *English* (from an earlier *Anglisc*, 'Anglian') as a name for all the tribes in England.

33. *The Scandinavians in England*

Before attempting to acquire some understanding of the place which the Scandinavian peoples have taken in the history of early England, it is necessary to enlarge upon what has already been said about them in Section 24. The Scandinavian, or North Germanic, branch may be termed the "great-aunt" of the Anglo-Saxon; and the four subdivisions, that is to say, the Swedish, Norwegian, Danish, and Icelandic, would then be "distant cousins" of the English. Philologists have employed the term *Old Norse* as a convenient general term for the Scandinavian language in its very early stages, before it was possible to distinguish the four subdivisions just mentioned. Even in historical times the earlier English chroniclers have apparently not always known whether they were talking about Danes or Norwegians; and since the literature of this northern branch is all relatively late, students of language are forced to take their examples of early Scandinavian from the richer Icelandic rather than from the Danish or Norwegian literature. Hence the student of English is likely to find used more or less indiscriminately the terms *Scandinavian, Old Norse, Norwegian, Danish,* and *Icelandic*; the Swedes do not come into this early history of the English language. But if Scandinavian be adopted as the more general term, Old Norse as the name of the earliest form of this general Scandinavian speech, and the other four, Swedish, Norwegian, Danish, and Icelandic as applying to the gradually separating subdivisions of the primitive northern branch, then it will be possible to discuss the subject with some clear understanding of the philological difficulties involved, as well as of the influences exerted by the great viking movement of these peoples.

The invasion of northwestern Europe, and particularly of Great Britain and Ireland, by these peoples must be understood in its general significance, as regards its extent and also its character, if one is to comprehend the manner in which the Anglo-Saxons were exposed during a period of some three centuries to their semibarbarous culture, and also the reason why so little impression has remained on our language as we know it today (see Sec. 25).

Just as the earlier historian Bede records the gradual invasion of England by the West Germanic tribes from Jutland, Schleswig, and Old Saxony, so the later writers of the long-continued *Anglo-Saxon Chronicle* insert here and there down through the years significant entries relating to the growing menace of these Norwegian and Danish vikings from farther north. Under the year 787 the writer of the *Chronicle* tells of the coming of three boatloads to the southwestern coast, as we have already noted. Year after year these pirates kept coming, plundering more widely each year through England but returning home in the autumn, until, finally, for the year 855 the *Chronicle* contains the significant entry "In this year heathen men first remained in Sheppey over winter." From this time on they increased their hold on England and Ireland and drove even the West Saxon kings back into their ever-narrowing borders, finally overrunning in the dark and anxious winter of 878 all the country except a little stronghold in the southwest at Athelney, where King Alfred made his last desperate stand. Fortunately the king was able to win back slowly all England south of the Thames, to force Christianity on some of the Danish leaders, and to make a treaty which held them in a part of the island north of London, the so-called Danelaw.

But one must read the early chronicles carefully and thoughtfully to appreciate the general significance of the westward movement of these vikings. They were settling in Mercia and East Anglia and Northumbria and becoming tillers of the soil; they were running up the rivers of France and settling, until finally Norsemen became Normans; they were setting up kings in Ireland and in parts of Scotland; and, at home in Denmark and Norway and in the more recently colonized Iceland, they were growing in culture and civil power. Finally, in the year 1016, they seized London, the last stronghold of the English, and Knut (or Canute) became king of all England as well as of Denmark. Perhaps the very manner in which the political power of the Danes in England became merged with that of the English may be taken as illustrating the merging with and absorption into the English language of the speech of these Danes and Norwegians in England. For after two reigns Edward the Confessor, who was a half-brother of the later Danish king Hardicanute, and at the same time a descendant of the old English royal house, was accepted by a united English and Danish people as their king. This intermingling, political and cultural, seems to have slowly subordinated the Scandinavian culture to the English, and eventually to that of the Normans, who had themselves earlier been Northmen.

After all, it is not surprising that this was the result of the western movement of these old vikings, if one considers a few outstanding facts that bear strongly on the situation. The Norwegians, and to a less degree the Danes, were confined, in their older homes, to narrow coastal strips of rugged and not very productive territory and were apparently driven to a life of seafaring and piracy in order to provide a living for their sturdy and rapidly increasing folk. When they seized the more fertile and productive lands of England and northern France, they almost immediately settled down and lost interest in the life of the seafarer, just as the Anglo-Saxons had done a few centuries earlier.

But while the Anglo-Saxon tribes had found in the Britons a decadent people, weakened and rendered subservient by centuries of Roman domination and helpless before the raids of the Picts and Scots, the Scandinavian vikings brought a pagan and relatively simple civilization into an England filled with Christian centers of learning and ruled by cultured kings like Alfred the Great; and as an inferior civilization usually yields in the long run to a superior, so the Scandinavians were apparently converted and educated and slowly absorbed into English life and culture. Exactly the same thing took place at the same time across the water in Normandy.

And, finally, and very important for an understanding of the reaction of the Scandinavian language to the Anglo-Saxon, the two tongues were so nearly alike that the Danes may have learned early to speak the Anglo-Saxon with only such modifications of the English as one might expect to find in some Scandinavian settlement in modern Minnesota. Where they were strongest, in northern England, they were most careless of Old English inflectional endings and were most likely to introduce here and there a word of their own. But if one will pronounce a page in any Old Norse glossary and a corresponding page in the glossary of an Anglo-Saxon reader, he will find a majority of words corresponding so closely that about all he has to do to interchange them is to modify the inflectional endings of the words. Why, then, should the Anglo-Saxons, already comfortably established in their homes and habits, try to conform to the semibarbarous life and speech of foreigners who were quite ready to settle down and become good neighbors, to marry their sons and daughters, and to learn many things which they didn't know before they came to England?

So the whole matter of early Scandinavian influence upon the English language may be summed up for the present (see Sec. 73) by the setting forth of a few significant facts. A few words occur in late Old English, such as *ceallian*, 'to call', in the poem on the battle fought by English and Danes at Maldon in the year 991, which scholars are inclined to consider early borrowings from the Scandinavian. Moreover, in Northumbrian literature some inflectional endings show a shortening similar to some in the Old Norse, as, for example, the infinitive *binda*, 'to bind', which is exactly the form used in the Old Icelandic speech. All through the counties once comprised in the Danelaw, place-names still occur which are plainly of Scandinavian origin. But, for the most part, scholars are not very sure about many English words that might have been introduced by these Scandinavian settlers, since similar forms may have already existed in Anglo-Saxon dialectal speech, and the inflectional forms observed particularly in literature emanating from northern England may have been due to the carelessness of the English themselves as much as to the influence of illiterate Scandinavian neighbors.

34. *The Anglo-Normans*

Before one can gain a distinct impression of an emerging and a growing English nation and English language, it is necessary to look into the origin, the character, and the coming to England of one more people, namely, the Normans. For these last invaders of Great Britain contributed most notably to the shaping of the character and genius of the English state; and though they did not make as marked an impression upon the language as one might expect, nevertheless they opened up the way for those very great changes in the character of the language which were to take place in the course of a few centuries.

Out of the many bands of Norsemen that wandered up the rivers of Belgium and France during the long years when England was suffering from their inroads, one band of them, under a leader called Rolf, or Rollo, had settled on the river Seine in the lands now known as Normandy; and only a few years after Alfred had recognized the Danelaw in England, they had laid the foundations of that great Norman dukedom which was to play so important a role in the history of both

France and England. In much the same way that the Danes in England had yielded to the hard-won culture of the Anglo-Saxons, these other Scandinavians in France had completely yielded to the Romanic culture of France and had become as strongly a Romanic people as the Danes in England had become a Low Germanic people. In both cases the strong characteristics of these vikings of the north had fitted them for political dominance, but their inferior culture almost immediately gave way to the superior Christian civilizations of the peoples among whom they had settled. Consequently, when Duke William of Normandy invaded England in the year 1066, defeated Harold, who had been chosen king of the now united Danish and English people of England, and finally persuaded the people that he should himself be made their king, while he introduced into their torn and discordant political life a strong and dominant leadership, he and his Normans had to recognize a culture and religious life fully equal to their own. So, while the Normans in England gradually replaced the English in as many of the political and ecclesiastical positions of importance as they could find excuse to seize, some of the upper-class English mingled with them and helped to carry on the affairs of the English Church and the English state.

In a short time two languages were being used in England by the Normans newly come and also by the upper classes and better educated of the English themselves, namely, Anglo-French and Latin. The Norman tongue became for a period of about a hundred and fifty years the speech of the court, of the legal profession, of schools, and of many a home where Anglo-Normans lived. Latin remained, as it had long been, the international language of the Church and of scholars in general. The native (Anglo-Saxon) tongue remained the speech of the common people, who had been either left undisturbed by their political conquerors or else forced to serve them. In other words, the vernacular speech was employed largely by illiterate and rustic dwellers on the land, and men and women of culture and learning wrote in Latin and Anglo-Norman almost altogether.

Even a very superficial inspection of the literature produced during this century and a half of Anglo-Norman supremacy should give the thoughtful student of English literary and linguistic history a fair idea of trends and accomplishments in England. While at most of the monastic centers of learning writers ceased to add to their local versions of *The Anglo-Saxon Chronicle* when the Normans flocked into England in 1066, at Peterborough, on the road from London to Lincoln, scribes kept an intermittent record of local and national happenings down to the accession of Henry II, in 1154, written in a degenerate Old English, with a scattering of the newer French words, such as *castle, prison, curse,* and *countess.* Moreover, preachers who had to preach to people of the lower classes, and other religious writers and teachers, occasionally modified some of the older Anglo-Saxon homilies or made some crude didactic and religious poems or translations of Biblical literature and church-service books in this same degenerate vernacular English. But the many writers, especially of twelfth-century England, such as Geoffrey of Monmouth, Marie de France, Gerald de Barri (often called Giraldus Cambrensis), Wace, who wrote histories of the Norman leaders of both earlier Normandy and later England, Walter Mapes (or Map), Geffrai Gaimar, and a great number of local chroniclers, wrote in the learned Latin or the courtly Anglo-Norman tongue.

It was only when King John lost his hold on the Norman and other possessions in France, shortly after 1200, that Englishmen seem to have become aware again of the possibility of utilizing the English language for the composition of important pieces of ecclesiastical and worldly literature. Perhaps the fact that the Angevin rulers of England preferred to be kings of England, primarily, rather than merely dukes of Normandy, gives a clue to a growing English national feeling and a gradual absorption of Norman life and culture by the native English life and culture. At any rate, about the beginning of the thirteenth century, several significant literary monuments took shape in the vernacular English, and once more English literature comes to the front. Out in western England a priest, Layamon, wrote a long metrical history of England which he entitled the *Brut* because of the growing popularity of the belief that the Britons could trace their history far back to a mythical Brutus, supposed to have come to Britain from the fallen Troy of Greek and Roman literature. Somewhere northeast of London a monk, Orm, made a long religious poem which he named his *Ormulum* and which he hoped would prove a helpful guide to better living and to improved spelling of the language. At the same time a prose *Ancren Riwle*, or *Rule of Nuns*, was composed in the south of England. A study of these three notable contributions to early Middle English vernacular literature supplies some interesting and valuable indications of the growth of the language during the long period while it had been submerged and subordinated to the Latin and Anglo-Norman, and at the same time helps to measure the size of the Norman vocabulary that had intruded into the native speech, and to some extent the Scandinavian borrowing, also.

In the western poem of Layamon, in spite of the fact that it contains over thirty thousand short lines, there are scarcely a hundred French words in the earlier version. Perhaps, however, it may be taken as testimony to the rapid influx of French words in the thirteenth century that the revision of the poem some fifty years later shows the insertion of various French loan-words in place of older native terms. In the contemporary long poem of Orm very few French words occur, but more Scandinavian words, as would be expected of a writer living in the vicinity of the descendants of the old Danish invaders. In the southern *Ancren Riwle*, however, several hundred French words can be found, possibly because it was written in the part of England most exposed to Norman French culture, and perhaps in part because the book was made for some women of culture and broader knowledge who were familiar with French and Latin. At any rate, the number of Norman French words that had worked into the English language by 1200 was very small compared with the great influx of other French words that the next two centuries were to experience.

In passing, then, from a period in which the English language maintained a strongly Germanic vocabulary to a later era of tremendous Romanic influence, it should be emphasized that just as the Danes in England failed to modify the language of the English as much as one might expect, so also the intrusion of Norman words into English was not nearly so great as some scholars have assumed in the past. But the reasons for this are quite different in the two cases. Whereas the Danes failed to modify seriously the language of their old Low German neighbors because they were so soon and so intimately merged with them in their new English home, the Normans failed to change the vernacular speech of the English because they kept to the higher walks of life, politically, ecclesiastically, culturally, using their own tongue in common with the upper classes of English people, and the vernacular was relegated to the illiterate and untaught folk, who continued to use it as they had been accustomed to. In this way the vernacular, no longer used extensively by writers and scholars and educated people in general, was deprived of the conservative and corrective influence that these classes would have exerted. This separation of the language of the upper classes, who used the Norman French, from that of the lower classes, who spoke the Anglo-Saxon vernacular, left the latter relatively free from Norman loan-words but also left it free to deteriorate grammatically in the mouths of careless and illiterate speakers. Consequently during this period the English language lost most of its grammatical niceties, particularly its inflectional endings, but preserved its old Germanic vocabulary, largely. So in the English of Layamon, of Orm, and of the writer of the *Ancren Riwle*, to cite these writers again as typical of a time of transition at the beginning of the thirteenth century, one still finds marked and fundamental Germanic characteristics, but with very badly worn-down inflectional forms, confused grammatical categories, uncertain spellings, and cross currents of dialectal and foreign influences, but no marked tendency as yet toward a standard literary English. The English of 1200 is still fundamentally the colloquial speech of the earlier Anglo-Saxon people.

35. The Age of Chaucer

From the death of that famous crusader Richard the Lionhearted, in 1199, until about 1500, England had such a variety of experiences, politically, socially, and culturally, that it is impossible to give to the period a title which will indicate in itself the nature of the period. So it is, perhaps, not altogether inappropriate to name the period, more particularly from about 1300 to 1500, for that great poet Geoffrey Chaucer, who, living as he did from about 1340 to 1400, illustrates in his work the cultural influences of the time, both as they earlier worked in his own life and as they later emanated from him to work upon many others after his day. For Chaucer used the English language more artistically and effectively than any other poet in England before Shakespeare's day; and while he did not create literary English, as some have mistakenly supposed, he helped to make his London English so popular and so impressive that since his time no other form of English has had an equal popularity.

To understand the development of the English language during this period of three centuries it is necessary to revert to our very first definition, namely, that of language as "the expression of thinking and emotion", and to consider the important political and social events of this medieval period which led to or allowed the expansion of English culture, to mark certain stages in the growth of this new culture, and, finally, to note the rapidly increasing vernacular literature which expressed this new culture. For, after all, the language could not have expanded and deepened so remarkably unless the thinking of the English people had expanded and improved likewise. It was the importation of new things and new ideas that forced the English people to adopt new words in such great numbers.

So many important political and social events and developments took place during this most important epoch of English history that we cannot hope to do more than indicate a few of the most significant. When King John lost the dukedom of Normandy in 1204, he decided for all time that England should be for Englishmen, a nation in itself and no longer an over-sea province of the French. Apparently from that time on Englishmen began to think more seriously of developing an English culture and expressing it in an English language. But many an Englishman had joined in the Crusades, had been to the Holy Land, and had seen strange sights and brought home to England a wealth of new ideas and experiences. Moreover, these same Crusades had slowly brought to western Europe the culture of the East, and much new literature sprang up because of it. At home, also, about the end of the Norman period, the two great universities at Oxford and Cambridge began to take shape, and learning of a high order spread from them. Shortly thereafter members of the newly established mendicant orders, particularly the Franciscans and Dominicans, wandered into England to visit and work among the lower classes, carrying with them as time passed an increasing wealth of songs, sermons, bits of scientific lore, and much more that would edify and enlighten the common man. About the end of the thirteenth century the wars began with the Scottish people which were ultimately to result in Scottish independence, in the beginnings of a separate Scottish literature, and in the realization that their far-northern dialect of Early English might now be deemed a separate national tongue. Moreover, the French soon became involved in these wars, so that for a hundred years the English and French peoples carried on a desultory warfare which even the poet Chaucer took part in at one time in his career. During this three-century era, also, the great guilds of tradesmen developed until they had to be reckoned with by kings and prelates everywhere. And not only did the common man of the city seek greater liberty and power through organizations of this kind, but the very peasants themselves rose up toward the end of the fourteenth century and for a moment almost overpowered the king and his counselors in London. Just at this time the teaching of Wyclif and his followers culminated in a break with the Church which came near to being an English Reformation. Over the country wandered Lollard preachers, haranguing against the friars and ecclesiastics in general, demanding that the common man think for himself and believe as he might see fit. While these movements for political, economic, and religious reform proved to a large degree premature, and England slipped back for another century into dissension and seeming retrogression, especially during the thirty-year period of the Wars of the Roses, nevertheless the intellectual horizon of the Englishman had been widened tremendously, and he was doing more real thinking than ever before in the history of the race.

It is a curious but natural feature of English cultural development during this age that as people gradually gave up the use of Norman French, slowly ruling it out of the schools and law courts, French literature was translated or paraphrased into the vernacular English in increasing quantities. Scores of long romances came in from the French, some of them very plainly the literary offspring of the Crusades. In the year 1352 Ralph Higden complained of the impairing of the native tongue because "children in school, against the usage and manner of all other nations, be compelled for to leave their own language and for to construe their lessons and their things in French, and so they have since the Normans came first into England." But change of program was already under way, and when John Trevisa translated Higden's Latin *Polychronicon* into English a short time later, he remarked that "now, the year of our Lord a thousand three hundred four score and five, and of the second king Richard after the conquest nine, in all the grammar schools of England, children leaveth French and construeth and learneth in English." Already, in 1357, a statute had been passed requiring that English should be employed in the law courts. So, gradually, there developed such an ignorance of French, even on the part of gentlemen's children, that it became necessary to translate into English such literature as people might desire to borrow from their French neighbors; and it was probably the difficulty that the translator had in finding equivalent English words for many ideas and things which forced him to take over bodily many of the French words that he found.

Certain it is that during this time more French words came into English than have ever been adopted during any other period of equal length.

But other reasons gradually developed for the introduction into English of more words and phrases. A religious drama slowly grew up and spread from the church to the streets and other public places. A growing taste for popular ballads glorifying Robin Hood and other heroes of England added to the literature of the land. By the time Chaucer had occasion to make a diplomatic visit to Italy, Dante and Petrarch and Boccaccio and other Italian writers had brought about an intellectual awakening which, while it did not sweep England until a century after Chaucer's death, must have had a marked influence upon the thinking and writing of this greatest of Middle English poets. And, finally, and by way of summing up the whole trend of this age, it should be noted that by the time Wyclif, "last of the schoolmen", died in 1384, scholasticism had largely ceased to heap up as conclusive evidence in any argument the opinions of the writers and thinkers of the past, and already men were beginning to question and reëxamine and often to discard the long-held and venerated old ideas that had been passed down from generation to generation after the manner of the Middle Ages.

In 1258 the first proclamation in English was issued by Henry III. About 1380 or a little later John Wyclif and his assistants brought out the first complete English version of the Bible. In 1386 the first petition in London English was addressed to Parliament. About this time there began to write in the English of London the first notable authors of that long line of literary Englishmen who have given to the world the greatest of all literatures — the English. Chaucer's friend John Gower made his first long poem in French, then he tried Latin in another, and finally he gained courage to put his third into his own London English. But Chaucer seems to have clung to the vernacular from the very start, and after his day a great many admirers and imitators in both England and Scotland carried on in the Chaucerian tradition, using his verse forms, his ideas, often his very words and phrases.

About the year 1476 William Caxton came to London and set up a printing press at Westminster, and for some years gave to the British public the best of the older English literature and many translations from the French which he himself had made. Perhaps no better testimony to the state of English culture and of the English language at the end of this age of Chaucerian influence can be found than in the prefaces of this earliest printer of London, who so admired Chaucer and his later imitators Hoccleve and Lydgate. At the beginning of the thirteenth century, as we have already observed, so few French words had entered into the English vocabulary that in all the long poem of Layamon (as he wrote it at first) not more than a hundred could be found, whereas in the vocabulary of Chaucer approximately half of the words had come from other languages, particularly the French. And as Caxton labored away at his long translations from French literature, he had occasion frequently to use some new French word for lack of an English equivalent. Moreover, as he selected words to express those exotic ideas for his fellow countrymen, he was apparently troubled at times by the realization that he was introducing words which some of his friends and fellow critics did not altogether approve of. For he says, in the preface to his translation of a French version of the story of Æneas, made in 1490, just a year before he died:

And when I had advised me in this said book, I deliberated and concluded to translate it into English, and forthwith took a pen and ink and wrote a leaf or two, which I looked over again to correct it. And when I saw the fair and strange terms therein, I doubted that it should not please some gentlemen which lately blamed me, saying that in my translations I had overcurious terms which could not be understood by common people, and they desired me to use old and homely terms in my translations. And fain would I satisfy every man, and to do so, took an old book and read therein. And certainly the English was so rude and broad that I could not well understand it. And also my Lord Abbot of Westminster had shown to me lately certain evidences written in Old English, for to reduce it into our English now used. And certainly it was written in such wise that it was more like to Dutch than English. I could not reduce it nor bring it to be understood. And certainly our language now used varyeth far from that which was used and spoken when I was born. For we Englishmen are born under the dominion of the moon, which is never steadfast but ever wavering, waxing one season and waneth and decreaseth another season. And that common English that is spoken in one shire varyeth from another.*

And so, with this note of uncertainty and perplexity, the first great printer of England leaves us just on the border line of that new era of English culture, the English intellectual Renaissance and the English religious Reformation, with a language that was still absorbing foreign terms most greedily, and converging toward a standard literary form, but still used with marked dialectal differences by the people of England.

36. *The English Renaissance*

While it has been possible to divide that great millennium of English linguistic history before 1500 into fairly definite periods because of sudden changes and breaks in the political life of Great Britain, with the coming of the English Renaissance, or rebirth, or revival, or awakening, as it has been variously called, it becomes necessary to look henceforth for continuous developments and movements in English cultural history and in the growth of the English tongue, and to take up, in turn, in the next three sections, the results of that awakening as they appear, first, in their earlier phases, in literature, art, and religion; next, in science and scholarly activity; and, thirdly, in increased commercial activities and political conquests. For a steady progress in each of these lines of human activity has resulted in a steady and healthy growth in that language which is today generally conceded to be the most interesting and promising and versatile of all the tongues of earth.

Students of the history of English culture have placed the beginnings of the English Renaissance at about 1500, and have often restricted the term to mean classical Renaissance because its earliest important manifestation was a new interest

* For a facsimile of the original text of this passage see the frontispiece of this book.

in the so-called classical, or pagan, literature of Greece and Rome; but we shall use the term here in a broader sense, as it connotes a protest against the medieval acceptance of authority in religion and in philosophy of life in general, on the one hand, and, on the other, a desire to improve every line of human endeavor. In Chaucer, already, one can observe this tendency in a dissatisfaction with the conventional forms of literature, such as the metrical romance and the love lyric, with the acquiescent philosophy of the old Boethius, with the exclusive interest taken by literature in the upper classes of society, and with the dogmatic religion of the Church of Rome. Chaucer's interest in the common man, his creation of new metrical forms, his jibes at many religious characters, and his quickened interest in the work of the Italian cultural leaders like Dante and Petrarch, all lead on to a greatly changed attitude in the sixteenth-century thinking of Englishmen in general. From the time Caxton faced the question of how one could best express new ideas in English, various writers for more than a century argued among themselves as to whether it was better to "improve" the language and "embellish" it by bringing in foreign terms (see Sec. 25) or whether it was better to keep it "pure" by using only the good old native words. During the sixteenth century, especially, many translations were made of the older literature of Greece and Rome, and the interest aroused by writers like Wyatt and Surrey in Italian art and literary theory led to marked changes in English literary productivity. The religious reform movement, which hung fire at the time of Wyclif, exploded with a bang in the time of Henry VIII, scattering the old monastic institutions of learning, with their great and precious libraries, and clearing the ground for the new Puritan movement in England and America. While the coming of printing tended to fix and conventionalize the spelling of the English language, it also gave wide currency to new forms of literature; a great dramatic movement spread over Elizabethan England, and Spenser, Shakespeare, Jonson, Milton, and a hundred other writers brought forth a wealth of new prose and verse such as the world has never seen since. With the capture of Constantinople by the Turks in 1453, the coming of printing to England about 1476, the discovery of America in 1492, and the separation of the English Church from Rome in 1531–1534, the awakening in England may be regarded as fully accomplished.

37. *Scientific and Scholarly Growth*

Perhaps the greatest manifestation of this new attitude toward thinking and the expression of this intellectual awakening may be seen in the new English scholarship which became prominent about the beginning of the sixteenth century. Scholarly work by men like Erasmus, Colet, and Sir Thomas More led to the improvement of teaching and the editing of old texts, notably the Bible. Teachers of Latin and Greek, French and Spanish, and other foreign languages began to publish bilingual dictionaries and to make grammars for the various foreign languages. From these bilingual textbooks it was only a step to the promotion of dictionaries and grammars for the English language itself. In 1604 Robert Cawdrey published his *Table Alphabeticall*, and for a century thereafter a succession of these little dictionaries of hard words appeared for the aid of those "more-knowing women and less-knowing men, or indeed for all such of the unlearned, who can but finde in an alphabet, the word they understand not", as the lexicographer Thomas Blount remarked in 1656. Already, late in the sixteenth century, Richard Mulcaster and William Bullokar had begun the making of English grammars; and if one desires to mark the progress of interest in the subject, he has only to follow the publication of that long series of school grammars which found their greatest popularity in the grammars of Noah Webster (1784) and Lindley Murray (1795), books which sold by the millions of copies. The ambition to collect all the words of the language in one dictionary did not show itself seriously until Samuel Johnson brought out his great two-volume folio dictionary in 1755, and the true attainment of the ideal may be said to have been realized, as nearly as it ever will be, only in the completion of the monumental ten-volume * New English Dictionary on Historical Principles, published at Oxford from 1884 to 1928.

It is customary to give to Francis Bacon (1561–1626) much of the credit for arousing enthusiasm for the new learning and putting the study of science on the modern foundation which it occupies today. It is interesting to note that Bacon was not quite sure of the permanence, even yet, of the English vernacular speech and so entrusted some of his greatest works on the new learning to the Latin language, just as Milton, a little later, continued to employ it in some of his more learned dissertations. Latin as an international and permanent vehicle for the expression of learned thinking had had so long and so honorable a career that it required a great deal of courage for the earlier English writers to set it aside and use only their own vernacular English tongue. But it is a most noteworthy testimonial, as already suggested (Sec. 27), to the growth of the use of the English language by scholars and scientists that many Dutch, Scandinavian, and other learned writers have swung to it within the past few decades and given up the use of German and French to a marked degree.

It is hardly necessary to call attention to the great number of highly technical scientific terms that have swarmed into the English dictionary during the last century or two. Many have become quite popular at times, such as *radio, telephone, phonograph, sulphur, humor, mercurial*; thousands of others are available for the scientific speaker when he needs them; and new ones are steadily coming into use as they are evoked by progress in scientific invention.

38. *Modern Trade and Conquests*

While it is true that a great part of the vocabulary increase since 1500 has resulted from the intellectual activity of literary men, scholars, and scientists, a steady growth must also be ascribed to the spread of British commerce over the world and the conquest and settlement by Englishmen of great tracts of land here and there, as already outlined in Section 27.

---

* A supplementary volume, published in 1933, brings the total to eleven.

MODERN TRADE AND CONQUESTS

British colonization of the new world of America between 1607 and the middle of the eighteenth century gave to the English language *moccasin, tomahawk, tomato, tobacco,* and various other new terms; early traders to the Orient brought back to England *cockatoos, tea,* and *teak* wood; from Dutch neighbors came many terms of the sea; and in later times the foods and fashions of Paris have left their imprint on the English-speaking world. Though the traders who have helped to coin the great jargons already discussed (see Sec. 17) have not brought back so many new terms from their voyages, nevertheless the very existence of Chinook jargon in the Pacific Northwest, of pidgin English in the Oriental lands, and of Beach-la-Mar in the great island region of Oceania has contributed to the growing importance of the English language.

Moreover, from the lands that the English have conquered there have come a great variety of new words: bush terms from Australia and Africa, Boer words like *trek* and *veld* from South Africa, words from the dialects of India, such as *coolie, mahout,* and *thug,* and from the polyglot vernacular of North America *muskeg, coyote, prairie, blizzard,* and many others.

The Englishman has been a wanderer over the earth, a pioneer in adventure, in trade, and in religious missionary effort from very early times. Chaucer, that realistic portrayer of the society of his day, illustrates well the wanderers of the Middle Ages in his "verray parfit gentil knight", who had seen service in many lands, both Christian and heathen, in the buxom Wife of Bath, who had done all the most expensive pilgrimages in her time, in the Pardoner, "that streight was comen fro the court of Rome", and in the cosmopolitan Friar, who was an education in himself as he wandered from tavern to tavern and home to home. But for an appreciation of the cultural contributions of the wandering Englishman of the later era one needs to follow the explorers and traders, such as the Cabots, Drake, Raleigh, and Frobisher; one needs to follow in the footsteps of the great Hudson's Bay Company, to go with Captain Cook to the islands of the Pacific, to follow Livingstone into darkest Africa, and to know something of the exploits of more recent explorers like Shackleton and the American Byrd.

And, finally, and not least in importance for an understanding of world wanderings which have been conducive to important growth in the English language, as well as to the spread of English into other lands, the work of missionaries, particularly in Africa, in India, and in the South Sea islands, has during the past two centuries been of great moment. For the missionary has been not only an adventurer but also a practical scholar, and wherever he has come into contact with an unknown foreign tongue, he has straightway learned the language and then proceeded to compile bilingual primers, grammars, and dictionaries until now there is scarcely a language spoken anywhere in the world for which one cannot find foreign-English, and frequently Anglo-foreign, textbooks of this kind, — Zulu-English, Hindustani-English, Portuguese-English, Sioux-English, and so on.

39. *The British Empire Today*

Perhaps enough has been said already in the discussion of the spread of English (Sec. 27) so that it is not necessary, in concluding this survey of the growth of English civilization, to enlarge upon the subject of the present-day scope of the use of the English language by those two great English-speaking powers, the British Empire and the United States of America. But it will throw further light on some aspects of the growth of English if the more important steps in the enlargement of the British Empire be reviewed briefly. Before entering into a discussion of this later growth of the Empire, it is in order to sum up the progress of the language in a few great steps or changes that it has experienced. In the first place, it was the transplanting of a group of Low German dialects from the shores of the Baltic to the island of Britain that marked the beginning of the Anglo-Saxon, or Old English, period. Secondly, it was the breaking down of the inflectional system of this Germanic Anglo-Saxon that introduced the Middle English period of our tongue. Thirdly, the great accomplishment of this later period may be said to have been the tremendous increase in the English vocabulary through the introduction of a great Romanic element, totaling nearly half of the entire body of English words. Finally, the language having been definitely established in England and having been then smoothed down inflectionally and built up in vocabulary, it has remained for the great Modern English period to accomplish two noteworthy things, namely, to refine and standardize the language, and to spread it abroad over the earth and make it an imperial language known to a large part of the population of the civilized world.

It is not necessary to go back farther than the year 1603 to find the beginnings of imperial English, for at that time James VI of Scotland came to London and assumed the title of James I of England as well. The significance of this event, linguistically speaking, has not always been fully appreciated. The loss of the court in Edinburgh meant the end of any serious competition at that time and for at least three centuries to come between Northern and Southern English, since all writers tended toward London and the use of the Southern English in their writings. It is true that the Northern Scots language has colored noticeably the speech of Canada and parts of the United States in later times. But the language that was to be spread throughout the British Empire during the next three centuries was the Southern English used around London and by the graduates of Oxford and Cambridge, of Eton and Rugby, and other centers of learning.

During the reign of this same James I (1603–1625) two great colonial developments took form which were to have very important bearings on the spread of the language during the Modern English period: the East India Company, already organized in 1600 under James's predecessor, Elizabeth, began to plant its trading posts in India; and in America settlements were made in Virginia and New England by the Cavaliers and the Puritans. In India this movement gained momentum and strength until the company became so thoroughly intrenched that it was able to conduct the government of many millions of natives speaking nearly a hundred and fifty different languages. It was not until the year 1858 that the British Crown assumed control directly of the government of these peoples of India. During the three hundred years of British control in India, traders have gone back and forth between India and England in increasing numbers, and a relatively small number of Englishmen have carried on in India, introducing their language here and there and adopting numerous native locutions to aid them in their intercourse with the polyglot population of the country. During the same period the culture of England was carried to the American colonies increasingly, but without any very great counter influence from the natives of America. The story of the later political and cultural growth of the British colonies now comprised in the United States of America is so important as to deserve separate consideration in a following discussion (Sec. 40).

In Canada, however, the British became more permanently established, with the winning of the land from the French at the end of the French and Indian War, in 1763; and today in places like the city of Victoria, Canadian life and culture are essentially British in spite of a strong coloring given by the American Indian and Canadian French populations. The outstanding peculiarity of the Canadian linguistic situation is that in some parts, such as Quebec, French has survived and is spoken as commonly as English. This bilingual situation, with the strong immigration of Scotch and Irish, has given to Canadian culture a coloring quite different from that of any other part of the British Empire.

As early as 1787 a colony was sent from England to establish itself in that part of New South Wales in Australia where Sydney now stands, and from that time on until the formation of the Commonwealth of Australia in 1900 a succession of exploring expeditions and settlements drove back the natives and built up this most distant part of the Empire. While the natives have contributed to English a few terms like *boomerang* and *kangaroo*, their linguistic influence has never been great, and such dialectal or provincial peculiarities as have appeared are probably due as much to the isolation of the Australians as to any native influence.

In the West Indies and British Guiana the language of Great Britain and the United States has played an important part in the cultural growth of the people from a very early time; and though the white people are relatively few, the influence of the English must be recognized both because of its official use and because of its intrusion into native dialects and jargons.

The question of language has assumed a very different form in South Africa, again, because of the triple relationship of natives, Dutch (Boers), and English. Inasmuch as the Boers had held much of this part of Africa since the middle of the seventeenth century, with a gradual increase of English influence during the same period until it culminated in the conquest of the whole country at the end of the Boer War in 1902, it is not surprising to find in the present Union of South Africa a population largely bilingual, speaking British English and that older provincial form of Dutch known as the Boer language, or Afrikaans. In the article on South Africa, written in 1910, shortly after the formation of the Union, the Encyclopædia Britannica said:

Officially throughout the Union of South Africa both languages are now on a footing of equality. Throughout South Africa a number of words, mainly Dutch, are in general use by the English-speaking inhabitants and also, to a great extent, among the natives.

Among the most common of these the writer went on to name *daal*, 'valley', *dorp*, 'village', *kopje*, 'little hill', *kraal*, 'inclosure', *rand*, 'border', *trek*, 'to take a journey', *uitlander*, 'foreigner', and *veld*, 'field'. Dutch place-names are, of course, fairly numerous, and Dutch weights and measures were also said to be in general use at that time. Whether the Boer element in the speech of the South Africans will maintain its place or ultimately yield to the English of the British remains to be seen.

Since the World War the British Empire has gained new prestige and new opportunities for the spread of the English language through the assumption of protectorates in various parts of the world, notably in former German colonies, such as German East Africa and German Southwest Africa, in Egypt, in Nigeria, in Palestine, and elsewhere.

It is interesting to note, in conclusion, that only in the oldest of the additions to the British Empire, in Ireland, has there been a tendency to withdraw completely from the Empire and to attempt to substitute for the use of Irish English the Celtic Gaelic tongue used in the past and now to be made a symbol of a new Irish independence culturally as well as politically. Whether the Irish patriot will succeed in restoring to general use the Irish Gaelic, which has been slowly losing its place to the English for a long time, remains, like the language question in South Africa and, in some degree, in eastern bilingual Canada, to be solved in the years to come. In all three countries the English language has been imposed upon the vernacular of conquered people, and the outcome of the contest for supremacy between the rival tongues will to a certain extent throw light upon the power and virility of English.

40. *American Speech*

In order to understand the linguistic relations of the British Empire and the United States of America, it is helpful to survey the cultural relations of the Englishman at home and the American as they have developed over a period of some three hundred years since the first colony was established in Virginia during the time of that greatest of English poets, William Shakespeare. For a century and a half the Englishman at home regarded the Englishman in the American colonies in much the same way as he regards those Englishmen of today who have occasion to go to the British colonial possessions and take up their residence there. He provided the American Englishman with most of his literature, from contemporary writers dating from Shakespeare to Samuel Johnson; he furnished him textbooks for his schools, especially grammars and dictionaries; and much of his own best philosophical and theological thinking he made available for the colonial Americans. The American schoolmen did not take up seriously the task of making their own grammars until

Noah Webster and Lindley Murray set the pace, after the American Revolution, and the first American dictionary was not published until 1798. Various British textbooks were reprinted in American editions, and doubtless many were shipped from England. Even the teachers and preachers were for some time men who had come over from England in a more or less missionary spirit. Not infrequently a man who had spent his active years in the colonies would return to England to finish his life, thus helping to maintain a sympathetic contact between the two countries.

With the political loss of the colonies, however, the attitude of the Englishman changed, and from a tolerant approval he shifted to a suspicious disapproval of the habits and life of his renegade countrymen. During the earlier part of the nineteenth century, especially, English visitors to America had much to say about the barbarous idiom that they heard spoken by the Yankees, by the Western pioneers, by the river men of the great inland waterways and valleys, and even by the townsmen of New York and Pennsylvania.[199] Much of this criticism was of a superficial nature, for the traveler did not stop to consider that the speech of these American users of English was no worse grammatically than much that he would hear in Yorkshire or Somerset or any other rural district of England; nor did he consider that different physical and political and geographical conditions must necessarily call for many different words and phrases. Perhaps, moreover, he failed altogether to examine the language of the educated and cultured American, so intent was he on the more colorful and cruder life of the frontiersman of the United States. Although Noah Webster insisted in the introduction to his great dictionary of 1828 that "the genuine English idiom is as well preserved by the unmixed English of this country, as it is by the best English writers", nonetheless British writers continued to dwell upon the barbarous slang and colloquialisms of American speech.

With the twentieth century there has come a strong effort on the part of American scholars and writers to counteract British criticism, and at the same time there has been a more earnest effort on the part of British students to differentiate between that which is standard and reasonably permanent in American English and that ephemeral slang and crude speech of illiterate foreigners and native pioneers which the United States of America has been especially afflicted with. In 1921 Tucker turned the tables on British critics by showing that many so-called Americanisms, such as *I guess*, had been used in England long ago.[200] At about the same time Mencken published a linguistic declaration of independence under the title *The American Language*.[201] In 1925 Krapp brought out under the auspices of the Modern Language Association of America a scholarly and thoroughgoing historical study entitled *The English Language in America*;[202] and when Craigie's *Historical Dictionary of American English* and the projected Dialect Dictionary of the American Dialect Society shall have been completed, American speech will have received sufficient scholarly recognition so that its real relationship to the English of the British Empire will be more clearly and satisfactorily understood than heretofore. At present those who regard it as a hopelessly barbarous dialect of English and those who extravagantly prophesy for it a separate linguistic career are about equally numerous and equally undependable as guides for the student of the English language.

Three centuries of separate growth have not produced as great a difference between British English and American English as one might reasonably expect. The most marked differences are with respect to pronunciation and can, therefore, be fully appreciated only as speakers of the two forms of English come together or are heard over the radio.[207] The pronunciation of certain classes of sounds is not difficult of analysis. The long [ō] in such words as *oh, know,* and *over* is a closer sound in the mouth of educated British speakers, so that to an American it sometimes seems tense and strained. In words spelled with the letter *o* followed by a single explosive consonant, such as *not, lot, hot,* British English has the short vowel [ɔ], whereas the vowel [ɑ] is generally heard in the United States. In words like *grass, path,* and *dance* British

English is likely to use the lower more open [ū] sound, just as some New Englanders and Southerners of the United States do, whereas the Westerner is wont to use the sound [æ]. It is also true of the *r* in words like *year, car,* and *part* that the consonantal *r* is a distinguishing feature of Western American pronunciation, whereas in England, as also in New England and the American South, the *r* is vocalized until a word like *fear* sounds like [fīʌ]. In certain types of words British English has its preferences: in *versatile, reptile, fertile, juvenile,* etc. the *i* is diphthongal, as in *file*; in *process* and the noun *progress* one can usually assume British pronunciation when he hears the sound [ō] instead of the usual American [a]. In the pronunciation of certain individual words, also, the two countries display striking differences, as, for example, in the British [lɛfténənt], [ʃédʒʊl], [bīn], [wɛr], where the American would say [luténənt], [skédʒul], [bɪn], and [wɜr]. Many British speakers tend to change the sound of the ending *-ing* from [ɪŋ] to [ɪn] as in *comin', sportin'* ; but this is not exclusively British.

In addition to pronunciations such as these, which are characteristic of the speech of the better-educated Englishman, the average American expects to hear in British speech the cockney misuse of initial [h], as in *hever* for 'ever' and *'eavy* for 'heavy', and the diphthongal [ɑɪ] in such words as *lidy* for 'lady' and *'Imarket* for 'Haymarket'. But the careful student of British English realizes that cockney-English pronunciation is one of the numerous British local dialects and should not be confused with the speech of the educated Englishman, just as the East Side dialect of New York City cannot fairly be regarded as typical American speech.

In various longer words British accentuation differs very strikingly from the American; in their pamphlet *Broadcast English* [216] the committee of the British Broadcasting Corporation (B. B. C.) have recommended, for example, that *centenary, doctrinal, intestinal, laboratory, quandary,* and *rotatory* be pronounced as if spelled *sentéenary, doctrýnal, intestýnal, labóratory, kwondáiry,* and *rotáytory*. Similar British pronunciations are *aluminium* (with an additional syllable)[28], *calíbre* [217], *cantónment,* and *coróllary.**

The American pronunciation of other longer words such as *decorative, dictionary, literary, necessary,* and *secretary* differs, in general, from the British pronunciation of such words in that the British speaker tends to stress strongly one syllable, usually the first, and hurry over the rest of the word, while American speakers are likely to pronounce every syllable more distinctly, putting not only a primary accent on the first syllable but also a secondary accent on a later syllable, as in *décoràtive.* Various explanations have been offered for this more careful pronunciation by American speakers. Doubtless it is to a certain extent a result of the teaching of spelling in spelling matches and spelling bees, where the common practice a generation ago was to build up a word syllable by syllable. A speller would say, for example, "*S-e-c,* 'sec', *r-e,* 'secre', *t-a,* 'secreta', *r-y,* 'secretary'." Moreover, the promotion of education in pioneer days in little isolated schools by young teachers who depended largely upon the printed page must have forced many of these teachers to employ spelling pronunciations just because they never had opportunity to hear other people of education pronounce such words. And, finally, a more conscious endeavor to maintain the integrity of words has probably arisen in America because of the need of counteracting the careless and ignorant pronunciation of a great swarm of foreigners who have immigrated to the United States. Nowhere else in the world have people purchased grammars and spelling books and dictionaries by the millions of copies as the Americans have bought the textbooks of Murray and Webster and Worcester, for example.

In a third respect, and one more difficult of analysis, the pronunciation of British English sounds slightly — sometimes very noticeably — strange to American ears. This difference lies in the lower pitching of the voice of the cultured Englishman, in the varying inflections of the voice in continuous speech, and in a somewhat different speech

* It should be noted, however, that opinion differs in both countries regarding the accentuation of most of these words.

rhythm in general. The individual vowel and consonant sounds may be the same, the accentuation and pronunciation of individual words may be the same; but when the British speaker strings them together in consecutive and unaffected speech, he produces a different effect from that produced by an American using the same sounds and words.

In the printed literature of British and American English one does not notice so many differences. Yet there are a few that stand out on the printed page. On the whole, the British speller has preferred *-our* in words like *colour, favour,* and *honour* rather than the *-or* commonly employed in America; he has clung to the verb suffix *-ise* in words like *civilise* and *humanise*, largely, although it should be noted that there is at present a strong movement in England to adopt the *-ize* spelling more commonly used in the United States; and in certain special spellings such as *cheque, gaol, kerb* ('stone edging to pavement'), *plough, shew, storey* (of a building), and *tyre* British English differs from the American *check, jail, curb, plow, show, story,* and *tire.* Perhaps the British speller may be considered somewhat more conservative in retaining the *æ* in words like *mediæval* and *æther.* But in the matter of spelling it is most unwise to attempt to establish hard-and-fast differences between British and American practice, because in both countries strong organizations for the reform of English spelling have agreed for some years on some of these matters, because many Americans choose to imitate the Englishman in writing words like *cheque* and *kerb*, and because much of the current literature of the two countries is being steadily reprinted or carried across the Atlantic.

To the student of the English language the most interesting phase of this comparative study, perhaps, is concerned with the vocabulary differences of British and American speech. It is about words, mostly, that the bitterest warfare has been waged by critics of American English. One can forgive differences in pronunciation when he has been accustomed to many dialectal variations such as have existed in England from Anglo-Saxon days on, and one can expect that individual caprice will account for peculiarities in spelling. But it has been very hard for many Englishmen to forgive the American for taking liberties with old and well-established words, changing meanings, substituting other words, or clinging tenaciously to words that they have dropped from their own speech at home in England. Until very recently Americanisms have been collected and published in lists or glossaries without much attempt at discrimination or classification either by the American student or by the British critic. But in fairness to the educated speaker of American English such discrimination should be made. For the lists of so-called Americanisms that have appeared have contained all sorts of locutions, originating in a great variety of ways and from various causes.

Tucker has compiled from the glossaries of Americanisms more than eleven hundred expressions which he has been able to find in earlier English literature but which have been modified in or lost altogether from the speech of present-day Great Britain,—such locutions as *baggage* (Brit. *luggage*), *ice cream*, *to guess*, *poorly* (adj.), and the like.[200] For various reasons the separately developing life and culture of America have evolved other distinctly American forms like *campus*, *coal oil* or *kerosene* (Brit. *paraffin*), *elevator* (Brit. *lift*), *pitcher* (Brit. *jug*), *street car* (Brit. *tram*), and the letter name *zee* (Brit. *zed*). Different physical features of the United States have added to American speech topographical words like *bluff*, *butte*, *canyon*, *prairie*, and, along with these, other words like *blizzard*, *chinook wind*, and *Indian summer*. From differing fauna and flora the English language in America has acquired *basswood*, *coon*, *cottonwood*, *hickory*, and *opossum*. Of course the American Indians have contributed numerous common nouns and place-names, such as *squaw*, *tomahawk*, *wigwam*, *Nebraska*, *Oklahoma*. Moreover, the presence of the negro in the United States has given currency to words like *banjo*, *cakewalk*, *darky*, *mammy*, and *pickaninny*. The colorful growth of American political institutions has had, also, a very marked influence on the vocabulary of the American, adding to it *caucus*, *congress*, *federal*, *filibuster*, *lobby*, *mugwump*, *platform*, and numerous others. The many foreigners coming to the United States, from Europe particularly, have introduced into American speech words like *bayou, calaboose, coleslaw, cookie, hamburger,* and *loafer* (see Sec. 16, *b*).

In the course of three centuries, as might be expected, the meanings of various old English words have gradually diverged in the two countries. In America *bloody* and *bug* have retained a social status of respectability, but in England they are not admitted to polite conversation; in America *corn* has been narrowed so as to mean only the Indian corn, or maize; *fraternity* in America is a more narrowly technical term; *sick* in American English is replaced by *ill* in British speech; a *store* in America is usually equivalent to a *shop* in England; the *first storey* of a British building is the *second story* in America.

In certain trades and professions the linguistic usages of British and American speakers have drifted rather far apart during recent years, largely, perhaps, because the workmen of the two countries have not gone back and forth as frequently as travelers of the higher social classes. Where the American railroad man speaks of *bumper, cowcatcher* (or *fender*), *fireman, freight train, roadbed,* and *to switch,* the English worker would use *buffer, pilot, stoker, goods train, permanent way,* and *to shunt*. In the automobile industry the American uses *gasoline, hood, truck,* and *wrench,* which appear in British English as *petrol, bonnet, lorry,* and *spanner* [203]. In the English theater the American finds his familiar *balcony, lobby, orchestra,* and *usher* renamed *dress circle, foyer, stalls,* and *attendant*; he seeks a *cinema* rather than a *movie*; he secures his tickets at a *booking office* rather than a *ticket office*. Shopping in London, he would have to ask for *biscuits, boots, sweets,* or *treacle* rather than *crackers, shoes, candy,* or *molasses,* and he would look for a *chemist* rather than a *druggist*.

But the greatest departure of American English from the speech of England has been due to the very pronounced tendency of Americans to coin slang and colorful colloquialisms of many kinds. This tendency can be ascribed largely, no doubt, to the ingenuity and resourcefulness of pioneers living a life from which many of the inhibitions common to life in an older and more settled country have been removed. It has also been influenced, probably, by the intermingling of foreigners from a great number of other lands. From every phase of American life these colloquialisms and slang expressions have come: from the miner, *to pan out* and *pay dirt*; from the gambler, *to ante up, to bluff,* and *to stack up*; from the hunter, *to bag* and *to miss fire*; from the underworld criminal, *to beat it* and *to hook*; from the woodsman, *to backtrack, bee line, logrolling,* and *tenderfoot*; and so on (see also Sec. 11).[204] So involved does this American slang become at times that the British speaker of English almost needs a glossary to make clear to him its meaning, as in the case of a very slangy popular drama which was played in London some years ago.[205] It is true that the Englishman too has his favorite colloquialisms and slang expressions, such as *bally, blighter, gaspers, right-o, rotter, swank*; a certain type of British novel abounds in locutions like *buzz along, loopy, squiffy, tootle off*; and the British schoolboy has always managed to vary and embellish his intimate speech with slang and schoolboy dialect not unlike that of his American cousins. On the whole, however, there is a noticeable difference between the constant and varied production of slang in the United States and the more restrained and limited British practice.

In a few points of syntactical usage English and American practices differ somewhat. While the American uses *different from*, in British English *different to* is preferred. The American uses *aim* with the infinitive form, as in 'He aims to go today', while in England the construction is not so popular. On the other hand, one often hears 'Aren't I?' in England, and some Americans have been inclined to adopt it as a convenient, even though illogical, shortcut in speech. Most of the variations in syntactical usage, however, which one might cite as examples of a separate American practice are to be found either in the language of the more illiterate and ungrammatical speaker or else in certain dialects of the United States.

Inasmuch as the stronger scholarly interest in American speech since about 1900 has resulted in the publication of whole volumes of so-called Americanisms, in the collecting of many glossaries of local American idioms by the American

Dialect Society, and in the printing of innumerable brief studies in *American Speech* and elsewhere about phases and trends in the language of the United States, it would be obviously impossible to do full justice to the subject in this summing up of the development of the American form of English. But the following chapters will naturally contribute more details for the study of American speech, and the student should expect to sort out for himself those locutions which can be regarded as distinctively American rather than British.

If such detailed information concerning American speech be sought and carefully and thoughtfully appraised according to the standards already presented in Section 8, perhaps one will feel himself more nearly ready to answer certain questions that are being asked with increasing frequency and growing interest by present-day students of language. An attempt has been made in the foregoing discussion to establish the fact that American speech does differ somewhat from the standard speech of England. One might list certain general causes for this difference, notably: the greater freedom in linguistic practice resulting from the removal of many inhibitions among pioneers in a new country; the dominance of certain social classes in well-defined areas, such as the Puritans in New England, the Cavaliers in Virginia, the Dutch in New York, the Quakers and Germans in Pennsylvania; the flocking together in colonial America of people speaking certain dialects of England, especially the Essex dialect, rather than the standard speech of London; the retention of Elizabethan English by isolated groups, such as the mountaineers of the South; the counter influence of races established in or bordering upon the United States, notably the American Indians, the Negroes, the Mexicans, and the Canadian French; and, finally, the contaminating influence of hordes of foreigners immigrating in later times to various communities of North America. Having examined the influences that have brought about separate linguistic tendencies in America, one can hardly avoid being carried along to a point where he will ask himself what the future has in store for American speech. And this questioning will take the form of four major questions, perhaps, namely: Just how great is the difference between American speech and standard British English? Will this difference increase as time goes on? Does American English need standardizing and stabilizing? and, finally, Is it likely that American speech will eventually replace British English in the preference of the world at large?

As to the first question, the matter may be summed up by the statement that the pronunciation of the American Westerner and the educated Englishman differ rather more noticeably than that of the New Englander and the Westerner or the Southerner and the Westerner; the written language of educated writers of the two countries varies relatively little, as any American reader of a British novel can see for himself; but the tremendous vogue of slang and social and other dialect in America constitutes a real difficulty for the speaker familiar only with British English. It should be said, however, that the Englishman has really no more need to fear the intrusion of this ephemeral slang and these vulgar colloquialisms into his standard speech than the American of culture and linguistic pride has, for to the speaker of standard American English the menace seems, probably, just as great as it does to the Englishman.[206]

It does not seem likely that British and American English will become more unlike than they are at present, since the causes that have induced differentiation in the past have been slowly yielding to other causes that favor unification. The old pioneer freedom of life and pioneer indifference to established habits and practices have slowly given way to a more settled and conservative mode of life; the rapid succession of new experiences peculiar to the American scene, experiences which called for new words and idioms, has largely ceased; the powerful waves of foreign immigration have likewise diminished since the passage of drastic laws of restriction, and more and more the communities of foreigners have been Americanized and absorbed into the life and culture of the United States. On the other hand, more intimate relations between the Americans and other English-speaking peoples of the earth are being constantly multiplied through the improvements of communication and travel. Indeed, it is not easy to foretell the probable unifying effects of the development of the radio, the sound pictures, air travel, telephone service, and world-news agencies.

Before an answer can be given to the third question, it is necessary to make some attempt to separate the enduring and conservative speech of the better-educated speakers of American English from those slang and dialect locutions that have shocked the Englishman. Moreover, we must recognize that although the New England and Southern dialects are outstanding, the Western, or General, type has been slowly encroaching upon the other two throughout the United States in much the same way that the American form of English has encroached upon British English in other lands. Undoubtedly the efforts that actors of the stage and screen and speakers over the air are making to get together and to agree upon some standard pronunciation of our language will have an important part in the standardization of American speech. Certainly it is becoming constantly harder for dialects to exist in America, just as the dialects of Great Britain have been slowly succumbing before the inroads of education and communication and linguistic conformity.

When it comes to the fourth and last question, namely, that of whether American speech will ultimately supersede British English, one can only set forth some of the facts pertinent to the question and then draw his own conclusions. At present the American people are more than twice as numerous as the inhabitants of the British Isles; American traders and travelers have gradually penetrated to every corner of the earth; American scholars and scientists are today influential in every civilized country to an extent not dreamed of a generation ago; and, finally, the aggressiveness and exuberance of American life seem to be appealing very strongly to the peoples of other lands. This question of supremacy may gradually cease to assert itself if the two forms of English should converge and become unified instead of drifting farther apart. The chances of their unification seem at the present time fully as good as the chances of continued differentiation.

CHAPTER VI

PRONUNCIATION OF ENGLISH

IN EXAMINING the sounds that are made use of in the pronunciation (or phonology) of Current English, it should be remembered that while the individual vowels and consonants, and certain combinations of them into diphthongs and consonant groups, can be distinguished and classified and studied separately, nevertheless they occur normally in a continuous flow of speech (see Sec. 19) wherein they are likely to be affected both by the strength or weakness of accentuation (see Sec. 22) and by the proximity of certain neighboring sounds which exert a modifying influence upon them (see Sec. 23). It should be borne in mind that it is not always easy to draw a line between long and short vowels and between voiced and voiceless consonants, and the rough classification made in Chapter III must be regarded, not only in the study of phonetics in general but also in the more detailed study of English sounds, as only an approximation of existing speech conditions. Strictly speaking, vowel length (or quantity) does not involve quality of sound at all but is a relative matter dependent largely upon the amount of accentuation of the vowel under consideration and the kinds of consonants that accompany it. It may be a long, a half-short, or a very short accented vowel, or, if it is unaccented, in quantity it may be slightly long, short, or so weak as to be almost nil as a vowel.

And not only does one person speak the same word differently at different times and under varying conditions of speech, but even speakers of the best standard English and the dictionaries differ among themselves to such an extent in their recognized pronunciation of certain words that for years the editors of Webster's unabridged dictionaries have deemed

Sec. 41] ENGLISH VOWELS AND DIPHTHONGS 167

it advisable to give a comparative tabulation setting forth the opinions of some seven of the leading dictionaries on several hundred words (see the 1934 edition, p. lix).

And, finally, an effort should be made from the very outset to think of these English sounds as they are spoken rather than as they are represented in spelling, since the spellings of Current English are so various and unphonetic and erratic that one can stand on firm ground only when he pronounces a sound and then represents it by the accepted phonetic symbol given in Section 21.

41. *English Vowels and Diphthongs*

Since even very slight changes in tongue positions, either upward and downward or forward and backward, will produce changes and variations in the quality of vowels, their relations to one another may be best kept in mind by means of the following diagram:

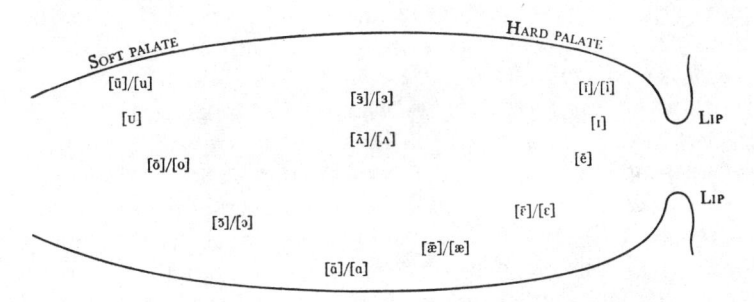

[ū]/[u]   [ə̄]/[ə]   [ī]/[i]
[ʊ]   [ɪ]   LIP
[ō]/[o]   [ʌ̄]/[ʌ]   [ē]
[ɔ̄]/[ɔ]   [ɛ̄]/[ɛ]   LIP
          [ǣ]/[æ]
   [ō]/[ɑ]

SOFT PALATE   HARD PALATE

A. ACCENTED VOWELS AND DIPHTHONGS
1*a.* *Long* [ā]

This sound is found in present-day speech most often in words containing a single *r* immediately following the vowel, as in *army, bark, barter, car, cargo, far, guard, hard, harp, hearken, heart, mar, martyr, parson, sergeant, star, starve, tartar,* and *yard.* In England *Berkeley, clerk,* and *Derby* are given this [ā] sound, but with the *r* not pronounced. And in America, sometimes, the dialectal pronunciation of *certain, dursin't, sermon, serpent,* and *service* has employed this same long vowel; it was also present in the early American *larn, tarnal,* and *varmint* (or *varmin*). The word *varsity* is, of course, a form of *university*. The pronunciation of *hearth* has gradually shifted from a once common [hɜrθ] to a present-day [hārθ].

In a number of words which had formerly a pronounced medial [l], the [l] has become silent and the vowel has lengthened to [ā], as in *alms, balm, palm, psalm, qualm*. There has been a tendency to lengthen similarly the *a* in *almond* and *salmon*; but, while the [l] seems to be gradually becoming silent, the [æ] sound is also commonly heard in both words.

A few other words like *father, baa, khaki, kraal, spa, lava, saga, garage, mirage, suave* (American pronunciation), and *errata* have, usually, [ā], either long, as indicated, or half long.

Variables.* Another group of words, estimated by Kenyon (p. 100)[212] at about a hundred and fifty in all, are variously pronounced with long [ā], with short [æ], and with an intermediate short vowel which the more exact phoneticians represent with the roman-type letter [a]. In this group are included mainly words with *a* before the continuants [f], [θ], [s] (alone or in combination), as in *half, staff, craft, laughter; bath; class, ask, clasp, aghast, master,* and before the nasals [m], [n] (in combination), as in *example, command, advance, answer, can't, aunt, advantage, stanch*; one should include here also *drama, piano*. Many British speakers use long [ā] in these words; in the General, or Western, American dialect short [æ] is very generally used†; but for about a century lexicographers and many teachers of speech have endeavored to distinguish in these words the short [a] which is a compromise between [ā] and [æ] and which has been rather difficult to teach to speakers accustomed to the Western American [æ].

* Inasmuch as the lists of variables in this chapter are intended to illustrate both earlier and later trends in the pronunciation of English words, colloquial and standard pronunciations will be found intermingled. Since no special effort has been made to distinguish them, the dictionaries should be consulted for help in determining good usage.

† A Georgia friend writes: "Southern American also. I use [æ] in every one of these words."

And, finally, in American dialect literature of an earlier period one finds such words as *bar* and *har* (for 'bear' and 'hair'), indicating a substitution of [ā] for the more usual [ē].

1b. *Short* [ɑ]

This sound is very commonly heard in American speech; in many words, however, it has not been universally accepted but is used interchangeably with [ɔ]. Perhaps there is no class of words in which American pronunciation varies so much as in this one. In *wanton, was, what, quality, quantity, swan, swallow, squad, wattle,* and *waddle,* for example, and in words spelled with *o* before double *r*, such as *borrow, horrid, morrow, sorrel, sorrow,* and *sorry,* the two pronunciations are heard commonly, and the authorities on pronunciation differ greatly.

In other words, such as *block, body, collar, college, copper, policy, politics,* the [ɑ] is quite generally heard. Not infrequently, in a longer derivative form of a word, this short [ɑ] replaces the long [ō] or [ū] of the briefer form of the word, as, for example, *locative* (cf. *locate*), *telephonic* (cf. *telephone*), *tonic* (cf. *tone*), *vocative* (cf. *vocal*), and *folly* (cf. *fool*).

Before [l], [m], [n], and [r] both short vowels are heard, also, as in *doll, follow, dromedary, honorary, coroner, forest, forehead, hollow, orange, foreign,* and also before other continuants, as in *coffee, Gothic, hospital, novel,* and *ostrich.*

Variables. Occasionally, however, the variation is between the short vowels [ɑ] and [ʌ], as in *bomb, grovel, hovel, monetary, nothing, was, what,* and *wont*; indeed, some words of this group are pronounced with all three of these short vowels.

One of the noticeable differences between American and British pronunciation is to be observed in monosyllables ending in stop consonants, such as *got, hot, lot, not, rob, rod, sod, stock,* the American using the short [ɑ] sound and the British speaker the [ɔ].

In a few common monosyllables, such as *daub, dog, frog, God, hog, log,* both pronunciations are common; but there has been a tendency on the part of literary people to assume that the [ɔ] pronunciation is dialectal and, sometimes, slightly vulgar. So, when they have wished to present the speech of certain illiterate characters, they have spelled these words *dawg, Gawd, hawg,* and so on, making the pronunciation appear worse than it really is.

2a. Long [ǣ]

This long vowel is theoretically the lengthened form of the vowel heard in *at, fan, fat,* and occurs only in words with final [r] or, sometimes, a medial [r], such as *air, fairest, fare, glare, glaring, hair, Mary,* and *parent.* Many speakers, however, use the higher long vowel [ē] instead and do not prolong the sound enough to make it much more than a half-long vowel (see 3a, below).

2b. Short [æ]

While this sound has always been common in English, it may be said to be at the present time characteristically Western American, as already noted. It is found regularly in monosyllabic words before the explosive consonants, as in *back, bad, bag, bat, cab, cap, plaid* (Scottish [plēd]). It occurs before the nasals in *band, clam, man, Sam, slang, span, spangle, Spokane.* It is found before other consonant combinations, as in *adz, badge, catch, lapse, lax,* and *Max.* In polysyllabic words before [l], particularly, this [æ] is often heard, although some of the dictionaries assume that the regular pronunciation has [ɑ]. Examples are *alibi, alimony, allegory, alley, alligator, anecdote, balcony.*

In other words of more than one syllable this vowel [æ] is commonly employed, as in *alum, ascertain, battery, caddy, captain, flattery, happy, hydrangea,* and *radish.* Often, in a longer derivative form of a word, it replaces the long [ē] which is heard in the shorter form of the word, as in *fabulous* (cf. *fable*), *tabulate* (cf. *table*), *national* (cf. *nation*), *gravity* (cf. *grave*), *depravity* (cf. *deprave*), and *declamatory* (cf. *declaim*).

Variables. As we have already observed, the Western American regularly employs this [æ] before the nasals [m], [n], and the continuants [f], [θ], [s] (alone or in combination), in such words as *dance, France, salmon* [sæmən], *demand, sample; have, laugh, lath, plaster, rafter, task, waft.*

In a few polysyllabic words with a very weak second syllable, practice is still divided or slightly uncertain. In *apricot* the short vowel seems to be giving way to the long; in *patriot* the pronunciation with the short is regarded as old-fashioned; in *patent* the short vowel is reserved for the noun function of the word, usually; in *rational* the short vowel is preferred, as in *national* and *patronage*, also; but in *stationary* the longer vowel is preferred; in *rations* usage is still divided, as also in *glacier*. The short [æ] sound is used in *chasm*, *spasm*, *protoplasm*, *gravel*, *cavil* (but long [ē] in *naval* and *navel*), *rapine*, *spavin*, *davit*, *habit*, *rabid*, *rapid*, *vapid* (but long [ē] in *David*, *naked*).

In dissyllabic words, before medial [r], this lower vowel [æ] is generally recommended by the dictionaries and is employed by many speakers, although some use the higher [ɛ]. Examples are *carry*, *farrier*, *narrow*, *sparrow*, *wheelbarrow*. Probably the same people who would use long [ǣ] in words like *fare* [fǣr], as noted above, would use the lower short [æ] in these words.

In some recently borrowed Latin words usage is divided between the long [ē] and this short lower [æ], as in *data*, *lapis lazuli*, *rabies*, *status*, and *strata*; and even in some of longer standing in English, such as *drama* and *satyr*, the pronunciation is still unsettled.

3a. Long [ɛ]

This long vowel is theoretically the lengthened form of the vowel heard in *bet*, *bless*, and *men*, and occurs chiefly in words with final [r]; perhaps it may sometimes be heard before medial [r], though in such instances its length is hard to prove. In such words as *air*, *fairest*, *fare*, *glare*, *glaring*, *hair*, *Mary*, *parent*, and numerous others not already mentioned, such as *bear*, *care*, *chair*, *heir*, *pear*, *prayer*, *there*, *wear*, and *where*, this long vowel is probably more often used than the lower [ǣ], discussed already in connection with some of these same words (see 2a, above).

Variables. Some speakers distinguish between such pairs as *bare* and *bear*, *fair* and *fare*, *hair* and *hare*, *stair* and *stare*, *ware* and *wear*, by utilizing the lower [æ] sound for the one and the higher [ē] sound for the other; but by most speakers these words are pronounced without appreciable difference in normal English speech.

3b. Short [ɛ]

This sound has always been common in English, and, because it is lax and neither high nor low, it is very popular today. It is found in monosyllables and many polysyllabic words, and, as already suggested, before [r] frequently. Before the explosives it occurs in words like *bed, bread, said, bet, wet, threat, neb, depth, jeopardy, leopard, step, egg, keg, wreck*. It is used commonly before the continuants, as in *clef, effort, Evans, bless, question, fez, says, breath, leather, digression, pleasure*. It is even popular for clipped words like *deb* (for 'debutante'), *ex* (for 'examination'), *jell* (for 'jelly'), *pep* (for 'pepper'), *pleb* (for 'plebeian'), *prep* (for 'preparatory'), *reb* (for 'rebel'), and *vet* (for 'veteran'). It is commonly used with [l], [m], and [n] in words like *realm, yelk, bell, hemorrhage, semaphore, Thames, mention, friend* (but not *fiend*), *bend, member, Leonard*, and *rennet*.

This short vowel occurs in many other polysyllabic words, such as *asafetida, Bethlehem, metaphor, nebulous, telephone, Texaco*. Often, in a longer derivative form of a word, it replaces the long [ī] or [ē] of the briefer form of the word, as, for instance, in *bestial* (cf. *beast*), *breakfast* (cf. *break*), *Denmark* (cf. *Dane*), *heather* (cf. *heath*), *metrical* (cf. *meter*), *stealthy* (cf. *steal*), *wealthy* (cf. *weal*), *zealous* (cf. *zeal*), and British *waistcoat* [wɛskət] (cf. *waist*).

Although vowels are, as a rule, likely to lengthen in open syllables (see Sec. 23), when the second syllable of a dissyllabic word consists of some weak form like *-id*, *-y*, or vocalic [l̥], [n̥], [r̥], the *e* (or other spelling) in the first syllable of the word generally stands for this short vowel [ɛ], as in *fetid, tepid, bevy, heavy, any, many, devil, bevel, level, metal, ethyl* (but long [ī] in *evil*), *clever, ever, feather, heifer, never, sever* (but long [ī] in *fever, meter*, and often in *lever*), *felon, heaven, seven, weapon* (but long [ī] in *Ethan* and *even*). Other vowels are similarly variable before weak syllables.

Variables. As already remarked, this short vowel (ε) is commonly used in dissyllabic (and even in polysyllabic) words before medial [r], varying with short [æ] (see 2b, above). Examples are *arid, carry, charity, clarinet, fairy, garret, meritorious, narrow, parrot, sparrow*, and *terrible*. As in the case of the long vowels before [r], an attempt is made also to utilize the two short vowels [æ] and [ε] to differentiate pairs such as *Barry* and *berry, fairy* and *ferry, hairy* and *Harry, marry* and *merry, vary* and *very*; but by some speakers the vowels in these words are pronounced alike or with only slight variations.

There is a marked difference of opinion as to whether long [ī] or short [ε] should be used in a number of words in common use. The tendency seems to be toward the use of short [ε] in *deaf, economics* (but long [ī] in college clipped *econ*), *ephemeral, genealogy, legend, lever* (British pronunciation with long [ī]), *scenic*; but the long vowel is preferred by many, especially American speakers, in *egoist, egret, Elizabethan, fetish, leaped, leisure, penalize*, and *seamstress*. In dialectal usage one often finds short [ε] in place of the regularly employed [æ], as in *ketch* (for 'catch'), *gether* (for 'gather'), and, in Yiddish-American, *esk* (for 'ask'), *pens* (for 'pants') (see Sec. 16, b).

4a. Long [ē]

This vowel occurs frequently in open syllables and in closed syllables whose former openness is indicated by the retention of a final silent *e* in present-day spelling; it occurs also in numerous other words of Current English. In open syllables it occurs in words like *ague, Asia, basic, chaotic, crochet, halo, Malay, Paley, salable*, and *salient*. In closed syllables with final silent *e* it may be found before all the explosive and all the continuant consonants, in such words as *babe, ape, made, lemonade, fate, fete, vague, ache, make*; *save, safe, staves* (but singular *staff*), *bathe* (but noun *bath*), *lathe, daze, glaze* (but noun *glass*), *ace, erase*; and before -*g* in *age* and -*ste* in *paste*.

In many words its length is indicated by the use of silent consonants or by vowel digraphs, as in *aye, faith, gauge, geisha, obey, pay, sleigh, straight, straits, they, waist, way,* and *weight.* In a number of standard-English pronunciations the digraph *ea* has this sound instead of that of the next higher vowel, as in *break, great, sleazy, steak*; and in the Irish-English dialect one frequently hears this vowel in words like *clean, dream, leave, mean,* which the dialect writer is likely to indicate by respelling these words as *clane, drame, lave,* and *mane.* Such Irish names as *Eames, McLean,* and *Yeats* are usually spelled with *ea,* though sometimes they appear as *Ames, McLain* or *McLane,* and *Yates.*

With [l], [m], and [n] this long vowel is common, as in *gaol, gale, pale, pail, feign, deign, main, name, claim, blame, range, mange* (but short in *flange*); even before [r] the more usual sound [æ] or [ɛ] is sometimes raised to this vowel [ē] when a word is prolonged and stressed, as in *chary, dairy, Mary, vagary* [vēgērɪ], and *wary.*

In an open syllable followed by a weaker syllable containing vocalic [l̥], [m̥], [n̥], [r̥], this long vowel is also commonly used, as in *cable, hazel, sable, acre, labor, neighbor, squalor* (but also [skwɑlr̥]), *tailor, vapor* (but short [æ] in *clamor, glamour, manor,* and *amorous*), *maelstrom, Salem* (but short in *Adam, atom, chasm, spasm,* etc.), *bacon, basin, craven, nation, raven.*

Variables. This long [ē] is generally preferred in such words as *apparatus, aviator, gala, gratis, ignoramus, patriot, phalanx, radio,* and *status,* though the use of the short [æ] in these words is not uncommon. Likewise both long [ē] and the Latin [ū] are to be heard in *aria, armada, promenade, tirade, tomato,* and *ultimatum.*

Perhaps more than any other long vowel this [ē] is likely to become a diphthong medially in an open syllable or in short words or at the end of a word, [eɪ] being heard in words like *day, Haymarket, lady, say, take, yesterday, way.* Quite often, moreover, this dipthong [eɪ] is lowered in pronunciation to [æɪ], and in the cockney dialect of London it goes even lower yet to the very open diphthong [ɑɪ], so that the dialect writer usually spells such words as *dy, 'Imarket, lidy, sy, tike, yesterdy, wy.*

5 a. Long [ī]

The tendency in English during the past millennium to raise the pronunciation of long vowels has resulted in the accumulation of a great number of English words with this highest front vowel. It appears in open syllables in many words, such as *ægis, bee, cohesion, expedient, he, key, lethal, mosquito, people, phœnix, precinct, quay, sea, subpœna, tepee, trio*. It is used before all the explosive consonants, as in *grebe, deep, heap, deed, read, beat, beet, complete, suite, fatigue, league, clique, creek, meek, sleek, siege, beach, beseech*, and (sometimes) *breeches*. It occurs regularly before the continuants, as in *believe, eve, receive, chief, leaf, freeze, frieze, trapeze, geese, fleece, caprice, police, seethe, teeth*, and *beneath*.

Before the liquid [l] and the nasals [m] and [n] this long [ī] is also commonly found, as in *anneal, feel, beam, cream, deem, bean, machine, ravine, seen*, and *intervene*. Before [r] it may be heard sometimes when a speaker makes a special effort to pronounce the word distinctly and carefully, as in *cereal, dear, dreary, eery, era, hero, near, query, serial, serious, weary, weir*. But usually in such words, before [r], the vowel becomes the relaxed and shorter [ɪ]. Occasionally, though by no means uniformly, this long [ī] occurs before the lengthening combinations [ld], [nd], and [st], as in *field, shield, fiend* (but [ɛ] in *end* and *friend*), *beast, least, priest* (but [ɛ] in *best, chest, vest*, etc.). Theoretically this long [ī] should be pronounced before [rd] in such words as *beard, feared*, and *weird*; but, as a matter of fact, most speakers use the short [ɪ] in their ordinary, unstudied speech.

In open syllables followed by weak syllables with vocalic [l̥], [m̥], [n̥], [r̥], the long [ī] is common but by no means universal. The vowel is long in *evil, needle, weevil, wheedle* (but short in *devil* etc.), in *freedom, besom, Edom*, and *sedum*, in *demon, reason*, and *season* (but short in *felon, seven*), in *ether, Peter, teeter*, and *heater* (but short in *ever, feather*).

Variables. As in the case of most other long vowels in English, there is some difference of usage in respect to long [ī]. It varies with the diphthong [ɑɪ] in a number of words, being preferred in *Argentine, either, neither* [219], *oblique,* by most American speakers, but apparently yielding gradually to the diphthong [ɑɪ] in *angina, appendicitis, iodine, tonsillitis.* As already noted, this long [ī] is more often heard in *amenable, egoist, leisure,* etc., but gives way to short [ɛ] in similar words, such as *legend* and *petrol.* In a few common words, such as *depot, detour, feeze, inveigle, jeans,* and *sheik,* both [ī] and [ē] are heard; and in the Irish dialect of English, as already illustrated (see Sec. 16, *a*), the usual [ī] is frequently changed to [ē] in such words as *leave, receive,* and *tea.* In a few words there has been a tendency to relax the vowel to short, lower [ɪ], particularly in *breeches* (spelled *britches* by the dialect writers), *creek, clique, sleek,* and *steelyards.* Indeed, the variant forms *crick* and *slick* are in common use in America, with slight changes in meanings. The "*crick* in the back" probably comes from *creak,* whereas the same form, when applied to a small stream of water, is a variant of *creek*; *slick* is a more general term than *sleek.* In the case of *been,* Americans use the short vowel, but in England the long one is often heard. *Creature* becomes *critter* in vulgar American speech.

5b. Short [i]

While it has been customary to say that the short form of long [ī] is the relaxed, lower [ɪ], which will be discussed later (see 6, below), it must be recognized that frequently in certain kinds of words there is a half-short or wholly short sound, [i], which is slightly tense but not held so long as the long vowel just considered. Of course speakers vary greatly in their pronunciation of such words, and the degree of shortening is very hard to determine, often because the accent is secondary rather than a strong primary accent. In the end syllables of *alumnæ, apostrophe, coffee, employee, strophe,* and in *magazine, gasoline,* and *vaseline,* where the last syllable certainly has a strong secondary accent, this short [i] is usual. Likewise in the pronunciation of certain prefixes, such as *pre-* and *re-,* the vowel length varies according to the stress laid upon the prefix. Examples are *prepay, presuppose, pretext, recount, regain, retail.* Much might be said regarding the fine shades of vowel quantity, of accentuation, and of meaning that are often produced in the pronunciation of words with these prefixes. But these words are so numerous in English that the student must make a separate study for himself in order to appreciate this phase of the subject.

6. *Short* [ɪ]

This short vowel, one of the higher front vowels, is also very commonly used. It occurs before the explosive consonants in such words as *rib, clip, bid, bit, counterfeit, dig, tick, ridge, ditch, fix*. Its use before the continuants may be seen in *give, sieve, if, with, pith, myth, fizz, bliss, this, wish*, and *risk*. It is used commonly before [l], [m], [n], and [ŋ], as in *build, fill, guilt, him, hymn, limb, been, lint, sin, bring, England, ink*.

Before certain consonant combinations, particularly [ld], [mb], [nd], there is usually lengthening to the diphthong [ɑɪ] in such monosyllabic words as *child, wild, climb, kind, wind*; but in a few such words as *build, guild, limb, wind* (noun), the short vowel is used, and in the longer words it occurs very consistently, as in *bewilder, children, wilderness, timber, hinder, kindle, kindred, linden*, and *window*.

In open syllables in polysyllabic words this short [ɪ] is common, as in *familiar, lyricist, miniature, pinafore, sycamore, synagogue*, and *trilogy*. Before weak final syllables of some other words, such as *-ic, -id, -y*, and those with vocalic [l̥], [m̥], [n̥], [r̥], this short [ɪ] is also frequently found, as in *lyric, satiric, timid, vivid, busy, city, dizzy, pity, pretty, witty* (but [ɑɪ] in *tidy*); *little, initial, pistol, victuals, whittle* (but [ɑɪ] in *vital*), *idiom, schism* (but [ɑɪ] in *whilom*), *decision, million, mission, vision, women, bitter, blizzard, liver, titter*, and *river* (but [ɑɪ] in *miter*). Not infrequently this [ɪ] corresponds to the diphthong [ɑɪ] of some shorter form of the word, as, for example, in *fifty* (cf. *five*), *derivative* (cf. *derive*), *wisdom* (cf. *wise*), *children* (cf. *child*), *hidden* (cf. *hide*), *blissful* (cf. *blithe*), and *vilify* (cf. *vile*).

Variables. Before [r], however, in short words like *dear, fear, near, queer, fierce*, and *weird*, there is also divided practice;

and, while these words are more often spoken with this short [ɪ], at times the longer and higher vowel [ī] can be heard, as already remarked above (see 5 a). In the longer words, such as *dirigible, period, serious, tyranny, cereal,* and *miracle,* this short vowel is regularly used. It appears frequently in *sirup,* although the more common pronunciation is with the vowel [ə], as [sərəp], in some parts of the United States.

Sometimes a following nasal raises the vowel [ɛ] to this [ɪ], particularly in the Irish English dialect, as already noted (see Sec. 16, *a*). So *men, meant, sent, went, any,* and *many* are occasionally spelled by the dialect writer *min, mint, sint, wint, inny,* and *minny;* and *Gwinn* and *Guinevere* are the usual forms from older *Guenevere.*

And, finally, there are numerous other words in which this short [ɪ] is not universally accepted. It varies with the diphthong [ɑɪ] in *feminine, juvenile, masculine, paradigm, primer, simultaneous,* and *virile;* it varies with long [ī] in *chagrin, chlorine, tangerine,* and *vaccine,* and sometimes in *breeches, clique, creek,* and *sleek,* as we have already noted; and it replaces [ɛ] sometimes in such dialectal words as *giddap* (for 'get up'), *git* (for 'get'), *kittle* (for 'kettle').

7a. Long [ɔ̄]

This vowel, often known as "open *o*" because it is spoken with the lips somewhat wider apart than is true of the regular [ō], is unusually variable and uncertain in many English words because it is so likely to be confused with the higher [ō] or the lower [ū], because its length is often difficult to ascertain, and because it is rarely employed in other modern languages, and consequently foreigners are troubled to remember in which English words it should be used. If the reader is inclined to differ as to the pronunciation of many of the examples given below, it will not be surprising, considering the uncertainty often manifested by even the best modern lexicographers.

It appears spelled as *a* before *l* plus a consonant in such words as *bald, ball, call, false, falter, hall, halt, halter, malt, palsy, salt,* and, even though the *l* is silent, in *balk, chalk,* and *talk* (but short [æ] in *shall, shally,* and *talcum*). Likewise the *a* is commonly given this long sound after [w], alone and in the combinations [kw] (= *q*) and [sw], in such words as *quart, quartz, squall, swan, swarm, swarthy, walk, Walter, war, warm, warp, wart, water.*

This long [ɔ̄] sound is heard frequently before the voiceless continuants and, in America especially, before [ŋ] and even [g], sometimes, as in *aloft, cough, off, soft, broth, cloth* (but [ō] in *clothes*), *moth, wroth* (but [ō] in *both*), *moss* (but [ō] in *gross*), and in *long, song, strong, wrong,* and, frequently, in *dog, frog, hog,* and *log.*

Before a pronounced *r* it would be safer, perhaps, to call this vowel half long, particularly in *born* (but [ō] in *borne,* usually), *cork, for, forlorn, horse, lord, north, orb, orthopedic, ward, warrant,* and *Warsaw*; when the *r* is vocalized so that it is not heard distinctly, the vowel is likely to be quite long, so that dialect writers sometimes write *hawss* for 'horse', and it is not always easy to distinguish in the speech of some persons between *cork* and *calk, lord* and *laud.*

This vowel is frequently found spelled *au* or *aw,* as in *awl, cauliflower, cause, claw, dawn, fault, launch, law, Paul, straw, taunt,* and *tawdry*. In some American place-names like *Choctaw, Kennesaw, Omaha, Utah* it is fairly long, even though it has only secondary accentuation.

Before silent *gh* this vowel occurs in words like *aught, caught, naught, taught, bought, ought, thought, wrought.* In *naughty* it is shorter and sometimes gives way to short [ɑ].

Long [ɔ̄] is fairly common in dissyllabic words before final syllables with vocalic [l̩], [m̩], [n̩], [r̩], and other weak syllables, such as *-y*. Examples are *aural, moral, autumn, Van Doren, auger, daughter, drawer, saucy;* and it is sometimes heard in words like *oral, glory, story,* and *Tory,* which usually have close [ō].

Variables. In certain American dialects one frequently hears *road* pronounced with open [ɔ̄] like *abroad* and *broad.* Likewise the word *God* is sometimes spelled *Gawd* by the dialect writers to show this pronunciation. This open [ɔ̄] is also frequently heard in words with a more usual close [ō] before

[r], such as *door, floor, fort, forth, four, oral, portion, report,* and *store*. This peculiarity of pronunciation is especially noticeable in some New England forms of dialect.

7b. Short [ɔ]

As already remarked (in 1 *b*, above), this sound is interchanged so much with short [ɑ] that there is a great deal of variation in American speech with respect to [ɑ] and [ɔ]. Before *ss* and *st* this [ɔ] sound seems to be more commonly spoken, as in *boss, Boston, frost, gloss, loss, lost, moss, toss* (but in *jostle* and *throstle* the [ɑ] is preferred). As already noted, the British speaker uses this short [ɔ] in words like *not, hot,* and *lot*; and in words like *Laura, morrow,* and *sorrow* both vowels are commonly used in the United States.

8a. Long [ō]

This so-called "close o" is, again, one of the more common vowel sounds of Current English.* It is found often in open syllables, naturally, as in *beau, bow, doe, foe, glow, know, lo, low, no, oh, owe, sew, show* or *shew, so, though,* and in longer words like *coyóte, hautboy, hobo, phonograph, potent, pronoun, quotient, toward, yeoman,* and *zoölogy*. It is found before all the stop consonants, as in *robe, rope, load, lode, note, oats, rogue, coke, folk, coach, brooch* (or [brūtʃ]), *hoax*. It likewise occurs before the continuants in such words as *rove, stove, loaf, loathe, both, oath, froze, rose, close, gross*. It is common, also, with the liquids and nasals, as in *bowl, coal, role, roll, soul, Holmes, home, roam, comb, lone, loan, floor, more, pour, store, ore,* and *o'er*.

Before certain consonant combinations which have exerted a lengthening influence on preceding vowels, in past centuries, notably [ld], [lt], [mb], [nt], [rd], [rn], [rs], [rt], and [st], this long close [ō] is very common. Examples are *bold, soldier, told; colt, bolt, molt, poultry; comb* (but [ɑ] or [ʌ] in *bomb*); *don't, won't; board, hoard* (but [ɔ] in *cord, lord); bourn,*

---

*As a matter of fact, this [ō] is very generally pronounced as a slightly diphthongal sound (which may be represented by [oʊ], especially at the end of a word such as *no, throw* (see page 197)).

mourn, shorn (or [ʃɔrn]), *torn*; *coarse, course, divorce*; *fort* (but [ɔ] in *cohort, short, sort*); *boast, ghost, host, roast* (but [ɔ] in *frost* and *lost*).

In dissyllabic words this long vowel appears before weak syllables, especially those with syllabic [l̥], [n̥], [r̥], and with -*y*, in such words as *noble, oval, total*; *notion, ocean, Odin, open, stolen* (but [ʌ] in *oven*); *clover, osier, over* (but [ʌ] in *cover, lover, plover*, etc.); *cony, Doty, gory, hoary, holy, pony*, and *wholly*.

Variables. In many words in which this close [ō] occurs commonly, other sounds are heard as variant pronunciations. While the British speaker generally uses this [ō] in *docile, process, progress*, the American is likely to use short [ɑ]; for long close [ō] in *sloth* and *wroth* one hears, also, the more open [ɔ]; for *scone* short [ɑ] is also used; for *courteous* and *courtesan* both [ō] and [ɜ] are used.

8b. Short [o]

While it is sometimes said that the English language lacks the short form of close [ō] which is heard so much in some other modern languages, there are numerous instances in which a shortened, or half-long, form may be heard in syllables bearing only a partial or secondary accent. In the first syllable of *grotesque, mobilization, molest, motorization, phonograph*, and in the many words with the prefix *pro-*, such as *proclaim* and *protest*, and in the last syllable of words like *cantaloupe, château, ozone, plateau, telephone, trousseau*, the sound is likely to be shortened [o], although some speakers take the trouble to stress it and prolong it in some of these words, such as *château* and *protest*.

In the varying pronunciation of nouns ending in -*o*, (-*oe*, etc.), such as *aloe, echo, folio, mosquito, negro, potato*, and *volcano*, this shorter [o] can be distinguished. For *cantaloupe* and *zoölogy* some speakers use [ū] instead of [o]; and for the *o* in the first syllable of the prefix *homo-*, as in *homonym*, the short [ɑ] is also heard.

9a. Long [ū]

This highest and most rounded of the back vowels (heard in *food*) should, for the sake of this study, be carefully distinguished from the diphthong [ɪu] (heard in *feud*), even though speakers do not keep the two sounds very well distinguished in actual practice. In the following lists of examples of the pure vowel [ū] there will be found words which are sometimes heard with the diphthongal pronunciation; each student of English pronunciation should, in going through these lists, test his own pronunciation with reference to this point. This long [ū], frequently spelled *oo*, is found in open syllables, as in *accrue, blew, canoe, coupé, crew, cuckoo, do, glue, gruesome, hoodoo, rue, shoe, taboo, too, two, voodoo, who* (but diphthongal, [ɪu], in *hew, hue,* and *Hugh*), *woo,* and *you*. It is used before the explosive consonants in such words as *boob, coop, group, food* (but diphthongal *feud*), *mood, rood, rude, chute, root, route, soot, fluke,* and *Luke*. Before most of the continuants it occurs commonly, as in *move, prove, aloof, roof, soothe, Ruth, uncouth, tooth, lose, ooze, bruise, goose, juice, rouge, douche,* and *scrouge*. It is used before the liquids and nasals in *fool, ghoul, school, boom, boon, boor, moor* (but diphthongal *immure*), *poor* (but diphthongal, [ɪu], in *pure*), and *spoor*.

Before the lengthening combinations [ld], [mb], [nd], and [st] long [ū] occurs only occasionally, notably in *Goold* or *Gould, tomb, womb, wound, boost,* and *roost*. But when it is followed by a final weak syllable with *-y* or syllabic [l̥], [m̥], [n̥], [r̥], it is found more often, as in *booby, brutal, cruel, noodle, scruple, bosom, brougham, Reuben, woman, accouter, cougar, maneuver*.

Variables. There are several variant pronunciations of words with this long [ū]. The most common, of course, is the diphthongization already noted. This diphthongal pronunciation, [ɪu], is commonly favored by lexicographers and teachers of speech in the case of words spelled with *u, eu,* and *ew* after the dentals [d], [t], [θ], [n], [z], [s], [ʃ], [dʒ], [tʃ], such as *assume, chew, deuce, due, duke, dune, duty, enthusiasm, Jew,*

Sec. 41] ENGLISH VOWELS AND DIPHTHONGS 183

June, knew, neutral, new, nuisance, presume, sewer, steward, suit, suitable, the prefix *super-, thews, tube,* and *Tuesday.* However, it is also true that many educated Americans prefer the simple long [ū] in such words, and failure to use the diphthongal pronunciation is by no means an indication of carelessness on the part of the speakers. Indeed, in some instances the dictionaries differ among themselves, and the student may be forced to select some one authoritative dictionary to the exclusion of all others in order to avoid confusion and uncertainty regarding such words.

After [l] and [r] some speakers still use the diphthongal pronunciation [ɪu], as in *alluvial, blue, delusion, lieu, lunar, rude, rule,* though usage is divided, many other speakers preferring the simpler [ū]. In some words, spelled with *ou* or *ow,* such as *acoustic, Cowper, Houston, route, scrouge,* and the noun *wound,* the diphthong [ɑʊ] is also heard.

Besides these diphthongal variations, there is a very common shortening of [ū] to the relaxed [ʊ] in the pronunciation of *bosom, Cooper, hoof, hoop, Hooper, jury, penurious, poor, proof, roof, room, rooster, root, soon, soot, spoon, sure, woman,* and the like. This relaxing and shortening of an especially high vowel is not surprising when one considers that it was standardized long ago in other similar words, such as *book, good,* and *hook.* In the case of *soot* the vowel is not only shortened but sometimes given the [ʌ] sound; in *joust* this short [ʌ] is preferred to long [ū] by most speakers.

9b. Short [u]

In syllables with secondary accent or in longer words even in the main accented syllables, a half-long or even shorter form of [ū] is sometimes heard, [u], as in *fortuitous, Housatonic, Hindu, lunatic, Lusitania, routine, suitable, tutorial.* The degree of difference between the sound in these words and the longer [ū] sound previously discussed is so uncertain and vacillating that it is unnecessary to do more here than call attention to the difference and insist that there is this short [u], which must not be confused with the more relaxed short vowel to be considered next.

10. Short [u]

This short relaxed vowel, made with more rounding of the lips than [ʌ], the other so-called "short *u*", is found only in limited circumstances. It is kept chiefly after the labial consonants [b], [p], [f], and [w], and is usually followed by [l] or [ʃ], as in *bull, bullet, bush; pull, pullet, push, put; foot, full, fulsome, Fulton; wolf, wool;* and *butcher*. It also occurs before [d] and [k], as in *book, brook, cook, could, good, hood, hook, look, shook, should, wood,* and *would,* and also in *cushion*.

Variables. In present-day pronunciation there is a marked tendency to use this shorter vowel, [u], before [f] and [t] also, as in *proof, roof, root, soot,* and after some other consonants, as already explained (see 9*a*, above). Moreover, this short [u] is commonly heard before [r] in words like *boor, cursory, endure, jury, lurid, Moorish, rural, sure,* and *your*.

A few words show variable pronunciation in standard English. Instead of [u] the short vowel [ʌ] is also used in *brusque, fulsome, supple;* instead of [u] the slightly lower but longer [ō] is sometimes heard in dialectal speech in such words as *poor, sure,* and *your*. Indeed, the dialect-writers often spell these words *pore, shore,* and *yore,* and for the same reason the proper name *Moore* is also spelled *More* at times.

11a. Long [ɜ]

This vowel is heard only before the consonant [r] and chiefly in monosyllabic words ending in [r] or in [r] plus a consonant. It occurs in *burr, confer, cur, err, fir, fur, her, purr, slur; berth, bird, birth, burst, curse, dirt, earn, earth, first, girl, hearse, learn, myrrh, pearl, purse, turn, verse, worm,* and *worse*.

Variables. Occasionally this sound is heard in other words with [r], in place of the proper vowels, especially in *darn, for, or,* which is not surprising when one remembers that in all of the words with this long [ɜ] the vowel was earlier pronounced differently and has gradually been changed to this sound through the influence of the [r].

11 b. Short [ɜ]

It is not easy to distinguish between the long and short forms of this vowel, but the short [ɜ] is generally to be heard in words of more than one syllable, before [r], as in *burden, burrough, courage, early, flourish, hurry, personal, purlieu, sirup, sterling, thorough, tournament, Turkey,* and *worry.*

12 a. Long [ʌ̄]

This long sound does not occur often in English; but in words like *bulk* and *hulk* the vowel is lengthened, usually; and when the tongue is dropped in the pronunciation of such words as *bird, curse, girl, hearse, hurt, nurse,* and *worse,* the [r] is likely to be vocalized and to disappear altogether, leaving a long vowel, [ʌ̄], so that the dialect-writer often spells *curse* as *cuss, nurse* as *nuss,* and *worse* as *wuss,* for example. This long [ʌ̄] is, therefore, for the most part a variant of long [ɜ̄], previously discussed (see 11a, above); when the [r] is strongly pronounced, the long [ɜ̄] is heard, but when the [r] is not spoken, this long [ʌ̄] is likely to result. A few people retain the [r] but drop the tongue a little so as to produce this longer [ʌ̠], as in [nʌ̄rs], [gʌ̄rl].

12 b. Short [ʌ]

This very common short vowel, already characterized as the "laziest" of all the short vowels and sometimes mistakenly called a "short *u*" just because it is usually written with that letter, is found in monosyllabic words before the explosive consonants, as in *cub, cup, bud, blood, but, rug, duck, judge, crutch, such, crux;* before the continuants in such words as *glove, love, cuff, tough, other, doth, does* (verb), *buzz, bus, fuss, hush, rust,* and *tuft;* before [l], [m], and [n], as in *cull, hum, honey, run,* and *son;* and when followed by weak syllables with vocalic liquids or nasals, or *-ed, -et, -y,* etc., in such words as *bundle, muzzle, stubble, custom, Rustum, button, cousin, dozen, lover, rudder, wonder, hundred, puppet, putty,* and *cubby.*

Variables. Since this is one of the vowels most easily made, various other vowels are likely to assume this sound when they are pronounced hurriedly and without much stress. So one hears [hʌlō] instead of [hɛlō], [jʌ] instead of [jū], [ʌv] for the preposition [av], [ʃʌfər] instead of [ʃōfзr], [wʌnt] instead of [wōnt], [ðʌ] instead of [ði], [fʌlo] instead of [fɛlo], [rʌðr̥] instead of [raðr̥], [hwʌt] instead of [hwat], [fʌðr̥] instead of [fзrðr̥], and [wʌz] instead of [waz].

13. *Diphthong* [aɪ]

Of the four common diphthongs of present-day English, this is perhaps the best established, although it is also likely to be most often misunderstood by the student of English sounds because it is usually represented by the simple letter *i* (or *y*). It is found regularly in open syllables, as in *aye* ('yes'), *bayou, biology, buy, by, eye, fie, giant, idea, island, lie, lye, sigh.* In closed syllables it is found before the explosive consonants in such words as *jibe, ripe, abide, guide, alight, height, like*; before the continuants, as in *I've, shrive, knife, lithe, writhe, blithe, size, assize,* and *vise*; before the liquids and nasals in words like *aisle, isle, style, mile, gentile, I'm, thyme, time, fine, stein, turpentine, choir, fire, quire;* and before the lengthening combinations [mb], [nd], and [ld], as in *climb, find, kind, child;* also in *Christ.*

In open syllables followed by weaker syllables with vocalic [l̥], [m̥], [n̥], [r̥], with -*y*, etc., this diphthong is frequently found, as in *final, idol, idyl, title, vital, item, whilom, lichen, bison, geyser, liar, tiger, visor, tidy,* and *crisis.*

Variables. In the cockney dialect of London the long [ē] of words like *lady* and *take* becomes a diphthong which sounds so much like this [aɪ], as already remarked (see 4*a*, above), that the dialect-writer usually spells the word with an *i* or a *y*; hence *lidy* and *tike.* Moreover, the slightly higher diphthong [ɔɪ] is sometimes lowered a little so that it sounds like [aɪ] in other dialects of English, especially the Irish, and instead of *boil, boy, join, roil,* and *spoil* the dialect-writer spells them *bile, bye, jine, rile,* and *spile.* Both [kaɪóte] and [káɪot] are heard in America.

On the other hand, this diphthong as it appears in such words as *fine, like,* and *mind* is sometimes raised to [ɔɪ], so that the dialect-writer spells these words *foine, loike,* and *moind.* In the dialect of the Southern negro this diphthong is frequently simplified to [ā], and so the pronoun *I,* for example, becomes *Ah.*

Of course there are numerous other instances of variation from the use of this diphthong [ɑɪ]. As already indicated (see 5*a*, above), there is a difference of opinion as to whether long [ī] or [ɑɪ] should be used in words like *geyser* and *either.* In numerous other words this diphthong is used interchangeably with short [ɪ] (see 6, above); in *dynasty, isolate, quinine,* and *sinecure,* for example, the preference seems to be for [ɑɪ], whereas in the case of *agile, futile, hostile, infantile, juvenile,* and *reptile* American speakers prefer the short vowel [ɪ], although American dialectal pronunciation often introduces [ɑɪ] into the syllable *-ine* in words like *engine, feminine, genuine, masculine,* and *strychnine.*

14. *Diphthong* [ɑʊ]

This diphthong resembles the combination just discussed in that it is made up of the very low [ɑ] plus a high vowel; but while the high vowel of the preceding diphthong was the front one, in this it is the high back [ʊ]. This diphthong is also heard commonly in Current English; and since *ou* and *ow* are used both for the diphthong [ɑʊ] and for the simple long vowel [ō], there is much confusion of the two sounds, particularly on the part of young children and foreigners learning the English language. As a general rule the spelling *ow* is used in monosyllabic words at the end and medially before [l] and [n], and in dissyllabic words when followed by syllables like *-el, -en, -er,* and *-y.*

This diphthong is found in open syllables, such as *bough, bow* ('to bend'), *chowchow, cow, dhow, haymow, how, Howe, plow* or *plough, row* ('quarrel'), *Show, sow* (the animal), *thou,* and *vow* (but long [ō] in *bow* ('weapon'), *mow* ('to cut'), *row* ('line', 'rank', 'file'), *show, sow* ('to plant'), *tow,* etc.). Its use before explosives is confined to the consonants [d] and [t] almost exclusively, in such words as *crowd, loud, about,* the German loan-word *kraut, lout, out, rout,* and *stout;* and it is found only before the continuants [θ], [z], and [s], as in *drouth, mouth, south* (but [ū] in *uncouth* and *youth*), *browse, carouse, rouse, spouse, douse, house,* and *mouse.* It occurs commonly before [l] and [n] and [r] (but not before [m]), in such words as *cowl, fowl, foul, howl, prowl* (but [ō] in *bowl, soul,* and *Towle), brown, clown, renown, town, flour, hour, our, sour* (but [ō] in *pour* and [ū] in *dour* and *tour).* It is also found before the lengthening consonant combinations [ns], [nd], [ndʒ], [nt], and, rarely, [st], as in *bounce, flounce, ounce, bound, hound, sound, wound* (past of *to wind), lounge, count, fount, mount,* and *oust.* It will be observed that this diphthong is used in closed syllables almost exclusively before dentals and [l] and [r].

In open syllables followed by weaker syllables with vocalic [l̩], [m̩], [n̩], [r̩], with *-y, -ard,* etc., this diphthong is common, as in *rowel, towel, chowder, cower, shower,* the verb *to lower* (but [ō] in the adjective *lower),* in the German loan-words *bauer* and *sauerkraut,* in *blowsy, drowsy, doughty, coward,* and *Howard* (but [ō] in *toward).* It is also found in a few polysyllabic words, such as *Bowditch, foundation, McDowell,* and *roustabout.*

Variables. There are certain variables associated with this diphthong, as we have already noted. This diphthong, [aʊ], and the long vowel [ō] are both heard in the pronunciation of *enow, jowl,* and *trow;* this diphthong, [aʊ], and long [ū] are variously used in *blouse, caoutchouc, gouge, slough,* and other words already noted (see 9*a,* above); this diphthong, [aʊ], is sometimes simplified to [a] in words like *coward, Howard, our.*

15. *Diphthong* [ɔɪ]

This diphthong differs from [aɪ] only in that the first part of it is made in a slightly higher position. It is usually spelled with *oi* medially and *oy* finally. It occurs in open syllables like *ahoy, boy, buoy, cloy, joy,* and *toy.* It is found before [l] and [n], as in *broil, coil, oil, turmoil, coin, join,* and *purloin;* and before [nt] in such words as *anoint, aroint, joint,* and *point;* and before [st] in *foist, joist, moist,* etc. It occurs before the dental explosives [d] and [t] in words like *avoid, Lloyd, sloyd, void, Detroit, exploit,* and *quoits*; and before the dental continuants [z] and [s] in *noise, poise, turquoise, choice, invoice, rejoice,* and *voice*; it is also used in *coif*. And it is found in various other words of two or more syllables, such as *anthropoid, boisterous, buoyant, goiter, hoity-toity, hoyden, loiter, oyster,* and *toilet*.

Variables. Attention has already been called (see 13, above) to a dialectal tendency to raise [ɑɪ] to this diphthong, [ɔɪ], in words like *fine, like,* and *mind*. A peculiar diphthongization of the [ɜr] of such words as *bird, girl,* and *hurt* has led writers of the dialect of the East Side of New York City to indicate this peculiarity by spelling these words *boid, goil,* and *hoit*.

16. *Diphthong* [ɪu]

This diphthong differs from the other three already discussed in that it requires a slight backward tongue movement from a very weak front [ɪ] to a back [u], whereas the movement in the others is upward from a stronger [ɑ] or [ɔ] to a weaker [ɪ] or [ʊ]. That doubtless accounts for the very frequent interchange of this diphthong, [ɪu], with the simple vowel [ū] (see 9*a*, above). Since there is this frequent variation, it is necessary to recognize also varying quantity and quality in the diphthong as well as in the simple vowel; in *fuse* a longer diphthong, [ɪu], is undoubtedly spoken; in *virtue* a shorter sound of [ɪu] may be assumed; but in *fury* the diphthong is not only shorter but more relaxed, hence [ɪʊ]. Also illustrative of the first, strongly accented form of this diphthong are *acuminate, acute, beauty, feud, few, hew, hue, humid, humor, mule, pew, pewter, queue,* and *view*; the diphthong without primary accentuation is found in *Eureka, issue, revenue, statue, value,* and *unique*; with a more relaxed and shorter sound the diphthong occurs in *bureau, Europe, fury, pure,* and *Puritan*.

This diphthong sometimes occurs at the beginning of words with various spellings, but is practically the equivalent of [j] + [ū], in such words as *eucharist, union, use, yew,* and *youth*. When words are spelled with the letter *u* or the digraphs *eu* and *ew* immediately following the labial consonants [b], [p], [v], [f], [m], and [sp], the diphthong [ɪu] is generally heard, as in *abuse, puling, view, feud, future, music,* and *sputum.* It is also heard before [r], as in *curious,* but this is not always true. After [l] and [r] the diphthong is rarely heard except in very precise speech in such words as *rule* and *lute.* After *c* (= [k]) the diphthong is heard in words spelled with the letter *u,* such as *acute, cubic,* and *cuneiform;* and by analogy the word *coupon* is often given this diphthong, although the dictionaries still recommend the simple vowel [ū].

B. Unaccented Vowels and Diphthongs

In the foregoing discussion of vowels and diphthongs it has been assumed that the sounds under consideration occurred in strongly accented syllables or at least in those syllables of polysyllabic words which bear a secondary accent. But of vowels and diphthongs having less accentuation or none at all, the sounds are much harder to define, so that some writers speak of them as "the obscure vowels". In pronouncing words of several syllables, speakers of English spread their accent over the words so differently that it is possible to indicate here only a few general and very roughly defined groups of unaccented vowels and diphthongs.

1. Every one of the vowels and diphthongs just discussed can be heard, but in somewhat weakened or obscured form, in the unaccented syllables of polysyllabic words, particularly at the beginning of long words, as, for example, [ɑ] in *particular,* [æ] in *panegyric,* [ɛ] in *characteristic* or *stenography,* [e] in *vacation,* [i] in *reality,* [ɔ] in *Laurentian* or *dogmatic,* [o] in *topography* or *pillow,* [u] in *neuritis,* [ɜ] in *personification,* [ɑɪ] in *vitality* and, sometimes, in *biography,* [ɑʊ] in *foundation,* [ɪu] in *futurity,* and so on.

2. As already noted (see 12 *b*, above), numerous vowels tend to become [ʌ] when there is little or no stress on the syllables in which they occur, as, for example, in [hʌló] for [hɛló].

In British speech and in the dialect of many Southerners and New Englanders of the United States, the unaccented final [ɜr] in such words as *father, never, over*, is vocalized and the consonantal [r] of Western American speech is not heard, but instead the syllable becomes merely a weak form of [ʌ], as in [fūðə], [nɛvə], [ōvə]. This is one of the most noticeable dialectal variations in English speech.

3. However, some of the higher front vowels tend to become an obscure [ɪ] in unaccented syllables, as in *demented* [dɪmɛ́ntəd]; and this is the sound heard regularly in the second syllable of such words as *city, honied, hurried, levies, money, pity,* and *tepid*.

4. In many words there are unaccented syllables in which the vowel is even more weak, or obscure, than those just illustrated. If, for example, such a word as *topógraphy* be analyzed, at least four grades of vowels may be distinguished; in the second, or accented, syllable is heard the strong vowel [ɑ]; in the first, as already remarked, a slightly reduced form of [o]; in the last syllable, the [ɪ] just discussed; and in the third syllable, *ra*, the obscure vowel [ə]. Not only can this obscure vowel be found in polysyllabic words, but even monosyllabic words are likely to be weakened to it when they are passed over hurriedly in continuous speech, as already illustrated in *the top of the hill* [ðə tɑp 'v ðə hɪl].

5. When the liquids and nasals [l], [r], [m], and [n] form entire syllables of themselves ([l̥], [r̥], [m̥], [n̥]), as in *oval, father, chasm,* and *even*, several grades of vowel quality are likely to be detected in the pronunciation of such words by various speakers or under various conditions. Usually, if we assume the weakest of values, these words may be written [ōvl̥], [fūðr̥], [kæzm̥], and [īvn̥], circles being placed under the letters merely to call attention to the fact that in these words they are consonantal vowels (or vocalic consonants). But some phoneticians would write the obscure vowel character with each word, representing the four words, then, as [ōvəl], [fūðər], [kæzəm], and [īvən]. Sometimes, however, a speaker will vocalize these syllabic liquids and nasals so strongly that one may hear [ōvʌl], [fūðɜr], [kæzʌm], and [īvɪn]. Indeed, it sometimes happens that one of the liquids or nasals used as a consonant ordinarily is vocalized so strongly that it be-

comes a separate unaccented syllable, thus making two syllables out of one, as in *alarum* (from *alarm*), *atheletics* (from *athletics*), *elum* (from *elm*), *filum* (from *film*), *warum* (from *warm*), and *woruld* (from *world*). In the stronger vocalization of these vocalic consonants, as illustrated, it will be observed that [l̥] and [m̥] assume the quality of [ʌ], while [r̥] is likely to become [ɜr], and [n] tends to become [ɪn].

When one is in doubt, however, as to the exact quality and degree of quantity of a vowel in an unaccented syllable, the best he can do is to treat it as the general obscure vowel and employ the phonetic symbol [ə]. It should be added that it is usually better to pronounce unaccented syllables with this obscure vowel than to attempt to give them stronger vowel sounds, as some speakers do in words like *autumn, blessed, evil, rugged,* and *stomach.*

42. *Causes and Processes of Vowel Change*

In the discussions of the various vowels and diphthongs, certain tendencies to change have been remarked, and to a certain extent the causes and processes have been indicated. But a clearer understanding of these can be gained by a summarizing of each cause or process as it affects various vowel sounds and combinations.

1. *Influence* of [r]

The influence of [r] immediately after a vowel has long been one of the outstanding causes of change and variation in the pronunciation of English vowels. On the whole, the tendency in English has been for many different vowels to assume the sound [ɜ] before [r], as in *her*, a development peculiar to the English language and likely to prove strange and troublesome to foreigners attempting to learn English. But, as already illustrated, instead of this [ɜr] one may find [ūr], as in British [klūrk] (*clerk*) and American dialectal *larn* (for 'learn') and *tarnal* (for 'eternal'); in earlier American dialect [ɛ] becomes [ū], as in *bar* (for 'bear'); [ɛ̄] and [ǣ] are used varyingly in words like *fair*; long [ī] is frequently shortened and relaxed to [ɪ], as in [dɪr] (*dear*); [ō] and [ɔ̄] are likewise used interchangeably, as in *four*; long [ū] is likely to be shortened and relaxed to [ʊ] in such a word as *sure*; and even [ɔ] may become [ɜ] in a few words like *for* and *or*.

2. *Influence of* [l]

This sound, [l], immediately following *a*, has caused that vowel to retain the sound [ɔ̄], as in *bald* and *talk*. Moreover, [l] in polysyllabic words like *alibi* has occasioned some uncertainty as to whether [ɑ] or [æ] should be spoken before it.

3. *Labialization*

Labialization has caused some development or survival of back vowels, owing to the fact that both the higher back vowels and the labial consonants involve the use of the lips. So after [w] the letter *a* is likely to mean the [ɔ̄] sound, as in *war*; and the short [ʊ] is generally heard after the labials [b], [p], [f], and [w], if it is in turn followed by [l] or [ʃ], as in *pull* and *bush*, whereas in other words which formerly had short [u] the sound [ʌ] has replaced the [u].

4. *Nasalization*

Similarly the influence of nasals has been and is still the cause of some vowel change, particularly of [ɛ] to [ɪ], as in the Irish English dialectal pronunciation of *mint* and *wint* (for 'meant' and 'went'). The name *England* shows this change already standardized, although the earlier spelling is still kept.

5. *Influence of consonant combinations*

Certain combinations of consonants have tended to cause vowel lengthening in English, especially liquids and nasals combined with certain stops, namely, [ld], [lt], [rd], [rt], [mb], [nd], [nt], and also with some other consonants, as in [ns], [ndʒ], [rn], [rs]. And before [st] lengthening has sometimes taken place. So we have observed long [ī] in *fiend*; we have noted the diphthong [aɪ] in *bind*; we have found long [ō] in *board*; and the diphthong [ɑʊ] is evidence of an earlier lengthening in words like *bounce* and *count*, as is also the long vowel [ē] in *change* and *haste*. However, exceptional short-vowel forms are also found before these consonant combinations, such as *friend*, *bomb*, and the noun *wind*. Lengthening before these combinations has not worked uniformly.

6. *Influence of following light syllables*

A similar lack of consistency in vowel quantity has been observed in dissyllabic words ending in light syllables, particularly syllabic [l̥], [m̥], [n̥], [r̥], and *-y, -ic, -id, -ard*. In a few words, such as *rations*, the variation is a personal one, depending on the speaker; but we have also found long [ē] the standard pronunciation in *tailor*, and the short vowel [æ] in *glamour*; likewise the long [ī] of *evil* is offset by the short [ɛ] in *devil*; the diphthong [ɑɪ] is heard in *tidy*, but short [ɪ] occurs in various others like *city*; the diphthong is spoken in *coward*, but long [ō] in *toward* (or sometimes long [ɔ]).

Indeed, much of the inconsistency in the use of long and short vowels in English is due to the two causes just discussed, namely, the lengthening influence of following consonant combinations and the unsettling influence of certain following weak syllables.

7. *Effects of word increase*

Another cause of change of vowel quality or quantity, or both, lies in the frequent increase of a word through derivational and inflectional addition of prefixes and suffixes. Sometimes the accent does not shift from the syllable at all, but the vowel shortens and relaxes, anyway; so [ī] and [ē], for instance, become short [ɛ], as in *heather* (cf. *heath*) and *breakfast* (cf. *break*); [ō] and [ū] become short [ɑ], as in *vocative* (cf. *vocal*) and *folly* (cf. *fool*); and the diphthong [ɑɪ] becomes short [ɪ], as in *fifty* (cf. *five*). When, however, the accent shifts from one syllable to another as a result of increasing the number of syllables in the word, shortening is still likely to result; so an unstressed [ī] may become short [ɛ], for instance, when the syllable containing it becomes more strongly stressed, as in *preparation* (cf. *prepare*) and *declamation* (cf. *declaim*), and unstressed [ō] may become short [a], as in *proclamation* (cf. *proclaim*) and *provocation* (cf. *provoke*); and when, on the contrary, the accent is removed from the syllable containing the vowel or diphthong, there is a tendency to shorten the diphthong [aɪ] to [ɪ], as in *finality* (cf. *final*) and *typography* (cf. *type*). An interesting phase of this is the bringing to life of a final silent *e* when a suffix is added after it. When the plural ending *-s* is added, it often becomes necessary to revive the silent *e* in order to make the plural form pronounceable, as in *bridges, changes, faces, horses*. Likewise the *e* is pronounced in *aloetic* (cf. *aloe*), *lineage* (cf. *line*), *nicety* (cf. *nice*), *phraseology* (cf. *phrase*), *rarefy* (cf. *rare*), and the colloquial *surety* (cf. *sure*).

8. *Lengthening*

The process of lengthening is, perhaps, not so common in Current English as that of shortening; but in the past it has been much more common, and the results can still be noted in certain classes of words already discussed. In compensation for the silencing of a medial [l], long [ā] is heard in words like *palm*, long [ɔ] in *talk*, and long [ō] in *folk*. When the accent is placed somewhat heavily on the last syllable of words like *employee* and *referee*, as sometimes occurs, the [i] sound is lengthened somewhat. And when foreigners attempt to pronounce our words with the short, relaxed [ɪ], as in *big, fish*, and *pig*, they often produce a higher, more tense [ī], so that dialect-writers try to show the difference by spelling these words as *beeg, feesh*, and *peeg*.

9. *Shortening*

Various examples of shortening, usually accompanied by a shift in vowel quality also, have been given in the foregoing discussion of causes of vowel change. Two which cannot be ascribed to any of those causes are, nonetheless, very common today, namely, the relaxing of long [ī] to [ɪ] in words like *creek*, and of long [ū] to [ʊ] in such a word as *roof*. In both of these cases the vowels are very high, and that doubtless accounts for the tendency to relax and shorten them.

10. *Raising and lowering*

Naturally the most common process of all is that of raising or lowering the vowel position. A great many differences in pronunciation of groups of words are due to different placing of the tongue, as, for instance, [ū] versus [æ] in *path* and *dance*; [æ] versus [ɛ] in *care* and *carriage*, and in the dialectal *kag* for 'keg', *ketch* for 'catch', *esk* for 'ask'; [ɑ] versus [ɔ] in *not* and *toss*; [ē] versus [æ] in Latin words such as *data*; [ē] versus [ɛ] in *again* and *against*; [ī] versus [ē] in words affected by the Irish English dialect, such as *clean*; [ē] versus [ū] in *tomato*; [ō] versus [ɑ] in *progress* (noun) and in the prefix *homo-*. In American dialectal and colloquial speech one not infrequently hears [ɪ] for [ɛ], as in [gɪt] (*get*), and in [gɪdæp] (*get up*), as spoken to a horse; or [ō] for [ʊ] in *pore* and *shore* (for 'poor' and 'sure'); or [ɑɪ] for the higher diphthong [ɔɪ] in the dialect-writer's *bile* and *ile* (for 'boil' and 'oil'); or, on the other hand, [ɔɪ] for the lower diphthong [ɑɪ] in the dialect-writer's *foine* and *moind* (for 'fine' and 'mind'). The varying use of [ō] and [ū] in *zoölogy* is also an example of this raising and lowering process, although the cause in this case is more likely to be mental confusion regarding the *oo* spelling than physiological inexactness.

11. *Vocalization*

The process of vocalization of [l], [m], [n], and [r] occurs in Current English with varying results. In accented syllables, as we have seen, [r], as in *curse* and *horse*, is often so completely vocalized that the dialect-writer spells these words *cuss* and *hawss*. But in present-day British English and also in the New England and Southern dialects of the United States, the vocalization of [r] in stressed syllables produces a diphthong, the [īr] or [ɪr] of *fear* becoming [īə], the [ɛ̄r] of *their* becoming [ɛ̄ə], the [ɑʊr] of *our* becoming [ɑʊə], and so on. In final unaccented syllables, as we have also noted, syllabic [l̥], [m̥], [n̥], and [r̥] may be strengthened until they become the vowels [ʌ], [ɪ], and [ɝ], as in *oval, chasm, even,* and *father*; and sometimes in consonantal combinations they are vocalized so much that *elm* becomes *elum* and *world* becomes *woruld*. Final syllabic [r̥] in words like *father* and *never* is regularly vocalized to the obscure vowel [ə] (or weak [ʌ]) in British speech and in the dialects of New England and the American South, giving [fɑðə] and [nɛvə].

12. *Diphthongization*

The processes of diphthongization of a simple vowel and, on the other hand, of the simplification of a diphthong are also very common ones and result in numerous discrepancies in present-day pronunciation. One hears both [ī] and [ɑɪ] in *either*, [ɪ] and [ɑɪ] in *isolate*, [ū] and [ɪu] in *Tuesday*, and [ū] and [ɑʊ] in *acoustic*. There are various diphthongizations in dialectal English, such as [æɪ] for [ē] in *today*; [ɑɪ] for [ē] in the cockney pronunciation of *lady* [lɑɪdɪ]; [ɔɪ] for [ɜr] in the East Side speech of New York, as illustrated by the dialect-writer's *boid* and *goil* (for 'bird' and 'girl'); and a shift of diphthongs in the substitution of [æʊ] for [ɑʊ] in Southern and New England dialect, as indicated by the dialect-writer's *caow*, *haound*, *haow*, and *naow*. There is no doubt that most people break simple [ō] into the diphthong [oʊ] in words like *no* and *throw* and [ē] into [ei] in *day*.

Simplification, on the other hand, is more rare and is to be observed chiefly in the tendency to use long [ū] instead of the diphthong [ɪu] in words like *new*; in the negro's *Ah* for *I*; and in a fairly common simplification of the diphthong [ɑʊ] to [ɑ̄] in words like *coward*, *Howard*, and *our*, producing forms that might be spelled *card*, *Hard*, and *ar*.

13. *Indifferentiation*

The process of indifferentiation, which is merely letting any vowel lapse into that indifferent and lazy position where the result is [ʌ], we have already discussed in its various aspects and workings. Long [ū] sometimes becomes [ʌ] in the accented word *soot*, as well as in the unstressed *you*; short [ʊ] sometimes varies with [ʌ], as in *supple*; either with loss of the consonantal [r] or occasionally with it retained, the vowel [ɜ] of words like *girl* and *nurse* is often relaxed into the indifferent vowel [ʌ]; and in dialectal speech one hears also [hʌm] (*home*). When words are pronounced carelessly and with little or no stress, they frequently assume this vowel, giving [wʌnt] (*won't*), [hwʌt] (*what*), and the like.

14. *Hiatus*

A few examples of hiatus have been given in the preceding lists, but without special remark, because the bringing together of two distinct vowels or diphthongs in this way is not uncommon in English. As already suggested (see Sec. 23), hiatus is often more apparent than real, because so often "glides" develop between the two vowels; but there are enough actual occurrences of hiatus to make it necessary to take some pains to distinguish between the pronunciation of a digraph representing a simple vowel or a diphthong, as in *foolish, nail,* and *season,* and two separately spoken vowels, as in *medieval* and *naïve.* When the two vowels are spelled with the same letter, as in *coöperate, coördinate, preëminence, preëmpt, reëvaluate,* and *zoölogy,* confusion arises unless the hiatus is indicated by means of the hyphen (*pre-empt*) or else (as here) the generally utilized diæresis (*preëmpt*). Even with the indication of hiatus in this way, the first vowel in *zoölogy* is often mispronounced as though it were *oo* (=[ū]), and *zoo* is the now generally used word for *zoölogical garden*; similarly the '*coop*' is sometimes used in college circles for 'the *coöperative store*'. However, there are numerous examples of hiatus which are not so troublesome, such as *archaic, bias, biology, chaotic, coincide, deity, inchoative, Leo, parietal, phaëton, riot*; and less troublesome still are those cases of hiatus wherein the two vowels are in unaccented parts of words, as in *cafeteria, cereal, oriole, period,* and *trillium.*

In the use of the indefinite article *a* (and *an*) hiatus is avoided before vowel-beginning words by using the older form *an,* as in *an apple, an expert.* In the past, speakers have generally used *an* before *h*-beginning words also, as in *an historical work,* and those who weaken the *h* in their pronunciation prefer to use it thus, even yet. But when the *h* is more strongly pronounced, its consonantal value obviates the need of the transitional *n* of *an*; hence many speakers now say *a historical work*.[418]

15. *Mutation* (German *Umlaut*)

The process of mutation is no longer active in English; but the effects of its earlier activity are still apparent here and there in the language and will demand some attention in a later chapter. Hence it should be defined and thoroughly understood by those who intend to study the more primitive stages of the development of the English language. Mutation is a vowel change which has resulted from the influence of some other vowel in a following syllable. The formation of the plural of nouns like *tooth* (plural *teeth*) is an example of the working of mutation. Likewise mutation is responsible for the peculiar comparison of *old, elder, eldest*, and also for much of the irregularity in such a verb as *teach, taught, taught*. Many words like *drink* and *drench*, *fox* and *vixen*, *full* and *fill*, *gold* and *gild*, can be more easily traced back to their common originals if this process of mutation be taken into account. But mutation must not be confused with that other, even more primitive, form of internal change of vowels which appears in the principal parts of the so-called strong verbs, such as *sing, sang, sung*, and which is named gradation (German *Ablaut*) because of the use of several "grades" of vowels.

43. *English Consonants*

The consonants of Current English are, as a group, much more stable and simple than the vowels and diphthongs. But because of many silent letters and inconsistent and ambiguous spellings, it is necessary to emphasize again the importance of always thinking, during the following discussion, of sounds rather than of the spelling of those sounds. In order to establish in the mind as clearly and definitely as possible the entire group of English consonantal sounds, apart from their spellings, one must ignore the fact that they shift somewhat according to the vowels with which they are spoken and the individual speech habits of the speaker, and one must classify them somewhat arbitrarily. Hence, in the following tabulation of the English consonants, a position is assigned to each according to its usual and general formation in the mouth:

	Explosives		Continuants		Liquids	Nasals	Semivowels
Labials . . .	[b]	[p]				[m]	[w]
Labiodentals .			[v]	[f]			
Dentals . . .	[d]	[t]	[ð]	[θ]		[n]	
			[z]	[s]			
			[ʒ]	[ʃ]			
Palatals and							[j]
velars . . .	[g]	[k]			[l], [r]	[ŋ]	
Breath sound [h]							

A. The Explosives

1. *Voiced labial* [b]

This consonant is used initially in *bite, blow, bowl, brown,* and *bye*; medially in *able, amber, arbor, cupboard, debit, hobble, neighbor, robin, rubber, warble*; and finally in *Cobb, ebb, jibe,* and *rob.*

It occurs in the combination [bz], as in *clubs, ribs.*

2. *Voiceless labial* [p]

This consonant is used initially in *pane, pelt, pew, place,* and *prow*; medially in *apron, couple, happy, open, spill, sprawl, tipple,* and *wiping*; finally in *Bopp, carp, clasp, help, hiccup* (or *hiccough*), *nap, nape.*

It occurs in combinations: as [ps] in *lapse, lips,* and as [pt] in *helped, slept, warped,* and other past-tense forms of verbs.

3. *Voiced dental* [d]

This sound is initial in *dill, disclose, do, drill,* and *dye*; medial in *adder, beadle, biding, Odin, odor, oodles, ridicule, saddle, shoulder,* and *solder*; final in *add, bead, could, Judd, lode, ride.*

It occurs in the combination [dʒ] (spelled regularly with *j, g,* or *dg*): initially in *general, Giles, gin, gist, gyrate, gyves, jail, jealous,* and *judge*; medially in *adagio, advantageous, aged, agile, badger, engine, grandeur, injure, majesty, orgy, pigeon, region, soldier, widgeon,* and in certain dialectal forms, such as *idjut* (for 'idiot'), *immejut* (for 'immediate'), *Injun* (for 'Indian'), *medjum* (for 'medium'), *odjus* (for 'odious'); *tedjus* (for 'tedious'); and finally in *age, allege, courage, edge, forge, Greenwich* (England), *Norwich* (England), *plunge.* It occurs also in the combinations [dθ] in *breadth, width*; [dz] in *adz, bids, odds*; and [dw] in *dwell, dwindle.*

4. *Voiceless dental* [t]

This consonant is initial in *till, tome, thyme, Thomas, try, tyrant, phthisic, ptomaine*; medial in *after, aster, beetle, alter, canter, batten, Esther, extend, fetid, futile, filter, daughter, octet, otter, patent, pity, putty, rattle, settle, stand, subtle,* and *atrocious*; final in *at, beat, oft, court, splint, bolt, cost, act, apt, next, orbit, spelt, worked, fixed.*

It should be noted that the *t* is likely to be silent in the combinations [ft] and [st] when medial and when followed by syllabic [l̥] or [n̥], as in *chestnut, fasten, often, soften, listen, jostle, whistle, wrestle.* It should also be noted that when the *-ed* suffix of past tense is added to verbs that end in voiceless consonants, such as [f], [p], [k], [s], the *d* is always pronounced [t] and sometimes spelled *t*, as in *laughed, lapped, lacked, passed* (or *past*), *blessed* (or *blest*); and sometimes this *d* is pronounced [t] and even spelled *t* after [l] and [n], as in *dwelt, spilt,* and *burnt.*

This explosive [t] is commonly heard in the combination [tʃ] (spelled regularly *ch* or *tch*): initially in *chase, child, chum*; medially in *anchovy, Atchison, bachelor, creature, culture, kitchen, nature, orchard, question, righteous,* and *teacher*; and finally in *beach, bench, birch, catch, filch, niche, rich,* and *which.* It occurs also in the combination [ts] in *bits, lots, rites*; there is even a slight tendency on the part of a few overcareful speakers of English to strain for a [tj] combination and to say *futyure, indentyure, natyure,* for 'future', 'indenture', and 'nature'. Moreover, the combination [tw] is heard in *between, twain, twig,* and *twilight.*

5. *Voiced palatal and velar* [g]

There is no tendency in Current English to distinguish between the front palatal and the back velar [g] (and [k]), since the difference exists only to the extent that the vowels with which the two consonants are used may be either front or back vowels. This [g] is found initially in *gherkin, ghost, gill* (of a fish), *Ginn, give, glow, go, grow, guard, guilt,* and *guy*; medially in *agriculture, angle, angry, blackguard* [blægərd], *figure, finger, haggle, Helga, hungry, niggard, Ogham, ogre, ragged, recognize.* and *vigorous*; and finally in *bag, beg, big, bog, bug, decalogue, egg, league,* and *rogue.*

In combinations it occurs as [gz] in *eggs, exact, exhort, figs,* and in other *ex-* words having the accent right after the *x*; as [gw] in *anguish, guava, Guido, Guinevere, Gwendolen, languid,* and *unguent.*

Variables. Since initial and medial *g*'s are more often pronounced as the double consonant sound [dʒ] when followed by *i, e,* and *y*, both sounds of *g* can be heard in a few words, such as *flagellant, gerrymander, gibberish, giblets, Giles, gyroscope,* and *oleomargarine.*

Initially in the combination *gn* this letter is always silent, as in *gnaw,* and likewise medially or finally in words of French or Italian origin, such as *benign, champagne, feign, poignant.*

6. *Voiceless palatal and velar* [k]

The two positions of [k] may be observed in the use of the sound initially, as in *cat, chaos, character, chasm, clerk, coal, cord, crock, cut, keg, khaki, kill, kin,* and *queue*; medially in *accomplish, acre, actor, anchor, Becket, chequer, crocodile, cycle, echo, hiccup, lacquer, lichen, liquor, ocher, pickle, scandal, school, skill, soccer, trekking, uncle,* and *weakling*; finally in *ache, back, balk, bilk, cardiac, check* (or *cheque*), *duke, grotesque, hock* (or *hough*), *irk, milk, oak, pique, reek, risk, took, traffic,* and *unique.*

In combinations it occurs as [ks] (often spelled *x*) in *accede, accelerate, ax, box, chicks* (rarely *chix*), *ecstasy, exercise, extant, locks, mixture, socks* (or *sox*), and *vixen*; as [kʃ] in *action* [ækʃən], *complexion, connection* (or *connexion*), *direction, friction, inflection* (or *inflexion*), *noxious,* and *ruction*; as [kt] in *act, fact, licked, octoroon, packed,* and *soaked*; as [ktʃ] in *lecture, stricture,* and *structure*; as [kw] in *acquiesce, acquire, acquit, adequate, choir, conquest, cuisine, liquid, queen,* and *quick*.

B. THE CONTINUANTS

1. *Voiced labiodental* [v]

This consonant is, curiously, almost never doubled, and is rarely written at the very end of a word. It is used initially in *vail, veal, view, vile, volt*; medially in *abbreviate, advocate, avocation, cavil, David, even, flivver, heavy, level, navy,* British *navvy* (abbreviation of *navigator,* meaning 'a laborer engaged in digging etc.'), *oval, pivot, river, seven*; and finally in *delve, have, live, nave, objective, of, swerve*. British pronunciation generally uses [v] in *nephew*.

2. *Voiceless labiodental* [f]

This sound is initial in *fail, fall, file, flow, frame, frown,* and, spelled *ph,* in numerous words of Greek origin, such as *philosophy, phonetics,* and *physics*; medial in *baffle, cipher, diaphragm, naphtha, offer, orphan, siphon, sphinx, telephone,* and *tiffin*; final in *cliff, half, laugh, leaf, loaf, lymph, off, puff, serf, tariff, triumph, trough,* and *wolf*.

The only combination in which [f] is commonly found is [ft], as in *aft, drift, laughed, muffed, oft, puffed, soft*. It is to be noted that it has replaced the voiced [v] in the past tense of several verbs, notably *bereft* (cf. *bereave*), *cleft* (cf. *cleave*), and *left* (cf. *leave*).

However, in the plural of nouns like *leaf, life, loaf, wife,* it is in turn replaced by the voiced form, giving the plurals *leaves, lives, loaves, wives*. Likewise the voiceless [f] of a noun may appear as the voiced [v] in the corresponding verb form, as in *life* and *live, rift* and *rive, shrift* and *shrive, thrift* and *thrive*.

3. Voiced dental [ð]

This voiced sound is heard at the beginning of a few common words, such as *that, the, them, then, there, they, this, thus*; medially in *bother, brother, either, fathom, leather, other, rhythm, southerly, swarthy, whither*, and in plural nouns like *baths, laths, mouths*, and *oaths*; finally in *bathe, bequeath, breathe, lathe, mouth* (verb), *scythe, seethe, with, writhe*.

4. Voiceless dental [θ]

This sound occurs in more words, initially, than the voiced form. Examples are *thane, thank, Thebes, theology, thick, thin, think, thought, thrill, throw*, and *thyroid*. While this dental continuant is more likely to be voiced when it comes medially between two vowels, as illustrated above, it is found in this voiceless form in some shorter words and more frequently in longer words of Greek origin, as, for example, in *author, catholic, diphtheria, ether, frothy, method, mythology, nothing, ornithology, pathological*, and *pathos*. At the end of words, naturally, this voiceless form is more commonly heard, as, for example, in *bath, berth, breadth, fifth, filth, forth, heath, labyrinth, length, mouth, myth, plinth, smith, teeth, wealth, width*, and *zenith*.

It will be found that often two slightly different forms of a word exist, one the noun with the voiceless [θ] and the other the verb with the voiced [ð], as, for example, *bath* and *bathe, breath* and *breathe, cloth* and *clothe, mouth* and *to mouth*.

This consonant is found rarely in combination, mainly in [θw], as in *thwack* and *thwart*.

5. Voiced dental [z]

This consonant is fairly common with the *z* spelling, but it is very much more often found spelled with an *s*. It is found initially (but never spelled with an *s* in standard English) in *zeal, zero, zodiac, zone, zoölogy, czar, Xenophon*, and *Xerxes*. In some dialectal speech of southern England, particularly in Somerset, as we have already observed (see Sec. 16, *a*), initial [s] is frequently voiced to [z], as in *zay* (for 'say'), *Zomerzet* (for 'Somerset'), and *zore* (for 'sore'). Medially this sound is also very common and with both the *z* and the *s* spelling, as in *anxiety, artisan, asthma, blizzard, bosom, busy, dazzle, dessert, discern, disease, dizzy, eczema, exact, flimsy, gosling, hazel, husband, Isabel, lazy, lizard, misery, Missouri, muzzle, proposal, raspberry, razor, scissors, spasm, venison, visor, weasel, wisdom.*

Occasionally the medial *x* stands for the sound [z], as in *anxiety* [æŋzɑɪətɪ], or for [gz], as in *exact, exert, exist,* when the accent rests on the following syllable.

At the ends of words, also, both spellings, *z* and *s,* occur: the less common is with *z* or *ze,* as in *adz, analyze, authorize, bronze, buzz, criticize, doze, freeze, furze, jazz, ooze, prize, raze,* and *whiz*; the more common, by far, is with *s* or *se,* as in *as, amuse, bruise, chastise, cheese, close, clothes* (colloqial [klōz]), *ease, his, to house, lose, Mrs., raise, rise, Thames, whose,* and *wise.* And *x* = [z] in *beaux, Esquimaux* (also *Eskimos*), *tableaux, trousseaux,* as generally pronounced in English. The verb ending *-ise,* however, is more often spelled *-ize* in America, and even in England the tendency is toward the latter spelling, as in *authorize,* the *-ise* being in reality a French spelling adopted by many Englishmen, and without justification in most instances, since the Greek suffix should be spelled *-ize* in English. Of course some words like *advertise, advise, comprise, surprise,* do not contain this Greek suffix and hence should not be changed for this reason merely.

Many occurrences of final *-s* pronounced as [z] arise through the inflection of noun or verb, as in the noun plurals *echoes, horses, leaves, news, pains, roses, rows, sales, tolls,* and *wives,* and the verb forms *ails, bids, brags, does, gains, goes, is, snares,* and *was.*

This voiced sound [z] is found in combination only before [d], as in the past-tense forms of such verbs as *buzzed, braised, cruised,* and *razzed.*

Variables. There is, as one might expect, a good deal of variation in the English-speaking world in the use of the voiced or the voiceless sound of *s*. Foreigners have much trouble in remembering always just which should be used, and in numerous instances British and American speakers, or even Americans themselves, differ, as, for example, in *discern, dishonest,* and other words with the prefix *dis-*; in *geyser, greasy, hussy, mistletoe, parse* (British [z]), *rise* (noun), *sacrifice, suffice, transact, transfer,* and other words with the *trans-* prefix; in *usage, vase, vaseline.*

6. *Voiceless dental* [s]

Of all the English consonants none has been more generally used or has proved more enduring than this voiceless [s]; and though it has become voiced in many words as the centuries have passed, the occurrences of the voiceless form of this continuant are still very numerous. It is initial in *sale, seal, side, so, soil, soul, suit,* and *syllogism.* With the *c* spelling it is also used initially before *e, i,* and *y,* as in *ceiling, Celt* (also *Kelt*), *cinch, cist, city,* and *cycle.* With different spellings it occurs at the beginning of *psalm, psalter, pseudo-, scenic, schism, science,* and so on. Medially it occurs in *acid, chestnut, conceit, crescent, defensive, disorder, Easter, fresco, jostle, lapse, lesser, listen, muscle, officer, passive, receive, stoicism, tassel, wassail,* and *wrestle.* Finally it is heard in *bass, chase, deuce, dice, dose, erase, face, grace, lease, miss, once, pace, pass, space, toss, verbose,* and *worse.*

While this voiceless [s] does not occur as often through the inflection of noun or verb as the voiced form does, still it is fairly common, in words ending with [p] and [f], [k], [t] and [θ], especially, as in *cups* and *hops, roughs* and *scoffs, checks* and *creaks, notes* and *hits,* and *fifths.*

As in the case of [f] and [v], and of [θ] and [ð], previously commented upon, so also with [s] and [z] it will be found that pairs of words exist of which the noun employs the voiceless [s] and the verb the voiced [z], as, for example, *abuse* and *abuse* (= [z]), *advice* and *advise, device* and *devise, glass* and *glaze, grass* and *graze, loss* and *lose,* and, with shift of accent also, *réfuse* and *refúse.*

This voiceless [s] is found in more combinations than any consonant heretofore considered. It appears as [sk] in *scandal, scheme, school, skill, skull, ask,* and *risk;* as [sl] in *slander, slime, sloop*; as [sm] in *small, smoke*; as [sn] in *snail, sneak, snoop*; as [sp] in *spare, special* (and *especial*), *spore, spy* (and *espy*), *aspirin, clasp, lisp*; as [skw] in *squall, squeak, squire* (and *esquire*), *disquisition*; as [st] in *state* (and *estate*), *steal, sting, stop* (and *estop*), *strain, stroll, aster, bolster, roster, Worcester, best, cast, taste*; and as [sw] in *swell, swear, swollen, swoon, assuage, Lasuen,* and *persuade.*

7. *Voiced dental* [ʒ]

The voiced continuant [ʒ] is not heard at the beginning of English words, and only at the end of borrowed French words, such as *camouflage, garage, mirage,* and *rouge*. It is fairly common medially; but almost without exception it results from the combinations [sɪ], [tɪ], [zɪ], [sɪu], [zɪu], as in *abrasion, abscission, Asia, azure, bijou, casual, Crozier, derision, equation, evasion, Frazier* (and sometimes *Fraser*), *freesia, glazier, leisure, luxurious, Mosher* (and sometimes *Moser*), *occasion, osier, Persia, pleasure, régime, scission, treasure, usual,* and *visual*. It is obvious that this continuant results either from direct borrowing of a French sound in French words or else from a peculiar combination of sounds arising from the addition of certain derivative suffixes, especially *-ier, -ion, -ual,* and *-ure*. Its only common use in combination with another consonant is in [dʒ], which has already been discussed (see page 200). It is true that whenever a French verb ending with this [ʒ] is inflected with a past-tense suffix, the combination [ʒd] results, as in *camouflaged* and *rouged*; but this is not a native English combination and is not very common.

8. *Voiceless dental* [ʃ]

This voiceless [ʃ] is not restricted to the middle of the word, as the foregoing voiced form of the sound is, nor does it seem to owe its existence to certain peculiar sound combinations in quite the same degree. It occurs initially in *schist, shape, shell, ship, shock, shriek,* in *sugar, sumac, sure,* in *pshaw,* and in words chiefly of French origin, with the *ch* spelling, such as *chagrin, chef, chevalier, chiffon, chivalry, chute,* and names such as *Charlotte, Cheyenne,* and *Chicago*.

It is heard in the final position in *ash, cash, crush, dish, harsh, mesh, mustache, Welsh,* and *wish.*

Medially the spelling *sh* occurs in a few words, such as *ashen, bishop, crusher, fashion, Flushing,* and *usher;* and some more recently borrowed words, largely French, have *ch* or *sch,* as in *brochure, crochet, machine, meerschaum* (German), and *sachet.* But the preponderatingly large number of occurrences of this medial [ʃ] are, as was found true also of the voiced form in the previous discussion, developments from the combination of [s] or [t] with the palatal, or front, vowels [ɛ] and [ɪ]. Accordingly this is the sound of *-ce-* in *ocean,* and in words with the suffix *-aceous,* such as *herbaceous;* of *-ci-* in *ancient, gracious, musician, social,* and *vicious;* of *-sci-* in *conscience, luscious,* and *omniscient;* of *-si-* and *-ssi-* in *ascension, discussion, fuchsia, passion, Russia, session;* of *-se-* in *nausea;* of *-ti-* in *addition, expeditious, satiate;* of *-s-* before the diphthong [ɪu] in *censure, luxury, sensual;* and of *-ssu-* in *fissure, issue, pressure, tissue.*

Again, it is obvious that this continuant likewise results either from the borrowing of a French sound or else very often from a peculiar combination of sounds in the middle of a word arising from the addition of a derivative suffix such as *-ia, -ial, -ian, -ion, -ious, -ual, -ue, -ure.* Likewise this sound is used in combination with a preceding dental, giving the combination [tʃ], as already discussed (see page 201). But it is also combined with a final [t] in the past tense of various verbs, such as *fished, lashed, splashed,* and *washed.*

Variables. There is some variation in the pronunciation of words with this sound; British English uses it commonly in *schedule,* but in America the word is more often given initial [sk]; speakers use both this simple French sound and the more usual English combination [tʃ] in *chivalry.*

C. The Breath Sound [h]

This consonant, though it varies greatly among speakers of English, is spoken generally at the beginning of words like *hale, hall, hand, hew, his, hold, hoot, who, whole, whoop,* and like *human, humble, humiliate,* and *humor.* In careful pronunciation it is sounded medially in *Ahab, behemoth, behind, childhood, dishearten, inhabit, inhale, household, Lehigh, perhaps,* and the like; but in hasty speech it is likely to be lost from most of these words. At the beginning of a number of words it is regularly silent, as, for example, in *heir, herb, honest, honorarium,* and *hour.* It is not usually spoken in such words as *Bingham, exhaust, exhibit, exhort, forehead, gingham, posthumous, shepherd.* At the end of words such as *ah, bah, hallelujah, high, howdah, hurrah, oh, sleigh,* and *verandah,* the *h* is, naturally, silent and sometimes omitted in spelling, even.

In the cockney dialect of London the initial [h] is likely to be dropped from a word which should have it and be added where it does not belong.

The only combination formed by this consonant in general use is [hw], made by pronouncing [h] with rounded lips at the beginning of a word, as in *whack, whale, what, when, where, whither, whittle,* and *why.* Some people regularly simplify this combination to [w] alone, saying *wen, were, wy,* and so on, and everyone does it to some extent in hasty and careless speech. Some speakers, it is true, intensify the diphthong [ɪu] after initial [h] so as to produce a combination [hj] in such words as *Hewlett, huge, Hugh, human, humor*; and then, just as in the case of [w] above, the [h] is lost, and such pronunciations as [jumr] and [jumən] result.

D. Liquids and Nasals

Of the five liquids and nasals, four, namely, [l], [r], [m], and [n], can be either vowels or consonants according as they are used: they are weak, unaccented vowels when they are used with consonants to form syllables, as in *ta-ble, la-bor, spa-sm,* and *puri-tan*; but they become consonants when the process of adding derivative suffixes brings them next to fairly strong vowels, as in *tab-let, labo-rious, spas-modic,* and *puritan-ical.* The palatal and velar nasal [ŋ] is used only as a consonant, never as a weak vowel, differing in this respect from the other nasals.

1. Liquid [l]

This sound occurs initially in *land, leal, lily, Lloyd, lore,* and *lunatic*; medially in *almost, bellows, daily, felon, filly, grilling, mallet, police, Stella, tattler,* and *valet*; and finally in *all, belle, crawl, deal, fill, gazelle, hell, kiln, quill,* and *soil.*

It occurs in many combinations: [lb] in *Elbe*; [ld] in *bewilder, old*; [ldʒ] in *bilge, bulge*; [lf] in *dolphin, elf*; [lg] in *Calgary, Helga*; [lk] in *elk, silken*; [lm] in *elm, palmetto*; [ln] in *ulna, vulnerable*; [lp] in *Alps, help*; [ls] in *false, holster*; [lʃ] in *compulsion*; [lt] in *holt, Sultan*; [lv] in *Culver, elves*; [lj] in *bullion, million*; and [lz] in *bells, palsy.*

Variables. In a number of words the *l* is pronounced by some speakers and omitted by others, particularly in *almanac, almond, falcon, golf* (Scottish [gɑf]), *psalter, salmon,* and *yolk.*

2. Liquid [r]

This consonant occurs initially in *rabbit, real, rhetoric, rhizome, rhythm, ritual, rob, rule, wrath, wren,* and *wroth*; medially in *Arion, carriage, charity, children, courage, dreary, flourish, garage, hemorrhage, moron, Norwich, nourish, porridge, story, worried, yarrow,* and *zero*; and finally in *are, bear, burr, catarrh, err, fair, for, myrrh, par, shire,* and *your.*

It occurs in many combinations: [rb] in *garb, orbit*; [rd] in *border, card*; [rdʒ] in *forge, George, orgy*; [rf] in *orphan, wharf*; [rg] in *burg, burglar*; [rk] in *irksome, mark*; [rl] in *earl, twirl*; [rm] in *harm, squirm*; [rn] in *burn, colonel, corner, kernel*; [rp] in *carpenter, sharp*; [rs] in *bursar, curse, fierce*; [rʃ] in *marshal, partial, portion*; [rt] in *court, martyr, porter*; [rv] in *carve, service*; [rks] in *barks, Marx*; [rj] in *courier, merrier*; [rz] in *cars, furze*; and [rʒ] in *excursion, version.*

3. Labial nasal [m]

This consonant is used initially in *many, mean, mint, moon, moor,* and *mule*; medially in *coming, diamond, grimace, hames, hummock, mimic, nominal, primer, salmon, summer, terminal,* and *timid*; and finally in *arm, calm, damn, diaphragm, dime, home, hum, lamb, lime, loom, phlegm, plum, realm,* and *ream.*

In combination with other consonants [m] is rarely found at the end of a word, except when the accompanying consonant is silent. It occurs in the following combinations: [mb] in *humble, somber, timber* (but with the *b* silent in *comb, dumb, limb*, etc.); [mf] in *Bamfield, Banff, comfort, cramfull*; [ml] in *Daimler, hamlet*; [mn] in *autumnal, condemnation, hymnal* (but with *n* silent in *autumn, condemn, hymn*); [mp] in *ampere, ample, camp, pumpkin* (dialectal [pʌ́nkɪn]), and *sump*; [mr] in the actual hurried pronunciation of words like *hamm(e)ring, simm(e)ring,* and *stamm(e)ring,* although the shortening of the second syllable is not ordinarily indicated in the spelling, and in careful and deliberate speech the full three syllables are maintained; [mst] in *Amsterdam, teamster*; [mθ] in *warmth*.

In the pronunciation of the past-tense form of such verbs as *hummed, limned,* and *roamed,* the combination is in reality [md], despite the spelling; and in the inflectional forms of noun and verb which take the ending *-s*, such as *limes, numbs,* and *slams,* the combination is [mz]. These are the most numerous [m] combinations used finally.

4. Dental nasal [n]

This nasal is found at the beginning of such words as *navy, need, nil, no, noon, knack, knee, gnaw, gnome, mnemonic, pneumatic,* and *pneumonia*; medially in *any, banish, comptroller, cranny, dinner, granary, money, penetrate, piano, pinafore, planet, poignant, tenor, tunnel,* and *vanish*; and finally in *Anne, been, bin, cane, deign, den, impugn, inn, Lincoln, moon, on, sign, train, vein,* and *wine*.

It occurs in various combinations: [nd] in *and, bundle, thunder*; [ndʒ] in *angel, harbinger, plunge*; [nf] in *confer, inference, unfurnished*; [ng] in *penguin* (or [pɛŋgwɪn]), *sanguine*; [nk] in *increase, inquiry*; [ns] in *once, pencil, sincere, spinster, wince,* and usually in such inflectional forms of nouns and verbs as *aunts, slants, wants*; [nt] in *bantam, bent, lantern, winter*; [ntʃ] in *bench, cinch, ranch*; [nv] in *anvil, Danvers, unveil*; [nz] in *banns, frenzy, pansy*; and [nj] in *canyon, lorgnette, union.*

5. *Palatal and velar* [ŋ]

This nasal is used only before the spellings *g* and *k* and is, like the two consonants for which those letters stand, palatal after front vowels and velar after back vowels. The simple sound is heard in *Bingen, bring, hang, hangar, long, ringer, rung, sing,* and *wrong.*

It occurs in various combinations: [ŋg] in *anger, angle, English, finger* (cf. *singer*), *hunger, languor, strongest, tango*; [ŋgw] in *anguish, language, linguist*; [ŋk] in *anchor, ankle, bronchial, plank, sinker, think, trinket, Yankee*; [ŋks] in *Bronx, jinks, minx,* and in other inflectional *s* forms of nouns and verbs like *rinks* and *thinks*; [ŋkw] in *banquet, relinquish, vanquish*; [ŋʃ] in *anxious, function, unction*; [ŋtʃ] in *punctual, tincture*; [ŋθ] in *length, strength.*

Variables. For many words with *n* there is variable pronunciation; in hasty speech they are spoken with this palatal or velar [ŋ], but when speakers are influenced by observing the appearance of a word, then the dental [n] is likely to be used instead. Many such words are derivative forms with prefixes ending in *n*, as, for example, *conclave, congregation, inquest, tranquil.* Other examples are *penguin, relinquish, vanquish.*

It has already been remarked that in British speech the final *-ing* of verbals like *going* and *seeing* is likely to be spoken with the dental [n] rather than with this palatal [ŋ]; and it should be added that this is not uncommon in careless or dialectal American speech, as well as in British English.

E. THE SEMIVOWELS

In an earlier discussion (Sec. 20) an attempt has been made to show how the palatal [j] (regularly spelled *y*) is likely to accompany a strongly palatal vowel, and the labial [w] a back vowel with much rounding of the lips. They are, by their very nature, unstable and elusive and hence not always written, even though spoken, as in *unite* and *one* ([junɑɪt] and [wʌn]), or else they are written but not spoken, as in *pay* and *know* ([pē] and [nō]). Spelling is not a very good indication, since *u* and *w* and *i* and *y* are used interchangeably to represent both the vowels and the consonants. And, finally, in the same word the vowel will be heard sometimes and the consonant at other times, as, for example, in *curious, follower, hallowèd,* and *serial,* which are sometimes so spoken that they might just as well be written *cur-yous, foll-wer, hallo-wed,* and *ser-yal,* whereas at other times they would need to be written *cu-ri-ous, follo-er, hallo-èd,* and *se-ri-al.* They are, very often, about half vowel and half consonant; hence the name *semivowels.*

1. *Semivowel* [j]

The palatal semivowel [j] occurs initially in *Yale, yawl, Yellowstone, yore, youth, Yule, ewe, unite, useful,* and rarely in *humor*; it is medial in *Arabian, behavior, Ethiopian, expedient, Fabian, hallelujah, immediately, lawyer, medium, odious, ruffian, Sawyer,* and *Vesuvius,* although many speakers will insist that they pronounce a distinct vowel [ɪ] in unstressed endings such as *-ian* and *-ious.* Doubtless some do pronounce this vowel; but in the hurried speech of most people the sound is certainly the glide consonant [j] rather than the more awkward hiatus of one vowel next to another. Consonantal [j] does not occur at the end of a word; when the letter *y* is used finally, it is either part of the spelling of a stressed vowel, as in *hay,* or of a diphthong, as in *boy,* or it represents the unstressed [ɪ], as in *city.*

There are no combinations of [j] with a following consonant; but with a preceding liquid or with the nasal [n] it is combined in important English words: [lj] in *ameliorate, collier,* the colloquial *colyum* (for 'column'), *cotillion, Elliott, familiar, folio, hellion, million, pavilion, trillium,* and *William*; [rj] in *barrier, burial, chariot, Harriet, heriot, interior, Marryat, superior, terrier,* and *warrior*; [nj] in *annular, banyan, Bunyan, canyon* (or *cañon*), *cognac, companion, leniency, lorgnette, mignonette, minion, onion, signor, union, venial,* and *vignette.*

Variables. Sometimes a meticulous pronunciation of the diphthong [ɪu] results in [ju], producing such affectations as *fig-yure, fut-yure, nat-yure,* and *sched-yule* for 'figure', 'future', 'nature', and 'schedule'.

2. Semivowel [w]

The labial semivowel [w] occurs initially in *wail, wall, weal, went, were, winter, one, once, won, woo, wore*, and frequently instead of [hw] in such words as *when, where*, and *why*, when they are carelessly spoken. It is heard medially in *backward, Brunswick, coward, cruel, froward, fuel, Howard, memoir, power, reservoir, sandwich, Sewell, stalwart, tower*, and *Wentworth*, although it is true here also that some speakers do manage to pronounce words like *cruel* with hiatus rather than with this labial glide consonant between the vowels. Often this [w] is present in the pronunciation of a word merely because, in adding a vowel-beginning suffix to a word ending in a back lip-rounded vowel, the speaker unconsciously and quite unintentionally, but very naturally, speaks this labial transitional, or glide, consonant, as in *brewer* (from *brew*), *fewest* (from *few*), *going* (from *go*), *owing* (from *owe*), *sawing* (from *saw*), and *slower* (from *slow*). There is no final consonantal [w]; when the letter appears at the end of a word, it is either entirely superfluous, as in *know*, or else it helps to indicate a special vowel or diphthong, as in *few, how*, and *law*.

There are no combinations of [w] plus a following consonant, although the *wr* of words like *wren, wring, wrong*, indicates that such a combination was spoken in earlier centuries. There are numerous combinations, however, with a preceding consonant; but in such combinations the [w] is little more than a quick rounding of the lips, a labialization, as in [dw] in *dwell, dwindle*; in [tw] in *twain, twit, between*; in [gw] in *anguish, Guelph, Guinevere, languid*; in [kw] in *queen, acquit, quondam*; in [hw] in *when, while, why*; in [sw] in *suave, swear, Sweden, swine, swollen, swoon, assuage, desuetude, persuade*; and in [θw] in *thwack, thwart, pathway*.

The gradual loss of [w] in past centuries of the English language is indicated by the number and variety of words which still retain a silent *w* in consonant combinations; silent *w* occurs initially in *who, whole, whoop*, etc., and in the spelling group *wr*, already mentioned, as in *wreck, wrench, wring*, etc., and medially in *answer, Greenwich, Norwich, sword, two*, etc.

44. Combinations and Changes of Consonants

It is necessary to know something of the interrelations of consonants before one can understand the changes that take place in many consonants or have already taken place in centuries past.

1. Combinations

Interesting light is thrown on the phonetic preferences of speakers of English when the many combinations noted in the preceding studies of the various consonants are brought together and tabulated and studied. Some may be considered characteristic of English; others, such as *hl, hn, hr, wl, wr*, have been simplified to single consonants.

a. Explosives and continuants + liquids and nasals

[bl]	blow	[br]	brown
[pl]	place	[pr]	prow
		[dr]	drill
		[tr]	try
[gl]	glow	[gr]	grow
[kl]	clock	[kr]	crock
[fl]	flow	[fr]	frown
[sl]	slow		
		[ʃr]	shrill
		[θr]	thrill

Also: [sm] in *small*, [sn] in *snail*. In earlier English initial [gn] and [kn], and [hl], [hr], and [hn], were also used; but the *g* and *k* are silent now in *gnat* and *knee*, though still written, while the *h* has vanished altogether from *loud, roof,* and *nut*. Likewise initial *pn* has silent *p* in words of Greek origin, such as *pneumatic*. Initial [wl] and [wr] of earlier English seem also to have proved unpleasant to later English speakers, as the *w* remains only in the spelling of words like *wren* and has been dropped altogether from *lisp*.

b. Explosives + continuants

[bz]	ribs		
[ps]	lips		
[dz]	adz	[dʒ]	gist, judge
[ts]	lots	[tʃ]	chase, batch
[gz]	exact, eggs		
[ks]	box, locks	[kʃ]	action

Also: a few combinations of explosives + explosives, namely, [bd] in *robbed*, [gd] in *nagged*, [pt] in *slept*, [kt] in *fact*, and [ktʃ] in *lecture*.

c. *Continuants + explosives*

[vd]	loved	[st]	stand, last
[ft]	quaffed, aft	[sk]	skill, ask
[ðd]	bathed	[skw]	squire
[θt]	frothed	[ʒd]	rouged
[zd]	buzzed	[ʃt]	rushed
[sp]	spare, clasp		

This kind of combination is not very popular in English, except insofar as the addition of the verb ending -*ed* produces numerous examples. The four combinations with [s] are used initially, but the others seem to have proved too awkward for such use.

d. *Liquids and nasals + explosives and continuants*

[l]	[lb]	Elbe	[m] [mb]	somber
	[ld]	old	[md]	hummed
	[ldʒ]	bulge	[mf]	comfort
	[lf]	elf	[mp]	camp
	[lg]	Olga	[mst]	teamster
	[lk]	elk	[mθ]	warmth
	[lp]	help	[mz]	gleams
	[ls]	false		
	[lʃ]	compulsion	[n] [nd]	and
	[lt]	bolt	[ndʒ]	plunge
	[lv]	silver	[nf]	confer
	[lz]	palsy	[ngw]	penguin
			[nk]	increase
[r]	[rb]	garb	[ns]	once
	[rd]	card	[ntʃ]	bench
	[rdʒ]	forge	[nv]	anvil
	[rf]	wharf	[nz]	frenzy
	[rg]	burg		
	[rk]	mark	[ŋ] [ŋg]	anger
	[rp]	sharp	[ŋgw]	anguish
	[rs]	curse	[ŋk]	ankle
	[rʃ]	harsh	[ŋkw]	banquet
	[rt]	court	[ŋks]	Bronx
	[rv]	carve	[ŋz]	anxiety
	[rz]	furze	[ŋʃ]	anxious
	[rʒ]	version	[ŋtʃ]	puncture
			[ŋθ]	length

e. Palatalization and labialization of consonants

The use of the palatal [j] is responsible for the combinations [tj] in the artificial pronunciation of words like *fortune* [fɔrtjūn]; [hj] in *humor* (when pronounced as though it were spelled *hyumor*); [lj] in *million*; [rj] in *burial*; and [nj] in *mignonette*.

The palatal combination [dɪ] frequently becomes [dj] in words like *hideous, idiot, immediate, Indian, tedious*; and in past usage and sometimes in present-day dialectal speech this combination is further palatalized into [dʒ], giving such forms as the dialectal *hidjous, idjut, immejut, Injun, tedjous,* and even *tremendjous.*

The rounding of the lips after certain consonants produces the combinations [dw] in *dwell*, [tw] in *twain*, [gw] in *guava*, [kw] in *queen*, [sw] in *swell*, [θw] in *thwart*, and [hw] in *when.*

A thoughtful appraisal of the five groups just discussed will afford some interesting results. For one thing, consonants are combined in speech, as illustrated above, in three quite different ways: some form a permanent phonetic unit, as in *blow* and *ridge*; others come together just because their two syllables happen to bring them into neighboring positions, as [ŋg] in *anger* and [nf] in *confer*; still others are the result of adding inflectional endings, as [st] in *blest* and [ks] in *locks.*

Those of the first combination group, such as *blow,* are regularly used initially, may come together by accident medially, but never occur finally as consonants.

The explosives + continuants, of the second group, such as *eggs,* may be brought together loosely in the middle of a word, but are mostly heard at the end as inflectional forms. The sounds in *jeer* and *chip* ([dʒ] and [tʃ]) are exceptional in that they can occur in any part of the word.

The continuants + explosives, of the third group, such as [zd] in *buzzed,* are usually final combinations resulting from inflectional processes, but may come together medially. The four [sp], [st], [sk], and [skw] are often used initially as well as elsewhere in a word.

The liquids and nasals + explosives and continuants, of the fourth group, never occur initially, but are found medially, and in most instances finally.

The fifth group, of palatalized and labialized consonants, are used as units initially, as in *queen,* are more accidental medially, and never occur at the ends of words.

2. Voicing

The *s* ending of noun plurals and of the verb in the present tense is regularly voiced after voiced consonants and after vowels, as in *adds, goes, roses,* and *tolls.* Very often in plurals formed of nouns ending in [f] and [θ], as *bath, loaf, wife,* these two continuants become voiced to [v] and [ð], giving the plural forms *baths, loaves, wives.* In certain other words, also, there is a tendency toward voicing, as in [gūzbɛrɪ] for *gooseberry,* the frequently heard *pardner* for 'partner,' [ræzbɛrɪ] for *raspberry.* In the dialectal pronunciation of southern England there has long been a tendency to voice the unvoiced initial continuants, giving *vane, vat, vixen* (as feminine form of *fox*), and in the Somerset dialect *zay* and *zure* for *say* and *sure.*

3. Unvoicing

When the ending *-ed* of the past tense is added to a verb ending in a voiceless consonant, the [d] of the suffix is regularly unvoiced to [t], as in *chafed, fished, past, slept.* As already noted, the voiceless form in a noun frequently corresponds to a voiced form in the closely related verb, as in *bath* and *bathe, grass* and *graze, life* and *live, shrift* and *shrive.* In longer derivative forms of certain words, also, the voiced consonant of the shorter word becomes unvoiced in the longer, as in *absorption* (from *absorb*), *fifteen* (from *five*), and *thrifty* (from *thrive*). The colloquial [hæftə] for *have to* has already been mentioned, and to this might be added [jūstə] for *used to.* In the compound *newspaper* the *s* is often unvoiced, although *news* has the [z] sound.

4. Assimilation

Occasionally, through the process of voicing or unvoicing or some similar change, two neighboring sounds merge into one, or become more nearly identical.* So the usual pronunciation of *blackguard* is [blægərd], of the nautical *boatswain* is [bōsn̥], of *cupboard* is [kʌbərd], of *gunwale* is [gʌnl̥]; in collo-

---

*Assimilation is generally understood as applying to that process whereby two different sounds become identical. But usually, as in the examples given above, the process has gone farther even, and the two sounds have merged into one, so that the *pb* of *cupboard* is now pronounced not as [bb] but as [b].

quial speech *clapboard* often becomes [klæbərd], and *grandma* becomes [græmɑ]. But in pronouncing *comptroller* as though it were *controller*, one is not assimilating an [m] to an [n] but is merely ignoring an earlier bad spelling; the word should be *controller*. Assimilation, since it makes easier the pronunciation of two dissimilar consonants, is naturally very common in colloquial and dialectal English, as illustrated by [nɔrɪdʒ] for *Norwich*, and the dialect spellings *gimme* for 'give me', *innards* for 'inwards', *lemme* for 'let me', *reconnize* for 'recognize', and *supprise* for 'surprise'.

5. *Reduction of consonantal vowels*

The consonantal vowels, [l̥], [m̥], [n̥], and [r̥], are often reduced to mere consonants when other syllables are added to words in which they occupy the final unaccented syllables. So vocalic [l̥] of *am-ple, sta-ble, ta-ble, ti-tle*, becomes consonantal [l] in *am-plify, sta-bility, tab-ular,* and *tit-ular*; [m̥] of *prism, rhythm, schism, spasm,* becomes [m] in *prismatic, rhythmical, schismatic,* and *spasmodic*; [n̥] of *garden, leaven, lighten,* becomes [n] in *Gardner, leavening,* and *lightning*; and [r̥] of *anger, center, theater, winter,* becomes [r] in *angrily, central, theatrical,* and *wintry*.

6. *Revival of silent letters*

In words with certain forms of silent letters, the addition of a suffix will often revive the silent letter. So silent *b* of *crumb* and *thumb* is spoken in *crumble* and *thimble*; *g* of *malign, phlegm, resign,* and *sign* is revived in *malignant, phlegmatic, resignation,* and *signal*; final *n* of *autumn, condemn, hymn,* and *solemn* becomes alive in *autumnal, condemnation, hymnal,* and *solemnity*; *t* in *apostle* and *epistle* is heard in *apostolic* and *epistolary*. The [w] which is merely the unconscious rounding of the lips at the end of *go, hoe,* and *row* not infrequently becomes a transition consonant in *going, hoeing,* and *rower*.

7. *Loss of consonants*

A tendency to drop consonants is observable in some words; in others it has become established already. Medial [d] is lost in *brand-new* [brænnu], *grandson* (colloquial [grænsʌn]), *Wednesday* [wɛnzdeɪ], and *Windsor* [wɪnzər]. It is frequently dropped after [l] in such words as *child*, *old*, and *told*, especially in some American dialectal speech. The explosive [b] has already been dropped from actual pronunciation in words like *dumb*, *lamb*, and *thumb*. Initial [h] comes and goes in the cockney dialect of England, and medial [h] is generally lost in the standard English pronunciation of such words as *Chatham*, *exhibit*, *exhort*, *forehead*, *Graham*, and *shepherd*. Medial [l] has already grown silent before the nasals in *palm*, *qualm*, and the like, and is gradually vanishing from *almond* and *salmon*, today. In some words like *February*, *library*, *reservoir*, and *secretary* careless speakers omit the first [r]; and the final [r] of such words as *bar* and *never* is vocalized out of the class of consonants altogether by a large proportion of speakers in England, New England, and the Southern states. For centuries it has been the common practice in English dialectal and colloquial speech to drop the final consonant from certain prepositions, as in *i' the house, John o' Lincoln, o'clock, Tam o'Shanter*.

8. *Addition of consonants*

There has long been a tendency in English to add a final stop consonant after [n] or [s]. This has brought about the final [d] of *kind*, *round*, *sound*, and today *drownd* (infinitive) is often heard from careless speakers, while *acrost*, *clost*, *oncet*, *twicet*, and *wisht* are merely following in the footsteps of *against*, *lest*, and others now standardized. A dialectal tendency to prolong a final vowel by means of an [r] seems to be responsible for such forms as *Hanner* (for 'Hannah'), *holler* (for 'hollo'), *idear* (for 'idea'), *lawr* (for 'law'), *Noar* (for 'Noah'), *winder* (for 'window'), and *yaller* (for 'yellow'). Somewhat like this is the pronunciation of a medial [r], producing [kārm] for *calm*, [wōrʃ] for *wash*.

9. *Metathesis*

The liquid [r] frequently slips over on the other side of a vowel, and the result is *apern* for 'apron', *childern* for 'children', *hunderd* for 'hundred', *iern* for 'iron', *perscription* for 'prescription', *perty* for 'pretty', *prespiration* for 'perspiration', and so on. By a similar form of metathesis the [sk] of *task* has become [ks] in the doublet form *tax*, and in illiterate colloquial pronunciation the verb *ask* sometimes becomes *ax*. Sometimes an entire syllable is added or misplaced, as in *calvary* for 'cavalry', *diary* for 'dairy', *revelant* for 'relevant'. A form of metathesis which is not phonetic but merely one of spelling is to be observed in such spellings as *centre* and *center*, *ochre* and *ocher*, *metre* and *meter*. This process of metathesis of sounds is one of the features of slovenly and confused speech and is especially likely to appear in the prefixes *per-* and *pre-*

10. *Substitution of different consonants*

Sometimes the addition of suffixes like *-able*, *-al*, *-an*, *-ion*, *-ous*, and *-ure* results in the substitution of a different consonant in place of the final sound of the simpler word. So final [t] becomes [ʃ] in *admission* (cf. *admit*), *creation* (cf. *create*), *inflection* (cf. *inflect*); [t] becomes [tʃ] in *creature* (cf. *create*), *factual* (cf. *fact*), *righteous* (cf. *right*); [k] becomes [s] in *criticism* (cf. *critic*); [k] becomes [ʃ] in *musician* (cf. *music*), *politician* (cf. *politic*); [s] becomes [k] in *practicable* and *practical* (cf. *practice*); [s] becomes [ʃ] in *facial* (cf. *face*), *gracious* (cf. *grace*), and *vicious* (cf. *vice*); [g] becomes [dʒ] in *analogy* (cf. *analogue*).

45. *Accentuation in English*

Much has been said in the preceding sections about the changes of vowels and of consonants resulting from shift of accent or weakening of accent; and it must be emphasized that such changes are fully as numerous and important as those that result from the interrelations of sounds, already summed up at the ends of the studies of vowels and consonants. Before summarizing, however, the various effects of accentual change that have already been touched upon, and introducing here some other aspects of the working of accentuation, two important fundamental facts should be reaffirmed: first, that the accent or accents of a word are but a portion of the larger plan of accentuation of the sentence as a whole, and, secondly, that in the accentual ups and downs of continuous speech a longer word, that is, a polysyllabic word, such as *còmplicátion,* has at least three degrees of accentuation — secondary, weak, primary, and weak again. The weakly accented syllables are generally said to be without accent. Moreover, it must be recognized further that while one speaker will make fairly obvious distinctions between primary and secondary accentuation, as in *còmplicátion,* or between accent and no accent, as in *táble,* another speaker will so spread the accentuation of a fairly long word, such as *philology,* that it will be difficult to determine whether the accent is stronger on one syllable or almost equally strong on two succeeding syllables. It is the tendency to center the stress on the one syllable which leads to the pronunciation [fɪláləd ʒɪ] by one speaker; the spreading or scattering of accentuation leads to the differing pronunciation [faɪləled ʒɪ] by another speaker. This accent-scattering, or accent-leveling, as some prefer to name it, is fully as important for the understanding of variation in vowel quantity as is accent-shifting; but it is much more difficult to measure and appreciate. In *cóllect* and *colléct* the shift is reasonably clear; but in *complication* there may be a strong primary accent on the *cóm* or on the *cá,* or there may be a spread of accentuation over both the first and the third syllable, so that the student may hesitate to say just where the accent rests most heavily in the word. Lindelöf has recently gathered a large number of examples like *biography, direction, philology,* and *typography* in which the preaccent *i* (or *y*) is differently pronounced by different speakers[221]. On the whole, the American tendency seems to be to pronounce the sound [ɪ] and put slightly more stress on the following syllable; but the dictionaries do not always agree on this point.

    a. In an earlier discussion of the characteristics of English (Sec. 28) attention was called to the Germanic tendency to put the accent as near as possible to the beginning of a word, a method of accentuation in marked contrast to that of the Romanic languages, especially French, where the accent is likely to fall farther along in the word. Whenever a French or a Latin word has been borrowed and dropped into the stream of English speech, the accent has usually begun to move back toward the first syllable, as can be seen today in the pronunciations *álloy, álly, álternate, chástisement, cóntemplate, cróchet, détails, énvelope* (noun), *éxtirpate, finance, gárage, íllustrate, inquiry, mústache, píanist, précedence, résearch*[222], *rómance, tróusseau*.

Variables. However, so many cross currents of influence are at work upon some of these words that quite the opposite tendency may be observed at times[223]. The verbs *ádvertìse, chastise, dispúte,* and *revóke* naturally influence one to say *advertísement, chastísement, dispútable,* and *revócable*; sometimes ignorance or a perverse feeling that one pronunciation is more "elegant" than another will be responsible for such counter tendencies in accentuation as *deficit, dirigible, envélope* (noun), *haráss, mischievous, theáter*.

b. Since the earliest Anglo-Saxon period, words of two or three syllables with prefixes have frequently illustrated the English rule or principle that the accent should be placed on the first syllable of such words when they are used as nouns, and on the second syllable when they are verbs or adjectives.

Noun	Verb	Noun	Verb
ábsence	absént	†ínvite	invíte
†áddress	addréss	†pérfume	perfúme
†cómbine	combíne	†pérmit	permít
cómpress	compréss	prémise	premíse
cóntest	contést	présent	presént
cóntract	contráct	próduce	prodúce
cónvert	convért	prógress	progréss
cónvict	convíct	próject	projéct
désert	desért	prótest	protést
†détail	detáil	récord	recórd
dígest	digést	†réfund	refúnd
†díscharge	dischárge	réfuse	refúse
éxports	expórt	rélay	reláy
éxtract	extráct	†súrvey	survéy
†fínance	fináince	†súspect	suspéct
ímpress	impréss	tránsfer	transfér
ínsult	insúlt	tránsport	transpórt

Noun	Adjective	Noun	Adjective
ábstract	abstráct	cóntents	contént
†ádept	adépt	éxpert	expért
†ádult	adúlt	ínstinct	instínct
cómpact	compáct	ínvalid	inválid
cómplex	compléx	mínute	minúte
cóncrete	concréte		

Variables. Pronunciations marked with a dagger in the preceding lists are still unsettled; some of them are regarded as colloquial or of somewhat doubtful propriety; most of them, however, are commonly used in colloquial speech, even though they may not be recommended by the dictionaries. The working of this principle of twofold accentuation is so strong still that in spite of the endeavors of teachers and lexicographers to keep the accent on the second syllable of certain nouns, such as *adult*, the shift to the first syllable goes steadily on. See also Krapp's discussion of *abject*, with his presentation of other reasons for the variable accentuation of such words.[17]

c. Accentual changes resulting from or accompanying the processes of derivative change are various and, as already noted here and there in the foregoing sections, are likely to lead to changes in vowels and even in consonants.

(1) When the accent shifts, the vowel to which it moves is likely to become shortened, as in *prèparátion* (from *prepáre*), *pròclamátion* (from *procláim*); and if it be vocalic [l̥], [m̥], [n̥], or [r̥], a stronger vowel results, as in *centrífugal* (from *cénter*), *probabílity* (from *próbable*), and *spasmódic* (from *spásm*).

(2) When the accent shifts, the vowel from which it departs is also likely to be weakened: the diphthong [aɪ] becomes [ɪ] in *àdmirátion* (from *admíre*), and long [ē], [ō], etc. weaken to the obscure vowel, as in *máintenance* (from *maintáin*), *próvidence* (from *províde*), *pròvocátion* (from *provóke*). While the accent rests on a vowel immediately following the consonant combination [gz] (= *x*), the combination remains voiced, as in *exált, exhórt, exúlt*; but when the accent is moved to the vowel just preceding the combination, it is unvoiced to [ks] (= *x*), as in *èxaltátion, èxhortátion, èxultátion*. Likewise, when the accent is removed from a syllable containing a silent g, this g generally comes to life, as in *phlegmátic* (from *phlégm*), *rèsignátion* (from *resígn*).

(3) When the accent does not shift, but is somewhat scattered, or leveled, because of the increase in syllables over which it must be spread, the accented vowels and diphthongs usually become shortened, as in *annùnciátion* (cf. *annóunce*), *chíldren* (cf. *chíld*), *Dénmark* (cf. *Dáne*), *deprávity* (cf. *depráve*), *fábulous* (cf. *fáble*), *héroine* (cf. *héro*), *lócative* (cf. *lócal*), *tèlephónic* (cf. *télephòne*).

The varying effects of the addition of suffixes are interestingly shown in the variant forms *depóse*, *depósitory*, and *dèposítion*; *províde*, *provísion*, and *próvidence*; *resíde*, *resíduary*, and *résidence*.

Variables. Numerous polysyllabic words still show variation in the placing of the accent in Current English, notably *advertisement*, *arbutus*, *cafeteria*, *clematis*, *commandant*, *communal*, *demonstrate*, *despicable*, *elegiac*, *exigency*, *gladiolus*, *gondola*, *hospitable*, *incomparable*, *indisputable*, *inexplicable*, *kilometer*, *mischievous*, *nomenclature*, *obligatory*, *recondite*, *respiratory*, *superfluous*.

Curiously enough, British and American speakers are both quite inconsistent in their pronunciation of two somewhat similar groups of words. As already shown (see Sec. 40), in American speech words like *nécessary* and *décorative* are usually given a secondary accent on the third syllable, whereas the British accent is placed strongly on the first syllable and the rest of the word is hurried over; but, on the other hand, Americans tend to give less value to the last syllables of such words as *fértile*, *téxtile*, *and vérsatile*, while the British speaker uses a fairly strong diphthong [ɑɪ] and consequently spreads the accentuation more uniformly over the entire word.

The accentuation of compound words, and of terms and proper names (especially place-names) made up of more than one word, varies greatly. For the compound word fits into the rhythm of the sentence in just the same manner as any polysyllabic word: it may have fairly level stress, or accentuation spread out or scattered over the various syllables of the compound, as in *road house* or *topcoat*; it may have its primary accentuation first, as in *lúnch time*, *póorhouse*, and *wáistcoat* (now often pronounced [wɛskət]); or it may start with a weaker accent and end with a primary stress, as in

Nèw Yórk and Sòuth Dakóta. It is interesting to see how speakers differ in their placing of the stress in such placenames as Sánta Fè (or Sànta Fé). Contrasting accentuations can be observed in the stressing of the letter name as dóuble-u for the labial consonant w and double ú for the doubled vowel uu.

In concluding this discussion of accentuation it is necessary to revert again to the thought expressed early in this book that the current of one's speech is being constantly modified by the thinking that underlies it; for along with the changes in the quality and quantity of sounds, variation in the stressing, or accentuation, of these sounds is equally important. The varying accentuation of words, of phrases, and of sentences as a whole not only helps to distinguish certain parts of speech, aids in the processes of derivative change, and gives finer shades of meaning, but also constitutes an important element in the flow, or rhythm, of speech.

46. Rhythm and Pitch

In the course of the discussion of the sounds of speech in general (Secs. 19, 20) and of English speech sounds in particular (Secs. 41–44), there have been several allusions to "the continuous flow of speech", this flow arising naturally from the fact that speech is made up of a succession of vowels and consonants; and gradually to this conception of the flow of speech we have added as equally necessary that of the measured sequence of accentuation, "the tendency of the speaker to stress syllables or words at frequent intervals". To understand thoroughly the rhythm, or flow, of speech it is plainly necessary to have all the information possible concerning the succession of long and short and unaccented vowels, of voiced and voiceless consonants, of the continuity of accentuation and its effect upon the sounds of speech, and of the interrelations of sounds generally; and until such information could be supplied, there was little use in endeavoring to analyze and appreciate the rhythm of English speech. Even after a scientific foundation has been laid in this manner, there still remains the more difficult task of comparing the rhythm of prose speech with the more consciously developed rhythm of poetry and of considering the art of rhythmical speaking. Happily it is not the purpose of this book to appraise the art of English prose and poetry, and so this study of English rhythm can be restricted to an examination of a few fundamental facts of English prose rhythm.

Of the numerous terms long used by the student of metrics, only two need be brought into this brief consideration of prose rhythm: namely, trochaic measure, with its falling stress, as in the dissyllabic *chásm, óver, táble,* and iambic measure, with its rising stress, as in *abóut, seléct, untíe.* Of course the accent is not always definitely on the one syllable or the other, but may be so spread or scattered over the syllables of a word as to be deserving of the name *level stress,* already illustrated in the discussion of the accentuation of such terms as *road house,* and heard also in *Santa Ana, sun room, twofold, uproar,* and so on.

The English language has been said to be predominantly trochaic in rhythm because of its Germanic tendency to stress the first syllable of each word, and this has been largely true in the past and may, perhaps, be so regarded still if allowance be made sufficiently for numerous changes and exceptions resulting from the loss of inflectional endings and the influx of a strong Romanic element which has brought with it both trochaic and iambic words. When *hadde* and *times* were still spoken as two-syllable words, to a certain extent they gave a trochaic swing to speech; when, however, they became monosyllabic, they could fit into either trochaic or iambic rhythm, leaving the speaker of English to use them as he might choose or chance to do. Numerous polysyllabic words have come into English with their so-called rhythmical accent, such as *còntemplátion, còrrespóndence, èxultátion, incidéntal, institútion, revèrberátion, trànscendéntal, translìterátion, ùnivérsal.* But by means of phrasing or by compounding simpler words, either native or borrowed, one can produce practically the same rhythmical effect, as in *in the mórning, òn the ríver, ópen-hànded, sùnny wéather, táble còver.*

Studies have been made of the various rhythmical pairs of words connected with *and* which English speakers are fond of using, such as *bag and baggage, free and easy, hammer and tongs, hill and valley, paper and ink*; and though the majority are so arranged as to give the trochaic effect, Scott has found, in a list of his own compiling, about 42 per cent of the *paper and ink* type, ending with the accented syllable rather than with the unaccented.[226]

In the lists of words given in Section 41 many dissyllabic words were included which had a weak second syllable, such as *able, clover, devil, number, rapid,* and *witty*. These are both native and borrowed, as to origin, but always trochaic. On the other hand, lists of words have been given which are regularly trochaic when nouns but iambic when used as verbs, as, for example, *contest, insult, refuse*; and this accentual distinction reaches back to the very earliest Old English usage. So it is plain that the English language never was entirely trochaic in its rhythm; and the words that have come into the language later have not been predominantly iambic, even though French accentuation of many words did for a while make them iambic in English.

As a matter of fact, one can, if his ear be attuned to the rhythm of music and poetry, also produce rhythmical effects in his everyday speech, and many speakers do at times. One hears sentences, for example, which can easily be labeled, such as

[Trochaic]
Mòther's táble hàs a cólor thàt is lóvely ìn the súnlight.

[Iambic]
He tóok the dìme and wálked awày.

[Trochaic]
Fáther sàid he'd gíve me Fìdo if I'd féed him évery mòrning.

[Iambic]
Look óut! He's còming dòwn the fíeld!

[Either]
And none the less he came up smiling.

Undoubtedly, successful writers and orators produce more strongly rhythmical prose, on the whole, than the ordinary speaker, because, in the first place, they use the longer, more rhythmical literary words, whereas the shorter and commoner ones are used colloquially, and, secondly, because they compose more artistically, and in the heat of composition or oratorical inspiration are more likely to be caught up into a rhythmical flow of English.

Then, again, some speakers have more rhythm than others, as one can observe while listening to various public speakers. Just as some people possess an ear for music, others (or the same people, perhaps) might boast of an ear for rhythmical speech.

And, finally, the rhythm of speech depends to some degree upon the mood of the speaker. Words of affection, especially diminutives, such as *baby*, *Willie*, *sonny*, are largely trochaic, with gently falling accent; words of warning and command are frequently iambic, with sharply rising accent, as in 'Get out', 'Look out', and 'Stand back'.

But in the last examples of iambic rhythm it should be remarked that there is also a rise in pitch as well as an increase in stress. This change in pitch is due to an increased vibration of the vocal cords and undoubtedly has its part in the expression of thinking and emotion, though it is even more difficult to dissociate it from vowel quantity and stress than it was to differentiate those two. Speakers undoubtedly modify the pitch of their speech, or at least of certain words and phrases, when they are under emotional strain; higher pitch is likely to be characteristic of the speech of a highly nervous person. Whether differences of pitch can also be regarded as due to racial differences is not so certain. That the refined British speaker pitches his voice lower than the American of similar educational advantages is noticeable to all who have an opportunity to compare the two classes of speakers of the English language.

CHAPTER VII

ENGLISH SPELLING

AMONG the characteristics of the English language most noticed by foreigners, the only one to be seriously criticized is its "antiquated spelling". Such a criticism is a definite challenge to the Englishman and the American, and can be met only by a thoughtful examination of the system of spelling employed to represent the sounds of Current English. This examination can be best made by summarizing the great variety of spellings that have been carefully indicated in the discussions of the sounds of English in the preceding chapter, by presenting in a series of notes such rules or principles as can be found for the guidance of spellers of English, and, finally, by attempting to appraise briefly the various outstanding features of the system as set forth in these summaries and notes.

In making an examination of Current English spelling, however, it is well to keep in mind Henry Bradley's assertion that "The ultimate end, and for most purposes, though not for all, the only important end, of written language is to convey meaning"[229]. In rapid silent reading people do not usually pronounce the written word, but, as Bradley suggests, they jump over the middle step which pronouncing aloud would necessitate and derive the meaning directly from the printed word. Consequently spelling must be regarded as accomplishing two general purposes: namely, helping to indicate the pronunciation of the sounds that make up the words in continuous speech and conveying the meanings of words and sentences.

Hence, in summarizing English spelling, it is necessary to show not only how individual sounds are represented, but also how words as a whole are treated.

47. *Summaries of English Spellings*

A. LONG VOWELS

[ū] *a** in *far*, *ea* in *heart*, *e* in *serjeant*, *au* in *aunt*.
[ǣ] or [ɛ̄] *a* in *fare*, *ai* in *fair*, *e* in *there*, *ea* in *bear*, *ei* in *heir*, *ay* in *prayer*.
[ē] *a* in *fate*, *e* in *fete*, *ai* in *main*, *ay* in *pay*, *ei* in *sleigh*, *ey* in *they*, *ea* in *break*, *ao* in *gaol*, *au* in *gauge*, *ae* in *maelstrom*, *aye* in *aye*.
[ī] *e* in *eve*, *ee* in *bee*, *i* in *machine*, *ea* in *sea*, *ei* in *receive*, *ie* in *chief*, *ey* in *key*, *æ* in *ægis*, *œ* in *subpœna*, *eo* in *people*, *ay* in *quay*.
[ɔ̄] *o* in *off*, *a* in *false*, *au* in *cause*, *aw* in *dawn*, *ou* in *cough*, *oa* in *broad*, *ah* in *Utah*.
[ō] *o* in *note*, *oa* in *load*, *oo* in *floor*, *ou* in *pour*, *ow* in *bowl*, *oe* in *doe*, *owe* in *owe*, *eau* in *beau*, *ew* in *sew*, *au* in *hautboy*.
[ū] *oo* in *taboo*, *u* in *flume*, *o* in *do*, *ou* in *group*, *eu* in *Reuben*, *ew* in *sewer* (variable), *oe* in *shoe*, *ue* in *accrue*, *ieu* in *lieu* (variable), *ui* in *bruise*, *œu* in *manœuvre* (spelled also *maneuver*).
[ɜ̄] or [ʌ̄] *u* in *burr*, *e* in *err*, *i* in *fir*, *ea* in *earn*, *o* in *worse*, *y* in *myrrh*.

Note 1. Of the various methods of indicating vowel length in English, the oldest and most familiar is based upon the general assumption, already discussed in some detail (Sec. 23), that the vowel will be long in an open syllable and short in a closed one. With the fixing of English spelling late in the fifteenth century and subsequent sound changes incidental to the breaking down finally of the inflectional system of English, many exceptions to this rule have come to stay; but it is still useful as a guide to spelling, especially when a vowel-beginning suffix, such as *-ed*, *-er*, *-ing*, is added to a brief verb or noun. So the variation in vowel quantity is indicated by

---

* The first spelling in each instance is the one most commonly used in present-day English, and generally it serves also (often with certain variations) as the symbol employed in the so-called "Websterian system" to indicate the pronunciation of the vowel or diphthong or consonant or consonant combination.

the single consonant, on the one hand, and by the double consonant, on the other, of such pairs as *crater* and *chatter*, *diner* and *dinner*, *framed* and *hammock*, *noted* and *otter*, *occasion* and *cassock*, *pining* and *pinning*, *smoking* and *locker*, *tuner* and *tunnel*. Unfortunately *coming* does not conform to this principle of spelling, and consequently many persons misspell it by doubling the *m*. There are also three notable groups of exceptions:

a. In most of the vowel studies of Section 41 attention was especially called to the frequent variation in quantity of vowels in open syllables followed by weaker syllables, as seen in *clover* and *cover*, *demon* and *lemon*, *tidy* and *city*, *vapor* and *clamor* (Sec. 42, 6).

b. Likewise numerous examples have been given to show the variation in vowel length before the so-called lengthening combinations, such as *-ld*, *-mb*, *-nd*, *-st*, as in *beast* and *best*, *boast* and *cost*, *fiend* and *friend*, *wild* and *build* (Sec. 42, 5).

c. The fact that the letter *v* is rarely doubled also causes confusion as to vowel length, as seen in *clover* and *cover*, *fever* and *sever*, *shaved* and *avid*.

Note 2. Final silent *-e* is used very commonly to show that a preceding vowel in a closed syllable is long (or diphthongal); and the moment this final *-e* is dropped, one inclines to pronounce the vowel short, as can be observed in the pairs *bathe* and *bath*, *bide* and *bid*, *fate* and *fat*, *note* and *not*, *robe* and *rob*, *tube* and *tub*. At present this method of indicating vowel length seems to be gaining in popular favor, since words are occasionally respelled by this method, as, for example, *complete* (for eighteenth-century 'compleat'), *flite* (for 'flight'), *nite* (for 'night'), *rite* (for 'right'). Unfortunately a misleading final silent *-e* is retained on a number of words with the short vowel, such as *bade*, *come*, *comrade*, *done*, *give*, *have*, *live*, *love*, *none*, *one*, and *sieve*.

Note 3. Gemination, or doubling, of a vowel has also been used in the case of *ee* and *oo* to show vowel length, as in *seed* and *food*. In a few names, such as *Aaron*, and in other borrowings like *kraal*, the double *aa* appears; but in such words it appears as an exotic spelling rather than as English.

Note 4. Much more popular and varied is the use of other vowel digraphs, especially *ai* in *fair* and *main*, *ei* in *vein* and *receive*, *ie* in *chief*, *ea* in *steak* and *steal*, and others listed above in the long-vowel spellings. Unfortunately for this kind of representation of vowel length, certain digraphs are also used frequently for short vowels, as *ea* in *breast* and *thread*, *ie* in *sieve*, *ei* in *heifer*.

Note 5. Through the gradual silencing of certain medial consonants it has become fairly common in English for the length of a vowel or diphthong to be indicated by the presence of a silent *l* or *gh*, as in *night*, *palm*, *talk*, and *thought*. In a few instances a final -*h* has been added to indicate a prolonged vowel, as in *ah*, *bah*, *eh*, *oh*, *pooh*.

Note 6. The digraph *ei* is used rarely, chiefly after *c* as in *ceiling*, *conceive*, *deceit*, *receive*, but also in *either*, *neither*, *seize*, *weir*, and *weird*. The *ie* is much more common; hence the old jingle

>   Use *i* before *e*, except after *c*,
>   Or when sounded like *a*, as in *neighbor* and *weigh*.

Note 7. Medial *au* appears as *aw* before *l* and *n*, and sometimes before *d*, as in *crawl*, *dawn*, and *tawdry*. And medial *ou* appears as *ow* before *l* and *n*, as in *bowl*, *known*, and *thrown*. There are exceptions, however, such as *Boult*, *fraud*, *haul*, *Paul*, and *soul*.

Note 8. The æ and œ of Latin loan-words have gradually been simplified to *e*, until only a few words still retain these digraphs. Some, like *ægis*, *æsthetic*, *æther*, *encyclopædia*, *mediæval*, *amœba*, *fœtus*, *phœnix*, and *subpœna*, have been slowly yielding to this process of simplification, but are still spelled in both ways.

Note 9. The letter *u* representing the long vowel [ū] is never used at the beginning of a word; when the letter *u* appears in that position, as in *union*, it is pronounced as [ju], unless the vowel is short, as in *us*, *usher*, or has the [ɜ] sound of *urn*. The few words of English that begin with this vowel sound are spelled with *oo*, as in *oodles* and *ooze*.

B. Short Vowels

[ɑ] *o* in *block*, *a* in *what*.
[æ] *a* in *bad*, *ai* in *plaid*.
[ɛ] *e* in *bet*, *ea* in *bread*, *ai* in *said*, *eo* in *leopard*, *ei* in *heifer*, *ie* in *friend*, *a* in *many*, *ay* in *says*, *œ* in *asafœtida* (also spelled *asafetida*), *æ* in *æsthetic* (also spelled *esthetic*), *u* in *bury*.
[ɪ] *i* in *bid*, *ei* in *counterfeit*, *ie* in *sieve*, *y* in *myth*, *ui* in *build*, *ee* in *been*, *e* in *pretty*, *u* in *busy*, *o* in *women*.
[ɔ] *o* in *Boston*, *au* in *Laura*.
[o] *o* in *phonography*. *eau* in *tableau*, *ou* in *cantaloupe*, *oe* in *aloe*.
[ʊ] *oo* in *book*, *u* in *bush*, *ou* in *should*, *o* in *wolf*.
[ɜ] *e* in *personal*, *u* in *burden*, *ou* in *courage*, *ea* in *early*, *y* in *syrup* (also spelled *sirup*), *o* in *worry*.
[ʌ] *u* in *cup*, *o* in *glove*, *ou* in *tough*, *oo* in *blood*, *oe* in *does* (verb).

Note 10. When *ea* is used to represent the short vowel [ɛ], it is usually before the dentals *d, t, n, s, th*, as in *bread, threat, cleanse, peasant, breath*, before *l* as in *health*, and sometimes before *m, f, v*, as in *dreamt, deaf, leaven*.

Note 11. When *oo* represents short [ʊ], it is usually before *d* and *k*, as in *wood* and *book* (see Sec. 41, A, 10).

C. Diphthongs

[ɑɪ] *i* in *ripe*, *y* in *style*, *ei* in *height*, *ai* in *aisle*, *ey* in *geyser*, *ay* in *bayou*, *oi* in *choir*, *oy* in *coyote*, *ie* in *tie*, *eye* in *eyes*, *uy* in *buy*, *ye* in *lye*.
[ɑʊ] *ou* in *house*, *ow* in *how*, *owe* in *Howe*, *au* in *kraut*.
[ɔɪ] *oi* in *coil*, *oy* in *boy*, *uoy* in *buoy* (variable).
[ɪu] *u* in *mule*, *eu* in *feud*, *ew* in *few*, *eau* in *beauty*, *eue* in *queue*, *iew* in *view*, *ieu* in *lieu* (variable), *ue* in *value*, *ou* in *coupon* (colloquial), *ui* in *suit* (variable).

Note 12. While the spelling *ow* is regularly used at the end of a word (except *thou*), it is used medially only before *l* and *n*, as in *fowl* and *town* (exceptions are *foul, Broun*), and before a weak syllable such as *-er* or *-y*, as in *bower, frowsy*.

Note 13. The diphthongal -*y* is used regularly at the end of monosyllablic words like *cry, dry, fry*, although a few end in -*ie*, particularly *die, hie, lie, pie, tie, vie*. All these are spelled with a *y* before the suffixes -*ing*, -*ly*, -*ness*, as in *trying, dying, slyly, dryness*; but the *y* is replaced by an *i* before the suffixes -*ed, -er, -es, -est*, as in *cried, lied, drier* (or *dryer*), *frier* (or *fryer*), *sprier* (or *spryer*), *cries, dies, shiest* (or *shyest*). The spelling *oy* is regularly used at the end of a word but is rare initially or medially (as in *oyster* and *Lloyd*).

D. Unaccented Vowels

[ɪ] *i* in *rapid*, *y* in *city*, *ie* in *cities*, *ey* in *money*, *ie* in *reverie*, *ee* in *coffee*, *e* in *demand* and *apostrophe*, *ei* in *forfeit*, *ui* in *conduit*, *ia* in *carriage*, *u* in *lettuce*.

[ə] *a* in *acute* and *climate*, *e* in *claret*, *o* in *anatomy* and *purpose*, *u* in *campus*, *ou* in *copious*, *oi* in *porpoise*, *æ* in *propædeutic*, *œ* in *œsophagus* (also spelled *esophagus*), *ea* in *sergeant*.

[l̥] *le* in *double*, *al* in *animal*, *el* in *hovel*, *il* in *devil*, *ol* in *vitriol*, *yl* in *idyl*, *ile* in *puerile*, *ule* in *capsule*.

[m̥] *m* in *chasm*, *am* in *Adam*, *em* in *tandem*, *emn* in *solemn*, *um* in *conundrum*, *umn* in *autumn*, *om* in *bosom*, *ome* in *handsome*, *im* in *Ephraim*.

[n̥] *an* in *Puritan*, *ain* in *captain*, *en* in *dozen*, *in* in *cabin*, *ion* in *translation*, *ine* in *feminine*, *on* in *London*.

[r̥] *er* in *brother*, *re* in *theatre* (also spelled *theater*), *ar* in *liar*, *or* in *color*, *ir* in *fakir*, *our* in *saviour* (also spelled *savior*), *eur* in *grandeur*, *ure* in *measure*.

Note 14. An exact list of spellings of unaccented vowels cannot be compiled, because, on the one hand, as already explained (Sec. 41, B, 1), every one of the accented vowels and diphthongs can be heard also in somewhat weakened or obscured form, as *eu* in *neuritis*, and, on the other hand, words included in the foregoing list, such as *capsule, coffee, feminine, forfeit, grandeur, measure*, and *solemn*, are often pronounced with a stronger unaccented vowel and are so recommended in the dictionaries. The tendency to pronounce unaccented syllables according to spelling is fairly strong in English.

Note 15. The only consonant vowel used alone in a syllable is *m*, as in *cha-sm*.

Note 16. In American usage unaccented *-or* is generally used, while *-our* is still distinctively British spelling, although British spelling-reformers recommend *-or*.

Note 17. One of the most irritating difficulties in the spelling of these unaccented syllabic consonants, [l̥], [m̥], [n̥], [r̥], in final syllables lies in the differing practice with regard to *-er* and *-or*, as in *keeper* and *editor*. In general the suffix *-er* is used with words of Anglo-Saxon origin and some French words, whereas *-or* is Latin and occurs in some French words also. The dictionaries explain these more fully and must be consulted whenever an individual word causes trouble.

Note 18. The French spelling *-re*, as in *centre* and *metre*, is still felt to be the more elegant spelling by some people but has been slowly yielding ground to the more characteristic English spelling *-er*.

Note 19. In connection with the accentual changes accompanying the derivative process and the resultant vowel changes, as set forth in Section 45 (p. 224), it can generally be assumed that a vowel digraph will become a simple vowel letter when it loses the accent, as in *a* from *ai* in *exclamation* (cf. *exclaim*), *e* from *ee* in *succession* (cf. *succeed*), *e* from *ai* in *maintenance* (cf. *maintain*), and even when the accent does not completely shift but when the word is lengthened, as in *u* from *ou* in *pronunciation* (cf. *pronounce*), and when the accent remains, as in *e* from *ei* in *reception* (cf. *receive*).

E. Consonants

[b] *b* in *bite*, *bb* in *hobble*.
[p] *p* in *pelt*, *pp* in *happy*, *gh* in *hiccough* (also spelled *hiccup*).
[d] *d* in *do*, *dd* in *adder*.
[t] *t* in *tome*, *tt* in *batten*, *th* in *thyme*, *d* in *worked*, *bt* in *debt*.
[g] *g* in *go*, *gg* in *haggle*, *gh* in *ghost*, *gu* in *guard*, *gue* in *rogue*.
[k] *k* in *kill*, *c* in *coal*, *ck* in *black*, *cc* in *hiccough* (also spelled *hiccup*), *kk* in *trekking*, *ch* in *chasm*, *kh* in *khaki*, *qu* in *liquor*, *cqu* in *lacquer*, *gh* in *hough* (also spelled *hock*).
[v] *v* in *veal*, *vv* in *flivver*, *f* in *of*, *ph* in British *nephew*.

Sec. 47] SUMMARIES OF ENGLISH SPELLINGS 237

[f] *f* in *fall*, *ff* in *offer*, *ph* in *cipher*, *gh* in *laugh*.
[ð] *th* in *that*, *either*.
[θ] *th* in *thin*, *ether*.
[z] *z* in *zero*, *zz* in *dazzle*, *s* in *busy*, *cz* in *czar*, *x* in *Xenophon*, *c* in *sacrifice* (verb); less often for the noun), *sth* in *asthma*, *ss* in *dessert*, *sc* in *discern*.
[s] *s* in *sale*, *ss* in *passive*, *c* in *city*, *ps* in *psalm*, *sc* in *science*, *sch* in *schism*, *st* in *chestnut*, *z* in *quartz*.
[ʒ] *zi* in *glazier*, *si* in *evasion*, *z* in *azure*, *s* in *casual*, *ti* in *equation*, *sh* in *Mosher*, *ss* in *scission*, *g* in *régime*.
[ʃ] *sh* in *shell*, *sch* in *schist*, *s* in *sugar*, *psh* in *pshaw*, *ch* in *chef*, *ce* in *ocean*, *ci* in *social*, *sci* in *luscious*, *si* in *ascension*, *ssi* in *passion*, *chsi* in *fuchsia*, *se* in *nausea*, *ss* in *issue*, *ti* in *nation*, *xi* in *anxious*.
[h] *h* in *hale*, *wh* in *who*.
[l] *l* in *land*, *ll* in *mallet*, *ln* in *kiln*.
[r] *r* in *rob*, *rr* in *sorrel*, *rh* in *rhetoric*, *wr* in *wren*, *rrh* in *catarrh*.
[m] *m* in *moor*, *mm* in *summer*, *lm* in *calm*, *gm* in *diaphragm*, *mb* in *lamb*, *mn* in *damn*.
[n] *n* in *need*, *nn* in *dinner*, *kn* in *knee*, *gn* in *gnaw*, *mn* in *mnemonic*, *pn* in *pneumatic*, *mp* in *comptroller*, *ln* in *Lincoln*.
[ŋ] *ng* in *sing* and *singer*.
[j] *y* in *yore*; *i* in *onion*; "unwritten" in *useful*, *ewe*, and rarely *humor*; *j* in *hallelujah*.
[w] *w* in *wall*, *u* in *assuage*, "unwritten" in *one* and *going*.

Note 20. Consonant-doubling, or consonant gemination, is both erratic and untrustworthy in English in that a consonant is often doubled in spelling, as in *dinner*, when, as a matter of fact, it is rarely pronounced as a double sound, even though one might expect it from such a spelling. As indicated in the preceding tabulation, twelve consonant letters are regularly doubled in the middle of a word when it seems desirable (*bb*, *pp*, *dd*, *tt*, *gg*, *ff*, *zz*, *ss*, *ll*, *rr*, *mm*, *nn*). Of the remaining consonant letters, digraphs, and trigraphs the following deserve mention: double *k* is regularly written as *ck* (although a few foreign words have introduced *kk*, as in *chukker* and *trekking*), double *v* occurs only in a few newer

238 ENGLISH SPELLING [Chap. VII

words like *flivver*, the voiced and voiceless *th* and the palatal and velar *ng* cannot very well be doubled, since they are already digraphs, and, finally, three others, *h*, *j*, and *w*, are never doubled in English. As already suggested, the failure of English spelling to provide for the doubling of the letters representing [v] (except as noted above), [ð], and [θ] causes a great deal of uncertainty as to the proper pronunciation of such words as *lever*, *blithe*, and *pathos*. At the ends of words only five consonants are regularly doubled, namely, *-f*, *-k*, *-z*, *-s*, and *-l*, as in *scoff*, *check*, *razz*, *pass*, and *will*. But for further remarks on the doubling of a consonant at the end of a word see pages 248-249.

Note 21. When to a word ending in one of the doubling group of consonants there is added a vowel-beginning suffix, such as *-er*, *-ed*, *-ence*, *-es*, or *-ing*, trouble is likely to descend upon the speller of English words if he fails to appreciate the principle explained in Note 1 (p. 231), namely, that when the vowel preceding the consonant is short, the consonant should be doubled if possible. The five consonants just mentioned above, *-f*, *-k*, *-z*, *-s*, and *-l*, are likely to be already doubled at the end of the word, and so they do not offer any difficulty; but when a suffix is added in this way to words ending in the other eight "doublers", then the application of this principle should give such forms as *barren*, *bidding*, *fitted*, *rigger*, *robber*, *slammed*, *tapped*, and *thinnest*. Of course a consonant should not be so doubled when it is preceded by a digraph, as in *beamed*, *leaden*, *leader*, *leaped*, and *reaped*.

But while this rule of doubling works out fairly well for words of only one syllable, in longer words of two or more syllables ending in but one consonant syllable-accentuation takes the place of vowel-length as the determining factor. Then the following rule generally holds, that when the last syllable is accented, the final consonant should be doubled before a vowel-beginning suffix, as, for example, in *allotted*, *bedimmed*, *compelled*, *confessor*, *equipped*, *japanned*, *occurrence*, *patrolled*, and *referred*; but when the last syllable is not accented, then either the final consonant should not be doubled, as in *buffeting*, *caromed*, *conference*, *differing*, *evening*, *Japanese*, *offered*, and *specialize*, or else it need not be doubled if the speller does not wish to do so, as in *bias(s)ed*, *diagram(m)ing*, *dial(l)ed*, *gallop(p)ed*, *level(l)er*, *quarrel(l)ed*, *travel(l)er*, and *worship(p)ed*. Words ending in unaccented -*ic*, however, are exceptional in that the *c* is usually increased to *ck* before a vowel-beginning suffix, as in *panicky*, *picknickers* (also spelled *picnickers*), and *trafficking*, in order that the *c* may not be pronounced wrongly as *s*, as it might be if such a form as *traficing* were used.

And, finally, to what has just been said about consonant gemination should be added the warning that sometimes the mere act of adding a prefix ending in a consonant, such as *dis-*, *mis-*, or *un-*, or a suffix beginning with a consonant, such as -*ly* or -*ness*, will naturally result in doubling, as in *dissect*, *unnamed*, *misspell*, *finally*, and *evenness*.

Note 22. When, however, a consonant-beginning suffix or word is added to a word already ending in a double consonant, quite the opposite thing is likely to happen, and the double consonant may become single, as in *almost*, *already*, *always*, *chilblain*, *elbow*, *enrolment* (also spelled *enrollment*), *fulfill*, *instalment* (also spelled *installment*), *pastime*, *skilful* (also spelled *skillful*), *welfare*, and *wilful* (also spelled *willful*). This is by no means general, however, and in such words as *gruffness* and *stillness* the double consonant is regularly used.

Note 23. In a group of nearly fifty verbs the ending of the past tense and the past participle is commonly or regularly spelled with -*t* instead of -*ed*, as in *bought*, *dwelt*, *felt*, *lent*, *meant*, *spilt*, *thought*, and *went*; and reformers of English spelling and some of the earlier nineteenth-century poets have made a practice of writing others with this final -*t* when the -*ed* was so pronounced (see Sec. 128).

Note 24. The letter *c* can be used to represent the [k] sound only before the back vowels *a*, *o*, and *u*, and in the consonant combinations *cl* and *cr*, as in *car*, *cold*, *cute*, *clock*, and *crown*. Otherwise, before *e*, *i*, and *y*, it is pronounced *s*.

Note 25. For many years there has been a real need of replacing the *ph* of Greek-Latin words like *phonetic* with the simpler and more typically English letter *f*. This has been accomplished in a few words that have come in via the French, such as *fancy, frantic,* and *frenzy;* in some others like *fantom* and *fantasy* the substitution is under way; and if the suggestion of the reformers of English spelling should prevail, some day the *ph* spelling for *f* may be dropped from the language altogether.

Note 26. When an inflectional final *-s* is added to a word ending in *-f* or *-fe,* such as *leaf* and *life,* the *f* is changed to the voiced form *v* and is regularly followed by *-es,* as in *leaves* and *lives.* This is, of course, merely a recognition of the sound change that has resulted from adding the inflectional ending *-s* or *-es* (see Sec. 43, *B,* 2).

Note 27. The American tendency to spell verbs with the Greek suffix *-ize* rather than with the French form of it, *-ise,* as is often done in England, has added a fairly large number of verbs to the more phonetic *z* spellings (see Sec. 43, *B,* 5).

F. Consonant Combinations

[dʒ] *j* in *jail,* *g* in *gist,* *dg* in *badger,* *dge* in *edge,* *ge* in *pigeon,* *gi* in *region,* *di* in *soldier,* *de* in *grandeur,* *ch* in *Norwich* (England).

[tʃ] *ch* in *chase,* *tch* in *kitchen,* *t* in *culture,* *te* in *righteous,* *ti* in *question.*

[gz] *x* in *exact,* *gs* in *figs.*

[ks] *x* in *ax,* *cks* in *locks,* *cs* in *ecstasy,* *cc* in *accede,* *xc* in *excise,* *xs* in *exsect.*

[gw] *gw* in *Gwendolen,* *gu* in *guava.*

[kw] *qu* in *queen,* *cqu* in *acquire,* *cu* in *cuisine,* *ch* in *choir.*

[hw] *wh* in *when.*

Note 28. Of a hundred consonant combinations illustrated in section 44, only the few listed above have been given distinctive spellings in English, such as *j, ch, x, qu,* and *wh,* and they are not spelled very consistently.

Note 29. The pronunciation [dʒ] is heard only when *g* appears before the front vowels *e, i,* and *y,* and even then there are exceptions, such as *gelding, get, gimlet, give,* which have the sound of *g* in *go.* In order to make sure of retaining this [dʒ] pronunciation when a suffix is added to a word ending in *ge*, the final silent *e* must be retained (or modified to *i*) if there is the least danger of confusion with the other value of *g*. Examples are *arrangement, collegiate, courageous, pageant, singeing, vengeance.*

Note 30. Usually, in the middle of a word or at the end, the spellings *dge* and *tch* are employed after short-vowel monographs, as in *budget, hedge, crotchet,* and *patch*; and *ge* and *ch* are used after long vowels, after vowel digraphs, and after other consonants, as in *cage, besiege, fringe, each, bench*. However, a number of familiar words do not conform to the latter part of this rule as they should, particularly *college, frigid, pigeon, rigid, attach, bachelor, much, niche, rich, such,* and *which*. All these have short vowels spelled with one letter only, but nevertheless they take the shorter *ge* and *ch* in defiance of the general practice.

Note 31. The convenience of using the single letter *x* for more complicated sound combinations has led to such spellings as *connexion* (for 'connection'), *coxcomb* (for 'cockscomb'), *coxswain* (for 'cockswain'), *genuflexion* (for 'genuflection'), *inflexion* (for 'inflection'), *pox* (for 'pocks'), *reflexion* (for 'reflection'), and the popular coinings *chix* (for 'chicks'), *high jinx* (for 'high jinks'), *sox* (for 'socks'), and the trade name *Westclox*.

G. Silent *e*

In the first subdivision (p. 231) of this section on spelling, vowel digraphs have been listed in which the letter *e* forms the second element, such as *æ, œ, ue,* and so on. But if a passage of Modern English prose be examined, it will be found that, in addition to this use of *e* in such vowel digraphs, a silent *e* is used also after consonants which has become so important a feature of Current English spelling that at least 15 per cent of all the words on any printed page contain it. Since it is quite indispensable in some words, and in others merely a superfluous conventionality of spelling, it is taken up below under seven different heads according to the circumstances of its use. It is used in the following ways:

a. Finally after a single consonant to show that a preceding vowel monograph in an accented syllable is long, as in *bathe, bide, fate, rode* (already discussed on page 232).

b. Finally after a single consonant, but usually unnecessarily, since the accented vowel or diphthong is written as a digraph, as in *awe, breeze, cease, cheese, geese, grouse, heave, moose, noise, owe, please, receive, route, souse,* and *troupe.* In most of these the *-e* is superfluous; but in a few like *please* the final *-e* helps to distinguish the word from a similar one, in this case the noun plural *pleas.*

c. Finally after a single consonant in an unaccented final syllable, as in *collective, departure, feline, feminine, infantile, justice, moderate, palace, promise, schedule, synonyme* (archaic), and in the suffix *-some* of such words as *bothersome, handsome.* In words like *infantile* and *feminine* the tendency to pronounce the unstressed *i* as [ɪ] makes the *-e* not only superfluous but misleading, while in others like *feline* it is needed to give the proper [aɪ] sound in the pronunciation (see Note 36, below).

d. Finally after a consonant digraph or trigraph in either an accented or an unaccented syllable, as in *absolve, admittance, belle, bronze, condense, curse, curve, dialogue, dunce, glimpse, grilse, judge, omelette* (also spelled *omelet*), *programme* (also spelled *program*) (see Notes 35 and 37, below).

e. Finally after unaccented syllabic [l̥] and [r̥], as in *addle, angle, ankle, cattle, epistle, fickle, muffle,* and the scores of words in *-able* and *-ible,* such as *capable* and *horrible*; in *acre, massacre, metre, mitre, reconnoitre, theatre* (see Note 18, above).

f. Before syllabic [l̥], [m̥], [n̥], and [r̥] in final unaccented syllables, as in *hovel, solemn, dozen,* and *bother.* Judged by the ordinary pronunciation of such words, this *e* is also superfluous and sometimes leads to a meticulous attempt to pronounce it, as is occasionally heard in *solemn.*

g. In some suffixes, notably *-ed* and *-es,* where the *e* is silent or pronounced according to the kind of sound at the end of the word to which the suffix is affixed, there is of necessity some variation in the pronunciation of the *e.* In the past tense and past participle of weak verbs (that is, regular verbs), the *e* is silent except when the verb ends in *-d* or *-t.* Accord-

Sec. 47] SUMMARIES OF ENGLISH SPELLINGS 243

ingly the *e* is not pronounced in *accrued, banned, buzzed, chafed, chilled, dragged, faced, hallowed, hopped, judged, locked, passed, pitched, raged, rammed, robbed, rushed, served, stirred, writhed,* and *wronged;* but it is of necessity spoken in *bonded, abated,* and *flitted.* In the use of *-ed* to form adjectives the same practice prevails, as in *ridged, flat-topped, antlered, four-wheeled,* and *red-headed* and *deep-rutted.*

Curiously, to distinguish more clearly between participles in *-ed* that are strongly verbal and those that are felt to be strongly adjectival, the *e* is sometimes revived in pronunciation for the adjectival function, and such pairs result as *áged* and *ágèd, belóved* and *belóvèd, bléssed* and *bléssèd, cúrsed* and *cúrsèd, cróoked* and *cróokèd, plágued* and *pláguèd, striped* and *stripèd, winged* and *wingèd,* the first of each pair being pronounced as one syllable, the second as two. Some adjectives, moreover, are given this pronounced *e,* although no corresponding verbal form exists, as in *long-léggèd, nákèd, péakèd,* and *rúggèd* (see *-ed,* suffix 2, in the New English Dictionary [20]).

As already explained in Note 26, silent *e* occurs in the plural forms of nouns in which *f* has been converted to *v* during the inflectional process, as in *leaves* and *lives.* A few other nouns have the *-ve* in the singular, such as *cove, hive,* and *wave,* and others have the silent *e* after other consonants, as in *lathe, ode, rate, strike;* to these only *-s* is added to form the plural. Whether the *e* be added or already present in the singular form, it is always spoken in such words as *basses, busses, buzzes, houses, judges, latches,* and *rushes.* Consequently there is no such abundance of words with silent *e* among the noun plurals as there is among the past-tense forms of verbs.

Note 32. Usually a final silent *-e* is dropped when a vowel-beginning suffix, such as *-able, -age, -al, -ance, -ed, -er, -ible, -ing, -ous, -y,* is added to the word, as in *desirable, movable, milage* (or *mileage*), *storage, final, refusal, grievance, pursued, pursuer, fusible, owing, pursuing, tracing, grievous, greasy, icy,* and *conducive.* The exceptions to this rule, such as *acreage, canoeist, noticeable, shoeing,* and *tingeing,* are clearly due to the need of keeping the sound just before the *e* from being confused with some other sound that might be suggested (see

Note 35, below). Words ending in *-ie*, such as *lie*, *vie*, change *ie* to *y* before *-ing*, as in *lying*, *vying*. In a few words like *lineage*, *lineal*, *phraseology*, the *e* is retained and pronounced when a suffix is added.

Note 33. Usually, on the contrary, a final silent *-e* is retained before a consonant-beginning suffix, such as *-ful*, *-less*, *-ly*, *-ment*, *-ness*, *-some*, or *-ty*, as in *baleful, doleful, useless, lonely, serenely, advancement, chastisement, likeness, terseness, nicety* (but with the *e* pronounced), *safety*. In a few words the *e* has generally been omitted, contrary to this rule, notably *awful, ninth, woful*, and adverbs like *duly, only, probably*, and *wholly*; of another little group now commonly used without the *e*, Ramsey protested many years ago: "*Judgement* is now almost universally written *judgment*. *Abridgment* and *lodgment* are also common, a violation of general usage poorly compensated by the economy of a single letter" [230]. To these three should be added the shortened *acknowledgment* and *argument*.

Note 34. In an accented syllable final *-e* is used after the ambiguous consonant spelling *th* to show that the sound is voiced [ð], as in *bathe, breathe, clothe, wreathe*.

Note 35. Because of the two very different sounds of *c* and also of *g*, it is always necessary to indicate the [s] or [ʃ] sound of *c* and the [dʒ] sound of *g* by retaining silent *e*, whether medial or final. An understanding of this principle will help in the correct spelling of such words as *change-able, courage-ous, notice-able, ocean, outrage-ous, singe-ing, tinge-ing, trace-able*, and *venge-ance*. Attention has already been called to the fact that the *e* in the verb suffix *-ed* is silent when affixed to a verb that ends in *-ge* or *-ce*; but it must be added that though the *e* is silent, it cannot be spared after these two letters in such verb forms as *alleged, caged, faced, paced*, and *traced*; and of course it cannot be spared from the end of the simple words *cage, face, garage, tinge*, and *wage*.

When, however, the suffixes *-al* and *-ous* are added to words ending in *-ce*, such as *face, grace, office, race, space*, and *vice*, the *e* is changed to *i*, as in *facial, gracious, official, racial, spacious*, and *vicious*. Final *-e* is likewise changed to *i* before *-ty* in *scarcity*, and in *density, diversity, intensity, perversity*.

After *ch* the *e* is used in such words as *luncheon, scutcheon,* and *truncheon.*

Note 36. There is a tendency in Current English to slough off this useless final silent *-e* from words ending in *-ide, -ile, -ine,* and *-ite,* particularly. So one finds *fertil, fragil, versatil,* etc.; from *antonym, dactyl,* and *homonym* the *-e* has fallen away; the chemical terms *bromid, glycerin, oxid, saccharin,* and numerous others are losing it; and *perquisit, preterit,* etc. are well on the way. So far, the peculiar rule that *v* cannot end a word has prevented a general removal of this silent *-e* from the *-ive* words like *elective.*

Note 37. There is also a noticeable tendency in Current English to simplify the endings of certain groups of words having silent *-e* after a consonant digraph. This applies especially to some of the more recent French borrowings with their exotic spellings. The *-me* is being dropped from *gramme, programme.* In many words like *coquette, etiquette, leatherette, lorgnette, mignonette,* and *rosette* there is as yet little tendency to drop the *-te*; in a few, however, particularly *banquet, epaulet, omelet, quartet,* and *sextet,* the longer form has nearly disappeared from use. The shortened forms *catalog, decalog, dialog, monolog, pedagog,* and *prolog* are widely used. It is more difficult to spare the *-ue* from words like *brogue, fatigue, meringue, morgue, plague, tongue, vague,* and *vogue,* because the stressed vowels might be mispronounced.

Note 38. Nouns ending in a vowel + *o* form the plural by adding *-s* only, as in *folios, rodeos, studios.* But with nouns ending in a consonant + *o* the matter of plural formation is much more troublesome because of a badly divided practice with regard to the entire group. Some nouns take *-s* only, such as *banjos, halos, octavos, pianos, pueblos, sombreros, stilettos,* and *zeros*; not nearly so numerous are those that require *-es,* such as *buffaloes, echoes, heroes, mosquitoes, negroes, potatoes, tomatoes,* and *vetoes.* Both spellings are permissible for *Dago, desperado, fiasco, hobo, portico, volcano,* and others.

Note 39. When a noun ends in a vowel + *y,* only *-s* need be added to form the plural, as in *bays, guys, toys*; when, however, it ends in a consonant + *y*, the *y* must be changed to *i* and the *-es* plural ending added, as in *berries, cities, dailies,* and *ecstasies.* This is, of course, true also of verb forms in the present tense, such as *hurries* and *pities.*

H. SILENT CONSONANTS

In the fifth subdivision of this section (p. 236) certain two-letter combinations have been listed which serve for single consonant sounds, particularly *ch* (= [k]), *ph* (= [f]), *th* (= [ð] or [θ]), *sh* (= [ʃ]), and *ng* (= [ŋ]). But in many English words a consonant will be found which has at one time been pronounced in English or in the foreign language from which the word has been borrowed, but which is now silent. Of the twenty-one consonant letters in use in English, all but five (*f, j, q, v, y*) can be found as silent letters, either in individual words here and there or else in whole groups of words. They are found silent as follows:

b Regularly at the end of a word after *m,* as in *limb;* occasionally elsewhere, as in *debt, doubt, redoubt,* and the variables *subpœna, subtile* (more often spelled *subtle,* in which case *b* is always silent).
c, ch Regularly in the combination *sc,* as in *muscle, science;* also in a few words like *Connecticut, drachm, fuchsia, indict, victuals.*
d Rarely as in *handkerchief, handsel* (variable), *handsome, Wednesday;* often in the prefix *ad-* before *j,* as in *adjourn.*
g Regularly in the initial combination *gn,* as in *gnaw;* also medially as in *deign;* before *m,* as in *apothegm;* commonly with *h,* as in *taught* and *though.*
h Occasionally at the beginning, as in *honest;* also after *g,* as in *ghost;* also after *r* in Greek words like *rhetoric,* and medially as in *hemorrhage* or finally as in *catarrh;* sometimes medially, also, as in *forehead, Graham, John, posthumous,* and finally as in *ah, bough, through,* and *verandah* (spelled also *veranda*).
k Regularly before *n* at the beginning of a word like *knee;* sometimes medially, as in *blackguard.*

Sec. 47] SUMMARIES OF ENGLISH SPELLINGS 247

l Regularly before *m*, as in *calm*; before *v*, as in *salve*; before *f*, as in *calf*; before *k*, as in *falcon* (sometimes), *folk*, and *talk*; and before *d*, as in *could*, *should*, *solder*, and *would*.
m Rarely before *n*, initially, as in *mnemonics*.
n Regularly at the end of a word after *m*, as in *autumn*, *damn*, *limn*; also in *kiln*.
p Regularly initially in Greek loan-words with *s*, as in *psalm* and *psychic*, and with *n*, as in *pneumatic*; sometimes medially, as in *comptroller*, *corps*, *raspberry*, and *receipt*. Before *t* it is silent at the beginning of a few learned words like *phthisic*, *ptarmigan*, *ptero-*, *Ptolemy*, and *ptomaine*; and it is either silent or very slightly pronounced between *m* and *t*, as in *empty*, *exempt*, *prompt*, *sumptuous*, and *tempt*.
r Regularly vocalized by British and some American speakers so as not to be heard as a consonant in such words as *far*, *hard*, *hear*, and *rather*; also in *Worcester*, *worsted*.
s Occasionally, as in *aisle*, *demesne*, *island*, *viscount*; also at the end of recent French loan-words, such as *apropos*, *chamois*, *corps*, *débris*, and *rendezvous*.
t, th Regularly medially after *f* and *s* when followed by [l] and [n̥], as in *apostle*, *chasten*, *glisten*, *often*, *rustle*, *soften*, *whistle*; also in *asthma*, *bankruptcy*, *hautboy*, *isthmus*, *mortgage*; and at the end of a few French borrowings, such as *buffet*, *depot*, *sobriquet*, *valet* (sometimes).
w Regularly at the beginning of a word before *r*, as in *wrath*, *wrench*, *wrong*; also before *h* in a few words like *who*, *whole*, *whoop*; sometimes medially, as in *answer*, *Norwich*, *sword*, *two*.
x Only in French plurals like *beaux*, *Esquimaux* (also spelled *Eskimos*), *tableaux*, and *trousseaux*, and even in these the [z] sound is commonly given to the *x*.
z Only in a few French loan-words, such as *rendezvous*.

Note 40. The revival of some of these silent consonants through the derivational change of words has been touched upon before and summarized for *b*, *g*, *n*, *t*, and *w* (see Sec. 44, 6). In some old words like *would* and *palm* the consonant became silent only when a following vowel was lost.

I. WORD ENDINGS

With the long and uninterrupted development of the English system of spelling, certain conventions, or customs, have become established, in the matter of ending words, which must be taken into consideration if one is to secure a complete understanding of the system as a whole. Many spellings in English are retained "just to make the word look right." In the following survey the chief points have been arranged according as words end in vowels, in consonants, and in silent *-e.*

a. The vowel digraphs containing *i* and *u* medially regularly take *-y* and *-w* at the end of words, as in *gray, joy, key, pay,* and *blow, claw, crew, how.* Likewise the accented diphthongal *-i* becomes *-y* finally, as in *cry, my, thy.* Exceptions are *thou* and *you,* and *die, hie, lie, pie, tie, vie.*

b. The accented double *-ee* and *-oo* are fairly common at the end of words, as in *absentee, see,* and *woo.* Various common words form exceptions, especially *do, go, Jo, lo, no, so, to, two,* and *who;* also *café* and *Santa Fe.* Final stressed *-a* and *-aa,* as in *spa* and *baa,* are both rare; but in the digraph *-ea* the final *a* is found in such words as *sea* and *tea.* The letters *-i* and *-u* (almost never doubled) occur at the end of words only in a few foreign words like *ski, gnu,* in the exceptional native *thou* and *you,* and in the colloquial *flu.*

c. Unaccented vowels occur at the end of words as follows: *-a* frequently, as in *drama, opera; -e* in various loan-words like *apostrophe, facsimile,* and *strophe,* and *-ee* in legal and other words of the type of *committee* and *employee* (see Note 41, below); *-i* usually written as *-y,* as in *pity* and *victory* (see Note 42, below), with such exceptions as *alibi, alkali, houri, khaki, mufti; -o* in a large group of nouns like *folio* and *negro;* but *-u* never in English except in modern loan-words like *emu, parvenu.*

d. Five consonants are regularly doubled at the end of monosyllabic words containing a simple vowel, namely, *-ff* as in *cuff, -ck* in *back, -ll* in *bell, -ss* in *less,* and *-zz* in *buzz.* The other consonants do not ordinarily double in the final position.

Sec. 47]   SUMMARIES OF ENGLISH SPELLINGS   249

Exceptions to this rule of doubling are *clef, if, of*; *roc*; *nil, pal*; *as, bus, gas, has, is, plus, this, thus, was, yes*; *quiz* and *whiz* (see Note 43, below).

The letters *j* and *q* (never doubled) are not used at the end of words; the letter *-v* (rarely doubled) is not found at the end of a word, except in borrowings like *Slav*.

e. Of the consonants not usually doubled at the end of words several are doubled in a few short words like *add, banns, butt, ebb, egg, err, inn, odd, purr*, and in the more archaic spelling of some personal names such as *Ann, Barr, Clegg, Clubb, Dunn, Hamm, Knott, Ladd, Pratt, Robb*. However, in spite of their shortness, there is not doubling of the final consonant in *an, in, on, or*.

f. After a vowel digraph or another consonant, a final consonant never doubles, but is always single, as in *barn, beat, feel, film, nook, soap, went*.

g. At the end of a word of two or more syllables the use of the double consonant is less strictly adhered to than in the shorter words already discussed in paragraph *d*. One finds *-ff* commonly, as in *bailiff, tariff*; *-ss* is regularly used in the suffixes *-ess, -less*, and *-ness*, as in *giantess, waitress, speechless*, and *loneliness*, and is common in other words like *albatross, canvass* (noun, in certain meanings, and verb), *carcass, compass, discuss*, and *windlass*, but the single final *-s* is also very common, as in *atlas, canvas* (noun), *circus, discus, fracas, glaucous, lustrous*; the double *-ck* (= *kk*) appears in *bullock, hammock*, and *tamarack*, but more often the single *-c*, as in *attic, bivouac, critic, music, picnic*, and *shellac*; *-ll* is sometimes used, as at the end of *idyll* (also spelled *idyl*) and the proper noun *Marshall*, but the single *-l* is more common in such dissyllabic words, as in *awful* and other words with the suffix *-ful*, in *civil, enrol* (also spelled *enroll*), *evil, excel, marshal, partial, ravel, travel,* and *vowel*; *-z* is never doubled at the end of a final unaccented syllable, as in *Alcatraz* or *topaz*.

h. The consonant digraphs *-ng, -ph, -sh*, and *-th* are commonly found at the end of words, as in *pilfering, sing, epitaph, graph, bush, succotash, path*, and *monolith*. But the use of *-ch* and *-tch* (= [tʃ]) is much more complicated: *-tch* is used at the end of a monosyllabic word containing a simple vowel, as in *Dutch, hitch, notch, patch,* but there are exceptions, such as *much, rich, such,* and *which*; *-ch* is used at the end of a monosyllabic word containing a vowel digraph or a single vowel followed by another consonant, as in *beach, bench, birch, each*; *-ch* is also used at the end of longer words, as in *Greenwich, Norwich, sandwich,* but there are exceptions, such as *eldritch, potlatch.*

i. Final silent *-e* is used after a single consonant to show that a preceding simple vowel is long, as in *jade* and *ride*; this has already been discussed in connection with methods of indicating vowel length, but is one of the conventional English word endings.

j. Final silent *-e* following another vowel as part of a vowel digraph also comes at the end of words frequently, as in *die, doe, glue, true*; *reverie, argue, revenue, Arapahoe.*

k. In the spelling out of syllabic [l̥], [m̥], [n̥], [r̥], there is so great a variety of usage that only a few general tendencies and practices can be distinguished at the end of words. The only consonant vowel used alone in a final syllable is [m̥] as in *chasm*; the only two followed by silent *-e* are [l̥] as in *table* and [r] as in *centre* (see Note 18, above); [r̥] appears in three troublesome suffixes, *-ar* as in *liar*, *-er* as in *taller*, and *-or* as in *editor.*

l. Final silent *-e* is very generally employed at the end of a final unaccented syllable, following a single consonant, as in *adjective, apposite, avarice, delicate, furniture, juvenile, masculine, pinnace,* and *promise* (see Note 36, above).

m. Final silent *-e* is also very generally employed after two consonants, in both accented and unaccented syllables, as in *absinthe* (also spelled *absinth*), *absolve, acknowledge, aigrette*, attendance, carve, collapse, false, hoarse, intense, judge, programme* (also spelled *program*), *reverence.* The *-e* is almost altogether superfluous and unnecessary but is maintained for the sake of the appearance of the words involved (see Note 37, above).

* A plume of feathers; also spelled *aigret.* The name of the bird is commonly spelled *egret.*

n. Final silent *-e* is not normally written after final double consonants such as *-ch*, *-ff*, *-ll*, nor after *-w*, *-x*, and *-y*; but it occurs occasionally, as in *niche, giraffe, belle, gazelle*; *awe, ewe, owe, axe, aye,* and *good-bye.* *Ax* and *good-by*, however, are often spelled without *-e*, and there are signs that *-e* is dropping away from *aye* and *gazelle.*

o. Final silent *-b* after *m*, as in *lamb, limb, numb,* silent *-gh*, as in *plough* (also spelled *plow*), *slough* (noun), *though,* and the pronounced *-gh* of *cough, laugh, slough* (noun and verb), *trough,* are also regular word endings of English of the present day.

Note 41. The unaccented final *-y* of such words as *country* and *history* was earlier written *-ee* or *-ie*, as in *countree* and *historie*; now the *-ee* ending is attached chiefly to legal terms like *employee* and *mortgagee*, indicating the person affected, and only a few words here and there, like *reverie* and the nicknames *Annie, Johnnie*, etc., retain the older spelling. This final *-y* is usually changed to *-i* before suffixes, as in *accompaniment, business, cozily, easier, glorious, iciest, laziness, pitiful,* but not before *-ing*, as in *studying*, or before *-ist*, as in *copyist*.

Note 42. The confusing use of both *-y* and *-ey* to represent the final unstressed vowel [ɪ], as in *donkey, funny, glory, happy, journey, memory, money, valley,* constitutes one of the difficulties of present-day spelling. No rule can be laid down for distinguishing the two spellings.

Note 43. In words of more than one syllable the modern tendency is to simplify the final *-ll*, even in accented syllables, as in *compel, control, excel, idyl, patrol,* and *until.* Lexicographers disagree about *distil, enrol, fulfil, instil,* some still preferring *-ll*.

J. Hyphenation

The varying use of the hyphen in English causes great perplexity. Not only do writers differ widely as to the words that should be hyphenated, but great variation and disagreement will be observed in the recommendations of dictionaries and printers' stylebooks. Hence in the following concise presentation of the subject an attempt is made merely to suggest a few rules that may be of some use as practical guides.

As was found true in the case of variable pronunciations, so also in the matter of spelling, and most of all in the matter of hyphenation, the student will probably have least trouble if he adopts as his guide some one authoritative dictionary and follows it consistently and persistently.

The hyphen is used in two quite different ways: namely, to tie together two or more words that are felt to constitute a unit, but a unit not yet sufficiently fused together to be written as one word; and to indicate the division of a word at the end of a line when it becomes necessary to carry over part of the word to the next line below.

The Hyphen for Compounding. In the use of the hyphen to tie words together, the following general phases may be observed:

a. In compounds composed of two nouns that have not been merged long enough to be written as one word, as, for example, *barrel-organ, fellow-countrymen, fishing-license, folk-lore, hero-worship, place-name,* and *window-shopping.** The compounds *today, tomorrow,* and *tonight* no longer require the hyphen.

b. In a few compounds made with an adjective and a noun, such as *great-aunt, hard-tack, rough-house, still-hunt.*

c. In *self* compounds like *self-control, self-sustaining.*

d. In compound numerals like *fifty-four, twenty-six.*

e. In prepositional-phrase compounds, such as *Carmel-by-the-Sea, sister-in-law, Stratford-on-Avon,* and the adjectival *out-of-the-way* (when used in the attributive position).

f. In certain compounds, to insure hiatus when the addition of prefix or suffix brings together two letters so that they are likely to be mistaken for a single vowel or diphthong, as in *co-operative, co-worker, re-establish, re-examine.* In the case of *e-e* and *o-o* the diæresis is very frequently employed, as in *reëxamine.*

g. To emphasize a prefix, as in *ex-wife, co-respondent* (cf. *correspondent*), *pro-German, quasi-scientific, re-collect* (cf. *recollect*), *super-elegant, ultra-stylish.**

* Most of the words hyphenated in paragraphs *a* and *g* are printed differently in some of the dictionaries: some, such as *folklore* and *ultrastylish,* being printed as one word; others, such as *place name* and *quasi scientific,* being treated as separate words. In this book the hyphen has generally been used in conformance with the editorial policy of the publishers.

h. In compound adjectives, when they are not too long-established, such as 'a *much-exercised* horse', '*election-day* returns', '*fifth-century* writers', '*far-reaching* consequences', 'a *two-thirds* vote', and 'on a *cost-plus* basis'.

Note 44. As fast as compounds become firmly established in English, they are likely to be written as one word, as in the case of *football, newspaper,* and *taxpayer.* But as for unquestionable compounds that have not yet reached this advanced stage in spelling, the writer should feel free to hyphenate whenever he wishes to make it quite clear that they function as single units, as in '*a well-planned* and *up-to-date round-up,* or cattle drive'. If the first word merely modifies the second, as in *Chicago politics,* no real compound exists, and the hyphen is not used.

The Hyphen for Division. In the use of the hyphen in dividing words at the ends of lines, while the basic principle is that words must be divided between syllables, for determining where the division should come three different and sometimes antagonistic kinds of rules prevail:

a. A single medial consonant follows the hyphen if the preceding vowel is long or diphthongal, as in *Pe-ter, do-tard, hoy-den,* or unaccented, as in *po-liti-cal, poli-tics,* but precedes the hyphen if the vowel is short and accented, as in *polit-ical, pol-itics.* This rule depends upon pronunciation and may be termed a phonological-type rule.

b. A double medial consonant is divided by the hyphen, as in *pil-lage, pret-ty, sin-ner,* and distinct adjoining consonants are usually so split, as in *produc-tive, whim-per.* This rule is somewhat more arbitrary and might be termed a mechanical-type rule.

c. A digraph representing a simple sound, or a diphthong, or a consonant combination of the word-beginning type (see page 217) is usually not divided by a hyphen, as in *cata-clysm, ging-ham, ortho-graphic, poi-son, sea-son, with-er.* This rule is somewhat arbitrary or mechanical, but still it is logical too.

d. A prefix or suffix, or other derivational element like *graph* and *phone,* is usually separated from the rest of the word by the hyphen, as in *arch-angel, bare-ness, be-side, ortho-*

graphic, and *use-less*. This rule is based upon etymological considerations, and sometimes goes counter to the others.

e. A one-letter syllable like *a-* of *alone* and *-y* of *many* is not separated; the second syllable of words like *James's, spasm*, is not separated, even though it is pronounced separately. These rules are, again, entirely arbitrary.

Note 45. Unfortunately, for the use of the hyphen at the end of a line no such clear-cut principles prevail as in compounds, but one word is governed by one principle and another by a quite different principle. In *orthog-raphy* can be seen, for example, an insistence on the phonological-type rule instead of the mechanical rule or the etymological rule, since the *g* is kept with the accented short *o* in spite of the fact that *gr* is a common word-beginning combination, and also in spite of the fact that *graph* is a common derivative element. Again, we read "*C* and *g* soft are not to end" a line;[26] but exceptions are made before a suffix (*rang-er*), after a short accented vowel (*prec-ipice*), and in a digraph (*judg-ment*) — that is, these letters end a line if another letter in their place would end it. Mawson says, "As a working rule, divide by the ear and not by the eye"[339]; and Seward has well said, "It is desirable to divide a word so that the part that ends one line will suggest the word being divided rather than another word"[402]. Further than this one cannot go except to recommend constant reference to a good dictionary in times of uncertainty.

K. Abbreviation and Contraction

As the hyphen may be considered the chief mechanical aid in the compounding and syllabication of words, and the diæresis the last resort in indicating hiatus in pronunciation, so the period and the apostrophe are generally — though not always — utilized as indications of abbreviation and contraction. Very commonly the term *abbreviation* is applied to shortening, or contraction, in the spelling of a word, and *contraction* is limited to shortening in pronunciation; while this is an arbitrary distinction, it is a convenient one. So

Sec. 47] SUMMARIES OF ENGLISH SPELLINGS 255

numerous are these shortcuts in writing or speaking that it is possible to indicate here only a few of the most general phases of this shortening process:

a. The names of the days of the week, as *Sat.* (*Saturday*), the months of the year, as *Feb.* (*February*), the year dates, as *'92 (1892)*, and such general terms as A.D. (*Anno Domini*), B.C. (*Before Christ*), A.M. (*ante meridiem*), P.M. (*post meridiem*).

b. Names of American states and English counties, such as *Calif.* (*California*), *Hants* (*Hampshire*), *Lancs* (*Lancashire*), *N.Y.* (*New York*), *Ore.* (*Oregon*).

c. The books of the Bible, such as *Gen.* (*Genesis*), *Matt.* (*Matthew*).

d. Christian names, as *Chas.* (*Charles*), *Jno.* (*John*).

e. Surnames, as *McDonald, St. John.*

f. Titles of honor and respect, such as *Mr.* and *Mrs.* (rarely spelled out), *Dr.* (*Doctor*), *Esq.* and *Jr.* (always postpositive), *Gen.* (*General*), *Rev.* (not properly used with a surname alone).

g. Common commercial terms, as *advt.* (*advertisement*), *Co.* (*Company*), *Ltd.* (*Limited*); names of measures and weights, as *gal.* (*gallon*), *lb.* (*pound*, Latin *libra*); scientific terms, as *arith.* (*arithmetic*), *C.* or *Cent.* (*centigrade*); geographical and local terms, as *long.* (*longitude*), *St.* (*Street*); literary terms, as *ed.* (*edition*), *etc.* (*et cetera*), *MSS.* (*manuscripts*), *pp.* (*pages*); philological nomenclature, as *adv.* (*adverb*), *AS.* (*Anglo-Saxon*), *etym.* (*etymology*), *ME.* (*Middle English*), *vb.* (*verb*).

h. Titles and the names of organizations, by the use of initials only, as *A.B.* (*Bachelor of Arts*, Latin *Artium Baccalaureus*), *B.B.C.* (*British Broadcasting Corporation*), *C.O.D.* (*collect on delivery*), *D.A.R.* (*Daughters of the American Revolution*), and *N.E.D.* (*New English Dictionary*).

i. The use of letters instead of syllables, a favorite device in the coining of commercial names, as in *Bar-B-Q* (*Barbecue*), *Ken-L-Ration* (*Kennel Ration*); also in *Xmas* (*Christmas*) and *Xtian* (*Christian*), although the *X* is used here not for its sound but for its symbolism, standing, as it does, for the cross of Christ.

j. The use of signs, such as *$* (*dollar*), *&c* (*et cetera*), *%* (*per cent*).

k. Contractions of a few words favored by poets, chiefly, as in *e'en* (*even*), *e'er* (*ever*), *ne'er* (*never*), *o'er* (*over*), *'tis* (*it is*), and *'twas* (*it was*).

l. And, finally, colloquial contractions of the auxiliary verbs with a preceding pronominal subject, as in *I've, we've,* and *you've* (from *have*), *he's, she's,* and *it's* (from *is*), *we're, you're,* and *they're* (from *are*), *he'll, we'll, you'll,* etc. (from *will* or *shall*), *he'd, I'd, you'd,* etc. (from *had* or *would*); and with a following negative, as in *can't, don't, haven't, mustn't, shan't, won't,* etc. (from *not*). While these are excluded from standard literary English, they are used very generally in standard colloquial speech. But *ain't* is regarded with disfavor by most careful speakers of English because, while it is the logical form for *am not,* it is too often misused for the third person *is not* instead of *isn't.* The British use of *Aren't I?* is entirely illogical but nonetheless has received some approval by American speakers desirous of avoiding the illiterate *ain't.* The contraction *let's* (*let us*) is also commonly used.

L. Capitalization

The capital letter is an essential feature of the English system of spelling. It distinguishes the individual from the group or generality, and our language has no other means of accomplishing this clearly and at the same time concisely; it also helps to indicate a complete thought as expressed in the sentence, and the complete expression of emotion as embodied in interjection, phrase, or exclamatory sentence; and, finally, it is utilized in an artistic way to produce certain effects for the eye principally, as in lines of poetry, titles, and so on.

a. To distinguish the proper noun or adjective appropriated to the individual from the common noun or adjective applied to an entire class, personal names are capitalized, as in *Samuel Johnson*; place-names, as in *Africa, Baltimore, Hampshire*; special groups or bodies of people, as in *Dutch, Liberals, Romanticists* (frequently also lower case, *romanticists*), *Rotarians*; titles of books, essays, and the like, as in *A Tale of Two Cities, Idylls of the King.*

It would be difficult to do without the capital letter when a common noun is to be subjected to personification, as in *Truth, Liberty*; when a word applied to some outstanding individual in a group is used constantly in address by members of the group, as *Chief, Judge, Mother*; or when a special group is to be given distinct recognition, as in *Catholics* (cf. *catholic*), *Masons* (cf. *masons*), *Odd Fellows* (cf. *odd fellows*), *Quakers* (cf. *quakers*). When a proper noun is commonized, as often happens, the importance of this distinction effected by the use of capitals is apparent, as in *atlas* (cf. *Atlas*), *macadam* (cf. *McAdam*).

b. To distinguish the completed thought as expressed in a sentence, the initial capital letter is useful, though not essential, since the period at the end helps to define the beginning and ending of sentences in a paragraph. But much of the ease of reading would be sacrificed if this capital were done away with.

c. To set off each line of verse or each item in an outline, the user of English has long preferred the capital letter for the sake of the appearance of the whole; but of late some poets have chosen to drop most of the line-beginning capitals in writing their verse. The capitalization of the pronoun *I* and the interjection *O* is also a matter of appearance, largely, or, perhaps better, of convenience, since the lone letter would be easily passed over in reading if it were too insignificant in appearance.

48. *General Comments on English Spelling*

a. An inspection of the various spellings of the different vowel and consonant sounds tabulated in subdivisions *A* to *F* of the preceding section will show that numerous letters of the English alphabet are capable of representing a variety of sounds. The most noticeable of these sound values are as follows:

a in *far, fare, fate, false; what, bad, many.*
e in *eve, fete, there, err; bet, personal, pretty.*
i in *machine, fir; bid; ripe, union.*

o in *off, note, do, worse; block, women, Boston, phonograph, wolf, glove.*
u in *flume, burr; bury, bush, burden, cup; mule; assuage.*
y in *myrrh; myth, syrup* (also spelled *sirup*); *style.*
ai in *aisle; main, fair; plaid.*
oo in *too, book; floor, blood.*
ou in *house; pour, group; should, courage, tough.*
c in *coal, city, sacrifice.*
d in *do, worked.*
f in *fall, of.*
g in *go, régime, gist.*
s in *see, busy, sure, leisure.*
t in *tome, culture, nation.*
x in *ax, luxury, Xenophon; exact, luxurious.*

Of course various other digraphs could be added to this list, such as *ea, ng, th*, and spellings of unaccented vowels would increase the variety of sound values.

b. Purely conventional spellings have become numerous in English. Final silent *-e* is kept in a great variety of such spellings; *i* and *u* must be written *y* and *w* at the end of words; *k* itself cannot be doubled, its doubling being represented by *ck*; five consonants should be doubled at the end of short words and the others should not, ordinarily; to give the word a proper appearance, *dg* and *tch* should not be used after vowel digraphs; three consonants, *j, q*, and *v*, cannot be doubled and cannot be used at the end of a word; the plural noun suffix *-es* should not follow an *o* preceded by a vowel, as in *rodeo*; *Mr.* and *Mrs.* cannot be written out; *k* can end a short word, but *c* a longer one; and so on. Such conventions, useful or useless, as the case may be, make very difficult any radical attempt at changing or improving English spelling.

c. Many of the less common spellings of English impress the thoughtful observer as exotic still, because their peculiarities do not, even after centuries of use, harmonize with the general pattern of English orthography. Survivals from Greek and Latin, such as *æ* in *mediæval, th* in *Thomas, ph* in *physics, ch* in *character, x* (= *z*) in *Xenophon*, and *rh* in *rhetoric*;

from the French, such as *g* in *régime*, *gn* and *tte* in *mignonette*, *qu* in *queen*, final *re* in *metre*, *lle* in *gazelle*, *mme* in *programme*, initial *gu* in *guard*, and the plural *beaux*; and such unusual spellings from other languages as *caoutchouc*, *chukker*, *czar*, and *jaguar* — these all detract seriously from such uniformity and systematic simplicity as the language might otherwise possess.

d. There are many variant spellings in English, partly because the British and Americans cannot agree on such questions as the use of *-or* or *-our* in *favour*, *-ize* or *-ise* in *civilise*, *tire* or *tyre*, and *curb* or *kerb* (stone edging to pavement), and partly because other variants have just accumulated down through the years, as, for example, *axe* and *ax*, *grewsome* and *gruesome*, *idyl* and *idyll*, *inflection* and *inflexion*, *plow* and *plough*, some of them due to a conservative sentimentality on the part of certain spellers, others due to an attempt to naturalize exotic forms, and still others the result of carelessness so widespread and so prolonged that they have become standardized eventually.

e. Some English spellings are mere makeshifts which should be replaced by reasonable spellings, as, for example, the writing of *th* for both the voiced [ð] and the voiceless [θ]; the retention of silent *e* after *g* and *c* in such words as *singeing* and *ocean* to prevent confusion with other values of the two consonants; the frequent use of *u* for the diphthong [ɪu], as in *mule*, and initially for [ju], as in *unite*; the use of *ng* for the simple consonant [ŋ], as in *singer*, and also for the consonant combination [ŋg], as in *longer*; and the juggling about of five vowel letters to express sounds for which at least nine are needed.

f. While some of these conventions and makeshifts of English spelling seem without much value or justification, there are words here and there which must be regarded as utter absurdities. Such are, for example, *asthma*, *choir*, *colonel*, *debt*, *doubt*, *hiccough* (also spelled *hiccup*), *hough* (also spelled *hock*), *once*, *phthisic*, *physique*, *pshaw*, *quay*, *Sioux*, *subtile* (also spelled *subtle*), *victuals*, *women*, *Worcester*, *worsted*, and *yacht*;[232] final *gh* (=*f*) in such words as *cough* and *laugh*;

and the use of *e* in *precede* and *secede* but *ee* in *proceed* and *succeed*. Whether it is more absurd to insert silent consonants in words like *debt*, *doubt*, and *island* or to continue to use other spellings that have long been left behind by changes in pronunciation, as in *laugh*, *subtile* (also spelled *subtle*), and *women*, is a question for the thoughtful student of language.

g. Not only does personal prejudice lead many British writers to object seriously to certain American spellings, such as *curb* (British *kerb*) and *tire* (British *tyre*), but even among Americans prejudice for certain forms tends to preserve such spellings as *cheque, comptroller, mediæval, metre, programme, Saviour*, and *theatre*. If prejudice for certain individual word spellings be added to insistence upon those conventions of spelling which are retained merely to make the word "look right", the fixity of the body of English orthography can be better appreciated.

h. If the International Phonetic Alphabet be accepted as a criterion, then English spelling cannot be called phonetic, or even predominantly so. Of the thirty-five phonetic symbols regularly employed in this book (see Sec. 21), English can provide only twenty-two, since *j* and *q* and *x* represent combinations of other sounds, namely, [dʒ], [kw], and [ks], and *y* has been discarded as unnecessary. Consequently thirteen more letters have had to be provided, either by making up new forms or else by adapting a few from other fonts of English type. Even with these thirty-five only a rough segregation of English vowels and consonants can be made.

i. But English spelling is wasteful in that it not only has the four unnecessary consonant letters just named, but also uses so many digraphs, as *ea* in *breath* and *ph* in *physics*, when one letter would suffice. It is wasteful, too, in the frequent doubling of certain consonants when, again, one letter would be enough, as in *fill, miss*; and, most extravagant of all, in the remarkable use of final silent -*e*, as illustrated above. At least 10 per cent of all the words on the printed page end with this final silent -*e*, and about half as many more have silent *e* within suffixes. Of course part of these silent -*e's* cannot be spared under the present system of English spelling. If to these wasteful features there be added the frequently used silent consonants, it becomes apparent that if English were absolutely phonetic, the number of letters required to spell the same words would be greatly reduced.

j. In many respects English spellings are misleading. For example, in the tabulation of sound values given above (p. 257), each of the vowel letters can represent at least four different sounds, and some more than four; of the consonant letters the average is more than two sounds to the letter. Moreover, the various silent letters, including final *-e*, come to life frequently to cause additional uncertainty, as illustrated by *g* in *signer* and *signal*, and by *-e* in *loathe* and *apostrophe*. Even when spellings are not positively misleading, they fail too often to be helpful in indicating pronunciation, as can be seen in the case of *s*, which can be either voiced or voiceless in *house* and *rise*, or of *th*, likewise, in *mouth*, or of the four *o's* in *homophonous*.

k. But the most serious weakness in English spelling is that it is unsystematic — a miscellaneous aggregation of rules and principles, no one of which can be applied thoroughly and few even with partial success. There are, as observed, at least five methods of indicating vowel length (see Notes 1–5, pp. 231–233). To represent the sounds a great variety of spellings are used. These spellings have been listed: for the ten long vowels, 66 spellings; for the nine short vowels, 45 spellings; for the four diphthongs, 29 spellings; and for the twenty-two consonants, 91 spellings (without counting doublings). Of course many of these can be eliminated from serious consideration on the ground that they are rarely used; but even after such elimination the number of variant spellings is very considerable. Furthermore, there is no uniformity in the practice of doubling consonants, but some double and others do not, and some double in one position and not in another.

There is but one conclusion at which any thoroughgoing study of English spelling can arrive, and that is that failure to settle upon a uniform plan of procedure in the spelling of English words, and lack of uniformity in the application of such rules as do exist, cause the student of English more uncertainty, and because of this uncertainty force him to spend more time in looking up words in the dictionary, than could be charged either to the unphonetic nature of our spelling or to the great number of silent and superfluous letters. He finds *belle* but *well*, *coffee* but *syncope*, *conference* but *occurrence*, *cranky* but *monkey*, *double* but *gavel*, *evidence* but *offense*, *feel* but *veal*, *filibuster* but *philosophy*, *folio* but *embryo*, *humming* but *coming*, *pianos* but *heroes*, *proceed* but *precede*, *receive* but *believe*, *whole* but *holy*. He cannot go far in the application of any one general rule; he must depend primarily upon his memory for details.

Many phoneticians have lamented the fact that in Modern English the representation of sounds, particularly the vowels, differs so markedly from that of other familiar modern languages; but that would not be so serious a matter if the English representation were consistent and systematic. For, after all, a phonetic alphabet is merely a set of symbols generally accepted by those who use them, and any set of symbols would be phonetic if they were used consistently by a large enough body of writers.

Other critics of our language have grieved over the wasteful extravagance of English spelling and have computed in dollars and cents the great gain that could be effected merely by the elimination of silent *e's*, to say nothing of unnecessary letters in digraphs and of other silent letters; but the gain that would come to both the older users and the younger learners as a result of the elimination of uncertainty would be much more important than even the dropping of superfluous letters.

CHAPTER VIII

THE CLASSIFICATION OF WORDS

HAVING left those smaller units of language, the sounds, and the letters by which they are represented graphically, we now approach the study of words in the following chapters and need, therefore, to establish a better understanding and appreciation by noting the various ways in which words may be classified. But before these methods of classification are considered, it should be emphasized that just as the sounds of speech cannot be said to have real significance except in words and continuous speech, so also the words themselves must be studied in sentences and continuous speech if they are to be properly classified and their meanings exactly defined. It is true that a separate word can express a simple idea; but the setting of a sentence is needed to give definiteness and exactness to the word and the idea that it expresses.

Words may be classified according to their general functions in speech, as nouns, which name; verbs, which assert action, state, or being; pronouns, which stand in the place of nouns; and so on. These are usually known as the parts of speech, and this method of approach to the study of words is as old as the earliest studies of grammar. Moreover, most of these classes may be subdivided into smaller groups, since the general function varies according to the circumstances and the object to be accomplished. One adjective, for example, modifies a noun by way of description, as in *the green tree*; another merely limits or restricts, as in *the second tree*. One verb shows action complete, as in 'He falls'; another demands that the recipient of the action be expressed, as in 'He felled a tree'. But the form of a word will not always show which part of speech is employed, since the same form may function as different parts of speech; *ride*, for example, may be either noun or verb according to the way it functions in speech. Consequently a thoroughgoing study of the parts of speech will consider both the derivative forms and the functional uses of words.

Words may be classified also according to their separate dictionary forms and the manner in which they were composed in earlier times. This etymological study of the derivation of words often involves the student in the history of his language, since forms tend to change as time passes and become blurred, sometimes almost beyond recognition. Moreover, since new words are being constantly coined, a knowledge of derivational categories or methods is imperative. Shall the new word be made up of stem and prefix or suffix, or shall certain combining elements like *graph* or *phone* be employed, or shall two old words be put together to form a new compound, as in *airship*? Such questions arise.

Or, again, words may be classified according to certain outstanding methods of inflection commonly employed in English to show their relation to other words in continuous speech, as, for example, those nouns that form the plural in *-en*, those verbs that have a past tense in *-ed*, or those adjectives that can be compared only by an irregular change of form, such as *good, better, best*. These inflectional categories have been greatly reduced in English during the past eight or nine centuries, and for the student of Modern English they play a relatively unimportant role in the classificational study of the language. It is only when one works back toward the Anglo-Saxon, or even farther back into the primitive Continental forms of our language, that one finds these few inflectional categories becoming more distinct and more numerous.

When we pass from the study of the single word to a consideration of continuous speech as it involves also phrases, clauses, and sentences, we must also classify words — or groups of words, sometimes — as they are used in sentences; and these classes may be named syntactical categories, since they are determined by the use of a word in a sentence, as its subject, its predicate, a modifier of its subject or predicate, a connective, and so on. It is obvious that one cannot draw any very clear-cut line of demarcation between a word as it functions in general and as it functions in a given sentence, since the sentence is a unit of speech in general just as the word is a somewhat smaller speech unit. Any attempt at a classification of words is sure to incur difficulties arising from the peculiar relations of form and meaning, of form and use, and of use in general and use in the sentence. A word may be either a noun or a verb, as illustrated by *ride*; it may be a pronoun and at the same time the subject of a sentence; it may be a pronoun like *who*, standing in general in place of some antecedent noun like *father* and at the same time serving as a connective in the sentence.

And, finally, words may be classified according to certain general semasiological categories, as, for example, those with figurative meaning, those of a highly specialized meaning, those "taboo" words avoided by some speakers because of unpleasant connotations, and so on. But since meaning is, after all, about the only excuse that most words have for their existence, variation in meaning attaches to each of the parts of speech (Chap. VIII), it accompanies each derivational change of form (Chap. IX), it is involved in even the simplest inflectional changes of form (Chap. XI), and any syntactical use of a word is bound to express a different shade of meaning from any other use in the sentence (Chap. XII). Consequently, and this should be recognized in all attempts at classification of words, semasiological usages cannot very well be kept separate from these other classificational studies.

49. *The Parts of Speech*

More than nine hundred years ago the West Saxon scholar and teacher Ælfric, in his Latin grammar written for his Old English countrymen, said, "There are eight parts of speech," and if allowance be made for just one discrepancy, the general practice in present-day grammar is still to name exactly the same list. Ælfric followed a practice already long established, and there is not much reason for changing the number today, since the classification is a logical one and rests on distinctions which constitute fundamental categories.

The *noun* is the name of a thing, quality, collection, or action.

The *pronoun* is a word used instead of a noun.

The *adjective* is a word that is used to limit or qualify a noun, and sometimes a pronoun.

The *verb* is a word that asserts action, state, or being.

The *adverb* modifies verbs, but also adjectives and other adverbs.

The *preposition* shows the relation of its object to some noun or verb, usually.

The *conjunction* connects words, phrases, or clauses.

The *interjection* stands apart from the other seven, because it expresses strong feeling or emotion, whereas they are concerned with the expression of thinking.

It is helpful to remember that these eight fall into four fairly distinct groups, the noun, pronoun, and adjective being associated with the function of naming, the verb and adverb working together to predicate something about the noun or its substitute. the preposition and conjunction being concerned chiefly with making connections for the other parts of speech, and the interjection having its separate place in the expression of emotion. Any attempt to increase this number of parts of speech is likely to prove illogical. Sometimes the article has been named separately; but it functions as any other adjective does. Sometimes the participle or infinitive or both have been distinguished; but since they are both forms of the verb and function either as parts of the verb or else as adjective and noun, respectively, they do not constitute separate logical categories. Sometimes the numeral has been separately classed as one of the parts of speech; but it usually functions as a pronoun or as an adjectival or adverbial modifier. And, finally, and with possibly the best reason of all, the expletives *it* and *there* are sometimes said to be a separate part of speech, because they perform a function in introducing sentences quite different from that of any other of the eight;

but they can be accommodated, one under the pronoun and the other under the adverb, and so it seems hardly worth while to set up a ninth class just for two little words. For some reason Ælfric did not name the adjective, but included instead the participle; after that one oversight or misunderstanding has been corrected, however, there remains little more to be said now than he said long ago, in the very beginning of English grammar-making.

50. *Nouns*

Nouns fall into two great classes, common and proper, and, as has already been said (Sec. 47, p. 257), this distinction between generality as expressed by the common noun and individuality as expressed by the proper noun (or name) is of very great importance in any language. It is interesting to observe that in the development of the English language the Latin-French loan-word *noun* has been retained as a technical term for the entire class of words, while the cognate English form *name* has been restricted very largely to the proper noun.

The term *substantive* is often used instead of *noun*; but the word has a much broader connotation inasmuch as it applies to any word, phrase, or clause used as a noun, particularly the pronoun and verbal noun. The adjective can be substantivized, as in the case of *a brief, elders, the rich and the poor.* Indeed, almost any part of speech can be substantivized, or converted to the function of the noun (see Sec. 58, p. 317).

A. Common Nouns

Common nouns name classes of objects and persons, whatever is tangible or definite, and are then known as concrete nouns, as *plow, store, teacher, wheat*; they name qualities, conditions, actions, things intangible and more vague, as *racing, strength, weariness,* and are abstract nouns; or they name collections of persons, objects, animals, and so on, and are then termed collective nouns, as *army, covey, multitude.* The distinction between these three kinds of common nouns is not always clear-cut: *shaving* may be an abstract noun (a process) or a concrete noun (a tangible result of the process); *battery* may be an abstract noun (an action punishable before the law) or a collective noun (a group of big guns); *circle* may be a concrete noun (a tangible ring of metal, perhaps), or it may be a collective noun (a gathering of people). Happily many nouns are still to be distinguished by certain inherited suffixes, as in the concrete noun *worker*, the abstract *goodness*, and the collective *citizenry*, so that to such nouns the two distinguishing tests, of meaning and of form, can be applied; but in general, meaning, or functional value, is the safer criterion of the two.

a. **Concrete nouns.** Names of persons and animals are particularly numerous, such as *bishop, friend, guard, horse, man, slave, son*; derivative forms indicating the doer, or agent, are *assistant, baker, beggar, buccaneer, drunkard, gamester, governess, lawyer, punster, socialist*, and *tailor*. Others are names of objects, geographical terms, and so on, as *aquarium, church, hill, house, hurdle, jewelry, peninsula, river, sail*, and *window*. Here should be included names of materials and measure, such as *acre, cupful, mile, oil, ounce, silver, sunshine, wheat*.

A few nouns, largely legal terms, may be termed passive nouns because they indicate the recipient of action rather than the doer. Of these the most noticeable end in *-ee*, as *employee, lessee, payee, referee, trustee*. Other passive nouns, fairly common in present-day usage, end in *-er*, as *attainder, broiler, bunker, drawer, fryer* (or *frier*), *locker, porker, roaster* (a fowl), *waiver*.

Diminutives have always been common in English and employ a variety of endings, as in *auntie, booklet, bullock, goatee, gosling, hillock, lambkin, lordling, nestling, ringlet*.

A large number of nouns, however, lie on the border line between the concrete and the abstract, — such words as *geometry, mathematics, music, philosophy*, — and are so hard to classify satisfactorily that it is well not to attempt to put every noun into a distinct class of its own. *Music*, for example, can connote in the mind of the speaker notes and bars and, in general, the physical representation of music, or it can be a very abstract and indefinite and intangible something, very difficult to define.

The categories of concrete nouns mentioned above do not exhaust the possibilities; various other categories could be made if necessary.

b. Abstract nouns. Many abstract nouns expressing qualities or conditions have been derived from verbs, as *action, growth, patience, sight, speech, terror, work.* Others are plainly to be associated with adjectives, as *breadth, drouth, filth, freedom, redundancy, sickness, truth, wealth, wisdom.* Some, of course, are derived from other simpler nouns, as *friendship, manhood, ownership, priesthood.* Others express ideas or certain general phenomena, as *autumn, honor, hunger, need, night,* and may give rise to verbs or adjectives rather than derive from them. The numerals, such as *two thirds, three, forty, million,* are usually classed as abstract nouns when they are employed in mathematical computations.

The words naming action are derived by three outstanding methods, and often three forms of the same word are given slightly different values, as *stealth* (cf. *to steal*), a *steal,* and *stealing.* The first is derived by means of the suffix *-th,* the second is converted from the verb, but the third is a verbal form, a so-called gerund, and can be distinguished, like the second, only by the way it is used in a sentence. Indeed, some grammarians hesitate to classify the gerund with the noun unless it has so far given up its verbal qualities that it can be pluralized as a noun, as in *feelings, shavings.* But since, in the sentence 'Stealing is wrong', the word is plainly subject of the sentence, whereas, in 'He was stealing', the word plainly functions as part of the verb, the classification of the words seems too certain to be seriously questioned. So in *motion,* a *move,* and *moving; frost,* a *freeze,* and *freezing; collection,* a *collect,* and *collecting,* three forms occur, of which the second in each trio tends to become so definite and at times concrete, even, that in the case of *collect,* for example, the word must be put over into the concrete class of nouns. But all three are primarily verbal nouns.

c. **Collective nouns.** These nouns are regularly singular in form but plural in meaning, as *army, committee, crowd, dozen, family, group, jury, mob.* Most of these collective nouns pertain only to highly specialized collections, in earlier times to birds and animals especially [235]; and the purists have long objected to the misapplication by uninformed persons of words such as a *bevy* (of maidens), a *brace* (of ducks), a *cluster* (of grapes), a *covey* (of quail), a *drove* (of cattle), a *flock* (of sheep), a *swarm* (of bees), and a *team* (of horses). Particularly abused are *bunch, couple, flock,* and *gang.* A writer in *Word Study* has remarked that "we have reduced the number of group designations of birds and beasts to about four — herds, packs, flocks, and coveys" [236]. Doubtless this tendency is the result largely of unfamiliarity with the world of nature in recent years; the earlier use of a greater variety of collectives of this kind may be due in part to the fact that game names such as *deer, grouse, pickerel,* and *quail* have generally had no separate forms for singular and plural, and so their number could be distinguished only by the words that accompanied them.

Some very familiar collective nouns are used as plurals, ordinarily, and a plural verb is required, as with *cattle, clergy, folks* (colloquial), *gentry, intelligentsia, kindred, militia, nobility, peasantry, people,* and *vermin.* When *folk* and *people* are used with either a singular or a plural verb, their meanings are somewhat different in each case.

B. Proper Nouns (Names)

Individual sentiment and caprice play so large a part in the formation and preservation of names (proper nouns) that the subject is a difficult one, and often only long and persistent research will throw much light on the history of a name. The court or the immigration officer is often responsible for a very radical change in the form of a personal name; and the influence of an earlier settler, public enthusiasm for a new national hero, or the more practical needs of the Federal postal authorities may be largely responsible for the present form of a place-name. For some time, philologists and genealogists have been working at the problem of clearing up and recording the histories of names; but many an American name which has been suddenly metamorphosed from a good Slavic or Oriental form to a very ordinary and unexpressive English commonplace will probably never be satisfactorily explained. Names that can be traced back throw so much interesting light on the various peoples that have settled in England and America, and on the earlier habits and life of those peoples, that every effort should be made to put their individual histories on record; and this is especially true at the present moment as regards the place-names in the newer American communities, where early settlers still dwell who could give personal testimony, ofttimes, about the origin of names of places here and there. In any study of proper names, two questions are likely to arise at the very outset: namely, "Whence came the name into English?" and "What is its significance?"; and while it is not always possible to answer both, in the following discussions both will be kept in mind.

a. Christian names. Before the coming of the Normans to England in 1066, family names were not commonly used. The old Germanic names of individuals, like *Alfred*, *Bertha*, and *Edward*, were composed usually of one or two common elements with meanings such as 'bright', 'friend', 'good', 'noble', 'war', 'wolf'. When the Christianizing of England brought an inclination toward Biblical names, such as *Esther*, *Judith*, *Matthew*, *Peter*, probably their earlier significance was not ordinarily apparent to the English, although an occasional scholar like Bede may have taken the trouble to hunt out that significance from the Bible in such a passage as the Old Testament story of the change of Jacob's name when the unknown wrestler said, "Thy name shall be called no more Jacob, but Israel: for as a prince hast thou power with God and with men, and hast prevailed" (Genesis xxxii, 28), or as the more familiar renaming of Simon when Christ remarked to him, "Thou art Peter, and upon this rock I will build my church" (Matthew xvi, 18). Those who are familiar with the literature of the American Indians will remember that the young braves often acquired significant names with such meanings as 'Hungry Wolf', 'Sitting Bull'; or a maiden might be called the Indian equivalent of 'The Fawn'. Various Latin names, like *Alma*, 'kindly, genial', *Augustus*, 'majestic, august', *Lupus*, 'wolf', *Sextus*, 'sixth', crept into English; and flower names for girls have long been favored, particularly *Lily*, *Rose*, and *Violet*. The most interesting names, perhaps, during the Puritan period in England and New England were those of a religious nature, such as Bardsley collected in his *Curiosities of Puritan Nomenclature*, like *Faith*, *Hate-Evil*, *Hope*, *Preserved*, and *Search-the-Scriptures* [237]; a few of these, mostly the shorter ones, have remained in use to the present day.

Early in the seventeenth century the English antiquary Camden wrote that "two Christian names are rare in England"; but since that time the need of defining the individual more exactly has led to so general a practice of giving two Christian names to a child at baptism that now in America about 90 per cent of the nonforeign population possess both. In numerous instances the second name is nowadays the mother's maiden name, and one writer in a Continental journal has lately erroneously assumed that the very common middle initial in American names always indicates the mother's family name. Moreover, Americans have frequently adopted the device of merging two Christian names of a girl into one, as in *Annamarie*, *Emmalou*, *Claribel*, *Laurabel*. It should be remarked that in the choice of Christian names the caprice of the individual plays an important role; surnames, or family names, are inherited. But even Christian names, especially those of boys, are not infrequently handed down from generation to generation in families.

b. Surnames. Even before the introduction into England by the Normans of the general practice of using surnames, various methods had undoubtedly been employed to separate one *John* of the village from another *John*. Eventually *John* the smith and *Thomas* the weaver and *William* at the well became officially *John Smith*, *Thomas Weaver* (or *Webster*), and *William Atwell*; many of the old names of occupation, like *Miller*, *Taylor*, *Wright*, are still in general use. Some names are derived from everyday words of early English life which have later lost much of their popularity, such as *Chandler*, 'the candle-maker', *Cutler*, 'the knife-maker' of the community, and *Fletcher*, who was employed in making arrows.

Men were also often called according to their earlier places of residence, as *Britton, Cornwall, England, Field, Swede, Woods*. Sometimes, even in very early England, epithets and nicknames became attached to families, and 'long *Will*' and 'black *Thomas*' became *Will Long* and *Thomas Black*. *Walter* was nicknamed *Wat*; and little Wat, his son, became *Watkin*, and Watkin's *John* ultimately *John Watkins*. A foundling might even be named for the day of his birth or discovery and be *William Monday*, in much the same way that Robinson Crusoe named his savage *Friday*.

Most varied and suggestive still of racial differences are the patronymics, those names derived from parents or ancestors. The Anglo-Saxon suffix *-ing*, meaning 'descended from', persists in a few like *Billings, Browning,* and *Channing*. The Norman *fitz*, 'son of', occurs in *Fitzgerald* and *Fitzpatrick*, the Irish *o*, 'a descendant', in *O'Keefe* and *O'Reilly*, the Welsh *ap* in *Powell* (from *Ap-Howell*) and *Price* (from *Ap-Rhys*), corresponding to the Irish and Highland-Scotch *mac* of *McFarland, McGinnis, Mackay, Macmillan,* the Norwegian or Swedish (also English) *-son* of *Erickson, Johnson, Williamson,* and the Danish *-sen* in *Larsen* and *Olsen*.* In the earlier English, also, William's *John* kept the genitive ending *-s*, sometimes, and as a consequence many *s*-ending names persist in modern English, such as *Graves, Williams, Woods*. Similar to these patronymics, but with prefixed or separate prepositions indicating 'place from which', are the French *Delaborde, Delatour, Descartes,* and the German and Dutch names with *von* and *van*, as *Von Arnim, Von der Leyen,* and *Van Buren* and *Van Dyck*.

* The Scandinavian practice of giving to the son a surname formed in this manner from the father's Christian name has sometimes appeared in American Scandinavian communities, and it has been a source of confusion to their American neighbors when John Anderson's son was named *Hans Johnson*, his grandson assumed the name *Ole Hanson*, and his great-grandson became *Peter Olson*.

Many cognate forms may be seen in present-day American nomenclature, such as *Anna* and *Hannah*; *Frank* and *Francis*; *Smith, Schmitt,* and *Schmid*; *Weaver* and *Webster*; and doublets due to changes in spelling, as *McLean* and *McLane, McVeagh* and *McVey*. The most popular of all Christian masculine names, *John* (Latin *Johannus*), also appears in a French form *Jean*, Russian *Ivan*, Scottish *Ian*, Welsh *Evan*, and even in a shortened Dutch and German *Hans*. Its derivatives appear as *Jennings, Johnson, Jones*, and so on. But some names have become so corrupted that they seem to have no relation to existing forms, notably *Attlebury* (from *at*, French *le*, and *bury*), *James* (from *Jacobus*), *Prothero* (from *Ap-Roderick*).

Various attempts have been made to estimate the relative number of occurrences of the most common surnames, and perhaps the estimate of Barker for the United States of 1924 may be accepted as a reasonably close guess. He finds the first ten in order of numbers to be (1) *Smith*, (2) *Johnson*, (3) *Brown*, (4) *Williams*, (5) *Jones*, (6) *Miller*, (7) *Davis*, (8) *Anderson*, (9) *Wilson*, (10) *Moore*; he estimates the total number of Smiths to be almost one and a third millions.[246] And yet, in spite of this, we must still insist that these are proper nouns rather than common.

If, instead of being content to estimate the more important individual surnames in this way, we should make an attempt to arrive at the proportions of the various groups according to their origins, the problem would, of course, be very much more difficult. Bardsley studied the surnames of a London directory of about the year 1879 and concluded that the five main groups could be estimated as follows: names from place-names, about 37.5 per cent; patronymics, 27 per cent; names from occupations, 14.5 per cent; names from nicknames, 10.2 per cent; and foreign and doubtful names, 10.8 per cent. Other places and other times might give somewhat different results, as regards figures.

c. **Place-names.** Because of the light it throws on the history of places and districts and countries, place-name study has been receiving much attention of late. There are in Great Britain still many names of places which were bestowed by the Celtic Britons and retained by the Romans during their occupation; indeed, most English river-names are said to be of Celtic origin. Often these Celtic names can be recognized by primitive compounding elements, such as *aber*, 'river mouth', in *Aberdeen, Aberford*; *avon*, 'river', in *Stratford on Avon*; *caer*, 'fortress', in *Caerleon, Cardiff, Carlyle*; *dun*, 'hill', in *Doncaster, Dumbarton, Dunbar, Dundee, Dunkirk*; *inch*, 'island', in *Inchcape, Inchcolm*; *inver*, 'river mouth', in *Inverary, Inverness*; *kill*, 'church', 'cell', in *Kildare, Kilkenny, Kilpatrick*; Welsh *pen* = Gaelic *ben*, 'mountain', 'summit', in *Pendleton, Ben Lomond, Ben Nevis*.

Roman occupation of England left its mark on various place-names, especially those with *chester* or *caster*, 'camp', such as *Chester, Dorchester, Lancaster, Worcester*; with *strat, streat*, 'street, road', such as *Stratford, Stratton, Streatham*; with *wall*, 'wall', such as *Wallsend*. The Roman *Londinium* appears as *London*; *Eboracum* is thoroughly disguised in modern *York*.

Of course the Anglo-Saxons gave many names to English places as they made their settlements here and there. *Borough, burgh*, or *bury*, 'town', appears in *Peterborough, Edinburgh, Canterbury, Salisbury*; *bridge* is common, as in *Cambridge, Uxbridge*; *ton*, 'town', as in *Hampton, Middleton, Repton*; *ford*, 'crossing', as in *Hartford, Oxford*; *ham*, 'home', in *Fordham, Waltham*; and *wich* or *wick*, 'dwelling', as in *Greenwich, Norwich, Sandwich, Berwick*, and *Warwick*. The county, or shire, names of England are mostly Anglo-Saxon, and mostly reflect the period of Anglo-Saxon invasion and settlement, *Saxon* being included in *Essex, Sussex, Wessex*; the "north folk" and "south folk" of the Anglians are responsible for the names *Norfolk* and *Suffolk*; and the northern Angles above the river Humber, for *Northumbria*. Those who "sat" or "settled" have left a record of that fact in *Dorsetshire* and *Somersetshire*. In other county names various elements like *ford* and *ham* appear.

The Danes have left their mark largely through the eastern strip of England running north of London. In Lincolnshire there are said to be still no fewer than three hundred Danish place-names, and others occur in Yorkshire and elsewhere. These can often be recognized by certain suffixes like *-by*, 'town', as in *Derby, Grimsby, Whitby*; *-thorp*, 'village', as in *Althorpe, Kingsthorpe*; *-thwaite*, 'piece of ground', as in *Hallthwaite, Stonethwaite*; *-toft*, 'a clearing', as in *Lowestoft*.

It is interesting to compare the naming methods of the Celts, the Anglo-Saxons, and the Danes in early England with those of the American pioneers and frontiersmen, and to find that they have all used name elements of nearly the same kind. In the United States one will find very commonly *burg*, as in *Julesburg, Swedeburg*; *city*, as in *Iowa City, Union City*; *crossing*, as in *Beaver Crossing*; *hill*, as in *Morgan Hill*; *town*, as in *Allentown, Uniontown*; *ville*, as in *Louisville*; *wood*, as in *Greenwood*. *New* has played a great part in the naming of American places, as in *New Haven, New London, New York*. Moreover, just as many of the Anglo-Saxon names were derived in part from the names of persons, so in American place-naming, famous men, early settlers, prominent pioneers, railroad-builders, and others have been honored.

When the French came to England to live, they did not find much need to name or rename places; but a few French names have come down through the years, such as *Beaulieu* (pronounced [bɪúlɪ]), *Pomfret, Richmond*, and *Shotover* (from *Château Vert*). In North America they are much more numerous, extending especially from *Montreal* through the Great Lakes country, with its *Charlevoix, Des Plaines* (pronounced [dē plēn]), *La Salle, Presque Isle*, down the Mississippi Valley, with its *Des Moines, Dubuque, St. Louis*, to *Baton Rouge, New Orleans*, and the home of an early French colony in *Louisiana*. Moreover, this French influence can be traced west even as far as the old trading region of Oregon and Washington in such names as *Bordeaux* (Nebraska), *Choteau County* (Montana), *Coeur d'Alene* (Idaho), the *Deschutes River* (Oregon), and *The Dalles* (Oregon).

But in North America a much more striking element in place nomenclature is that of the names of American Indian origin. Such names have often been modified by French pronunciation. Half the state names are of Indian origin, notably

Dakota, Kentucky, Nebraska, Ohio, Oklahoma, Tennessee, as well as the Canadian *Manitoba, Saskatchewan,* and so on. Many tribal names have been repeatedly used for both county and city names, particularly *Cherokee* (at least twenty times), *Cheyenne, Muskegon, Oneida* (sixteen times), *Ottawa* (twenty-one times), *Pawnee* (fifteen times), and *Sioux.* Many lakes, rivers, and mountains have been given Indian names, such as *Chautauqua, Mississippi, Niobrara, Okoboji, Mt. Shasta, Mt. Tamalpais,* and the *Appalachians.* Prominent among the city names are *Alleghany, Chicago, Erie, Omaha,* and *Wichita.*

In California and the Southwest the influence of the Spanish and Mexicans has left its lasting imprint along the highways and byways in names like *Albuquerque, La Junta, Paso Robles,* but most noticeably in the many names of religious association, such as *San Jose, San Pablo, Santa Ana, Santa Fe.* Of the California county names, more than half are of Spanish origin, and a fourth are Indian.

America is curiously spotted with specially selected groups of place-names. In New York State the classical scholar has left his lasting mark in names like *Athens, Carthage, Ithaca, Rome, Troy,* and numerous others.[254] In Nebraska and states north of it Sweden is suggested by *Gothenburg, Swedeburg,* and *Upsala,* while in California the various Spanish saints are well represented, as, for example, *San Anselmo, San Francisco, San Rafael, Santa Rosa,* and others already named.

To appreciate the varied and unsystematic and altogether haphazard nature of American place-names, one needs only a brief journey in almost any part of the country. One will find, of course, many places named after early settlers or pioneers, such as *Axtell, Beulah, Ogden;* he will find descriptive names, such as *Greenwood, Mirage Flats, Red River, Salt Creek, Warm Springs,* and *Weeping Water;* many names will appear as obvious borrowings or transplantings from older countries, as in the case of *Berlin, Boston, Bristol, New London, Oxford,* and *Venice;* history and literature will doubtless have suggested others like *Council Bluffs, Hebron, Runnymede, Waterloo,* and *Waverly;* and the heroes of American military and political life have been remembered in the naming of many other places, such as *Franklin, Grant,* and *Sheridan.* Indeed, aside from Indian names, the many counties of the United States are named mainly from well-known English surnames,* and especially those borne by America's noted men, such as *Washington* (in thirty states), *Lincoln* (in at least twenty-one states), *Grant* (in eleven states), *Clay, Jefferson, Sheridan, Adams, Sherman, Webster,* and *Polk.* The unimaginative choice of local names is manifested, also, in the monotonous use of certain other names for which even the excuse of hero worship is lacking. McKnight says that there are in the United States thirty-four *Florences,* nineteen *Genevas,* thirty-six *Libertys,* twenty-nine *Troys,* and thirty-eight *Unions.*[298] Probably these figures do not include all the townships or precincts to which such names are likely to be given.

One of the most unusual features of American place nomenclature has been the blending of two state names to furnish a name for a border town. Heck has collected about fifty such names representing at least twenty-six different states; examples are *Calexico, Dakoming, Mexicali, Texarkana,* and *Wyuta.*[253] Other ingenious blendings are *Ohiowa* and *Wynot* (said to be from *Why not?*). *Amerind* (= *American Indian*) and *Eurasian* (= *Europe* + *Asia* + *-an*) are of similar origin.

d. **Collective names.** The gregarious nature of the human race has been responsible for the development down through the centuries of a great range and variety of names of collections of people. These are mostly substantivized adjectives, made with such endings as the Anglo-Saxon *-ish* and the Romanic *-an* and *-ese,* especially. They are still being coined as need arises, and show differing degrees of substantivation; those in *-ish,* like *English,* are still incapable of use in the singular, while those in *-an* can be either singular or plural, as *Roman, Romans*; but those in *-ese,* like *Genoese,* have led to some confusion, so that speakers sometimes insist upon making new and unwarranted singulars like *Portugee* and *Chinee,* because of a feeling that the ending *-ese* is a plural

---

* When the surname is also an old English place-name, as in the case of *Lincoln* and *Washington,* the American place may sometimes have been named after the English place rather than the American person.

suffix, which it really is not. On the whole, these proper collective nouns differ from the common collective nouns in that the latter usually have a singular form with a plural meaning, whereas the former are used about like any other substantivized adjectives. A collective common noun designates a group or collection as a whole (*team*), whereas a collective name designates one or more individuals belonging to a collection (*Athenian*).

As a rule the continental collective names show a preference for *-an*, as in *African, American, Australian, European*; but the form for Asia is *Asiatic*. The very general use of *American* for inhabitants of the United States has caused not a little dissatisfaction and discussion, and occasionally someone has attempted to coin a new special term, such as *Usonian* (from *U.S.A.*) or *Fredonian* (from *freedom*), in order that a name might be available coördinate with *Canadian* and *Mexican*. But in this book, as generally, the term *American* has been used for citizens of the United States, and sometimes in a broader sense to include all people of the Western continents. This use of *American* is not always definite and exact, but on the whole there is not much danger of misunderstanding.* In naming Celtic and Germanic races the suffix *-ish* or some form of it is usually employed, as in *British, Dutch, English, French* (from *Frankish*), *Irish, Scotch* or *Scots*, and *Welsh*. Romanic influence can be seen in *Anglo-Saxon* and *German*, and elsewhere in *Belgian, Italian, Roman, Rumanian; Hittite, Israelite; Chinese, Japanese, Portuguese*. And some simple stems are used, notably *Dane, Goth, Scot, Slav, Swede*, and *Wend*.

In the names of citizens of American states the suffix *-an* is generally employed, as in *Californians, Iowans, Minnesotans*; but there are a few exceptions, such as *Marylanders, New Jerseyites, Vermonters, Wyomingites*. In naming the

* More than a century ago John Pickering wrote in his *Vocabulary* of Americanisms (Boston, 1816) : "The general term *American* is now commonly understood (at least in all places where the English language is spoken) to mean an inhabitant of the *United States*; and is so employed, except where unusual precision of language is required. *English* writers in speaking of us always say, the *Americans*, the *American* government, the *American* embassador, &c."

inhabitants of cities and towns a similar variety of suffixes are employed, as in *Londoner, Long Islander, New Yorker; Bostonian, Chicagoan, Neapolitan, Philadelphian, San Franciscan, Venetian; Milanese, Viennese.* But the majority of American local names, such as *Des Moines, Kansas City, Montreal, Quebec, Santa Fe,* do not lend themselves readily to this derivational process, and it is necessary to use a more roundabout locution, speaking, for example, of *the citizens of Des Moines.*

Followers or admirers of certain noted persons are often named, in the same manner, *Chaucerians, Elizabethans, Hitlerites, Jacobites, Rousseauists, Shavians* (from G. B. Shaw), *Wycliffites.* Religious differences have, of course, long been responsible for such collective nouns as *Baptist, Catholic, Lutheran, Mennonite, Methodist,* and *Unitarian.* Political parties have given rise to *Conservative, Democrat, Know-Nothing, Mugwump, Republican, Tory, Whig,* and so on. The growth of the fraternal orders or groups, in college and out, has given to the world such names as *Knight of Columbus, Mason, Odd Fellow, Phi Beta Kappa, Rotarian,* and the long-established religious orders, such as the *Benedictines, Carmelites,* and *Franciscans.* Finally, and of growing importance in the scheme of national nomenclature, the increased interest in athletic competition has popularized a great number of team names, like the *Cardinals* and *White Sox* in baseball, the *Broncs, Indians,* and *Trojans,* in football.

e. **Names of animals and objects.** Since the animal pets of mankind also need names, there have been gathered, gradually, names for cats and dogs and horses which are chosen with humor and caprice, often, but often also with as great care as personal names. *Bowser, Bucephalus* (favorite horse of Alexander the Great), *Fido, Grimalkin, Malkin, Rex, Rover,* and *Tabby,* these and many similar names have become almost standardized as names of animal pets.[257] In olden times the knight sometimes named his favorite sword, as King Arthur did *Excalibur* and as Beowulf did *Nægling;* and men also named their boats. With the growth of navigation famous series of names, like *Aquitania* and *Lusitania,* have become prominent, and the naming of men-of-war has become a matter of national concern, states and cities contending for the honor of giving their names to battleships and cruisers. The names selected for Pullman cars are varied and interesting; and one of the more recent phases of name-choosing has to do with the many summer cottages and resorts that dot the wilds of America with such names as *Idlewild, It'lldo, Resthaven,* and *Tumble-Inn.* The names of the old inns of England, such as *The Bull, The Tabard, The White Horse,* owe their fame not so much to any imaginative richness as to the very important role which they have played in English life and literature.

f. **Chronological names.** The names of our months are, as a whole, to be credited to the Romans; but they were fixed in the calendar at different periods of Roman history, hence their variety. *March* honored Mars, god of war. *April (Aprilis)* has been somewhat fancifully but doubtfully explained as the "opening" month of the new spring season. *May* was dedicated to the goddess Maia, and *June* has been generally supposed to be derived from a family name famous in Roman history, Junius. The summer months *July* and *August* were named to honor the great emperors Julius and Augustus Cæsar. But the autumn months were named at a time when the Roman year began with March; hence the names of the months *September* to *December* were once merely the Latin ordinal numerals 'seventh' to 'tenth'. *January* was the month of the two-faced god Janus, and *February* the month of *februa,* the Roman feast of purification and expiation.

For the days of the week, Germanic names have been used mainly; the sun and moon are honored early in the week with *Sunday* and *Monday,* the Teutonic deities Tiu, Woden, Thor, and Freya are commemorated by *Tuesday, Wednesday, Thursday,* and *Friday*; but *Saturday* is named for one of the classical gods, Saturn.

Since the English *holiday* originally meant 'holy day', one need not be surprised to find in earlier centuries a great number and variety of such days observed by the medieval English churches and generally named after the saints commemorated.

Of these the best known even today, perhaps, are *Christmas, Saint Patrick's Day* (March 17), *Easter, Whitsuntide,* and *Michaelmas* (September 29). *Halloween* is the eve before *All Saints' Day* (November 1). Others generally celebrated by Americans are *Independence Day* (July 4, hence often known as *The Fourth*), *Thanksgiving Day* (in late November), and *Memorial Day* (May 30, known also as *Decoration Day*). Special communities of the English-speaking world have, of course, their more local holidays: in New Orleans such a holiday is the celebration of *Mardi Gras*; in Canada, *Dominion Day*; in the British Empire as a whole, *Empire Day*; in California, *Admission Day*; in Nebraska, *Aksarben,* whose name was found by reversing the state name. For the smaller units of time (morning, afternoon, etc.), common nouns are used in English.

g. **Trade names.** Too important among Current English names to be ignored in such a study as this are the many proper names that have been coined by the trade and applied to a great variety of commercial products. In the making of these new names special trends can be observed, such as the use of certain favorite endings, particularly *-ex,* as in *Kleenex, Cutex, Kardex, Pulvex, Pyrex, Sealex, Vapex*; *-ox,* as in *Clorox, Hydrox*; *-ine,* as in *Absorbine, Danderine, Dentyne, Opaline, Ovaltine, Vaseline, Zerolene*; *-eum,* as in *Congoleum, Linoleum*; *-ola,* as in *Grafonola, Mazola, Motrola, Radiola, Victrola*; *-ite,* as in *Alemite, Bathite, Masonite, Sillimanite, Warrenite.* Most of these pseudosuffixes have no linguistic significance like the suffixes of common nouns, but are often selected, apparently, because they contribute a quasi-scientific or euphonious tone to the name. The use of alliteration in trade names has long been a favorite device, as in *Big Ben Clocks, Brakeblok, Ground Gripper Shoes, Kiddie-Kar,* and among the automobile manufacturers, as in *Aëro-Eight, Salient Six, Silent Six.* Another device is the blending of the initials or initial syllables of the company name, as in *Arco* (from *American Radio Co.*), *Nabisco* (from *National Biscuit Co.*), *Socony* (from *Standard Oil Co. of New York*). Other blends, of two words only, are more common, as in *Duco* (from *Du Pont Co.*), *Elcar* (from *Elkhart Co. car*),

Philco (from a *Philadelphia company*), and *Texaco* (from *Texas Co.*). Phrases of two or three words are also made frequent use of, as in *Dri-Brite, Eversharp, Gainaday, Kantleek, Wearever*. And, finally, throughout this whole business of manufacturing distinctive trade names runs the practice of changing the conventional spelling of words so as to give the new name a more striking appearance, as in *Hi-Heat Coal, Ken-L-Ration* (a dog food), *Pennzoil, Stixall Glue, Uneeda Biscuits*.

In this class of names, more than in any other, commonization (see page 320) is likely to occur, since a trade article has only to become sufficiently popular to be looked upon as common and for its name to become a common noun. Either the patent expires or the public forgets that the name is a trade name and hence a proper name. This is true of *celluloid, kodak, linoleum, listerine, tabloid, vaseline*.

h. **Titles of respect and social distinction.** Any consideration of names inevitably leads to the subject of titles of respect and social distinction. The most nearly universal titles of respect in English are *Sir, Madam, Mr., Mrs.,* and *Miss.* In England *Mr.* is used to a limited extent in addressing business communications, and the abbreviation *Esq.* (for 'Esquire') is generally placed after the name when a gentleman is addressed who does not possess some special title pertaining to religious orders or higher social rank; but in the United States the title *Mr.* is used almost universally when the man addressed is not known to have any official or honorary title, and the use of *Esq.* after a man's name is limited mainly to legal practice. *Master* is often used in addressing a boy, instead of *Mr.*; *Mademoiselle* is still regarded as French and not English.

When the makers of the American Constitution decided that "No title of nobility shall be granted by the United States: And no person holding any office of profit or trust under them, shall, without the consent of the Congress, accept of any present, emolument, office, or title, of any kind whatever, from any king, prince, or foreign state," they greatly simplified future American procedure in this respect. In England the titles *Sir, Lord,* and *Lady* are, of course, in common use. Moreover, of late, *Earl, Marquis, Duke*, and others have been used more commonly in newspaper discussions, so that Fowler protestingly said in his Dictionary of Modern English Usage (under "Titles")[16]:

A curious & regrettable change has come about in the last twenty or thirty years [before 1926]. Whereas we used, except on formal occasions, to talk & write of Lord Salisbury, Lord Derby, Lord Palmerston, & to be very sparing of the prefixes Marquis, Earl, & Viscount, the newspapers are now full of Marquis Curzon, Earl Beatty, Viscount Rothermere, & similarly Marchioness this & Countess that have replaced the Lady that used to be good enough for ordinary wear. We have taken a leaf in this as in other matters from the Japanese book; it was when Japan took to European titles that such combinations as *Marquis Ito* first became familiar to us, & our adoption of the fashion is more remarkable than pleasing.

A few political and legal titles have become popular in the United States, however. Almost any person who has served as a judge or justice of the peace is likely to continue to be addressed as *Judge*. The title *Honorable* is frequently retained by persons in England who have occupied official positions of trust and honor; it is applied more especially to the children of earls and viscounts and barons; in the United States it is attached to the more important state and Federal offices, such as the governorship or a place in the cabinet of the President. In almost any deliberative gathering *Mr. Chairman* is used, except when some special term such as *Moderator* is required.

Most titles used regularly in America pertain to the ecclesiastical, the academic, or the naval and military phases of our national life and are merited rather than inherited titles. *Bachelor of Arts (A.B. = Artium Baccalaureus), Master of Arts (A.M. = Artium Magister)*, and *Doctor of Philosophy (Ph.D. = Philosophiae Doctor)* are generally granted by the universities, but only the last carries with it a form of address, *Doctor. Professor* is often applied to any male teacher, but is properly applicable to those persons only (male or female) who have been elected to a position carrying with it the official title of professor[261]. In the same way the term *Doctor* has been widely and often wrongly applied to people in a great variety of professions. Its widespread use is more to be expected, however, since the degree of *Doctor* pertains also to medicine, dentistry, divinity, law, literature, and so on. Of other ecclesiastical titles the most familiar are *Reverend, Father, Bishop, Mother, Brother, Sister,* and, in the case of at least one order of nuns, *Madam*. Of the military titles the most familiar are *General, Colonel, Major, Captain, Lieutenant,* and *Sergeant*; naval titles vary somewhat from these. There is an almost universal tradition that in Kentucky and elsewhere in the South since the Civil War most white men of good social standing have been and should be addressed as *Colonel* without regard to military considerations.

An interesting and unusual development in titles arose long ago through the use of abstract nouns in addressing kings, prelates, and judges, as in *Your Majesty, Your Highness, Your Grace, Your Honor*.

Of course various other social distinctions are likely to result in titles, relationship giving *Aunt, Cousin, Darling, Father,* and the various other affectionate terms and relationship names. A favorite in the lower classes is *Boss*, and likewise *Chief* seems to have appealed to the American public. Fortunately for the learner of English, the many and exotic titles used by the various fraternal orders do not generally have much currency outside the lodge rooms.

i. **Nicknames.** Originally *a nickname* was *an ekename*, that is to say, an 'also', or additional, name and not necessarily either affectionate or disparaging; nowadays it is likely to be either the one or the other, at least to some degree, since the use of a nickname implies familiarity on the part of the user. Nicknames are mostly of two kinds: namely, those abbreviations and diminutives that are merely modified forms of standard English names, as *Jim* (for 'James'), *Betty* (for 'Elizabeth'), and those epithets that characterize the persons to whom they are applied, as *Slim Jones, Fatty Williams*. Both kinds have played an important part in the development of surnames, since the only second names possessed by the Anglo-Saxons were epithets, mostly of a complimentary nature, such as in *Alfred the Great, Edward the Confessor, Eric the Red,* and *Harold Harefoot.*

In place of the standard collective names applicable to nations, states, and lesser groups of people, certain nicknames have sprung up which are often regarded as somewhat uncomplimentary, although not always so. Some of the more famous are *Boche,* 'German soldier', *Dago,* 'Italian' usually, *Greaser,* 'Mexican', *Mick* or *Paddy,* 'Irishman', *Sambo,* 'negro', *Sandy,* 'Scotchman', *Spick,* 'Mexican', *Wop,* 'Italian' or 'southern European', *Yankee,* 'New Englander' or sometimes 'American'. To these should be added the fanciful *Uncle Sam* and earlier *Brother Jonathan* for the United States of America and *John Bull* for England, and perhaps *Dixie,* the Southerner's affectionate name for that part of the United States south of the old Mason and Dixon's line.

Most of the American states have nicknames, such as *Badger State* (Wisconsin), *Bay State* (Massachusetts), *Buckeye State* (Ohio), *Empire State* (New York), *Hawkeye State* (Iowa), *Hoosier State* (Indiana), *Keystone State* (Pennsylvania), *Prairie State* (Illinois), and *Sunflower* or *Jayhawker State* (Kansas).[263]

There is a strong tendency to select nicknames of a descriptive and often complimentary nature for cities of some distinction. Boston has long been known as *The Hub,* Chicago as the *Windy City,* Minneapolis and St. Paul as the *Twin Cities,* Philadelphia as the *Quaker City.* This practice is, of course, neither very recent nor strictly American; Rome, it will be recalled, has been named the *Eternal City,* and Edinburgh is *Auld Reekie.*

American life has not yet progressed to the point where municipal rivalry has led to the fixing upon smaller communities of epithets of this kind; but writers in *Word-Lore* have recently compiled lists of nicknames for English townsmen, as, for example, the *Dickybirds* of Dartmouth, the *Horseheads* of Totnes, the *Jackasses* of Hartland, the *Scads* of Penzance.[267] Of course the *Cockney* of London is well known.

Of the two kinds of personal nicknames, the abbreviated forms and diminutives are more generally used. The commoner Christian names have long been reduced to familiar or diminutive forms, such as *Clem* (for 'Clement'), *Dick* (for 'Richard'), *Bess, Lizzie, Betsy, Beth,* and *Betty* (for 'Elizabeth'), *Mollie* (for 'Mary'), *Will, Willie, Bill,* and *Billie* (for 'William'), and *Johnnie, Jack, Jackie,* and the Scottish *Jock* (for 'John'), though, as a matter of fact, the form *Jack* was originally a variant of the French *Jacques* and should really be the nickname of 'James' or 'Jacob' rather than of 'John'. Occasionally the entire English or American nation has formed the temporary habit of speaking familiarly of one of its noted leaders by some nickname of this kind, as, for example, *Cal* for President 'Calvin' Coolidge, *Dizzy* for Benjamin 'Disraeli', *Tay Pay* for 'T. P.' O'Connor, the Irish statesman, and *Teddy* for 'Theodore' Roosevelt.

Many epithets of a special kind have been applied to famous Englishmen or Americans from earliest times, notably *Beau Brummell,* the *Black Prince, Good Queen Bess, Honest Abe,* the *Iron Duke* (Wellington), and *Richard the Lionhearted.* Moreover, certain epithets are now or have long been common linguistic stock, such as *Black, Bud, Dutch, Fatty, Junior, Limpy, Shorty, Skinny, Slim, Sonny, Red, Swede, Tiny,* and the affectionate *Dad* and *Mother* applied to persons not necessarily related to the speaker.

The common noun, because it names a class composed of many individuals, can be modified by a variety of adjectives; but the proper noun or name can be modified only by such adjectives or titles or nicknames as the peculiar nature of the individual may warrant. When once a particular trait or characteristic of a person has been hit upon and an appropriate nickname bestowed, the nickname may persist throughout the remainder of the life of that individual. Consequently the study of titles and nicknames may be justified as of fully as much importance for the proper noun as the study of adjectives is for the common noun.

While the nickname has not been the most important element in the formation of English family names, it was undoubtedly one of the earliest factors in name-making.

51. *Pronouns*

Pronouns stand in place of nouns; they are linguistic shortcuts, colorless words used to avoid repetition of the more striking proper nouns or common nouns, but always something more than mere shortcuts. The variation in this "something more" makes it necessary to distinguish six kinds of pronouns, as italicized in the following sentences:

a. Mr. Smith missed his three companions because *he* took the lower road.

b. Mr. Smith missed his three companions, *who* had taken the other road.

c. Who took the lower road and who took the upper?

d. That man went by the lower road; *these* took the other.

e. The one man took the lower road; the *others* took the upper one.

f. Three of them took the lower road.

In *a*, above, the personal pronoun *he* avoids renaming the person *Mr. Smith*; in *b*, the relative pronoun *who* not only relates to an antecedent, *three companions*, but it also joins a subordinate thought to the main statement; in *c* the interrogative *who* has to be used because the antecedent is unknown; in *d* the demonstrative *these* avoids the repetition of *man* (in its plural form, *men*); in *e* the indefinite *others* cannot well be called an adjective, because there is no noun present which it could modify, and because, unlike an adjective, it takes the plural ending *-s* and must therefore be regarded as an indefinite pronoun referring to *men* (understood); in *f* the more definite numeral *three* also avoids repetition of an antecedent *men*. In each sentence the simple pronoun avoids a more cumbersome mode of expressing the idea involved in its antecedent.

It should be plain, however, that some of these words — namely, *these*, *others*, and *three* — are used as pronouns but might at other times be simply adjectives modifying nouns (*others* being changed to *other*, of course). They can be either adjectival pronouns or pronominal adjectives. Function, and not form, determines their classification, for the most part.

a. **Personal pronouns.** The personal pronouns are *I, we, you* (singular and plural), *he, she, it,* and *they.* Inasmuch as the genitive forms like *my* and *his* function as adjective modifiers, they will be discussed more fully in Section 52, below, and all the inflectional forms of these pronouns will be summed up in Section 88. The older pronouns of address, *thou* and *ye,* are still used occasionally in religious and poetic language. *You all* is a colloquial term of the southern United States, addressed usually to more than one person.[268]

While *it* is ordinarily a personal pronoun, in spite of the fact that it is neuter and refers to some thing rather than person,* it has varying degrees of definiteness, the most important of which are as follows:

With definite antecedent: 'He took the book and read *it.*'
With vague antecedent: '*It* is my turn now.' '*It* is I.'
As impersonal pronoun: '*It* is raining.' 'Go *it!*' 'They are roughing *it.*'
As an expletive: '*It* is a pity that you spoiled the picture.' '*It* is wrong to steal.'

The compound pronouns made with *-self* and *-selves* and used as intensives to emphasize or as reflexives to refer back to the subject fall into two troublesome groups according as they are formed with a genitive (possessive) form, as in the first person, *myself, ourselves,* and the second person, *yourself, yourselves,* or with an objective form, as in the third person, *himself, herself, itself,* and *themselves.* It is not strange that the logically minded but ignorant speaker wants to say *hisself* and *theirselves,* since the other forms of these compounds seem to be made with genitives.

b. **Relative pronouns.** The relative pronouns are *who, which, that,* and the so-called double relative *what,* which sometimes seems to be equivalent to *that which,* as in 'I saw *what* you were looking at.' Sometimes *as* and *but* function as relative pronouns, as in the sentences 'I gave him such books *as* I had on hand'; 'There was not a person *but* looked sick.' In Eng-

---

* For a definition of the grammatical property commonly called person, see Section 88.

lish dialect *as* is used sometimes instead of the generally preferred relative pronouns *who* and *that*: 'There's some *as* picks 'em up only to lose 'em again.' Since, as already observed, the relative pronoun joins a subordinate clause to its antecedent, as in 'The man *who* was hurt has recovered', some grammarians do not recognize *what* as a double relative but insist that it introduces an embedded, or indirect, question. They would say that in the sentence given above to illustrate *what*, the clause '*what* you were looking at' is merely the indirect form of an implied question, '*What* were you looking at?'

The compound relatives are *whoever, whosoever, whichever, whichsoever, whatever,* and *whatsoever.* They are often used like the double relative *what* with no antecedent actually expressed, as, for example, in the sentence '*Whoever* left the book evidently had no more use for it', where *whoever* means 'that person who'.

c. **Interrogative pronouns.** The pronouns used in asking questions are *who, which, what,* and, in earlier times, *whether.* Sometimes the compounds *whoever* and *whatever* are used interrogatively, as in the question '*Whatever* did you do with my book?' This use is said to be more common in British English and is often expressive of surprise or impatience.

d. **Demonstrative pronouns.** The demonstrative pronouns, which are frequently used as adjectives also, are *this* and *that,* with their plurals *these* and *those.* *The former* and *the latter* are also used as demonstratives, and, in much the same way, *the first* and *the second.* Occasionally *such* and *so* serve as demonstratives, as in the sentences 'He is a foe to high tariff and as *such* will seek reëlection', 'I told you *so.*'

Slightly different from these demonstratives is the so-called identifying pronoun *same,* which is correctly used in such a sentence as 'The *same* was true of his brother also', and in legal language generally, but is not correctly used as a substitute for *it,* as too often it is used in modern business English.

As we have observed in discussing Scottish dialect, *yon* is still used as a demonstrative pronoun in Modern Scots.

e. **Indefinite pronouns.** The indefiniteness of the pronouns usually classified under this head varies; the most commonly used of them are as follows:

all	everybody	nothing
another	everyone	one
any	everything	other
anybody	few	several
anyone	many	some
anything	much	somebody
both	neither	someone
each	nobody	something
each one	none	such
either	no one	

All of these can be used also as adjective modifiers except those compounded with *-body, -one,* or *-thing.* Two other indefinites (phrasal), *each other* and *one another,* are known as reciprocal pronouns and can never be adjectives in the reciprocal sense. There is also a compound *oneself,* which is used as a reflexive pronoun, as in the sentence, 'It was not easy to save *oneself* in the storm.' And, finally, the personal pronouns *they* and *you* are often used as indefinites in such colloquial sentences as '*They* say the man was insane' and '*You* never can tell what a crazy person will do', where *they* refers to some very indefinite antecedent *people* and *you* is the equivalent of the indefinite pronoun *one.*

f. **Numeral pronouns.** The cardinal numerals *one, two, three, four,* and so on are pronouns — and pronouns of a more definite kind than those just considered — when they stand alone in the stead of nouns understood, as in the sentence 'Some took the course, but only *five* passed in it.' The ordinal numerals *first, second, third, fourth,* and so on can in the same manner be used as pronouns.

52. *Adjectives*

For the sake of convenience in considering them, adjectives can be roughly grouped as common descriptive, common limiting, and proper. They usually answer the questions

What kind? Which one? How many? One of the most profitable studies of language growth is that of adjectival functions. *High*, for example, is descriptive in *a high hat*, but it is used largely for the sake of limitation in *the highest peak of all*. On the other hand, the proper adjective *Utopian* is largely limiting, or restrictive, in the expression 'the *Utopian* theme in literature'; but it becomes a common descriptive adjective in '*utopian*' dreams. Any adjectival modification of a noun limits somewhat the noun's meaning; adding the descriptive adjective *white* to *horses* restricts one's attention to a certain number of horses in a given herd. On the other hand, the popular slang use of the limiting adjective in 'He's *some* runner!' makes a highly suggestive and descriptive adjective out of *some*, even though it might be difficult to define exactly its descriptive qualities. Certainly when one says that an athlete is '*some* runner', there is nothing indefinite about the adjective *some*. To revert to a thought stressed earlier in this book, the thinking that lies behind the use of such a locution determines its function in speech.

a. **Descriptive adjectives.** There are many simple descriptive adjectives in Current English, such as *brown, dull, high, little, old, queer, round, straight, wet*, and *white*. There are many derivative adjectives of this kind, like *awful, beautiful, beneficent, godlike, golden, gracious, moody, polyglot, subordinate*, and *valiant*. Compounds are also made frequently, such as *gilt-edged, long-drawn-out, played-out, stuck-up*, and *three-sided*. Some older amalgamated phrases and compounds persist, such as *aglow, alight, alive, enough*. And just as the verbal called the gerund is used as a noun, so those other verbal forms called participles are regularly used as adjectives, such as '*dried* fish', '*running* water', '*watered* stock'.

Some colloquial or slangy adjectives have been developed from phrases by the use of prepositional adverbs, as *all in*, 'exhausted, tired out'; *all up*, 'finished'; *down and out*, 'reduced to penury' or 'completely incapacitated'; *hard up*, 'impoverished'; *over with*, 'ended'; *well off*, 'thriving, prosperous.' Numerous other slangy adjectives are formed with the suffix *-y*, such as *nifty, ritzy*, and *spiffy*.

b. Adjectives of limitation, quantity, and number. The articles, *a, an, the,* belong in this class; likewise all the pronominal words which are capable of being used as modifiers of nouns. The possessive forms of the personal pronouns *my, our, thy, your, his, her, its,* and *their* are used only as adjectives; but it is unnecessary to say that they cease to be personal pronouns when they are so used, just as it is unnecessary to call a possessive form of the noun, as in '*man's* estate' or '*Smith's* store', an adjective because it is used to modify another noun. The confusion in the naming of these possessive pronouns is an old one and goes far back to the Anglo-Saxon period, when two distinct sets of words of possession actually existed, one the genitive form of the personal pronoun and the other a separate possessive adjective which was regularly declined as an Old English adjective. Happily that state of ambiguity has vanished, and it is only necessary to insist today that the possessives are inflectional forms of the personal pronouns used as adjective modifiers. The so-called absolute forms of these possessives, namely, *mine, ours, thine, yours, hers,* and *theirs,* and the dialectal *hisn* and *hern,* are likewise adjectival in function but are used when the speaker wishes to avoid repeating the noun modified by the possessive, as in 'This book is *yours* (= *your book*)', 'His paper is better than *mine* (= *my paper*).' Like the personal possessives, the other possessives *whose, whosever, either's, neither's, another's, other's, one's,* the possessive forms of compounds with *-one* and *-body,* and the troublesome *someone else's* are used as adjectives.

The other pronouns discussed in Section 51, when they are used as adjectives, may be said to be actually converted into adjectives for the time being. So the relatives *which* and *what* and their compounds *whichever* and *whatever* become adjectives in such constructions as '*which* man' and '*whatever* book'; these four words may also be used as interrogative adjectives in direct or indirect questions; the demonstratives *this, that, yon,* and *yonder* become adjectives when they modify nouns, as in '*this* man' and '*yonder* house'; most of the indefinites, as indicated above, are just as often adjectives, as in '*any* word', '*both* boxes', '*either* city', '*few* letters', and '*many* people.' A few indefinites are seldom or never pronouns, but regularly adjectives, used with nouns or pronouns, such as *certain, considerable* (colloquial), *every, no, respective,* and *various*. The adjective *very* is intensive in 'the *very* day', and there are three common identifying adjectives in English, namely, *identical, same,* and *selfsame*.

The more definite numerals are often grouped with the indefinite number words already discussed; but it is possible to draw a distinct line between the two groups. The cardinals, *one, two, three, forty,* etc., and the ordinals, *first, second, third, fortieth,* etc., are as often adjectives as pronouns. Moreover, the multiplicatives, *single, double, duplex, twofold, threefold, triple, quadruple, manifold, hundredfold,* etc., are also regularly adjectives. With these definite numerals are often associated the less definite adjectives *farther, foremost, former, hindmost, last, latest, latter, next, utter,* which pertain rather more to order or sequence than to actual number.

c. Proper adjectives. Most of the collective names already discussed, such as *Athenian, Benedictine, British, Chaucerian, Genoese, Jacobite, Roman, Rousseauist, Tory,* began as proper adjectives derived from names and are commonly adjectives. Proper adjectives are, at the outset, limiting rather than descriptive; but gradually, as the characteristics of the persons or movements or groups which they indicate become better known, they are likely to assume some of the qualities of descriptive adjectives. So the adjectives *Bohemian, Christian, Mid-Victorian, Olympic, Philistine, Pickwickian, Pre-Raphaelite, Puritan, Quixotic,* and *Spartan* have become strongly descriptive in the understanding of those persons who use them frequently. If this process of gathering semantic moss should continue long enough, these words might conceivably become mere common descriptive adjectives like *erotic, jovial, mosaic, stentorian,* and *titanic,* all of which were once proper adjectives. It is difficult sometimes to decide whether an adjective of this kind should still be capitalized or be written as a common adjective.

53. *Verbs*

Of all the parts of speech the verb is perhaps the most important in the expression of thinking; but it is also most difficult to classify satisfactorily, because it can be viewed from so many different points of view. The distinction of strong and weak verbs depends upon inflectional forms and belongs therefore in a later discussion of the conjugation of verbs (see Sec. 90); the study of complete and incomplete, of transitive and intransitive, verbs must be made as a part of the study of sentence structure, and belongs with the later consideration of the syntax of the sentence (see Sec. 94); and the contrasting of simple and phrasal verbs belongs in the syntactical treatment of the English verb (see Sec. 106). There remains for consideration here the verb as it functions in expressing action, state or condition, and being, either by means of its peculiar form or because of the way it is used.

a. **Verbs of action.** Both physical and mental activity are expressed by the numerous verbs of this first class, such as *bellow, breathe, calculate, fall, fly, gravitate, hold, pulverize, raise, sink, think, travel, wriggle.*

b. **Verbs of state, feeling, condition.** Under this head may be included such verbs as *deteriorate, grow, hate, increase, lie, recline, sicken, waste away,* and *weaken.*

c. **Verbs of being.** The main verb of this class is the verb *be,* with its various forms. Very close to it in meaning are *become, consist in, exist, hang around* (colloquial), *result in, seem,* sometimes *stand,* as in 'he *stands* ready to help', *wait,* and a few others.

d. **Auxiliary verbs.** A little group of auxiliary, or helping, verbs have become of very great importance in the general plan of Current English usage, because, when they are used variously with the verbal forms (the infinitive and the participles), a great variety of modifications of meaning can be produced in a single verb. These are *be, have, do; can* and *may, shall* and *will, must* and *ought.* To these may be added *dare,* in such a use as 'I *dare* say', *let,* as in '*Let* us begin', *need,* as in 'You *need* not bother', and *used,* as in 'He *used* to go often.' Of the nine commonly used auxiliaries, four are also frequently used as notional verbs, namely, *be, have, do,* and *will.* In 'He *is* working' the use of *is* with a verbal (that is, participle) constitutes it an auxiliary; but in 'He *is* sick' or 'He *is* behind' it has no verbal form depending upon it, and so it cannot be called an auxiliary. The same is true of *did* in 'He *did* go' and 'He *did* the work.' For a discussion of the various uses and accomplishments of the auxiliaries in the sentence see Section 106.

e. **Impersonal verbs.** If the subject of a verb be impersonal, the verb itself may be called impersonal. So one must expect to find, as the subject of such verbs, the impersonal *it* already discussed (Sec. 51) or, occasionally, the interrogative *what.* The only important group of impersonal verbs are those concerned with weather conditions, such as *it blows, it hails, it snows, it thunders.* There are a few other verbs that have been called impersonal by some grammarians when used after the expletive *it,* particularly *appears, behooves, looks, seems,* as in the sentence 'It *seems* to me that he is mistaken.' But the expletive is merely a filler in anticipation of the real subject *that he is mistaken,* and this clause is too definite a subject to be called impersonal, or to warrant calling these verbs impersonal. So it is better to distinguish between those verbs that follow a truly impersonal *it* and those that follow the expletive *it.* The trouble in classifying impersonal verbs is due largely to an earlier change from an Old English use of purely impersonal verbs without any subject at all, as in *methinks,* to the later adoption of *it* as the subject of all sentences where the real subject is vague and uncertain. In the question 'What *ails* you?' the verb is similarly impersonal.

f. **Active-passive verbs.** Sometimes a verb is active in form but so utilized that it must be regarded as passive, since the subject of the verb is not the doer but the recipient of the action. In Current English many verbs of action are employed in this way, as in 'It *adds up* correctly', 'It *cleans* easily', 'That meat *will keep*', 'His book *reads* well', 'This machine *operates* easily', 'An article that *sells* readily', 'Silk that *washes* well', and 'Putty that *works* easily.' Of course the passivity must be quite obvious when a verb is so used, or else the construction is not a success. Not all verbs are capable of being used in this way.

g. **Verb-adverb combinations.**[269] The use of the verb-adverb combination has developed so gradually in English, and over so long a period of time, that many philologists fail to appreciate even yet how important a place it has assumed in Modern English. Indeed, there has been much sputtering about it and superficial criticism of the so-called "parasitic preposition," as the prepositional adverb has been termed in such combinations as *heat up, look out, throw over, win out*. But in order to appraise these many combinations in a satisfactory manner, it is necessary to understand them, and such understanding can result only from a careful and detailed examination of various aspects of the usage.

In earliest English, compound verbs were regularly composed, or made up, by the use of adverbial prefixes, such as *at-, be-, for-, on-, out-, over-, to-, under-, up-, with-*; and later, as Latin and French words were borrowed, verbs came into use in English with Romanic prefixes like *ex-, pre-, trans-*. Many of these verbs were later dropped from the language, but many still persist, such as *belittle, express, forgive, induct, outrun, overtake, prefer, translate, undergo, withhold*. For the most part, English has ceased to coin new compound, or derivative, verbs of this kind and has changed to the practice of using certain of these particles — not all of them, be it said — loosely after the verbs rather than prefixed to them. So clearly has this differentiation in practice manifested itself in later times that today pairs of such verbs exist which employ the same adverbial particle with quite different meanings, as in *forbid* and *bid for, forgo* and *go for, outrun* and *run out, overtake* and *take over, overwork* and *work over, understand* and *stand under, uphold* and *hold up* ('rob'), *upset* and *set up, withdraw* and *draw with*. But the number of survivals among the older type of verb compounds has decreased, while there has been a steady increase in the number of such combinations as *bring out, get over, give up, go under, lay by, pull through,* and *run down*. To distinguish the older type of derivatives, as well as other compounds like *back-fire, black-ball, triple-plate, welcome,* and *whitewash,* from the newer combinations with the more loosely used adverbial particle, the term *verb-adverb combination* has been adopted for the latter.

It is not always easy to distinguish between a verb modified by such an adverb, as in *stand up,* and a verb so closely combined with the adverb that the two words merge, or fuse, into a new and often quite different meaning from that of the modified verb, as in *bring round,* 'resuscitate'. Two tests can be helpfully applied: If the adverb gives to the verb a shade of meaning which it does not possess when used as a separate adverb, or if the combination of verb and adverb produces a meaning which can be translated by some other verb alone, then the adverbial use of the particle can be said to have largely disappeared. So in '*carry out* a plan', *doze off,* '*dust up* a room', '*eat up* a cake', and '*line up* for tickets', the adverbial values of the separate particles *out, off,* and *up* do not stand out distinctly. Likewise when *blow in* means 'spend', *call down* 'rebuke', *get on* 'prosper', and *go off* 'explode', the combination is fairly well established. The punster loves to play upon the two possible meanings (literal and derived) of such pairs of words, emphasizing humorously their literal meanings in such contexts as 'the man was *broken up* over his loss', '*blow up* a lazy servant', '*cough up* a dollar', 'friends *falling out*'. One of the greatest dangers in this modern use of verb-adverb combinations lies in the ambiguity resulting from giving so many shades of meaning to a few word pairs.

Some sixteen prepositional adverbs are regularly used in combination, namely, *about, across, around* (or *round*), *at, by, down, for, in, off, on, out, over, through, to, up,* and *with.* The use of these with just the familiar verbs *back, blow, break, bring, call, come, do, fall, fix, get, give, go, hold, lay, let, look, make, pull, put, run, set, shut, take, turn,* and *work* will produce nearly two hundred different combinations, which are susceptible of about a thousand fine shades of meaning.

After what has been said about the difficulty of distinguishing between a verb modified by a prepositional adverb and a verb-adverb combination, it would, of course, be rash to attempt an exact computation of numbers of combinations and meanings; but the figures just given can be tested somewhat by making a rough estimate with the aid of any unabridged modern dictionary. The articles in the original edition of Webster's New International Dictionary (1909), for example, treating of these twenty-five verbs, show that on the average each of them could, at the time they were listed, be combined with seven or eight out of the sixteen adverbs given above; *get*, as might be expected, led the list with at least fourteen such combinations;* *go*, *come*, and *put*, each with almost as many; *lay* and *take*, each with nine; *fall*, *run*, and *turn*, with eight each; and the rest with fewer.

The verbs *take*, *put*, and *go*, used in all the combinations possible, were each capable of expressing more than sixty meanings, *get* over fifty, *turn* and *lay* at least forty each, *set*, *run*, *make*, and *fall* over thirty, and the others of the list not so many. For the one combination *make up* the dictionary listed fourteen different meanings, although one of them, it is true, was labeled "*Obs.*"

During the quarter-century that elapsed between the publication of the first edition of the New International Dictionary and the appearance of the second, other combinations have become popular and other meanings have developed, so that the new edition of the dictionary shows an increase in the number of combinations and meanings. Probably some of this increase has come about through a more liberal attitude on the part of the editors toward the presentation of colloquialisms in the dictionary; but also, undoubtedly, forms and meanings of verb-adverb combinations have gained during the twenty-five years a more widespread approval in general usage which has forced the lexicographer to recognize them by including them.

Some of the peculiarities in the use of verb-adverb combinations are worthy of notice. Intransitive verbs or verbs ordinarily intransitive, like *bawl*, *cough*, *look*, *talk*, and *work*

* These figures do not include combinations with two adverbs, such as *put up with*, *go in for*.

become transitive in combination. A calf *bawls* but an employer *bawls out* his helper; one *coughs* from throat irritation but *coughs up* a dollar; we *look* at a picture but *look up* a friend; *talk* about a book but *talk up* one we especially like; *work* steadily to *work up* a case at law. The reverse may also be true, a transitive verb becoming intransitive in combination, as in *dig in, give in* ('yield'), *keep out, own up*, and *pull through*. Sometimes the verb alone will take one kind of object, but quite a different kind when used in combination; so one *burns* a paper but *burns off* a field, *does* work but *does up* a garment or an opponent or a house, *lives* his life but *lives down* a disgrace, *signs* a paper to *sign away* property.

The semasiological effects of combining in this way vary greatly. The most frequently used adverb is *up*, and beyond the purely adverbial use of it in *brick up, spade up, stand up*, there are various shades of meaning. It may express forward motion, as in *move up, speed up*, or motion to a certain position or standard, as in *grade up* (fruit), *join up* (pipes), or making tight or secure, as in *close up, lock up*, or bringing into prominence, as in *pipe up* (for 'speak up'), or, most commonly of all, it may give to the combination merely a perfective sense, as in *dress up, muddle up, polish up*. Next in importance is *out*, with its implication of removal or separation in *back out, pick out*, of completeness or finality in *feather out, peter out, measure out*.

An analysis of some hundreds of these combinations brings to light several interesting facts. In the first place, about 90 per cent of all the combinations are made with verbs of one syllable, like *get, lay, put*. When longer ones are used, they are generally common dissyllabic verbs like *barter, measure, polish*, and *settle*. A very large percentage of the verbs so used are, moreover, of native Anglo-Saxon origin. Then, again, a few dozen of these combining verbs are seldom or never used alone without the adverb. So one can say *chirk up, eke out, jot down, peter out, side with*, but cannot or commonly does not use these verbs alone. And, finally, when the object of a verb-adverb combination is a pronoun, it is usually placed between verb and adverb, as in 'I will *look* him *up*';

but when the object is a noun, it is more often put after the adverb, as in 'I will *look up* the book.'

The verb-adverb combination is often nearly synonymous with a loan-word of Romanic origin and in Current English tends to supplant it. Sometimes the combination is merely a translation of the general idea, as in *blow out* (for 'extinguish'), *crumble up* (for 'disintegrate'), *get down* (for 'descend'), *give in* (for 'acquiesce'), *own up* (for 'confess'). In other instances the verb of the combination is the exact equivalent of the verb of the Romanic compound, and at times the adverb also translates the Romanic prefix, as, for example,

blow up	inflate	gather up	collect
bring in	introduce	light up	illuminate
call off	revoke	put off	postpone
call out	evoke	put out	extinguish
catch on	apprehend	take up	assume

The older English compound with adverb prefixed is used for the noun, and the verb-adverb combination for the verb, in *downfall* and *fall down*, *income* and *come in*, *intake* and *take in*, *outlet* and *let out*, *output* and *put out*, *thoroughfare* and *fare through*, *upturn* and *turn up*. The nouns *offset* and *overthrow*, however, are represented by both kinds of verbs, namely, *to offset* and *to set off*, *to overthrow* and *to throw over*.

Nouns and adjectives have gradually developed from these verb-adverb combinations as the verbs have become more firmly established in the language, through the process of conversion, as in a *clean-up*, a *cut-out*, a *dugout*, a *gadabout*, a *holdup*, the *Passover*, a *send-off*, a stylish *turnout*, a *write-up*. Some have gone so far in this direction that derivative and inflectional forms are used, as in a *dressing-down, hangers-on, leftovers, pop-overs, runabouts*, a *thinning-out*, and others listed above. Adjectives are common in Current English, such as *bang-up, battered-up, broken-down, cast-off*, a *closing-out* sale, a *coming-out* party, a *grown-up* son, *long-drawn-out, played-out*, a *wearing-down* process.

The causes of this increase in the use of verb-adverb combinations are, apparently, of several different kinds. At first, figurative change seems to have led to the popularity of such locutions as *blow in, come off, dry up*; a desire to strengthen or emphasize the idea expressed by the simple verb probably causes many speakers to add such particles as *out* and *up* in combinations like *add up, pay up, stretch out*; the ever-present desire to vary the expression of an idea doubtless leads to the coining of new combinations, so that instead of *add up* one may say *figure up, foot up, reckon up,* or *sum up*; a desire for rhythmical effect seems at times to account for the making of a trochaic phrase out of the monosyllabic verb, as in *hush up, lead off, look out, slow down,* or perhaps of an iambic if the stress is put on the adverb, as often happens when *look óut* and *slow dówn* are used as exclamations; and, finally, mere linguistic laziness undoubtedly influences many people to use these simpler combinations rather than take the trouble to learn the more highly specialized derivative verbs like *comprehend, corroborate, extinguish.*

The ever-increasing tendency to use verb-adverb combinations in modern speech is resulting in several important changes in the character of the English language. Most obvious is the amazing increase in the number of combinations and uses, as already illustrated, and the resultant forcing of the hearer to depend upon an intimate knowledge of the meanings, since he can no longer trust to differences in forms to make clear the distinctions. One may *get off* a joke by perpetrating it on his friends or by mailing it to a publisher, or one may *get* it *off* his mind by *writing* it *down* and *laying* it *away*. The locution is concise and handy, but it is often, as in this case, slightly ambiguous. Then, again, this growing tendency to combine is increasing the number of synonymous or nearly synonymous combinations which a writer can employ, as illustrated in a statement in Oman's *England before the Norman Conquest* (p. 489) that "the army had not utterly *broken down* the English nation" but "instead it had been itself *broken up.*" One can *buy in* or *buy up* property, and the exact meaning of each combination must be determined by the context or the circumstances accompanying the act of buying. And last of all, but not least in importance, increased use of these verb-adverb combinations is resulting in crowding out of the writer's and speaker's used vocabulary many derivative verbs of more highly specialized meaning, such as *acquiesce* ('give in'), *continue* ('go on'), *quarrel* ('fall out'), *relinquish* ('give up'). In so far as these combinations make for greater versatility and richness in English, they must be deemed acceptable and a gain to the language; but when they are but further evidence of intellectual sluggishness and linguistic laziness, as is unfortunately too often the case, they are to be avoided, and the old well-established and more exact verbs should then be sought out and used.

h. **Verb aspects.** A verb aspect may be defined as one of the ways in which an action or change of condition or state is viewed or contemplated. It is only recently that grammarians have been attempting to contemplate in more exact ways the action or change of condition or state expressed by English verbs, and there is still some difference of opinion as to the number of verb aspects in English and the definition and naming of each. Sometimes the aspect of a verb depends upon the peculiar nature of the verb, sometimes on the fact that a specially made phrasal verb is used to show aspect; and often it depends upon the words, particularly the adverbs, that are used with the verb. The most obvious aspects of the English verb are as follows:

The verb has a *terminate* aspect when it simply indicates the action as a whole, without regard to beginning or ending or duration or repetition. So the simple verb has this aspect in 'He *went* to town', 'She *went* blind.'

The verb has an *ingressive* aspect when it points to the beginning of an action, as in 'He *began to work*', 'The mill *ran at last*', 'He *took possession* of the house', and 'She *fell to weeping*.'

The verb has, on the contrary, an *effective* or *conclusive* aspect when it implies the ending or completion of an action, as in 'My watch *suddenly stopped*', 'She *ceased speaking*' and 'The rumor *turned out* false.'

The aspect of the verb is called *durative* when the action is presented as continuous. Statements of general truth have verbs of this aspect, as in 'Wheat *grows* in Canada', 'Steel *is harder* than lead.' The so-called progressive phrasal verb is usually durative in aspect, as in

'He *is walking* along the street', 'He *was sowing* wheat all last week.' The simple verb may become durative when some adverbial modifier helps to indicate the continuity, as in 'The mill *ran all summer long.*'

The aspect of the verb becomes *iterative* when repeated action is indicated, as in '*Every day* he *went* to the office', '*Each night* the old man *would walk* slowly to town.'

It is hardly necessary to remind the reader that so much depends upon the words and phrases accompanying the verb that many verbs can scarcely be said to possess aspect independently. In 'He *ran* the mile yesterday' the aspect is terminate; in 'It *runs* at last' the aspect is ingressive; in 'My watch *has run* down' the aspect is effective; in 'The mill *runs* day and night' the durative aspect is present; but in 'It *ran* intermittently' the iterative aspect is indicated.

The main excuse for introducing the study of aspect here lies in the interesting fact that English actually possesses a phrasal verb of progression quite different from anything found in most other languages (see Sec. 106). To this might be added the excuse that recently the fashion of classifying English verbs has been passing into a new phase. At the beginning of the nineteenth century the chief grammarians, such as Noah Webster and Lindley Murray, classified verbs as "active, passive, and neuter", meaning by "neuter" verbs of being or state of being. A half-century later grammarians like Harvey and Reed and Kellogg presented them as words that "assert action, being, or state of being", and in accordance with this practice an attempt has been made in the beginning of this section on verbs to distinguish three such groups. But in 1923, when Malone protested that "the distinction between act and state seems unsatisfactory", he went on to suggest a reclassification according to the various aspects of action;[270] and now the recently compiled grammars of English are devoting more space to this phase of the study of verbs. Consequently it has seemed advisable to begin this classification of verbs from the older point of view and conclude it from the more recent one. Each is useful, and neither is quite conclusive.

54. *Adverbs*

The adverb has already been described as modifying verbs, adjectives, and other adverbs; it might be further characterized as showing place, time, manner, degree, and so on; and, finally, it often answers the questions Where? When? How? How much? and Why? To a marked degree the ending *-ly* has become the adverbial suffix in English, as in *directly, naturally*; in a few adverbs the old endings *-ward, -wards, -wise*, and the genitive ending *-s* have survived, as in *downward* (or *downwards*), *upward* (or *upwards*), *crosswise*, and *always, nowadays*. Moreover, there are numerous amalgamated phrases in common use, such as *aboard* ('on board'), *adrift, aloft, astray*. But many of the older native adverbs have no such distinguishing endings or forms and must be recognized through their meanings and syntactical use in the sentence. Occasionally such an adverb is facetiously or confusedly given the *-ly* ending, as in *illy, muchly, overly, thusly*.

a. **Adverbs of place and direction.** *Aboard, aft, alongside, back, backward, below, far, farther, here, hither, north, southwest, thence, there, thither, upstairs, where, wherever, yonder.* Many of the prepositions can be used as adverbs, particularly *about, across, around, by, down, in, off, on, out, over, through, under, underneath,* and *up*.

b. **Adverbs of time, succession, and distribution.** *Afterward, again, always, anon, by and by, early, eventually, ever, finally, hitherto, late, lately, never, now, often, since, sometime, soon, still, then, today, until, when, whenever, yet.* The numeral multiplicatives *once, twice, thrice,* etc., the ordinals *first* (*firstly*), *secondly, thirdly, fourthly,* etc., and the distributives *one by one, two by two, by tens,* etc. are adverbs of this class. Other distributive adverbs are *individually, jointly, respectively, separately, severally,* although these sometimes appear to be almost adverbs of manner rather than of time.

c. **Adverbs of manner.** These are by far the most numerous of the adverbs, largely because they can be made from adjectives simply by adding *-ly*. The more common examples of the older native adverbs of manner are *alike, anyhow, as,* *astride, how, so, somehow, thus, well, worse.* Many are formed with *-ly,* such as *badly, brightly, dully, gracefully, keenly, miserably, nicely, openly, suddenly,* and a few with other suffixes, such as *headlong, lengthwise, likewise, piecemeal,* and *unawares.* Participles can be made into adverbs likewise, as in *chokingly, devastatingly, heatedly, pointedly,* and even compound adjectives made with *-ed,* as in *single-handedly, whole-heartedly.* Some adverbs have the same forms as adjectives, particularly *better, hard, late, right, straight, well, worse, wrong,* and some have both forms, as, for example, *hard (hardly), loud (loudly);* and because of this there is confusion and difference of opinion about the use of such forms. This is true of some others in such sentences as 'Drive *slow*', 'He paid *dear* for it', 'Come *quick*', 'He's doing *fine*', 'It's running *good*', 'He did *noble*', 'It will open *easy.*' The context often determines the usage.

d. **Adverbs of degree and measure.** Among the common simple adverbs of degree and measure are *about, all, almost, altogether, how much, less, little, much, quite, so, somewhat, too, too much, very,* and the colloquial or dialectal *real* and *right,* as in *real good, right well.* Those made with *-ly* are fairly numerous, notably *barely, completely, entirely, equally, exceedingly, extremely, greatly, hardly, nearly, partly, scarcely, thoroughly.* Some adverbs of manner have been so weakened by exaggeration in colloquial English that they have become mere intensifying adverbs, particularly *awfully, badly, dreadfully, horribly,* and *terribly.* Sometimes degree is expressed for an adjective by prefixing a noun or other adjective, as in *brick-red, dead-tired, dirt-cheap, dog-cheap, grass-green, pitch-dark,* and *stone-dead.* The colloquial use of *kind of* and *sort of* as adverbs of degree, as in '*kind of* funny,' '*sort of* stupid,' is of doubtful propriety.

e. **Adverbs of cause.** Simple adverbs of cause are not numerous, since cause is usually expressed by an adverbial clause. But there are a few, such as *because, consequently, hence, therefore, wherefore,* and *why.*

f. **Adverbs of assertion.** A number of adverbs assist in assertion through affirmation or negation or the indication of probability or doubt. They are sometimes called modal adverbs, because they contribute to the manner of assertion. The most commonly used are *assuredly, certainly, doubtless, indeed, not, perhaps, possibly, probably, really, surely, truly, undoubtedly,* and *yes* and *no.* The adverbs *aye, nay,* and *yea* are archaic. The use of *likely* instead of *probably* is colloquial. The use of *sure* instead of *surely* is still avoided by careful speakers, as dialectal or slang, even though the use of it has become very general in the last few years. Speakers of the best English do not say, 'I *sure* did enjoy it.' Beside the standard forms *yes* and *no* various other colloquial forms exist which resemble interjections in the way they are used, which the dictionaries sometimes call adverbial particles, and which are usually explained as the equivalents of entire sentences. Popular substitutes for *yes* are the colloquial *all right, O.K.* (or *okay, okeh*), *uh-huh, yah, you bet*; and for *no* may be heard *nix, nixy, no sirree, unh-unh,* and the like.

g. **Introductory and parenthetical adverbs.** A few adverbs are used mainly to introduce clauses or sentences, particularly *accordingly, anyhow, consequently, furthermore, however, indeed, likewise, moreover, nevertheless, still,* and *yet.* Since these are in reality a loose kind of illative conjunction, they will be discussed somewhat more fully below (see Sec. 56, *c*).

A smaller number of adverbs, notably *as, especially, namely, notably, particularly, scilicet, (sc.* or *scil.), specifically,* and *videlicet (viz.),* are used as introducing or specifying words, as in this sentence (see page 482).

Of course the classifications just given are not final in every instance. The adverb of place *about* expresses degree in '*about* finished'; the adverb of time *immediately* also expresses degree in '*immediately* behind'; the adverbs of manner *hard* and *thoroughly* are degree adverbs in '*hard* by' and '*thoroughly* wet'; and *assuredly* is an adverb of assertion when one replies, 'Most *assuredly* I will come,' but an adverb of manner in 'He spoke *assuredly.*' *Truly* is an adverb of manner when it modifies a verb, but an adverb of assertion when it belongs to the entire sentence.

55. *Prepositions*

Prepositions join their objects normally to preceding words, especially nouns and verbs. But they also show relationship of some sort between their objects and the preceding words just mentioned. If one says 'a house and a mill', he merely connects two nouns; but if one says 'a house *above* the mill', he at least establishes a relationship of position between the two buildings. As prepositions have in various instances evolved from other parts of speech, it will be helpful to arrange them in at least four different classes according to their primitiveness.

a. **Primary prepositions.** Among the oldest and simplest prepositions of English are *after, at, by, down, for, from, in, of, off, on, over, since, through, till, to, under, up,* and *with.* Most of these can be used also as adverbs or in the verb-adverb combinations. *But* is also a preposition in constructions where it is followed by an objective case and has the meaning of 'except' (see page 539).

b. **Compound prepositions.** Some compound prepositions are made with *a-*, as *aboard, about, above, across, amid, around,* and the archaic *anent*; others are formed with *be-*, as *before, behind, below, beside, between, beyond.* Other compound prepositions are *despite, into, throughout, toward(s), until, unto, upon, within,* and *without.* While phrases like *in by, down through, down on,* and *up to* are not written as single words, they function in much the same way that *into* and *upon* do.

c. **Secondary prepositions.** These are largely participial forms that have lost their verbal force. The most common are *barring, concerning, considering, during, except* and *excepting, including, notwithstanding, past, pending, regarding, respecting, saving* (and *save*), *touching,* and the Latin *versus.* While *like* is generally considered a preposition in such constructions as 'Acquit yourselves *like* men', it was in earlier English an adjective or an adverb; and it causes some trouble today because speakers use it as a conjunction, a use alien to it in earlier times.

d. **Phrasal prepositions.** It is often better to treat a prepositional group, such as *by reason of,* as a prepositional unit, particularly when it equals another already recognized, such as *because of*, than to attempt to analyze it carefully into its component elements. Phrasal prepositions of this sort are *according to, apart from, as far as, as for, as regards, by dint of, by means of, contingent upon, for the sake of, in accordance with, in addition to, in case of, in compliance with, in lieu of, in opposition to, inside, in spite of, on account of, out of, outside, owing to, with reference to, with regard to.* In the phraseology of the law, political procedure, and business such prepositions are frequent, as, for example, *by virtue of, in consideration of, with reference to.* The phrase *in terms of* is widely and carelessly used. Many Americans are using *due to* as a preposition, as in '*Due to* his illness he could not come'; but careful users of good English still insist upon keeping *due* an adjective, as in 'His illness was *due* to carelessness'.*

The phrasal preposition *in back of* seems to be gradually winning acceptance as a colloquial idiom, possibly because of its resemblance to such phrases as *in front of, on top of, at the bottom of.* The shortened form *back of* is used colloquially as the equivalent of *behind.*

The Latin noun *via* in the ablative case has become a simple preposition in English but has the meaning of a phrase, 'by way of'. The Latin preposition *per* is used mainly in scientific and commercial language.

The use of the preposition *up* in certain phrases is strongly colloquial or slangy: in 'It's *up to* you' the meaning is 'incumbent upon' or 'dependent upon'; in 'What is the child *up to* now?' the phrase very often means 'doing mischievously'; in *up against* the meaning is 'confronted with'.

56. *Conjunctions*

Conjunctions connect words, phrases, or clauses; but they are more than mere connectives, usually, and it is this additional value which necessitates their separation into several classes.

* See "The Dangling Participle *Due*", in *American Speech*, Vol. 6 (1930), pp. 61–70.

310   THE CLASSIFICATION OF WORDS   [Chap. VIII

a. **Coördinating conjunctions.** By means of these conjunctions, words, phrases, or clauses are coördinated: *and* merely connects; *or* and *nor* indicate alternation; *but*, contrast; and *for*, cause. All but the last can be used, with the aid of certain other words, to correlate more closely coördinate pairs of words, phrases, or clauses; these correlative conjunctions are *both . . . and, either . . . or, neither . . . nor*, various combinations with *but*, such as *not only . . . but also*, and a few other similar constructions.

b. **Subordinating conjunctions.** These connectives always introduce clauses subordinate to the rest of the sentence. Some of them have already been classified as adverbs, but some of them never function other than as connectives. The most important groups are employed as follows:

To introduce a substantive clause: *that, what, whatever*. (See the remark below on the conjunctival use of the relative pronouns.)

To introduce a causal clause: *because, inasmuch as, since, why*. (For the classification of *why* as a conjunction see the remark below on relative adverbs.)

To indicate purpose: *that, so that, in order that*, and the negative *lest*.

For comparison: *than, as, as if, as well as, as . . . as*, and *so . . . as* (with negatives). (See also below.)

To introduce a condition: *if, unless, whether, in case that, provided (that), providing, on condition that, in the event that*, and the correlative *whether . . . or* (see page 541).

To express result: *that, so that, so . . . that*.

To introduce a temporal (time) clause: *after, as long as, as soon as, before, ere, since, when, whenever, while*.

To indicate concession: *although, though*, and the correlative *though . . . yet*.

To indicate place and direction: *where, wherever, whence, whither*.

To indicate manner and hypothetical comparison or concession: *how, however, as if, as though*.

To indicate degree and extent: *as far as, as much as, as little as, as few as*.

To introduce an adjectival clause: the relative pronouns *who, which, that, whoever, whichever, as*.

To introduce an adjectival clause immediately after a preposition, the compound relative adverbs, such as *wherein* ('in which'), *whereby* ('by which'), *whereupon* ('upon which'), *whereof* ('of whom', 'of which'), are substituted for a relative pronoun and a preposition governing it.

There is no difficulty involved in the conjunctival use of the relative pronouns, since they normally function as both parts of speech at once; the trouble comes when connectives are employed which may ordinarily be simple interrogative adverbs, like *how, when, whence, where, whither, why,* or simply prepositions, like *after, as, as far as, before, since, till, until.* All of these connecting words which can be employed as adverbs also are generally called relative adverbs. Occasionally the simple adverbial modifiers *once, directly, immediately,* are used as conjunctions, as in the sentence '*Directly* he arrives, I will leave.' Sometimes nouns indicating periods of time are also used as temporal conjunctions, as in '*The day* he comes, I will go' or '*The moment* he sails, I will notify you.'

c. **Illative conjunctions.** There is a form of thought connection which is not usually recognized as a grammatical construction but rather as a feature of rhetorical art, because the words used to make the connection do not tie together words, phrases, and clauses within a sentence, as do the conjunctions already discussed, but they bind together various separate sentences into those larger units known as paragraphs. These conjunctions are called illative because they carry on the train of thought by introducing inferences drawn from other thoughts already expressed in foregoing sentences. The chief illatives are *accordingly, anyhow, anyway* (colloquial), *besides, furthermore, hence, however, indeed, likewise, moreover, nevertheless, still, then, therefore, wherefore,* and *yet.* Most of these illative conjunctions have already been classified as introductory adverbs; but it must be recognized also that they help to join sentences in a grammatically loose fashion by implying that inferences have been drawn. A number of adverbial phrases are also commonly used as illatives, especially *at any rate, at the same time, in like manner, in other words, in short, on the contrary, on the other hand, then again.*

When writers attempt to use in this same loose fashion at the beginning of sentences other conjunctions listed above in *a* or *b*, such as *and, because, but, or, since, so that, which,* many grammarians protest. But it is sometimes a temptation to carry on a train of thought in this way, and Sweet has recognized the practice by naming them "detached" conjunctions and citing writers, like Shelley, who have used them thus loosely.

57. *Interjections*

Interjections are exclamations. While they are all characterized by a certain amount of emotion or feeling, it must not be assumed that they are always so utterly devoid of idea or thought as to be absolutely distinct from the other seven parts of speech. Sudden and strong emotion may evoke simple sounds like *ah* and *oh* and *ouch*, or it may merely raise to a higher emotional plane words that are not originally exclamations at all, such as *help* and *horrors*. On the other hand, mild exclamations like *good night* and *hello* generally possess more thought content than emotion or feeling. The test of function in the case of interjections is primarily that of emotion or feeling; nevertheless the exclaiming of words when the emotional content is not especially marked also constitutes them a form of interjection. So in the following groups of interjections an attempt has been made to arrange them in a descending scale of emotional importance.

a. **Primitive emotional interjections.** Many sounds which are not recognized as standard English words are used to express the emotions, while others have long had a place in the dictionaries. Hills has gathered an extensive and varied collection from contemporary American usage, such as *ah, aw, bah, boo, ha, heigh, hoohoo, humph, hush, oh, ouch, pooh, pshaw, ugh, wow*.[282] A few, such as *fie, heigho, la,* and *lo*, are archaic today, although *la* probably lives on in the dialectal *law* and *lawsy*. The different vowel sounds are made to express different feelings, — surprise, pleasure, sorrow, contempt, disgust, pain, and so on. Often the *h* sound is produced with the vowels through the excessive use of breath incidental to exclaiming, and the labials *f, p,* and *w* are also commonly used with the vowels.

But individual speakers differ in their preferences, and consequently these primitive interjections do not have the general acceptance in language that the other parts of speech have. Yet they are so spontaneous and have been used so long in all languages that a theory has been evolved by some historians of language that man's first speech consisted solely of such interjections.

b. **Secondary emotional interjections.** Other parts of speech are sometimes converted into interjections under strong emotional stress. This is true especially of *bravo, fire, good, help, horrors, murder, nonsense, shame,* and *splendid,* as well as some less dignified interjections commonly used by audiences at baseball games, by rooters at football games, and the like. The literary exclamation *alas* once meant 'ah, wretched me (or one)'. In modern slang usage *yes* is pronounced *yeah,* and with an inflection of the voice that implies scorn or doubt. Sometimes the same effect is produced with *no.*

c. **Imperative interjections.** The imperative form of the verb is often converted into an interjection, especially *behold, bless us, hurry up, look, look out, stop,* and the slang exclamations *beat it,* 'depart', *skiddoo,* 'depart', *step on it,* 'hurry', and the like.

d. **Exclamatory and courteous phrases.** Many colloquial and dialectal expressions and sentences are used in exclamation, such as *amen, dear me, do tell, good gosh, goodness gracious, great guns, holy smoke, I declare, I want to know, what do you know about that, you don't say.* The British *I say* is usually shortened to *say* in American usage. Of the terms of courtesy the most common are *excuse me, forgive me, pardon me, please,* for the older 'If it please you', *sorry* (British), *thanks* and *thank you* and (recently) *thanks a lot,* and *you're welcome.* The phrases which depend upon emotions or feelings almost never become standard literary English, but, like the other interjections already discussed, are very common and varied in colloquial English. The expressions of courtesy are naturally of a higher order.

e. **Oaths and imprecations.** An oath, says the dictionary, is "a solemn attestation in support of a declaration or a promise, by an appeal to God or to some person or thing regarded as high and holy"; but it is also defined as "a frivolous and blasphemous use of the name of the Deity or of any sacred name or object, as in appeal or ejaculation".[27] It is the frivolous abuse of the "solemn attestation" which has resulted in so great a number and variety of oaths in English, and consequently in a frequent protest against their use. As Chaucer's pilgrims made their imaginary journey down to Canterbury, notwithstanding the sacred goal of their journey they thoughtlessly invoked most of the saints of the calendar; they swore by Christ and his body and his wounds until the irreverent Host's "For God's bones" and "By God's dignity" drove the earnest Parson to protest, "What aileth the man so sinfully to swear?" Three centuries later Uncle Toby remarked in *Tristram Shandy*, "Our armies swore terribly in Flanders, but nothing to this." Since Chaucer's day the kinds of oaths that so shocked the good Parson have largely disappeared from English usage, just as the many saints themselves are no longer generally familiar to English and American speakers. But three kinds of oaths still persist: one, the thoroughly blasphemous use of the deity names *God, Jesus, Christ*; another, the very general use of euphemistic substitutes by people not willing to indulge in unrestrained profanity but nevertheless in need of mild oaths of some kind; and the third, a more imaginative but more faddish indulgence in curious rhetorical inventions which, like other varieties of slang, live out their day and then pass out of use.

In place of the more blasphemous forms of oaths, various conventional substitutes have developed and persisted in popular usage: for 'God' the expressions *by gad, by golly, by gum, by Jove*, the older *pardie* (from French *par dieu*), and *zounds* (for 'God's wounds'); for 'Jesus' the shortened *gee* and *jeeze*, and the longer *Jerusalem, gee whillikins, gee whizz*; for 'Christ' *cripes, jiminy Christmas, for crying out loud*; for 'Lord' *lor, lawdy, law sakes*, and the archaic *lud*; and so on. Though the words *damn, devil*, and *hell* are not technically profane oaths, since they do not name the Deity, they have long been felt to be in the same general category, and consequently milder substitutes have been employed for them too, such as *I'll be blamed, bless me, I'll be blowed,* and *darn* for 'damn'; *the deuce* and *the dickens* for 'the devil'; and for 'hell' *hades, Helen Maria, go to Halifax, Oh heck,* and the like.

The fad for exclamatory inventions of a striking or flamboyant kind dates back at least as far as the period of Elizabethan drama. Swaen has cited from the literature of that time such oaths as *by the foot of Pharaoh, by my matins cheese, by the arms of Robin Hood, by this air*; [281] and the fashion has persisted in the use by individuals here and there of certain favorite interjections, such as *by the great horn spoon, jumping Jehoshaphat, not on your tintype, sizzling Susan,* and the more recently popular *hot dog.*

f. **Animal calls.** A phase of human speech which differs from ordinary standard English because its purpose differs from that of ordinary communication between human beings is the language of man to his domestic animals. Bolton has remarked [280]:

The driver who stops his horses by crying *whoa!*; the teamster who directs his oxen to the right or to the left by the terms *gee* and *haw*; the farmer's lad who calls the scattered cattle *boss, boss, come boss*, or the timid sheep with the musical *ko-nanny, ko-nanny,* and the grunting hogs with the prolonged *chēē-ōō-ōō*; the playful child who calls her pet *puss, puss,* and drives it away with *scat!*; the farmer's wife who calls to feed the peeping chickens and clucking hens with *coo-chee, coo-chee,* afford familiar illustrations of a language having peculiar characteristics. The words of this language are chiefly monosyllabic and dissyllabic, and are generally repeated in groups of three; although entirely devoid of grammar, consisting exclusively of exclamations and words in the imperative mood, and although, with a few exceptions, the words are omitted by the most comprehensive dictionaries, the language serves as a ready and sufficient means of communication between man and the many races of animals under his subjection. This language has but little in common with that used by the animals themselves. The hen clucks, the duck quacks, the dog says *bow-wow,* the cat *meow,* the horse neighs, the ass brays, and the sheep cries *baa*; but man, in responding, does not confine himself to imitations of these dialects of the several races; he forces upon them original sounds better adapted to his own vocal organs, and by constant repetition compels their comprehension.

So one says also to the horse *giddap* ('get up'), to the dog *sickem* ('seek him (or them)'), to the restless cow *soh boss,* and one gives orders to other animals in other ways.

g. **Exclamations of greeting and farewell.** These words of salutation usually exemplify still in some measure the original meaning of the word *salutation,* namely, wishing someone good health, prosperity, and happiness. Those that are used upon meeting are either, like *hello, hullo,* and their older form, *halloo, ship ahoy,* and the more elementary *heigh* or *hey,* merely intended to attract attention, or else expressions of good will like *welcome* and inquiries concerning the health of the newcomer, such as *howdy* (for 'how do you do?') and *how are you, how goes it,* whereas the interjections used at parting are mostly expressions of good wishes, such as *farewell* ('may you fare well'), *good-by* ('God be with you'), and the borrowed French *adieu* (meaning 'I commend you to God'). "These words," says the Century Dictionary, "have completely lost their original meanings." Much the same thing could be said today of the colloquial *so long* and *see you later,* which sounds like an American paraphrase of German *auf Wiedersehen* and French *au revoir.* Five common interjections, *good morning, good evening, good day, good night,* and *good afternoon,* are a peculiarly ambiguous group in Current English; they are variously used, some to persons coming and some to those departing, but with some very fine distinctions about which English speakers do not altogether agree. The Biblical and religious *amen* has persisted in a limited way; but sometimes it is used in a broader way today as an indication of hearty approval, as in 'I'll say *amen* to that.'

58. *Conversion and Confusion of the Parts of Speech*

One of the chief results of the foregoing attempt at a systematic classification of the eight parts of speech and their various subdivisions should be a realization that all words do not lend themselves at all times to clear-cut distinctions.

Words shift from one part of speech to another by the process of conversion; at times a word becomes a sort of hybrid, functioning as two different parts of speech at the same time and fusing them together; and sometimes a word is so utilized that this fusion or confusion produces uncertainty in the mind of the speaker or writer. Numerous examples have been given in the previous discussions in this chapter which should have called attention to the frequent conversions and confusions of the parts of speech in Current English; but the process of conversion has become so important a characteristic of English, as already remarked (p. 119), that further discussion and summarizing of the matter seem worth while.

When Sweet used the word *conversion* in his *New English Grammar* in 1892, he was one of the first grammarians to employ the term in its more restricted grammatical sense and perhaps one of the first to revolt against a tendency to put every word into a hard-and-fast classification as a part of speech. Since that time there has been a more general recognition of the shifting character of the Modern English parts of speech and of the almost puzzling flexibility that this one characteristic of Current English gives to the language. Consequently it is hardly possible to lay too much stress on the subject or to spend too much time in grouping its various manifestations in present-day English.

A. Conversion

Conversion has already been defined as "a shift from one part of speech to another." But this functional change has also been observed in a shift from one kind of noun to another, or one kind of verb to another, or one kind of adverb to another, and it seems logical to regard conversion as functional change not only between the parts of speech but also within each part of speech. It should be insisted also that conversion and derivational change are two distinct processes; derivational change by the use of prefixes and suffixes shifts words between the parts of speech, and also within each, by producing different forms, as, for example, the adjective *wide*, the noun *width*, and the verb *widen*, whereas conversion makes no change in the form of a word but only in its general functions. And, finally, it is necessary to recognize various stages of conversion; in 'The *poor* are with us always' the adjective is not completely converted into a noun, but in 'He sold his *goods* finally' the adjectival value of *good* has disappeared so completely that the word can take the plural ending *-s* like any other noun. When a word has changed its function to such an extent that it is capable of taking on new inflectional endings, then the process of conversion may be considered complete. Moreover, conversion may be regarded as complete when a word has been substantivized to the point where it can be modified by adjectives, as in *the others, a lunatic, good reading*; or verbalized to the point where it can be modified by adverbs, as in *telephone soon, motor often*.

a. Interchange of nouns and verbs in Current English is so common a form of conversion, as in *a run* and *to run, a try* and *to try*, 'to make *a go* of it' and *to go*, that further discussion should be unnecessary.

b. The substantivation of adjectives has always been an important process in English and is active today. Some of the earlier substantivations have been so long established as nouns that English-speakers no longer realize that they ever were adjectives; in many instances, however, the substantival use of the adjective is only temporary, and as soon as the need is past, the word reverts to its usual adjectival function. Three ways have been suggested by which adjectives become nouns: the adjective is adopted for the name of the thing itself because it indicates some especially striking quality of the thing, as *blacks*, 'black people', *gold*, 'the yellow metal', *shorts*, 'short pants', *wheat*, 'the white grain'; or the modified noun is dropped, and the adjective then functions as noun, as in *the Almighty (God), the good (people), in high (gear)*; or the adjective may become an abstract noun naming a quality which it already indicated as an adjective, as *evil, good, for better or worse*.

There are two stages in the substantivation of adjectives: the more complete, when the word can be declined like any other noun; and the less complete, when declension is not yet possible. The most advanced stage has been reached by the old native or borrowed adjectives in *aliens, the ancients, belles, the commons, elders, goods, innocents, negro spirituals, nobles, pagans, privates, a quarterly, the ritual, sides* (early meaning as adjective 'wide'), and *toughs*. All the collective names like *American, Asiatic, Bostonian,* and *Chinese* are substantivized proper adjectives. Many older participles are today nouns, such as *a compact, the deceased, a drunk, dugout, fact, fiend, friend, a grown-up, The Illustrated, her intended, leftovers, Occident, Orient,* and *primate*. Sometimes even the compound adjectives are so completely substantivized as to be capable of declension, as, for instance, *Black and Tans, handmades, two-year-olds*.

Adjectives are usually still in the indeclinable stage when they become collective nouns like *the aged, the dead, the halt and the blind, the infirm, rich and poor, the wealthy, young and old*.

English avoids substantivation very often by placing after the adjective the so-called prop word *one*. So we say 'a *good one*', 'the *best ones*', 'He's a *clever one*'; and we also avoid the repetition of a noun with two adjectives, in the same manner, using such expressions as 'an *old* business and a *sound one*', 'a *new* bank but a *large one*'.

c. The interchange of concrete, abstract, and collective nouns, such as *battery, circle,* and *shaving,* has already been commented upon. The verbal nouns in *-ing* often take the plural *-s* ending when they become concrete, as in *earnings, filings, findings, shavings, sweepings*.

d. The verbal noun in *-ing,* often known as the gerund, is sometimes confused with the verbal adjective, known as the participle. Ordinarily there is no real reason for confusion when the gerund is used in nominative constructions, as in '*Seeing* is *believing*'; but in objective constructions, after a verb or a preposition, there is often a fusion of adjectival (participial) and nominal (gerundial) functions which causes uncertainty regarding both the proper classification of these *-ing* words and the correct syntactical uses of them. Indeed, it is necessary to view the gerund from both the classificational and the syntactical points of view if there is to be any general agreement about its nature and use, inasmuch as syntactical usage generally determines the classification of these *-ing* words. In some sentences the nominal function is clearly apparent, in others the adjectival; but between these two extremes of relative certainty lie numerous constructions which cannot be so definitely classified, as can be observed in the following progressive series:

'Excessive *speeding* on this highway is severely punished.' *Speeding* is a gerund used as subject of the verb.

'He sought to check his *son's speeding*.' *Speeding* is unquestionably a gerund used as object of the infinitive. It has a genitival modifier (or subject), *son's,* and this fact helps to identify it as a gerund.

'I saw *them speeding* along the highway.' In this sentence *speeding* may be classed as a gerund on the ground that it is used with the subject accusative *them*, just as the infinitive *speed* is used in 'I saw *them speed* along the highway'; but grammarians have generally considered it a participle modifying *them*.

'He held up a hand *trembling* with age.' *Trembling* is certainly an adjectival modifier of *hand*, and hence participial.

This unfortunate confusion of the *-ing* verbals has arisen, in the first place, because the distinctive endings of the Anglo-Saxon verbal noun (*-ung*) and the participle (*-ende*) have become merged in the *-ing*, and, in the second place, because the verbal function of each has become more and more important, sometimes almost crowding out their earlier, more purely nominal and adjectival functions. (See also Secs. 102, p. 514, and 107, p. 531.)

e. Commonization is merely the process of making a common noun (or a verb or a common adjective) out of a proper noun (name). Since it has added largely to the English vocabulary, it will be considered in detail later (Sec. 67). But it is too important a phase of conversion to be entirely passed over in this present survey. At first some familiar name of history or literature is used figuratively, and a man is called a gay *Lothario*, a *Shylock* of greed, or a *Solomon* of wisdom. If the idea needs frequent expression, the term becomes more and more common, until we find embedded in the English vocabulary such words as *a guy* (from *Guy Fawkes*), *to hector, a jehu*, or *maudlin* (from *Magdalen*). So place-names likewise yield common nouns, giving, for example, *buncombe*, spelled also *bunkum* (from *Buncombe County*, North Carolina), *currants* (from *Corinth*), *wienies* (from German *Wien*, English *Vienna*).

f. When the relative and interrogative pronouns *which* and *what*, the demonstratives *this, that, yon*, and *yonder*, and various indefinites like *many, some*, and *each* are used as modifiers of nouns, the conversion may be regarded as complete and the term *pronominal adjective* an appropriate one. They are pronouns when they stand in place of nouns, and adjectives when they modify nouns, and it is always possible to distinguish clearly between the two functions.

g. The varying use of *who, which*, and *what* as relatives introducing subordinate clauses, as in 'I saw the man *who* brought it', and as interrogatives introducing questions, as in '*Who* brought it?', may well be considered in a discussion of conversion, since their functional shift changes their pronominal classification.

h. The same thing may be said of those compound pronouns like *myself* and *themselves* which function as intensives when they follow in apposition, as in 'I *myself* will go' or 'I will go *myself*', but as reflexives when they become the objects of verbs, as in 'They have hurt *themselves*.' While the change in use is largely a syntactical one, that is to say, a change in sentence construction, yet there is a general functional distinction between emphasis or intensification, on the one hand, and the reflexive use, on the other, which merely indicates that the object refers to the same person or persons as the subject.

i. When the same form is used for both adjective and adverb, as in the case of *better, high, low, right, well,* and *wrong,* only the function of the word determines which part of speech it is. So the adjective of 'He looks *well*' is converted into an adverb of manner in 'He sings *well.*'

j. The auxiliary verbs *be, have, do,* and *will* can be converted into notional verbs by a simple change of construction. As long as they are used with verbal forms, as in *be going, have finished, do wish, will come,* they are auxiliary, or helping, verbs; but when they are used with nouns, pronouns, adjectives, or adverbs, as in *be sick, be away, have need, do well,* and *will a thing,* they become notional verbs.

k. Active verbs are converted into passives when they are used in such a manner as to indicate that the subject is really acted upon, as in 'How *did* it *clean*?' and 'It *dyes* beautifully.'

l. When a preposition such as *about, by, down, in, on,* or *over* has an object, as in '*in* the box', its prepositional status is unquestioned; but when it has no object, as in 'Come *in*', it is certainly an adverb. General change of function is not so clearly the cause of conversion in these words as the very simple syntactical change involved in the mere addition of an object or omission of it.

m. The gradual conversion of adverbs of manner like *awfully, likewise, simply,* and *surely* into adverbs of degree or of assertion is a fairly common process in English. From the careful use of the word *simply* as an adverb of manner in 'He spoke *simply* and clearly' it is but a step to the colloquial use of it to show degree of intensity in 'He was *simply* wild.' But it is well to bear in mind that this simple step sometimes carries a speaker from good literary English over into the realm of questionable colloquial speech, as in the illative use of *anyway* in '*Anyway* he didn't get it' (see Krapp [17], p. 46).

n. Several conjunctions become prepositions when they are followed by objects instead of clauses or other coördinate constructions. Some grammarians call the coördinating conjunction *but* a preposition in 'I saw no one *but* his father', although others consider it still a conjunction (see page 539): certainly *for* is a preposition in 'tea *for* seven'. Likewise the subordinating conjunctions *after, as far as, before, ere, since,* and *until* become prepositions in such constructions as *after dark, before night,* and *until noon.* It is this interchangeable character of these words, no doubt, that is responsible for the objectionable use of the prepositions *except, like,* and *without* as conjunctions in such sentences as 'Don't take it *except (unless)* I give you permission', 'He plays *like (as)* I do', and 'He couldn't come *without (unless)* I brought him'.

B. Confusion of the Parts of Speech

Some groups of words never change their functions so completely that the process of conversion drives out altogether one function, to make room for another. So they are really hybrid parts of speech, fusing together or confusing two different functions.[286]

a. The possessive, or genitive, forms of nouns and pronouns regularly function as adjective modifiers, as in '*Smith's* house', 'one *man's* interests', and '*my* notebook'; but they always retain the distinguishing characteristics of nouns and pronouns. The very fact that *one* modifies *man's* is evidence that *man's* is a noun, since an adjective does not normally modify another adjective; the fact that *my* has within itself the properties of person and number seems to warrant classing it with the pronouns, since adjectives do not normally possess either property. Since, however, possessive pronouns are used only as adjective modifiers, as already remarked (see page 293), and the fusing or confusing of pronominal properties and adjective functions is so complete, it is not illogical to call them either possessive pronouns or possessive adjectives. Indeed, the very fact that grammarians use these terms so interchangeably attests the hybrid state of these forms.

b. Participles are sometimes used after verbs in such a manner as to leave one with the impression that they describe the subjects of the verbs in adjectival fashion and at the same time show the manner of the action as adverbial modifiers of the verbs. So in 'A tiny stream went *babbling* down the valley' one can insist that it is a *babbling stream* or else that *babbling* tells how it ran. But is it necessary to decide between the two?

c. The relative pronouns, *who, which, that, what, as*, as in 'He saw the man *that* struck him', and relative adverbs, such as *when, where, why*, as in 'He asked *why* we came', meet the usual tests of pronouns and adverbs but at the same time function as subordinating conjunctions. They are hybrid parts of speech when so used.

d. Sometimes adverbs like *now, then, tomorrow, tonight, here*, and *there* are used as nouns, as in *until now, from here, by tonight*; but it is better to recognize a twofold, or hybrid, functioning of the word than to insist that the adverb becomes purely a noun just because it serves as a noun. When an adverb takes on an inflectional ending of a noun, as in 'the *ups* and *downs* of life' or 'the *whys* and *wherefores* of the matter', or when an adjective modifier is used with it, as in 'just *this once*', '*the wherefore* of it', then it is safer to assume that the adverb has been fully converted into a noun.

Uncertainty as to how the grammarian should regard certain usages or constructions causes serious difficulty in the classifying of some other words. In the practice of diagraming sentences one has often been forced to assume that something is "understood" in order to be able to decide where certain words should be placed in the diagram. That is a weakness of the otherwise helpful process of diagraming; it forces one to make clear-cut distinctions when usage does not bother to make such distinctions. Sometimes it is better to allow speakers and writers of English — or of any language, for that matter — a little latitude and inexactness in their expression of ideas rather than insist upon too exact definition and limitation.

e. There has always been some uncertainty in the minds of grammarians as to whether or not adverbial nouns actually become adverbs. Krapp says, for example, in his *Modern English* (p. 310), that in 'I am going *home*' the word *home* "is to be regarded simply as an adverb". Probably he is right, since the use of the word here does not bring to mind a distinct image of the home but rather indicates general tendency or direction after the usual habit of certain adverbs of place. But in most instances of the adverbial use of nouns to express space and time the noun remains definitely a name word, as in 'He came *last Wednesday*', 'Step *this way*', 'I go *every year*', 'It cost *two dollars*'; that is to say, the test of the noun is its ability to have an adjective modifier, such as *last* or *every*. There is a strong colloquial tendency to use various other nouns as adverbs of place, as in 'to go *places*', 'to go *the upper road*', 'to come *the short way*'; but the more careful speaker usually prefers to insert a preposition and make an adverbial phrase, as in 'to go *by the upper road*'.

f. There is also confusion in the classification of the so-called double pronoun *what*, as already suggested, and of double adverbs like *when, where, whither, why*, when, in the capacity of relative pronoun and relative adverbs, they introduce subordinate clauses. In the sentences 'I did not learn *what* he wanted', 'I saw *where* the box had stood', and 'I know *when* he came', one may say, as some grammarians have said, that these words are really "double" because antecedents are "understood", so that *what* = *that which, where* = *the place in which*, and *when* = *the time at which*; or, as other grammarians have insisted, one may argue that these words are interrogatives and that questions are implied, such as '*What* did he want?', '*Where* did the box stand?', and '*When* did he come?' It is more likely that speakers are not conscious of either possibility but are fusing the two functions into a hybrid construction not readily analyzable.

g. Adjectives such as *large, round, tall, white*, are normally descriptive; but when one undertakes to point out an object by saying, 'I mean the *tall* building', he limits by means of description, so that he unconsciously employs the adjective in two different functions at the same time. Likewise, when one says of an active business man, 'He is *thé* man in the office', one implies more by the simple article *the* than mere limitation.

h. Adjectives sometimes assume adverbial functions while continuing to describe adjectivally, when they follow verbs which can be regarded as either complete or linking, as in 'Hope springs *eternal* in the human breast', 'The day dawned *bright* and *clear*', 'He stood *straight* and *fearless* before his accusers', 'The child went away *happy.*' There is poetical economy in being able to say in this concise manner that 'Hope is eternal' and 'It springs eternally.'

i. Since for centuries certain participles have been functioning as prepositions, forming what we now call secondary prepositions, such as *concerning, except,* and *respecting,* there is likely to be at times serious doubt as to whether the word shall be classed as preposition or as participle still. In the sentence 'He had doubts *respecting* the man' the word is prepositional; but in '*Respecting* the man as he did, he could not very well doubt his veracity', it is unquestionably participial. In like manner some of the phrasal prepositions like *contrary to, in view of,* and *owing to* very easily cease to be prepositional entities when used as in 'It was *owing to* his bravery' and 'It is *contrary to* our practice', where *owing* and *contrary* are merely adjectival, and in 'He worked in plain *view* of all', where *view* is clearly a noun. It is this fusing tendency that is sweeping the adjective *due* over into the phrasal preposition *due to* in such colloquial sentences as '*Due to* his illness, he could not come.' Sometimes foreigners go in the opposite direction when they fail to recognize that these phrasal prepositions are completely fused, and insist upon saying 'on *the* account of' or 'with *regards* to'. Curiously the article *the* is still retained in 'for *the* sake of', and in the latest edition of Webster's New International Dictionary (1934) both *in stead* (commonly *instead*) *of* and *in the stead of* are recognized.

j. Adverbs are at times used as adjectives, as in 'in *after* years', 'an *out*-and-*out* failure', 'our *sometime* queen'. But some writers still hesitate to use *above* adjectivally, as in 'the *above* quotation'. Since the adverb, though it may function as an adjective in this manner, never loses its adverbial quality altogether, such conversions are not common and are not encouraged in English. In the case of certain adjectives and adverbs which were originally phrases, such as *afloat, alive, askew, astray,* it is not always easy to distinguish adjective from adverb when they follow some form of the verb *be*; but in 'The man was *alive*' the adjective describes the *man,* whereas in 'He was *abroad*' the adverb modifies *was* and answers the question Where? The dictionaries do not agree on *galore* in 'He had books *galore*.'

It is not necessary to assume that an adverb loses its adverbial nature when it is placed immediately after a noun or in the predicate position after the verb *be*; consequently one can say 'That man *there* is my friend', using *there* as a kind of elliptical or parenthetical locution. But one should not say 'That *there* man', because the placing of the adverb in the attributive position makes of the word an attributive adjective.

k. The fusion of thought and emotion which takes place in the exclamatory use of verbs like *hold up, look out,* and *stop* presents a different aspect of this process. Any simple word may become an interjection if strong emotion or feeling is added to the idea which it usually expresses. If one shouts *back, indeed, murder, never, quit, run,* or *thief*, the original meaning of the word is retained as an element in the new hybrid.

l. The use of the pronoun *it* and the adverb *there* as mere expletives, or fillers, at the beginning of sentences is worthy of further comment, since some grammarians are inclined to set them apart from the other parts of speech, as already noted. In the sentence '*It* was wrong to take the car' a subject is anticipated which later proves to be *to take the car*; and in '*There* was no truth in the rumor' the words *no truth* may be regarded as the real subject of the sentence. In *it* the pronoun and in *there* the adverb are lost sight of, largely, in the sentences just given; and yet their original functions show faintly still, since *it* stands in place of a deferred subject and *there* anticipates some sort of answer to the question Where? They are hybrids of a sort.

m. Inasmuch as we have refused to accept the numeral as a separate part of speech, treating it instead under four of the foregoing heads, as noun, pronoun, adjective, or adverb, its characteristic features may be summed up as follows:

Cardinal numerals are used as pronouns, as in '*Three* of his friends waited'; as adjectives, as in 'He had *three* friends'; and they are commonly regarded as abstract nouns in mathematical usage, as in '*Seven* and *six* make thirteen.'

Ordinal numerals are also used as pronouns, as in 'The *second* was his son'; as adjectives, as in 'He had a *third* book'; and as fractional nouns, as in 'Add a *third* and a *fifth*.' An ordinal adverb is made by adding *-ly*, as in *thirdly*.

Multiplicative numerals are used as adjectives, as in 'a *twofold* error'; other multiplicatives are adverbs, as in 'It stopped *twice*.'

Distributive numerals (adverbs) are formed as phrases, as in 'The animals went in *two by two*.'

n. Because the word *most* is used as an adverb of degree in making superlatives like *most beautiful*, *most kind*, it is often incorrectly substituted for *almost* in such colloquialisms as *most all*, *most everyone*, *most finished*, *most well*.

o. The comparative conjunction *than* has long been a source of trouble because of a tendency to use it as a preposition and, as such, governing the objective case. Grammarians generally agree that

'He is stronger *than I*' is correct because *am* is understood after the nominative *I*.

The use of the objective *whom* in 'Napoleon, *than whom* no greater general ever lived', commonly found in earlier literature, is now archaic and awkward.

The objective case is correct in 'He chose you rather *than me*' because some form of the verb *choose* is implied before *me*.

If the student of language, in attempting to classify words, will recognize the two possibilities presented in this section, namely, that words may be completely converted or that they may be fused into hybrid categories so that sometimes their classification becomes almost hopelessly confused, his thinking will be much clarified, and much useless argument about the classification of the various parts of speech will be done away with.

On the whole, it is not difficult to separate words into those eight general classes known as the parts of speech. Many words, as indicated at the beginning of this chapter, can be distinguished by their forms, as the noun *strength* and the verb *strengthen*; some must be classified after consideration of their syntactical uses, as verb in 'to *ride* a horse' and noun in 'to take a *ride*'. And without consideration of either form or use the grammarian feels that certain words fall into their proper classes because of their essential and normal meanings, as, for example, the pronoun in '*He* has come', the adverb in 'It was *there*', and the conjunction in 'one *or* two'. It is not often that after the application of one or more of these tests (of form, of use, and of meaning) there is still uncertainty as to the proper classification of a word.

There has been of late some dissatisfaction on the part of grammarians with the whole business of classifying words into the eight general categories discussed in this chapter because, with the change from the older dependence upon distinctive forms to the more modern dependence upon function, much confusion and uncertainty have arisen. But all grammatical study is based so largely on a recognition of the parts of speech as generally defined that the use of the terms *noun, pronoun, adjective, verb,* etc. is still almost imperative if the grammarian wishes to speak a language which other grammarians will generally understand and appreciate. Hence it seems better to attempt to agree on some workable basis for discussion and classification which will still employ the long-established terminology than to attempt to shift to an entirely new basis of classification which only a few theorists can hope to comprehend. For it is as true of the language spoken by grammarians as it is of language as a whole that generality of usage is the prime test of linguistic value and usefulness. To throw overboard a generally workable scheme for a new and unproved one is not likely to promote understanding and agreement by students of language.

CHAPTER IX

THE DERIVATION OF WORDS

SO MUCH has been said in Chapters VI and VII about the changes in sounds and spellings that result from the processes of derivation, particularly in the addition of prefixes and suffixes, that little more need be said here regarding those aspects of the matter. In consequence of derivational changes in words we have observed changes in the length of vowels and the voicing of consonants, changes involving a shift of accent, the doubling or simplifying of consonant letters, the dropping of final silent -*e*, the bringing to life of silent consonants, and various other changes too numerous to review here. Assuming, then, an understanding of these processes incidental to the making or remaking of words in English, we shall consider in this chapter the broader aspects of the subject, particularly the general methods employed in the building up of a vocabulary and some of the more general processes that constitute English derivation.

The term *etymology* has already been introduced (see page 11) and has been defined as "that branch of philology which treats of the derivation of words." Moreover, the need of distinguishing between derivational and inflectional processes has been emphasized, with the insistence that derivational changes give rise to new and permanent words, whereas inflectional changes serve only the temporary needs of syntactical usage.

But etymology takes cognizance of more than changes in form; it has to do with changes in meaning as well. In the case of borrowed words it is necessary to add a third consideration, namely, the question of whether a word could have come into the English language from a certain other language at a given time. Changes in form may be studied as processes; changes in meaning must be regarded as results.

Consequently it is possible to view the many changes in English words from those two differing points of view, and that is our chief justification for attempting to deal with them in two separate chapters. This chapter will be concerned largely with derivational processes and forms; Chapter XIII will attempt to survey the changes in meaning that result from various processes, phonetic and psychological, formal and functional[291].

English etymology has generally followed two aims and methods in the past: it has taken up English words one by one and has sought their individual life histories with a view to gaining from them interesting and valuable information concerning the earlier life and thought of the English people; on the other hand, it has looked for derivational processes and tendencies and has sought groups of words to illustrate them, gaining thereby better insight into the manner of growth of the English language itself. Both are profitable and interesting, but in this chapter it has seemed better to adopt the latter method, since it gives a more clearly defined view of this aspect of the English language, namely, the development of the vocabulary as we know it today.

59. *Creation and Adaptation versus Borrowing*

There are two chief methods of increasing a vocabulary: one, the process of creating new words from old material already in the language, and the other, the simple expedient of reaching out to other languages and borrowing whatever may be needed. In the Anglo-Saxon period new ideas were generally expressed in the vernacular tongue by adapting or combining native words. A *miracle*, for example, was called a *wonder*, and a *disciple* was a *learning-youth*. But during the Middle English period, as we have already noted, such a flood of foreign words poured into the language that the English people became quite accustomed to borrowing instead of manufacturing the words needed. It was only with the awakening of the English people to a greater interest in cultural matters at the end of the Middle Ages that English writers and critics began to debate, as we have seen (p. 100), about the relative advantages of the two methods of embellishing and improving the language. Caxton's perplexed remarks have already been quoted (p. 144); but he was only one of a long line of thoughtful Englishmen who for some four centuries have kept the debate alive. Said Roger Ascham, one of the earliest of the purists, in his *Toxophilus*, published in 1545:

He that wyll wryte well in any tongue, muste folowe thys councel of Aristotle to speake as the common people do, to thinke as wise men do; and so shoulde every man understande hym, and the judgement of wyse men alowe hym. Many English writers have not done so, but usinge straunge words as latin, french and Italian, do make all thinges darke and harde.*

But a little later the pamphleteer Thomas Nash said in the 1594 preface to his *Christ's Tears over Jerusalem*:

Our English tongue of all languages most swarmeth with the single money of monasillables, which are the onely scandall of it. Bookes written in them and no other seeme like Shop-keepers boxes, that containe nothing else save halfe-pence, three-farthings, and two-pences. Therefore what did me I, but having a huge heape of these worthlesse shreds of small English in my *Pia maters* purse, to make the royaller shew with them to mens eyes, had them to the compounders immediately, and exchanged them foure into one, and others into more, according to the Greek, French, Spanish and Italian? †

Since the controversy began, in the days of Roger Ascham, the borrowing of words has gone steadily on, and by the use of a variety of derivational methods the vocabulary has grown to a most remarkable degree. Sometimes, it is true, things have been made "darke and harde" for the ordinary man by the swarm of "straunge words" that have descended upon us; but often we have been the better off for exchanging some of our simple little words, "foure into one," for the more elaborate and highly sophisticated foreign words.

* Arber's edition, p. 18.   † McKerrow's edition, Vol. II, p. 184.

I. CREATION AND ADAPTATION OF WORDS

In the creation of new words by various methods which are to be discussed in the following sections, the English people have utilized without much discrimination both the native Anglo-Saxon stock already on hand and the materials borrowed from numerous foreign languages. In the long process of building up the English vocabulary through the creation and adaptation of words, four outstanding methods have been employed, namely, creating entirely new words, changing the forms of old ones, converting words so that they function in various ways, and changing word meanings. These four methods may be observed still in use, though in differing degrees, in the vocabulary-building of the twentieth century.

60. *Original Creation*

The creation of brand-new words which have no connection with any material already existing in the language is, of course, possible and does occasionally occur; but it is hard to adduce examples with any degree of certainty. It is so much more likely that the maker of a new word has followed some familiar method, such as the use of an old word with a new meaning or the use of a common prefix or suffix, that the philologist usually looks askance at any suggestion of original creation in the sense of creating something out of nothing, as it were. The Belgian chemist, Van Helmont, is said to have invented the word *gas*; but etymologists have guessed that he may have had in mind some similar Dutch or Flemish word when he used it. Weekley says that *kodak* is "a trade-name coined arbitrarily".[297] A few words like *quiz** and *skew-gee* have not been explained satisfactorily. Some of the words popularized by the author of *Alice in Wonderland,* such as *burble, chortle, frabjous, galumph, jabberwocky,* and *vorpal,* have had wide currency; but they have always been considered nonsense words, and Lewis Carroll's imitators have been regarded as

---

* Perhaps a mere abbreviation of *inquisition,* however.

contributors to "nonsense English". Swift's coinings in *Gulliver's Travels*, especially *Brobdingnagian, Lilliputian*, and *Yahoo*, have become quite standardized and show what an individual writer can do for the language if he happens to produce a literary classic. Just at present certain authors and newspaper "columnists" are attempting to promulgate new and original terms; but James Joyce's weird coinings and revivals of old words, such as *aresouns, inverecund, jellibees, lutulent*, and *proliferant*, are too subjective and too incomprehensible to most people to gain much popularity, and the coinings of the newspaper writers usually partake too strongly of the nature of ephemeral slang to stand much chance of living on in the language. An occasional original creation of this sort may possibly strike the popular fancy and persist, like the few in Swift's *Gulliver*; but the majority will pass on into the limbo of the useless and unwanted.

But though writers and speakers generally fail in their attempts from time to time to introduce original creations of their own, by a curious irony of fate a few words which Skeat has named "ghost words" have maintained a place in the dictionaries, although they have apparently never had any legitimate place in the language because they came into existence as misprints or other strange misunderstandings. Skeat has cited as ghost words the old *abacot, desouled, encortif, golk, nalle, panfray, rendit*.[304] Weekley adds *collimate* and *syllabus*.[297] The well-known *aroint* of the witches in Shakespeare's *Macbeth*, which was later taken up by the Brownings and Walter Scott, might almost be classed as a ghost word, although the etymologists have tried hard to legitimatize it; and likewise Spenser's *derring-do* and the misunderstood *help meet* of the Authorized Version of the Bible might be considered as ghost words. It is not unlikely, moreover, that some of the "hothouse words" that have already been alluded to (p. 97) never really existed in actual use but have dragged out a ghostly existence down through the years merely because some early lexicographer like Thomas Blount saw fit to include them in his dictionary, in Blount's case in his *Glossographia* of 1656[139].

If, then, there have been few linguistic magicians capable of rolling up their sleeves and reaching out into thin air and producing tangible words, the like of which no one has ever before heard or known, the question may well be asked, Why devote any space to this subject of original creation in a study of Current English? The reply is that there are two kinds of words in English — as in all languages, presumably — which are as old as the language itself, apparently, and yet perennially new. These are the simple interjections and the so-called onomatopœic words and phrases.

Enough has been said about the primitive interjections expressing emotion purely (Sec. 57), so that it should not be necessary to enlarge upon the matter here. Those exclamations like *ah, alas, oh, pshaw,* and *wow* that have become fairly well standardized are numerous, and there are others which never get into the pages of dictionaries but which individual speakers use regularly. These possess some measure of originality, since they are often spontaneous.

Onomatopœic (or onomatopoetic) words are vocal imitations, linguistic echoes, as it were, of the sounds of nature and are usually simple, often uninflected words. If they ultimately gain admittance to standard English, they assume less simple forms and are inflected according as they become nouns, verbs or some other parts of speech. Some of the more familiar of these primitive words are *bang, boom, buzz, clank, click, crash, croon, fizz, growl, honk, hum, puff, purr, roar, snap, squeak, whoop, zip, zoom.* The childish *baby, daddy, mamma,* and *papa* go back to the first attempts of a little child to address its parents. Various popular bird names are of this kind, also, such as *bobolink, bobwhite, chewink, cuckoo, pewee, phœbe, touraco,* and *whippoorwill.*

Besides these simpler primitives, all languages possess to a greater or lesser degree word pairs which, while they do not necessarily arise through the process of onomatopœia, do possess a primitive simplicity very like that of the onomatopœic words just discussed. There are three kinds of these reduplicated, or doubled, words, namely, those with both parts exactly alike, such as *tom-tom,* those which alliterate with the same initial consonants but vary the vowels, such as *singsong*, and those which rime but begin with different initial consonants, such as *hurdy-gurdy*. Most of the first kind come from children's speech, as *baa-baa, choo-choo, moo-moo, quack-quack*, and *woof-woof*, or else from foreign languages, as *bulbul* (Persian for 'nightingale'), *sing-sing, tom-tom*, and *Walla Walla*. As already noted (see Sec. 17), this type of reduplication is favored in English jargons, as in *chin chin, chop chop*, and *chow chow*. The alliterative type is much more common, and more varied in use and origin. Examples are *bric-a-brac* (French), *chitchat, crisscross, dingdong, flimflam, flipflop, jim-jams* ('delirium tremens'). *knickknack, ping-pong, riffraff, seesaw, singsong, teeter-totter, ticktack*, and *zigzag*. In *hippity-hop, kitty-cat*, and *pitapat* (or *pitypat*) the rhythm is somewhat different. The third, or riming, kind of reduplication is even more common. Examples are *boohoo, bowwow, claptrap, falderal, harum-scarum, heebie jeebies, helter-skelter, higgledy-piggledy, to hobnob, hocus-pocus, hodgepodge, hoity-toity, hoodoo* (or *voodoo*), *hubbub, hurdy-gurdy, namby-pamby, pell-mell, picnic* (French *piquenique*), *rat-tat*, and some coined names like *Piggly Wiggly* stores. Words of this kind are very slow in winning a place in standard English, and many of them have never attained to the status of literary English.

61. *Word Composition: Suffixes and Prefixes*

Word composition, or word-compounding, is merely the process of composing new words by the utilization of certain compounding, or derivational, elements. There are three outstanding kinds of word composition: first, that form of derivation which adds suffixes or prefixes to older root words (Sec. 61); secondly, the putting together of certain compounding elements which are somewhat more than mere prefixes and suffixes but not quite separate words (Sec. 62); and, thirdly, the bringing together of two or more distinct words to make a new compound word (Sec. 63). It is not always easy to distinguish these three types of compounding, because many of the prefixes and suffixes were at one time distinct words and are sometimes used separately still; the free compounding elements included in the second group are mostly borrowed from foreign languages in which they were separate word forms; and in the third group the very unsettled use of the hyphen makes it difficult to say whether two words are really compounds or merely neighboring words syntactically related, as noted in Section 47 (p. 251). But it is worthy of emphasis that whether a suffix, a prefix, a free compounding element, or a distinct word is added, it brings to the compound some new shade of meaning of its own, and the rough classification into these three groups is merely an attempt to indicate the degree of dependence or independence of the compounding factor. For that reason the rather senseless reduplicated words just discussed have not been regarded as compounds; in them the doubling does not add meaning.

Three aspects of this study of word composition need to be emphasized in any discussion of the matter, as already indicated in preceding chapters: (1) many of the elements employed are borrowed, as will be shown in the following subdivisions; (2) most of them are used to make new nouns, adjectives, verbs, and adverbs, as already set forth in Chapter VIII; (3) and some of them are no longer active in Current English usage. In so far as suffixes and prefixes are still active, that is to say, regarded as easily available for the coining of new compounds, they will be indicated in the following tables by dagger marks. Perhaps it would be well to add to these three considerations a fourth, namely, that some individual suffixes have been employed to make special kinds of nouns, adjectives, verbs, or adverbs; these received attention as they came up for consideration in Chapter VIII and will receive further consideration in this chapter.

Only the most commonly used suffixes and prefixes are listed below, with the forms recognized in Current English rather than their more primitive forms. Some suffixes represent several earlier forms. The inflectional suffixes have not been included, except when they can also be used as derivational suffixes.

A. Suffixes: Nouns

a. Noun suffixes from Anglo-Saxon

-ar: *beggar, liar.* A variant of *-er.* Also a French suffix.
-craft: *handicraft, witchcraft.*
-dom†: *Christendom, earldom, freedom, wisdom.* New words like *fandom, moviedom,* are often of doubtful propriety.
-en: *chicken, kitten, maiden.* Mostly diminutives; but *vixen* is the old feminine form of *fox.*
-er†: *builder, crooner, Hollander, tinner.* Nouns naming the agent, or doer, or an inhabitant are made with this suffix more commonly than with any other.
-ful†: *armful, cupful, pocketful, spoonfuls, trunkful.*
-hood†: *knighthood, manhood, priesthood.* An older variant form *-head* occurs in a few words like *Godhead.*
-ie†, *-y*†: *Annie, auntie, baby, granny, Johnny, kitty.* A diminutive ending often used to make familiar nicknames and other colloquial words like *the funnies, the heebie jeebies, movies, wienies.*
-ing†: *running, shavings, stuffing; Billings, Browning, farthing; Dorking, Reading.* A suffix very active in forming gerunds, or verbal nouns; formerly used to make patronymics and to show origin; found also in a few place-names.
-kin†: *bumpkin, lambkin, manikin; Perkins, Wilkins.* A diminutive suffix occasionally employed to make affectionate terms like *daughterkin, Peterkin.* Most family names with this suffix will be found to have grown out of earlier diminutive nicknames, *little Will* having been the progenitor of the *Wilkins* family.
-le, -el: *beadle, fiddle, ladle, kernel.*
-ling: *darling, hireling, weakling, yearling.* A suffix used to form diminutives, sometimes in a depreciatory sense.
-ness†: *goodness, redness, smallness.* Abstract nouns are still formed with this suffix from almost any descriptive adjectives, and sometimes even from *-ing* forms, as in *cunningness, knowingness, willingness,* though the latter are often awkward and of doubtful propriety.
-ock: *bullock, hillock, hummock.* A diminutive suffix.
-ship†: *friendship, ownership, township.*
-ster†: *gamester, huckster, roadster, spinster; Baxter, Webster.* This suffix is still being used to form such words as *dopester, gangster, slangster, tonguester.*
-t: *drift, flight, weight.* Abstract nouns.

-th: *birth, breadth, filth, wealth.* Abstract nouns made in earlier times from the stems of adjectives or verbs.

-yer: *lawyer, sawyer; Bowyer.* A variant of *-er.*

b. Noun suffixes from French, Spanish, Italian*

-ade†: *cannonade, cascade, promenade; lemonade, orangeade; brigade, cavalcade, parade.* The recently made *motorcade* is based on the false assumption that *-cade* is the suffix just because it happens to occur in *cavalcade.*

-age†: *acreage, baggage, language, mileage, shrinkage, voyage, yardage.*

-ance, -ence: *acceptance, resistance; diligence.* These are verbal abstract nouns, and come from verbs of different conjugations in Latin; hence the two forms. Sometimes used with native stems, as in *forbearance, hindrance.*

-ancy, -ency: *brilliancy, hesitancy; agency.* The Century Dictionary calls the *y*-ending form "a modern extension" of the preceding *e*-ending form and adds that "the two forms seldom differ in force". Deciding between such pairs as *acceptance* and *acceptancy* constitutes one of the little niceties of English usage.

-ant, -ent: *dependant, descendant, servant; accident.* Sometimes, as in the case of the adjectives *dependent* and *descendent*, there is an attempt to distinguish noun from adjective by using *-ant* for the noun and *-ent* for the adjective; but there is not much uniformity in the practice.

-ard, -art: *coward, drunkard, mustard, sluggard; braggart.*

-cle: *article, miracle, spectacle.*

-ee†: *absentee, devotee, lessee,* and a recent coining, *tryoutee,* "one who tries out for a place in orchestra, drama, etc."

-eer†: *auctioneer, gazetteer, profiteer, racketeer.* One of the most recent is *fountaineer.*

-el: *bushel, libel, pommel.*

-er†, *-or*†: *butler, officer; sailor.* When *-or* is added to stems with *-t-*, like *aviation*, a double suffix, *-tor*, results, as in *aviator, executor, realtor.*

-ery†, *-erie*: *archery, grocery, slavery, menagerie,* and some recent coinings like *beanery, bindery, booterie* (or *bootery*), *creamery, fish-hatchery, haberdashery.*

-ese†: *Chinese, journalese.*

---

* Suffixes included in this list were, for the most part, originally Latin. They have been listed here because they came into English directly from these Romanic languages, and also because they have usually assumed forms somewhat different from those of classical Latin.

Sec. 61] SUFFIXES AND PREFIXES 339

-*ess*†: *actress, laundress, waitress.* This feminine suffix is used sometimes to create new forms, such as *championess, doctress.*[311]
-*et*†, -*ette*†: *anklet, ringlet; aigrette, farmerette, kitchenette, leatherette, yeomanette.*
-*ice*: *armistice, justice, notice, service.*
-*ine*†: *benzine, chlorine, discipline, heroine, Josephine,* and many recently made trade names like *Danderine.*
-*ism*†: *Buddhism, criticism, egoism, Gandhiism, realism.*
-*let*†: *booklet, leaflet, playlet.* Diminutives.
-*oon*: *balloon, cartoon, saloon, spittoon.* Augmentatives.
-*ry*†: *foundry, jewelry* (British *jewellery*), *revelry*; also collectives like *citizenry, peasantry.* Recent creations are *pheasantry, rabbitry,* perhaps through the influence of *poultry* etc.
-*teria*†: *cafeteria, drugeteria,* 'drugstore', *groceteria, roadateria,* 'road house'. The present American tendency to form names for self-service business houses by the use of -*teria* shows a confused use of an older suffix -*eria,* apparently, found in Spanish-American *barbería,* 'barber shop', *carnicería,* 'butcher shop', etc.[312]
-*ty*: *celerity, quality, safety.*
-*y*: *army, glory, history, victory.* When words like *accurate* and *primate* take this ending, a double suffix, -*acy,* results, as in *accuracy, primacy, privacy.*

c. Noun suffixes from Latin and Greek*

-*al*: *animal, dismissal, missal, refusal.*
-*an*†, -*ian*†: *African, artisan; cosmetician, mortician, Philadelphian, statistician.*
-*ana*†: *Californiana, Shakespeariana.*
-*ar*: *bursar, vicar.*
-*arium*†: *aquarium, columbarium, sanitarium.* Usually this suffix appears in the form -*ary,* as below.
-*ary*: *notary, secretary; aviary, dictionary, granary.*
-*aster*: *criticaster, poetaster.* Terms of disparagement.
-*ate*: *consulate, delegate, mandate, nitrate.*
-*ation*†, -*ition*: *acclamation; admonition.* Sometimes used colloquially, as in *botheration, thunderation.*
-*ic, -ics*: *critic, mechanic; acoustics, classics, physics.*
-*ion, -sion, -tion*: *suspicion; fusion; action, adoption, selection.*
-*isk*: *asterisk, basilisk.* A Greek diminutive suffix.

* In this list are included suffixes which might also have appeared in the preceding list, since they may be regarded as French as well as Latin.

-ist†: *bigamist, Darwinist, motorist, oculist, pianist, royalist, socialist, theorist.* This suffix often comes via the French, and the form *-iste* is retained in *modiste* and *artiste* and other borrowings not yet fully naturalized.

-ite†: *Alemite, anthracite, Canaanite, lydite, Warrenite,* and various other trade names and collective names.

-ment: achievement, argument, judgment.

-mony: alimony and *matrimony.*

-or†: *aviator, chiropractor, doctor, educator, governor, motor, realtor; arbor, clamor.*

-orium†: *auditorium, crematorium, sanatorium, suitatorium.*

-ory: accessory, dormitory, observatory.

-osis†: *hypnosis, neurosis, tuberculosis.*

-trix: aviatrix, executrix. Feminine of *-tor* (see *-or*)

-tude: attitude, gratitude, multitude.

-ure: adventure, creature, ligature.

B. Suffixes: Adjectives

a. Adjective suffixes from Anglo-Saxon

-ed†: *crooked, straight-edged.* This old participial suffix is regularly used to make compound adjectives (see *-ed,* suffix 2, in the New English Dictionary [20]).

-en: ashen, brazen, wooden, and colloquial or dialectal *boughten, proven.*

-fold: Duofold, threefold.

-ful†: *awful, playful, wonderful.*

-ish†: *boyish, Flemish, foolish, grayish, latish.*

-less†: *homeless, hopeless; reckless, tireless.*

-like†: *homelike, manlike.* These compounds are often composed for special occasions to give emphasis or definiteness to comparisons, as *coatlike, elephant-like, Topsy-like, treelike.*

-ly: goodly, lively, lonely. Older adjectives, and sometimes confused with adverbs in *-ly.*

-some: frolicsome, lonesome.

-teen: thirteen to *nineteen,* only. A form of *ten.*

-th: fourth, fiftieth. Ordinal numerals.

-ty: twenty to *ninety,* only. Another form of *ten.*

-ward: awkward, backward. Often used adverbially.

-y†: *creamy, flighty, hilly, roomy.* Often used in the making of colloquial adjectives like *cranky, daffy, doggy, hunky-dory, ritzy, scratchy, touchy, uppity.*

b. Adjective suffixes from French, Latin, Greek

-*able*†, -*ible*†: *eatable, tolerable; dirigible.*
-*ac*, -*ic*: *cardiac, elegiac; dramatic, evangelic, poetic.*
-*aceous*, -*acious*: *foliaceous; veracious.*
-*al*, -*ical*: *actual, naval; critical, pontifical.* There is a strong tendency in Modern English to simplify -*ical* to -*ic*, as in *epic(al), lyric(al), poetic(al)* (see Krapp [17], p. 314).
-*an*†, -*ian*†: *human, Texan; Chaucerian, Rotarian.*
-*ant*, -*ent*: *extravagant; eloquent, fluent.*
-*ar*: *regular, velar.*
-*ary*: *primary, sedentary.*
-*ate*, -*ite*: *delicate; definite.*
-*ern*: *eastern, Northwestern.*
-*escent*†: *obsolescent, quiescent.* Commonly used in scientific terminology, as in *arborescent, opalescent.*
-*ese*†: *Japanese, Johnsonese, journalese.* Proper adjectives, usually.
-*esque*†: *grotesque, picturesque, Turneresque.*
-*fic*: *beatific, soporific, terrific.*
-*ic*: see -*ac*, above.
-*id*: *acid, humid, stupid.*
-*ile*, -*il*: *juvenile, servile; civil, fossil.*
-*ine*, -*in*: *canine, feminine, Florentine, saccharine* (or *saccharin*).
-*ive*: *creative, elective.*
-*ory*: *hortatory, introductory.*
-*ose*: *adipose, grandiose, verbose.*
-*ous*: *famous, poisonous, sumptuous.*

C. Suffixes: Verbs

-*ate*: *regulate, tolerate.* A Latin suffix.
-*en*: *harden, toughen, widen.* An Anglo-Saxon suffix added to adjectives to create verbs.
-*esce*: *coalesce, effervesce.* A Latin suffix used to make inchoative, or ingressive, verbs (see Verb aspect, p. 303).
-*fy*†: *beautify, codify, electrify, terrify.* A Latin suffix meaning 'make', 'arrange', etc.
-*ise*†, -*ize*†: *botanize, criticize, Hooverize, mesmerize, motorize, oxidize, simonize.* Originally a Greek suffix.
-*ish*: *abolish, famish, polish.* A French suffix, -*iss*, -*is*, originally.
-*le*: *babble, cobble, dribble, topple, wiggle.* An Anglo-Saxon frequentative suffix.

D. Suffixes: Adverbs

-long, -ling: endlong, headlong, darkling, sideling.
-ly †: evenly, oddly, rationally.
-meal: piecemeal.
-ward, -wards: backward(s), upward(s).
-wise: clockwise, endwise, lengthwise, otherwise.

For genitival adverbs in *-s* see page 516.

E. Prefixes

a. Prefixes from Anglo-Saxon

a-:   abroad, arise *
be-: belittle
by-†: byplay
down-†: downpour
for-: forgive
fore-†: foresee
in-†: income
mis-†: mistake
n-: none

off-†: offset
on-†: onlooker
out-†: outlook
over-†: overtake
un-†: unfurl
under-†: understand
up-†: upturn
with-: withstand

b. Prefixes from French

a-: average
counter-: counteract
en-: enroll
em-: embody

mis-: miscreant
par-: partake
sur-: surmount

c. Prefixes from Latin

NOTE. In this list are included prefixes which might also have appeared in the preceding list, since they may be regarded as French as well as Latin.

ab-: abrupt
abs-: abstract
ad-: advocate
ac-: accept
af-: affix
ag-: aggregate
al-: allude

an-: annex
ap-: applaud
ar-: arrogant
as-: assist
at-: attention
ambi-, amb-: ambition
ante-†: antebellum

* Since the prefix *a-* has developed from numerous earlier forms — prepositions, verb prefixes, etc. — every occurrence of it should be examined with the help of a good dictionary.

Sec. 61] SUFFIXES AND PREFIXES 343

bene-: benefactor
bi-†*:* biplane
circum-†*:* circumscribe
cis-: cisalpine
com-: complete
  co-†*:* coexist
  col-: collect
  con-: connect
  cor-: corrupt
contra-: contradict
de-†*:* debunk
dis-: dislocate
  di-: diverge
ex-†*:* ex-secretary
  e-: evoke
  ef-: effect
extra-†*:* extraordinary
in-: ('in'): inspire
  il-: illuminate
  im-: imbibe
  ir-: irradiate
in- ('not'): infallible
  il-: illegitimate
  im-: impossible
  ir-: irresponsible
inter†*-:* interstate
intra-: intramural
intro-: introduce
juxta-: juxtaposition
mal-†*:* malpractice
multi-†*:* multicolored

non-†*:* nonnegotiable
ob-: obscure
oc-: occur
of-: offer
op-: oppose
per-: permit
post-†*:* postwar
pre-†*:* preëlection
preter-: preternatural
pro-†*:* pro-German
re-†*:* refill
retro-: retrograde
se-: seduce
semi-†*:* semifinals
sub-†*:* subcontract
suc-: succeed
suf-: suffer
sug-: suggest
sum-: summon
sup-: support
sur-: surrender
sus-: sustain
subter-: subterfuge
super-†*:* supersensitive
supra-: supraliminal
trans-†*:* transcontinental
tri-†*:* tristate
ultra-†*:* ultra-violet
uni-†*:* unicellular
vice-†*:* vice-regent

d. Prefixes from Greek

a-: aseptic
  an-: anarchy
amphi-: amphitheater
ana-: anagram
anti-†*:* antidote
  ant-: antarctic
apo-: apostrophe
arch-†*:* archvillain

cata-: catalogue
  cath-: cathedral
di-: dilemma
  dis-: dissyllabic
dia-: diagram
dys-: dyspepsia
en-: energy
  el-: ellipsis

epi-: epigram	*hetero-:* heterogeneous	*pro-:* prologue
ep-: epoch	*homo-:* homonym	*proto-:* prototype
eph-: ephemeral	*hyper-:* hypersensitive	*pseudo-*†*:* pseudoscientific
eu-: eulogy	*neo-*†*:* Neoplatonism	
ev-: evangelist	*para-:* paradox	*syn-:* syntax
ex-: exodus	*par-:* parody	*sy-:* system
ec-: eclipse	*pen-:* peninsula	*syl-:* syllogism
hemi-: hemisphere	*peri-:* perimeter	*sym-:* sympathy

Although it cannot be said that there is evidence of any very extensive original creation in the English vocabulary of today, it must be admitted that the splendid variety and versatility of that rich body of words that constitute the best literary English are the result of a long-continued and skillful manipulation of the more than two hundred suffixes and prefixes that are contained in the foregoing lists. Whether the words as we now have them were first given these suffixes and prefixes and then introduced into English or were made up after the simpler forms had been borrowed does not concern us here; we are able to appreciate their variety and importance if we take even the briefest time to analyze them. A measure of the remarkable derivational expansion of the two elements in the English vocabulary, the native and the foreign, can be best gained by collecting the derivative forms for some characteristic root words. For the Anglo-Saxon the familiar verb *bear* and for the Romanic contribution the Latin verb *cedo*, 'I go,' will serve our purpose well. The principal variations of *bear* are as follows:

bear	bier	inborn	unbear
bairn	birth		unbearable
barm	bore	overbear	unbearably
barrow	burden	overbearing	unborn
bearable	burdenless	overbearingly	
bearably	burdensome		unburden
bearance (archaic)	burdensomeness	overburden	
bearer		overburdensome	upbear
bearing	abear (dialectal)		upbearer
bearings		rebirth	
berth	forbear	reborn	
	forbearance		

SUFFIXES AND PREFIXES

These thirty-six forms of the old native word make use of seven different prefixes and at least twelve suffixes, some of which are combined in double or triple suffixes.* One of the prefixes, *re-*, and the two suffixes *-ance* and *-able* are not native but originally Latin forms.

But the variations of the Latin root, *ced-*, with its participial form, *cess-*, and a form derived from the French, *cease*, are much more numerous. There are at least eighty forms in English, as follows:

cede
cessation
cession

cease
ceaseless
ceaselessly

abscess

accede
access
accessary
accessible
accessibility
accession
accessory

antecede
antecedent
antecessor
ancestor
ancestral
ancestress
ancestry

concede
concession
concessionaire
concessive

decease
decedent

exceed
exceedingly
excess
excessive
excessively

incessant
incessancy
incessantly

intercede
intercession
intercessor
intercessory
intercedingly

precede
precedence
precedent
precession
precessional

predecease
predecessor

proceed
process
procedure
proceedings
procession
processional

recede

recess
recedingly
recession
recessional
recessive

retrocede
retrocession

secede
secession
secessionist
secessionism (and the Civil War colloquialisms *secesh, seceshdom, secessionizer*)

succeed
success
successful
successfulness
succession
successional
successive
successiveness
successor

unceasing
unceasingly

cess (a shortened form of *success*, used in the Irish imprecation "Bad *cess* to you!")

* The figures given for *bear* and *cedo* must be taken as only rough approximations, inasmuch as no effort has been made to analyze the modern prefixes and suffixes comprised in the foregoing lists into their more primitive elements.

These eighty forms of the Latin root word make use of fifteen different prefixes and some twenty-five suffixes, which are often combined to form double or triple suffixes, such as *-iveness* and *-ionizer*. Of the prefixes only *un-* is of Anglo-Saxon origin; but of the suffixes at least eight are native, two are Greek in origin, and one, *-ionaire*, is plainly French.

If one were to list in like manner the forms of other native words like *lay, set, strong, take,* or of such Latin roots as *duc-* (participle *duct-*), *ger-* (participle *gest-*), *pon-* (participle *pos-*), *port-, vert-* (participle *vers-*), and *voc-*, he would be amazed at the number of derivative forms that he would gather for a very few main root words, and he would appreciate more fully the manner in which the English vocabulary has been enriched in the past by the composition of words by means of suffixes and prefixes.

62. Word Composition: Free Compounding Elements

There is a group of compounding elements that deserve separate consideration because they are largely the stock in trade of scholars and scientists. In Current English they appear usually in combination; but they were originally distinct words in the Greek and Latin from which they were borrowed and are sometimes so used in Current English. They differ from suffixes and prefixes in that they can be used freely in any part of a word. Only some of the most generally used need be noticed here.

a. Greek compounding elements

-anthrop-, 'man': *anthropology, philanthropy*
-arch-, 'ruler': *monarch, squirearchy*
-aut-, 'self': *autocrat*
-drom-, 'running': *dromedary, motordrome*
-gen-, 'born': *eugenics, genetic*
-gram-, 'writing': *gramophone, telegram*
-graph-, 'writing': *graphic, telegraph*
-lith-, 'stone': *lithograph, monolith*

-log-, 'word': *logic, decalogue*
-mega-, 'great': *megaphone*
-met(e)r-, 'measure': *metronome, diameter*
-micro-, 'small': *microphone*
-mono-, 'one': *monograph*
-pan-, -pant-, 'all': *Panhellenic, pantheon; pantomime*
-path-, 'suffering': *pathology, homeopath*
-phil-, 'loving': *philosophy*
-phon-, 'sound': *phonograph, telephone*
-photo-, 'light': *photograph, telephoto*
-poly-, 'many': *polygamy, polyglot*
-scop-, 'seeing': *telescope*
-trop-, 'turning': *tropic, heliotrope*

b. Latin compounding elements

-cultur-, 'cultivation': *agriculture*
-fer-, 'bearing': *auriferous, conifer*
-form-, 'form': *formality, uniform*
-spec(t)-, 'see': *spectacle, circumspect*
-vers-, -vert-, 'turned': *universe; introvert*

c. Anglo-Saxon compounding elements

Lists have been given already of the compounding elements employed in the making of proper names (Sec. 50, p. 275). Others are so often utilized in common nouns, verbs, and elsewhere that they are worthy of special notice.

-after-: *afterglow, hereafter*
-al(l)-: *always, all-American, carryall*
-back-: *backgammon, half-back*
-body-: *everybody*
-ever-: *Eversharp, whatever*
-high-: *high-toned, highway*
-self-: *self-starting, myself*
-side-: *sideswipe, sidewalk, ringside*
-smith-: *blacksmith, songsmith*
-soever-: *whatsoever*
-stead-: *steadfast, homestead*
-wright-: *Cartwright, millwright, playwright*

63. Word Composition: Distinct Words

In an earlier discussion of hyphenation (Sec. 47, p. 251), the difficulty of determining always when two words are compounded was commented upon, and certain kinds of compounds were illustrated. The putting together of two or more words to express a special idea is as old as the English language, and still as active a process as ever, today. The proportion of such compounds on any printed page is not large; but the dictionaries are full of them, and new compounds can be made on the spur of the moment if they seem to be required. Some of the chief methods of compounding are as follows:

a. Compound nouns are formed most commonly by the mere juxtaposition of two simple uninflected nouns. Usually the first limits the meaning of the second, somewhat; hence *bonehead, furniture store, house dog, race horse,* and *truck horse* do not mean the same as *head bone, store furniture, dog house, horse race,* and *horse truck.* Other compounds of this first kind are *apple tree, catbird, fellow citizen, handbook, newspaper, place-name,* and *schoolhouse.* Sometimes, however, the first noun names that which is affected by action implied in the second noun, as in *bookseller* ('a seller of books'), *dressmaker, storekeeper, windbreak, windshield-wiper,* and *wonder-worker.*

b. Compound nouns have been formed very far back in the history of English by the use of the genitive, or possessive, form of a noun plus another noun, such as *adder's-tongue, bull's-eye, herdsman, kinsman, money's worth,* and *sheepshead.*

c. Compound nouns are made with an adjective plus a noun, as in *blackbird, broadside, busybody, shortcut,* and *sixpence.*

d. Compound nouns consist sometimes of adverb plus verb, as in *downpour, outcry, outlay, undertow.*

e. Some very expressive compound nouns have been coined from time to time by the use of a verb and its object, as in *breakfast, carryall, cutthroat, forget-me-not, killjoy, Know-Nothing, makeshift, marplot, pickpocket, scarecrow, scofflaw, spitfire,* and *turncoat.*[313]

f. Compound nouns and adjectives result when the verb-adverb combination is converted, as in *bang-up, blowout, cave-in, frame-up, hoedown, holdup, jollyup, kick-off, knock-out, make-up, Passover.*

g. Nouns and adjectives are compounded of gerund or participle plus adverb, in words like *bringing-up, calling-down, closing-out, dried-up, goings-on, leftovers, sawed-off.*

h. As already explained, the practice is frequently resorted to of making an adjective by compounding an adjective with a noun and then inflecting the compound with the suffix *-ed*, as in *broad-shouldered, golden-haired, sad-eyed, thin-lipped.*

i. Compound adjectives result when adverbs or nouns are used to qualify simple adjectives, as in *all-powerful, cocksure, dirt-cheap, headstrong, iron-gray, lemon-yellow, overfat, stone-cold.*

j. Adjectives are compounded of adverb plus participle, as in *farseeing, forthcoming, full-blown, long-lost, rough-hewn, seldom-traveled, slow-moving,* and *well-bred.*

k. Compound adjectives and nouns result from the use of a participle or a gerund preceded by the noun that it governs, as in *ear-splitting, epoch-making, heart-breaking, money-making,* and *oil-bearing.*

l. Some compound verbs are still made — though not nearly as many as in centuries past — by the use of adverb plus verb, as in *broadcast, gainsay, overlay, undertake, upend, withstand.*

m. Compound verbs are also made from adjective plus noun, as in *double-cross, sidetrack, triple-plate,* and *whitewash.*

n. Compounds are sometimes merely worn-down phrases like *coat of arms, father-in-law, fly-by-night, hand-me-downs, jack-o'-lantern, linotype, man-of-war, ne'er-do-well.*

o. Compounding in personal names and place-names is, of course, fairly common. The double family name, such as *Beach-Thompson, Bolton-Smith,* is more frequently found in England than in America. Compound adjectives like *French-Canadian, German-American,* and *Indo-European* are coined whenever needed.

Various tests have been suggested for determining whether two or more words actually form a compound. Compound adjectives and verbs are usually recognizable without much trouble, because they function distinctly as units, as in *overgrown, whole-hearted,* and *to sidestep,* and also because they are either hyphenated or written as solid words. But compound nouns are not so readily established. Some writers recognize three stages in their merging — when they are still separate words, such as *cash register,* when they are hyphenated, as in *lawn-mower,* and when they are written solid like *handbook.* It has been suggested that when the words forming the compound are so completely merged that only one main accent can be detected, as in *vineyard, workman,* the compound is far enough along to be written solid. But many compounds, such as *place-names, loan-words,* cannot be so tested; in the many cases of doubt the dictionaries must be consulted.

64. *Amalgamated Compounds*

As time passes, the parts of a compound tend to become so closely amalgamated, or welded together, and their meanings so fused into one newer meaning, that one rarely suspects the word of having been at one time a compound. The following list contains a few of the more important of these old amalgamations:

alone	all-one	*Lammas*	Loaf-mass
as	all-so	*lord*	loaf-ward
avast	hold-fast	*marshal*	horse-servant
barn	barley-room	*neighbor*	nigh-dweller
bridal	bride-ale	*nightingale*	night-singer
Christmas	Christ-mass	*nostril*	nose-opening
daisy	day's-eye	*orchard*	garden-yard
dandelion	French *dent de lion*	*pastime*	pass-time
doff	do-off	*rigmarole*	ragman-roll
don	do-on	*sheriff*	shire-reeve
garlic	spear-leek	*steward*	sty-ward
good-by	God-be-with-you	*stirrup*	step-rope
gospel	good-story	*walnut*	foreign-nut
gossamer	goose-summer	*walrus*	whale-horse
gossip	God-relation	*wanton*	without-training
holiday	holy-day	*window*	wind-eye
husband	house-dweller	*woman*	wife-man
hussy	house-wife	*world*	man-age
lady	loaf-kneader	*yeoman*	district-man

The compounds *blackguard, clapboard, cupboard,* and the nautical compounds *boatswain, coxswain,* and *gunwale* are well along toward similar amalgamation. If they were spelled as they are usually pronounced, their amalgamation would be even more clearly apparent (see Sec. 44, p. 218).

Some of the best examples of amalgamation are to be met with in English place-names, such as *Essex* (from *East Saxons*),

Leicester (from *Legionis Castra*), *Lincoln* (from *Lindum Colonia*), *Norfolk* (from the *North Folk*), and *Shotover* (from *Château Vert*).

In connection with these amalgamated compounds, numerous adjectives and adverbs with the prefix *a-* might well be listed, since they were originally prepositional phrases. Some of the best known are *abed, aboard, abroad, adrift, afire, afoot, aglow, ajar, akimbo, alive, aloft, apace, ashore, astern,* and *awry.* Sometimes the original phrase is also used today, as, for example, *on board, on fire, on foot, on shore.*

65. Blends

Blending differs from amalgamation of compounds just discussed because in blends the fusing of two words is immediate and final, and there is no preliminary stage of word composition to be reckoned with. The amalgamated compound *cupboard* may nowadays indicate neither 'cup' nor 'board', but in its earlier history as a compound it undoubtedly signified 'a board on which to put cups', whereas the blend *Ohiowa* was coined outright by the simple process of putting together *Ohio* and *Iowa* and was intended to continue to suggest the two state names. Lewis Carroll named these blends "portmanteau words" and coined some for *Alice in Wonderland* and other books, which, as we have already remarked, have had wide currency in the years since. Carroll's very definition, "words into which two meanings are packed as in a portmanteau", recognizes the existence of two meanings in the blending and so distinguishes them from the amalgamated compounds in which the two meanings have long ago fused into one new meaning. Since the motives that inspire the making of blends are usually apparent, blends may be classified according to the most important of these motives as follows:

a. Jocular and Confused Blendings. *Alcoholiday* ('alcohol' and 'holiday'), *anecdotage* ('anecdote' and 'dotage'), *animule* ('animal' and 'mule'), *bumbersoll* ('umbrella' and 'parasol'), *bungaloafer* ('bungalow' and 'loafer'), *dollarature* ('dollar' and 'literature'), *gerrymander* ('Gerry' and 'salamander'), *happenstance* ('happening' and 'circumstance'), *hellophone* ('hello' and 'telephone'), *insinuendo* ('insinuation' and 'innuendo'), *scandiculous* ('scandalous' and 'ridiculous'), *slanguage* ('slang' and 'language'), *slaughtoist* ('slaughter' and 'autoist'), *slickery* ('slick' and 'slippery'), *solemncholy* ('solemn' and 'melancholy'), *stuffocate* ('stuffy' and 'suffocate'), *swellegant* ('swell' and 'elegant'), *yellocution* ('yelling' and 'elocution').

b. **Scientific and Technical Coinings.** *Autobus* ('automobile' and 'omnibus'), *avigator* ('aviator' and 'navigator'), *cablegram* ('cable' and 'telegram' or perhaps merely a compound with *gram*), *confectaurant* ('confectionery' and 'restaurant'), *dextrose* ('dextro-glucose'), *electrocute* ('electro-' and 'execute'), *electrolier* ('electro-' and 'chandelier'), *fruice* ('fruit' and 'juice'), *futhorc* (first six letters of the runic alphabet), *limequat* ('lime' and 'kumquat'), *plumcot* ('plum' and 'apricot'), *pomato* ('potato' and 'tomato'), *travelogue* ('travel' and 'monologue'), *turkhen* ('turkey' and 'hen').

c. **Trade Names.** *Autel* ('automobile' and 'hotel'), *Hupmobile* ('Hupp' and 'automobile'), *Katy Line* ('K.T.', from Missouri, Kansas and Texas Railway), *Mobiloil* ('automobile' and 'oil'), *Motel* ('motor' and 'hotel'), *Patapar* ('Paterson' and 'parchment'), *Pennzoil* ('Pennsylvania' and 'oil'), *Stacomb* ('stay' and 'combed'), *Walkathon* ('walking' and 'marathon'). Names coined from initials and initial syllables, such as *Arco*, *Philco*, and *Socony* have already been discussed in an earlier analysis of trade names (p. 282).

In England it has been a popular practice to speak of national organizations by combining their initials, sometimes with the addition of a letter or two to make a more pronounceable word of the initials; so the Women's Royal Naval Service became the *Wrens*. In the United States the alphabetical age of American political history has seen the coining of a few such blends, as in *Nira* (National Industrial Recovery Act) and *Hokies* (bonds of the Home Owners' Loan Corporation). In American college circles the Delta Kappa Epsilon fraternity is known as the *Dekes*. A notable blending of the World War was *Anzac*, from Australia and New Zealand Army Corps.

d. **Personal Names and Place-names.** *Calipatria,* California ('California' and 'patria'), *Calistoga,* California ('California' and 'Saratoga'), *Calneva,* Nevada ('California' and 'Nevada'), *Calvada,* California ('California' and 'Nevada'), *Dakoming,* Wyoming ('Dakota' and 'Wyoming'), *Dorena,* Washington ('Dora' and 'Rena'), *Elmonica,* Washington ('Eleanor' and 'Monica'), *Lewanna,* Nebraska ('Lewellen' and 'Anna'), *Mayhen* ('May' and 'Henry'), and numerous other borderline place-names like those already discussed (p. 278). Some jocular blends have been made from existing place-names, such as *Chicagorilla, Michigander,* and *Omahog;* but for the most part the place-name blends have been seriously intended and have become permanent contributions to American nomenclature because they have often settled controversies by the method of compromise.

e. **Miscellaneous Blends.** A number of somewhat colorless words have resulted from the confusion of two similar words and have stayed on in the language because they have apparently satisfied a need. Such words are *blurb* ('blurt' and ?), *blurt* ('blare' and 'spurt'), *boost* ('boom' and 'hoist'), *brunch* ('breakfast' and 'lunch'), *chump* ('chunk' (?) and 'lump'), *doldrums* ('dull' or 'doleful' and 'tantrums'), *dumfound* ('dumb' and 'confound'), *flounder* ('founder' and 'blunder'), *flurry* ('flaw' and 'hurry'), *flush* ('flash' or 'flare' and 'blush'), *lunch* ('lump' and 'hunch' or 'bunch', if it is a blend at all), *squish* ('squirt' and 'swish'), possibly *straddle* ('astride' and 'saddle'). The pronoun *thon* ('that' and 'one') was proposed some years ago as a third person pronoun of common gender to obviate the awkwardness of saying "he or she", "his or hers", and the like; but it failed to win favor. In most of these last-named blends there is some doubt about the derivation of the blend, — for example, *blow* and *blubber* have been suggested, as well as *blare,* for the blend *blurt,* — so that one can only guess at the probable sources of the blend, and consequently the lexicographers differ in their suggestions. Perhaps it is this very fact, that several different ideas are suggested by the blending, which has made this last type of blend live on when the jocular and confused ones have died.

It would appear from a study of these five classes of blends that when two words are thus telescoped in a humorous or stupid manner, the blend is not likely to find a permanent place in standard English usage; but when the blend represents a practical compromise, as in proper names especially, or when it has a suggestive comprehensiveness like those of the last group, then it is likely to live on in the language. As to trade-name blends, their span of life depends largely upon the life of the business promoting them. Some few live, but most of them do not outlive their patents or copyrights.

66. Clipped Words and Back Formations

The clipping, or shortening, of words is to be expected in colloquial usage in almost any language, and English has its full share of them. Ordinarily clipping a word does not increase the vocabulary but merely reduces a longer word. But sometimes it is necessary to take cognizance of this process of word-shortening in order to establish the etymology of a short word now in use in English, and sometimes both the longer and the clipped form live on in the language. This is just one more of the outstanding factors in the simplification and reduction of many English words to their present almost monosyllabic state. It is a very natural process and begins, as might be expected, early in life. The child uses shortened words like *dad* or *pop*, *gramp* ('grandpa'), *hanky* ('handkerchief'), *mom* ('mamma'), and *sis* ('sister'). The college student clips many of his most used terms, using *chem* ('chemistry'), *comp* ('composition'), *cords* ('corduroys'), *ex* or *exam* ('examination'), *gym* ('gymnasium'), *lab* ('laboratory'), *prexy* ('president'), *prof* ('professor'), *quad* ('quadrangle'), and others of a like nature.[318] Other terms are shortened by those workers who use them most, and we get such forms as *caps* ('capitals'), *mike* ('microphone'), *navvy* (British for 'navigator', in the sense of a laborer engaged in digging etc.), *props* (theatrical 'properties'), *super* ('supernumerary'), *tarp* ('tarpaulin'), and perhaps *cups* ('cupfuls') and *spoons* ('spoonfuls'). Some of the longer names of races and places assume clipped forms, such as *Frisco* (San Franciscans do not approve of it!), *Jap* ('Japanese'), *Kazoo* ('Kalamazoo'), *San Berdoo* ('San Bernardino'), and the *Soo Line* (for the Minneapolis, St. Paul and 'Sault' Ste. Marie Railway).

Of course, clipped words are characteristic of slang and the more colloquial English, such as *deb* ('débutante'), *doc* ('doctor'), *gent* ('gentleman'), *glads* (an evasion of an awkward 'gladioli' or 'gladioluses'), *pep* ('pepper'), *vag* ('vagabond'), and *vet* ('veteran'). In the colloquial speech of everyday life certain shortened forms have assumed a place as a matter of course, and few people question *ad* ('advertisement'), *auto* ('automobile'), *bike* ('bicycle'), *bus* ('omnibus'), *flu* ('influenza'), *gas* ('gasoline'), *knickers* ('knickerbockers'), *Peke* ('Pekingese' dog), *phone* ('telephone'), *photo* ('photograph'), *Pom* ('Pomeranian' dog), *pram* (British, 'perambulator'), *stage* ('stagecoach'), and *taxi* ('taxicab'). Beyond these lie others which are even more securely entrenched in standard English usage, such as *cab* ('cabriolet'), *cad* ('cadet'), *curio* ('curiosity'), *incog* ('incognito'), *mob* ('*mobile vulgus*'), *spats* ('spatterdashes'), *van* ('caravan'), *wag* (perhaps 'waghalter'), *wig* ('periwig'), and *zoo* ('zoölogical' garden). Indeed, some of the last group have become so well established as separate words that the older, longer form, if it persists, has a meaning quite distinct from that of the clipped form, as in the case of *cad* and *cadet*, *van* and *caravan*.

The shortening of the adjective ending *-ical* to *-ic*, as in *comic(al)*, *dramatic(al)*, *electric(al)*, *epic(al)*, *historic(al)*, *periodic(al)*, *polemic(al)*, is so erratic and uncertain in its working that it is hard to indicate any very definite trends. When the shorter form has become a noun, like *critic*, *logic*, *music*, *politics*, then the longer form is usually kept for the adjective, as in *critical* (see Krapp[17], p. 314).

Occasionally a clipped word is made on the false assumption that a shorter form is needed to correspond to some longer word form. Because this goes just counter to the derivative process discussed in Section 61, it has been named *back formation*. So the noun *enthusiasm* is given a shorter verb *to enthuse, to beg* is made from *beggar, to bootleg* from *bootlegger, to burgle* from *burglar, to canter* from *Canterbury, to edit* from *editor, to jell* from *jelly, to laze* from *lazy, to peeve* from *peevish, to rove* from *rover, to sidle* from *sidelong, to sub* from *substitute, to type* from *typewriter,* and *to vamp* from *vampire.* Such back formations are usually classed as barbarisms or slang, though a few have won a place in standard literary English.

A few words in English have been clipped through a misunderstanding of their true etymological forms. As the silencing of a final *-e* sometimes left a stem ending *-s* at the very end of a word, English speakers apparently made the mistake of assuming that the *-s* must be the plural ending and so removed it when using the word as a singular noun. Earle has remarked, in commenting upon this form of shortening in nouns, "The *s*-plural has had in English the effect of making the close of a word almost untenable by *s* unless the word be of the plural number."[8] French *cherise* has been cut to *cherry* (and later the word was borrowed again in the form *cerise* to name the color); *marquise,* 'tent', was reduced to *marquee;* an earlier *pese* has acquired a singular form *pea;* from *chaise* was made a dialectal *shay,* famous in the "One-Hoss Shay" of Oliver Wendell Holmes; and a colloquial form *corp* is occasionally made from *corpse* and *a specie* from *species.* In Anglo-Saxon the words *burial, eaves,* and *riddle,* all ended in *-s;* but only *eaves* has retained its *-s,* and it is treated as a plural in Modern English, with the *s*-less form only in *eave trough* (preferably *eaves trough*). The dialectal *Chinee* and *Portugee* are likewise examples of this tendency to make new *s*-less forms. *Bermuda* was formerly *Bermudez.*

Probably this clipping of commonly used words will go steadily on in colloquial speech, and from time to time a clipped word will become established in the standard literary language. But such shortenings will have to run the gantlet, just as slang in general does, before the speaker of good English will use them with entire confidence; for linguistic laziness is so obviously the prime factor in most clippings that the careful speaker hesitates to employ them.

67. *Conversion, or Functional Change*

Ordinarily the conversion of a word from one part of speech to another does not increase the English vocabulary but rather diminishes the number of word forms in actual use, as we have already remarked more than once. But when the conversion becomes so definitely permanent that different derivative forms come into existence, then conversion must be reckoned with as a vocabulary-builder. A review of Section 58 will bring to light a number of such contributions to the vocabulary of English. *Breadths* of cloth and *shavings* from a plane are too thoroughly concrete nouns to be longer classed with the abstract *breadth* and the verbal *shaving*; the nouns *descendant, dugout, elders, goods, lean-to, primate, privates, window-blind*, have traveled too far from their original adjective or verb forms and functions to be considered quite the same words; about the nouns *extras*, a *half-back*, the *ins* and *outs* of it, and the verbs *to down* and *to cold-shoulder* (a person) so much special meaning has gathered that the words must be accorded separate treatment in any dictionary.

Perhaps the most outstanding contribution of conversion to the English vocabulary, however, has been through the process of the commonization of proper names. This process has already been defined as merely the making of a common noun or verb or common adjective out of a proper name (Sec. 58, p. 320); but to appreciate more fully its effect on the vocabulary of today, one should examine in some detail the groups and kinds of names that have been most often commonized, and the derivative forms that are later made from them. When a proper name retains its capital initial and is used in a figurative way, as in Shakespeare's "A *Daniel* come to judgement!", there is no creation of a new word; but when from *Vulcan* develops a verb *to vulcanize*, and from *Jove* the adjective *jovial*, then the dictionary is the richer by two new words; and since we have forgotten that *dunce* was once the middle name of *Joannes Duns Scotus*, two distinct words may be said to exist. Most of our commonized names have come from the following sources:

a. **Biblical names:** *babel* ('Babel'), *bedlam* ('Bethlehem'), *to christen* ('Christ'), *jeremiad* ('Jeremiah'), *jezebel* ('Jezebel'), *lazar* ('Lazarus'), *nimrod* ('Nimrod'), *philistine* ('Philistine'), *simony* ('Simon' Magus).

b. **Names from classical literature:** *amazon, atlas, bacchanalian* ('Bacchus'), *calliope, Crœsus, to hector* ('Hector'), *herculean* ('Hercules'), *iris, mercurial* and *mercury* ('Mercury'), *myrmidon, panic* ('Pan'), *phaëton, stentorian* ('Stentor'), and *to tantalize* ('Tantalus').

c. **Names of places and peoples:** *assassin, champagne, china, cologne, copper* ('Cyprus'), *damask* ('Damascus'), *gauze* ('Gaza'?), *hamburger* ('Hamburg'), *italic* ('Italy'), *laconic* ('Laconia'), *magic* (the 'Magi'), *magnesia, to meander* (from the river 'Meander'), *morocco, morris dance* ('Moorish'), *muslin* ('Mosul'), *sardine* ('Sardinia'), *slave* ('Slav'), *spaniel* ('Spain'), *stoic, surrey, turkey, worsted.* Many of the commercial products brought into England during the great period of trade and conquest have since borne the names of places from which they were imported.

d. **Names of inventors and scientists:** *ampere* (French electrician, 'Ampère'), *begonia* (French patron of botany, 'Bégon'), *dahlia* (Swedish botanist, 'Dahl'), *derrick* (London hangman), *doily* (London draper, 'Doily'), *macadam* (Scottish engineer, 'McAdam'), *mackintosh* ('Macintosh' introduced the coat), *mesmerize* ('Mesmer,' German physician), *pasteurize* ('Pasteur,' French scientist), *pullman, shrapnel, volt* ('Volta', Italian physicist), and *watt* ('Watt', British inventor).

e. **Names of famous people:** *brougham, chesterfield,* a *derby* hat, *epicure* ('Epicurus'), *Hooverize, martinet, platonic* ('Plato'), *sandwich* (Earl of 'Sandwich'), *valentine, victoria.*

f. **Miscellaneous literary characters:** *bluebeard* ('Bluebeard', villain of a popular story), *braggadocio* (Spenser's 'Braggadocchio'), *knickerbockers* (Irving's 'Knickerbocker'), *malapropism* (Sheridan's Mrs. 'Malaprop'), *pander* (Chaucer's 'Pandare' or Boccaccio's 'Pandaro'), *quixotic* (Cervantes's Don 'Quixote'), *Shylock* (Shakespeare's famous Jew), and *utopian* (More's 'Utopia').

g. **Trade names:** *celluloid, kodak, listerine, vaseline.*

h. **Other names:** *bowdlerize* (Dr. 'Bowdler'), *boycott* (Captain 'Boycott'), *hillbilly* ('Billy'), *jockey* ('Jock', English 'Jack'), *to lynch* (probably Judge 'Lynch'), *maverick* ('Maverick'), and *tawdry* ('Saint Audrey').

68. *Semasiological Change*

The multiplication of the meanings of a word ordinarily tends to reduce the number of distinct words, since the one word carries in itself meanings enough to serve for several words. But sometimes, as the meanings of a word diverge, different forms develop also to accompany these divergent meanings, so that the semasiological change actually increases the vocabulary. If the semasiological, or meaning, content of a word becomes quite different under two differing sets of conditions, among two different classes of speakers, or at two different periods of the language, two different forms of the word are likely to develop also. In Chapter X many doublets and triplets will be considered as they are found in the vocabulary of present-day English; but it is the purpose of this immediate study to look into the process of semasiological divergence as it contributes to vocabulary-building, a process which is not intentional and deliberate but which works gradually and often quite unsuspected by the users of the language, fixing ultimately two distinct pronunciations or forms of a word. Often a professional or technical use of one form will keep it different from the popular use of the corresponding form, as in the legal use of *chattel, escheat,* and *estate* and the more popular *cattle, cheat,* and *state.* The barber uses a *strop,* but the ordinary piece of leather is a *strap.* The farmer *threshes* his grain, but *thrashes* his erring son. The judge condemns a murderer to be *hanged,* but a curtain is merely *hung.* A document is *inválid,* but a person recovering from illness is an *inválid.* Since the legal term *trustee* is specialized in meaning, the trusted man in a penitentiary is called a *trusty.* Long ago the form *parson* was employed for the chief religious 'person' of a town; but *person* has been retained for the broader meaning of the word. Medical science seized upon the two forms *cancer* and *canker* and defined them differently, so that it became necessary to preserve them both in English. While *sir* became a popular form of address, the form *sire* remained more restricted in meaning. *Cute* became so broad in meaning that its earlier form *acute* was able to hold its narrower place in English. The colloquial phrase *by dint of* has preserved the old pronunciation when *dent* has prevailed elsewhere. And in America today, the educated *negro* is winning a place of respect and responsibility in art and science while his illiterate and unprogressive fellow of the colored race may still be 'a *nigger* in the woodpile' or have to 'work like a *nigger*'. It will be interesting to see whether the two words will drift farther and farther apart until they both become embedded in the language or whether changing conditions will gradually eliminate the old colloquial *nigger*. Semasiological change is uncertain and erratic in its effects upon the vocabulary of English.

69. *Confused Etymologies*

Confused thinking by speakers of the English language has played its part in the development of certain words, just as it has in the classification of the parts of speech. Indeed, the historian of the language has been inclined to presume more intelligent direction in the making of words than can be justified in many instances. Confusion has led sometimes to the substitution of a familiar form for an unfamiliar one or to the gradual fusing of two words originally quite distinct in both form and meaning. Moreover, a certain amount of confusion still exists in the minds of the lexicographers themselves when it comes to explaining the source or origin of a number of still troublesome words of Current English. The first of these groups may be called folk etymologies, the second overlapping etymologies, the third controversial etymologies. Probably in some cases etymological science will never be able to explain in a final way the exact process of derivation of some of these troublesome words, since so many things could have happened to them in the course of some fifteen hundred years of English history, as the foregoing discussions should have made quite evident to all. A word could have been created (without reference or virtually without reference to a previously existing form), changed in form by various compounding methods, reduced in form, converted so as to function differently, or its whole semasiological content could have been changed, so that sometimes what actually happened to a word can only be conjectured by the lexicographer living in the twentieth century.

a. **Folk Etymologies.** People with little understanding of the history of English or of the foreign languages that have contributed to English are likely to jump at conclusions and assume erroneous relationships between words. Weekley uses the term *folk etymology* to include "all phenomena which are due to any kind of misunderstanding of a word"[295]. This would include the activities of both the very ignorant speaker and that somewhat-learned student of the language who happens to possess more philological enthusiasm than true understanding of the facts. The effects of this popular etymologizing may be seen in most of the phases of language examined and illustrated in preceding chapters and word lists.

Careless pronunciation of *an hour* frequently produces *a nour* by the transfer of the *n*, and while *hour* is not in serious danger of becoming *nour* by this process, *an once word* has become *a nonce word* and *an ekename* is now *a nickname*; on the other hand, older *nadder* and *napron* have become *adder* and *apron* by the loss of initial *n-*. People became confused as to just where the *n* belonged and so misplaced it. The respellings that have resulted from a smattering of etymological information are a troublesome lot: the *b* was put into *debt* and *doubt*, as already explained, by some overzealous persons who happened to know the Latin *debitus* and *dubitare*, but who unfortunately did not know Chaucerian English; so they also put an *s* into the old Anglo-Saxon word *iland* because they confused it with Latin *insula* and its Old French derivative *isle*; somebody also felt that a *hiccup* had some vague relationship to a *cough* and proceeded to spell it *hiccough*; and because *should* and *would* had naturally a medial *l*, a similar spelling seemed to be called for in *coude*, and so it became *could*. Much the same kind of semilearned and overzealous etymologizing produced certain changes of prefixes and suffixes: the French *a-* of *aventure* and *avocat* and similar words of Middle English suddenly became *ad-*, giving *adventure* and *advocate*, because some enthusiastic Latinists decided to change them; *surloin*, 'steak on the loin', was mistakenly made *sirloin*, and even a far-fetched story concocted about some steak-loving king's having dubbed his favorite steak "Sir Loin"; in a popular misconception of *shamefast* (cf. *steadfast*), the suffix *-fast* was replaced by *-faced*, since the idea to be expressed appeared to justify *shamefaced*.

The most interesting and widespread of folk etymologies, however, are those which change unfamiliar locutions, generally foreign loan-words or very old native words, into compounds that contain more familiar elements. So one hears *coldslaw* (for *coleslaw*), *crawfish* or *crayfish* (Old French *crevice*), *gooseberry* (see Weekley's Etymological Dictionary), *horehound* (Anglo-Saxon *harehune*), *isinglass* (perhaps Dutch *huysenblas*), *muskrat* (the Algonquin *musquash*), *pennyroyal* (earlier *puliall royal*), *pickax* (Middle English *pikois*), *primrose* (French *primerole*), *saltcellar* (*salt* + Old French *saliere*), *sparrowgrass* (Greek-Latin *asparagus*), *wormwood* (Anglo-Saxon *wermod*). In each compound one can see plainly the word guessed at by the ignorant person — *cold, fish, goose, hound, glass, rat, penny, ax, rose*, and so on, always a well-known old word. Hamlet's "I know a hawk from a handsaw" has long caused perplexity to Shakespearean critics; it is not unlikely that *handsaw* was merely Hamlet's humorous mutilation of Old French *heronceau*, 'a small heron'. Hamlet would have enjoyed indulging in the popular game of folk etymology of this kind.

Popular misunderstanding is also responsible for the dropping of a final *-s* to give certain words a more characteristically singular form, as in *Chinee* (from *Chinese*), *pea* (from Middle English *pese*), and *Portugee* (from *Portuguese*). Sometimes, again, an entirely different word is substituted because speakers do not recognize the older word. So *to curry favor* is substituted for *to curry favel*; and some people have insisted upon saying *a Welsh rarebit* instead of *a Welsh rabbit*, an unwarranted change inasmuch as it has long been customary for people in certain districts to give fanciful slang names to popular articles of food. Palmer characterizes such an expression as "the mock-heroic of the eating-house", an expression "in which some common dish or product for which any place or people has a special reputation is called by the name of some more dainty article of food which it is supposed humorously to supersede or equal".[324] Similar expressions are *African golf* for the game of craps, *Cape Cod turkey* for codfish, the London East End *German duck* for a sheepshead stewed with onions, *Irish apricots* for potatoes, *Jew's-harp* for a very elementary musical instrument, *Missouri meerschaum* for corncob pipe, *Norfolk capons* for red herrings, *Swedish Christmas turkey* for stockfish, and so on.

Sometimes a locution by this process of folk etymology has its meaning slightly changed, as well as its form, as in *belfry* (from *berfrei*, an earlier movable watchtower), *hangnail* (from *agnail* or *angnail*; see Skeat's Etymological Dictionary), and *humble pie* (from *umble pie*, a pie made from the entrails of deer etc.). The ideas of *bell*, *hang*, and *humble* have gradually become such important elements in these words as to crowd out entirely the original ideas. So, in the story of Cinderella, the slipper which may have been originally one of 'fur of squirrel' (Old French *vair*), or even one decorated with 'pearls' (Old French *veir*), became one of 'glass' (Old French *verre*), because the English people did not know their French very well. Other mistranslations might be cited which have brought similar results for English.

b. **Overlapping Etymologies.** In some instances Current English uses words in a confusing manner or is uncertain about their etymologies because two similar words of earlier times have tended to overlap and gradually coalesce in their forms and meanings. The adjective *afraid* is undoubtedly a participle, but probably influenced by both the native verb *afear* and the French *afrayer*; *bid* means in Modern English 'to command' and also 'to invite', 'to ask', and still maintains some duplicate forms, but in Anglo-Saxon there were two distinct verbs, *beodan*, 'to command', and *biddan*, 'to ask'; *bound* has gradually merged in itself the values of the participle of *bind* and also of an Old Norse-Middle English adjective *boun*, 'ready to go'; *cleave* means both 'to cut' and 'to adhere to' and still keeps some duplicate forms, but in Anglo-Saxon two distinct verbs existed, *cleofan* and *cleofian*; *dream* has the form of Anglo-Saxon *dream*, 'noise', but the meaning of Old Norse *draumr*; *fret* may have been affected by both Anglo-Saxon *fretan*, 'to eat up', and some foreign word like Old French *frette*; *havoc* may well be the modern form of Anglo-Saxon *hafoc*, 'hawk', but an Old French *havot* is generally considered the source of it; *let* now has only one form, but has survivals of two different meanings, in 'to allow' and 'to hinder', because it represents the gradual converging of two Old English verbs, *lætan*, 'to allow', and *lettan*, 'to hinder'; *mystery* sometimes confuses the historical student because one early form came from the Greek-Latin *mysterium*, 'secret religious ceremony', while another was derived from Old French *mestier*, 'trade', 'occupation'; *ravenous* is usually traced back to an Old French *ravinos*, 'rapacious', but it is not at all unlikely that English speakers have associated it with the more familiar bird, the *raven*, at the same time. Indeed, if by the process of folk etymology one word could be substituted for another because of a misunderstanding, certainly two similar words may well have been confused and at times merged until the modern result of the confusion can best be explained by this overlapping, which McKnight has named "compound etymology"[325].

c. **Controversial Etymologies.** But even after folk etymology has been convicted of making numerous wrong substitutions or of confusedly merging two similar words, there still remain a number of words whose pedigrees have not yet been established to the satisfaction of all. A few examples will suffice to make clear the difficulties that beset the lexicographer: *blizzard* is still in a state of etymological confusion because of a variety of suggestions regarding its origin, notably derivation from French *blézard*, relationship to native *blast* (as from a trumpet), modification of German *blitzartig*, 'lightning-like', with possibly some onomatopœic influence[326]; to explain *gull* 'a dupe', Weekley suggests an obsolete *gull*, 'immature fish', related to Dutch *gul*, or else a figurative use of *gull*, the name of the bird that swallows anything thrown to it,[297] while Webster's New International Dictionary (Second Edition) gives as probable origin the Old Norse *gulr*, 'yellow'[26]; the American slang *guy*, 'man', 'fellow', has been variously connected with *Guy Fawkes*, with *guy* (meaning a 'rope'), and with Yiddish *goy*[327]; the colloquial *a little shaver*, says Palmer,[324] came from Gypsy *shavie* or *chavo*, a 'child' or 'son', but some later lexicographers are content to explain it as meaning 'the youth just beginning to shave'; and the pronoun *she* has been regarded by some historical philologists as a mere mispronunciation of the Anglo-Saxon feminine pronoun *heo*, while others have insisted upon an analogical confusion with the old demonstrative *seo* as the explanation of its present form. In view of the overlapping etymologies previously observed, it is not unlikely that the etymologists will be compelled to compromise ultimately on an acceptance of several confused sources for various controversial words of this kind. If the student of language, to reword the concluding remark of the chapter just preceding this one, will recognize the two possibilities presented in this chapter, namely, that most English words can be clearly etymologized but that some few have had a most confused and confusing career in the language, his thinking will be much clarified, and much useless argument about the etymology of words will be done away with.

It is well, however, to compare the more credulous methods of the older etymologists with the exacter and more scientific work of up-to-date lexicographers; the older student of language was not much superior to the popular etymologist, and his folk etymology manhandled many an unfamiliar locution until its earlier users would no longer have recognized it as their own. Not infrequently he invented apt stories to account for words that he did not understand, as in the case of *sirloin*, already mentioned, and of that gem from John Minsheu's *Guide into the Tongues* (1617), in which the term *cockney* was ascribed to the ignorance of a little London boy who asked his father as they traveled in the unfamiliar country, "Doth the cocke neigh too?" The twentieth-century etymologists gather all the evidence available regarding sound changes, meaning changes, and the ways by which a word could have entered into the English language from the foreign world. Their chief sources of materials are the New English Dictionary on Historical Principles (the great Oxford Dictionary) and the period dictionaries; and when such books do not supply enough examples, they go to the literature of all periods of English linguistic history for more detailed information. They do not jump at conclusions, as did one shortsighted but enthusiastic etymological novice who not so long ago evolved the beautiful explanation for *niggard* that *ni-* was simplified spelling for an older *nigh* and that "a *niggard* was a *nigh-guard* because he kept close watch on his goods or money." His assumption of a reformed spelling was of the twentieth century, but his etymological methods smacked of the Middle Ages.

II. THE BORROWING OF WORDS

Concerning the borrowing of words by the English people so much has already been said in connection with other phases of the history of the language that the rest of this chapter will be devoted mainly to further word lists illustrating points already raised. It has been shown that at least three fourths of all the words in the English dictionary are borrowed words (Sec. 25). The times and sources of these borrowings have been roughly sketched in Chapter V. Those exotic spellings which English orthography has acquired from foreign tongues, and the foreign suffixes, prefixes and other compounding elements which are to be found in so many of the words of Current English, have been discussed in some detail. But it remains for the student of the English language to examine the various groups and kinds of words that have been borrowed, in order to appreciate more fully the great richness and versatility of the English language of the twentieth century.

It is well, however, before examining these borrowings in detail to remind the reader that very many of these words had long and interesting lives before they were ultimately absorbed into the English vocabulary. When the Latin language began to influence the Anglo-Saxons, it had already adopted many of the terms expressive of that rich Greek culture which the Romans admired and imitated; the French people had a primitive foundation of Frankish German upon which the Latin of colonial Gaul was imposed, and it is reasonable to suppose that they were further affected by the language of their High German neighbors; the Normans began as a tribe of Northmen and later were Romanicized; the Italians and Spaniards and Portuguese used other modified forms of the Roman Latin; and everywhere the peoples of civilized Europe went, during the period of exploration and colonization, they carried to the uncivilized portions of the world many Greek and Latin words to be adapted to new uses and made over, so that when such words finally came into English, they had already experienced manifold and interesting changes. Sometimes it is difficult for the English lexicographer to decide from just what point in its linguistic wanderings a word dropped into the stream of English speech. We are told, for example, that *baluster* was a Greek word which passed through Latin into Italian and thence via French into English, that *albatross* went from Greek to Arabic and then via Spanish through Portuguese to English, much as *apricot* started in Latin and via Greek passed through Arabic to Portuguese and thence through French came into English. *Sack*, says Skeat, is an Egyptian word which has traveled through Hebrew to Greek and then into Latin. and he adds[294]:

> This remarkable word has travelled everywhere, together (as I suppose) with the story of Joseph; the reason why it is the same in so many languages is because it is, in them all, a borrowed word from Hebrew. We find Du. *zak*, G. *sack*, Icel. *sekkr*, Swed. *säkk*, Dan. *sæk*,

Goth. *sakkus* (sack-cloth, Matt. xi. 21), Ital. *sacco*, Span. and Port. *saco*, F. *sac*, Irish and Gael. *sac*, W. *sach*.

With such situations, it is not surprising that there are many controversial etymologies in English.

70. *Latin Borrowings*

It is hardly possible to say too much about the part that Latin life and culture have played in the development of English culture and the English language. More than half of our words have come from the Latin, directly or through some other tongue, such as the French; even before the Anglo-Saxons came to England, Roman life had made inroads into the ruder culture of the Germanic peoples on the Continent and had been established for some centuries on British soil; much of our derivational apparatus, such as prefixes, suffixes, and other compounding elements of various kinds, is Latin, and in the building of new words in English the changes have been rung on these over and over again down through the later centuries; even today the scientist and the inventor depend largely on New Latin coinings for names of plants, commercial products, and so on. A steady and continuing influence of Roman culture, both pagan and Christian, over a period of almost two thousand years should convince the student of English that he cannot hope to understand English literature and the English language until he has made some study of Latin literature and the Latin tongue.

The earliest borrowings of the English language were probably Latin words. It is not unlikely that the Romans introduced to the Angles, Saxons, and Jutes a few of their everyday words while those semibarbarous tribes still dwelt in their older Continental homes; but since little is known of the English until they began to make history on the island of Great Britain, it is hardly worth while trying to distinguish their earlier Continental acquisitions from their later borrowings. Very early they were using *mile, mount, port, Saturday, street, wall, wine,* and were making place-names with

-caster and *-chester* and *wic-*. In the everyday life of early Anglo-Saxon England they made use of *anchor, butter, candle, chalk, cheese, chest, copper, cup, dish, drake, gem, kettle, kitchen, mill, mint, ounce, pepper, pile, silk, tile,* and a few adjectives, notably *crisp*.

With the introduction of Christianity a whole vocabulary of special terms was introduced, such as *ark, creed, font, mass, noon, nun, pope, prime, temple,* and *Vulgate*. Some of these religious terms the Romans had themselves already acquired from the Greek, particularly *bishop, church, devil, minster, priest, school*; and these must be considered again later in this chapter as an early phase of Greek influence, although they came into the English in Latinized forms, mainly, since the early scholars of England did not use the Greek language to any great extent.

Many animal and plant names were introduced in the process of translating Latin literature into Anglo-Saxon, such as *beet, camel, elephant, lily, lion, palm, pear, phœnix, plant, poppy, rose, tiger*.

A few verbs were early borrowings, such as *offer, pine, shrive, spend,* and *stop*; but most of the Latin verbs that have come into English entered later in shorter form through early French, as *cease, chase,* or in longer form more directly from the Latin, as *accentuate, coagulate, permeate*.

The great influx of Latin words that followed the English Renaissance should, to be properly appraised, have a careful and detailed classification according to the phases of culture represented by them. We have numerous terms of divinity and theology, like *carnal, foreordination, trinity, unitarian*; of philosophy, mathematics, and physics, such as *diameter, fundamental, mental, momentum, proposition, radius, vacuum*; of law and government, like *affidavit, alibi, coroner, habeas corpus, judicial, subpœna, veto*; of botany, especially, hundreds of terms recognizable as Latin, such as *calix, corolla, mallow, palmate, petal, stamen,* and the New Latin coinings like *dahlia, freesia, magnolia,* and *wistaria,* which owe their form to Latin but derive from proper names and other words not necessarily Latin; terms of medicine and surgery, like *anesthetic, cardiac, diagnosis, fibula*; many geographical and topographical terms, such as *equator, Capricorn, continental, insular, meridian, latitude, peninsula, tropical*.

Among the examples given several will be found which were originally Greek, and the difficulty of separating Latin from Greek words will be apparent in any study of philosophical, botanical, medical, and other scientific terms of Modern English, since the culture of Rome rested so heavily on that of Greece. Often the form of the borrowed word shows Latin use, even though the word can be traced ultimately to Greek. In the naming of newly discovered or hybridized plants in later times, it has been the general practice to Latinize the name of some botanist or horticulturist, as in *Sempervivum braunii* ('Braun's everliving'), *Berberis darwini* ('Darwin's barberry'). It is almost impossible to determine, moreover, whether certain words should be credited to the Latin directly or should be regarded as borrowings from the French and ultimately from the Latin. Who can say whether the scholar in medieval England, using as he did Latin as an international tongue and French and English as everyday languages, took his word from his Latin reading or from the French literature so commonly read at that time in England? When Gower, for example, made poems in three languages, he used for 'serve' a Middle English *serven*, a French *servir*, and a Latin *servire*; and he probably felt free to adapt words from any one of the three languages to any other, as occasion required. If one looks up in the dictionaries of today such words as *narration, nation, notation,* and *notion*, he will find that one lexicographer will suggest only the Latin form as the source of the word, another will indicate borrowing by "F. < L.," and another will evade the responsibility of indicating a direct source by naming both the French and the Latin form.

It is obvious, then, that it is often best for the student of Current English to be content with a recognition of the fact that a word was originally Latin. If he is familiar with the Latin language,— as he should be if he is to appreciate the vocabulary of English,— several aids to identification of Latin material in English are at his command. Embedded in our vocabulary are many important Latin words, such as *ager* 'field', *ago, actus,* 'do', 'act', *audio,* 'hear', *cedo,* 'go', *clarus,* 'clear', *duco,* 'lead', *frater,* 'brother', *gero, gestus,* 'bear', 'carry', *gradus,* 'step', *mors, mortis,* 'death', *pono, positus,* 'put', 'place', *scribo,* 'write', *signum,* 'sign', *tego, tectus,* 'cover', *vacuus,* 'empty', *verto, versus,* 'turn', *vir,* 'man', *voco, vocatus,* 'call', *volvo,* 'roll', 'turn'.

The many Latin suffixes and prefixes are also helpful in identifying Latin borrowings, although these cannot always be trusted because sometimes they have been added to words from Anglo-Saxon and other languages to make hybrids. Those that have been marked as being still active in Current English are the most untrustworthy, of course (see Sec. 61). But there are, for example, scores of verbs in English ending in *-ate* (Latin participial *-atus*), such as *actuate, dominate, placate, regulate, vibrate,* and many adjectives like *adequate, coördinate, obstinate, truncate,* which are unquestionably of Latin origin. Not many nouns retain (like *ratio*) the nominative form in *-io*; but English is full of Latin nouns with the longer form *-ion,* such as *action, creation, diction, nation, union.* Occasionally a Latin adverb is retained in literary English, notably *seriatim, verbatim,* and the adverbial ablative *gratis.*

Those Latin nouns which retain more purely still in Modern English their Latin inflectional endings are, of course, not hard to place. Some end in *-a,* such as *alumna* (plural *alumnæ*), *fuchsia, inertia, magnolia, vertebra*; others in *-us,* like *alumnus* (plural *alumni*), *animus, bonus, cactus, genus, gladiolus, radius*; others in *-um,* such as *curriculum, datum* (plural *data*), *desideratum, memorandum, stadium, vacuum.*

Some few Latin phrases are used by English speakers, usually without change in their forms, such as *alma mater, bona fide, et al.* (for '*et alii*'), *et cetera, ex cathedra, ex officio, magnum opus, per se, pro and con, sub rosa,* and *tertium quid*; but these are the embellishments of learned English and not standard colloquial expressions.

And, finally, one can generally assume that many words used in certain fields of modern English intellectual life, such as botany, medicine, horticulture, are of Latin origin. The more learned the terms are and the more highly specialized their use, the more likely they are to be of Latin origin or formed after Latin models.

71. *French Borrowings*

We have already credited the French with more than a fourth of all the words comprising the vocabulary of Current English. Most of these were originally Latin, but received the peculiar stamp of French before being handed on to English. The earliest of these borrowings were from the Norman French, mostly after the conquest of England in 1066, and pertain to that feudal form of medieval life which would need such words as *bailiff, banner, baron, battle, castle, count* and *countess, crown, duke, power, prison, tower, treasure, war,* and *warden.* The language of the law and politics was enriched early with terms like *chattel, country, heritage, judge, jury, justice, mortgage, peace, plaintiff, rent,* and *treason*; but no limited period for such borrowings can be established, since they continued to increase with English legal usage long after French ceased to be the official language of English courts. Beginning with the twelfth century, words of trade and everyday affairs were introduced, such as *barber, butcher, carpenter, chair, chamber, city, grocer, labor, mantle, mason, tailor.* And certain native words were supplemented by the use of similar French words, as in the case of *bacon* and *pork* (cf. AS. *swine*), *beef* (cf. AS. *ox*), *mutton* (cf. AS. *sheep*), *veal* (cf. AS. *calf*), *venison* (cf. AS. *deer*), and *alas* (cf. AS. *wellaway*), *to cause* (cf. AS. *do*), *dame* (cf. AS. *lady*), *sire* (cf. AS. *man*). Abstract and cultural words began to appear, such as *chaplain, chapter, faith, false, gentle, grace, grief, mercy, miracle, saint.*

As the demand for French literature in English translations grew greater, hundreds of words appeared, many of them pertaining to more erudite and complex culture and less to the everyday and commonplace life of the English. So one finds quite early in English literature such words as *abash, abundance, anoint, chase, claim, danger, embellish, enter-*

prise, gage, guard, guardian, homicide, joint, moral, point, and *ransom.* These are, of course, like most of the French words adopted before the English Renaissance, thoroughly assimilated into the English vocabulary and rarely thought of by modern speakers as foreign words.

But there are many French words in Modern English use that still suggest their French origin, usually by some little peculiarity of form or pronunciation — such words, for example, as *automobile, cadet, camouflage, caprice, chagrin, chamois, chaperon, débutante, depot, fiancée, foyer, garage, machine, prairie, résumé, role, technique.*

And, finally, there are certain French words and phrases which the more cultured or quasi-cultured English speaker likes to use but which are still on the border line and generally included by the lexicographer among the foreign words and phrases or else given a special mark in the general vocabulary to indicate their foreign status, such as *apropos, au revoir, bête noire, billet-doux, château, genre, laissez faire, nouveau riche, tête-à-tête.*

The many French place-names in America, such as *Bordeaux, Des Moines,* and *La Salle,* have already been discussed (p. 276), and the French personal names that can be found in the pages of British and American history are familiar to all readers of historical literature.

Aids to the identification of French words in English are relatively few and undependable, except in the case of the most recent borrowings. The Norman words are hardest to identify because they are simple in form and pertain largely to everyday life and thought. The later medieval borrowings from the Central French are likely to be less simple and more highly specialized in meaning and more learned or literary in their use. Since the French had difficulty with initial *w*, they changed it to *g*, which was later spelled *gu*; this gave us such words as *guarantee* (cf. *warrantee*), *guard, guardian, guerdon, guide, guile* (cf. *wile*), *guise.* The medial *s* of some earlier French borrowings, like *castle, feast, hostel, pasty,* was dropped from the later French pronunciation of such words; and so we have borrowed again these same words in modified forms as *château, fete, hotel,* and *patty.* Since the French had trouble also in pronouncing words with initial *sk, sp, st,* etc., they added an initial *e-* and gave us such words as *esquire, especially, estate,* although English tends to drop this initial *e* again, as in *squire, specially, state.*

Occasionally the pronunciation of a more recently borrowed French word helps to identify its parentage, particularly in the case of words with final silent *s, t, ue, x,* such as *apropos, depot, unique,* and *billet-doux.* When typically French sounds appear, such as the palatalization of *g* in *mignonette,* or the pronunciation of *g* as [ʒ] in *régime* and *ch* as [ʃ] in *chef,* or *e* as [ē] in *fete,* one generally senses the exotic nature of the word. Likewise the more exotic spellings of certain French words strike the attention, as *-re* in *centre, -lle* in *gazelle,* medial *-qu-* in *liquor, lacquer, -mme* in *programme.*

Some of the suffixes that have been brought in with French loan-words are so distinctively French as to mark them beyond question, such as *-age* in *homage, -ance* in *abundance* (Latin would have *-antia*), and *-ence* in *diligence* (Latin would have *-entia*), *-ee* in *devotee, -ese* in *journalese.* So, also, the prefix *Fitz-* in *Fitzpatrick* marks a Norman word, just as *(de) la* shows later French influence in Marquis *de Lafayette.*

And, finally, words pertaining to the culinary art, such as *café* and *hors d'œuvre,* to the business of the *modiste,* such as *basque, crêpe de Chine,* and *peignoir,* to literature and the fine arts, such as *bas-relief, beaux arts, belles lettres, bon mot, brochure,* and to various other phases of modern French life and culture, have permeated the English language to such an extent that the well-educated man or woman must needs take cognizance of them.

72. *Celtic Borrowings*

In spite of the fact that the Celtic peoples held all of Britain at one time, they have left only a slight heritage to the English language of today. The Britons fled before the Anglo-Saxons westward into Strathclyde, Wales, and Cornwall, chiefly; the Irish learned to speak English; the Northern form of English which we now call Lowland Scotch encroached more and more upon the Celtic tongue spoken by the Scotch Highlanders. And so today not much more than 1 per cent of the English vocabulary can be traced to these Celtic peoples. Attention has already been called to the almost complete lack of early British Celtic words (Sec. 30); only a meager handful are listed by the etymologists, of which the most important are *bard, bin, brat, brock* (badger), *crock* (?), *down* (hill), *dun*, and *slough* (?). To these may be added some Latin words borrowed by the early Celts and handed on to the English, particularly *bannock, Christ, cross, pillion*, and *plaid*. Some words of the Continental Celts of Gaul were adopted by the French and later handed on to the English; but since scholars are almost as doubtful of the Gallic remains in the French language as of the British Celtic remains in English, only a few such Celtic-French loan-words are reasonably sure. The most probable are *ambassador, attack, budge, carpenter, carry, charge, chariot, druid, gab, javelin, lay* (a song), *varlet*, and *vassal*. So there remain as evidence of the actual presence of Celtic people in England and Scotland mainly the Celtic place-names, already discussed, such as *Aberdeen, Ben Lomond, Caerleon, Dunbar, Inverness*, and *Kildare*.

The later borrowings of Celtic words are more easily recognized, usually, and are traceable to certain branches of the language. From the Welsh come *coracle, cromlech, eisteddfod*, and *flannel*; from the Irish, *banshee, bog, brogue, galore, ogham, shamrock, shillelagh, spalpeen*, and *Tory*; and from the Highland Scotch, *cairn, clan, claymore, crag, glen, loch, mackintosh, reel* (a dance), *slogan, tartan*, and *whisky*. Some others, such as *colleen* and *mavourneen*, of the Irish, and *cairngorm* and *coronach*, of the Scottish, are likely to appear in dialectal literature but can hardly be said to hold places in standard English. The purely Celtic tongues of modern times, namely, Welsh, Irish Gaelic, and Highland Scotch, have proved difficult for English speakers to acquire.

73. Scandinavian Borrowings

The difficulty of distinguishing those words in Modern English which came from the Old Norse tongue as spoken in the time of the viking invasion and occupation of England has already been discussed in Section 33, and because of the very simple character of the words acquired at that time scholars still feel much hesitation about ascribing to Scandinavian influence words and forms and meanings that might conceivably have arisen through developments within the Northern dialect of the Anglo-Saxon people themselves. Certainly not more than 5 per cent of our present vocabulary is of Norse origin, and possibly somewhat less, even. The fragmentary nature of the Old English literature that remains today leaves always the possibility that while a word may not be found by us in the extant literature, nevertheless it may have existed in the native speech of that early day. So in seeking Old Norse loan-words we can list only such words as seem to have been unknown to the early English or such as appear unlike the forms that they would be likely to have used. Of Old Norse origin, probably, are the nouns *anger, bank* (cf. AS. *bench*), *brae* (cf. AS. *brow*), *dirt, fellow, gait, husband, lad* and *lass, law, leg, root* (cf. AS. *wort*), *scale* (of a balance), *skid, skill, skin, skirt* (cf. AS. *shirt*), *sky, thrall, wing*; the verbs *bask, busk, call, cast, die* (cf. AS. *starve*), *happen, hit, raise* (cf. AS. *rear*), *ransack, scare, scrape, take, thrive*; the adjectives *bound,* 'ready to go', *flat, ill* (cf. AS. *sick*), *loose, low, meek, Norse, odd, ugly*; the adverbs *aloft* and *fro* and the preposition *till*; and the pronominal forms *they, their,* and *them*. Probably Old Norse forms have superseded the Anglo-Saxon forms in *egg, get, give, welcome,* and perhaps in *wrong*.

The numerous place-names that are to be found in the old territory of the Danelaw in northeastern England, such as *Derby, Kingsthorpe, Lowestoft,* are readily recognized by the Old Norse suffixes *-by, -thorp, -toft, -thwaite,* as already shown (p. 276), and these constitute by far the most satisfactory evidence of the early Scandinavian occupation of England. Scholars have been enabled by means of the many place-names of this kind scattered throughout Lincolnshire, Yorkshire, and neighboring counties to determine with fair accuracy the dwelling places of the Danes in medieval England.

The Scandinavian loan-words of more recent times are relatively few, but they are usually more easily identified with the different Scandinavian countries. Modern scholarship has revived a few Old Norse terms, such as *berserker*, *Edda*, *saga*, *skald*, *troll*, *valkyrie*, and *viking*. From Icelandic comes *geyser*; from Swedish, *dahlia*, *gantlet*, *sloyd*, *tungsten*; from Norwegian, *fiord* and *ski*; and a few others not so easily localized, particularly *auk*, *floe*, *flounder*, and *narwhal*, must be loosely credited to the Scandinavian group. Personal names ending in *-sen* and *-son* (meaning 'son'), such as *Gibson*, *Larsen*, *Olsen*, and *Peterson*, are of Scandinavian origin, although many have been current in northern England since the viking invasions.

Attempts have been made to list distinguishing features of these Norse words in English; and if such criteria be accepted with a recognition of their inadequacy, they can be useful to the etymologist. In general it can be said that words with *sk* (*sc*) are likely to be of Norse origin, since Old English generally developed *sh* in similar native words. Such borrowings are *bask*, *busk*, *scald*, *skill*, *skin*. But a few words of French origin also have this same consonant combination. Then, again, various Norse words have *g* or *k* (*c*) when the corresponding native forms would have regularly developed some other form of the consonant, as in *drag* (cf. native *draw*), *dregs*, *flag*, *keg*, *kid*, *kirtle*, *leg*, *log*, and perhaps the Scottish *kirk* (cf. *church*). Roughly speaking, words with *ai* (*ay*) and *ei* (*ey*) are likely to be of Norse origin when they correspond to similar English words with *o* or some other vowel. Such Norse borrowings are *bait* (cf. AS. *bite*), *gait* (cf. AS. *gate*), *hail* (cf. AS. *whole*), *nay* (cf. AS. *no*), perhaps Northern *raid* (cf. AS. *road*), *raise* (cf. AS. *rear*), *sleigh*, *swain*, *wail*. One needs, of course, to know the earlier history of English words as a whole in order to appreciate more fully the extent to which native Anglo-Saxon forms and meanings have been affected or replaced by the very similar Norse words.

74. Greek Borrowings

As a whole, the most learned and highly specialized of all the words that have been borrowed in the course of the growth of English culture are comprised in that 10 per cent of the English vocabulary of today which bears strongly the stamp of Hellenic life and thought. While there has been no direct contact between the Greeks and the English, a fairly steady stream of cultural and scientific terms has flowed through the Latin or New Latin into English for the entire period of almost two thousand years during which Roman culture has been influencing English. The ecclesiastical words which the Roman Church gave the English after the Conversion, in 597 A.D., were largely of Greek origin, as already remarked, particularly *alms, angel, bishop, church, deacon, devil, episcopal, martyr, minster, monk, priest, psalm,* and many sacred names, such as *Bible, Christ, Peter.*

Until the English Renaissance few Englishmen read Greek. Nevertheless many Latin words of Greek derivation will be found in Middle English literature, such as *abyss, barbarous, character, clerk, distich, harmony, organ, paradise, patriarch, philosopher, physic, school, spasm.* Gradually proper names of Greek mythology and literature have become commonized in English, giving such words as *amazon, atlas, calliope, erotic, panic, platonic, plutocrat, psychical, tantalize.* At the same time various personal names from the Greek remained in general use in England, such as *Catherine, Dorothea, George, Helen, Homer, Margaret, Phœbe, Stephen,* and *Theodore.*

But to appreciate fully the importance of Greek words in the vocabulary of English science and scholarship, we need to consider the various fields of learning, one by one. In English literary terminology, for example, are to be met such words as *antithesis, chorus, comedy, drama, hexameter, hyperbole, lexicon, poet, rhythm, tragedy*; in philosophy and mathematics, *basis, category, diagram, enthusiasm, ethics, hypotenuse, pentagonal, theory, thesis*; in botany, *balsam, bulb, cactus, cotyledon, delphinium, heliotrope, organism, parasite, phlox*; in the realm of physics, *dynamo, hydraulic, pneumatic, thermometer*; in medical terminology, *chiropractor, diagnosis, diaphragm, esophagus, homeopathy, neuralgia, rheumatism*; in the naming of modern inventions, *bicycle, cinematograph, phonograph, photograph, telegraph, telephone.*

Except for the very earliest borrowings, Greek words are not very hard to identify in English. For one thing, the spellings *ch, ph, pn, rh*, as in *chasm, phone, pneumatic, rhetoric*, are outstanding in English; certain Greek suffixes have remained fairly distinct, particularly *-ics, -id, -isk, -ism, -ist, -ize, -oid, -osis*, as in *acoustics, Leonid, asterisk, organism, bigamist, philosophize, asteroid, neurosis*; and the various compounding elements listed in Section 62, such as *-arch-, -graph-, -log-, -path-, -phil-, -phon-, -scop-, -trop-*, can scarcely be mistaken.

75. *Borrowings from Other Germanic Languages*

Since the Anglo-Saxon tribes brought the Low German linguistic stock to Britain and there exposed it to the later influence of the Norse vikings, the English language has not been strongly affected by any other Germanic tongue. But there have been minor borrowings from time to time, which, taken as a whole, make up a more formidable body of English words than all the Scandinavian borrowings together.

In the first place, it should be borne in mind that the Merovingian rulers of France were originally Franks, a West Germanic tribe, and though these Franks yielded largely to the Romanic culture and speech of the country which they conquered, nevertheless a fairly large number of old Germanic words remained in French speech and were imported into medieval England, such as *belfry, butcher, gain, gallant, gallop, garden* (cf. AS. *yard*), *garrison, guard* (cf. AS. *ward*), *guide, hardy, heron, pocket, random, riches, rob, seneschal,* and *sturdy*.

Then the Dutch have contributed numerous simple words to the English vocabulary, such as *boor, brandy, drum, isinglass, knapsack, landscape, scrabble, sled, wagon* (cf. AS. *wain*), and numerous nautical terms, such as *avast, boom, deck, dock, hoist, jib, lighter, marline, reef, skipper, sloop, splice, yacht*, and *yawl*. The Boer dialect of South African Dutch has more recently been contributing a few terms, such as *Boer, kopje, kraal, rand, trek, veld,* and *wildebeest*.

From modern German life and thought a few expressions have been transferred to the English, notably *cobalt, dachshund, Fahrenheit, fuchsia, kindergarten, meerschaum, mesmerism, minnesinger, poodle, quartz, sauerkraut, shale, wienerwurst* (American *hot dog*), *Yiddish*, and *zinc*.

76. *Borrowings from Other Romanic Languages*

In their influence upon the English language, the other Romanic languages have exerted a far smaller and a much later influence than the French. Their political and cultural contacts with the English people have been chiefly of the Modern English period of the language, and usually the borrowings have resulted from the adventures of scholarship and trade or conquest outside of Great Britain. Frequently these borrowings have been at second hand, the French having taken them over first and put their own stamp upon them before passing them on to the English.

The influx of Italian culture into England came pretty early in the sixteenth century and without much preliminary preparation; for while Caxton, in the preface of his 1490 translation, the *Eneydos*, refers mainly to French words when he mentions his "fair and strange terms", a half-century later Roger Ascham specifically protests against the influx of "straunge wordes as latin, french, and Italian". Very early *alarm, brigand, ducat, florin, pilgrim* had been introduced. At first the English Renaissance borrowings from the Italian were general and literary, such as *alert, attitude, ballot, bravo, bulletin, cadence* (cf. Italian *cadenza*, borrowed later), *canto, fiasco* (cf. French *flask*), *gazette, influenza* (cf. French *influence*), *isolate, macaroni, motto, ruffian, stanza, umbrella*. Various architectural terms have come from the Italian, such as *arcade, balcony, colonnade, corridor, piazza, portico*; for words pertaining to music and painting and other arts English is especially indebted, as, for example, *aria, cameo, finale, fresco, opera, piano, prima donna, replica, soprano, staccato, studio,* and *violin.*

There are others which even today are still felt to be slightly strange, although they are quite generally used, such as *campanile, cognoscente, dilettante, extravaganza, Fascist.*

A little later in the sixteenth century the Englishman began to come into closer political contact with the Spaniard; he translated Spanish literature, and gradually his explorations and commercial expansions brought him into touch with Spanish colonies and Spanish culture everywhere over the world. So we find such early borrowings as *armada, cargo, comrade, desperado, mulatto, negro, renegade;* others that have been borrowed as they were needed are *anchovy, bravado, cigar, embargo, guerrilla, mosquito, tornado.*

Spanish American life has utilized numerous other words, such as *alligator, armadillo, calaboose, chinchilla, rancho,* and *vanilla;* some are Spanish or Mexican in form but American Indian in origin, such as *alpaca, barbecue, chocolate, guano, tobacco;* and Spanish place-names, such as *Colorado, Eldorado, Florida, Sierra,* are common. In the western part of the United States, especially, many Spanish words have been used which are not so familiar elsewhere, such as *adobe, bonanza, broncho, canyon, chaparral, corral, lariat, manzanita, mesquite, patio,* and *sombrero.*

The Portuguese words in English are not always readily distinguishable from the Spanish, nor are they very numerous. Skeat has estimated that there are only about fifty, the most important of which are *albatross, buffalo, caste, cobra, dodo, fetish, joss, junk, Madeira, molasses, palaver, veranda, zebra,* and perhaps *banana, flamingo, peon, pimento, tank;* some of these might well have come through the Spanish. It is interesting to observe that these Portuguese words, as well as many of the Spanish borrowings, reflect a life of exploration and trade on the outskirts of European civilization, which has often brought to the Englishman new and unusual experiences, — with the *banyan tree* of Hindustan, the *emu* of Australia, the *pagoda* of the Orient, and *sargasso* of the open seas.

77. Miscellaneous Borrowings

In the foregoing sections we have discussed that preponderatingly large part of the English loan element which has come from the four great branches of the Indo-European family, the Hellenic, the Romanic, the Celtic, and the Germanic. Most of it we have found to have entered the English language by way of the Latin or one of its offspring, namely, French, Italian, Spanish, or Portuguese, or else by way of the Norse, Low German, or High German tongues. A few old Greek and Latin words we have traced by roundabout courses far afield in other languages and then ultimately back into English, as, for example, the Latin word *apricot*, which went into Arabic at one time; another example is the Greek *effendi*, which went over into Turkish before the Englishman had occasion to use the word.

But there is a miscellaneous though highly interesting scattering of words in the English vocabulary — possibly not more than 7 or 8 per cent of the whole — which have come to the English people partly through their reading but more largely through their widespread living and trading and traveling. The most interesting and suggestive groups of these are as follows:

a. **Hebrew.** One of the earliest non-Indo-European tongues from which English words have been drawn is that branch of the Semitic family of languages known as Hebrew. Naturally, because they were almost all Biblical words, they were gained through reading rather than first-hand contacts with the Hebrew-speaking people. Most nearly unchanged are such words as *alleluia, amen, cherub, hallelujah, Jehovah, jubilee, leviathan, mammon, Messiah, Pharisee, rabbi, sabbath, Satan, seraph, shibboleth,* and the many other Biblical names that have been commonly used by English people. Words dealing with everyday life have been more commonly employed, and sometimes much modified, especially *ass, bedlam* (from *Bethlehem*), *camel, cider, cinnamon, damson* and *damask* (from *Damascus*), *earnest* ('pledge'), *ebony, gopher, jack* and *Jacob, Jesuit, Jew, kosher, lazar, maudlin* (from *Magdalen*), *sapphire,* *simony*, and *sycamore*. Our Hebrew words do not make a long list, but they have played an important part in the history of English life and thought.

b. Arabic. The Arabic branch of the Semitic family of languages has contributed rather more freely to English because it has not been restricted to literary contact so narrowly; during the Middle Ages Arabic learning and life left a most marked impress upon our language as well as upon the other tongues of Europe. A few words begin with the Arabic article *al* ('the'), particularly *albacore, albatross, alchemy, alcohol, alcove, alfalfa, algebra*, and *alkali*. Other technical terms are *caliber, cipher* (or *zero*), *nadir, zenith*. From the literature and everyday life of the Arab have come *admiral, arabesque, artichoke, camphor, coffee, cotton, crimson, fakir, ghoul, harem, hegira, houri, Koran, magazine, Moslem, sheik, sherbet, sirup, sofa*.

c. Sanskrit, Indian. When the English etymologist cannot find the source of a word nearer at hand, he sometimes goes to that very old sacred tongue of India, the Sanskrit, for a possible original. So Sanskrit is usually cited for *candy, chintz, indigo, loot, mandarin, pepper, sapphire*, and *sugar*. More recent borrowings from India are *bandanna, bungalow, curry* (the food), *juggernaut, polo, shampoo*, and *toddy*.

d. Persian. The relatively small number of words taken by the Englishman from that other old branch of the Indo-European family, the Persian, illustrate most admirably the manner in which English life and thought have been enriched from outside life and culture. Foods and plants are represented by *jasmine, lemon, lilac, orange, rice* (?), perhaps *spinach*, and *tulip*; other words pertaining to the home life and everyday life of Persia are *azure, bazaar, borax, caravan* (and the clipped *van*), *check, checkers* and *chess, divan, magic, pajamas* (spelled also *pyjamas*), *scarlet, shawl, taffeta, turban*; and such political terms as *mogul, shah, Tartar* (spelled also *Tatar*).

e. Slavic. Of all the greater branches of the Indo-European family of languages, the Slavic has made least impression on English down through the centuries, largely, no doubt, because of the relative isolation of the Slavic peoples and the difficulty that Westerners have with their languages. An occasional term has appeared in English literature, such as *argosy, Cossack, droshky, howitzer, knout, mammoth, Polack, rouble, slave, steppe*; and some few fads and fashions have brought words into use in English, particularly *cravat, mazurka, polka, sable, samovar,* and *vodka.* The political developments of Russia in more recent times have familiarized English speakers with such terms as *Bolshevism, czar, duma, ikon, intelligentsia, muzhik, pogrom, soviet,* and *ukase.* But even yet most of the English discussion of the Russian political situation employs Romanic words, such as *bourgeois, communism, Internationale* (spelled also *International*), and *proletarian* — words which have not yet been Russianized.

f. American Indian. It is interesting to observe that the natives of America (so-called Amerinds) have contributed to the English vocabulary only words to name the unusual features of a very primitive life, such as names of animals and plants and personal possessions, almost exclusively nouns. From the North American Indian languages come *caucus, chinquapin, Eskimo, hickory, hominy, moccasin, moose, muskrat, opossum, papoose, persimmon, potlatch, powwow, raccoon* (and *coon*), *skunk, squaw, Tammany, toboggan, totem, wampum, wigwam,* and many place-names like *Dakota, Kentucky, Okoboji* (see page 277).

From Mexico and the West Indies have been contributed *barbecue, buccaneer, cannibal, canoe, cassava, chili, coyote, guava, hammock, hurricane, maize, potato, savannah, tobacco, tomato,* and *yucca.*

South American native terms are *alpaca, cacao* and *cocoa, caoutchouc, cayenne, condor, Inca, ipecac, llama, mahogany, pampas, petunia* (Latinized), *puma, quinine, tapioca,* and *tapir.*

g. African. Out of Africa have come into English some of the oldest and also some of the most recent of our borrowings. From Egypt, it is generally agreed, have come *ammonia, fustian, gypsy, ibis, Leo, lion, oasis, paper, papyrus,* and possibly *sack* and *satchel.* Elsewhere in Africa have originated *banana, chimpanzee, fez, gnu, gorilla, morocco, voodoo* (or *hoodoo*), *yam,* and *zebra*; recent interest in African life is introducing gradually other words like *quagga, tsetse.* But just as the earlier

Egyptian culture was superseded by Hebrew, Greek, and Roman, so that few Egyptian words have come through to English, so likewise in later times the foreigner has introduced words into Africa instead of adopting words from the languages of the scattered and varied native tribes. Many more words have been carried into African usage than have come out of it.

h. **Other sources.** In concluding our survey of the contributions of the world to English life and thought, we shall pass hurriedly through the lands of the Far East and the South Seas, using as stepping-stones in such a journey numerous words that have become established in English since traders began to visit those lands, some of them through the influence probably of the two great jargons, pidgin English and Beach-la-Mar. Of Chinese origin are *china, chop suey* (San Francisco Chinese), *chowchow, ginseng, kowtow, kumquat, loquat, mah-jongg, pongee, serge, silk,* and *tea.* A few Japanese words have become familiar in English, particularly *banzai, geisha, jinricksha* (spelled also *jinrikisha*), *jiu-jitsu* (spelled also *jujitsu*), *kimono, mikado, satsuma,* and *soy.* From Hawaii come *lei* and *ukulele.* For India can be cited, besides words already named, *coolie, ginger, thug*; and from the Malay country a fairly long list, notably *amuck, bamboo, caddy, cockatoo, gingham, gong, gutta-percha, ketchup, launch, mango, orangoutang* (spelled also *orang-utan*), *rattan, sago, teak, trepang,* and possibly *tom-tom.* In Java the English traveler met *bantam*; in the islands farther south *atoll, taboo, tattoo*; and, finally, in Australia he learned *boomerang, kangaroo,* and *wombat.* Far from the influence of Greek and Roman, untouched by the Germanic and Romanic culture of later Europe, he has found various words here and there which he has fitted into his vocabulary of World English.

78. *Hybrid Words and Phrases*

It was inevitable that the application of the various methods of word-compounding to the great body of native and foreign words accumulated in English should produce a vast number of hybrid words and phrases — those combinations of materials from two or more different languages which are bound to occur when the compounding elements are in active use and have been so long in the language that English speakers have ceased to feel any incongruity or strangeness between them. Scholars have frequently protested against this hybridizing process, in the case of certain elements, arguing, for example, that one's sense of propriety or congruity should prevent the adding of a Latin termination to a word "that is not obviously Latin". But the student of Current English knows that only occasionally is an English word "obviously Latin" or *obviously* anything else than English, nowadays. In composing new words, then, we do not look into the racial ancestry of our materials so much as we do consider whether our new compound is made in such a manner as to avoid awkwardness of form and incompatibility of ideas and to conform to the patterns usually employed in English for the making of such words. Critics have objected to such coinings as *racial* and *scientist*; but the words have become established in good English, nonetheless. Certainly no other language has been able to fuse so many words, from such varied sources, with as much ease as the English language has.

Some of the more obvious forms of hybridization of elements alien to each other are as follows:

a. **Alien prefixes and stems**

interloper	*Latin + Dutch*
interwoven	*Latin + English-*
nonbreakable	*Latin + English + Latin*
surname	*French + English*
unceasing	*English + French + English*
unrelated	*English + Latin + English*

Most of the prefixes still in active use, such as *pre-* in *prewar* and *over-* in *overemphasis*, are freely used today without much regard for the origin of the words to which they are prefixed; one does not ordinarily stop to think that one may be manufacturing a hybrid.

HYBRID WORDS AND PHRASES

b. Alien stems and suffixes

awkward	*Norse + English*
beautiful	*French + English*
falsehood	*French + English*
forbearance	*English + French*
martyrdom	*Greek + English*
pacifist	*Latin + Greek*
plainness	*French + English*
teachable	*English + Latin*

c. Alien compounding elements

cablegram	*Latin + Greek*
dictaphone	*Latin + Greek*
marconigram	*Italian + Greek*
saxophone	*Germanic + Greek*
speedometer	*English + Latin*
television	*Greek + Latin*
vitascope	*Latin + Greek*

d. Word compounds of different origin

alarm clock	*Italian + French*
asafetida	*Persian + Latin*
callithumpian	*Greek + English + Latin*
ginger ale	*Greek + English*
heirloom	*French + English*
ill-tempered	*Norse + French + English*
joss house	*Portuguese + English*
marigold	*Hebrew + English*
nutmeg	*English + French*
polo field	*Indian + English*
saltpeter	*English + Greek*

Sometimes a tautological compound has been produced by combining two different words which had essentially the same meanings, as in *brickbat* (Fr. + Engl.), *cabbage head* (Fr. + Engl.), *Glendale* (Celt. + Engl.), *pea-jacket* (Du. + Fr.), *piecemeal* (Fr. + Engl.), *pussycat* (Engl. + Engl.), *saltcellar* (Engl. + Fr.), *sledge hammer* (Engl. + Engl.), *solan goose* (Scand. + Engl.), *turtledove* (Lat. + Ger.), and possibly *orchard* (Lat. + Engl.). Of course these are not all hybrids.

As an example of the gradual coalescing in a single word of very different materials, Skeat has cited *macadamized*, inasmuch as *mac* is a Gaelic prefix, *adam* a Hebrew name, *iz* a French or originally a Greek suffix, and *-ed* the regular English verb ending. Only a trained etymologist would have become conscious of the curious intermingling of foreign elements in such a hybrid word, and it is not surprising that the average speaker of English takes no thought of the origins of the materials that he chooses to put together for the expression of some new or unusual idea. To him they are all English of the twentieth century; and the long processes of derivation and borrowing with which this chapter has been concerned are as a closed book to him. He is more interested, as a rule, in the various aspects of the Modern English vocabulary as we shall view them in the following chapter. The more apparent results, rather than the long and intricate processes of derivation, are likely to impress him.

CHAPTER X

THE MODERN ENGLISH VOCABULARY

NOW that we have examined in some detail the various methods by which English words have been derived and the varied sources from which the English language has borrowed, it should prove interesting to stop for a brief time to see what has been accomplished by all this derivational expansion, to examine and appraise and make some broad classifications of the vocabulary of Current English. Among the outstanding characteristics of English, as we have said in Section 28, its cosmopolitan vocabulary has been most often commented upon; and the preceding studies of English borrowing will surely have impressed this cosmopolitanism on the mind of the reader beyond any shadow of doubt. But while the student of present-day English cannot avoid paying some attention to the methods by which the English vocabulary has increased during this period of nearly two thousand years, he should also spend some time in an appraisal of the results, as they may be found set forth in the pages of the best of the Modern English dictionaries.

79. *Size and Nature of the Vocabulary*

If we could stop at this point for a detailed study of the history of English dictionary-making since 1500, we should have a most suggestive and useful index to the growth of the English vocabulary, as well as to the growing interest of the English people in their own language as a whole. But since we are not making a historical survey, we can only pause to notice some of the outstanding phases of English lexicographical history, particularly as it throws light on the size and nature of the Modern English vocabulary. In the sixteenth century most lexicographers were busy making bilingual lexicons of English and foreign tongues — English and Latin, English and French, English and Spanish, English and Greek, and so on; and the borrowing of words was at its height, still. But in the seventeenth century the average educated Englishman was becoming conscious of a great need of explication of the many strange terms that had been dragged into his language. By 1656 Thomas Blount deemed it necessary to justify his new *Glossographia* by explaining:

> After I had bestowed the waste hours of some years in reading our best English Histories and Authors; I found, though I had gained a reasonable knowledge in the Latine and French tongues, as I thought, and had a smattering both of Greek and other Languages, yet I was often gravelled in English Books; that is, I encountred such words, as I either not at all, or not throughly understood, more then what the preceding sence did insinuate.

So he proceeded to compile a little dictionary of hard words, containing some sixteen thousand entries, to explain those words, such as *janizarie*, *infanta*, *dictator*, *obelisk*, *Quakers*, *shibboleth*, and *piazza*, which had puzzled him in his reading.

But dictionaries like Blount's were mere makeshifts, and as late as 1742 David Hume wrote in his "Essay on Civil Liberty", "We have no dictionary of our language, and scarcely a tolerable grammar." Finally, five years after Hume said this, Samuel Johnson set to work to make a more comprehensive presentation of the English vocabulary and "drudged" for eight years at the business, bringing out in two large folio volumes in the year 1755 a dictionary so far in advance of anything that had been produced before that time that for a century thereafter Englishmen swore by Johnson's Dictionary of the English Language in much the same way that Americans came later to believe in the infallibility of Noah Webster's American Dictionary. Johnson's two volumes contained some fifty thousand words, and more than a century after its first appearance Wheatley was still able to say of it [342]:

It has, however, three grand characteristics, of which no time or successor can ever deprive it.

1. It was the first English Dictionary that could in any way be considered as standard, all its predecessors being mere lists of words in comparison.

2. Johnson was the first to illustrate his meanings by quotations from standard authors.

3. His definitions are above all praise in their happy illustration of the meanings of words. It is possible to quibble at them now, but this department is one of the most difficult in Lexicography, and he had no assistance from his precursors, whose explanations are usually miserable in the extreme.

To appreciate the fresh personal touch which Johnson gave to the writing of definitions, one has only to consult such articles as those on *excise, Grub Street, lexicographer, oats, patriot, patron, pensioner, Tory,* and *Whig.*

In 1828 the American educator Noah Webster brought out in two large quarto volumes his American Dictionary of the English Language, which he claimed to have founded upon the best scientific progress since Johnson's day and which contained seventy thousand words. Since the appearance of this epoch-making American dictionary in 1828 so many revisions and condensations and imitations have appeared that it would be quite impossible to list them all. The influence of Webster's dictionaries in American schools, publishing houses, courts, offices, libraries, and homes has been almost beyond measure.

More recently two other notable American dictionaries have appeared in the field of Modern English lexicography and from time to time have increased their offerings of words and phrases; the encyclopedic Century Dictionary was published first in 1889–1891, and the Standard Dictionary of the English Language in 1893–1894.

It was not until members of the English Philological Society became dissatisfied with the plan of dictionaries in general use, about 1857, that the society undertook to publish A New English Dictionary on Historical Principles, which should give all words that have at any time appeared in English literature, with an orderly array of quotations chronologically arranged to show the progress of the English vocabulary from the earliest Anglo-Saxon times down to the present. It appeared in parts from 1884 to 1928, making ten large volumes when complete, and even before the publication of the last part so many new words had appeared that it needed the additional supplementary volume, which was added to the set in 1933, to bring it up to date. The ten volumes are said to contain 414,825 words in all. But inasmuch as numerous supplementary word lists have been published since the first part of this dictionary was edited, and various new words have entered the language, the supplement has brought this number somewhat nearer to the half-million mark.[346]

But this does not yet bring us a satisfactory answer to the question, How many words are there in present-day English? Perhaps it may not be possible to give an exact answer to that question, because of the various elements involved in our vocabulary as a whole. A writer associated with the editing of the Standard Dictionary said in 1926[68]:

> It is no flight of fancy to state that there are between 1,000,000 and 1,250,000 words in our language today. At least two-fifths of these are ultra-scientific terms used only in the recesses of a laboratory; they are not to be found in standard dictionaries. Many other words are obsolete or antiquated. . . . The American dictionary of today contains nearly half a million terms.

The writer just quoted goes farther in throwing light on our problem by stating that there are in the editorial office of the dictionary more than fifty thousand trade terms, few of which have been admitted to the dictionary because few have as yet gained public approval.

It is plain, therefore, that when those two splendid American dictionaries, Webster's New International Dictionary and the New Standard Dictionary, are each credited with about four hundred and fifty thousand "living vocabulary" terms, there remains much still to be said as to the many ultra-scientific and trade terms not included, as well as the many locutions of a somewhat questionable sort that have been recorded.*

It is not likely, however, that philologists will ever agree on the size of the English vocabulary until they decide what shall be counted as separate words. How many italicized forms, for example, in the following colloquial sentence shall be considered distinct words?

> If the *laundry* gets a good *do* on his shirts and collars, it *does* not *do* for a *well-to-do* man like Mr. *Warren* to make too great a *to-do* over the *launderer's* charges for *doing up* the shirts; he should send the *washing*, and the *washing* and *ironing* should be done satisfactorily.

Shall derivative forms like *laundry* and *launderer* be counted as separate words? Shall converted nouns like *do* be counted? Shall compounds like *well-to-do* and combinations like *doing up* be regarded as words? How many proper names like *Warren* shall be included? And shall concrete nouns like *washing* (meaning 'clothes') be separated from verbal nouns like *washing* and *ironing*? If these be rejected, as Ramsay has recently suggested[347], then the count may be reduced to half the number which the lexicographers have been inclined to claim for their recent "complete" dictionaries. But there must be some sort of agreement on such matters before we can hope to arrive at a satisfactory estimate.

The making of a Modern English dictionary is a more complicated matter than the average person realizes, who usually takes for granted the essential unity of English as he reads it and hears it spoken day by day. In any practical dictionary must be comprised so much of the colloquial and slang usage of the day as may be met with commonly in speech or in current literature; but it is obviously not all included, for Farmer and Henley's *Slang and its Analogues* runs to seven large volumes, and the third volume of Thornton's *American Glossary* is still under way. On the other hand, the "complete" dictionary must include all the more important archaic and

* Since this statement was prepared a Second Edition of Webster's New International Dictionary has appeared, with 600,000 entries.

obsolescent words that the student of history and literature may run across in his reading. We have already estimated, moreover, that of the older living words in the dictionary fully half the meanings are obsolete or archaic (Sec. 13). Yet the dictionary would lose much of its value if these old words and old meanings were omitted, since so many people like to live in the past as well as in the present.

There is still in use much dialect which should be entered in the dictionary. And yet the lexicographer cannot go too far in including dialectal variations of standard English. The great English Dialect Dictionary makes six large volumes, and the collections of the American Dialect Society will also make a large book, to say nothing of the various other dialects and jargons of present-day English which are not recorded.

Moreover, it is not an easy thing to decide just when a foreign locution has become sufficiently naturalized so that it can be moved from a supplement to the body of the book and be left there without the encumbering mark of its foreign strangeness still before it on the printed page. The noun *camouflage*, to illustrate, still has the double bar sinister in one recently edited dictionary, while in another it has been accepted with only the label "recent" to deter it from feeling quite at home. It is not easy to determine just the exact moment when a foreigner of this kind attains to full citizenship in the English language.

And, finally, the educated user of the dictionary expects to find indicated, at least briefly, for each word its history, its genealogy, as it were. This is, in some respects, the most difficult thing of all that a lexicographer has to do, because opinion regarding the source and time and method of the borrowing of a word may vary so much that no one can say with entire assurance how the word became English. The author of the separate etymological dictionary can devote his entire space to supplying information on this point exclusively, and leave the reader to draw his own conclusions; but the maker of the general dictionary must give a definite and concise answer, or else evade it in some simple manner, such as omitting its etymology altogether or indicating doubt as to its origin.

In order to appreciate in even a fairly intelligent way the remarkable complexity and versatility of the vocabulary of Current English, one must consider derivative processes and word-borrowings, as we have attempted to do in the foregoing chapter. Hence we may pause for a moment to summarize very briefly the borrowings discussed in that chapter.

English has drawn most largely from the Romanic tongues, primarily Latin and secondarily French, and to a lesser degree Italian, Spanish, and Portuguese. One who is familiar with the Romanic languages can conceive in some measure of the peculiar contribution that these languages have made to English as we know it today. But English has also drawn somewhat heavily on the classical Greek, and the stamp of Hellenic culture is strongly impressed on English culture and speech. The more simple speech of the Old Norse peoples, with some later Dutch and Scandinavian words, has strengthened the original Germanic character of English. Beyond these, sprinklings of Celtic and Slavic and Hebrew and Arabic and Malay and American Indian have enriched the language in their own peculiar ways.

Then, again, we can throw some light on the present complex character of English by noting the relation of the different periods of borrowing to the cultural developments that were taking place over the world. Christianity, after 597 A.D., brought much of the first Latin that England received. Upon a mingling of Latin and Anglo-Saxon were then superimposed some Norse and some Norman French. But the simplicity of the earlier Norman French terms is in marked contrast with the more learned and sophisticated character of the later French borrowings. In the modern period the successive influences of literary and scholarly activity, of exploration and conquest, and of trade the world over have imposed on the vocabulary layer after layer of varied foreign words.

If we regard these borrowings again from a different point of view, we may gain still more understanding of our most complex vocabulary by noting that the character and purposes of our different borrowings have varied greatly. The early borrowing of Latin was almost entirely through the channels of ecclesiastical thought and literature; the Latin that was borrowed during the English Renaissance was of a more worldly cultural sort; the Latin gained in recent centuries has been more and more narrowly scientific. The Greek loan element can be said to correspond closely to the Latin in that it was first ecclesiastical, then cultural in a more worldly way, and latterly strongly technical and scientific. But both languages have contributed to the expression of the Englishman's most erudite and abstract thinking — ecclesiastical and theological, artistic and critical and philosophical, scientific and technological. The Italian words came in response to artistic and literary needs of the English Renaissance; the Spanish and Portuguese contacts and borrowings resulted from trade and exploration, largely, and the more recent borrowings from other tongues have often been through the intervention and assistance of Spanish and Portuguese pioneers and traders who have acquired the words in various lands and then passed them on to the English.

Nevertheless, in spite of these periodic and purposeful borrowings, the vocabulary of almost any one of the arts, crafts, sciences, or other phases of human need is most amazingly diffuse and heterogeneous in its origins. One has only to consider the most common words in any group of this kind to appreciate how various and widespread have been their origins. A few lists will suffice.*

a. **Plants and flowers**

bamboo	*Malay*	lily	*Greek*
banana	*African*	marigold	*Hebrew + English*
cotton	*Arabic*	mignonette	*French*
dahlia	*Swedish*	petunia	*South American*
fuchsia	*German*	poppy	*Latin*
hickory	*North American*	potato	*West Indian*
kohlrabi	*German*	shamrock	*Irish*
lilac	*Persian*	sycamore	*Hebrew*

* It is, of course, impossible to label all of these words with final accuracy, since they have traveled through so many different languages. *Buffalo*, for example, could be labeled "Greek"; others, such as *fuchsia*, have the stamp of New Latin upon them.

b. Animals

buffalo	*Portuguese*	gorilla	*African*
calf	*English*	kangaroo	*Australian*
camel	*Hebrew*	lion	*Egyptian*
chamois	*French*	mosquito	*Spanish*
dachshund	*German*	raccoon	*North American*
gelding	*Scandinavian*	turtle	*Latin*

c. Minerals and woods

bronze	*Italian*	emerald	*Greek*
coal	*English*	mahogany	*South American*
copper	*Latin*	nickel	*German*
corundum	*Sanskrit*	rock	*French*
diamond	*Greek*	teak	*Malay*
ebony	*Hebrew*	tungsten	*Swedish*

d. Foods and drinks

brandy	*Dutch*	sauerkraut	*German*
candy	*Sanskrit*	sirup	*Arabic*
cider	*Hebrew*	sugar	*Sanskrit*
coffee	*Arabic*	tapioca	*South American*
ketchup	*Malay*	tea	*Chinese*
macaroni	*Italian*	toddy	*Indian*
molasses	*Portuguese*	whisky	*Celtic*
mutton	*French*	wine	*Latin*
salt	*English*	yam	*African*

e. Clothing

bandanna	*Indian*	shirt	*English*
cravat	*Slavic*	silk	*Chinese*
kimono	*Japanese*	skirt	*Norse*
mackinaw	*North American*	sombrero	*Spanish*
shawl	*Persian*	tartan	*Gaelic*

f. Music

coronach	*Gaelic*	organ	*Greek*
drum	*Dutch*	piano	*Italian*
flute	*French*	polka	*Slavic*
harp	*English*	saxophone	*Germanic + Greek*
lute	*Arabic*	tuba	*Latin*
music	*Greek*	zither	*German*

All these studies, however, are concerned still with the ways the English vocabulary has grown and the sources from which it has drawn. But there are several very interesting and important aspects of the vocabulary of the present day which are the results of this growth and which must be appraised if one is to understand and appreciate Current English. In the first place, English is today the common meeting place of numerous cognate or related words, some native and some foreign. Then, again, much confusion has resulted from the fact that homonyms arise through the development of similar or identical forms, and synonyms accumulate through the association of various words with similar or identical meanings. And last of all, the tremendous accumulation of words in English, as we have just observed and estimated it, has led to some very serious questioning as to the usefulness and usableness of a great part of this vocabulary preserved within the covers of the latest "complete" dictionaries. These lines of research we shall pursue in the following six sections of this chapter — relationships of words, resemblances of words, and relative importance of words.

80. *Cognate Words in English*

In an earlier discussion of cognate languages (Sec. 24), it was demonstrated that there are words common to the more modern Indo-European languages which are evidently closely related to one another. But since it is not our purpose to go farther into the comparative study of these languages which are related to English, we shall restrict the following consideration of cognate words to those found in the English language today as the result of both inheritance and the manifold borrowings described in the preceding chapter. Moreover, since the derivative processes of English have also been discussed in detail in the same chapter, we shall, for the most part, exclude English derivative forms from this discussion in order that the material to be considered may be kept within reasonable limits. The subject of cognates is,

Sec. 80]   COGNATE WORDS IN ENGLISH   399

in so far as the study of English is concerned, almost a worldwide one, and so we must be content to exclude from this present consideration both what happened to them before they came into English and also those derivative changes which they underwent after they became English. By tabulating at the end of Section 61 the numerous forms derived from English *bear* and Latin *cedo*, we have already illustrated the almost unlimited possibilities of derivational expansion in both our native and our borrowed words. So we shall examine here only a few of the most striking of those words which, starting in primitive times from a common Indo-European ancestor, developed differently in different languages and then were directly inherited and also borrowed at one time or another by the English people. These are the cognates in which we are interested for the moment.

In the following list a few of the more familiar native Anglo-Saxon words are arranged in alphabetic order, together with the most striking of the cognates, or related words, that have later appeared in English, the cognates being labeled with the names of the languages from which they have come:

acre: Lat. *agriculture;* also Engl. *acorn.*
bear (verb): Lat. *fertile, suffer, translate,* and the suffix *-fer* as in *cruciferous;* Gr. *phosphorus;* also Engl. *bier, birth, burden* (see the list on page 344).
bite: Lat. *fissure;* Fr. *abet, bet;* Norse *bait;* Engl. *beetle, bitter.*
bloom: Lat. *Flora, floral, florid;* Fr. *flour, flourish, flower;* Ger. *Blumenthal;* Engl. *blossom, blow* ('to bloom').
bow (verb): Lat. *centrifugal, fugitive, refuge;* Fr. *fugue;* Low Ger. *bout;* Eng. *bight, bow* ('weapon').
break: Lat. *fraction, fracture, fragile, fragment, refract;* Fr. *brick, frail;* Du. *brake;* Engl. *brake* ('thicket'), *breach.*
brother: Lat. *fraternal, fratricide;* Fr. *fraternity, friar.*
burg: Fr. *bourgeois, burgess, burglar;* Du. *burgomaster;* Engl. *barrow* ('mound'), *borough, Canterbury.*
corn: Lat. *granary, granular;* Fr. *garner, grain;* Engl. *kernel.*
do: Lat. *facile, fact,* and the suffix *-fy;* Fr. *treasure;* Gr. *anathema, apothecary, epithet, synthesis* (and similar compounds), *theme, thesaurus, thesis;* Engl. *ado* (Northern), *deed, deem, deemster, doff, don, indeed, to-do.*

eat: Lat. *edible*; Du. *etch*; Ger. *delicatessen*; Engl. *fret*.
edge: Lat. *acid, acrid, acute*; Fr. *ague, eager, vinegar*; Gr. *acacia, aconite, acme, acrobat, Acropolis*; Norse *awn*; Engl. *ear* (of corn).
father: Lat. *paternal, paternoster*; Fr. *patrician, patriot, patron*; Gr. *patriarch*; Du. *patroon*; Span. *padre*.
fee: Lat. *peculiar, pecuniary*; Fr. *feud, fief*; AN. *fee*.
food: Lat. *pabulum, pastor*; Fr. *companion, pantry, pasture*; Engl. *feed, fodder, foster*.
foot: Lat. *biped, pedal*; Fr. *centipede, expedite, impede, pawn, pedestrian, pedigree, pioneer*; Gr. *antipodes, chiropodist, podagra*; Norse *fetlock*; Span. *peon*; Engl. *fetch, fetter*.
four: Lat. *quadrant, quadruped, quarto*; Fr. *quadrille, quarry, square*; Gr. *tetrarch*; Ital. *squad, squadron*; Span. *quadroon*; Engl. *forty, fourteen, fourth*.
guest: Lat. *hostile*; Fr. *host* ('army'), *hostility*. Cf. *hospitable, hospital*; Fr. *host* (of guests), *hostel, hotel*.
hall: Lat. *cell, cellular, occult*; Fr. *cellar, cellophane, celluloid, cellulose, conceal, helmet*; Gr. *eucalyptus*; Engl. *hell, helm*.
head: Lat. *capital, capitulate, occiput*; Fr. *cabbage, chapter, chef, chief, chieftain, kerchief*; Ital. *cape* ('headland'); Engl. *headlong* (and similar compounds).
hen: Lat. *cant*; Fr. *chant, chanticleer*; Ital. *cantata, canto*.
holy: Norse *hail*; Engl. *hale* (Northern), *halibut, halidom, Halloween, heal, health, holiday, hollyhock, whole*.
horn: Lat. *corn* (on the foot), *cornucopia*; Fr. *cornet*; Engl. *hornet*.
kin: Lat. *cognate, genius, gentile, genus, progenitor*; Fr. *genteel, gentle*; Gr. *cosmogony, genesis*; Engl. *kind, kindred*.
know: Lat. *ignore, narrate*; Fr. *cognizance, noble, recognize*; Gr. *agnostic, agnosticism*; Ital. *incognito*; Engl. *can* (verb), *keen, ken, knowledge, uncouth, kith*.
mother: Lat. *alma mater, maternal, matrix*; Fr. *matron*.
murder or **murther:** Lat. *mortal, mortician, mortify, mortuary*; Fr. *amortize, mortgage*.
night: Lat. *nocturn, nocturnal*; Gr. *nyctalopia*; Engl. *nightingale, nightshade*.
sad: Lat. *sated, satiate, satisfy*; Engl. *sadiron*.
shear: Norse *sca(u)r* (a 'rock'), *score, sheer* (adj.), *skirt*; Du. *sheer* (verb); Engl. *shard, share, shears, shirt, shore, short*. Cf. Lat. *curt*, Fr. *curtail*, Engl. *kirtle*.
sit: Lat. *sedate, sedentary, sediment, sessile, session, supersede*; Fr. *assess, assiduous, assize, besiege, insidious, possess, president, reside*.

residence, seize, siege, size; Gr. *cathedral, chair, chaise;* Engl. *seat, set, settle, soot.*

stand: Lat. *stamen, station, status;* Fr. *consist* (and similar compounds), *constant, distant, establish, estate, obstacle, solstice, stable, stage, stanchion, state, statue, statute, stay;* Gr. *ecstasy, metastasis, static, system;* Ital. *stanza;* Engl. *stool, stow, understand.*

stick: Lat. *instigate;* Fr. *etiquette, ticket;* Gr. *stigma, stigmatize;* Du. *stoker;* Norse *steak;* Span. *stockade;* Engl. *stake, stickleback, sting, stitch, stock, stocking, stuck-up* (colloquial).

tame: Lat. *dominate, dominie* (Scotch), *domino;* Fr. *dame, danger, daunt, demesne, domain, dungeon;* Span. *don;* Du. *domineer.*

teach: Lat. *dictate, diction, dictionary, index, indicate;* Fr. *ditty, indict, judge, syndic;* Ital. *ditto;* Engl. *token.*

ten: Lat. *December, decimal;* Fr. *decalogue;* Gr. *decasyllabic, dekagram;* Engl. *-teen, tithe, -ty.*

thin: Lat. *attend, extend, tenacious, tender, tendon, tense;* Gr. *hypotenuse, tone* (and its compounds); Fr. *dance, tent, tune.*

tooth: Lat. *dental, dentist;* Fr. *dandelion;* Engl. *tine.*

tow (verb): Lat. *conduct* (and similar compounds), *ducal, duct;* Fr. *adduce* (and other compounds), *conduit, duchess, duchy, duke;* Norse *tug;* Ital. *doge, ducat.*

weigh: Lat. *vehicle, viaduct, viaticum;* Fr. *voyage;* Du. *wagon;* Norse *wag* (verb); Engl. *wain.*

wit: Lat. *advise, visible, vision;* Fr. *guide, guise;* Gr. *idea, idol;* Engl. *twit, wise, witness, wizard;* Du. *wiseacre.*

yard: Lat. *cohort, horticulture;* Fr. *court, courtesy, curtain, garden;* Engl. *gird, girdle, girth, orchard.*

yoke: Lat. *conjugal, conjugate, conjunction* (and other compounds), *jugular, junction, juncture;* Fr. *adjoin* (and other compounds), *join, rejoinder;* Span. *junta.*

In giving this list of cognates, no attempt has been made to discuss problems of interrelationship that arise from even a hasty survey of the words listed. The student of linguistics should pursue the subject for himself, if he becomes interested, and it is probable that he will feel challenged to do so when he comes across such striking relationships as that of the plebeian *hen* and the learned *canto* of the poet or the *cantata* of the musician. But such researches will lead him far afield and will involve him in fairly intensive philological research, for he will find that some of the younger languages, such as French and Italian, have themselves drawn heavily from the older Greek, Latin, and Arabic, that some of the cognates within English have been developed by means of derivative processes now obsolete and obscure (such as *i*-mutation and breaking) and that some have come from a blending or confusion of the Germanic and Romanic elements in English. If the student is familiar with any of the foreign languages, he will even be tempted to compare cognates as they live on in the various tongues today. Moreover, after he has repeatedly come across certain consonant correspondences, such as that of Latin *t* and English *th*, he may even become ambitious to tabulate them and prove for himself that primitive shift of consonants which we have merely touched upon in concluding our earlier discussion of cognate languages (see Sec. 24, at end). But these are studies lying outside the province of our present study of Current English and cannot be pursued here.

81. *Doublets and Triplets*

There is one sort of simple analysis of English cognate words which deserves some passing comment; that is concerned with those pairs of related words in English which are generally known as doublets. We have omitted from the foregoing section most of the fairly numerous doublets because they have, as a group, certain peculiar limitations which warrant giving them separate consideration here. Doublets are pairs of words (or groups of three, sometimes called triplets, or even more) which have arisen from the same original form but have gradually diverged in both form and sense. It has been customary to list as doublets only those pairs that function alike as the same part of speech (for example, as noun or adjective or verb), and consequently we shall not include in the following lists the noun-and-verb pairs (like *cóllect* and *colléct*) which are distinguished chiefly by a shift of accent (see Sec. 45), or those participle-and-adjective pairs (like *áged* and *ágèd*) which vary the suffix (see page 243).

While many of these pairs of doublets are due to borrowings from different languages, or arise from the same foreign language at different times or through different dialects, sometimes a native English word has split in the course of time in such a manner as to provide two different words ultimately. So it will be most useful to classify the doublets and triplets of Current English according to the sources or diversifying influences responsible for their existence today. But it should be noted that the existence of two different spellings of the same word (as *gaol* and *jail* or *gray* and *grey*) does not entitle the word to a place among doublets, nor do doublets result from the ordinary derivational or inflectional processes; doublets are the outcome of semasiological differentiation, and of borrowing from different languages or at different times from the same language.

a. **Doublets from Different Languages**

English and Latin

| eatable/edible | kin/genus | naked/nude | thin/tenuous |
| foam/spume | mother/mater | nine/noon | thole/tolerate |

English and French

beard/barb	fresh/frisky	wile/guile
bench/bank	lapel/label	wise/guise
brother/friar	mark/march (*boundary*)	wit/guide
coffee/café	name/noun	word/verb
corn/grain	ward/guard	worm/vermin

English and Scandinavian

brow/brae	hale/hail	shirt/skirt
draw/drag	no/nay	shriek/screech
edge/egg on	rear/raise	stake/stack
from/fro	road/raid	tow/tug
gate/gait	saw (*saying*)/saga	yard/garth
girdle/girth	shabby/scabby	

English and Dutch

eat/etch   slide/sled   thatch/deck   thrill/drill   wain/wagon

Latin and French

- abbreviate/abridge
- amicable/amiable
- arc/arch
- balsam/balm
- calix/chalice
- camera/chamber
- cancer/canker
- cant/chant
- capital/chapter
- captive/caitiff
- comprehend/comprise
- compute/count
- concept/conceit
- delectable/delightful
- deposit/depot
- elect/élite
- fact/feat
- faction/fashion
- florid/flowery
- fragile/frail
- lobby/lodge
- major/mayor
- masculine/male
- monastery/minster
- native/naïve
- oration/orison
- pauper/poor
- pause/pose
- pope/papa
- potion/poison
- pungent/poignant
- radius/ray
- rotund/round
- scandal/slander
- secure/sure
- separate/sever
- spirit/sprite
- strict/strait
- tabernacle/tavern
- vast/waste
- wine/vine
- zealous/jealous

French and Italian

- aptitude/attitude
- brave/bravo
- duke/doge
- flask/fiasco
- influence/influenza
- madame/madonna
- porch/portico
- sovereign/soprano
- study/studio

French and Spanish

- army/armada
- charge/cargo
- musket/mosquito

Greek and French

- basis/base
- cathedral/chair
- deacon/dean
- papyrus/paper
- paralysis/palsy

Some other interesting international pairs are

- banjo (*Span.*)/mandolin (*Ital.*)
- cipher (*Arab.*)/zero (*Fr.*)
- insulate (*Lat.*)/isolate (*Ital.*)
- pitcher (*Fr.*)/beaker (*Scand.*)
- ship (*Engl.*)/skiff (*Ger.*)
- tremor (*Lat.*)/temblor (*Span.*)

b. Doublets from Different Periods of the Same Language

Earlier and later French

- adamant/diamond
- antics/antiques
- blame/blaspheme
- carmine/crimson
- castle/château
- chief/chef
- demesne/domain
- entry/entrée
- feast/fête
- feeble/foible
- hostel/hotel
- pasty/patty
- roll/role
- saloon/salon
- sergeant/servant
- suit/suite
- ticket/etiquette
- veil/voile

Sec. 81] DOUBLETS AND TRIPLETS

Earlier and later borrowings from Latin

camp/campus
chest/cist
cross/crux

devilish/diabolical
inch/ounce
plum/prune

sanatorium/sanitarium
street/stratum

Most of the older forms have been in the English vocabulary since Anglo-Saxon times.

c. Doublets from Different Dialects of a Language

French dialectal variants

canal/channel
card/chart
catch/chase
cattle/chattel

cavalry/chivalry
convey/convoy
reward/regard
task/tax

wage/gage
warden/guardian
warrant/guarantee

Northern and Southern English forms

ado/to-do
bosky/bushy
fox/vixen
hale/whole

kale/cole
kirk/church
laith (*Scotch*)/loath

lurk/lurch
mickle (*Scotch*)/much
scatter/shatter

d. Doublets from Various Changes within English Itself

Loss of an initial syllable

abet/bet
acute/cute
adventure/venture
amend/mend
appeal/peal
astray/stray
defense/fence

despite/spite
disport/sport
Egyptian/gypsy
escheat/cheat
especially/specially
esprit/sprite
espy/spy

esquire/squire
estate/state
estop/stop
example/sample
exchequer/checker
history/story
ribald/bawd

Change of vowel

an/one
born/borne
clench/clinch
cloths/clothes
creek/crick
daft/deft
dale/dell
deal/dole

farther/further
font/fount
inapt/inept
master/Mr.
mode/mood
outermost/uttermost
parson/person
peck/pick

preen/prune
resin/rosin
shade/shed
slack/slake
sleek/slick
snob/snub
strap/strop
thresh/thrash

Difference in word stress or sentence stress (see page 85).

a/one	gállant/gallánt	of/off
as/also	gentle/genteel	urban/urbane
divers/diverse	human/humane	than/then

Change of consonant

baluster/banister	hunch/hunk	stitch/stick
caliber/caliper	kill/quell	wake/watch
cud/quid	scrub/shrub	whippletree/whiffletree
dike/ditch	scuffle/shuffle	

Metathesis

through/thorough   wight/whit   worked/wrought

Revival of an older form

fancy/fantasy   Frank/French   later/latter

Making of clipped forms (see page 355)

bus/omnibus	cad/cadet	van/caravan
cab/cabriolet	canter/Canterbury	varsity/university

Variation of spelling

flour/flower	metal/mettle	ton/tun
load/lode	to/too	travail/travel

Use of different inflectional forms

macaroon/macaroni	morn/morrow	shade/shadow
mead/meadow	peer/pair	twain/two

Derivation of causative transitive verbs

bind/bend	drink/drench	sing/singe
bite/bait	fall/fell	sit/set
blind/blend	fare/ferry	swing/swinge
blink/blench	lie/lay	wind/wend
brood/breed	rise/rear	

See also doublet noun plurals, p. 442.

e. Triplets from Various Sources

acute (*Lat.*)	cute	aguish (*Fr.*)
cadence (*Fr.*)	chance (*Fr.*)	cadenza (*Ital.*)
capital (*Lat.*)	chattel (*Fr.*)	cattle (*Fr.*)
corpus (*Lat.*)	corpse (*Fr.*)	corps (*Mod. Fr.*)
debit (*Lat.*)	debt (*Fr.*)	due (*Fr.*)
dragon (*Fr.*)	dragoon (*Fr.*)	drake (*Engl.*)
estate (*Fr.*)	state	status (*Lat.*)
hospital (*Lat.*)	hostel (*Fr.*)	hotel (*Fr.*)
legal (*Lat.*)	leal (*Nor. Fr.*)	loyal (*Fr.*)
place (*Fr.*)	piazza (*Ital.*)	plaza (*Span.*)
regal (*Lat.*)	real (*Fr.*)	royal (*Fr.*)

f. A Few Words now appearing in Four or Five Forms

gentle (*Fr.*)	plan (*Fr.*)	sca(u)r (*Scand.*)	stack (*Scand.*)
genteel (*Fr.*)	plane (*Fr.*)	score (*Scand.*)	stake (*Engl.*)
gentile (*Fr.*)	plain (*Fr.*)	share (*Engl.*)	steak (*Scand.*)
jaunty (*Fr.*)	piano (*Ital.*)	shore (*Engl.*)	stock (*Engl.*)

discus (*Lat.*)	parabola (*Gr.*)	senior (*Lat.*)
disk (*Lat.*)	parable (*Fr.*)	sire (*Fr.*)
dish (*Engl.*)	parole (*Fr.*)	sir (*Fr.*)
desk (*Ital.*)	parley (*Fr.*)	seigneur (*Fr.*)
dais (*Fr.*)	palaver (*Port.*)	signor (*Ital.*)

Many doublets are to be encountered among personal names, such as *John* and *Jean*, *Walsh* and *Welsh*; but this phase of the subject is too complicated and difficult to permit of discussion here.

82. *Homonyms*

Turning now to a countertendency in English, we find that as the vocabulary has increased through the various methods of derivation and borrowing, in numerous instances two or three words quite different in origin and meaning have assumed identical forms or forms so nearly identical as to cause some confusion and trouble. These words of similar or identical form are generally called homonyms, but philologists disagree as to the exact meaning of the term. It is used in this book to include both words pronounced alike (homophones) and words spelled alike (homographs). Hence it is necessary to consider them under three heads, namely, homophones spelled differently, homographs pronounced differently, and those homonyms that are identical in both sound and spelling, that is, homographic homophones.

In earlier sections of this book, pairs of words have been discussed which were pronounced alike or spelled alike or both; but nonetheless these are not to be regarded as homonyms, because they are not of different origin, nor do they vary greatly in meaning. So we must exclude from this section those pairs of words like *abuse* (noun) and *abuse* (verb), where the *s* is voiced to distinguish the verb (see page 206), such pairs as *cóllect* (noun) and *colléct* (verb), where the accent is shifted to distinguish the verb (see page 223), and other pairs like *léarned* (verb) and *léarnèd* (adj.), where the silent *e* in the suffix is revived to indicate the adjective (see page 243), because these are all closely akin, derived from common ancestors. Moreover, all those pairs like *hold* (noun) and *hold* (verb), which are identical root words merely converted to function as different parts of speech, must be excluded (see Sec. 58). Even when quite different meanings develop from a word, as in the case of *fast*, which caused the Frenchman so much trouble, we do not have homonyms but merely words of ambiguous meaning.

But after all these word pairs of similar or identical form or sound and of identical origin have been excluded, there are still almost innumerable possibilities of confusion among English words which sound alike or look alike or both, but which are not alike in meaning and are not related etymologically or only distantly so. Indeed, this confusing of such words is, though it was not emphasized in our hasty study of foreigners' English, one of the chief obstacles to a foreigner's acquisition of a complete familiarity with the English language. Bridges has listed eight hundred of these homophones which are to be found in the simpler dictionaries of everyday English; and he estimates that since each form stands for two or three different words, there are nearly two thousand of these confusing words in common use in English.³⁵² And these, it must be remembered, are distinct dictionary forms that do not change, while beyond them lie countless other possibilities of confusion when words are inflected by the addition of endings like -(e)d, -(e)r, -(e)s, producing other temporary homophones like *banned* and *band*, *liver* (noun) and *liver* (comparative adj.), *freeze* and *frees*.

One of the chief difficulties of the etymologist, as we have already observed, lies in the gradual overlapping and confusion of two old words of similar form and sound in English, as illustrated by *afraid, bid, bound, cleave, fret, havoc, let, mystery,* and *ravenous*. Some of these old pairs have merged their meanings completely; others still keep the two at least reasonably distinct. In *gull* and *guy*, as noted, the etymologists are still insisting upon a twofold origin, and in the colloquial use of *crick* there are apparently still to be detected the two older forms *creek* and *creak*.

The homonyms that have maintained their separate meanings most generally are the pairs that have been derived from foreign tongues in part or altogether, such as

air/ere
arm (limb)/arm (weapon)
bark (of trees)/bark (of dogs)
bass (music)/bass (fish)
better (a wagerer)/better (adj.)
cast (to throw)/caste (class)
duck (bird)/duck (canvas)
feeze/phase
friar/fryer
hall/haul (to draw)
lesson/lessen (to diminish)
mass (lump)/Mass (a service)
mine (to dig)/mine (pron.)
mood (temper)/mood (manner)
peer (to look)/peer (equal)
prune (fruit)/prune (to trim)

Within the English language itself the changes in pronunciation and inflection have brought together various pairs of words, thereby increasing the confusion, as

bear (animal)/bear (to carry) and bare (adj.)
bee/be
hide (skin)/hide (to conceal)
know/no
lead (metal)/lead (to conduct)
saw (to cut)/saw (a saying) and saw (viewed)
son/sun
sow (hog)/sow (to scatter)
tear (a drop)/tear (to rend)
wind (air)/wind (to turn)

In some of these homonyms the difference in spelling has been maintained in order to give at least the appearance of distinction, even though they sound alike.

Inflectional changes produce temporarily a great number of identical pronunciations, although very few are spelled alike. So we have, as the result of making certain noun plurals, the pairs *daze* and *days, nose* and *noes, rose* and *rows* (and *roes*), and one might even have remarked in the days of the Barbary pirates that "their *crews cruise* and *seize* the *seas.*" Of verbs the present-tense forms ending in *-s* frequently correspond in sound to other words, as in the case of *braise* and *brays, frays* and *phrase, freeze* and *frees, hoes* and *hose, seize* and *sees.* Forming the past tense of verbs produces the pairs *clove* (spice) and *clove* (cut), *dove* (bird) and colloquial *dove* (dived), *new* and *knew, through* and *threw.* In the comparison of adjectives homonyms arise, such as *bowlder* and *bolder, grater* and *greater, planer* and *plainer.*

Much might be said about the speakers of English, both the dialectal and the out-and-out careless ones, who make different words sound alike by their peculiar habits of speech. Bridges has shown some concern over the tendency of speakers of the so-called Southern English of Great Britain to vocalize the *r* out of their speech, producing such pairs as: *alms* and *arms, cork* and *caulk, farther* and *father, laud* and *lord, roar* and *raw.*[352] But speakers elsewhere in the English-speaking world produce many homophones because of other peculiarities of pronunciation. Attention has already been called in Chapter VI to some of these matters. The vowels heard before *r* are pronounced by some speakers so that they sound practically the same in pairs like *berry* and *Barry, hairy* and *Harry, merry* and *marry, vary* and *very,* although other speakers clearly differentiate these words. Those who pronounce *wh* as *w* also produce homophones, with such pairs as *whale* and *wail, what* and *watt, when* and *wen, where* and *wear, while* and *wile.* If for no other reason, the danger of producing more homonyms in English should make speakers more careful of their pronunciation of such words.

There are many pairs of words in Current English that

can be traced back to common ancestors if one presses the matter far enough, and yet one is inclined to include them as homonyms because they have separated so completely in their meanings and sometimes even in spelling. Bridges has named these "false homophones," and after trying to be consistent in his adherence to definition, has nevertheless been tempted to the extent of including in his study of homophones a few of these very remotely related homonyms, such as *bit* (of a bridle) and *bit* (of a plane), *cousin* and *cozen*, *deck* (of cards) and *deck* (of a boat), *metal* and *mettle*, *patent* (noun) and *patent* (adj.), *shear* (verb) and *sheer* (adj.), *smart* (to pain) and *smart* (clever). Obviously there are numerous doublets that might be called homonyms, also.

The difficulty with the use of homonyms in English speech is plainly a twofold one. The few homographs scattered through the foregoing lists which are pronounced differently cause trouble primarily to the reader; it is only the homophones that make trouble in spoken English. But spoken English is much more important for the average man, and consequently the fact that homophones are so much more numerous than homographs is a fact worthy of serious thought. Words that sound alike cause not a little hindrance to telephone conversations, and the scientists associated with the Bell Telephone System have devoted much attention to them.

The making of puns depends very largely, of course, on homonyms, since a pun is, as the dictionary explains, either "a play on words of the same sound but different meanings" or else a play "on different applications of a word." When Chaucer's Squire remarked apologetically,

> Albeit that I cannot sound his *style*,
> And cannot climb over so high a *stile*,

his pun was good literary form still. Even the great Shakespeare was not above making the Duke of York passionately exclaim in the first scene of the second part of *Henry VI*,

> "For *Suffolk's* duke, may he be *suffocate*,
> That dims the honor of this warlike isle!"

But since Shakespeare's day it has been more and more the humorous writer who has utilized the English stock of homonyms for punning, and the more serious poets have grown distrustful of them, until the late poet laureate of England, Robert Bridges, took the stand in his monograph "On English Homophones", in 1919, "that homophones are a nuisance"[352]. Indeed he even went somewhat farther than that in his insistence that many good words have been crowded out of use because of the confusion arising from their use. Not only has there been a decided tendency to increase the number of homophones through careless pronunciation of unlike words, but some reformers of English spelling have threatened to add numerous homographs by changing the spelling of verbs in the past tense, making *chilled* like *child*, *grinned* like *grind*, *guessed* like *guest*, *leased* like *least*, and *milled* like *mild*.

Occasionally there is a slight tendency to offset the increase of homonyms by a change in spelling, as in *metal* and *mettle*, *plum* and *plumb*; or by a slight variation in pronunciation, as in the case of the vowel sounds in *bare* and *bear*, *Mary* and *merry*; or by an insistence, for example, on the sounding of the *t* of *often* where there is danger of confusion with an *r*-less *orphan*. But the chief solution of the difficulty resulting from the confusion of homonyms is still to be found in the very simple expedient of dropping one of the pair from use; and there is no better illustration of this evasive method than that of the story of the Englishman who enjoyed the humorous explanation of the American fruit-grower that "we eat what we can and what we can't we can", but later reported to his friends at home that "they eat what they can and what they can't they put up in tins". The pun suffered from the loss of the last *can*, but clarity of meaning gained in the process; and in English generally the serious need of clarity is likely to break up the confusing identity of homonyms somehow, either through changes in spelling and pronunciation or else through the complete abandonment of one of the pair of words. Homonyms will undoubtedly continue to occur; and they will disappear again as often as they cause trouble, since the need of clear expression of thought will tend to reduce them.

83. *Synonyms and Antonyms*

Synonyms are somewhat ambiguously defined by the dictionaries as words in the language "having the same or nearly the same essential meaning". As a result of this ambiguity of attitude toward the numerous synonymous words of English, some students endeavor to find words exactly the same, while others seek to learn the fine distinctions in meaning which the part of our definition "or nearly the same" implies. Antonyms are words which are opposite in meaning; and naturally any list of antonyms should parallel and contrast with a similar list of synonyms, so that the study of the two presents merely two contrasting aspects of the same thing.

For the foreigner, as already remarked in Section 26, English synonyms offer a serious difficulty in the acquiring of a perfect understanding of our speech; but to the English-born speaker and writer our unparalleled wealth of synonymous words presents opportunities for versatility and exactness in the expression of thought and emotion seldom fully appreciated by the ordinary student of English. Indeed, many a writer has discovered that he never really thought clearly until he began to use synonyms discriminatingly.

Both the difficulty of the foreigner and the opportunity of the native user of English can be easily emphasized by a careful examination of the words that center about any important idea or concept. The insistence of the Standard Dictionary that a synonym is "oftener, one of a number of words having one or more meanings in common" stresses the determining factor in the selection of any group of synonyms. Just what is that meaning which a given group of synonymous words have in common, and just what are the different finer shades of meaning which distinguish them and force one to study the entire group before he can find "just the right word" for the expression of his idea? Let us examine a typical synonym-antonym group centering about the contrasting ideas "Increase" and "Decrease", as it has been compiled from a number of different word books and word lists:

414   THE MODERN ENGLISH VOCABULARY   [Chap. X

Increase		Decrease	
Nouns			
accession	elaboration	abatement	diminution
accretion	enlargement	abridgment	extenuation
accrual	exacerbation	anticlimax	lessening
accumulation	exaggeration	coarctation	mitigation
aggrandizement	extension	declension	reduction
aggravation	growth	decline	reflux
amplification	improvement	decrease	shrinkage
ascent	increase	decrement	subsidence
augmentation	increment	deduction	subtraction
betterment	inflation	deflation	thinning out
development	multiplication	depreciation	wane
dilatation	rise	derogation	waste
distension	spread	descent	
Verbs			
accrue	extend	abate	lessen
accumulate	gain	abridge	lower
add to	get ahead	attenuate	melt away
advance	grow	belittle	mitigate
aggrandize	heighten	crumble	reduce
aggravate	improve	decay	run low
amplify	increase	decline	shorten
ascend	inflate	decrease	shrink
augment	intensify	deflate	subside
better	magnify	depreciate	subtract
broaden	multiply	descend	thin out
deepen	progress	die away	wane
dilate	prosper	diminish	waste away
distend	raise	discount	weaken
enhance	rise	drop off	wear
enlarge	run up	dwarf	withdraw
exacerbate	shoot up	dwindle	
exaggerate	spread	ebb	
exalt	strengthen	extenuate	
exasperate	wax	fall away	
expand	widen	fall off	
expatiate		languish	

A similar list of synonymous adjectives and adverbs might be compiled.

Such a list as this clearly demands a long and minute study, word by word and idea by idea, if one is to do full justice to the subject. It is possible here to touch only upon some of the more obvious features of this particular synonym-antonym group. The essential meaning, that meaning which the entire group possesses in common, is that of 'becoming greater', on the one hand, and of 'growing less', on the other. The various distinctions in meaning which give rise to the various words in the group under "Increase" are indicated in the definition in Webster's New International Dictionary, that *to increase* is "to become greater in size, quantity, number, degree, value, intensity, power, authority, reputation, wealth, etc." In terms of the foregoing list of words, this definition might be rewritten so as to read: "To enlarge, magnify, multiply, progress, accrue, intensify, gain, aggrandize, get ahead, prosper, etc." Each synonym has within it the "essential meaning" which binds it to the group; but each synonym also carries a distinctive meaning which makes it somewhat different from every other word in the group.

Since earliest times the English people have been fond of using pairs of words connected by *and*. This practice is stylistic and general; we are interested in it at this point because not infrequently the two words will be found to be synonymous. Some of these synonymous pairs are rhythmical and often alliterative, such as '*bag* and *baggage*', '*hale* and *hearty*', '*kith* and *kin*', '*might* and *main*', '*modes* and *manners*', '*safe* and *sound*'. Some of them seem to be the result of a very general habit that translators have always had of giving a pair of synonymous words when they could not decide on some one word. Probably this accounts for the tendency to use synonymous pairs in ecclesiastical and religious phraseology, such as '*defender* and *keeper*', '*meek* and *lowly*', '*picking* and *stealing*', and especially in early translations of the Bible, where the translator's uncertainty gave rise to such pairs as '*enter* and *come in*', '*gladden* and *delight*'. In legal phraseology there have always been many synonymous repetitions, such as '*aid* and *abet*', '*metes* and *bounds*', '*pray* and *beseech*', '*ways* and *means*', '*will* and *testament*'.

Certain English writers have been especially prone to use synonymous pairs, such as Stevenson's '*batter* and *bemaul*'.

The indiscriminate heaping up of synonymous adjective modifiers, as in '*aged old* man', '*great big* house', '*little tiny* girl', '*same identical* book', is a notable weakness of some careless speakers and should be avoided.

As one would naturally expect, the great increase in the number of English synonyms since the Norman Conquest has been due largely to the bringing in of foreign words meaning about the same as some already in the language. Borrowing has given such pairs as

acknowledge/confess   foregoing/preceding
act/deed   humble/lowly
allow/permit   meet/assemble
apt/likely   mirth/jollity

But the pairs of words of similar meaning that have been developed as the result of derivational processes already discussed (see Chapter IX) are likely to give more trouble to the speaker of English, and often only close study of the dictionary will make him aware of their fine differences in meaning. Pairs of this kind are *accrual* and *accruement*, *admission* and *admittance*, *amiable* and *amicable*, *conformance* and *conformity*, *duration* and *durability*, *illumine* and *illuminate*, *vicinage* and *vicinity*.

As a consequence of the growing use of verb-adverb combinations, it is now possible to express an idea, very often, by means of a combination or else by the use of a verb of somewhat more distinctive meaning. So we have such pairs as

blow out/extinguish   fall out/disagree
break in/interrupt   get on/prosper
call down/rebuke   give in/acquiesce
come about/happen   go off/explode

In the expression of certain ideas the ingenuity of newspaper writers and modern slangsters has been responsible for the existence of veritable swarms of terms. The sports writer who was able to marshal eighteen different verbs to express football defeat has been mentioned (see page 45). Another journalist has listed 288 words that can be used in place of the word *said*, beginning with *added, assented, amended, approved, agreed, asked, asserted, assured*, and including many that could be used only under very special conditions.[360] One of the most fertile ideas for the growth of slang has been that of intoxication; more than a hundred slang expressions meaning 'drunk' have been sent in to *American Speech*, such as *blotto, ginned, lit, pie-eyed, stewed*, and *tipsy*, and more are available.[359]

Perhaps the most nearly synonymous words of all are those popular slang terms which have been variously called dyslogistic words or terms of disparagement or derogatory terms — often terms of abuse, such as *applesauce, blah, boloney, bosh, hokum, hooey, hot air, humbug, piffle, poppycock, rubbish*.[362] Equally numerous and perhaps equally lacking in individual distinction are the eulogistic words, words that express approbation, such as *corking, peachy, rattling good, scrumptious, spiffy, swell*.[363]

Among the standard words of English there are doubtless a few pairs of synonyms whose members might be regarded as almost identical in meaning; but they are very few, and one is never quite certain that they are identical. In most cases one member of the pair is not used as commonly as the other and hence does not become a threat to the continued existence of the other. How nearly identical, one might inquire, are the following pairs?

annual/yearly	danger/peril
authentic/genuine	face/visage
buy/purchase	foreword/preface
congratulate/felicitate	hide/conceal
daily/diurnal	obstacle/hindrance

These are as nearly average samples of closely synonymous words as will be found in English, and yet there is probably not one pair in the list wholly unaffected by the prejudices and preferences that English speakers have for one or the other of the pair. Either one word is on the way to banishment from common usage or else it is moving toward greater security in a distinct and separate meaning of its own. Many pairs have remained in general use only because the meaning of one word has become narrower and special, as may be seen in the following pairs:

    affection/affectation   ought/should
    artist/artisan   shepherd/pastor
    die/starve   stool/chair
    foam/froth   travel/voyage
    kill/murder   unknown/uncouth

When the French brought into England certain words of their own for animals and plants, the native words did not give way to them but persisted so strongly that the newcomers became modified in use. In a number of instances the older native word names the raw material, animal or vegetable, and the new word is applied to the finished product. So we still have pairs only slightly synonymous today, such as the oft-discussed *calf* and *veal, deer* and *venison, flax* and *linen, ox* and *beef, sheep* and *mutton.*

If the student of English will take up occasionally a single group of synonyms and antonyms, such as are to be found helpfully set forth in books like Roget's Thesaurus [356] or March's Thesaurus [355], and will seek both their common and their different meanings, he will greatly gain by the practice; for he will enhance the clarity and logic of his thinking, and he will acquire precision and flexibility in the expression of his thoughts. No better practice in the fitting together of ideas and words can be found anywhere than in this particular phase of language study. Indeed, in concluding this study of synonyms and antonyms, we can do no better than go back to the remarks of that clever and versatile lady of the eighteenth century, Hester Lynch Piozzi, who published in 1794 under the title of *British Synonymy* a series of essays which reflected her personal feelings as well as her broader thinking on a number of groups of synonymous words. Her method can be sufficiently illustrated from two of the shorter essays [353]:

Dusky, Cloudy, Obscure,

Is the spot we inhabit, using these adjectives in a literal sense, according to their just and natural synonymy: *dusky, cloudy,* and *obscure* will of course be our reasoning on subjects above our powers of understanding; for so in a figurative sense we accept these epithets most expressive of that which is acknowledged most difficult to express — *unintelligibility* — half-comprehended notions of half-distinguished, indistinct ideas, like silent shadows fleeting by in a *dusky* night, when *cloudy* vapours conceal the moon, and an *obscure* cavern exhibiting total blackness is all which convinces us that we enjoy even partial illumination. But too much of these gloomy synonymes... (pp. 112–113).

Illusion, Delusion, Phantasm,

Though not synonymous, are near enough to be very easily confounded, at least by strangers; while we natives know so certainly how to place these words, that we say properly enough, that if a person is under so strong a *delusion* as to believe himself removed for some strange crime or fancied excellence beyond the common limits of humanity, he may soon come to imagine himself surrounded by sad or gay *illusions*, out of the ordinary course of nature; and if he feeds such notions in solitude, nor seeks recourse from medicine in due time — his friends (as one's relations are popularly called) will soon pronounce him statutably mad — and, contenting themselves with enjoying his real estate, leave our *deluded* friend to converse with *phantasms* in a perpetual and strict confinement (p. 186).

For the thoughtful student of English, unhampered by dusky, cloudy, and obscure thinking, and free from illusion, delusion, and phantasms, there is no better thoroughfare to an appreciation of English life and thought than an intelligent study of the synonyms of the present day. As the race has progressed culturally, its thinking has been less generally concerned with the personal needs of food, clothing, shelter, with other people and with the physical world around, while more and more it has been devoted to characteristics and qualities, to mental processes and attitudes, to personal and social relations. Hence, in all the books of synonyms, from Mrs. Piozzi's vivacious and readable studies down to the latest edition of Roget's Thesaurus, the largest groups of synonyms have pertained more to the abstract type of thinking than to the definite and concrete. For the key to the cultural growth of the English people is an appreciation of the development of abstract terms rather more than of the concrete.

84. *Individual Vocabularies*

Previous consideration of the size and nature of the English vocabulary as a whole will have paved the way for a more intelligent study of the size and nature of the vocabulary of the individual speaker of English, inasmuch as the problems are the same in both cases and the vocabulary of any one speaker must expand in somewhat the same manner and for the same reasons that the dictionary of the English language has expanded. Estimates, however, of the size of the vocabulary of the individual have been much more varied and uncertain even than those of the English vocabulary as a whole, because, while the entire vocabulary is largely a matter of written record, it is not so easy to record individual usages in sufficient numbers to establish dependable averages. Indeed, the subject of individual vocabularies is too challenging and difficult to warrant doing more here than setting forth a few of the many varying opinions regarding size and presenting the various considerations that the investigator must keep always in mind.

Years ago that famous philologist Max Müller accepted the very superficial judgment of a clerical acquaintance that "some of the laborers in his parish had not three hundred words in their vocabulary", and this very low estimate has been quoted and bandied about almost down to the present day. In 1897 Wood remarked that "the average man uses about five hundred words". We have already cited the opinion of Whipple that "the average three-year-old child makes use of 1000 words"[78]. For many years studies of certain famous writers have been made the basis of conjecture as to the size of individual English vocabularies; Shakespeare has been variously credited with from 15,000 to 24,000 words altogether, and Milton has been allowed from 8000 to 14,000 words in his writings. In 1880 Professor E. S. Holden reported that he had made a test of his own vocabulary and found that he used 33,456 words.[364] A few years later Professor E. H. Babbitt estimated that he knew about 65,000 English words well enough to define them, although he did not pretend to use all of them.

In 1915 Frank H. Vizetelly, editor of the Standard Dictionary, summarized the findings of various scholars and investigators in his *Essentials of English Speech* (p. 219) as follows [366]:

Every well-read person of fair ability and education will be able to define or to understand as used nearly or quite, perhaps more than 50,000 words. And the same person in conversation and writing will command not fewer than 15,000 to 20,000, and can add 5,000 to 10,000 to these numbers if he be literarily inclined. The plain people, as Lincoln liked to call them, use or read understandingly from 8,000 to 10,000 words according to their general intelligence and conversational power, while a person who can not read, but who has a good degree of native mental ability, will command about 5,000.

It is apparent from the preceding estimates that those who attempt to measure the "average individual vocabulary" go about it in quite different ways. First of all, it is necessary to recognize three different vocabularies: that of common colloquial speech, which uses far fewer words because it is generally concerned with the concrete rather than the abstract; that of the more formal written or literary English, which deals with abstract thinking to a much greater degree and naturally employs a greater variety and number of words; and, finally, that vocabulary some of which one recognizes but does not often employ. In this last vocabulary there are said to be at least three times as many words as in the used vocabulary, since people are likely to be familiar through their reading with many learned and technical terms, with archaisms, and even with slang, much of which they never use themselves. Then, again, before attempting to estimate the number of words known to the average speaker of English, it is also necessary to decide which word forms are to be counted and which ignored as mere variants of others. Shall the pronominal forms *I*, *my*, *me*, for example, be regarded as separate words or merely inflectional variants? Are *amiable* and *amicable*, *come* and *coming*, *epic* and *epical*, *gray* and *grey*, *metal* and *mettle*, *small* and *smallest*, separate words? How many of the eighty forms of the Latin word *cedo*, listed near the end of Section 61, should be counted separately?

Even after some sort of definition and basis of selection have been worked out, there are other considerations of importance. The environment of the individual must be considered, for his intellectual development and the linguistic expression of that development vary according to environment. The findings of psychologists studying children through their vocabularies have sometimes been seriously criticized on the ground that children had been chosen for study who had been reared by educated parents. The isolated peasant will certainly have fewer opportunities to acquire words than the city man; and in a bilingual community, such as a Swedish-American town of Minnesota, the vocabulary of purely English words is bound to be dwarfed by the use of foreign words.

Moreover, the age and experience of the individual must be considered. Terman has concluded after many tests of individuals that the numbers of words recognized at different ages are approximately as follows [367]:

Eight years	3,600	Fourteen years	9,000
Ten years	5,400	Average adult	11,700
Twelve years	7,200	Superior adult	13,500

But later studies seem to indicate that these figures are not high enough. Certainly there is a great discrepancy between Terman's 13,500 words recognized by the superior adult and Vizetelly's guess of 50,000.

Perhaps this remarkable increase in the estimates of the more recent investigators is not altogether the result of superior methods and better understanding of the problem; perhaps it may fairly be assumed that the working vocabulary of the average individual has actually increased during the past half-century. Certainly the English vocabulary as a whole has grown steadily during that period. Nowadays the individual undoubtedly needs a more elaborate vocabulary for any profession or art or trade that he may follow. Moreover, the words that have come into very general use as the result of inventions such as the automobile, the radio, the airship, the moving picture, and the ideas that are broadcast everywhere through the agency of improved communication and transportation, have extended greatly the intellectual horizon of the average man and woman and child. The increase in the number of words needed for twentieth-century life has been most marked.

While for some time efforts at measuring the vocabularies of individual users of English were inspired mainly by philological curiosity, more recently the importance of knowing the vocabulary scope of individuals, both younger and older, and of large groups of speakers and readers of English, has been brought home to scholars and scientists in various lines of educational and sociological endeavor. The psychologist makes use of vocabulary tests to measure the intelligence of individuals of various ages; for he stresses that truth which is the fundamental and guiding motive for this entire analysis of Current English, namely, that language is the expression of thinking. The teacher is interested in knowing the size of the child's vocabulary at various ages and stages of development because the knowledge aids him in measuring school efficiency and in deciding what spellings should be stressed and what literature should be utilized and how much foreign-language study should be undertaken at various stages in the child's scholarly career. Even the general sociologist should realize the importance to him of a study of the speech of any individual whose social conditions he is endeavoring to appraise, since vocabulary reflects so well social environment.

Very different methods of estimating the size of individual vocabularies have been employed since people became seriously interested in the matter. At first observers, like the English clergyman cited, based their estimates on guesses resulting from years of intercourse with persons of certain social status, such as the ignorant peasant. Then philologists began to count the words used by authors like Shakespeare and Milton and to guess at their probable total vocabularies on the basis of their recorded ones. Later still, many interested parents recorded laboriously and carefully the words used by their little children, year by year. These all had to do with the used vocabularies of individuals.

Quite recently Terman and others developed the test based upon a selection of approximately one hundred words chosen from dictionaries by various systematic methods. But their findings have varied, in the estimate of vocabularies of children and adults, from 9000 words to as high as 43,680 words. Apparently these variations have been due to the fact that the dictionaries on which they based their selections were of different sizes. At Colorado College a list of one thousand words was compiled, and the test consisted in choosing for each one the correct meaning when three out of the four meanings offered were false.[368] All of these tests aimed at measuring the vocabulary of words recognized, which has been said to be about three times as large as the used vocabulary.

And, finally, some investigators have undertaken to count their own vocabularies by going laboriously through certain dictionaries and recording the words which they recognize. This last type of vocabulary test is perhaps the most satisfactory, even as it is the most difficult to apply. It is the kind of test that can be commended to any one who is sufficiently interested in measuring his own individual culture as expressed in his use of words.

However, any serious and conscientiously applied test of the vocabulary of an individual is certain to prove interesting and illuminating. A better understanding of the words that a person uses day by day, informally and formally, and the words that he reads and understands will throw light on his intellectual development. For his language is the surest indication of his thinking.

85. Relative Frequency of Words

When one has come to realize how relatively few words in the dictionary are commonly used by even the best educated persons, he is likely to ask himself what the words are which people use most frequently. The attempts made lately at answering this question should have real interest for any student of twentieth-century English. Before considering, however, the various classes of commonly used and more rarely used words in the vocabulary of present-day English, we can appreciate better the attitude of recent investigators toward the matter of word frequency if a hasty survey be made of the growth of interest in the subject. The older lexicographers were not concerned about the commonly used words of English; they made their dictionaries of hard words for people who, like Thomas Blount himself, were "gravelled" by the many learned and exotic terms that had crept into the language. Even after the dictionary-maker had become obsessed with the idea of making his dictionary as big and as widely comprehensive as possible and had begun to boast about the number of words offered in his latest edition, still the common word was not taken very seriously but was plainly put in to pad out the book or else to aid in displaying the erudition of the etymologist. Such entries as "Cabbage. A plant", "Dog. A well-known domestick animal," "Hog. The general name of swine," "Horse. A neighing quadruped, used in war, and draught, and carriage", "Man. Human being. Not a woman. Not a boy", "Potato. An esculent root", "Rose. A flower", all found in Johnson's English Dictionary as Improved by Todd and Abridged by Chalmers, in 1842 — these and numerous others help to swell the numbers and do not serve any real need. Indeed, the statement in a 1914 abridged dictionary for elementary-school use that a *hog* is "A swine, esp. an adult one" still indicates that the lexicographer was not very much interested in the common word.

But gradually the educator and the scientific investigator have begun to realize that knowing just what words are commonly employed by all of us may aid greatly in compiling more helpful dictionaries and spelling books for school use and even in understanding some of the more influential factors in the development of sounds and words. In 1921 Thorndike published in his *Teacher's Word Book* a list of 10,000 words to assist the teacher in determining what should be stressed in teaching the younger student;[373] in 1926 Horn published, after a similar careful study, a *Basic Writing Vocabulary* of 10,000 words most commonly used in adult writing;[374] and in 1930 French, Carter, and Koenig presented, in *Words and Sounds of Telephone Conversations*,[376] their list of the 737 words most commonly heard over the telephone.

Upon examination of the studies just named and of some of the more limited studies already summarized in this book, it becomes apparent that the words most commonly employed by the average speaker of English are largely of certain kinds. The studies of the used vocabularies of Shakespeare, Addison, Tennyson, and others (see page 98) indicate that from 70 per cent to as high as 94 per cent of occurrences are of native Anglo-Saxon stock.

Naturally the less striking words that are used in putting together sentences have an important place in these lists of common words, notably the pronouns (*I, you, his, them*, etc.), the numerals (*one, second, forty*, etc.), the prepositions (*about, in, over, with*, etc.) and such conjunctions as *and, or, but*.

Some of the nouns found in most common use by these investigators are

account	answer	bottom	eye	fellow
afternoon	bag	error	face	news
age	ball	exchange	fact	night
air	basket	expense	favor	number
animal	bone	express	feet	people

Some of the most commonly used verbs are

act	bow	complete	excuse	give	make
add	bring	contrast	fall	go	offer
allow	call	do	favor	guess	order
be	can	don't	feel	have	put
beat	care	doubt	fill	hope	read
bless	come	enjoy	get	lay	take

Sec. 85] RELATIVE FREQUENCY OF WORDS

The relatively small number of adjectives comprised in the first thousand most commonly used words in the lists cited impresses one immediately. Some of the most familiar are

afraid	different	eight	even	fat	great
black	direct	either	every	few	happy
blind	due	else	extra	fine	hard
cold	duplicate	enough	fair	first	high
dear	each	entire	far	good	past

Since the list compiled from telephone conversations does not depend upon written matter, as the foregoing lists do, but is derived from the everyday talk of people of varying social status, a closer examination of the list will give an even better idea of the words most frequently used today. The first hundred words, in order of frequency, are as follows:

1. I
2. you
3. the
4. a
5. on
6. to
7. that
8. it
9. is
10. and
11. get
12. will (*aux.*)
13. of
14. in
15. he
16. we
17. they
18. see
19. have
20. for
21. know
22. don't
23. do
24. are
25. want
26. go
27. tell
28. with
29. me
30. him
31. about
32. at
33. think
34. this
35. day
36. thing
37. say
38. can (*aux.*)
39. call (*verb*)
40. would
41. them
42. was
43. now
44. from
45. what
46. morning
47. an
48. just
49. over
50. be
51. or
52. take
53. am
54. come
55. make (*verb*)
56. give
57. very
58. send
59. as
60. right (*adj.*)
61. order (*noun*)
62. good
63. minute (*noun*)
64. price
65. here
66. car
67. had
68. time
69. can't
70. much
71. there
72. week
73. let
74. letter
75. any
76. did
77. more
78. didn't
79. talk (*verb*)
80. today
81. other
82. company
83. fine (*adj.*)
84. could
85. same
86. put
87. wait (*verb*)
88. has
89. anything
90. my
91. night
92. call (*noun*)
93. your
94. little
95. stuff (*noun*)
96. won't
97. last (*adj.*)
98. she
99. all
100. better

As the list stands, there are apparently 15 pronouns, 16 adjectives (including the articles), 10 prepositions, 25 different verbs (but 36 forms of them), 3 conjunctions, 14 nouns, and 6 adverbs.

In all of these lists classification according to the parts of speech is very uncertain, because so many of these commonly used words are convertible. Of the 25 nouns first listed at least 14 can be used as verbs; of the 36 verbs at least 23 can easily be used as nouns; of the 30 adjectives at least 17 are regularly used otherwise, and also there is a strong colloquial tendency to use *fine* and *good* as adverbs. If there is any doubt as to the importance of the part played by conversion in Current English, a study of the possibilities of conversion in the words listed by Thorndike and Horn should prove highly convincing.

Then, again, it will be observed that a very high percentage of these frequently used words are monosyllabic. In the hundred most commonly heard in telephone conversations there is no word of more than one syllable in the first thirty, and only thirteen in the entire hundred. In the larger collections of Thorndike and Horn monosyllabic words are fairly numerous, although the nature of the material analyzed and the inclusion of many inflected forms like *going, starter,* and *stitches* would lead one to expect a smaller percentage of monosyllabic forms. Indeed, despite this fact, about four fifths of the first five hundred words in frequency of use in Thorndike's list are monosyllabic. It is not unusual to find in almost any modern book entire lines which contain monosyllabic words exclusively.

Among these commonly used words of Modern English there are, of course, some much-abused "counter words", such as *awful, fierce, fine, funny, grand, horrid, keen, marvelous, nice,* and *pretty.* Krapp, in discussing these in *Modern English* (p. 202), remarked upon the very common use of *fair* in Shakespeare's day. In attempting to explain the remarkably small vocabulary of the English rustic of a later day, a writer in the London *Saturday Review* for 1869 (Vol. 28, p. 43) said:

In some circles all that is agreeable or successful is expressed by "comfortable"; all that is moving or pathetic, by "cutting". Each man selects some one epithet in harmony with his own temperament to express approval. With one it may be "pride" and "proud" as the one quality to be admired in man or beast. Another finds "tidy" of as universal application. Animation in man, woman, or child is being "fierce"; to be engaging and affable is invariably to be "free". With one all puzzle and dilemma is being "stagnated", while "odd" includes all that many have to say on all varieties of temper, character, and circumstances.

But while this may have been true of the use of "counter words" by the rustic speaker of 1869, among American writers of a later day these words are not a matter of individual choice; on the contrary, when such a word becomes popular, it is universally abused by all that great class of imitators alike who do little thinking and much writing. Almost every year some thoughtful person protests about the abuse of words in this indiscriminating manner; one writer listed recently *crass, culture, hokum, intrigue, lurid, meticulous, terse*, etc.; another thinks *motivate, outstanding, reaction*, and *superimposed* have been sadly overworked; and still another detests *anent, hectic*, and *meticulous*, also. Newspaper usage has so completely conventionalized expressions like *movie star, prominent clubman, rich heiress, savant*, and *society matron* that many a young reporter would find it hard to carry on his trade without them. And in the lists of common words which have been considered there will be found, of course, the makings of many verb-adverb combinations, those hard-worked little verbs *break, get, lay, put, throw, work*, etc. and the adverbial particles *at, in, out, over, up, with*, etc., on which the ordinary English speaker rings the changes day after day to the exclusion of more formidable and learned verbs like *disintegrate, precipitate*, and *succeed*.

If one turns, however, to the less commonly used half of either of the ten-thousand-word lists under consideration, he finds an entirely different array of words. He finds, instead of predominantly Anglo-Saxon and monosyllabic words, too often overworked and shopworn, many more of those special words of Latin or Greek origin that characterize the more formal standard literary English. In this more select class of words will be found such words as *alteration, anticipation, declamation, discrimination, environment, harmonious, justification, lamentable, misapprehension, paramount, sanguine,* and *supererogation,* excellent old words, high-sounding and dignified, but too awe-inspiring to the average speaker of English to be bandied about freely. There are also numerous words of a more narrowly technical nature, such as *diagnosis, intestate, nonparticipating, rhomboid,* and *spores,* which are regularly employed in the more restricted circles where they properly belong.

More remote still from the common mob of everyday words are those "hothouse words" which languish in the large dictionaries, apparently still alive, but rarely met with outside the shelter of the dictionary or the book of some writer who has been experimenting with exotics in his garden of words or endeavoring to revive obsolescent ones. A century ago they were still used in the writing of popular fiction and probably heard in the speech of the educated man; but now it is seldom that one hears words like *ablutions, arbitrament, desuetude, ejaculated, fraught with, habiliments, inspirit, perfervid, persiflage, physiognomy, pusillanimity,* and *sepulchral.*

There are, of course, in the unabridged dictionaries many words marked "*Archaic*" or "*Obsolete*" which only the poet or the newspaper humorist has the courage to disinter. These have already been examined at some length (Sec. 13), and they should not need further illustration. But it is pertinent to this study of word frequency to note that some archaic words are not entirely dead, just as some living words are surrounded in the dictionary with a fairly large number of antiquated meanings. Some words which would be quite obsolete otherwise are commonly heard in special stereotyped phrases, such as '*betwixt* and between', '*hale* and hearty', 'without *let* or hindrance', 'the *livelong* day', 'with might and *main*', '*metes* and bounds', 'for *weal* or woe', 'widows' *weeds*', and 'the *wherewithal*'. There are, moreover, a few archaisms which individual writers or speakers employ occasionally, especially *albeit, anent, 'bounden* duty', *forbears, forsooth, gainsay,* 'for the *nonce',* 'beyond *peradventure', perchance, save* (preposition), '*wax* old', and *whilom*. For poetical and religious usage the archaic element in the vocabulary still has some appeal; it is only to the historian and antiquarian that the purely obsolete vocabulary has a constant usefulness.

And, finally, most people could name a few words that they dislike, for one reason or another, and avoid, words that are taboo, as it were, in polite conversation. These are not merely the shopworn "counter words" and phrases, such as have been illustrated above; they are also words that society in general has agreed to ignore as far as possible in its conversations and writings. Among the more primitive races of Polynesia and elsewhere "taboo" was a prohibition not only of the speaking of certain words but also of certain acts and things; but "taboo" words in English are mainly those pertaining to the more intimate phases of personal life or to disagreeable happenings and conditions, and it is a common practice to euphemistically substitute less offensive words. Substitutions which have been made at one time or another are *abattoir* for *slaughterhouse, casket* for *coffin, cemetery* for *graveyard, cuspidor* for *spittoon, expectorate* for *spit, food* for *victuals, intoxicated* for *drunk, laundress* for *washerwoman, light-fingered* for *thievish, limbs* for *legs, nose* for *snout, to pass away* for *to die, perspire* for *sweat, smell* or *odor* for *stink* or *stench,* '*soiled* clothes' for '*dirty* clothes', *the white plague* for *tuberculosis*. It is not difficult to see why people avoid the use of some of these words in an endeavor to soften the impact of death or deadly disease or dire poverty, or the sordidness and squalor implied in others of the list. In the case of some of these taboos the aversion is quite universal; but in the case of some others it is more restricted. In England *bloody* and *blooming* can no longer be employed for their proper uses. In some districts of America one can *carry* a *pail* of water more elegantly than he can *fetch* a *bucket* of it. And there are, of course, various traditional solecisms and rhetorical abuses which are taboo to the more carefully educated, even though the generality of users may be quite tolerant of them; many dislike *ain't*, 'It's *me*', '*like* he did', *due to* (as a preposition), '*Who* did you see?' 'I *sure* did', and the pronunciation [ɛt] for the past tense of *eat*, and their taboo still stands quite firmly in the way of general acceptance of these locutions. On the whole, the verbal taboos of present-day English usage are reasonable and readily comprehensible; and while there have been some absurdities, such as *gentleman cow* for 'bull' and *unmentionables* for 'trousers,' most of our taboos have been preserved as a concession to decent social intercourse or long-established grammatical practice.

Early in this chapter an effort was made to estimate the gross number of words that are comprised in the current vocabulary of the English language, and the result was somewhat astonishing. But the conclusions reached regarding the number of words actually utilized by the average user of English contrast so markedly with the number which might be used — the great number which the average person might employ if he chose to study the dictionary and increase his own individual vocabulary — that one can only marvel at the proportion not ordinarily used. Between the estimated half-million of English words that might be used and the few thousands that ordinarily are used, there is so wide a margin of unappreciated possibilities that we cannot avoid the conclusion that our thinking is very greatly restricted, if language is to be regarded as an index to thinking. Ideas and facts lie buried, by the tens of thousands, in the unused portion of the vocabulary of Current English, and the best way of bringing to light these ideas and facts is through the systematic resurrection of the words that express them. Can one find any stronger argument for a careful and prolonged study of the English vocabulary as set forth in the splendid dictionaries and word books of the language? It has been customary to joke about the reading of the dictionary, but certainly no more illuminating educational method could be devised than this very practice. A few words a day and a few new facts and ideas would at least make it possible for the student desirous of broadening his intellectual horizon to say in the words of the famous Coué formula, "Day by day in every way I am getting better and better." Even the unsystematic method of the cross-word puzzle has probably widened the intellectual horizons of many people in recent years, and any systematic procedure such as the recommended study of groups of synonyms and the more historical investigation of the relationships of English words will certainly bring valuable results for both the thinker and the writer.

In the following chapters the expression of thoughts in sentences will receive attention, and thinking will be presented as a stage of intellectual growth higher and better and more complex than the mere collection and evaluation of ideas and words. But ideas are not to be scorned, since they are the bricks with which we build the more elaborate structure of thinking. They are the definite bits of knowledge necessary to the art of speaking and writing the English language.

CHAPTER XI

INFLECTION

INFLECTION (also spelled inflexion) is the process of changing the forms of words in order to indicate certain of their grammatical properties, such as gender, number, person, case, tense, mood, or to make clear their grammatical relations to one another. Inflectional changes, to repeat what has already been said on the matter, are temporary and give rise to forms not often separately listed in the dictionary; in these respects they differ from derivational changes, which are permanent and produce forms separately listed in the dictionary and treated as separate words. Inflection of nouns and pronouns is called declension; of verbs, conjugation; and of adjectives and adverbs, comparison. The other three parts of speech are not inflected.

86. *The Breaking Down of English Inflection*

Very early in this survey of the English language it became necessary, in discussing the relation of form to use, to notice the gradual loss of inflection in English and the substitution of syntactical usage (Sec. 3); throughout the various later discussions it has been necessary to touch upon the subject from time to time because of the important bearing that the breaking down of the inflectional system has had upon various features of English — its simplicity of grammar, its monosyllabism or laconicism, its many silent letters, its homonyms, and so on. Once English was largely a "synthetic" language, putting together stems and inflectional endings to express variations in meaning (as in Modern English *act-ed*); now it is more nearly an "analytic" language, since it commonly makes syntactical usage express the same variations (as in Modern English *did act*). The English inflectional system still shows in shreds and patches, here and there, it is true; but it is so nearly gone that the modern grammarian of English must shift his point of view almost completely and regard the above-mentioned grammatical properties (case, gender, etc.) as matters of syntactical usage rather than as inflectional matters, as the older Latin grammarians did. Where the Anglo-Saxon noun, such as *stan*, had six different inflectional forms, its Current English equivalent, *stone*, has but two, if the apostrophe be disregarded; where the inflection of an Anglo-Saxon verb like *hear* involved at least fourteen different forms, today the same verb has only four; where the Anglo-Saxon adjective required an elaborate twofold system of declension to fit it to its noun, today it is quite free from declension. Grammarians have clung long and stubbornly to the classical conception of the grammatical properties as inflectional; and even today opinion is still quite evenly divided as to whether case, for example, is a matter of inflectional forms or of syntactical usage [390]. The truth of the matter is that, except for the loss of adjective declension, the five inflected parts of speech have the same grammatical properties that they have always had; but whereas in Anglo-Saxon times inflectional changes were resorted to for almost all variations in case, number, gender, tense, etc., today inflectional change goes only a little way in performing this service, and syntactical usage finishes the work.

So it becomes necessary once more to warn the student of Current English that in these two successive studies of inflection and of syntax (Chaps. XI and XII) he must be prepared to recognize and take into account two cross currents in the growth of our language, just as it has been necessary in earlier chapters of this book to recognize other fusions and confusions of different and even discordant elements. When we talk of the genitive case, for example, in this chapter, we shall mean a word with a genitive ending, such as '*man's* life'; when we consider the genitive case in the next chapter, we may mean a genitival phrase, such as 'the life *of man*'. When we discuss inflectional tense, we cite a past form *worked*; but when we go on to consider a syntactical tense, such as the future, we find a phrasal verb *shall work*. When we look for an inflectional comparative adjective, *richer* is suggested; but syntactical comparison in the next chapter involves a phrase, such as *more wonderful*.

If the student of language in attempting to understand what we have called the "grammatical properties" will recognize the two possibilities, namely, that they may be manifested to some extent, still, through the use of inflectional forms, but that to a far greater extent they are manifested through the syntactical usages, his thinking on this subject too will be much clarified, and much useless argument about the meaning of case, tense, number, mood, etc. will be done away with. But he must know what inflectional forms are, and so in the following sections the few surviving ones of English will be presented as briefly as possible.

87. *Declension of Nouns*

Declension, insofar as it relates to nouns, is any inflectional change in the form of a noun which helps to show its gender, its number, or its case.

Gender. Gender is that grammatical property of a noun by which we indicate sex or lack of sex. There are, therefore, three grammatical genders: masculine (male), feminine (female), and neuter (neither). Some grammarians use as a matter of convenience the term *common gender* for nouns that may refer to either sex, such as *animal, bear, cousin, friend, person, singer, teacher*.

While Old English indicated a noun's gender to some extent by the use of certain long-accepted inflectional endings, as do various other languages still, notably Latin, German, and Italian, Current English has very few gender suffixes and depends for the indication of gender mainly on the syntactical context of the noun, as we shall show later (Sec. 116), as in the sentence 'The bird broke her own eggs'; or else on word-compounding, as in *billy goat, bridegroom, cock sparrow, he-goat, lady clerk, landlord, male cousin, manservant, mother bird, salesman, tomcat*. Indeed, there is some doubt as to whether the gender suffixes should be regarded as inflectional at all; the nouns that employ them are treated separately in the dictionaries, and some of them have been listed among derivational suffixes in Section 61. But because there is doubt as to which they are, inflectional or derivational, they will be summarized here also. The surviving gender suffixes are almost exclusively feminine and are as follows:

-en: vixen (masculine *fox*).
-ess: abbess, actress, authoress, baroness, benefactress, countess, deaconess, duchess, empress, enchantress, giantess, goddess, governess, heiress, hostess, Jewess, laundress, lioness, mistress, negress, patroness, princess, prioress, seamstress, tigress, waitress. The suffix is still used sometimes to form new feminines, such as *championess, doctress*.[311] On the other hand, numerous words have lost it, and their gender is indicated now by some other method.
-ine: Caroline, Clementine, Josephine, heroine. During the World War such forms appeared as *actorine, booberine, doctorine*, and more recently *chorine*, 'chorus girl', and *dudine*, 'lady at a dude ranch'.
-trix: adjutrix, administratrix, aviatrix, executrix, testatrix. In most instances this ending has tended to give place to some other form.

Practically all Christian names are gender words, and not infrequently one name has both masculine and feminine forms, as in the case of *Augustus* and *Augusta*, *Charles* and *Charlotte*, *Ernest* and *Ernestine*, *Francis* and *Frances*, *Henry* and *Henrietta*, *John* and *Joanna*, *Paul* and *Pauline*, *William* and *Wilhelmina*. Of course some of these forms are of recent borrowing from other languages.

A few foreign gender suffixes occur in such pairs as *alumnus* and *alumna, comedian* and *comédienne, czar* and *czarina, kaiser* and *kaiserin, sultan* and *sultana*.

Little more can be said regarding inflectional change in English to express gender. Beyond this lies, of course, the possibility of indicating gender by choosing certain words that possess gender meanings; these gender words occur as gender pairs, usually.

Fairly numerous gender pairs of distinct words have come down into Current English and are in common use, while others have been lost along the way. Some of the survivors are

bachelor/spinster	lad/lass
beau/belle	lord/lady
boar/sow	man/woman
boy/girl	master/mistress
bridegroom/bride	monk/nun
brother/sister	nephew/niece
buck/doe	ram/ewe
bull/cow	sir/madam
cock/hen	sire/dam
earl/countess	son/daughter
father/mother	stallion/mare
hart/roe	uncle/aunt
husband/wife	widower/widow
king/queen	wizard/witch

In some pairs one of the words becomes quite general in its meaning, while the other remains distinctly a gender word; *bee, duck, goose, horse,* are often used without regard for gender, but *drone, drake, gander,* are masculine, and *mare* is feminine.

On the whole, it may be said of these surviving gender forms that, while they generally persist quite stubbornly, here and there a feminine form tends to disappear. So *author-ess* is losing its suffix, *administratrix* is being superseded by *administrator*, and except in legal documents *spinster* has dropped out of general use.

Number. Number is that grammatical property of a noun by means of which we show whether one or more than one person or thing is named. There are only two numbers in Current English, singular and plural. Declension of nouns to indicate plural number is the most persistently surviving phase of English noun inflection. In Old English, nouns fell into some nine classes, according as they formed their plurals; today one of the nine is predominantly used, and there are a few survivors from some of the other classes.

a. The plural of most English nouns is formed by the use of the suffix *-s* or *-es*, as has already been explained in the earlier discussions of pronunciation and of English spelling (see especially Notes 26, 38, 39, in Chapter VII). So we have *bowls, cities, feats, horses, houses, husbands, negroes, pianos, wives*, etc.

b. A few old nouns survive with the plural ending *-en* or *-n*, namely, *brethren, children,* archaic *kine* (singular *cow*), *oxen,* and the archaic and dialectal *shoon* (singular *shoe*). A once-common medieval English *brethren and sistren* sometimes turns up in modern dialectal usage, especially in the negro dialect.

c. A few old nouns still have plurals with only mutation, or internal change of vowel: *dormice, feet, geese, lice, men* (and its compounds like *footmen*), *mice, teeth,* and *women*. The two plurals *kine* and *brethren* also have internal change as well as the addition of *-n.*

d. One old plural in *-er* survives in the Anglo-Irish *childer*; but in standard English *child* forms its plural with both the *-r* ending and the *-n.*

e. The most striking exception to the general rule of pluralization in Current English is to be seen in that fairly numerous class of nouns which have or may have the same form for both the singular and the plural. These nouns with uninflected plurals are of three general kinds: those that are commonly used without *-s*, those that are frequently used with *-s*, and those that are regularly used with *-s* in standard English. Since, however, these categories are not very well defined, it is better to group the nouns involved according to subject matter, and for information regarding the pluralization of the individual words refer to some good dictionary (see Webster's New International Dictionary, Second Edition, pp. 1895–1897).

(1) Names of animals, fish, and birds, mostly wild game:

antelope	elk	partridge	reindeer
bison	fish	perch	salmon
buffalo	grouse	pickerel	sheep
cod	mackerel	pike	swine
deer	moose	quail	trout

(2) Some collective nouns and numerals:

billion	gross	million	span
brace	head	pair	thousand
dozen	horse (*cavalry*)	sail (*vessels*)	twain
foot (*infantry*)	hundred	score	yoke

(3) Some measure words still used colloquially without any ending in the plural, such as *acre, foot, hundredweight, mile, rod, ton, yard*; but most of these are given the *s* ending in standard English usage.*

The tendency is to use the *s* ending for some of this group of uninflected-plural nouns with a slight difference in meaning, as in the case of *braces, fishes*[385], *spans*, and *yokes*. When numerals like *billion* and *hundred* take *s*, they name groups.

f. The most troublesome plurals in Current English are those of foreign nouns which have not yet become completely naturalized; some foreign plural endings persist most stubbornly, while others are gradually going over to the English *s* plural. There are several thousand of these nouns, some with a well-established English plural like *spatulas*, some with the foreign-plural form used exclusively, as *alumni*, and some with both kinds permissible, as *cacti* and *cactuses*, or even necessary, as *genii* and *geniuses*. Words marked with the dagger in the following lists can have either form of plural ending.

Latin feminine nouns with plural ending in -æ:

alumna/alumnæ
† formula/formulæ
† larva/larvæ
minutia/minutiæ
† nebula/nebulæ
† vertebra/vertebræ

Latin masculine nouns with plural in -*i* or -*us*:

alumnus/alumni
† apparatus/apparatus
† cactus/cacti
† focus/foci
† fungus/fungi
† gladiolus/gladioli
† nucleus/nuclei
† radius/radii
stimulus/stimuli
† syllabus/syllabi

* Of course no plural ending is possible when these words are used in compound adjectives, as in 'a *five-yard* pole', 'a *ten-pound* weight', 'a *forty-acre* field'.

Latin and Greek nouns with plural in -es:

amanuensis/amanuenses
analysis/analyses
antithesis/antitheses
† apex/apices
† appendix/appendices
axis/axes
basis/bases
codex/codices
crisis/crises
† crux/cruces
ellipsis/ellipses
hypothesis/hypotheses
† index/indices
† larynx/larynges
oasis/oases
parenthesis/parentheses
synopsis/synopses
synthesis/syntheses
thesis/theses
† vertex/vertices

Latin and Greek nouns with plural in -a:

addendum/addenda
agendum/agenda
† automaton/automata
† candelabrum/candelabra
† criterion/criteria
† curriculum/curricula
datum/data
† delirium/deliria
desideratum/desiderata
† dictum/dicta
duodenum/duodena
† emporium/emporia
erratum/errata
† genus/genera
† gymnasium/gymnasia
† medium/media
† memorandum/memoranda
† millennium/millennia
† moratorium/moratoria
phenomenon/phenomena
referendum/referenda
† stadium/stadia
† stamen/stamina
† stratum/strata

French nouns with various plural endings:

bandeau/bandeaux
† beau/beaux
† bureau/bureaux
† madam/mesdames
monsieur/messieurs
† plateau/plateaux
† tableau/tableaux
† trousseau/trousseaux

Italian nouns with plural in -i:

† bandit/banditti
† dilettante/dilettanti
† Fascist(a)/Fascisti
† libretto/libretti
† seraglio/seragli
† virtuoso/virtuosi

Hebrew nouns with plural in -im:

† cherub/cherubim
† seraph/seraphim

Modern scientific usage still employs the foreign plurals of some of these nouns where general English usage shows a preference for the English *s* endings. Occasionally popular ignorance of the correct foreign endings results in the use of a foreign plural form as a singular in English; this is true especially of the Latin and Greek nouns with plural in *-a*, such as *data, insignia, memoranda, strata*.[386]

General comments on number. Confusion regarding the use of some of the less important methods of pluralization in earlier English has sometimes led to the use of two different methods in the same word; so *brethren* and *kine* show internal change, but they also take the plural *-n*; and the *-n* has also been added to the *-r* plural *childer*. In *breeches* internal change is reënforced by final *-s*.

Attention has already been called (p. 96) to the peculiar preferences that the various Germanic languages have shown for these plural forms, English preferring the ending *-s* (or *-es*), High German employing *-e*, *-r*, or *-en*, and frequently internal change, and Danish using *-e* or *-r*. In this matter it would be difficult to account for national tastes.

Sometimes, when two kinds of pluralization have produced two plurals for a word, different uses and meanings have resulted, and as a consequence the older form has not been crowded out by the *-s* form. This can be seen in such pairs as

brother/brethren, brothers
cherub/cherubim, cherubs
cloth/cloths, clothes
cow/kine, cows
die/dice, dies
fish/fish, fishes
genius/genii, geniuses
head/head, heads
index/indices, indexes
penny/pence, pennies
staff/staves, staffs
stamen/stamina, stamens

While purely abstract nouns like *growth* and concrete nouns of material like *silver* do not have plural forms, as such, yet they can often be used with somewhat different values which make pluralization possible, as in the case of

advice/advices
air/airs
beef/beeves
copper/coppers
force/forces
good/goods
grace/graces
honor/honors
iron/irons
pain/pains
refreshment/refreshments
respect/respects
salt/salts
sand/sands
virtue/virtues
water/waters
wit/wits
work/works

Some collective nouns are usually considered plurals because they are regularly used with plural verbs, notably *artillery, cattle, cavalry, clergy, gentry, infantry, intelligentsia, kindred, militia, nobility, peasantry, police, offspring, poultry,* and *vermin.*

A large number of other nouns rarely or never appear in the singular form; some are names of tools or clothing double by nature, others name diseases, others name sciences and special studies, some are verbal nouns become concrete, and so on. Among words of this kind are some that give rise to that troublesome syntactical problem of Modern English which pertains to number. One never can be quite sure whether a word like *thanks* should be used with a singular verb or a plural; words marked with a dagger *may* be used with a singular verb, though it is sometimes awkward to do so. The following are familiar, and many of them old in the language[389]:

† acoustics	doings	† mumps	shears
alms	doldrums	† news	† statistics
† amends	dregs	nuptials	suds
annals	eaves	† odds	† summons
† antipodes	† economics	pants	sweepings
arms	embers	† phonetics	tactics
ashes	† ethics	† physics	thanks
† athletics	forceps	pincers	tidings
† bellows	† gallows(es)	pliers	tongs
belongings	giblets	† politics	trappings
† billiards	† headquarters	proceeds	trousers
bowels	† mathematics	remains	tweezers
breeches	† means	resources	victuals
chap(arajo)s	† measles	riches	vitals
† civics	mews	savings	wages
contents	† molasses	scissors	† whereabouts

A few of the plurals given above, such as *alms, eaves, riches,* and *summons,* are pseudoplurals, inasmuch as the *-s* was originally the stem ending of the singular, just as we have already shown that a lost *-s* was the ending also of the earlier singular forms of *burial, cherry, minnow, pea, riddle,* etc. (see page 356).

One of the noticeable features of modern colloquial speech of a slangy character is the use of words which usually have no singular form, such as the *blues*, the *heebie jeebies*, the *jim-jams*, the *jitters*, his *nibs*, *oodles*, *scads*, the *willies*,— mostly vague and somewhat indefinite in meaning. These do not appear to cause syntactical difficulties as often as the more formal words of standard literary English. Perhaps this is to be ascribed to the fact that most of these slang words are used only in objective constructions.

The pluralization of compound words and of phrases also causes trouble sometimes. When the parts are separate or hyphenated, the chief element is usually pluralized; but if the phrase is such that no one word is the chief element, the -*s* is added finally. Rarely, both parts are pluralized. A few examples will suffice:

aides-de-camp	knights-errant
attorneys-general or attorney-generals	Knights Templars
battle-axes	lookers-on
brothers-in-law	man-eaters
coats of mail	men-of-war
courts-martial	menservants
editors in chief	passers-by
forget-me-nots	poets laureate
good-bys	sisters-in-law
hand-me-downs	vice presidents
hangers-on	will-o'-the-wisps
home-comings	

Compounds written solid are almost always pluralized by the addition of -*s* at the end or by internal change in the last word, as in *armfuls*, *busybodies*, *castaways*, *cupfuls*, *fishermen*, *maidservants*, *mouthfuls*, *pickpockets*, *shortcomings*, *spoonfuls*, *stepfathers*. The compounds with -*ful* cause special trouble because in spoken English they are confused with nouns followed by the adjective *full*; but *cupfuls* means certain measures even though cups may not be used at all, whereas *cups full* means 'full cups'. When titles and names are used together, either may be pluralized, as in the *Misses Brown* or the *Miss Browns*.

The plural of letters, figures, and signs is formed by the use of an apostrophe and -s, as in *6's, x's, 9's, e.g.'s*. When words are cited merely as forms, without reference to meaning, this method of pluralization is also employed, as in 'two *one's*', 'your *that's*'.

Case. Case is that grammatical property of a noun by which we show its relation to other words in the sentence. Since the earlier case forms have almost completely disappeared from English, case relations are generally indicated by syntactical usage, and grammarians have become very much confused as to what case really is. As Vickers has shown in his study *The Concept of Case in English Grammar* [390], during the past century English grammarians have been about equally divided as to whether case is inflectional or syntactical, with a few defining it as both form and use. Since an understanding of case relations is necessary for a thoroughgoing study of both nouns and pronouns, and since the student of the English language who goes from the study of Current English back into the past will find more cases with more distinct case forms, four of the more commonly recognized cases will be considered in this book. And since so much of the apparent aimlessness and confusion of modern grammar-making for English centers about this matter of case, it may prove helpful to both teacher and younger student of English if current opinion on the subject is summarized:

a. In most nouns there are but two inflectional case forms, the common and the genitive (possessive), and insistence upon case as merely inflectional would restrict the number of cases to two.

b. In many of the simpler English grammars, three phases of case are recognized, namely, nominative, possessive (or genitive), and objective, and for the more elementary study of the subject of case these three are perhaps quite sufficient.

c. In the more advanced study of grammar, as in the present discussion, a recognition of the four cases, nominative, genitive, dative, and accusative, is desirable because it leads to a more careful and appreciative study of the relation of Modern English case usage to earlier forms and uses, and also it throws light on case theory in other languages as well as in English.

d. Consideration of case entirely from the standpoint of the many case relations, as set forth in the next chapter of this book, would necessitate the naming of so many different cases that the study would be far too complex for any except the most advanced philosophical philological research into the subject.[391]

Consequently the definition of case for Modern English must be based largely on the decision as to how thoroughly one wishes to go into the matter; it would be as foolish to insist upon minute distinctions for elementary study as it would be shortsighted to ignore them in advanced philological study.

The nominative case indicates that a noun is used as the subject of a verb or in some way pertains to the subject. The genitive case expresses primarily the relation of source or possession and in Modern English grammar is often known as the possessive case, although the genitive usually covers more than just possession. The dative case is primarily the case of the indirect object and is usually merged in Modern English grammar with the objective case. The accusative case expresses primarily the relation of direct object of a verb or of a preposition and is often called the objective case.

In Current English the noun has only one distinctive case form, the genitive, or possessive; a common case form serves for the other three cases just defined. It is true that the apostrophe is placed before the *-s* in the genitive singular and usually after the *-s* in the genitive plural; but this is a visible and not a phonetic distinction. The scarcity of Modern English noun inflection can be seen in the following paradigms:

SINGULAR

Nom.	house	man	ox	city	wife
Gen.	house's	man's	ox's	city's	wife's
Dat.	house	man	ox	city	wife
Acc.	house	man	ox	city	wife

PLURAL

Nom.	houses	men	oxen	cities	wives
Gen.	houses'	men's	oxen's	cities'	wives'
Dat.	houses	men	oxen	cities	wives
Acc.	houses	men	oxen	cities	wives

There are no gender forms; for number and case there are two spoken forms for *house* and *city*, four for *man* and *ox*, three for *wife*. Spelling gives the appearance of more than there really are.

88. *Declension of Pronouns*

The declension of the personal pronoun includes, like that of the noun, gender, number, and case; but it goes farther and embraces also the property of "person". Person is that grammatical property by which the speaker shows whether he refers to himself, to the person addressed, or to some third person* or persons. The personal pronoun in its full present-day declension is as follows:

	First	Second		Third		
		Modern	*Archaic*	*Masc.*	*Fem.*	*Neut.*
Sing. *Nom.*	I	you	thou	he	she	it
Gen.	my	your†	thy	his	her	its†
Dat.	me	you	thee	him	her	it
Acc.	me	you	thee	him	her	it
Plur. *Nom.*	we	you	ye	they		
Gen.	our	your	your	their		
Dat.	us	you	you	them		
Acc.	us	you	you	them		

Besides the genitive forms given above, some longer ones, which are generally known as the "absolute" forms, namely, *mine, ours, yours, thine, hers,* and *theirs,* are regularly used when the pronoun stands alone, as in the sentence 'The book is *mine*.' At one time the forms *mine* and *thine* were used before vowel-beginning words, as in *mine eyes,* and before *h,* as in *mine host.* In vulgar colloquial speech the influence of *mine* and *thine* can be observed in such imitative or analogical forms as *ourn, yourn, hisn, hern, theirn.*

* While *person* usually refers to a human being, in its grammatical use it is more comprehensive, including anything that can be spoken about.

† In the writing of these genitives, *your* and *its* are sometimes confused with the verb contractions *you're* ('you are') and *it's* ('it is').

The intensive-reflexive compound with -*self* has the same gender, number, and person variations as the simple pronoun:

myself	yourself	thyself	himself	herself	itself
ourselves	yourselves	yourselves		themselves	

As we have already observed, the illiterate speaker often makes this entire set uniform by substituting *hisself* and *theirselves* for the two forms that are made with the objective instead of the genitive form of the simple pronoun.

With the declension of the personal pronoun the high point is attained in the inflectional system of Current English. On this pronoun depends much of the grammatical effectiveness of Modern English; for without it we should have no distinctions of person, indication of gender would be greatly diminished, and other syntactical usages would be less clearly defined, as we shall show in the next chapter. Even as it is, the capacity for exact expression has been somewhat lessened by the loss of the archaic second person and the use of *you* as a singular pronoun; for in such a sentence as '*You* are wrong', no indication is given as to how many persons are addressed.

As for the other pronouns, the tale of their declensional changes can be quickly told:

The interrogative and relative *who* (*whoever*) has the case forms *whose* and *whom*, and *whosever, whomever*, and *whomsoever*, in fairly general use. But the nominative forms are often carelessly substituted for the objective; for a fuller discussion of this practice see Section 104.

The demonstratives *this* and *that* have the plural forms *these* and *those*.

The indefinite and numeral *one*, being normally singular in meaning, can have only the genitive case form *one's*; but when it is used as a "prop word", as in 'a good *one*', 'the best *ones*', 'my other *ones*', then it can be pluralized like other substantives. The indefinite *other* can also be pluralized as *others* when it is used as a pronoun.

The compounds with -*body* and -*one* have the genitive forms *anybody's, anyone's, everybody's, everyone's, nobody's*, etc. When indefinites are followed by *else*, present-day usage prefers to give the genitive ending to the *else*, as in *someone else's*, *everyone else's*; and even the interrogative *who* is commonly used in this way, as in 'Who *else's* book?', although a few speakers endeavor to be logical by saying *someone's else* and *whose else* (see Fowler [16] and Krapp [17], under "else").

89. *Comparison of Adjectives and Adverbs*

Comparison is that property of adjectives and adverbs whereby degrees of quality, quantity, intensity, relation, and so on, can be indicated. The degrees of comparison are three: the positive, denoting the simple quality; the comparative, denoting a higher degree of the quality; and the superlative, denoting the highest degree.

a. Most monosyllabic adjectives and adverbs, and some dissyllabic ones, are compared by the addition of the inflectional suffixes -*er* (or -*r*) and -*est* (or -*st*). Examples are

fast	faster	fastest	able	abler	ablest
gay	gayer	gayest	empty	emptier	emptiest
ıard	harder	hardest	happy	happier	happiest
large	larger	largest	kindly	kindlier	kindliest
long	longer	longest	mellow	mellower	mellowest
loud	louder	loudest	narrow	narrower	narrowest
soon	sooner	soonest	often	oftener	oftenest
stout	stouter	stoutest			
tall	taller	tallest			
thin	thinner	thinnest			

b. A few of the most commonly used adjectives and adverbs are compared irregularly:

bad, ill, evil	worse	worst
good	better	best
late	later, latter	latest, last
little	less, lesser, littler	least, littlest
much, many	more	most
old	older, elder	oldest, eldest

While *elder* and *eldest* seem irregular today, in earlier English *old* was one of a small group of adjectives in which the process of comparison regularly involved not only the addition of comparative and superlative suffixes but mutation, or internal change of vowel, as well. *Old* is the sole survivor of this group.

The comparative and superlative forms of *bad* (*ill, evil*), *good, little,* and *much* (*many*) are "suppletive", filling in the comparison of the four adjectives irregularly, inasmuch as they are in reality quite different stems. *Latter* and *last* are due to vowel shortening.

c. A few adverbs are regularly used as adjectives in the comparative and superlative forms; in most instances the simple form can also function as an adjective:

far	farther	farthest
in	inner	innermost, inmost
near, nigh	nearer, nigher	nearest, next, nighest
(be)neath	nether	nethermost
out	outer, utter	outermost, utmost
up	upper	uppermost

The old superlative suffix *-most* is added also to the four adjectives of direction, producing *easternmost, northernmost, southernmost,* and *westernmost*; it also occurs in *aftermost, foremost, furthermost, hindmost, topmost.*

d. The Latin comparative form has been taken over bodily into the English in such words as *anterior, exterior, inferior, interior, junior, major, minor, posterior, prior, senior, superior,* and *ulterior,* and the superlative form appears in *extreme, maximum, minimum, supreme.*

e. Many dissyllabic adjectives and adverbs, adverbs with the suffix *-ly,* and almost all adjectives and adverbs of three or more syllables are compared syntactically by the use of the words *more* and *most,* as in *most beautiful, more cautious, more cheerful; most clearly, more evenly, most wonderfully; most indefatigably, most interesting, more irritating, more refreshing, more talented.* There is no very clear-cut rule as to when one should use the inflectional *-er* and *-est* and when the *more* and *most* method of comparison; such words as *handsome, lively, lonely, remote, serene,* and *tender* are commonly compared by both methods; a few monosyllabic words, such as *just, like, wrong,* are compared with *more* and *most.* Indeed, almost every short adjective or adverb is compared by the syntactical method at times, especially to emphasize the superlative degree, as in 'It is *most kind* of you.' On the other hand, colloquial usage permits the use of some very awkward comparisons with the inflectional endings *-er* and *-est*, as in *cheerfulest, correctest, cunningest,* '*curiouser* and *curiouser*', *wonderfuller,* although these are likely to be regarded as childish or else whimsical and humorous usages. Shakespeare's '*Most unkindest cut of all*' would be regarded today as unnecessary doubling of comparative methods.

f. There are, of course, many adjectives which theoretically are incapable of being compared, such as *dead, empty, infinite, parallel, perfect, square, unanimous, unique,* and adverbs like *completely, eternally, finally.* But in actual practice various words like *black, complete, dead, full, hopeless,* and *round* are compared, with a total disregard for logic. As a matter of fact, when one says *completest,* he is merely using a linguistic shortcut for *most nearly complete*; and in comparing words of this kind the very exact thinker is likely to use the phrases *more nearly* and *most nearly* instead of loosely comparing them by the usual methods.

90. *Conjugation of Verbs*

Conjugation, says the dictionary, is "a schematic arrangement of the inflectional forms of a verb" or "a class of verbs having the same type of inflectional forms" or "the act of conjugating, or inflecting, a verb".[28] But always, it will be noted, inflection is implied in conjugation. Consequently, in spite of the fact that some grammarians have printed many pages of schematic arrangements of English verbs which were largely syntactical, the term *conjugation* will be restricted in its application here to the forms that the verb assumes as the result of using inflectional endings, or other inflectional devices, such as internal change of vowel.

As far back as English grammar-making goes, it has been customary to pay attention to five verb properties, namely, person, number, tense, voice, and mood; the old grammarian Ælfric, in his Latin-English grammar written shortly before 998 A.D., discussed these five properties in connection with the four inflectional conjugations of the Latin language, and nine hundred and thirty years later (1928) an American grammarian stated that "Verbs may be inflected for Tense, Voice, Person, Number, and Mood." So it will be most convenient, in spite of the many differences between Latin grammar of

998 and that of Current English of the twentieth century, to recognize the existence of these five properties of the verb, and to base our treatment of the Modern English verb on these five properties, in continuous use by English grammarians for nearly a thousand years.

Person. Today the standard English verb has just one distinctive personal form, the third person singular of the present tense, which ends in *-s* or *-es*, as in *lifts, goes, grazes, lives.* If the verb has any other personal distinctions, they must depend entirely on the personal forms of the pronouns that accompany it.

Number. Today the English verb has just one distinctive number form in general use, and that employs the same *-s* or *-es* ending as shown in the verbs just given. Number, too, depends mainly upon the inflectional forms of the nouns and pronouns with which the verb is used, and so, if one is to regard a verb as having singular and plural number, it must be a matter of syntactical usage largely.

There is, however, a more elaborate archaic system of inflecting the verb which persists in some religious and poetic usage still. It is essentially that of the time of Shakespeare and the makers of the Authorized Version of the Bible, and contrasts in several respects with present-day usage, as may be seen from the following tabulation of indicative forms.

	MODERN			ARCHAIC	
I	*run*	*ran*	I	*run*	*ran*
you	*run*	*ran*	thou	*run-est*	*ran-est*
he	*run-s*	*ran*	he	*run-eth*	*ran*
we	*run*	*ran*	we	*run*	*ran*
you	*run*	*ran*	ye	*run*	*ran*
they	*run*	*ran*	they	*run*	*ran*
I	*am*	*was*	I	*am*	*was*
you	*are*	*were*	thou	*art*	*wast* (or *wert*)
he	*is*	*was*	he	*is*	*was*
we	*are*	*were*	we	*are*	*were*
you	*are*	*were*	ye	*are*	*were*
they	*are*	*were*	they	*are*	*were*

CONJUGATION OF VERBS

The six auxiliaries *can, may, shall, will, must,* and *ought* do not have even the ending of the third person singular.

Tense. But standard English usage of today, while it has lost most of its personal and number forms, still depends upon the inflectional form of the verb, either the simple verb or the auxiliary in the phrasal verb, to determine the time of the action, that is to say, the tense. Hence any discussion and classification of Modern English verbs from the standpoint of tense must take into consideration the different ways in which tense is indicated.

But before going into a more detailed discussion of English tense forms, it is necessary to define *tense* somewhat more exactly. There are two possible views of the matter: If *tense* is synonymous with *time*, then it would be logical to say that there can be only three general tenses, present, past, and future, as in *I go, I went,* and *I shall go*; but since the Latin language has six inflectional tenses with six different sets of endings, and since earlier English grammars grew out of the study of Latin grammar in England, it has long been customary to list six English tenses, namely, present *I go*, past *I went*, future *I shall go*, present perfect *I have gone*, past perfect *I had gone*, and future perfect *I shall have gone*. Inasmuch as English has never had inflectional endings for the last three and inasmuch as the only difference between the first three and the last three is the idea of completion present in the latter, if one takes a strictly logical stand (as above) on the simpler definition of *tense* as meaning 'time' (Latin *tempus*, Old French *tens*), then there are but three tenses in English, and syntactical verb phrases (phrasal verbs) indicating completion can be set apart, like those other verb phrases which are to be studied in the next chapter in connection with the ideas of progression, customary action, and the like (Sec. 106).

The expression *principal parts* has been customarily used in English grammar to include the simple-infinitive form with *to*, namely, *to go, to walk, to drive*, the past-tense form, *went, walked, drove*, and the past-participle form, *gone, walked, driven*. Sometimes grammarians give four principal parts by including the present-participle form, *going, walking, driving*; but since there is never any variation in this form, it is not worth while to bother to list it each time. If the principal parts of a verb are known, it is possible to form the various phrasal verbs without difficulty. But the changes in verb forms down through the centuries have made it desirable to list the principal parts, and most good grammars have included such lists.

If the English verbs be regarded from the standpoint of tense distinctions, two outstanding groups will be observed in Current English, the so-called strong verbs and weak verbs, besides a few miscellaneous or anomalous verbs that do not fit into either general category. It is true that the teacher of elementary Modern English grammar usually prefers a different alignment and classifies all verbs as regular or irregular, according as they are formed with the past tense in *-ed*, like *walked*, or irregularly, like *sang, drove, taught, led, hit, could*, and *went*. But while this simple classification may be adequate for the practical purposes of elementary-grammar teaching, for the more advanced study of the English verb one ought to go somewhat more deeply into the matter, because his study of the verb may well carry him back into the earlier stages of English verb history and may even necessitate some comparisons with verbs of cognate Germanic tongues.

Strong verbs. The term *strong* — a term which has little intrinsic meaning for the average student of Modern English — is applied to those verbs which do not take the *-ed* or *-t* ending for the past tense but which undergo internal change only, as in *sing, sang, sung*. Because there is no simple logical method of classifying these strong (or gradation) verbs in Current English, they will be presented below in seven groups to correspond to seven distinct strong-verb classes that long ago had their separate existence in Anglo-Saxon. Since some are generally weak verbs today, they are indicated by the dagger.

a. abide	abode, abided	abode
arise	arose	arisen
† bide	bode, bided	bided
bite	bit	bitten
drive	drove	driven

CONJUGATION OF VERBS

	ride	rode	ridden
	rise	rose	risen
	shine	shone, *arch.* shined	shone, *arch.* shined
	† shrive	shrove, shrived	shriven, shrived
	slide	slid	slidden, slid
	smite	smote	smitten, smit
	stride	strode	stridden
	strike	struck	stricken, struck
	write	wrote	written
b.	choose	chose	chosen
	† cleave (split)	clove, cleft, cleaved	cloven, cleft, cleaved
	† dive	dove, dived	dived
	fly	flew	flown
	freeze	froze	frozen
	† seethe	seethed	sodden, seethed
c.	begin	began	begun
	bind	bound	bound
	cling	clung	clung
	drink	drank	drunk(en)
	fight	fought, *dial.* fit	fought, *dial.* fit
	find	found	found
	grind	ground	ground
	† melt	melted	molten, melted
	ring	rang, rung	rung
	run	ran, run	run
	shrink	shrank, shrunk	shrunk(en)
	sing	sang, sung	sung
	sink	sank, sunk	sunk(en)
	sling	slung	slung
	slink	slunk	slunk
	spin	spun, *arch.* span	spun
	spring	sprang, sprung	sprung
	sting	stung, *arch.* stang	stung
	stink	stank, stunk	stunk
	† swell	swelled	swollen, swelled
	swim	swam, swum	swum
	swing	swung, *arch.* swang	swung
	win	won	won
	wind	wound	wound
	wring	wrung, *arch.* wrang	wrung

In this third group the vowel *u* or *ou* of a participial form has almost entirely driven out the older *a* of the past tense in a number of words, such as *bind*, *sling*, and *swing*, and in other words, such as *sing*, *spring*, *swim*, the *u* form seems to be gradually encroaching upon the *a* form; occasionally, on the other hand, an *a* form, such as the archaic *span*, *swang*, *wrang*, is revived, and illiterate speakers not infrequently use it as a participial form, as in *had sang*. This tendency to use one form for both the past and the participle is but the modern phase of that long-drawn-out leveling process which has been at work among the strong verbs for centuries.

d. bear	bore, *arch.* bare	borne, born
break	broke	broken
come	came	come
† shear	sheared, *arch.* shore	shorn, sheared
steal	stole	stolen
tear	tore	torn
e. bid	bade, bid	bidden, bid
eat	ate, *Brit.* eat [ɛt] *or* ate	eaten
get	got	got(ten)
give	gave	given
lie	lay	lain
see	saw	seen
sit	sat	sat
speak	spoke, *arch.* spake	spoken
tread	trod	trodden, trod
weave	wove	woven
f. draw	drew	drawn
forsake	forsook	forsaken
† grave	graved	graven, graved
† heave	hove, heaved	hove, heaved
† lade	laded	laden, laded
shake	shook	shaken
† shape	shaped	shapen, shaped
† shave	shaved	shaven, shaved
slay	slew	slain
stand	stood	stood
swear	swore, *arch.* sware	sworn

take	took	taken
† wake	woke, waked	waked
g. beat	beat	beat(en)
behold	beheld	beheld, *arch.* beholden
blow	blew	blown
† crow	crowed, *arch.* crew	crowed
fall	fell	fallen
grow	grew	grown
† hang	hung, hanged	hung, hanged
† hew	hewed	hewn, hewed
hold	held	held, *arch.* holden
know	knew	known
† mow	mowed	mown, mowed
† sow	sowed	sown, sowed
throw	threw	thrown

In this last group too there is trouble for the uneducated English speaker because the vowel of the participial stem is generally identical with that of the first, or infinitive, stem and also because five of the group have already become weak verbs with the *-ed* ending in the past tense and participle. Consequently there is a temptation to use the same vowel in all the principal parts, and so one frequently hears the colloquial *blowed, growed, knowed,* and *throwed* instead of *blew, grew, knew,* and *threw.*

A few verbs which either were weak in Anglo-Saxon or else came into the language after that early period have dropped into the strong-verb conjugation, at least partially. The most important of these converts are

† chide (*AS.* weak)	chid, chided	chid(den), chided
dig (*OF.*)	dug, digged	dug, digged
fling (*ON.*)	flung	flung
hide (*AS.* weak)	hid	hidden, hid
† prove (*AS.* weak)	proved	proven, proved
† rive (*ON.*)	rived	riven, rived
† show (*AS.* weak)	showed	shown, showed
† stave (*AS.* weak)	stove, staved	stove, staved
stick (*AS.* weak)	stuck	stuck
† strew (*AS.* weak)	strewed	strewn, strewed

string (*AS.* noun)	strung	strung
strive (*OF.*)	strove	striven
† thrive (*ON.*)	throve, thrived	thriven, thrived
wear (*AS.* weak)	wore	worn

These surviving strong verbs of English are an important part of the hardy, persistent Germanic element of the language and deserve careful and thoughtful appraisal, for they are, as it were, a high peak in the English language which has stubbornly resisted the erosion of the ages and from which one can look back over the history of our language. Hence a few comments are called for at this point:

The daggers indicate verbs which are generally weak in their inflection today rather than strong, as in the past, and they are intended also to serve as a warning, because the strong forms have been placed first, as in *molten, melted*, regardless of preferences in current usage, in order that the reader may see as clearly as possible that these verbs all have some claim to a place in this strong-verb list. When there is any doubt as to which form is preferred in standard English, a dictionary should be consulted. Our purpose here is not to determine good usage today, but rather to picture the breaking down of the strong-verb class in Modern English. The eighty-seven verbs listed (this includes a few compounds) in the seven classes are about all that remain of some four hundred Anglo-Saxon strong verbs; some have disappeared entirely from the language, and many others have become weak verbs altogether.

Of the daggered verbs listed above, several have been included merely because a strong participial form in *-en* or *-n* remains, as *molten, sodden, shorn*. When two participial variants exist, there is a marked tendency to distinguish them by using the older strong form as a pure adjective. This is true of *cloven, graven, swollen*, for example; and the legal use of 'not *proven*' is the chief justification for the retention of the strong form in that verb.

The wearing-down process can be observed in the gradual sloughing off of the *-en* suffix of the past participle, as in *beat(en), bid(den), drunk(en), got(ten), trod(den)*.

The feeling that English speakers still have for these older strong verbs can be observed sometimes cropping out in the tendency to give a strong-verb form to a weak verb, as the illiterate colloquial *brung* (for 'brought'), *drug* (for 'dragged'), *snuck* (for 'sneaked'), or in the resurrection of older strong forms like *clomb* (for 'climbed'), *swoll* (for 'swelled').

The etymological confusion and fusion which have already been discussed (Sec. 69) are responsible for some trouble today in the use of *bid*, *cleave*, *hang*, and *wake*; in each instance the modern verb stands for at least two different Anglo-Saxon verbs.

Weak verbs. Weak verbs are those very numerous English verbs which take the ending *-ed* or *-d* or *-t* in the formation of the past tense and the past participle. So much has been said in earlier chapters about the changes in pronunciation and spelling that result from the addition of the weak-verb suffix *-ed* that little more need be said about the class as a whole. With the few exceptions just listed, all verbs borrowed from other languages, such as *create*, *drag*, *reef*, *systematize*, have been put into this class; all newly coined verbs, like *motor*, *simonize*, *telephone*, take the *-ed* ending; older verbs formed by derivative processes from strong verbs, such as *bait*, *fell*, *lay*, *rear*, *set*, *wend*, always belong in this class; and most of the verbs that have been made in the course of the centuries since the Anglo-Saxons came to England have been inflected as weak verbs. The weak verb is a strictly Germanic development, and although it is not as old as the strong verb, in the Indo-European family of languages, it is nevertheless much more important for Current English.

A fairly large number of weak verbs have assumed irregularities of one kind or another because of certain phonetic changes that have taken place in English, and these are often, just for the sake of convenience, grouped with the strong verbs as "irregular" verbs; but this is not a farsighted policy, and in any ambitious study of English verbs these weak verbs should be analyzed and reclassified with a view to emphasizing their earlier history. Many of the verbs included in the following lists are marked with the dagger because they tend to assume the more regular forms of weak-verb inflection.

a. A little group of very old weak verbs look somewhat like strong verbs because they have undergone mutation, or internal change of vowel, in the present tense, leaving a different vowel form in the past tense and past participle; but their classification as weak verbs is decided by the fact that the dental ending -*t* (or -*d*) is also required. They are

beseech	besought	besought
bring	brought	brought
buy	bought	bought
catch	caught	caught
seek	sought	sought
teach	taught	taught
think	thought	thought
† work	wrought, worked	wrought, worked
† clothe	clad, clothed	clad, clothed
sell	sold	sold

b. Another group have vowel-shortening in the past and participle but also add -*d* or -*t*:

† bereave	bereft, bereaved	bereft, bereaved
creep	crept	crept
deal	dealt	dealt
† dream	dreamt, dreamed	dreamt, dreamed
feel	felt	felt
flee	fled	fled
† hear	heard, *dial.* heared	heard, *dial.* heared
keep	kept	kept
† kneel	knelt, kneeled	knelt, kneeled
† lean	leant, leaned	leant, leaned
leave	left	left
lose	lost	lost
mean	meant	meant
say	said	said
shoe	shod	shod
sleep	slept	slept
sweep	swept	swept

c. In a third group there is shortening of the vowel but no addition of a suffix. And yet these are historically weak verbs because they did have the suffix in earlier times in the form of -*de* or -*te*, as in Chaucer's *fedde, sette*, which later lost the final -*e*, becoming *fedd, sett*, and ultimately lost the last *d* or *t*.

† alight	alighted, *arch.* alit	alighted, *arch.* alit
bleed	bled	bled
breed	bred	bred

CONJUGATION OF VERBS

feed	fed	fed
lead	led	led
† light	lit, lighted	lit, lighted
meet	met	met
read	read (*pron.* red)	read (*pron.* red)
† speed	sped, speeded	sped, speeded

A vulgar form *het* (for *heated*) is sometimes heard also.

d. In a few verbs which end in *-ld*, *-nd*, *-rd*, no vowel-shortening is possible, but the *-d* is changed to *-t*:

† bend	bent, *arch.* bended	bent, *arch.* bended
† blend	blent, blended	blent, blended
† build	built, builded	built, builded
† gild	gilt, gilded	gilt, gilded
† gird	girt, girded	girt, girded
lend	lent	lent
rend	rent	rent
send	sent	sent
spend	spent	spent
† wend	went*, wended	wended

e. In the process of forming the past tense and participle of some verbs ending in *-l*, *-n*, *-s*, the suffix *-t* is commonly used, and double consonants simplified if necessary:

† bless	blest, blessed	blest, blessed
† burn	burnt, burned	burnt, burned
† dress	drest, dressed	drest, dressed
† dwell	dwelt, dwelled	dwelt, dwelled
† kill	killed, *dial.* kilt	killed, *dial.* kilt
† learn	learnt, learned	learnt, learned
† pass	past, passed	past, passed
† pen	pent, penned	pent, penned
† smell	smelt, smelled	smelt, smelled
† spell	spelt, spelled	spelt, spelled
† spill	spilt, spilled	spilt, spilled
† spoil	spoilt, spoiled	spoilt, spoiled

The regular form in *-ed* is generally preferred in verbs of this group; *kilt* is dialectal; others, like *smelt* and *spoilt*, are of less doubtful propriety. Of course *past* is merely a phonetic spelling of *passed*; and if spelling reform should be widely adopted, other verbs would be thrown into this group, such as *guest* (for 'guessed'), *least* (for 'leased'), *mist* (for 'missed').

* *Went* has been adopted as the past-tense form of *go*.

f. The last group of these irregular weak verbs is composed of words ending in *-d* or *-t* which usually remain the same in all three of their principal parts. They once had past endings in *-de* or *-te*, like the verbs of the third group, above; but the wearing away of the endings has left them with all forms alike. They are † *bet, bid, burst, cast, cost, cut, hit, hurt,* † *knit, let, put,* † *quit,* † *rid, set, shed,* † *shred, shut,* † *slit, spit, split, spread,* † *sweat, thrust,* and † *wet.*

Of these, *bid* and *spit* have also the more archaic past-tense forms *bade* and *spat*; *bursted* is heard occasionally but is considered "inelegant and dialectal"; *hurted* is sometimes heard in Irish English; and for *knit* and *shred* the longer participles with *-ed* are generally used adjectivally. There has been much discussion of late as to how the past and participial forms of *broadcast* should be made; at present, opinion seems to be that, since it is a compound of *cast*, it should logically take no ending, but that it may ultimately be standardized with the *-ed* ending because it is so often used with that ending nowadays.[393]

The daggers in the foregoing lists of irregular weak verbs mark those that may also be inflected with the regular weak forms in *-ed*; and, as in the case of the strong verbs, the daggers serve also as a warning, because the less regular forms have been placed first, regardless of preferences in current usage. The number of the daggers shows how strongly the regularizing tendency is at work among the slightly irregular weak verbs.

Miscellaneous verbs. A few verbs lack the infinitive and the participial forms; others (*be, go*) are irregular in having quite different (that is, suppletive) stems in their principal parts. They are chiefly the auxiliary verbs already studied (Sec. 53, p. 295), and most of them have been irregular in English as far back as they can be traced.

The most defective of all the English verb groups are the seven simple auxiliaries; the other auxiliaries are more fully inflected. This defectiveness is largely the result of a prolonged tendency in English to use certain past-tense forms as present, thus leaving no forms available for use in the past tense.

Sec. 90]   CONJUGATION OF VERBS   463

These anomalous verbs are as follows:

INFINITIVE	PRESENT	PAST	PRES. PART.	PAST PART.
------	can	could	------	------
------	may	might	------	------
------	shall	should	------	------
------	will	would	[willing]	------
------	must	------	------	------
------	ought	------	------	------
[to dare]	dare	[dared, durst]	[daring]	[dared]
to be	am	was	being	been
[to do]	do	did	[doing]	[done]
to have	have	had	having	had
to go	go	went	going	gone
to wit	wot (*arch.*)	wist (*arch.*)	witting	wist (*arch.*)
------	------	quoth	------	------
------	------	------	------	y-clept (*arch.*)

Bracketed forms are used only when the verbs cease to be mere auxiliaries and become notional verbs.

Voice. Voice is that property of a verb by which we are able to show whether the subject is acting, as in 'He *stopped* the man', or is acted upon, as in 'The man *was stopped* by him.' If the subject is acting, the verb is active in voice; if the subject is acted upon, the verb is passive in voice. Obviously not all verbs possess both active and passive voice, but only those that express action or, sometimes, feeling, as passing from the doer or agent (subject) to the recipient or product (object). Voice will be found to be entirely a syntactical matter, and therefore it belongs in the next chapter. But the subject has been introduced here because some other languages, such as Latin, actually inflect verbs to show voice, and consequently some students of language might expect to find inflectional voice in English as well. It is necessary to insist, therefore, that voice is not inflectional at all in English, but purely syntactical (see page 523).

Mood. Mood (sometimes pronounced and spelled as *mode*) is that property of a verb whereby the speaker or writer is able to indicate the manner in which he conceives of the action or state or being. If he regards it as actually occurring or to occur, the mood is called *indicative*; if he regards it not as a fact but merely as possible or conditional, it is *subjunctive*; and if the verb is so shaped or used that it expresses a command or request, it is in the *imperative* mood. There has always been more uncertainty among scholars regarding the nature and definition of mood than about any other of the so-called properties. As long as the conjugation of the English verb contained distinct subjunctive and imperative forms, as in Anglo-Saxon, definition was a much simpler matter; but since subjunctive and imperative endings have been dropped and it has become necessary to accomplish the same results by means of syntactical usage, — by means of phrasal verbs, commonly, — the moods are not so clearly distinguished.

There are no subjunctive endings in Modern English; the third person singular is regarded as subjunctive when it lacks even the *s* ending which the indicative does possess, as in the clause 'if it *come* out well'. But as a matter of fact the mood of *come* is indicated rather by the use of *if*, and under other circumstances the form *come* might be indicative or imperative or merely the infinitive. So, in the case of *be* and *were* in 'if it *be* true' and 'if I *were* in your place', the subjunctive mood is shown less by the verb-form than by its use. But this is matter for the chapter on syntax (see Sec. 106).

Some grammarians class the infinitive with the moods of a verb; but since it cannot assert action or state in a definite manner, it is not usually so classed.

91. *The Verbals*

By verbals are meant those forms of a verb which may be used as nouns or adjectives, on the one hand, or as parts of phrasal verbs, on the other. There are four of these verbals: the infinitive, the gerund, the present participle, and the past participle. The infinitive is merely the simple form of the verb (the so-called verb root or root infinitive), and can be used with *to* as a noun, as *to run, to economize**; the gerund is the verbal noun formed from the verb by the use of *-ing*, as in '*Seeing* is *believing*'; the present participle is the verbal adjective also formed by the use of *-ing*, as '*running* water'; and the past participle is the verbal adjective made with the strong-verb suffix *-en*, as *broken*, with the weak-verb suffix *-ed*, as *stuffed*, or by some other inflectional method, as *crept, dug, fed, shone*, etc.

It is unfortunate that the gerund and the present participle coincide in form; at one time they had different endings, but now they can be distinguished only by the way they are used (see Sec. 58, p. 319).

In the case of some verbs there has been a tendency to make a distinction between the past participle used as a descriptive adjective and the past participle used as part of a phrasal verb, by keeping two slightly different forms of the word. Among the strong verbs listed above, the form in *-en*, such as *molten, sodden, swollen*, has in some instances remained because of its adjectival function, while the rest of the verb has changed to the weak inflection. Of the strong verbs listed, almost two thirds retain the participial ending *-en* (or *-n*), but sometimes this is the only surviving strong-verb form that is retained. In some cases the weak-verb past participle has shown a similar tendency to distinguish between its use as adjective and as part of a phrasal verb; while the *e* of the *-ed* ending remains silent in the verbals *blessed, cursed, striped, plagued*, etc., when they are used as adjectives the *e* is pronounced.

When Richard Grant White in his *Words and their Uses* entitled his tenth chapter "The Grammarless Tongue", he obviously defined grammar so as to cover only the inflectional aspects of language. But our insistence upon a broader conception of grammar which includes both the inflectional and the syntactical methods of indicating the grammatical properties, if it be approved and thoroughly comprehended. should make the study of English syntax (to follow in the next

---

* The infinitive with *to* is sometimes called the *supine*.

chapter) a vitally important phase of the study and teaching of Current English grammar. For more and more the stress is being laid on the way words are used, and less and less on their individual forms. Those essential grammatical properties which have been defined and discussed in this present chapter — gender, number, and case, person and tense and voice and mood, and comparison — are just as necessary to an understanding of the relations of words as ever; but in expressing them speakers and writers of English have shifted the emphasis from inflectional form to syntactical usage. Hence it has become necessary for the student of Current English to take a broader view of the properties of the various parts of speech, as they have been presented in the chapter just concluded; to give up in very large measure that older conception of them as inflectional forms and assume more fully the modern conception of them as syntactical uses or constructions. For English grammar is still accomplishing the same things in the expression of thinking that it has always accomplished, but it is doing it in different ways.

CHAPTER XII
SYNTAX

THE last four chapters have been devoted primarily to the classification and analysis of words, those units of speech employed in the expression of individual ideas or concepts; now, however, we step up once more to the consideration of still larger units of speech and in syntactical usage deal with the processes of fitting words into phrases, clauses, and sentences to express complete thoughts — those larger speech units which we have earlier distinguished from the simpler expressions of ideas. Syntax has already been defined as "the putting together of words into phrases, clauses, and ultimately into sentences" (Sec. 4). It has been continually emphasized as the modern substitute for that more elaborate inflectional system which has gradually been almost completely lost from English. Nowhere in the study of Current English does the student come nearer to the heart of the understanding of Modern English grammatical usage than in the careful study of our syntax, and nowhere will he meet with more insistent demands for the settling of controversies over "correct" and "incorrect" English. The more recently compiled grammars are devoted largely to the syntax of English; studies have been published by teachers of English, based upon the results of widespread questioning of users of English; and in the study of those still larger units of speech and writing which form the material of courses in rhetoric and composition, syntactical matters constantly demand consideration. And so, now that we have carefully analyzed the phonological clay and the orthographical straws and have observed the making of word bricks from them, we come to the more challenging problems pertaining to the building of our grammatical house.

In concluding the systematic classification of words in Chapter VIII, it was found necessary to anticipate this chapter to some extent by showing how syntactical use is often the only criterion by which words can be judged and classified. But it is worth while to stress further the importance of that same syntactical use in helping to establish the various shades of meaning of a word in Current English. In such a sentence, for instance, as 'The *saw* that I *saw* on the bench was not yours', the only way one can decide which *saw* is noun and which is verb is through the help of the accompanying words *the* and *I* and of position in the sentence. Moreover, it is evident that that *that* that that sentence contains is a different *that* from the *that* in the preceding sentence, and it is clear that the succession of *that's* in this present sentence would be hopelessly confused if they did not have the benefit of sentence setting, or environment, to aid in making clear their meanings. Since much has been said in Section 58 concerning the conversions and confusions of the parts of speech through changes in their use, it will be taken for granted in this discussion of English syntax that the reader is fully aware of the possibility of great variation in the functioning of many English words, phrases, and clauses, and that he will not be surprised to find some further evidence of confusion, here and there, and some border-line cases where it is hard to decide which one of the parts of speech is involved.

In approaching English syntax, it should be made quite clear, again, that we are to consider what English speakers and writers usually do with words when they put them together into sentences, and not what they ought to do or what they might do if they took full advantage of their opportunities. The versatile literary artist will find countless possibilities of varying his syntactical practice; but in the limited space of this chapter only the ordinary things that ordinary people do in their sentence-making can be considered. In the study of syntactical questions, moreover, the emphasis is not to be laid on the determination of what is correct usage and what is incorrect usage, but rather on the constant seeking for better, more effective ways of expressing ideas and thoughts,

I. THE SENTENCE

In the presentation of the syntax of English it is hardly possible to avoid examining usages twice; for at one time it is desirable to observe the sentence and its parts (subject, object, etc.), and again it is worth while to summarize the uses of the parts of speech (noun, verb, etc.), taken up one by one. The subject of the sentence, for example, may consist of any one of several parts of speech or speech units; on the other hand, the noun may be used in various ways in the sentence. This is just one more illustration of the need of making numerous and varied surveys of that many-sided subject the English language; and while much of the second summing up may seem unduly repetitious, it is justified by this need of a broad survey.

92. *The Sentence in General*

In general, sentences accomplish four ends and are of four kinds: declarative, interrogative, imperative, and exclamatory. In classifying a sentence the determining factor is not the form of the sentence, primarily, though that sometimes helps in the classifying process; in the final analysis sentences must be classified according to their accomplishment.* A declarative sentence makes an assertion; an interrogative sentence asks a question; an imperative sentence expresses a command or a request; an exclamatory sentence expresses strong feeling. These sentences assume certain forms normally, which may be illustrated as follows:

Declarative: He has finished his work, and the manager has paid him.
Interrogative: Who inspected the box when it was finished?
Imperative: Bring me the inspection tag.
Exclamatory: How beautifully he has carved the box!

* Sentences can, of course, be viewed and classified from various other points of view: If the determining factor is emotion, they may all be classified as exclamatory and nonexclamatory; if the criterion is the manner of assertion, they are affirmative and negative; if, however, it is a question of what the speaker knows, they are declarative and interrogative.

Each of these sentences is complete to the extent that it has at least a subject and a verb, namely, *He has finished, Who inspected, (You) bring,* and *he has carved.* But it is often possible to accomplish the same results with locutions that are not so nearly complete sentences in form; hence the warning has already been given (Sec. 5) that "it is not safe to depend always on the form of the locutions in attempting to classify them as word, phrase, clause, or sentence". The phrase *out with you* may be used as an imperative sentence meaning 'Leave this room'; and the imperative sentence 'Look out' becomes an interjection, merely, when it is uttered with emotional force.

When the manager says to his assistant, "You will pay the man and dismiss him", his sentence is declarative in form; but it is understood by his underling as a command and so is an imperative sentence. One may even ask a question in the form of a declarative sentence, as in 'You saw the man leave the store?' Very often a sentence becomes exclamatory merely because it is made to express emotion or strong feeling; so the interrogative 'How could he be so careless!' is exclamatory if it becomes a so-called rhetorical question, that is to say, if it is uttered with no expectation of its being answered.

But it should be emphasized that the two essential elements of a sentence, namely, the subject, about which something is predicated, and the predicate, which predicates something about the subject, must be present in the form of the sentence or understood or implied by the circumstances attending the utterance of the locution if we are to assume that the locution is really a sentence expressing a thought, and not merely a word or phrase or clause expressing a single idea or a group of ideas. In a conversation between two persons, sentences are often cut to the barest essentials, as in "Why did he close out his business?" "Bankrupt." — "Who left the book on my desk?" "The principal." — "I suppose you are ready to quit." "Not at all." The first speaker knows that the much abbreviated answers mean, 'He is bankrupt', 'The principal left the book', and 'I am not ready to quit.' Answers are often merely elliptical sentences.

Sec. 92]   THE SENTENCE IN GENERAL   471

Various linguistic curiosities have been collected by students of the sentence; these freaks are amusing, even if they are not especially important. In a search for the longest sentence, for instance, one observer has noted the first sentence in Edward Phillips's Preface to *Theatrum Poetarum* (1675 A.D.), which contains 1012 words; another has cited Hazlitt's hundred-line sentence on Coleridge in his essay "The Spirit of the Age"; and still another example can be found in Wordsworth's "Character of the Happy Warrior", where two sentences of eighty-one lines contain over 600 words loosely strung together.[404] But these sentences are not recommended as models for present-day writers, for they are hopelessly rambling and cumbersome.

In marked contrast with these cumbersome sentences are the freakish sentences that have been collected by other observers or creators of linguistic curiosities, which economize to a ludicrous degree. A writer in *Notes and Queries* once contributed the following thrifty Scottish conversation [403]:

Careful Scotch Wife (examining material for winter wear) asks: "A' oo?" (= "All wool?")
Shopman (reassuringly): "Ou, aye! a' oo." (= "Oh, yes! all wool".)
She: "A' *ae* oo?" (= "All *one* wool?")
He: "Ou, aye! a' *ae* oo." (= "Oh, yes! all *one* wool".)

But this illustrates what one can accomplish with just a string of vowels, whereas the "alphabetic" sentences that went the rounds a few years ago show what can be done with just single letters in spelling out sentences. The best examples, perhaps, are the presumed dialogue between a Yiddish father and son who were visiting the aquarium, and the more doubtful one between customer and waitress in a Yiddish café; the jingles run as follows [405]:

A B, C D goldfish!   F U M N X?
L, M N O goldfish.   S, V F M N X.
O S, A R goldfish.   O K, M N X.
D L A R goldfish! M R sunfish!

Sentences are also classified according to the complexity of their make-up, as simple, compound, or complex. A simple sentence has one subject and one predicate, as in 'He has left his work unfinished.' A compound sentence is made up of two or more simple sentences (also called principal, or coordinate, clauses), which could be used separately, such as 'He finished the work, but the manager did not pay him.' A complex sentence also contains two or more clauses, but always one is a principal, or independent, clause, the other or others being subordinate to, or dependent upon, it, as in 'He left the house when his work was finished.' The subordination of one clause to the other in a complex sentence is generally accomplished by means of subordinating conjunctions like *when, why, who, because* (see Sec. 56). Sometimes, to go a little farther into the realm of the art of writing, one finds simple sentences joined in the similitude of compound or complex sentences by the use of semicolons and colons; this is a sentence of that kind, for example, and many others can be found scattered through this book, since it is a convenient method of tying together two thoughts that are somewhat akin or that contrast. When two sentences present strongly contrasting thoughts, a mere comma is often sufficient to tie them together, as in 'He went by the upper road, I took the valley trail.' But such joining is mainly a matter of punctuation, rather than of grammatical construction, and the sentences are not truly compound or complex, but are merely simple sentences joined by punctuation. In pseudocompound sentences of this punctuational variety, an illative conjunction is often used to introduce the second part, as in 'He finished his work most carefully and skillfully; nevertheless he was unable to draw any pay that week.'

93. *The Subject*

The subject of a sentence denotes that of which something is affirmed or predicated; it is in the nominative case. It may be a word or a group of words. In a declarative sentence it normally comes before the verb; in an interrogative sentence it normally follows the verb or at least the auxiliary part of a phrasal verb; in an imperative sentence it is regularly omitted, being expressed only when emphasis is desired; in an exclamatory sentence of the kind used for illustration early in the preceding section, the subject precedes the verb. Any part of speech or grammatical unit that can be used as a substantive can also be the subject of a sentence. Since there can be infinite variety in the subjects of sentences, only a few typical examples can be given:

Noun: *Men* came to see the dragon. (This is a simple subject.)

Verbal noun, or gerund: *Swimming* is good exercise.

Verbal noun, or gerund (deferred): There was good *fishing* in the deep river. (In this sentence the subject is deferred to a later position in the sentence, and the expletive *there* stands in the normal place of the subject, at the beginning of the sentence.)

Infinitive: *To see* is to believe.

Proper name, with noun in apposition: *Mr. Smith*, the *secretary*, read the minutes of the last meeting.

Personal pronoun: *He* finished the reading.

Impersonal pronoun: *It* was raining.

Compound relative pronoun: *Whoever* stole the book had little use for it. (In this complex sentence the pronoun *whoever* serves as the subject of *stole* in the subordinate clause and also of *had* in the principal clause.)

Indefinite pronoun: *One* cannot be sure of the outcome. (Purists prefer *one*; but in colloquial usage *you* is often employed in sentences of this kind. *They* is similarly used in ' *They* say he lost his fortune in the crash.')

Pronoun (for emphasis): *You* stay right there until I return. (In imperative sentences of this kind the pronoun is ordinarily omitted, being used mainly when emphasis is desired.)

Substantivized adjective: The *sick* soon recovered.

Infinitive phrase: *To keep the animals alive* was an awkward job. (A certain contemporary novelist has developed a striking but stilted style by putting into the mouths of his characters who speak colloquial English over many sentences beginning with *one* or with this type of infinitive phrase. In many of his sentences colloquial usage would show a preference for the deferred infinitive phrase, as follows:)

Infinitive phrase (deferred): It was an awkward job *to keep the animals alive*. (While older English usage, especially literary usage, has frequently placed the infinitive at the beginning of the sentence, modern colloquial English likes to begin the sentence in this manner, with the expletive *it*.)
Substantive clause: *That he had lost hope* was evident.
Substantive clause (deferred): It was evident *that he had lost hope*.
Compound subject: The *letter* and the *package* were lost. Mr. *Smith* and *I* will do the work.
Noun modified by a clause: The *man who lost his passport* was a foreigner. (In a sentence of this kind it is desirable to keep the modifying clause always as near to the subject noun as possible.)

Standard English syntax has been developed in conformance with certain generally accepted rules which the writer of good English hesitates to violate. Hence the compound personal pronouns made with *-self* and *-selves* are ordinarily used in apposition as intensives, as in 'I *myself* will do it' and the more colloquial, 'I'll do it *myself*', or as reflexive objects, as in 'You have hurt *yourself*'; but the intensive is not employed alone, in generally accepted Current English, either as a simple subject, as in the Irish dialectal '*Himself* said it', or as part of a compound subject, as in the colloquial 'Mr. Smith and *myself* will do it.' It is obvious that if these compound pronouns are to function effectively, they should not be utilized instead of simple personal pronouns, which are usually quite capable of serving their own long-established purposes. Indeed, the pattern of English grammatical usage is unnecessarily blurred by such confusion of different functions, inasmuch as a speaker can always intensify a simple pronoun merely by emphasizing it vocally. In a few exceptional constructions, chiefly objective, these compound pronouns are used alone, intensively, but with an effect of emphasis which is generally considered sufficient justification for violating the rule (see page 477).

Much more might be said about sentence subjects, but most of it would be concerned with the finer points of style, with the art of writing and speaking, and that is another story. It might be in order to remark that some of the so-called grammatical solecisms which receive so much attention in the current teaching of English are not violations of syntactical practice at all but are, rather, just instances of poor judgment in the choice of words — of using poorer locutions instead of the better, more effective ones.

94. *The Predicate*

Whatever is said about the subject, roughly speaking, constitutes the predicate of the sentence. It may be affirmation or denial; it may be asserted, asked, commanded, or exclaimed. It is, in the opinion of many grammarians, the more important part of the expression of a thought, because thinking as a process does not get under way until something is predicated about the subject. A predicate may be a simple verb or may become highly involved because of the necessity of recognizing the effects produced by the action or state or being in the verb — effects expressed by object, predicate nominative, or other complementary construction. Many of the more puzzling matters of English grammar pertain to the relations of the verb to the predicate as a whole, and so it will be best, perhaps, to indicate first the kinds of predication that can be expected of the many verbs of English. Insofar as verbs indicate relations and results, they can be most conveniently classified as

a. Complete verbs
b. Incomplete verbs
  (1) Linking
  (2) Transitive

a. **Complete Verbs.** In 'Time *flies*' the verb is complete. In 'Time *flies* fast' or 'The manager *is* away' the verb is still regarded as complete because any adverbial modifier, whether word, phrase, or clause, merely modifies the verb as to manner, time, place, degree, etc., of action and has nothing to do with relations or results. So one might add, 'Time *flies* fast in the summer when the weather is pleasant', and the verb would still be complete in itself.

***b.* Incomplete Verbs.** (1) *Linking verbs and the predicate nominative.* In 'Time *is* money' or 'The treasurer *became* president' or 'The tree *seems* dead', the verb links to the subject a noun or adjective, commonly called the predicate noun and the predicate adjective.* Since the words that follow linking verbs of this kind have been used in the nominative case from very early times, the term *predicate nominative* is a slightly better term for such constructions. Always the predicate nominative explains, defines, or describes somewhat more exactly the subject. While the most commonly used predicate nominatives are the predicate noun or the predicate adjective, as illustrated above, other forms of the construction are possible, such as

Pronoun: It is *I*. (Very generally in colloquial English the objective case is substituted, and 'It is *me*' or 'It's *me*' results. But in spite of the fact that the form *me* is so used by many speakers of good colloquial English, 'It is *him*' is not accepted as equally desirable, and the more careful speaker still feels it logical to use the nominative *I*, as well as *he*.)

Infinitive phrase: Our first duty is *to obey the laws.*

Clause: Our hope was *that he would surrender peacefully.*

Of course the chief linking verb is the verb *be* (often called the copula) and its various forms, *was, were, have been,* etc. Other verbs commonly used to link predicate nominative to subject are *appear, become, look, remain, seem,* and, less commonly, *go, lie, prove, smell, sound, stand, taste,* and *turn* (sometimes called copulative verbs). The last-named verbs are most often used with the predicate adjective, as in 'He *went* slack', 'It *sounds* good', 'The house *stood* empty', 'It *has turned* cold.' Indeed, there has been a curious development of special uses of certain verbs in later English, all of them expressing the idea of 'become'. These locutions are in various stages of standardization, as can be observed in 'to *fall* sick' 'to *take* sick', 'to *get* tired', 'to *run* dry', etc. Fully a score of English verbs are functioning in this way, mainly because one old verb, *worth*, has been lost.

* Various other names have been used by grammarians for this construction, notably *attribute complement, subjective complement, predicate attribute.*

Some adjectives can be used as predicate adjectives but cannot be used in the attributive position, in front of nouns; most of these have the prefix *a-*, and some also serve as adverbs sometimes. Examples are *ablaze, afire, afraid, aghast, agleam, aglow, akin, alive, amiss, askew, aware, awry, enough, loath*. These adjectives, used after the linking verbs, must not be confused with similar adverbs (such as *aboard, abroad, away*) which are used after the notional verb *be*, as in 'He is abroad', as well as after other verbs, as in 'He went abroad.'

When a possessive pronoun takes the predicate position, it assumes a longer form, as already explained; in place of the attributive modifiers *my, our, your*, etc., Modern English uses *mine, ours, yours*, etc., as in 'The book is *mine*.'

(2) *Transitive verbs and objective constructions*. When a verb indicates an action as passing over from the subject (the doer) to some object (the recipient of the action), it is called a transitive verb. Transitive verbs differ so much in their transitivity that grammar recognizes several outstanding kinds of objective constructions.

(a) *Direct object*. A direct object names the direct recipient or product of the action expressed by the verb, as in 'It struck the *workman*', 'Who saw *him*?', 'He wrote *poetry*.' Sometimes the direct object is cognate with the verb, as in '*fight* a good *fight*', *run races*, '*sing* a *song*'. Reflexive pronouns are regularly used as direct objects, as in 'He found *himself* at last.' Sometimes *myself* is used as part of a compound direct object as an intensive rather than a reflexive pronoun, as in 'He invited Smith and *myself*.' It is not correct to say that *myself* is merely a substitute for the simple pronoun *me* in this construction. It is used to emphasize the person of the speaker. Consequently the need of laying stress on *self* may be considered sufficient justification of this usage.[407] The impersonal use of *it* in an objective relation to the verb is seen in 'They have been roughing *it*', 'Go *it*, boy!'; but the verbs in these sentences cannot be called transitive because no action passes over to the objective pronoun *it*.

Other direct objects of the transitive verb are

Infinitive: He wanted *to go*.
Gerund: The house needs *cleaning* and *painting* throughout.
Substantive clause: I heard *that the owner had returned*. I do not know *why they could not come*.

In some sentences the verb has two objects, both apparently direct objects; although there is sometimes a possibility that one may have been in Early English an indirect object, there is no dative ending nowadays to prove that it is anything more than a simple direct object. Examples of two objects are

Pronoun and noun: I envy *you* your *wealth*.
Noun and clause: We asked the *man what he was doing*.

It will sometimes be very difficult to distinguish between this use of two direct objects and the next construction, in which an indirect object and a direct object follow the verb.

(b) *Indirect object.* An indirect object often accompanies the direct object following a transitive verb, naming the person or thing to whom or for whom something is done. Inasmuch as the older dative-case endings have been lost, the indirect object is generally indicated in Current English by its position just preceding the direct object or else by its use as the object of *to* or *for*. So one has a choice of constructions:

He brought *me* a gift, or He brought a gift *to me*.
They gave their *father* a set of books, or They gave a set of books *to* their *father*.

When the direct object is a phrase or clause, however, the phrasal dative is not as likely to be used, though it does occur:

I told *him* to close the gates securely.
They complained *to* the *manager* that he did not pay his men enough.
She wired *us* that she could not delay longer.

It is not unusual to change the indirect object into the subject of the sentence and make the verb passive, retaining the object, however, just as it was. So 'His brothers gave *him* a set of books' can be changed to '*He* was given a set of books by his brothers.' Other examples of the "retained object" are 'He was charged five *dollars*', 'We were allowed our *expenses*', 'They were not allowed *to go*.' It is possible, sometimes, to change the direct object into the subject and retain the indirect object, instead. 'My friend promised *me* a delightful surprise' can be changed to 'A delightful surprise was promised *me* by my friend.' So the indirect object is retained in 'A prize was given (*to*) *me* by the principal', 'The money was returned *to Mr. Smith* by the customer.'

(*c*) *Predicate objective.* Some transitive verbs of a factitive nature, such as *choose, elect, make, consider, call, name*, require at times not only a direct object but also a substantive or adjective as a predicate objective, to explain, define, or describe more fully the direct object.* Examples of this construction are

> They chose him *captain* of the team.
> They named him *Theophilus*.
> Keeping bad company made him *what he is today*.
> *What* did they name her?
> We found the man *trustworthy*.
> It made him *bitter* and *morose*.

(*d*) *Subject of infinitive.* Some transitive verbs permit of a construction in which the objective is the subject of a following infinitive, as in 'They wanted *him to run for Congress*'; the whole phrase composes the object of the main verb. It is possible to give a different verb aspect to the action expressed by the infinitive if it be changed to a gerund. So in 'I saw *them leaving*' an aspect of duration is suggested rather than the simple action, as in 'I saw *them leave*.'

It should be borne in mind that since the subject of an infinitive is put into the objective case, a linking verb used in the infinitive is logically followed by an objective case, as in 'You did not expect the visitor to be *me*.' Fortunately no difficulty arises in the use of nouns in constructions of this kind because the common-case form of a noun will fit into

---

* This construction is also called the *objective complement, adjunct object, supplement, factitive object*, etc.

almost any grammatical usage. But when a pronoun is used after the infinitive form of a linking verb, such as *be*, many speakers become confused and mistakenly use the nominative case, as in 'I supposed the real owners to be *they*.' Overlapping of the practice of using a predicate nominative after a linking verb and of that other practice of making the predicate noun or pronoun agree in case with the subject of the verb or verbal leads to a more confusing situation here than is usually met with in English grammar. Most people have to pause and debate this before they can feel sure which is correct.

Special Comments on the Predicate. *a.* A more thoroughgoing and detailed study of the constructions just illustrated will show that the use of incomplete verbs in Current English constitutes one of the most complicated and troublesome phases of syntactical usage, because not only choice of verbs is involved but also understanding of a great variety of complements used to complete the predication — predicate nominatives, direct objects, indirect objects, predicate objectives, and infinitive phrases.

b. Verbs differ greatly in the way they function in sentences: sometimes the same verb is used as a complete verb, as in 'It *stands* at the end'; sometimes as a transitive verb, as in 'He *stands* his cane in this corner always'; and sometimes as a linking verb, as in 'He *stands* ready to pay.' This is a form of conversion, and the meaning of the verb changes somewhat according to its use in the sentence. So the linking verb *be* of 'He *is* lonesome' may become a complete notional verb, as in Hamlet's well-known soliloquy '*To be* or not *to be*', or when used with an adverb, as in 'He *is* abroad at present.'

c. Many grammarians prefer to classify the verbs discussed above in a slightly different manner, calling them transitive or intransitive, and dividing the latter into complete verbs and linking verbs. This is merely a matter of attitude on the part of the classifier and does not change the essential values of the verbs. Many verbs can be either transitive or intransitive. These terms are regularly employed in the dictionaries, and very generally elsewhere, because they are convenient and are generally understood.

d. Only transitive verbs can be used in the passive voice, normally, because in the change from active to passive an object is needed for the subject, ordinarily: 'He wrote the *book*' becomes 'The *book* was written by him.' However, examples can be adduced wherein the indirect object of an intransitive verb becomes subject of the verb used passively, as in '*I* was told finally'; but such verbs, it will be noted, are usually capable of being used with direct objects also. Perhaps one might insist that some sort of object stands vaguely in the background, since one might say '*I* was told the *truth* finally', or one might go farther and call *me* the direct object in 'They told *me* finally.' Such passive constructions do not really invalidate the rule that only transitive verbs are normally used in the passive voice.*

e. There is occasionally some uncertainty in the minds of grammarians as to whether in an objective construction there is involved an indirect object or the subject of an infinitive or the object of a preposition. Because the case endings of earlier English have so generally disappeared, there is no longer any formal distinction by which one might determine the exact use. The following sentences will illustrate this difficulty:

1. I told *him* to leave the house.
2. I wanted *him* to leave the house.
3. You must abide by the *agreement*.
4. He took over the *business*.

In No. 1 the advice or command is given *to him* and the real object of *told* is *to leave the house*; and if a distinct dative form were still in use, there would probably be no doubt as to the construction. In No. 2 the thing desired is *that he should leave the house*, and the entire expression, *him to leave the house*, constitutes the object of the verb *wanted*. In No. 3 one cannot be so sure, again, as to whether *abide by* is the verb or *by* a preposition governing the noun *agreement*. But in

---

* Attention has already been called to the fact that an intransitive verb is frequently used with a following preposition in such a manner that a transitive verb-adverb combination may be said to result (see page 299, and also page 536).

No. 4 it is quite clear that *took over* is a verb-adverb combination meaning 'assumed', and *business* is clearly the direct object of the verb.

Grammarians often evade the issue in the case of verbs and prepositions, as illustrated in No. 3, by calling such expressions idioms, especially *abide by, account for, admit of, aim at, amused at, concerned with, confide in, consist of, cured of, deprive of, disagree with, excel in, indulge in, laugh at, meddle with, scoff at, tire of, yearn for,* etc. Many of these can be classed as verb-adverb combinations with the value of simple verbs, and the words that follow them can be considered direct objects of the verbs rather than objects of the prepositions alone. They are certainly speech units which conform to our earlier definition of idioms, inasmuch as they are not readily analyzable into distinct and separate ideas (see page 13).

f. Nouns can be used as appositives in most of the objective constructions, as, for example,

Direct object: We met Mr. Z. A. Smith, the *musician*.
Indirect object: He gave Mr. Z. A. Smith, the *musician*, some advice, or He gave some advice to Mr. Z. A. Smith, the *musician*.
Subject of infinitive: They want Mr. Z. A. Smith, the *musician*, to join in the benefit concert.

A noun in apposition has a descriptive or defining function not unlike that of an adjective modifier. It is often tied to the preceding noun by some introducing word or phrase or abbreviation, such as *as, especially, like, namely, or, particularly; for example, for instance, in other words, such as, that is, that is to say, to wit;* e.g. (*exempli gratia*), i.e. (*id est*), viz. (*videlicet*).

After such introducing elements the descriptive and defining function appears also in the use of adjectives, verbs, and other parts of speech, with or without modifiers, and in the use of phrases and even more elaborate constructions, especially when these are employed as simple explanations, as examples, or as illustrations of what precedes the interrupting comma or dash, as in the sentence 'They added two more criticisms, namely, *that a cellist and a drummer were needed and that the horns were too loud.*'

When the appositive is a detailed explanation or an enumeration of particulars, it is more often a phrase or clause, somewhat more elaborate than the word appositives first illustrated above, and is likely to be set off from the preceding part of the sentence by a warning colon or dash, as in the sentences 'He had but three ambitions: *to live in peace, to have a few good friends, and to finish his lifework successfully*' and 'They wished to do more exciting things — *to fly over the Pacific Ocean, to invade the Far North, and to rise to great heights.*' Appositives may be very simple constructions; but they may, on the other hand, be made very detailed, very elaborate, and, if well used, they may become effective artistic features of speaking and writing.

95. *Modifiers*

Modifiers are of two general kinds, adjectival and adverbial. The adjectival modifiers limit or qualify the meanings of substantives; the adverbial, those of verbs or verbals or other modifiers. The two parts of speech (adjective and adverb) have been defined and illustrated in an earlier chapter, and the importance of recognizing the two functions should be manifest by this time; for sometimes the nature of its modifiers has been the determining factor in deciding whether a word is used as a noun or as a verb, and sometimes, on the other hand, knowing what part of speech is modified enables one to decide which kind of modifier is involved. If, for example, *drawing* is modified by *poor*, it is a noun; but if it is modified by *poorly*, it is verbal in function. If, on the other hand, *wrong* modifies a noun, as in 'the *wrong* road', it is an adjective; but if it modifies a verb, as in 'to go *wrong*', it is an adverb.

But while the two parts of speech have been sufficiently established, there is much to be said concerning other parts of speech and larger speech units (phrases and clauses) which can be used as modifiers; for the meaning of a noun or a verb can be modified in a number of different ways.

Adjectival Modifiers

Adjective: *Careless* writers often use *poor* English. He had a *two-foot* rule and a *dull-edged* saw in his hand.

Possessive pronoun: I had *his* address.

Participle: *Running* water is sometimes *tainted* water.

Noun (genitival): *Shakespeare's* plays won the *queen's* approval.

Noun (uninflected): A *stone* house stood by the roadside. His house, *stone* below and *plaster* above, looked unfinished. A *vegetable* cellar belongs to the house. (The difficulty of drawing a line between the use of a noun as modifier of another noun and as part of a compound noun has already been observed (see page 253). Indeed, in view of the fact that one word in a compound generally limits the meaning of the other, it must be admitted that there is no clear-cut line of demarcation between the two uses. In the adjectival use of *stone* in *stone house* the meaning of *house* is consciously modified; in the compound *schoolhouse* the limitation of the meaning of *house* is already long established and is taken for granted. To go just one step farther, one must recognize in such a colloquial sentence as 'It was a *peach* of a game' that grammatically *peach* is a noun used as the predicate nominative, but logically it is just as strongly adjectival as though the sentence read 'It was a *peachy* game.')

Infinitive: Houses *to rent* are plentiful now.

Verbal noun, or gerund: He was a *fencing* teacher. (*Fencing* is not a participle; the expression is a shortcut for 'a teacher of fencing', in which the verbal noun is clearly object of the preposition.)

Participial phrase: *Running freely across the roads*, water barred our passage everywhere.

Prepositional phrase: The house *on the hill* is *on fire* (or is *afire*). She offers a course *in cooking*.

Relative clause. The house *that we built* was of stone. I know the house *whereof you speak*.

Adverbial Modifiers

Adverb: It ran *slowly* because it was *very* old. *Only once* did I see it run *by*. Think *hard*. He is *abroad now*.

Noun (or noun with adjective): They waited *months*. He left *this afternoon*. Walk *two blocks* and take the interurban car. (This "adverbial accusative" is as old as the English language and is common in other languages as well. Once it was distinguished by an accusative-case ending, but now it is no longer so easily distinguishable.)

Infinitive: He came *to stay*. (In earlier times this infinitive of purpose formed part of a prepositional phrase of purpose, as in the Biblical "What went ye out *for to see?*")

Participle: She departed *weeping*. (As already remarked (Sec. 58, p. 322), there is probably a confusion of adjectival and adverbial functions in this use of the participle, since it both describes the subject and tells the manner of the action.)

Prepositional phrase: It stands *by the river*; *in rebuilding the mill*, they did not move it.

Infinitive phrase: I came *to inspect your work*.

Participial phrase: He went *stumbling along the corridor*.

Clause: He went *because he feared to stay away*. (Most subordinate clauses introduced by the subordinating conjunctions listed in Section 56 are adverbial, except the substantive clauses and the adjectival clauses generally introduced by relative pronouns. Occasionally there is an exception, such as 'I cannot recall a day *when I have been free from anxiety*' or 'This is the house *where we once lived*.' These are adjectival modifiers.)

Sometimes adverbial modification is implicit in the verb itself. Just as the noun at times seems to have taken unto itself certain adjectival, or descriptive, functions, so also the verb frequently acquires within itself adverbial limitations. The difficulty of distinguishing between a verb plus an adverb, such as *stand up*, and a verb-adverb combination, such as *bring round*, 'resuscitate', has been discussed in an earlier presentation of the verb (Sec. 53, p. 298). But there are other English verbs more simple in form which contain within themselves both the action and the manner of the action: so *speed* means 'travel fast', and *crawl* implies 'go slowly' and sometimes 'go humbly'; *disintegrate* means 'fall apart'.

96. *Independent and Introductory Elements*

Outside of the essential parts of sentences comprised in subject and predicate, and not included as modifiers in the usual sense of the term, there are certain elements which, though they are not absolutely free from all connection with the rest of the sentence, do, nonetheless, have sufficient independence to warrant the use of the term *independent and introductory elements* of the sentence.

a. **Vocative.** When a noun or pronoun, with or without a modifier or modifiers, is used in direct address, it is generally said to be in the nominative case:

> *Mr. President,* I move to adjourn.
> *My friend,* you are badly mistaken.
> Say, *you,* what do you think you are doing?

b. **Exclamation.** Some interjections and exclamatory phrases are set apart from the rest of the sentence, by means of an exclamation point in writing, by a slight pause in speaking:

> *Pshaw!* He couldn't have crossed anyway.
> *The wretch!* He nearly ran them down.
> *What a pity!* There's scarcely a house left standing.

c. **Pleonasm.** In older English, and in some current colloquial English, the subject is sometimes repeated unnecessarily:

> *The Lord, He* will provide.
> *Thy rod and thy staff, they* comfort me.
> *John, he* hurt me.

Grammarians have often protested against this usage, and it is true that it has ceased to be standard-English usage — if it ever was. But after all, it is a stylistic matter and not really grammatical.

d. **Nominative absolute.** A noun and its modifying participle can be used absolutely, that is to say, as a unit of speech complete in itself, and yet with a certain connection with the rest of the sentence. The participle may be active or passive, but it is usually in the past tense; sometimes it is omitted:

> *The farmer having dumped the grain,* the elevator was started.
> *The matter having been settled,* the lawyer withdrew.
> *The lesson ended,* the teacher went away.
> *The estate being hopelessly encumbered,* the heirs dropped the lawsuit.
> *School over at last,* they ran to their games.

Usually a clause introduced by *as soon as, since, when, because,* or some similar subordinating conjunction could be substituted for this construction. But such a clause would be more closely joined to the principal clause and would commit the speaker to the idea of time or cause more definitely than might be desired. Consequently some speakers — or rather writers, for this nominative absolute is almost altogether a literary construction — like to use this construction because it is more nearly independent than any other speech unit. It is a speech unit lying in between the phrase and the clause, a syntactical shortcut of a somewhat noncommittal sort, just one more illustration of a fairly strong tendency in Current English to evade clear-cut classifications. It is a slightly dangerous construction for the younger writer because it is so easily confused with that other anticipatory participial construction wherein the participle starts the sentence but belongs to the subject, as in '*Having finished* the work, the man laid away his tools.' Indeed, the so-called dangling participle has become one of the chief bugbears of the teacher of English composition, since the writer starts with one idea and switches to another, producing such confused sentences as '*Having swelled* because of the rains, the workman was unable to remove the timber.'

e. Introductory word or phrase. Frequently an introductory word or phrase is used, especially in writing, which has no very close connection with the rest of the sentence but which helps to carry on the thought, to maintain continuity in a sequence of sentences. These introductory adverbial locutions have been considered under the head of illative conjunctions. A few examples will suffice to illustrate their relation to the rest of the sentence:

> *However,* he could not come.
> *Nevertheless* he had no excuse for delay.
> *And what is more,* he stole my coat.
> *The worst of it was,* I couldn't get away.

f. Parenthetical expressions. Sometimes a word, a phrase, or even a short sentence is inserted in a sentence by way of explanation or comment, with no close grammatical relationship to the sentence in which it is inserted. These insertions assume a variety of forms:

> There were, *indeed*, no friendly faces there.
> They were, *on the whole*, fairly comfortable.
> We were, *to tell the truth*, utterly helpless.
> The report was, *take it all in all*, fairly accurate.
> He has been, *you must admit*, reasonably careful.

97. *Phrases*

A phrase is composed of two or more words; it functions as a part of speech, such as noun, adjective, adverb; it expresses more than a simple idea, but it does not come so near to the expression of a complete thought as does a clause. From the very beginning, almost, of this study of Current English, attention has been called repeatedly to the tendency of the English people to use, increasingly, syntactical combinations of words instead of the older inflectional forms. But this use of phrasal constructions in English goes farther than merely serving the purposes of inflection; it sometimes replaces the simple uninflected parts of speech. Furthermore, phrasal idioms have become established in English usage which do not lend themselves to any kind of grammatical analysis. Many phrases have been cited[1] in the discussions of the parts of speech (Chap. VIII) and of the inflection of some of these parts of speech (Chap. XI); many more have been used and will of necessity continue to be used to illustrate the various syntactical usages explained in this present chapter. Consequently a brief summary of the kinds and functions of phrasal groups in Current English will help to clarify the whole subject of Modern English syntactical practice and will lead inevitably to a better appreciation of some of the finer points of style in speaking and writing English today.

The English grammarian usually confines his discussion of phrases to three kinds, namely, those made with prepositions, those made with participles, and those made with infinitives and gerunds. But it is obvious that the dictionary definition, of which a summary is presented at the beginning of this section, leaves the way open for the inclusion of all sorts of word groups; and if one is to understand certain developments in the English language of the past millennium, he must look at the matter in this broader and more inclusive way.

The three kinds of phrases according to the more restricted conception of the phrase mentioned above may be presented briefly as follows:

a. **Prepositional phrases.** The phrase composed of a preposition and its object is ordinarily used as an adjectival modifier, as in 'the house *in the woods*', or as an adverbial modifier, as in 'built *in the woods*'. These uses will be analyzed more minutely in the broader study of phrases soon to follow.

b. **Participial phrases.** Since a participle is a verbal (see Sec. 91), it can have both adverbial modifiers and the complementary constructions that verbs often require to complete their meaning. So it sometimes develops into an elaborate phrase, and this phrase is usually an adjectival modifier, because the participle is itself an adjectival form of the verb; for example, '*Running quickly and cautiously along the muddy path*, the smallest boy finally jumped the ditch.' It is clear that a participial modifier of this kind contributes something more to the sentence than a simple adjective modifier, such as *smallest*, can contribute; but that extra accomplishment must be recognized as innate in the verbal, as an essential part of its functioning. *Running* modifies *boy* just as *smallest* does, but because it is a verbal, it can be modified by the adverbs *quickly* and *cautiously* and by the prepositional phrase *along the muddy path*.

c. **Infinitive phrases.** Some grammarians have included under this head both the root infinitive (generally used with *to*) and the gerund, or verbal noun, ending in *-ing*:

> *To respect a man for his zeal in a wrong cause* is not necessarily *upholding him in his misplaced zeal*.

The first phrase (with the infinitive) functions as subject of the sentence, the second (with the gerund) as predicate nominative. In each instance the verbal contributes more than a simple noun could contribute, inasmuch as the infinitive has a direct object and is modified by a prepositional phrase, and the gerund has a similar object and modifier.

Looking at phrases somewhat more broadly, we may classify them according to their various uses as follows:

a. **Phrasal parts of speech.** (1) A prepositional phrase is sometimes the equivalent of a simple adjective; one can say 'garments *of silk*' or '*silken* (or *silk*) garments', 'a man *of intelligence*' or 'an *intelligent* man'. The phrase has the function of a predicate adjective in 'He is *in good health*', 'The house is *on fire*'.

(2) The verb-adverb combination, such as *put off, set out,* has been distinguished from other verbs and adverbial modifiers which do not function as special verbs (see Sec. 53, p. 297). Strictly speaking, the verb-adverb combination is a phrasal verb; but since, in a later study of the verb (Sec. 106), those phrasal verbs will be taken up which nowadays represent or replace older inflectional forms of the English verb, it is best to reserve the term for the latter.

(3) A prepositional phrase is sometimes the equivalent of a simple adverb; one can say 'to move *with rapidity*' or 'to move *rapidly*', 'come *at once*' or 'come *immediately*'. Such phrasal adverbs are usually employed by speakers who wish to avoid the awkward addition of the usual adverbial suffix *-ly* to those few old adjectives which retain the ending *-ly*, such as *deadly, friendly, homely, kindly, manly,* and *womanly.* Hence the evasive constructions *in a friendly manner* and *with a kindly expression* generally replace the more cumbersome *friendlily* and *kindlily.*

(4) Various phrasal prepositions have become standard in Modern English, such as *in accordance with, owing to* (see Sec. 55).

(5) Similarly phrasal conjunctions have come into use which are now generally employed without much thought of

their earlier meanings. Examples are *as well as, inasmuch as, in the event that, on condition that* (see Sec. 56).

(6) Phrasal interjections, such as the exclamatory and courteous phrases *dear me, pardon me,* are commonly used (see Sec. 57).

It would, of course, be possible to list many phrasal nouns (such as *will-o'-the-wisp* and *forget-me-not*) and names of people and places (like *Tam o' Shanter* and *Carmel-by-the-Sea*). Some are so thoroughly amalgamated that they are no longer easily recognized as phrasal, just as certain adverbs (*abroad, aloft*) and adjectives (*alive, akin*) and other phrasal parts of speech have long ceased to appear as phrases.

b. **Phrases as substitutes for earlier inflectional forms.** (1) The inflectional genitive, such as *Mr. Smith's,* and the phrasal genitive, such as *of Mr. Smith,* are both commonly used in Modern English and sometimes with a difference in emphasis or meaning. Several of the older uses of the inflectional genitive can be observed in the modern phrasal genitive:

(*a*) Possession is shown by the phrase, as in 'the property *of Mr. Smith*' or by the inflected genitive '*Mr. Smith's* property'. Sometimes both kinds are combined to form a double genitive, as in 'a book *of my father's*'.

(*b*) Authorship is also shown in either way, as in 'the plays *of Shakespeare*' or '*Shakespeare's* plays'.

(*c*) After certain nouns having a verbal quality an objective genitive is still used, as in 'fear *of the consequences*', 'love *of country*', 'need *of assistance*', 'the winning *of the race*'.

(*d*) After numerals and some indefinite pronouns a partitive genitive is commonly used, as in 'hundreds *of men*', 'some *of the money*', 'all *of the people*'.

(*e*) Some adjectives are followed by a phrasal genitive, such as *desirous, enough, forgetful, full, mindful.*

(*f*) Instead of a noun in apposition, a genitive phrase is sometimes used to accomplish the same appositional function, as in 'the city *of London*', 'the state *of California*'.

(2) The dative function of indirect object is expressed by a phrasal dative with *to* or *for,* as in 'sent *to him* for his own

use' or by the position of the uninflected dative just after the verb, as in 'sent *him* for his own use'. When a verb is followed by both an indirect and a direct object, the uninflected dative regularly precedes the direct object, as in 'I gave *him* a book'; but the phrasal dative can be placed before or after, as in 'I gave many books *to the new library*', and 'I gave *to the new library* most of my old books and magazines.'

(3) As already shown, the phrasal comparison of adjectives and adverbs, with *more* and *most*, is required for almost all adjectives and adverbs of three or more syllables, for many dissyllabic adjectives and adverbs, for adverbs in *-ly*, and even for monosyllabic adjectives and adverbs when emphasis is desired (see Sec. 89).

(4) Phrasal verbs formed by the use of auxiliaries with the verbal forms (infinitive and participles) are so important for the expression of the various properties of the verbs that they will be specially considered in Section 106.

98. *Clauses*

A clause contains a subject and a predicate and might often with a very little rewording be separated into a simple sentence; because it is not a distinct sentence, but is tied to one or more other clauses and embodied in a compound or a complex sentence, it is called a clause. It is a *principal* clause when it is grammatically or logically capable of standing alone; it is a *subordinate* clause when it functions as the equivalent of a noun, an adjective, or an adverb in such a manner as to be an essential part of the principal clause or else a modifier of it.*

Ordinarily, when the subordinate clause is used as a noun (as subject, object, or predicate nominative, for example), as in '*That he was ill* was apparent', the principal clause cannot

---

* Some grammarians use the term *independent clause* instead of *principal clause*; but the term is contradictory, since no clause can be entirely independent and still be a clause, as defined above.

be grammatically separated from the subordinate clause, because the complex sentence consists of a clause within a clause. When the subordinate clause is adjectival, but introduced by a compound relative, as in '*Whoever stole the book* had little use for it', the principal clause likewise cannot be readily separated from the subordinate clause, because both clauses are dependent upon the same pronoun. Nevertheless it is obvious that in both kinds of complex sentences there are embedded principal clauses, even though they are not grammatically independent.

a. **Principal clause.** *He walked to town* because he lacked money for carfare. *The house* in which I live *is new*, or, somewhat more colloquially, *The house* I live in *is new*.

b. **Subordinate noun clause.** *That he was ill* was apparent, or It was apparent *that he was ill*. (Whenever a direct statement or question is repeated as indirect discourse or as an indirect question, it becomes a substantive, or noun, clause, as in 'He told me *that he would come soon*', or, 'I asked *what he wanted.*' Object clauses are regularly introduced by *that, whether,* and the ordinary interrogative pronouns (or adjectives) and adverbs *who, which, when, where, why,* etc., and in colloquial English by *if.* In standard literary English this use of *if,* as in 'I do not know *if* he can come', is commonly avoided, because it is felt that *if* should be kept to introduce adverbial conditional clauses. The use of *lest* is not uncommon in good English, although it is considered nowadays somewhat formal.)

c. **Subordinate adjectival clause.** Subordinate adjectival clauses, introduced usually by the relative pronouns *who, which,* and *that,* are often classified as restrictive and nonrestrictive; the restrictive clause is generally introduced by *who* or *that,* the nonrestrictive by *who* or *which.* The nonrestrictive clause is set off by commas from the word it modifies.

Restrictive: The man *who pays his debts* is respected. The watch *that you recommended* has been sold.

Nonrestrictive: The old man next door, *who pays his debts always,* is a good business man. This watch, *which you recommended so positively,* has proved unsatisfactory.

It will be observed that the nonrestrictive clause, as it is set off by commas, has the effect of a mild aside or comment and can be used quite effectively sometimes, although many writers do not take the trouble to distinguish between restrictive and nonrestrictive clauses and consequently make no distinction between the two pronouns *that* and *which*.

d. Subordinate adverbial clause. Subordinate adverbial clauses are introduced by the subordinating conjunctions *as if, because, before, if, so that*, etc. (see Sec. 56). They are, therefore, various in their purposes, expressing or indicating

Cause: He left the house *because he was angry*.
Purpose: He stopped *so that he could hear the bell*. (Purpose is also expressed by infinitive phrases, as in 'He came *to look at my pictures*.')
Condition: I will go *if I can find the time*.
Result: He ran so fast *that he failed to see the ditch*.
Time: The senate adjourned *when the bill was passed*.
Concession: He paid, *although he was scarcely able to do so*.
Place: The hammer lay *just where it had fallen*.
Manner: He stopped *as if he were faint*.
Degree: Stretch it *as far as it will go*. He sees more *than I do*.

When comparison is implied by the wording of the principal clause, these clauses of time, manner, degree, etc. are sometimes called clauses of comparison, although the comparison is really expressed by the entire sentence.

Just as a simple adjective or adverb is expanded into an adjectival or adverbial phrase to produce certain effects, so also it is sometimes possible to expand even more, into an adjectival or adverbial clause. So one may say,

A *silken* robe, a robe *of silk*, or a robe *that is made of silk*.
He spoke *uncertainly, in an uncertain manner*, or *as if he were uncertain*.

But it must be emphasized that these varying forms of the adjectival and adverbial modifiers are not necessarily identical in meaning, and it is part of the art of a good writer to know their varying values or effectiveness.

99. *Concord*

Grammatical concord is the agreement of words with respect to gender, number, case, and person. As long as the English language had numerous inflectional forms, grammatical concord was of great importance, because the right ending must always be chosen in order that verb might agree with subject, adjective with the noun it modified, pronoun with its antecedent. But with the loss of most of the case endings, with the disappearance of grammatical gender, with the complete wiping out of the adjective declension, and with the elimination of most of the verb endings, concord demands far less attention in Current English. Indeed, most of the violations of the rules of agreement — or uncertainties as to what concord demands — are due to illogical and confused thinking, and to ambiguous use of words, rather than to inability to select harmonious endings, as in Anglo-Saxon times.

a. **Agreement of subject and verb.** (1) Collective nouns are the cause of uncertainty in the choice of the number of a verb because the speaker sometimes conceives of the group, such as a *committee*, a *family*, a *herd*, as a unit, sometimes as various individuals composing the group. One can say 'The committee *is* ready to report', but 'The committee *are* divided in their opinions.' In America one usually says 'the *government is*', but in England 'the *government are*' is frequently met with in papers and magazines. The choice in such cases must depend upon how the speaker thinks of the group.

(2) In the use of nouns like *deer, heathen, sheep*, where the plural form is always or usually the same as the singular, one can determine the number of the subject only by the form of the verb, as in 'The deer *runs*'; when the verb has no number form, as in 'The deer *ran*', the reader is dependent entirely on the general context of the sentence in deciding the number.

(3) In the use of nouns like *athletics, ethics, measles*, there is often uncertainty as to which number of the verb should be used; sometimes meaning decides, and sometimes Modern English usage has arbitrarily established one or the other

number as the correct one. In the list given in Section 87 (p. 443), those nouns that may be used with a singular verb are marked with a dagger; but when one cannot be sure, as in *ethics is* or *ethics are*, it is advisable to refer to a good dictionary.

(4) The worst grammatical traps are those sentences that contain a deferred subject or compound predicate nominative, where the speaker starts with a verb in the singular and then discovers that he needs a plural verb instead. If he starts his sentence without looking ahead to see what is to follow, he is likely to say 'There *is* a box, two letters, and a card in the mail'; but if he anticipates the whole predicate, he will be careful to start his sentence 'There *are* . . .'. In writing, a false start can be corrected; but in hurried colloquial speech such grammatical disagreement between subject and verb is hardly worth worrying about. The traffic department of the Burlington Railroad secured much publicity a few years ago by writing, "For within this tremendous area *is* produced: Two thirds the oats, more than half the corn, more than half the barley, half the wheat . . .", and then questioning some of the linguistic authorities of America regarding this use of the singular verb. The authorities disagreed among themselves.[409]

In Current English the singular verb is always used after the expletive *it*, even though the deferred subject is plural, as in 'It *is* the branches rubbing against the window that you hear.' Curiously, in Early English the speaker preferred the plural verb in such sentences; he would have said 'It *are* the branches', anticipating the plural that was to follow rather than stressing the number of *it* in making his choice. Which speaker would be logically right?

(5) Another grammatical trap is illustrated by such a sentence as 'The man with all his children *were* drowned.' Grammatically *was* should be used with the simple subject *man* because the phrase *with all his children* is only a modifier of *man*; but logically the speaker is thinking of 'the man *and* all his children' and would therefore feel justified in using the plural verb *were*. The speaker can accomplish what he

wishes and avoid an awkward situation by using *and* instead of *with*, as illustrated above; or he can rearrange the sentence to read 'The man *was* drowned, with all his children.'

(6) The use of *none* with a plural verb, as in 'None *were* saved', has often been criticized on the ground that *none* means 'no one'. Krapp says, "Usage justifies *none* also as a plural",[17] and the New English Dictionary[20] states that the plural construction is more common. Few speakers hesitate to use it. If the plural seems illogical, the use of *no one*, the uncontracted form, will settle the trouble.

(7) Another kind of grammatical trap catches the unwary speaker when he uses one of the indefinite pronouns, especially *one, each, each one, neither, everyone, another, another one*, with a following partitive-genitive phrase, as in '*Each one* of the men sitting in the store *were* hurt', '*Neither* of the books *are* bad.' Grammatically, and logically this time, the singular verbs *was* and *is* are plainly required.

On the other hand, the noun in the intervening phrase sometimes really governs the number of the verb which follows it, as in 'He wrote one of the best novels *that ever were written*', and it is illogical to make the verb singular, as though the clause were a modifier of *one* instead of *novels*.*

(8) There has always been confusion in English regarding the person of the verb *be* when two substantives connected by *or* and of different persons form the subject. Shall one say 'I do not know whether the *boys* or *I am* to blame' or 'whether the *boys* or *I are* to blame'? Curme says of this difficulty (*Syntax*, p. 60)[399]:

> Most grammarians prescribe that the verb should agree with the nearest subject... In our ordinary English, however, this construction is not now common, for most people desire to avoid the annoying necessity of making a choice between the two persons. Hence the most common usage now is to separate the sentence into two distinct propositions, each with a verb or one with a verb and one elliptical in form: 'Either *he is* in the wrong or *I am*.' 'We are not in the wrong, nor [*is*] *John* either.'

* But note 'Aunt Selma is the only one of my relatives who *has* ever been abroad.'

(9) In colloquial and dialectal usage, wrong uses of verb person or verb number are frequently heard, as in *I says* (for 'I say'), *you was* (for 'you were'), *he don't* (for 'he doesn't'). In contracting *am I not*, the colloquial *ain't I* is commonly resorted to and is, as we have already remarked (p. 256), the logical contraction, even though it is not regarded with favor by the more careful speakers of standard English. The British speaker has been driven by his dislike of *ain't* to use the more illogical *aren't I*, and to some extent this has been adopted by American speakers, recently.

b. **Agreement of pronoun and antecedent.** (1) The indefinite pronouns *another, anybody, anyone, each, each one, either, everybody, everyone, neither, nobody, no one, one, somebody, someone*, and the indefinite locution *a person*, cause much grammatical difficulty because a certain generality implied by or implicit in them leads many people to use plural forms later in the sentence in referring back to them, as in '*Everyone* has *their* work to do', '*A person* sometimes loses *their* interest in better things', 'If *anyone* doubts this, let *them* speak up.' One often feels that he is dealing with a plural subject, even though his grammatical training tells him that the subject is technically singular. Hence the generally approved practice of using a masculine form to refer back to one of these indefinite pronouns of common gender does not always seem quite suitable. Indeed, when the indefinite subject is known to mean a woman, rather than people in general, the feminine forms *her, hers*, and *she* should, of course, be used.*

(2) Some speakers get around this difficulty by saying '*Each one* has *his* or *her* work to do.' But this is a cumbersome solution of the problem, and most careful speakers of English are content to arbitrarily use the masculine pronoun.

---

* It is a curious inconsistency of Modern English usage that while one is advised to use the masculine singular pronoun after all other indefinite pronouns, one is not allowed to follow one's understanding of this rule when the simple indefinite *one* is used as subject; but one must either resort to a stilted and pedantic sequence of *one's* (as in this sentence), or else evade the issue by entirely reconstructing one's sentence. In deliberate violation of this senseless and inconsistent rule of the purist and the prescriptive grammarian, the author of this book has employed the masculine singular pronoun whenever he felt the need of a concise and clear-cut sentence beginning with an indefinite *one*.

(3) Another problem of pronominal agreement arises in such a sentence as 'I saw the river *whose* current had lately swept the village away.' Many grammarians would change *whose* to *of which* on the ground that *whose* is the genitive form of *who* only. As a matter of fact, *whose* has long been used as the genitive of *which*, as well as of *who*; and insistence on the phrasal genitive *of which* forces one to use what is sometimes an awkward construction, instead of the much simpler one.

Agreement of a pronoun with its antecedent in number or in gender is, of course, only a part of that broader subject generally called the "reference" of the pronoun. Many uses of pronouns are faulty because it is not clear what they refer to, as in the sentence '*He* met *his* pupil, and *he* tipped *his* hat to *him*.' When the pronoun is definite, the antecedent should be equally definite, and clearly indicated.

c. **Agreement of adjective and noun modified.** Inasmuch as adjectives have lost their older declensional forms, only the distinction of number still existing in *this — these, that — those*, many syntactical difficulties have been escaped which would probably greatly complicate the study of grammatical usage today if it were still necessary to fit the adjective to its noun in gender, number, and case. There is one grammatical trap under this head, however, into which slovenly thinkers fall; that is the use of the plurals *these* and *those* with the singulars *kind* and *sort*, mainly because the two nouns are conceived of as collective nouns, which in reality they are not.

d. **Sequence of tenses.** While our definition of concord would seem to exclude automatically from this discussion any consideration of agreement in the matter of tenses, nevertheless the two subjects are in reality closely enough akin to warrant the inclusion of the latter here.

In complex sentences the tense of the verb in the principal clause determines what tense the verb shall assume in a subordinate clause. In general the rules are as follows:

When the verb of the principal clause is in the present, the future, the present perfect, or the future perfect tense, any tense needed to express the thought can be used in the subordinate clause, as, for example,

> He *says* that he *has seen* the river Nile.
> He *has told* me often that he *will make* you his heir.
> *Has* he *told* you what he *was seeking*?

When the verb of the principal clause is in the past or the past perfect tense, a past tense should also be used in the subordinate clause, as in

> He *said* that he *had seen* the river Nile.
> He *had told* me often that he *would make* you his heir.

Sometimes the sequence usually required after a past tense is not used, but the tense is retained as it would be if the clause were entirely independent. This exception to the rule above is usually due to a desire on the part of the speaker to show that he is stating a general or universal truth, as in 'I *told* him that wheat *will grow* anywhere in this state', or, 'He *knew* that such disease *is* incurable.' But even in these sentences one could say *would grow* and *was*.

100. *Word Order*

With the gradual wearing away of English inflectional endings, it has become necessary to depend more and more upon the order of words for an understanding of the relationship of one word to another in the sentence. But the placing of a word or phrase in the sentence does more than merely provide a syntactical substitute for an Early English inflectional form; it is today, and has been from earliest times, our chief method of placing emphasis on an idea or group of ideas. The positions of chief emphasis are the beginning and the end of sentences, but any unusual placing of a word or phrase calls attention to it. And so the writer who pays close attention to stylistic effects frequently rearranges his words within the sentence so as to get the utmost advantage from word order.

As a result of the fixing of word order in the sentence, there is a general recognition of normal sentence arrangement; and the recognition of normal word order makes it possible to give emphasis to a word or phrase by putting it in an abnormal or exceptional position. Consequently the best way to approach the study of English word order is to attempt to define normal order and then examine the exceptions that are to be found. A normal arrangement of word, phrase, and clause may be seen in the following sentence:

I have found you a good high seat where you can rest comfortably and watch the finish of the race.

The normal arrangements illustrated in this sentence are

Subject + verb + indirect object + direct object
Adjectival modifier + noun modified
Verb + adverbial modifier
Noun + phrasal modifier
Principal clause + subordinate clause

a. **Subject and Verb.** The subject normally precedes the verb; but there are exceptions wherein the subject and verb are inverted, so that the subject follows all or at least part of the verb. Such inversions in Current English are due to several causes:

(1) In interrogative sentences, which are usually introduced by an interrogative pronoun or adjective or adverb or else by the verb itself, the subject usually follows, as in 'Why did *you* come?', 'Are *you* ready to go?', 'What have *they* there?'

However, when a direct question is incorporated in a complex sentence and thus made an indirect question, as in 'I do not know *why you came*', the subject is no longer inverted but is put back into normal position before the verb.

(2) In declarative sentences, when an adverbial modifier or a complement of the verb is placed first for emphasis, the subject sometimes follows the verb, as in 'Closely following her was *a pleasant-looking servant*', 'Never have *I* seen so great a failure', 'Wise was *he* in the ways of this world.'

Inversion of subject and verb was once quite generally practiced in sentences of this kind, but nowadays it is not so common. When an adverb or complement is placed first for emphasis, Modern English prefers to keep the verb after its subject, usually, as in 'Twice *he* stopped to examine his car', 'The tire *he* left lying by the roadside.'

(3) Perhaps the most commonly used and most nearly standardized form of inversion today is that which involves the use of the expletives *there* and *it* to start the sentence. When the inverted subject is a noun or pronoun, *there* is employed, as in 'There was *only one apple* left in the sack'; when the subject is an infinitive phrase or a subordinate clause, *it* is regularly used, as in 'It is easy *to start the radio*', and 'It was evident *that the tramp was ill*.'

(4) In narration the interpolated inversions 'says *he*', 'said *I*', etc. are still customarily used. In earlier English usage narration was often speeded along by the use of sentences beginning with verbs, as in 'Came *a day* when he no longer...'; occasionally a modern writer resorts to this trick of inverting when he wishes to emphasize the action expressed by the verb rather than the thing named by the subject.

(5) Sometimes a conditional clause is introduced by an inverted verb instead of the usual conjunction *if*, as in 'Had *I* known you would come, I should have been prepared', 'Were *I* in your place, I would resign.'

b. Indirect and Direct Objects. The simple dative pronoun or noun used as the indirect object regularly precedes the direct object, as in 'I have found *you* a good high seat' and 'I gave *my father* a new necktie.' The phrasal dative used as indirect object is generally placed after the direct object, as in 'Give that box *to me*' and 'I gave a new necktie *to my father*.' Any departure from these practices is likely to throw special emphasis on either the indirect or the direct object.

c. Adjectival Modifiers. Normally an adjective is placed before the noun it modifies, as in '*good high* seat', and the adjectival phrase is put just after the noun, as in 'money *to lend*', 'the finish *of the race*'. But when two adjectives are connected by *and*, or when several form a series, they may be used postpositively, that is, after the noun modified, as in 'The father, *tall* and *gaunt* and *gray*, stood just within the gate.' Indeed, whenever the adjectival modifier becomes expanded so that it is awkward to put it just before the modified noun, it is made a postpositive modifier, as in 'Mr. Smith, *weak from many months of suffering and want*, dragged himself to the station', 'a horse *ten years old*' (or 'a *ten-year-old* horse'). But there are some postpositive modifications which are not due to this cause:

(1) The use of postpositive adjectival modifiers in French and Latin has left its imprint upon the English language in a few formal expressions, such as *attorney-general, battle royal, body politic, bride elect, court-martial, fee simple, God Almighty, heir apparent, knight errant, money due, prince regent, proof positive, States-General, third person plural, time immemorial.*

(2) An earlier use of postpositive epithets has remained in such expressions as *Alfred the Great, Jack the Ripper, Jerusalem the Golden, Pliny the Elder.*

(3) Some adjectives, mostly old amalgamated phrases or compounds, are not regularly placed before the noun modified but are used as predicate adjectives (see p. 477), or they may be used as postpositive modifiers, as in 'The boat, *all ablaze*, was towed into port.' Others not already listed are *alike, alone, ashamed, asleep, athirst, pursuant, worth*. While *enough* is used before the noun modified, its use in that position is slightly restricted, and many speakers prefer to use it postpositively (see Fowler [16], p. 140). The adjective *else* is used only after the word it modifies.

(4) Many participial modifiers can be placed either before or after the noun modified; but when they are placed before, as in 'an *assumed* attitude', '*lost* time', '*unceasing* talk', their adjectival value is somewhat more clearly brought out, whereas their verbal quality is slightly stronger when they are placed after, as in 'the attitude *assumed*', 'the time being', 'money *needed*', 'talk *unceasing*'. Indeed, in some of these postpositive constructions the participle might easily be expanded into an adjectival clause, as in 'the money *that is needed*'. One is never sure which element in a participle is

stronger, the adjectival or the verbal. Consequently position sometimes helps to make its true function somewhat clearer.

(5) Numerals are used postpositively, as in 'Chapter *X*', 'page *50*', 'the year *900*'.

(6) In a few expressions the postpositive use of the adjective has become conventional in informal English, such as 'books *innumerable*', 'father *dear*', 'sister *mine*'.

When two or more adjectival modifiers precede the noun, the articles *a* and *the*, the possessives *my*, *our*, *his*, etc., and the demonstratives *this* and *that* are generally placed before any other adjectives, as in '*the* great flood', '*that* old gray barn', '*a* few horses'. In a few cases, however, other modifiers (adverbs and nouns, as well as adjectives) take precedence of these, as in '*all the* day', '*both their* books', '*half a* loaf', '*half the* price', '*how sad a* case', '*many a* day', '*so rich a* man', '*such a* storm', '*too sick a* man', '*what a* man'.

d. **Adverbial Modifiers.** It is not easy to generalize as to what the normal position of an adverbial modifier is or what it has been in the past. Some adverbs can be moved about in the sentence more freely than others; this depends somewhat on the kind of adverb and somewhat on the kind of word that it modifies. In general it can be said that

(1) An adverb modifying a verb (or verbal) can generally be placed quite freely in the sentence. So one can say 'Mr. Smith had *recently* rebuilt his store' or '*Recently* Mr. Smith had rebuilt' or 'had rebuilt his store *recently*' or, with the verb simplified, 'Mr. Smith *recently* rebuilt his store.' But the adverbs which were originally phrases, such as *aboard*, *abroad*, *adrift*, *aloft*, *astray*, *galore*, and prepositions used as adverbs, such as *along*, *around*, *below*, *by*, *in*, *out*, *up*, *within*, can be used only after the verb in a normal sentence, as in 'He has been *abroad*' and 'The captain went *below*.'

(2) An adverb modifying an adjective or another adverb should be placed as near as possible to the word it modifies. So one says, '*very* happy', '*truly* repentant', '*almost* dead'. Sometimes there is an accumulation of such modifications, each adverb modifying the word next after it, as in '*quite hopelessly* tangled', '*not so very well* done', '*most awfully* sur-

prised'. Occasionally such modifiers are used postpositively, as in 'longer *still*', 'five *only*', 'dead, *almost*'.

While the definition of an adverb would seem to exclude the modification of any other part of speech, as a matter of fact, adverbs of degree are frequently put before prepositions, as in '*just* across the border', '*nearly* through the rock'. But this should not be surprising, since, as has already been established, the preposition becomes an adverb very readily (Sec. 58, p. 321). Some grammarians maintain that the adverb modifies the entire phrase in such constructions.

(3) An adverb introducing a sentence usually comes first, as in '*Nevertheless* he could not hope to finish.' It is possible, however, to defer these introductory adverbs (which have also been called illative conjunctions because of their loosely connective character) and drop them into the sentence a few words farther along, as illustrated by the use of *however* in this sentence.

Vagueness as to just what one wishes to accomplish with an adverb, which of these three kinds of adverbial modification one is going to employ, often leads to careless and ineffective placing of adverbs. The haphazard use of *only, just, nearly, exactly*, etc. is an example of this careless word order. In 'He *only* sang two songs', the fact of singing is emphasized; in 'He sang *only* two songs', the number of songs is stressed. If the speaker is content to throw out his thought in a roughly shaped and unpolished form, then the placing of *only* does not matter much; but if he would shape and polish the expression of his thinking into as highly effective an instrument as possible, then the position of every little word makes some difference.

e. **Phrases and Clauses.** Since these word groups function as entities, it is desirable not to mar the unity of such groups; since they frequently function as modifiers, it is also desirable not to allow them to become too far removed from the words modified. When these two principles are not observed, it is necessary to justify the violation of them. "The unit of syntax", says C. Alphonso Smith, "is more often a phrase or a clause than an entire sentence. In other words, the normal tendency of English syntax, a tendency antagonized by impositions from the syntax of the classical languages, has always been toward short circuits rather than toward long circuits" (*Studies in English Syntax*[394], p. 34).

(1) To many careful users of English the "splitting" of an infinitive through the interpolation of an adverb between the sign *to* and the infinitive, as in 'to *rightly* amend', is an indication of poor literary taste. Possibly the objection to the practice arises primarily from the fact that the infinitive and its sign *to* form a compact and special kind of phrase, slightly different from any other in the language. At any rate, it has generally been considered bad practice *to thus split* the infinitive, even though very good writers have sometimes done it, and even though there is no very strong logical argument against it. Rhetoricians are gradually coming to realize that it is sometimes necessary to interpose the adverb in infinitives where no other order will prove quite so effective. If one wishes to stress the action, one can hardly avoid writing 'He built an altar *to just miss* the ceiling', 'He tried *to further improve* foreign trade', 'He failed *to fully comprehend* the problem.' For if the adverb be placed after the infinitive, as in '*to improve* foreign trade *further*', and '*to comprehend* the problem *fully*', the emphasis is no longer placed on the infinitive but now rests on the adverb, which has been moved to the end, where, as we have already noted, one of the chief positions of sentence emphasis is located; if the adverb be placed before the *to*, it may seem to modify the main verb, as in *tried further* and *failed fully*, giving quite different meanings to these sentences; and if the adverb be placed after the infinitive but before the direct object of the infinitive, as in '*to comprehend fully* the problem', the close relationship of infinitive and object is interrupted.

Curiously enough, there seems to be no objection to a similar interpolation when a gerundial construction is substituted for the root infinitive; one does not hesitate to say, 'He had hopes *of further improving* foreign trade' and 'He failed *in fully comprehending* the problem.' If, as Curme has insisted,[399] the infinitive construction is being used more and more as a convenient substitute for a more cumbersome finite verb, then the speaker must be allowed to place the adverb according to the amount of emphasis he wishes to give it, whether it be a modifier of an infinitive or of a finite verb. But in the opinion of many he should avoid splitting the infinitive if the adverb can be placed outside the group just as well.

(2) Likewise, when the object of a preposition is an interrogative or a relative pronoun, there is a strong tendency in Modern English to begin with the pronoun and postpone the preposition to the end, as in '*What* are you looking *for?*' and 'I saw the house *that* he had talked *about.*' Some careful users of English would insist upon placing the preposition before its object, as in '*For what* are you looking?' and 'I saw the house *about which* he had talked.' Again it is clear that two different syntactical principles or practices are clashing. On the one hand, it is desirable not to mar the unity of a prepositional phrase, and postponing the preposition does scatter the phrase; on the other hand, it is common in English to begin a question with an interrogative word, and a relative clause with a relative pronoun, but one forgets in beginning his sentence or clause that this is not always true. In other words, the very careful and farsighted speaker — and, more often, the writer — anticipates the entire sentence and so is able to use the preposition neatly at the beginning, where, perhaps, it logically belongs; but the hasty and more careless speaker plunges in with interrogative or relative and later finds that he must hang the preposition on the end of his sentence (see also p. 538).

It is the speaker who postpones his preposition who says, "*Who* did you give the book *to?*', incorrectly using a nominative *who* because he does not stop to think that it is to serve as the object of a deferred preposition *to*; if he were to bring together *to* and *who* as a phrase, he would of course say '*To whom* did you give the book?' It is the "long circuit", as Smith has called it, that causes the confusion in a construction of this kind. A similar confusion causes speakers to begin sentences with the adverb *where* and end with the superfluous and ungrammatical preposition *at*, as in '*Where* are you staying *at*?', although they would never say '*At where* are you staying?'

(3) Sometimes, in order to give special emphasis to a preposition, it is placed after its object; so one might say 'the world *over*', 'the whole town *through*', 'the clock *around*'.

(4) From these instances of postponed or postpositive prepositions — a contradiction in terms, if one insists on the original meaning of *preposition*, 'placed before' — it is but a step to the consideration of the verb-adverb constructions, such as *put up, get over, lay by, run down*. When the prepositional adverb is felt to be strongly adverbial, it may be separated from the verb, as in 'He *put* the shutters *up*', '*Take* the screen *down* again'; but when the verb and adverb or adverbs are closely combined so as to offer the equivalent of some simple verb, as in 'I cannot *put up with* his carelessness', and 'He will *get over* his disappointment', then separation is not usually permissible.

Perhaps no better conclusion can be offered concerning these matters of word order than Fowler's advice relative to the use of the preposition at the end. He says[415]:

Follow no arbitrary rule, but remember that there are often two or more possible arrangements between which a choice should be consciously made; if the abnormal, or at least unorthodox, final preposition that has naturally presented itself sounds comfortable, keep it; if it does not sound comfortable, still keep it if it has compensating vigour, or when among awkward possibilities it is the least awkward.

101. *Ellipsis*

Various forms of linguistic economy or linguistic laziness have already been discussed — word-shortening, use of one word instead of two, and so on. In syntax this takes the form of ellipsis, which is defined as the omission of a word or words ordinarily necessary to complete a sentence but omitted because their meanings or functions are taken for granted. Two extremes may be recognized in the practice of ellipsis: in an informal conversation, where the contact between two speakers is close, much can be taken for granted, and much ellipsis is justifiable; in formal writing, where little can be taken for granted, it is not safe to risk much ellipsis.

It would be wrong to suppose, however, that when a speaker indulges in what the grammarian would call ellipsis, he has a clear idea of that which he omits or neglects to express. It is more likely that the speaker very often has no definite idea of that which he is omitting — indeed, that he would rather not be forced to word the idea or thought too carefully and exactly. If, then, in the following examples, ellipses be assumed, it is because in each instance the complete grammatical construction would require more; it cannot be assumed that a speaker would necessarily fill out his construction, even in his own mind. The syntactical usages that have been presented in the foregoing sections (Secs. 92–100) have been gradually developed in standard English as normal practices toward which English speakers generally strive, but from which speakers and writers often depart just as far as they dare. Ellipses are shortcuts in syntactical usage, and often they are evasions as well. Some of them are standard English constructions by right of long usage.

a. **Omission of the Subject.** Since the subject of a verb in the imperative mood is always the personal pronoun of the second person, it is omitted except when it is needed for emphasis. In a colloquial reply to a question, the subject is often omitted when both speakers understand it clearly, as in "What did you do with my book?" "Gave it to the librarian." In business letters a sort of telegraphic style has been developed by some business men with a mistaken notion of economy; they effect some of their saving through the omission of the pronominal subject, as in "Received yours of the 16th inst." In a few locutions, such as 'Thank you', 'Beg your pardon', the pronominal subject is commonly omitted. These four omissions of the pronominal subject illustrate the range of ellipsis, inasmuch as one is standard and normal, another is colloquial and exceptional, the third is exaggerated and of very doubtful propriety, and the fourth might be termed idiomatic, since it is found only in special locutions.

b. **Omission of the Verb.** Sometimes the entire verb is omitted; more often, when it is a phrasal verb, the auxiliary is retained. Sometimes the omission is due to the fact that the verb is so familiar that it can be taken for granted; more often it is omitted to avoid unnecessary repetition in the same sentence.

(1) *Omission of a familiar verb.* Forms of *be* are often omitted, along with their subjects, as in 'He hurt his foot while swimming', 'He came to America when a boy of twelve'; verbs of going are often implied, as in 'I will away', 'After him!' 'The cat wants in'; in replies to questions, verbs are taken for granted, as in "Who broke the chair?" "[It was] Not I"; at auctions and under similar conditions a familiar verb and its subject are presumed, as in 'Six dollars for the chair.'

(2) *Avoidance of unnecessary repetition.* The entire verb may be omitted after a comparative, as in 'He is taller than his brother', 'He was older than I'; an infinitive is often represented merely by its sign *to*, as in 'He went, but I did not care *to*'; similarly the infinitive or participle may drop out of a phrasal verb, and its object or its modifier also, if it has one, leaving only the auxiliary, as in 'If you can't watch the gate, someone else should', 'Smith has done well in business, even though his brother hasn't.'

There is a tendency to utilize certain partial fillers in some of these ellipses; the verb *do* has long been used in this way, as in 'You may not care to read the book when I *do*' (= 'read it'); and the little adverb *so* is similarly employed in "Can you read this?" "I think *so*" (= 'I can read it').

c. **Omission of a Modified Noun.** When phrases such as *St. Paul's Cathedral* and *Meyer's Grocery Store* and *Brown's home* become very familiar, speakers consider the genitive sufficiently suggestive and drop the other noun, saying 'to see *St. Paul's*', 'buy at *Meyer's*', 'stop at *Brown's*'. Probably this same form of ellipsis is at the bottom of many substantivations of adjectives, as in 'The *poor* are with us always'.

d. **Omission of Connectives.** The relative pronoun is so commonly omitted that one might almost be justified in suggesting in the case of such sentences as 'I found the book you mentioned' that *book* is a syntactical hybrid, acting as both the object of *found* and the object of *mentioned*; but it has been customary to assume the omission of a relative *that* or *which* after *book*. Likewise, in such sentences as 'I told you I could not come', the conjunction *that* is sometimes said to be omitted before the subordinate clause *I could not come*, although it is not really needed in the sentence. The noun clause, which serves as the object of *told*, is clearly comprehensible as such. So also some grammarians would insist that *if* is omitted when a conditional sentence is introduced by a verb, as in '*Had* I *known* you would come, I should have been prepared.' But this is a matter of word order, as already explained; it is not necessary to assume ellipsis in such a sentence.

e. **Elliptical Clauses.** An adverbial clause is often shortened by the omission of both subject and linking verb or auxiliary, as in 'While running for office, he made many friends', 'When two years old, he came to America.'

f. **Elliptical Phrases.** In colloquial English it is not unusual to hear such shortened phrases as 'It stands [at the] *back* of the pole', 'He doesn't play [in] *the way* I do', 'He wasn't [at] *home* when I called.'

The subject of ellipsis is an important one for the ambitious student of English, and it is well to seek for a workable definition of the term. To some grammarians it means an omission in the sentence which should usually be filled out in good literary English; to others it means an omission which may be filled out for the sake of grammatical analysis and comparison with other constructions, but which does not need to be filled out even in good formal usage. Somewhere between these two extremes of overfussiness and excessive laxity there must be a happy mean. When the illiterate person says 'I asked him *could I borrow his book*', it is manifest to the mind of the average educated speaker of the English language that the speaker has made his meaning quite clear, but that his sentence does not conform to the pattern of accepted English grammatical usage. The illiterate speaker probably feels no need of an *if* or *whether* to introduce his indirect question; but the educated speaker, even though he is not a grammarian, does insist upon some kind of connective in the sentence quoted. For after all, the integrity of the English language must be maintained, even to the point of compelling the illiterate man to surrender some of his linguistic rights to the grammatical bourgeoisie.

Within reasonable limits, then, ellipsis is proper, both as a shortcut and as a means of avoiding unnecessary repetition, provided, of course, that the hearer or reader is able to make allowance for omissions. One must always consider how far he can safely go in making such omissions. When a person remarks 'I read where a factory blew up in Chicago yesterday', there is far too much implied between *I read* and *a factory blew up in Chicago yesterday* to be satisfactorily suggested by the one simple connective *where*. Much linguistic slovenliness and literary ineffectiveness result from allowing the hearer or reader to fill in gaps in sentences which should have been supplied by the speaker or writer while the sentences were in process of construction.

102. *Irrational and Hybrid Constructions*

Attention has been called to English idioms which cannot be rationally analyzed into their component elements; some discussion has been devoted also to parts of speech so hybrid in their functioning that they cannot be distinctly classified; and etymologies have been considered which are too badly confused for final and satisfactory explanation. In the study of English syntax, likewise, similar confusion and fusion can be observed in certain constructions of Current English which are the troublesome offspring of confused thinking and of indulgence in linguistic shortcuts or the crossing of two different functions. A few of the irrational constructions have become well intrenched in English in spite of their illogical character; but most of them are still outside the pale of good literary usage, and attention is called to them here chiefly to illustrate an ever-present tendency toward the irrational and evasive in the syntactical practice of colloquial English.

a. 'I will *try and* find it.' This is very generally used in colloquial English, but it does not say exactly what the speaker intends. One *tries to* do something.

b. 'It was the *richest of any* university in America.' This is an unfortunate compromise between *richer than any other* and *richest of all the universities*. It is very commonly used and illustrates the danger inherent in syntactical shortcuts.

c. 'That's *all the farther* it will reach.' While this is a colloquial equivalent of *as far as*, it seems to be also a confusion of a comparative form with a superlative construction, a hybrid construction, as it were.

d. 'He *could not help but* believe their story.' This colloquialism has not been favored by grammarians as an idiom of the language because it infringes on other uses of *help* and other similar constructions of a more clear-cut nature, such as 'He *could not help believing* their story.'

e. 'I always *have* and *shall continue to pay* my debts.' Since the auxiliary *have* requires a participle *paid*, the best way to insure the use of the proper verbal with such an auxiliary is to rearrange the sentence, as 'I always *have paid* my debts and *shall continue to do* so.' Many speakers are trapped through plunging too hastily into this use of two or more auxiliaries and then attempting to economize by using the main verb only once.

f. 'He found it *different than* he expected.' One may argue that *different* should be followed by a preposition, *from*, rather than a conjunction, *than*; but the shortcut *different than* is more direct and concise, so that many speakers of good colloquial English use it. It may become necessary to accept it as standard idiom, ultimately. It is still avoided by the most careful speakers and writers.

g. 'They asked *whether* he could skate as well as his father did.' If *whether* implies a choice of alternatives, then to be strictly logical the speaker should add *or not*—or strongly imply it. But often it would be very awkward to include the alternative, and so the sentence stands as a slightly irrational construction, although generally accepted as standard English.

h. 'To go *a little ways*'. This dialectal usage seems to have resulted from a confusion with such forms as *always*.

i. 'He played *as well or better than* his brother.' This is another grammatical trap resulting from the use of two different kinds of comparison. It would usually be avoided if the speaker completed the first comparison: 'He played *as well as* his brother did — *even better.*'

j. 'They heard the *boy call(ing)* for help and smiled at *his showing* such cowardice.' Unlike most of the constructions previously discussed, the two in this sentence are neither irrational nor objectionable to users of good standard English. They have been chosen in order that there might be included in this brief survey of present-day syntactical confusion and fusion examples showing how intimately two different constructions can be merged under certain circumstances. In *boy calling* there is the equivalent of subject accusative + infinitive; and at the same time one might rightly insist that *boy* is the direct object of the verb *heard*, with *calling* a participial modifier, merely. In *his showing*, on the other hand, two different functions of the genitive *his* blend; the older grammarians have been accustomed to parse *his* as a genitival modifier of the gerund, while more recently there has been a noticeable tendency to call *his* a genitival subject, on the ground that it embodies the subject of the action named in the gerund *showing*. Such hybridization is not unknown in language, and in gerundial and participial constructions of Modern English it has assumed a place of increasing but, at the same time, perplexing importance.[425]

The two types of troublesome constructions — the irrational and the hybrid — have been illustrated in the foregoing sentences in order that a distinction may be made between those that are avoidable and those others that must be accepted. In hybrid constructions such as those given in the last paragraph, there is a fusion of syntactical functions which must be accepted as inevitable; but since, as we have undertaken to demonstrate in the last few chapters, there is a reasonably clear-cut pattern of English grammatical usage which the grammarian and the literary artist endeavor to maintain, and since, moreover, it is desirable that the uses and values of words be kept well defined and intact, those who feel strongly the importance of preserving the integrity of the English language avoid as much as possible irrational constructions. If such syntactical constructions assume, ultimately, in colloquial usage, meanings so generally accepted that no one questions them longer, then, of course, they must be approved as idioms or converted locutions. This general acceptance has taken place in the case of the very illogical use of an accusative plural pronoun as a singular subject, as in '*You* are my friend', of the equally illogical use of the singular negative *none* ('no one') as a plural, as in 'There *were none* in the box', and of the use of an objective pronoun *himself* in apposition with a nominative form, as in '*He himself* told me the story.' But usually the English language has progressed along fairly logical and reasonable lines, and the irrational idioms that the language now possesses must be regarded as isolated survivals — as occasional contributions of the careless and unthinking element in the English race, linguistic fossils, as it were, smoothed and polished and now used to adorn our grammatical house.

II. THE PARTS OF SPEECH

Since the foregoing discussions of syntactical usage have constantly involved the seven parts of speech that enter into the make-up of the sentence (interjections are independent and expressive of emotion rather than thought), it will be sufficient, in most cases, to summarize the uses of the various kinds of words and stop with that. In a few instances, more must be said from the standpoint of the syntax of individual parts of speech; but on the whole, the sections that follow are intended to provide merely a final summing up of those categories of words that have been considered heretofore with reference to their general functions in language, their derivation, their inflectional forms, and their use in the sentence.

103. *The Noun*

The chief uses of the noun are as follows:

Subject: The *store* is closed.
Indirect and direct objects: I sold the *merchant* two *cars*
Predicate nominative: He was *president*.

Predicate objective: They chose him *secretary*.
Subject of infinitive: I saw *Sam* leave the office.
Subject of gerund: I saw *Sam* leaving the office, or, Do you approve of *Sam's* leaving the office so early? (See pages 319, 514, 531.)
Object of preposition: Step into the *office* of the *manager*.
Appositive: Thomas, the *manager*, dismissed Tom the *janitor*.
Vocative: My *friend*, what have you lost?
Nominative absolute: The *car* having burned, insurance was paid.
Adjectival modifier (genitival): The *manager's* house burned.
Adjectival modifier (uninflected): The *stone* house is mine.
Adverbial-accusative modifier: He went *home* last *Wednesday*.
Adverbial-genitive modifier: *Evenings* he would walk to town. (This may be considered a survival of a once-common adverbial genitive, since one hears also the phrasal-genitive equivalent '*Of an evening* he would walk to town.' *Unawares* is another example of the adverbial genitive.)

104. *The Pronoun*

The chief uses of the pronoun are as follows:

A. Nominative Case

Subject: *Who* arrived just now? *I* did. *No one* else?
Personal subject (implied): [*You*] Bring it to me.
Double subject: *Whoever* left the book did me a favor.
Compound subject: *He* and *I* lifted the trunk alone. (In vulgar speech, '*Him* and *me* done it', or '*Me* and *him* done it.')
Indefinite subject: *It* was I who left the book. *They* say he has made much money lately, but *you* never can tell.
Impersonal subject: *It* is raining, and *it* is turning colder.
Expletive subject: *It* is easy to misspell some words.
Appositive: We *all* tried to help. They *each* brought a box.
Emphatic appositive: I *myself* will report it, or I'll report it *myself*.
Vocative: *One* of you, please open the door.
Nominative absolute: *Some* of the men having been dismissed, the others resumed work.
Pleonastic subject: The Lord, *He* will provide.
Predicate nominative: Who was *that*? It was *I*. (The use of the accusative form, in 'It was *me*', is almost universal in colloquial English, but not yet generally approved for literary English, as

already remarked (p. 476). The nominative form is more likely to be used when a relative clause follows, as in 'It was *I* who left the book.')

B. Genitive Case

Adjectival modifier: That is *my* book.
Subject of gerund: I do not object to *his* having the farm.
Predicate nominative (absolute form): That book is *mine*.
Direct object (absolute form): He has his book, but I've lost *mine*. (It is in constructions like the last two that vulgar colloquial usage frequently employs the analogical forms *ourn, yourn, hisn, hern*, probably through the influence of *mine* and the archaic *thine*.)
Appositive: Willm Rose *His* Book. (This form of possessive modifier may be found on the flyleaf of many an old book.)

C. Objective Case

Direct object: I saw *you* yesterday. *Whom* did you see? (In colloquial English the form *who* is very generally used, largely, no doubt, because the nominative form seems more natural at the beginning of a sentence and also because no other interrogative pronoun has a separate objective form. Many careful writers avoid it, however.[416])
Reflexive direct object: He has hurt *himself*.
Reciprocal direct object: We have helped *each other* often.
Impersonal object: Go *it*! We were roughing *it* last summer.
Implied relative object: He lost the car [*that*] he had worked so hard to secure.
Indirect object: We lent *him* the copy. (But '*Whom* did you lend the copy?' is not very satisfactory to most speakers, and so the phrasal dative *to whom* is more likely to be used in this question by a speaker of good standard English. Of course the colloquial '*Who* did you lend the copy *to*' is very commonly heard. Likewise colloquial English does not favor the use of the simple dative of the indirect object before a pronominal direct object, as in 'You thought you could send *us* them', and so the dative of the phrasal type is used in preference, giving 'You thought you could send them *to us*.')
Reflexive indirect object: John bought *himself* a new hat. (In colloquial speech one frequently hears 'John got *'im* a new hat', a use of the simple pronoun which is even older than the compound

personal with *-self* but which is no longer approved in standard literary usage because it is not definite enough as to its antecedent.)

Subject of infinitive: I saw *him* leave the office.

Subject of gerund: I saw *him* leaving the office.

Predicate objective: Do you consider this *all* that you owe me?

Object of preposition: The top of *it* was in sight of *all*. Of *whom* did you buy the ticket?

Object of preposition (omitted): The man I bought your ticket of was a ticket broker. (This awkwardly composed sentence can be rendered much more effective if the pronoun *that* be inserted, giving 'The man *that* I bought your ticket of . . .'; and it can be still more improved if *whom* be used and *of* placed where it really belongs, as in 'The man of *whom* I bought your ticket was a ticket broker.')

Compound object of preposition: He bought a box for *you* and *me*. (Many people who have enough grammatical training to avoid the vulgar compound subject, as in '*Me* and *him* done it', do not have quite enough to carry them safely past this objective construction, and so they say 'for *you* and *I*', falling into another error while fleeing from the worse one.)

The most troublesome of all the pronouns, however, is the compound relative *whoever* (or *whosoever*), which serves a double purpose in the sentence, as part of the principal clause and also as part of the subordinate. In the following examples three different constructions are given:

Whoever took the book *failed* to return it.
Whoever you *saw must have gone* out again.
Whomever you *hire* you *must pay* well.

In the first sentence *whoever* is unquestionably nominative because it serves as subject of both *took* and *failed*; in the second *whoever* is considered correct because, while it is object of *saw*, it is at the same time subject of *must have gone*; but in the last sentence *whomever* is grammatically correct because it is the object of both *hire* and *pay*. However, as in the case of *whom* discussed above, general colloquial usage prefers the nominative form *whoever* in the last sentence also, mainly, no doubt, because sentences normally begin with the subject in the nominative case.

Naturally the mistakes made in the case forms of pronouns

are most troublesome because the pronouns retain more of their earlier inflectional forms than other parts of speech do. But it would be very difficult for the English-speaking people to get along without the pronominal forms because, as we have already attempted to make clear (Sec. 88), on these forms depends much of the grammatical effectiveness of modern English. Distinctions of person and of gender could not be indicated with the same facility, and mere position in the sentence would have to be depended upon even more often than it is now to show the syntactical use of a pronoun in the sentence.

105. *The Adjective*

There are three outstanding methods of utilizing an adjective in a sentence, namely, as an attributive modifier, as an appositive modifier, and as a predicate modifier. This applies mainly to descriptive adjectives, common or proper, and the three positions indicated are resorted to mainly in order to vary the amount of emphasis that the speaker or writer wishes to lay upon the adjective.

a. **Attributive Modifier.** Normally an attributive adjective is placed before the noun modified, and no special emphasis is laid on the attribute expressed, as in 'a *good* man', '*correct* spelling', 'very *bad* manners'. Adjectives of limitation generally assume this position before the nouns modified, as in '*this* chapter', '*some* people', '*more* influence'.

b. **Appositive Modifier.** Adjectives are placed just after the noun modified for two main reasons: they receive more emphasis in the postpositive position, as in 'The old father, *spare* and *gray*, stood by the gate waiting'; and when an adjective is accompanied by other words, as in 'The old father, still *hopeful* of saving his son, waited at the gate', it would be awkward to put the entire modifier in the attributive position before the noun. Sometimes slightly cumbersome phrasal modifiers are so placed, being generally tied together by hyphens, as in 'a *never-to-be-forgotten* day'. For a fuller discussion of postpositive modification see Section 100, p. 503.

c. **Predicate Modifier.** When an adjective is used in the predicate after a linking verb, as in 'The coat is *old*', or, 'It seems *empty*', the quality which the adjective expresses is predicated of the subject somewhat more positively and emphatically than if the adjective stood before the noun modified. So 'a *rude* man' assumes rudeness, but 'The man is *rude*' goes farther in that it predicates, or affirms, the rudeness of the man.

If one wishes to emphasize the rudeness of the man more yet, there are several other methods of increasing the emphasis further; the sentence can be inverted so as to throw the adjective to the very beginning, as in '*Rude* was the man and unkempt'; adverbs of degree can be employed, as in *very rude, exceedingly rude, unspeakably rude*; or a superlative form of the adjective can be employed, as in 'He is the *rudest* man I know', or, 'He was a *most rude* man.'

The last two sentences illustrate two different uses of the superlative degree of comparison. In 'the *rudest* man' the superlative indicates that a comparison has been made with other men; but in 'a *most rude* man' no comparison is indicated, even though a superlative form is used, and so it is called the absolute superlative.[419]

Two comparative adjectives are often used with the correlative adverbial *the* to emphasize more effectively the degree of intensity, as in *the more, the merrier; the darker, the better*.

106. *The Verb*

The conjugation of the English verb has always been a relatively simple one, and since the Anglo-Saxon period it has become even more so because it has dropped its person and number endings to so great an extent that it is necessary to depend almost altogether on the subject of a verb to determine its person and number. But during the same period of inflectional decline, the uses of the English verb have been increased and varied so greatly that today the syntax of the verb has become a highly complicated matter. In Old English there were comparatively few phrasal verbs; today a majority are phrasal, that is to say, made up of an auxiliary and a verbal form. In Old English a single simple form served a variety of purposes, indicating differences in aspect, tense, etc.; today the changes that can be rung on the English verb by syntactical variation are almost innumerable.

In this summary of the syntax of the Current English verb, only the most important uses of the verb will be listed. For convenience in arranging them, and in order to give some idea of the limited scope of the older, simpler verb, the uses of the simple verb will be listed first, and afterward those of the phrasal verb will be given. Before we take up these uses, however, it should be noted that

a. The auxiliary verbs regularly employed in making these phrasal verbs are *be, have, do; may, can; must, ought; shall, will*; and more rarely *dare, let, need,* and *used.*

b. The verbal forms used with these auxiliaries are the root infinitive (usually without the sign *to*) and the present and past participles.

c. A few idiomatic phrasal verbs have been developed which are not so readily analyzed into these two elements.

d. When the past-tense form of a verb is used to indicate present or future time, it may be considered subjunctive in mood. Indeed, this subjunctive use of a past-tense form to express present or future time has so completely preëmpted the auxiliaries *might, could, should,* and *would* that they are seldom used as mere past indicatives in Current English.

A. The Simple Verb

a. **Present tense:** He *teaches. Are* you cold?
b. **Past tense:** He *taught. Were* you there?
c. **Historical present:** Then he *brings* me the package and *stands* waiting. (Used in narration to make past events more vivid.)
d. **Command:** *Bring* me the book.
e. **Condition (possible):** If he *is* well again, the doctor deserves much credit. If it *meets* expectations, I will buy it. (Careful speakers use the older subjunctive form *be* in such conditions as 'If it *be* true, then he is lucky.')

f. **Condition (contrary to fact):** If I *had* his wealth, I would give liberally. (Careful speakers also use the older past subjunctive *were* in such conditions as 'If I *were* in your place, I would not wait.')

g. **Future tense:** Tomorrow we *leave* for Europe.

h. **Passive voice:** The car *cleans* easily (see Sec. 53, p. 296).

i. **Subjunctive survivals.** In a few stereotyped expressions an older subjunctive verb is retained, notably 'God *forbid*', '*Suffice* it to say', '*Perish* the thought', *Please* ('if it please you'), 'Far *be* it from me to interfere.'

B. The Phrasal Verb

a. **Future tense:** *shall* or *will* + infinitive

I *shall* go	we *shall* go
you *will* go	you *will* go
he *will* go	they *will* go

In colloquial English the form *will* is generally used in the first person also. But for a long time grammarians have endeavored to maintain the forms as tabulated above, when simple futurity is expressed. When, on the contrary, intention or determination is to be expressed, they would reverse the two auxiliaries, putting *shall* in the second and the third person and *will* in the first person. However, as Fries has discovered [423] (p. 1022), "A survey of the discussions of *shall* and *will* since the early 19th century and especially of those since 1900 reveals much conflict of opinion and *no thoroughly accepted views* concerning (*a*) the present state of the usage of these two words, (*b*) the meaning and trend of the development of that usage, (*c*) the causes which have given rise to it." There is no logical method of determining what is correct in this matter; there are fine distinctions in meaning which careful speakers, and more often careful writers, of English endeavor to indicate, and the student of the language can develop a feeling for them only by careful study and observation. Since the contractions *I'll, you'll, he'll*, etc. are generally employed in colloquial speech and do not show which verb is used, there is not much use in worrying about *will* and *shall* in colloquial English.

An idiom which also expresses futurity is made by the use of *be* + *going* + *to* + infinitive, as in 'We *are going to live* in New York next year.' This idiom, however, often expresses more than mere futurity; it expresses also intention, as in 'I *am going to report* him to the police.' [420]

Sometimes, in order to make sure that the idea of intention shall not overpower that of mere futurity, the idiom is reduced to *be* + *to* + infinitive, as in 'We *are to live* in New York next year.' But this idiom has acquired a slightly different shade of meaning from that of either of the other phrasal futures.

b. **Completion:** *have* + past participle. The so-called perfect tenses — the present perfect, *have worked*, the past perfect, *had worked*, and the future perfect, *will have worked* — really indicate completion of action rather than time of action. Indeed, the descriptive quality of the participle is often intensified by separating it from the auxiliary, as in 'I *have* my paper all *written*.'

c. **Passive voice:** *be* + past participle. It has generally been necessary to express passivity in English by a phrasal verb, as in *is painted, was being finished, will be hurt*. In such constructions the adjectival quality of the participle is often so pronounced that one ceases to feel the unity of the phrasal verb in such a sentence as 'The house *was* all *refurnished* throughout', and one thinks of the participle as descriptive rather than verbal.

d. **Progression:** *be* + present participle. The English language has gained greatly in flexibility and versatility through the development and broader use of the so-called progressive forms of the verb. Usually they give to a verb the durative aspect (see Sec. 53, p. 303), as in 'He *is walking* along the street', although the progressive verb can be given some other aspect if the context be changed somewhat [422]. Any tense in either the active or the passive voice can be put into the progressive form, as in 'He *has been running*', or 'The new floor *is being laid*.' A subjunctive construction can be made progressive, as in 'If the mill *were* still *running*'; and even an exhortation can be made progressive in colloquial English, as in '*Let's be going*.'

e. **Emphasis:** *do* + infinitive. Nowadays when *do* is used with the infinitive in a declarative sentence, as in 'He *did come* after all', or in a request, as in '*Do take off* your coat and stay a while', emphasis is intended. A few centuries ago, however, the use of *do* in the past tense with an infinitive was merely a feature of narrative style and meant no more than the simple verb would mean; so 'Then he *did praise* our musick' meant 'Then he *praised* our music.'

f. **Negation:** *do* + infinitive. In older English one could say 'He *came* not till the evening'; but today this would be almost invariably worded 'He *did* not *come* . . .' Forms of *be* and *have* are still regularly used alone in negation, as in 'He *was* not ready', and 'They *had*n't a penny left.' But to use most other verbs in this way would be considered archaic.

g. **Interrogation:** *do* + infinitive. About the same conditions are found in the asking of a question. Older English allowed such sentences as '*Saw* you my servant there?'; but Current English requires '*Did* you *see* my servant there?' Forms of *be* and *have* can be used alone, as in '*Were* you there?' '*Have* you a match?' The perfect tenses can, of course, be used without *do*, as in '*Had* you *seen* him before?', or any other phrasal verb, such as '*Am* I *dreaming*?', '*Could* you *wait*?' It is chiefly the simple verbs that cannot be employed alone in questions.

h. **Permission, possibility:** *may* + infinitive. One of the little niceties of English consists in the use of *may* (but not *can*) to express permission, as in 'You *may take* my book.' Much energy is expended in teaching children to use *may* correctly; but in spite of it all, *can* is very often used instead. When *may* is used to express possibility, as in 'It *may be* that the same man returned', there is less tendency to confuse it with any other word. Sometimes *may* is used in a conjectural way, as in 'He *may be learning* a trade.' In the Pennsylvania Dutch dialect, so called, the verb *dare* is used instead of *may* to indicate permission, as in 'You *dare take* the book if you wish.' This *dare* is also used regularly in a very colorless way in such expressions as 'I *dare say* you are right.'

When the past-tense form *might* is used, as in 'It *might be* the same man', the verb may be considered in the subjunctive mood and the possibility somewhat more remote than when *may* is used. Indeed, this subjunctive use of *might* has almost driven out the older indicative use of it with the simple infinitive; one must either say 'It *may have been* the same man', expressing the past tense by the phrasal infinitive, or else one must express the possibility by an adverb, as in '*Perhaps* it *was* the same man.'

i. Power or ability: *can* + infinitive. In 'You *can distinguish* mint by its square stem', a fact is stated in the indicative mood; in 'I suppose I *could* also *recognize* a plant of the milkweed family', the use of the past form *could* as present or future gives a less certain tone to the assertion and identifies the mood as subjunctive. Because *could* is so generally used to indicate the subjunctive mood, many speakers use as a past indicative to express power some form of *be able*, as in 'He *was able to pay* most of the bill.' To say 'He *could pay* most of the bill' would not necessarily determine the tense of the verb as past; it might point to the future.

j. Obligation: *ought* + *to* + infinitive or *should* + infinitive. 'I *ought to go* to the city tomorrow' and 'I *should go* to the city' both show the use of the past-tense form in the manner of a present-day subjunctive. But since *ought* is now thought of as exclusively a present-tense form rather than as the past tense of *owe*, which it was originally, it might well be classed as a simple indicative statement of fact. Indeed, this feeling concerning *ought* has become so strong that in dialectal and vulgar colloquial usage one sometimes hears *shouldn't ought* and *hadn't ought*, just as if *ought* could also be used as an infinitive or as a participle.

Very often, as in 'It *ought to come out* even', and 'The stage *should be* here by five o'clock', the obligation is very much diluted; it is rather probability or expectation that the speaker tries to express.

In colloquial American speech an idiomatic use of *want* expresses a mild obligation or command, as in 'You *want to go* slow or you'll get hurt.' It is less common in the third person, as in 'She *wants to take care* or she'll lose her money.'*

Since *ought* and *should* cannot be used as past-tense forms, it is necessary to use after them a perfect infinitive to indicate past time, as in 'He *ought to have attended* to the matter', or 'He *should have gone* last week.'

k. Necessity: *must* + infinitive. Like the auxiliary just considered, *must* can be used to indicate present time, as in 'It *must be* true', or it can be used with a perfect infinitive for past time, as in 'He *must have gone* while we were away.'

An idiomatic use of *have* (or *had*) + *to* + infinitive is a common substitute in colloquial English for the phrase with *must*; one can say, 'I *have to hurry* for my train', 'They *had to go* at six o'clock', and it is even possible to make a future with this idiom, as in 'We *have to leave* soon.' The limitations of *must* have gradually driven speakers to use this idiom.

Another colloquial idiom expressing necessity is made with *have got* + *to* + infinitive, as in 'We *have got to leave* promptly at seven', 'It's *got to be done* soon.' This idiom suddenly emerged into the limelight of newspaper publicity when President Franklin Roosevelt, in conference with the prime minister of England, remarked concerning the need of helping the world back to prosperity, "Mr. MacDonald, it is more than hope. We have got to do it", and Mr. MacDonald replied, "Yes, that good old Scotch word *got*. I will go along with you. We have got to do it."

Since there are nowadays no past-tense forms of *ought* and *must* to use in subjunctive constructions, speakers are forced to resort to some idiom or equivalent phrase to express subjunctive mood. So one has to say, 'If you *had to work* for a living, what would you do?' and 'If you *were under obligation* to remain, you would be informed.' It is awkward, sometimes, to eke out the very slender resources of such very deficient verbs as *ought* and *must*.

l. Customary action: *would* + infinitive. In such a sentence as 'Every morning the old man *would trudge* down to the store for his mail', the idea of intention in *would* has been so weak-

*See *American Speech*, Vol. 7 (1931), p. 450.

ened that the phrasal verb has come to signify merely customary action in the past tense. This same iterative aspect of the verb (see Sec. 53, p. 304) could be expressed by the simple verb *trudged*, but the effect would not be quite the same.

Customary action is also expressed by *used to* (pronounced [justə]), as in 'He *used to trudge* down to the store every morning'; but the iterative aspect of the verb is, perhaps, not quite so marked as in the other two constructions.

m. **Conditions**: simple verb or phrasal verb; indicative or subjunctive. Conditional propositions are of several kinds:

(1) Possible, in the future: 'If the story *proves* true, the town *will be* greatly astonished.' Sometimes the older subjunctive is used, as in 'If it *be* true . . .', 'If it *prove* true . . .'. But few speakers bother with the subjunctive nowadays.

(2) Possible, but somewhat less probable, in the future: 'If the story *should prove* true, the town *would be* greatly astonished.' In this sentence the phrasal subjunctive of the verb replaces the simple indicative or subjunctive of the preceding condition. If, instead of *should,* one of the other auxiliaries *could, might,* or *would* should be used in making one of these less vivid conditions, the possibility would then be with reference to power, permission, or willingness.

(3) Contrary to fact: 'If I *had* your talent, I *would turn* it to some useful purpose'; 'If I *were* you, I *would work* more'; 'If it *hadn't snowed* yesterday, they *would have returned* home'; ' *Had* I *seen* the man, I *would have reported* him to the police.'

Careful speakers still cling to the subjunctive form *were* in constructing conditions contrary to fact; in all of them a past or past perfect form of the verb must be used. It is important to adhere to this rule, since there is no distinguishing subjunctive inflectional form (except *were*, perhaps) in present-day English.

(4) Simple conditions of present and past time: 'If the report *is* true, the city *is* in bad condition'; 'If he *was* there, I *did* not *see* him.' There are, of course, various ways of making conditional statements without indicating futurity or implying doubt as to whether something is or has been true; the speaker or writer simply assumes a possibility and offers his conclusion, as in the two sentences just given. These may be termed simple conditions because they do not attempt to look into the future and they do not assume that the conditional clause is contrary to fact.

n. **Wishes.** Wishes are often expressed by using the conditional part of a conditional sentence as an exclamatory clause, as in 'If only the story *should prove* true!' (possible wish), or 'If only the story *had been* true!' (impossible wish).

Wishes can also be expressed by the use of a substantive *that* clause, some governing principal clause such as *I wish* or *I would* being vaguely understood, as in 'O that Ishmael *might live* before thee!' or 'O that we two *were* a-Maying!' This form of elliptical wish is generally regarded as archaic.

o. **Contingent propositions.** Similarly some propositions are given a slightly contingent tone by using the other part of a conditional sentence, as in 'I *should like* to see your library', 'It *would have been* a pity to miss it.' Sometimes the implied conditional clause could easily be supplied, as in 'I *should like* to see your library, if I might do so'; but more often it is probable that the speaker has very little thought of any condition when he uses the form of contingency. When Shelley wrote, "I *could lie* down like a tired child and *weep* away the life of care", one might argue that the contingency lay in some such mental reservation as 'If I were to allow myself'; but it would be grammatical pedantry to insist that all contingent propositions should be thus completed.

p. **Exhortations:** *let us (let's)* + infinitive. In formal literary English, and sometimes in deliberate colloquial usage, the uncontracted form is used, as in '*Let us see* what we can do about it'; but more often the informal contraction *let's* is employed, as in '*Let's stop* for the day.' This phrasal verb has almost completely superseded the earlier simple subjunctive of exhortation, which was used in Shakespeare's day in such sentences as '*Do* we all holy rites.'

It is, of course, possible to make various combinations of these phrasal verbs so as to give almost infinite variety in English verbal expression; one can express, for example,

    Futurity + completion + progression: *will have been working.*
    Possibility + completion + passivity: *may have been hurt.*
    Condition + power + completion: if he *could have stopped.*
    Condition + futurity + passivity: if he *were to be hurt.*

Sometimes grammarians have set up a special mood for verbs composed with *may, can, might, could, would,* and *should* and have named this the potential mood; but this is both unnecessary and illogical. With *may* and *can* the permission or power is asserted as a fact; hence the verb is indicative. With the other auxiliary forms, which are all past-tense forms, the permission, power, willingness, etc. are merely conceived of or contingent; hence the verb is subjunctive. The potentiality expressed by such verbs is inherent in their meanings and not due to the manner (or mood) of making the assertion.

At the beginning of this study of the syntax of the English verb, the assertion was made that a verb is usually subjunctive in mood when present or future meaning is given to a past-tense form. Most of the examples of verb usage will have borne out this contention; but when in indirect discourse or other subordinate clause the past tense is required to maintain the proper sequence of tenses, one cannot be certain always that the verb is subjunctive. Usually it is; but occasionally it is an original unchanged indicative, as in 'He remarked that he *was* in Chicago yesterday.' Distinction in mood is no longer as clear-cut as it was in an earlier day when conjugational endings were more numerous.

107. *The Verbals*

Since the four verbals play a very important part in the syntax of Current English, a brief summary of their functions will help to emphasize their importance.

A. ROOT INFINITIVE (WITH OR WITHOUT *TO*)

Subject and predicate nominative: *To see* is *to believe.*
Direct object (with subject accusative): We wanted *him to go.* I heard *him sing.* I watched *him leave.*
Direct object (alone): He wanted *to leave.* (Many verbs such as *ask, beg, desire, hope, plan, seek,* and *wish* take the infinitive in this construction. A few which are sometimes used as auxiliaries,

notably *dare, need, will,* may also be followed by *to* + infinitive, as in *dares to go, needs to buy, wills to live.*)

In phrasal verbs: One might *fail.* (The infinitive without *to* is used regularly after the auxiliaries *shall, will, do, may, can, must,* the idiomatic *let's,* and sometimes after *dare, durstn't, needn't*; but it is used with *to* after *ought* and in such idiomatic locutions as *is to stay, am going to leave, have to wait, have got to go, used to come.*)

After adjectives: He was *afraid to start.* It was not *fit to be seen.* (Various adjectives can be followed by *to* + infinitive, such as *anxious, apt, ashamed, eager, glad, hard, liable, prone, ready, slow, sorry, sure, unable, wont.*)

Adjectival modifier: Money *to lend* is scarce.

Adverbial modifier: They came *to stay* a week.

B. Gerund (or Verbal Noun in *-ing*)

The gerund is the only verbal form not used in making phrasal verbs; it is easily confused with the present active participle, in *-ing,* as can be seen from a comparison of the gerund in *dancing-teacher* ('teacher of dancing') with the participle in *dancing teacher* ('teacher who dances'). The gerund is frequently used as a substitute for the root infinitive; but after some verbs it cannot take the place of the root infinitive, and after some others it can be employed when the root infinitive cannot. This variable use of these two substantive forms of the verb makes English syntax particularly difficult for foreigners.

Subject and predicate nominative: *Seeing* is *believing.*

Direct object (with subject accusative): I saw *them leaving* the store. (Cf. 'I saw *them leave* the store.')

Direct object (with genitival subject): He praised *our singing.*

Direct object (alone): The boat needs *cleaning.* She taught *singing* and *dancing.* He delayed *starting.* (A study of the verbs that govern root-infinitive objects or gerund objects or both would reveal many curious inconsistencies and variations in English practice. If *cleaning,* in the first sentence, were changed to a root infinitive, the passive form would be required, as in 'The boat needs *to be cleaned*'; after *taught* the root infinitive cannot be used alone as object; and likewise after *delayed* the gerund is considered preferable, although one can say 'He *hesitated to start.*' While speakers prefer the root infinitive with *to* after *agree, ask, care, desire, expect, hope,* etc., they prefer the gerund after *avoid, endure, help* ('avoid'), *postpone, stop, tolerate,* etc. Why these distinctions are made it would be difficult to say, sometimes (see Kruisinga's *Handbook* [19], Pt. II, Vol. I, p. 251).

Object of preposition: He is accustomed *to* your *singing.* They were afraid *of losing* their places. He stopped the raid *by closing* the gates.

Object of an omitted preposition: You helped me greatly, [*by*] *holding* back the mob as you did. There's no use [*in*] *wasting* time. (It is also possible to construe *holding* as a participle.)

C. Present Participle

Attributive modifier: *Running* water filled the streets.
Postpositive modifier: Water, *running* across the roads everywhere, hindered our progress.
In phrasal verbs of progression: He *is failing.* (Sometimes the adjectival force of the participle after a form of *be* is so marked that one might well call it a predicate adjective.)
With nominative absolute: School *being* over at last, they ran to play. (The participle is often omitted in a sentence of this sort.)

The confusion of gerund and present participle has been discussed in an earlier attempt to clarify the problem of the classification of *-ing* words (Sec. 58, p. 319), and syntactical considerations necessarily entered into the discussion. But the syntax of these two verbals is more complex than our previous discussion would indicate, and it presents difficulties for all users of English, whereas only the grammatical theorist is seriously concerned about the careful classification of such forms. It has been suggested that much of the confusion of gerund and present participle can be ascribed to the fact that both have become more strongly verbal since the Anglo-Saxon period, and to the resulting uncertainty as to how the subjects of such verbals should be expressed. There is a tendency among certain grammarians to require a genitival subject when no awkwardness would result, as in 'They disapproved of the *king's riding* such dangerous horses', and to permit an accusative subject when awkwardness would result, as in 'What do you think about the *ruler* of a great land *riding* his own horse in a race?' And those speakers and writers who are careful in such matters usually endeavor to follow this rule, using the genitival subject with the gerund when they can do so without awkwardness, but employing the accusative subject when the construction is more elaborate and cumbersome; so they would say, 'I marvel at *his drawing such pictures*', but they would recognize the necessity which compelled a grammarian to write recently, "Special pleading of this kind can result only in people fighting shy of 'scientific' grammar." Generally speaking, the subject of the gerund is more often put into the genitive (possessive) case when it is a pronoun, and less often when it is a noun.

It will have been remarked, perhaps, that in the four examples of gerundial constructions used in this present discussion the gerund is the object of a preposition, whereas most of the gerunds previously discussed in Section 58 were employed as the direct objects of verbs. It would seem reasonable to assume, however, that if the gerund is sometimes used with a subject accusative when it is the object of a preposition, as in two of the sentences given above, it is likewise used with subject accusative after a verb, in such a sentence as 'I saw the *king riding* toward the palace.' Such an assumption would seem to disprove the argument of various grammarians (see page 320) that in such a sentence *king* is merely object of the verb *saw* and *riding* a participle modifying *king*. If one is accepted as gerundial with subject accusative, the other would seem to be gerundial also.

It is not easy to make satisfactory generalizations concerning the use of these verbals in *-ing*; the speaker will vary his constructions somewhat, according to the force or shade of meaning that he desires to produce. On the whole, it may be said that

1. When a gerund is strongly felt to be a noun, a genitival subject (also called a modifier) is likely to be used.

2. When a gerund is felt to be strongly verbal, an accusative subject is more likely to be employed, but

3. In a complicated or extended gerundial construction, the accusative subject will of necessity be used.

When a gerund is made from a transitive verb and is therefore capable of taking an object, this direct object can be expressed in two different ways:

When the gerund is preceded by a modifying article (*a, the*) or some other adjectival modifier, the object of the gerund assumes the form of a phrasal genitive, as in *a lessening of the danger* or *the burning of our forests*, whereas

An ordinary accusative object follows the gerund when no such modifier precedes it, as in *for lessening the danger* or *danger of burning our forests*.

When an *-ing* verbal is capable of taking either a genitival or an accusative subject, and when it may have either an accusative or a phrasal genitive as its object, there can be no doubt that it is a verbal noun, that is to say, a gerund. For if it were an *-ing* participle, it could not be used with a preceding genitive, nor with a preceding article or other adjective.

D. Past Participle

Attributive modifier: *Sawed* wood is more expensive.
Anticipatory modifier: *Having sawed* the wood, he left.
Postpositive modifier: Wood *sawed* in short lengths is best.
In phrasal verbs: to indicate completion, as in 'He *has left*'; to show passive voice, as in 'This box *was left* behind.' (It is often difficult to decide whether the past participle used after forms of *be* is more strongly verbal or more strongly adjectival. In 'The man *was unbalanced*', for example, the adjective *crazy* could easily be substituted.)
With nominative absolute: Winter *having come*, the birds left.

The English verbals are capable of assuming certain phrasal forms, just as the finite verbs themselves are. Completion is indicated by the use of *have*, in the perfect infinitive, as in *to have gone*, and in the perfect participle, as in *having gone*; passivity is indicated by the use of *be*, in the passive infinitive, as in *to be finished*, in the present passive participle, as in *being finished*, and in the perfect passive participle, as in *having been finished*.

The gerund may be used in the same phrasal constructions as the present participle.

108. *The Adverb*

The chief syntactical classes of adverbs are as follows:

a. **Simple modifiers.** Most adverbs can modify verbs to indicate place (*came back*), time (*came early*), manner (*came slowly*), etc. But only a limited number, namely, those of degree and measure. regularly modify adjectives and other adverbs. When others, such as *terribly, awfully, horribly*, do modify adjectives, as in *awfully slow*, they undergo some change in meaning, generally. There are a few adverbs of degree that careful writers do not like to use as direct modifiers of verbs and verbals, notably *very* and *too*; they would say '*very greatly* disappointed' rather than '*very* disappointed'; '*too much* disappointed' rather than '*too* disappointed'. For a fuller discussion of the positions of adverbs see Section 100 (p. 504).

The use of double negatives is still very common in colloquial Current English, although the practice is no longer tolerated in standard literary usage. This doubling occurs when the speaker uses a verbal negative contraction, such as *can't, won't*, or *ain't*, or the negative adverb *not* or *never*, and then intensifies his negation by the additional use of the negative pronouns *none, no one*, or *nothing*, the adjective *no*, the negative connective *but*, or an adverb like *hardly, only, scarcely*. Examples of this double negation are

> He *never* said *nothing*.
> I *don't* doubt *but* he did it, and I *couldn't* help *but* smile.
> He *couldn't scarcely* walk. She *hadn't only* five cents.

b. **Relative adverbs.** Any adverb that can be used to introduce a subordinate clause, such as 'He came *when* we called', belongs to this category. Some of the most commonly used are *although, as, because, before, since, unless, where, while, why* (see Sec. 56, p. 310).

c. **Interrogative adverbs.** The adverbs used commonly in asking questions are *how, when, whence, where, whither*, and *why*, as in '*Whither* did he go?', '*Where* was he?'

d. **Modal adverbs (of assertion).** These adverbs are not used as simple modifiers of verbs or adjectives or other adverbs; but they modify the entire assertion in a very general manner, as already indicated (Sec. 54, p. 306). They are such words as *certainly, doubtless, possibly, really, surely,* and *undoubtedly,* as in 'He has *certainly* lost ground.' The objectionable dialectal use of *sure* (instead of *surely*) in sentences of assertion has already been commented upon.

e. **Introductory adverbs.** Such adverbs as *accordingly, furthermore, however, moreover,* which can be employed as illative conjunctions, helping to carry on the thought from one sentence to the next, have likewise been presented already (Sec. 56, p. 311).

f. **Substitutes for pronouns.** By a peculiar idiomatic compounding of *there, where,* and *here* with such prepositions as *at, by, in, of, on,* substitutes are produced which can be used instead of the phrases composed of these prepositions and such pronouns as *it, which* and *whom,* and *this.* So the English speaker can say 'He spoke *thereof*' instead of 'He spoke *of it*'; 'The box *whereon* it lay' instead of 'The box *on which* it lay'; 'I *hereby* notify you' instead of 'I notify you *by this.*' These are felt to be rather formal and are not heard so generally in colloquial English now as at one time. On the other hand, it is regarded as vulgar usage to introduce a question with *where* and end it with *at,* as in '*Where* are you staying *at*?'

g. **Objects of prepositions.** Adverbs of time and place, particularly, are often used as objects of prepositions. Examples are *before long, by now, from there, in here, of late, until lately, until then.* In *from whence* the preposition is redundant because *whence* means 'from where'.

109. *The Preposition*

Inasmuch as the preposition has but one normal function in English, namely, to show relationship between its object and some other word in the sentence, the chief difficulties involved in the use of prepositions are those of selection and of position in the sentence. Insofar as prepositional phrases have become the accepted substitutes for earlier inflectional forms, there is little trouble; the *of* phrase is, of course, genitival; the indirect object is commonly indicated by *to* or *for*; the adverbial relations of time and place are indicated by phrases with *at* or *in,* chiefly; and so on.

It is not always easy to decide whether one has a preposition with its object, as in 'talk *to a customer'*, or a verb-adverb combination followed by a direct object, as in '*talk up* his wares'. But after the verb-adverb combinations have been carefully segregated (see Sec. 53, p. 297), there remain still numerous words (verbs, participles, adjectives, nouns) in Modern English which puzzle many speakers and writers because they must always be followed by certain special prepositions; or others that can change their meanings so as to require several different prepositions accordingly. A few of these words are of native Anglo-Saxon origin, but for the most part they are French or Latin in origin. Sometimes the peculiar meaning of the governing word shows which preposition is needed, but often there is little to aid in the choice except an understanding of the idiosyncrasies of the English language. (For the significance of the daggers in the following lists see page 537.)

a. **Prepositions used after verbs**

abound *in* or *with*
accede *to*
† accommodate *to* or *with*
† accord *in, to,* or *with*
acquiesce *in*
† admit *into, of,* or *to*
† agree *in, on, to, with,* etc.
burden *with*
† compare *to* or *with*
† confide *in* or *to*
† connive *at* or *with*
† consist *in* or *of*
contrast *with*
† convert *into, from,* or *to*
crave *for*

detract *from*
† differ *from, in, on,* or *with*
endow *with*
† guard *against* or *from*
hanker *after* or *for*
hint *at*
† laugh *at, over, about,* etc.
object *to*
† part *from* or *with*
reason *with*
† reckon *on* or *with*
revel *in*
tamper *with*
† treat *of* or *with*
trust *in, to,* or *with*

b. Prepositions used after adjectives or participles

addicted *to*
adept *in*
† apprehensive *for* or *of*
† averse *from* or *to*
capable *of*
characteristic *of*
† concerned *about*, *in*, or *with*
conducive *to*
devoid *of*
different *from* (Brit. also *than*, *to*, *from*)
empty *of*
envious *of*
fearful *of*
foreign *to*
fraught *with*

† good *at* or *for*
† grounded *in* or *upon*
heedless *of*
identical *with*
† liable *for* or *to*
negligent *of*
† overrun *by* or *with*
preparatory *to*
prior *to*
proficient *in*
† responsible *for* or *to*
unconscious *of*
worthy *of*
zealous *in* or *for*

c. Prepositions used after nouns

abhorrence *of*
adept *in* (not *at*)
† analogy *to* or *with*
attitude *toward*
confidence *in*
craving *for*
danger *of*
† difference *between* or *in*
† disparity *between* or *in*
distaste *for*
favor *of*

hatred *of*
† inclination *for* or *to*
interest *in*
laugh *at* or *over*
mania *for*
necessity *of* or *for*
† need *of* or *for*
† resemblance *between* or *to*
substitute *for*
variance *with*
view *of*

The words that have been marked with daggers often vary in meaning according to the accompanying preposition; the prepositions, on the other hand, are sometimes varied according to whether they are used after verb, adjective, or noun. Moreover, speakers of English sometimes differ among themselves in their choice of prepositions for the same construction. One of the most noticeable examples of this is the verb *differ*, with its adjective *different* and its noun *difference*; a person can *differ from* another in physique, he can *differ with* another on some matter of opinion, they can *differ* little *in* their views, or they can *differ on* certain questions. As regards the adjective, American usage is often *different from* British, and the British is *different to* (or *than, from*) the American practice. But in the case of the noun, there is no *difference in* use, nor is there any *difference between* British and American usage in this last respect.

When the governing word varies in its speech function, the preposition is sometimes varied; so one can use the verb to *laugh at* something, but with the noun have a great *laugh over* (or *at*) it; one may be *capable of* doing something, but have *capacity for* it; one can *fear for* his life, but be *fearful of* something or in *fear of* it.

The selection of the correct preposition in constructions of this kind involves many of the little niceties of speech which the speaker and writer of good English must take up, one by one, as they arise. The dictionaries do not give as much assistance in this matter as could be desired,* and so it is necessary to consult special guides, such as Krapp's[17], Fowler's[16], Weseen's[337], and Vizetelly's[427]. The choice of a preposition under these circumstances is not a matter of syntax merely; it is influenced by the meaning of the governing word and is also a matter of taste belonging to the art of expression.

d. **Postpositive and postponed prepositions.** The occasional postpositive use of a preposition after its object, as in *the world over* and *the whole day through*, is an old phase of standard-English usage employed to give emphasis to the preposition, as already explained (Sec. 100, p. 508). The postponement of a preposition to the end of a question or a subordinate relative clause is not so easily disposed of. More than a thousand years ago the English were saying 'the army that we spoke *about*', and this postponement of the preposition has been a feature of our speech ever since. The reason for its postponement has already been suggested (Sec. 100, p. 507), and the chief objection to its use stated. But the convenience of using it and its long-continued popularity in English must be recognized. In colloquial usage there can be little question

* The most helpful dictionaries in this connection are the New English Dictionary (Oxford English Dictionary) and the Century Dictionary and Cyclopedia.

as to its propriety, provided, of course, the use and meaning stand out clearly; in more careful, formal literary usage it may well be avoided, as a general rule.

e. **Wrong or superfluous prepositions.** In 'Where is he *at*?' the preposition is superfluous. In 'Where did it come *from*?' an adverb, *where*, is used as the object of a preposition, *from*, a use of an interrogative adverb not in keeping with the normal practice of literary English. In '*From whence* did he come?' both objections may be urged; *from* is superfluous with *whence* and also is not ordinarily used with an interrogative adverb as its object. Since *between* is ordinarily used of only two persons or objects, *among* should be used for more than two. A German-American use of *by* instead of *with* or *at* is sometimes heard in such sentences as 'He lives *by* his uncle' and 'She lives *by* Chicago.' To express 'place whither' the preposition *in* is sometimes incorrectly substituted for *into*, as in 'He went *in* the house.' Likewise *through* is occasionally heard where *throughout* would be better. To say 'I got the book *off of* the desk' is unnecessary, and to say 'I bought it *off* a peddler' instead of *from* is even worse.

In spite of the fact that *but* was generally a preposition in early English, today grammarians are inclined to consider it a conjunction in certain controversial constructions and consequently to recommend 'There was no one ready *but* I', rather than 'no one ready *but* me', basing their recommendation on the assumption that the sentence is elliptical and that *was ready* is implied after *I*. They would, therefore, prefer *except* or *save* as the preposition. Some few grammarians, however, argue that *but* in such constructions is equivalent to the preposition *except* and should therefore be followed by an objective, *me*. The uncertainty and confusion with regard to this construction is increased, no doubt, by the fact that when a noun is used after *but*, as in 'There was no one ready *but* the leader', it is impossible to determine the case of the noun, and that when an objective construction is used just before the *but*, an objective must follow it, as in 'They had no friend *but* me'. (See Fowler[16], Krapp[17], Weseen[337], Curme[399], and others.)

110. *The Conjunction*

The chief uses of the conjunction are as follows:

a. **As coördinating conjunctions, to connect**

Words: Wind *and* rain drive *both* man *and* beast within.
Phrases: He stood in the room *but* near the door.
Clauses: He did not see the gate *or* he could not stop in time.

b. **As subordinating conjunctions, introducing:** (1) *Noun clauses.* Noun clauses are introduced by the conjunctions *that, whether,* literary *lest,* and colloquial *if,* as in 'We saw *that* he was hurt'; by the interrogative pronouns, *who, which, what,* and the interrogative adjectives, *which, what,* in indirect questions, such as 'He asked *who* it was'; and by the interrogative adverbs *how, when, whence, where, whither, why,* etc., in indirect questions, such as 'He asked *why* they had not come.'

(2) *Adjectival clauses.* These are introduced by the relative pronouns* *who, which, that,* as in 'The house *that* Jack built'; by the relative adverbs* *when, where, while, why,* etc., as in 'The day *when* he left', 'The spot *where* the church now stands'; and by those peculiar adverbial substitutes for prepositional relative phrases compounded with *where,* such as 'The man *whereof* he spoke', 'The rock *whereon* it lay.'

(3) *Adverbial clauses.* Subordinate clauses expressing cause, purpose, condition, result, time, concession, place and direction, manner, and degree and extent, are introduced by such conjunctions as *although, as far as, as if, as much as, because, if, lest, so that, than, where,* and *while,* in sentences like 'He wrote *when* he could', 'It fell *where* he dropped it.'

c. **As correlative conjunctions.** A closer correlation between the two connected parts is effected by pairing certain conjunctions with certain pronouns or adjectives or adverbs. In the coördinating correlatives the conjunction is always anticipated by the other member of the pair, as in *both . . . and, either . . . or, neither . . . nor, not merely . . . but also, not only . . . but even;* in some subordinating correlatives the

---

* The fact that relatives are both connective and pronominal or adverbial has been emphasized in an earlier discussion of hybrid parts of speech (p. 323).

conjunction is also anticipated by its correlative word (for example, *as ... as, so ... as, so ... that, such ... as, such ... that*), as in '*as* far *as* he could throw', '*so* sick *that* he nearly died,' '*such* labor *as* he could hire'; but in other subordinating correlatives which are employed only when the subordinate clause is placed first in the sentence, the second word of the pair is added later in the sentence to intensify the effect produced by the adverbial clause just used. The most common of these pairs are *although ... nevertheless, although ... still, although ... yet, if ... then, though ... nevertheless, when ... then, where ... there, whether ... or.* Quite different from these correlative conjunctions is the use of two comparative adjectives or adverbs modified by the adverbial *the ... the*, as in '*The older* it grows, *the more beautiful* it becomes', and '*The more rapidly* you work, *the more carelessly* you proceed.' These various correlatives are a great help in giving balance and coherence to long sentences, when they are properly utilized.

For some reason not readily discernible, certain stylists have adopted the curious practice of using *as ... as* only in affirmative constructions, such as 'He did *as* well *as* could be expected', changing to *so ... as* in negative constructions, such as 'He did not do *so* well *as* could be expected.' This applies also to elliptical sentences in which the second verb is implied or wanting, as in 'Your sentence is *as* good *as* mine' and 'Your sentence is not *so* long *as* mine.' Most speakers and writers tend, however, to use *as ... as* in all these constructions.

d. **As illative conjunctions.** Adverbs used to introduce sentences and at the same time to bind them somewhat loosely together into the larger rhetorical units of discourse have already been discussed (Sec. 56, p. 311). They serve much the same general purpose as the correlative conjunctions, just considered; but while the correlatives connect parts of a sentence, the illatives connect complete sentences which are grammatically separate.* With the correlatives one may say, for example, '*Although* he had many relatives, *still* he lived a lonely

---

* Pseudosentences of the punctuational variety have already been discussed (p. 472), but it should be emphasized that in such sentences the two parts are grammatically separate, in spite of the use of illative and semicolon (or comma).

life'; with the illative construction the sentence would read 'He had many relatives; *nevertheless* he lived a lonely life.'

e. As either conjunctions or prepositions. As already observed, the prepositions *but* (colloquial) and *for* are also used as coördinating conjunctions, and the other prepositions *after, as far as, before, ere, since,* and *until* can easily be converted into subordinating conjunctions (see Sec. 58, p. 321). The use of the prepositions *like, except,* and *without* as conjunctions in such sentences as 'He walks *like* his father does' is still considered objectionable by the more careful speakers of English. But in the case of *like* it is very easy to fall into a trap by intending to stop with a prepositional object only (*father*, above) and then deciding to go farther and add the verb (as above).

Syntax and meaning go hand in hand. Often syntactical usage illuminates the meaning of a word or phrase; but not infrequently the more complicated meaning of a word offers a syntactical shortcut or even obviates altogether the necessity for a syntactical construction. On the one hand, the word *cut* tells little of itself; but in 'I *cut* last time' or 'a poor *cut*' it is possible to determine somewhat more fully what *cut* means because syntactical aids are given. On the other hand, in *capitulated, foreclosure,* or *matriculation* so much is suggested that by the use of these words numerous word combinations can be avoided, such as *gave up the fort* or *surrendered on certain terms, final seizure of a mortgaged estate,* and *enrollment as a member of a college.* It is well to insist again here that the parts of speech are best distinguishable on the basis of function; the modification of substantives, for example, is adjectival, that of verbs is adverbial. But the recognition of these functions depends sometimes on form, as in *golden, rapidly,* sometimes on syntactical use, as in '*cut* hand', 'drive *fast*', and sometimes on meaning inherent in the word itself, as in *moreover, rude,* and *wrangle.*

Throughout the foregoing discussions of English syntax, an effort has been made to mark out the generally accepted pattern of English grammatical usage. This pattern has been gradually changed during the past thousand years; but it is today more clearly defined in the minds of all intelligent speakers of English than it has ever been before, and it receives such general recognition today that one can reasonably assume that the logic of English grammar is dependent upon that pattern.

There are at the present moment three possible attitudes to take toward questions of grammatical usage: there are still many dogmatic grammarians who base their decisions on a dogma of grammar which has been developed from the usages of Latin and from other foreign grammatical practices; there are other modern grammarians who go quite to the other extreme in accepting common colloquial usages merely because many people favor them; but if the generally accepted principles of Modern English syntax mean anything at all, then there is a third attitude which should be taken by all thoughtful speakers of English, namely, that of the reasonable or rational grammarian. He understands that the grammar of Current English involves a minimum of inflectional grammar which cannot be reduced much more without a decided shift in the whole plan and theory of our grammatical usage; that it recognizes the importance of normal and abnormal order in the arrangement of words in sentences as a means of lending emphasis to ideas and thoughts; and that it recognizes values in words and phrases as they play their parts in the make-up of the sentence. If forms are lost, obviously something else must take their place; if word order is not stressed, then the effectiveness of the sentence will be lessened; and if words and phrases are used in a slovenly and irresponsible manner, then they cannot be trusted to perform their individual functions. If, in other words, the speakers and writers of the language do not cling to some kind of pattern in grammatical usage, such confusion will arise that no one will be sure just what a speaker or a writer is trying to say. The dogmatic grammarian bases his doctrines on an untenable past; but the modern adherent of the doctrine of *laissez faire* pins his faith too tightly to the practice of an ungrammatical and unthinking and changeable present.

CHAPTER XIII

SEMASIOLOGICAL CHANGE

SEMASIOLOGY is variously defined as "the science of meanings", "the significance of words and the development of their meanings", and "the science or study of growth and change in the meanings of words". It is with the changes in meanings that this chapter is concerned, and chiefly with the cumulative results of semasiological change as they can be summarized and observed in the vocabulary of Current English, rather than with the causes of this change.

Various changes in the meanings of words have been observed, as they enter into the conversion of the different parts of speech, particularly in the substantivation of adjectives and the commonization of proper names; as they have accompanied the derivative processes of the language and sometimes increased the number of words (see Sec. 68); as they have resulted in the numerous doublets and triplets of Modern English (see Sec. 81); as they have been produced frequently by the inflectional modifications of words; and, finally, as they are constantly arising from syntactical variations within the sentence. Nowhere in these studies of the classification of words has it been possible to ignore the semasiological changes that take place and have been taking place in the language from its very beginnings.

But after all it must be borne in mind that these formal changes are but the shoals and channels and sand bars produced in that great stream of English speech by the current of English thinking as it has gone steadily on down through the centuries, broadening and deepening and increasing its sweep from year to year. While these limitations of English grammatical form — classificational, derivational, inflectional, and syntactical — do have some temporary restraining effect on the current of English thinking, undoubtedly, in the long run it is necessary to seek for broader, more general trends in semasiological change if we are to appreciate the tremendous sweep of English life and culture as it is reflected in the infinite variety of our present-day vocabulary.

The enormous extent of the English vocabulary has been duly stressed in Chapter X, and to some extent an effort has been made to analyze it. But a much more detailed analysis would be required to make even reasonably clear its infinite variety and its abounding richness — its words for everyday things and activities, its highly poetical and dignified terms for use on formal occasions, its vague and noncommittal words for hasty speech [440], and its clear and incisive words for careful scientific use, — words that are often too technical for the man on the street, and other words that are too beautifully colored for mere everyday use. [443]

The histories of many words in the language taken one by one would repay the student richly for more careful study; and while such study would, for the most part, take the form of a series of little archæological researches into the past histories of individual ideas, yet the cumulative results of the study of a great number of individual English words would throw much light on the causes of change in meaning — on the backgrounds of English words.*

It would be interesting to attempt to classify the general causes of semasiological change. Some such general causes have been suggested here and there in the foregoing discussions: the effects of ignorance and carelessness in the transmission of meanings have been observed in the study of popular etymologizing; the weakening effects of exaggeration or hyperbole have been noted also; the results of shifting from inflectional forms to syntactical usage have manifested themselves frequently in the chapters just completed; and all through the discussions of English words the thoughtful historian of the language cannot fail to have remarked the

---

* In order that students especially interested in the study of meanings may have the benefit of this semasiological method, various special word studies will be referred to throughout this chapter.

many changes of meaning that have accompanied the gradual raising of the intellectual and spiritual levels of English life and culture.

It would also be most interesting to attempt to measure the number and range of meanings of which the great English vocabulary is capable. When the lexicographer has estimated the vocabulary as numbering a half-million or more distinct words, he has told only a part of the story; for attention has been called repeatedly to the fact that many individual words are capable of expressing a variety of meanings. Such words as *block, crown, draw, fast, get, hold, lead, order, power, raise, see, stick, stiff, stroke,* and *take* are credited in the dictionary with at least a dozen meanings each; some of the verb-adverb combinations, like *make up,* run to fourteen or more separate meanings; and in the process of conversion word forms multiply in meanings most surprisingly. This multiplication of meanings in words is not unlike what happens when potatoes are planted: in every hill at the end of a successful growing season the philological fork will turn up a cluster of meanings where the original planting had but one or two. Of course not every word multiplies meanings; in the studies of this chapter numerous examples will also be found of segregation and isolation of individual meanings. But on the whole, the multiplication of meanings has been fully as important as the multiplication of verb-adverb combinations (Sec. 53), of derivational forms like those of *bear* and *cedo* (Sec. 61), and of phrasal verbs (Sec. 106). All four methods of expansion have been important for the development of Modern English; but today the most active, undoubtedly, is that of semasiological multiplication.

However, such broad and sympathetic appraisal of the vocabulary of Current English as we have suggested is for the sensitive literary artist rather more than for the scientific grammarian and must be excluded largely from the following discussion. And the narrower, more detailed study of words taken one at a time is a form of semasiological research which must be excluded for lack of space. Moreover, any thoroughgoing attempt to discover the causes of semasiological change would demand a more intensive and detailed examination of the history of English meanings than our space will permit. Hence it is necessary to limit our consideration of semasiological change in this chapter to a summarizing of certain general results already produced or being produced now in the use of English words.

111. *Figurative Change*

There is, however, one cause of semasiological change so constantly present all down through the centuries and so clearly active that it must be considered before any attempt be made to summarize the effects of semasiological change. This is the figurative use of words. Figurative usage may be defined, for the purposes of this discussion, as the employment of words with meanings different from those properly or ordinarily assigned to them.

The metaphorical substitution of a special word in place of a common one in order to emphasize some one aspect of the idea to be expressed has long been practiced by English speakers, giving some well-established standard locutions as well as much slang. Many words pertaining to the animal world are used in this figurative way, such as '*bark up* the wrong tree', *bovine, bulldoze, buzzard, chicken-hearted, crane* (for lifting), *crocodile* tears, '*crow* over somebody', '*cub* reporter', *foxy, gull,* 'road *hog*', *jay,* 'the *lion* of the occasion' or 'the *lion's* share', 'play *possum*', 'loan *shark*', *sucker, swine, vixen,* '*whale* of a load' '*wolf* one's food', *worm.* Other words ordinarily applicable in a restricted sense are regularly used in other broader connections, as in '*cloak* or *mantle* of darkness', '*eye* of a needle', '*foot* of a ladder', '*hand* of a clock', '*head* of a valley', '*key* to a mystery', 'in the *lap* of luxury', '*shoulder* of a road', '*tail* of a procession'. Current English speech is full of such figurative expressions (mainly slang and colloquial) as *bonehead,* '*camp* on his trail', *crapehanger* ('pessimist'), *gold brick, gold-digger, hard-boiled,* '*hinge* on something', '*sail in* and do a task', *she-dragon,* '*sidetrack* a bill', and the many expressions for 'intoxicated', such as *boiled, half shot, tight, woozy*,[359] and for money, such as *cart wheel, dough, long green, rocks, tin*. In each use of metaphor the word introduced is supposed to suggest some quality or characteristic or aspect of that to which it is thus applied.

But in the figurative use which is called metonymy one word is substituted for another because they are ordinarily associated in the mind of the speaker or hearer. It is easy to see what the substituted word is meant to imply in the legal *bar*, in 'addicted to the *bottle*', *bluecoat, bluestocking*, 'to respect *gray hairs*', '*green* fruit', 'kind *heart*', 'enjoying *Ibsen*', 'the *kettle* boils', 'win *laurels*', *numskull*, 'the *pulpit*', '*red tape*'.

In a third type of figurative usage, known as synecdoche, one does not actually substitute, as in the two foregoing types, but he somewhat loosely employs a word that expresses a part when a whole is meant or he names the whole when only a part is meant or names the material instead of the thing made of it, as in 'the *ABC's*' ('alphabet'), 'daily *bread*' ('food'), *copper* ('penny'), *creed* (from 'I believe etc.'), 'to *dial*' ('telephone'), *flannels* ('clothing'), 'farm *hand*' ('laborer'), 'seventy *head*' ('cattle'), *mass* (from 'is dismissed etc.'), '*meat* and *drink*' ('sustenance'), *nickel* ('five cents'), *rubbers* ('overshoes'), 'fifty *sail*' ('sailboats' or 'sailing vessels'), *wheel* ('bicycle'), 'the *whole world*' ('people of the world').

And, finally, a desire to avoid disagreeable expressions by the euphemistic use of milder or more agreeable locutions has increased the figurative usages in English. The idea of death has always been expressed as mildly as possible by the use of such euphemisms as *answer the last summons, pass away, pass in one's checks*. A cemetery nowadays often contains a *columbarium*; the poorhouse has become the *county farm*; hostility is *aversion* or the *cold shoulder*; a lie is a *whopper* or a *fib*; the dead and wounded in war are *casualties*; and when the gangster kills nowadays, he *takes his victim for a ride* or *puts him on the spot*. Something has already been said of the verbal taboos which speakers of English observe, either generally or individually (p. 431); more examples might easily be found, for as often as a word acquires unpleasant associations, euphemistic substitutes are found for it.

112. Specialization in Meaning

The development of special meanings in words has been going on from the earliest times, and, as we have already observed, one result of this process has been an amazing multiplication of meanings in the English vocabulary, a multiplication so extensive that it is almost impossible to measure it with any degree of accuracy. In some words, however, there has been a narrowing in and a segregation of special meanings, so that the scope of meaning of the word is today less than it was a few centuries ago. In any well-rounded study of the working of specialization in meaning, both of these tendencies should, of course, be examined and appraised.

The development of various special meanings from an earlier simpler meaning has been named radiation because, in this process of multiplying meanings, the various special meanings all have fairly close relations to the central idea (see Greenough and Kittredge [432], p. 260, and McKnight [435], p. 207). Such words as *board*, *glass*, *hand*, and *head* have been cited as offering good examples of radiation of meanings; perhaps one of the best is *round*, which always has the central idea of 'circular' or 'spherical', but reaches out to include a *round* dance, a *round* table, a *round* robin, in *round* numbers, a *round* of applause, a *round* ('song'), a *round* of boxing, *round* steak, full *round* tones, *round* out a program, the *round* of a ladder, and so on.

Sometimes systematic specialization has led to the separation of certain groups of words in particular. This is true of English measure words, such as *acre* (once a field), *fathom*, *foot*, *hogshead*, *mile*, *rod*, *ton*, *yard*. It is also true of the development of various titles of nobility and official military terms, such as *captain* (cf. *chieftain*), *cavalry* ('horsemen'), *count* ('companion'), *duke* ('leader'), *general*, *major*, *prince*, *sergeant* (cf. *servant*).

This multiplication of meanings through specialization has, of course, been responsible for the gradual accumulation in the English language of many doublets and triplets (see Sec. 81). These divergent forms, such as *estate* and *state*, *cad* and *cadet*, *later* and *latter*, *legal*, *leal*, and *loyal*, *pity* and *piety*, *shade* and *shadow*, represent a more advanced stage of specialization of meaning than does the word *round*, because their separate forms are now considered distinct words and are treated in the dictionary as such; but they are, as has already been explained, "the outcome of semasiological differentiation", and they show what specialization in meaning can do for a language in the course of time.

However, multiplication of meanings is far too great a subject for consideration in detail in the space of a single chapter; and so the following list of examples of specialization in meaning will be limited, for the most part, to words whose special meanings have tended to become segregated or isolated. In each case the earlier, broader signification will be given, and then the more special meaning as it commonly appears.

bachelor: a novice, in arms etc.; now, often, an unmarried man.
beau: a dandy; frequently, an escort.
beef: ox; later, meat of the ox.
bereave: rob; generally, passive, to be robbed by death.
campus: a field; in America, the grounds of a college (see Mathews [444]).
car: a vehicle; often, a railroad coach or an automobile (see Foley [439], p. 61).
cattle: property; now, domestic animals, usually bovine.
chalice: a cup; now, generally, the consecrated cup.
chant: sing; later, intone.
chase: hunt or catch; later, pursue, merely.
colored people: of any color; in the United States commonly applied to negroes.
consumption: process of consuming; especially, tubercular.
corn: grain; in America, generally, maize.
cornet: little horn; a special kind of little horn.
deer: a wild animal; later, one of the smaller Cervidæ.
drowse: sink; later, sink into sleep.
eaves: edge or margin; now, lower edges of a roof.
engine: ingenuity or contrivance; later, a locomotive, machinery in an automobile, etc. (see Foley [439], p. 49).
ferry: carry; later, transport across a river.
flume: a river; now, generally, a conduit or chute for water.
fowl: any bird; now, usually, a domestic cock or hen.

SPECIALIZATION IN MEANING

ghost: a spirit; now, usually, a specter or phantom.
green: a color; but, often, unripe.
juice: fluid; in technical slang, electricity.
knell: sound of a bell; now, usually, sound of a tolling bell.
liquor: a liquid or fluid; usually, alcoholic beverage.
meat: food; later, usually, flesh of animals.
medium: middle, intervening; sometimes, one who is sensitive to spiritual agencies (see Ficke [445]).
miser: a wretched person; now, a covetous hoarder.
operate: perform any operation; more recently, perform a surgical operation (see Morse [446]).
overalls: a garment to cover other clothing; but in some sections of the United States, loose trousers of a special shape and material.
pall: a cloak or mantle; a coffin cover or other gloomy covering.
parson: a person; generally, a spiritual overseer, a pastor (see Joseph [447]).
pastor: shepherd; generally, a spiritual overseer.
poison: a potion or drink; now, a harmful drink or drug.
quell: kill; now, put down a riot etc.
scissors: shears etc.; now, only small shears.
speed: success, swiftness; now, only swiftness.
starve: die; now, die of or suffer acutely from hunger.
stool: seat; now, a simple backless seat, only.
veal: a calf; now, meat of the calf.
voyage: a journey; hence, a journey by water.
wade: advance; advance through water, mud, etc.
warden: a guardian or keeper; now, of a prison, chiefly.
wit: understanding; now, usually, humor, except in the plural, *wits*.
worm: serpent or worm; now, only the latter.
wort: a vegetable; now, only certain special varieties.

Many of these finer shades of meaning the lexicographer has difficulty in evaluating and emphasizing properly. The foreigner, especially, has trouble with these words of special meanings and sometimes fails to find a clear-cut setting forth of their manifold meanings in the dictionary; the dictionary must, as we have already observed, give room to many obsolete and obsolescent meanings of good old English words, and while the speaker who has been familiar with the idiom of English from infancy knows which meanings are in common use, which are central and which are minor radiations, one who lacks his linguistic experience will often be puzzled to sort out the various definitions listed by the lexicographer. One foreigner has already been quoted as saying, "One of the most perplexing features of the English tongue is the fact that, as a rule, the same word has different significations" (see page 106). The student of the English language must recognize that the ordinary dictionary cannot justly be expected to give sufficient space to each word to make clear all these fine shades of meaning; more detailed studies must be sought in the increasingly generous offerings of students of the English word like Greenough and Kittredge, McKnight, Vizetelly, Weekley, and others of similar interests. For ideas are too expansive to be fully accommodated in the limited pigeonholes that can be allotted to them in even the best of dictionaries.

113. *Generalization in Meaning*

Any long-used and well-developed language accumulates ultimately a supply of general-utility words which have such broad meaning and general application that they can be utilized in a great many different ways with no special change of meaning. Some of the most commonly used words of this kind are *affair, business, circumstances, concern, condition, fact, institution, matter, means, organization, person, place, situation, state, stuff,* and *thing.* The word *proposition* is becoming more general in its use; *dope* has broadened the range of its use in colloquial English greatly; *trash* has become a term of very general condemnation; *feature* is widely and loosely used; *damn* and the *devil* have ceased to lurk in the shadow of ecclesiastical condemnation and have become more general in use and meaning; and almost any little tool or fixture is a *gadget* nowadays.

Those words which Krapp has called "counter words", such as *awful, cute, fine, get, grand, great, keen, nice,* and *pretty,* show what a weakening influence this generalizing process can have on a word if it is too long continued.

Of course there are many words that have broadened their

GENERALIZATION IN MEANING

scope and yet have not been spread out so much that they have lost all their depth of meaning. A few of these will suffice to illustrate this tendency toward generalization in meaning:

barn: place for storing barley; building for horses, hay, vehicles, etc.

bootleg: sell alcoholic beverages illegally; later, sell other wares in similar fashion, such as gasoline.

box: box tree, that is, *Buxus*; later, a receptacle made of boxwood; then, a receptacle in general.

butcher: one who kills he-goats; now, one who kills animals for food, and, sometimes, a murderer of people.

butler: one who attends to bottles; usually, one who serves, at table or door.

capital: of or pertaining to the head or top; now, wealth, head of a pillar or of a person etc.

chamber: room or vault; later, room, legislative body, compartment in a gun, etc.

charge: load, burden; then, task, responsibility, price, etc.

citizen: a city dweller; now, inhabitant of state or nation, also.

clerk: clergyman; later, a learned man or scholar; then, one who could read and write; now, one who keeps accounts, records, etc.; in the United States, commonly, a retail salesman.

cupboard: shelf for cups; now, small closet with shelves.

discard: throw away a card; reject or throw away (anything).

dismantle: strip of dress or mantle; strip of furniture or other equipment.

frock: garment of a monk; later, various kinds of garments.

front: forehead; later, that which confronts or is directed forward, etc.

layman: one who is not of the clergy; tending now to return to an even earlier meaning, one who is not expert.

pipe: reed pipe or whistle; hence applied to many cylindrical objects (see Weekley [437], p. 90).

try: sift or select; hence, try before a court, render (that is, extract by melting, as fat), endeavor, etc.

walk: roll; now, generally, go on one's feet.

wretch: an outcast or exile; an unfortunate or base person.

By the process that we have named commonization (Sec. 67) a proper name applicable to an individual only is generalized so that it can be applied to an entire class. This is a simple and easy way of avoiding detailed explanation, because the word so commonized usually carries within itself certain well-defined ideas. For example, a woman can be called an *amazon*, with one word, whereas it would be necessary otherwise to characterize her as tall and strong, belligerent, feared to some extent by men, perhaps, and decidedly masculine in her attitude and habits. So one can likewise avoid much detailed explanation by the use of *bedlam, cupidity, dunce, herculean, jovial, maudlin, mesmerize, quixotic, vandal,* and the many other words that have been derived from proper names. This is not so much generalization in meaning as generalization in use for the sake of economy of expression.

To the thoughtful student of language it will be apparent that generalization is needed to offset overspecialization in meanings. If one were not able to cover a group of special words, such as *boy, carpenter, felon, grocer, parson, waiter,* by using some general term like *person, individual, somebody,* or the slang *some guy,* the burden of special words and special meanings would become so intolerable that most speakers of English would despair of being able to hold long conversations without the use of dictionaries. The danger of using too many "counter words" has already been discussed, and it is true that the person who possesses only a pair of adjectives like *keen* and *fierce* to express all degrees of approval and disapproval is sadly handicapped. But there is a certain amount of justification for the use of some of these general words, these coins of baser metal, in the more hasty give and take of colloquial speech. One wishes, for example, to say that the concert was *a good one,* and he does not care to take the time to explain that it was *restful* or *inspiring* or *harmonious* or *cheerful* or *of just the right length.*

One wishes, in other words, to avoid the necessity of expressing minutely specialized ideas, just as one sometimes likes to use the more careless syntactical shortcuts. For while careful writing calls for special meanings, colloquial speech is more often satisfied with generalizations. Indeed, it is in the choice of words that literary and colloquial language differ most generally and most fundamentally. Good writing is relatively free from colloquial generalizations.

114. Change from Concrete to Abstract

In the classification of nouns (Sec. 50) an effort has been made to differentiate between the so-called concrete nouns, which name objects, persons, whatever is tangible and definite, and the abstract nouns, which name qualities, conditions, actions, things intangible and more vague. In this present section and the following one, this arbitrary grammatical distinction between concrete and abstract will be applied also to some adjectives and verbs of a similar nature. The development of word meanings in such a manner that the expression of purely physical and material and personal attributes and qualities gradually gives way to the expression of more abstract and philosophical and spiritual concepts — this is a development in language so important and so significant that it must be recognized as of almost equal significance with the expansion of the vocabulary and the refining and enhancement of the syntax. The Anglo-Saxons were a relatively barbarous and simple people, with few words capable of expressing abstruse and erudite conceptions; in the course of a thousand years many learned words have been borrowed from the older, superior cultures of Greece and Rome, and at the same time the culture of the English-speaking people has been so greatly enhanced that many words have been stepped up from a very material and physical level to a highly philosophical and spiritual one. Much of this change is due, of course, to figurative usage, and it goes steadily on, often producing new slang usages of this kind. In some words it has occurred even before they were borrowed into English.

So *ambition* originally meant merely 'going around'; *anger* seems to have signified a 'choking'; *brains* is often used as the equivalent of 'intelligence'; *cheer* meant 'face'; *compunction* signified merely 'pricking'; a *curriculum* was a 'race course'; an *error* was a 'wandering' (cf. *knight errant*); *heart* is often used as the equivalent of 'affection'; *humor* was in medieval usage a 'fluid'; *outrage* meant 'going too far' (cf. modern slang 'Isn't that the limit?'); *spleen* is given the meaning 'malice' or 'anger'; and *sympathy* originally meant 'suffering with another'. In slang parlance *applesauce* is 'buncombe', *brass* means 'impudence', *pep* is used for 'vigor' or 'vitality', *sand* means 'courage', and *sprouts*, 'discipline'.

Many adjectives have ceased to express the more physical characteristics: *abject* once meant 'cast down'; *brazen* is often used for 'shameless', 'impudent'; *cross* is a figurative application of 'athwart' or 'opposed'; *current* meant 'running'; *dreary* was 'bloody' or 'gory'; *gentle*, 'of the family' or 'of the tribe'; *glad*, 'smooth', 'shining'; *grave*, 'heavy'; *horrid*, 'bristling'; *lunatic*, 'moon-struck'; *sad*, 'heavy'; *sinister*, 'left-handed'; *unctuous*, 'oily'; *urbane*, 'citified'; *versatile*, 'easily turned about'; and *wrong* (cognate with *wring*) meant 'twisted', 'crooked'. In the slang of the present day, *batty* means 'crazy', *crooked*, 'dishonest', *dumb* is often used for 'stupid', *haywire* means 'hopelessly confused', *locoed* is applied to people, sometimes, with the meaning 'crazy'.

Among the verbs there are numerous examples of this same change in meaning: *allude* once meant 'play with'; *appall*, 'make pale'; *apprehend*, 'seize' (cf. slang *catch on* and *I get you*); *blackball* is 'vote against'; *incline* meant originally 'bend'; *inculcate*, 'stamp in'; *ruminate*, 'chew the cud'; *tease*, 'pull apart'; *thrill*, 'pierce'.

As the thinking of the English people has been gradually raised from the level of the simpler and more commonplace everyday things and happenings of a primitive and crude life as it was lived by the three Germanic tribes that came into England long ago, so the words have been acquired, either by borrowing or by semasiological change, which have been needed to express this more abstract and abstruse thinking which has gradually but steadily brought the English-speaking peoples to their present advanced stage of life and culture.

115. *Change from Abstract to Concrete*

But there has been in English from early times a steady current in the opposite direction, making many abstract nouns and adjectives more concrete, more expressive of the physical

Sec. 115] CHANGE FROM ABSTRACT TO CONCRETE 557

and tangible and definite. This is particularly true of the verbal nouns in *-ing*: such concrete nouns have evolved as *bedding*, a *drawing*, *dressing* (in a turkey), *filling* (of a cavity), *flooring*, a *gathering*, a large *ironing*, *paling*, *railing*, *roofing*, *sheeting*, *washing*. Moreover, as we have already noted, these concrete verbals are often pluralized, as in the case of *leavings*, *lodgings*, *shavings*, *sweepings*, etc.

Other examples of this change in meaning are *audience*, the *authorities*, *bead* (originally a prayer), a *beauty* (or a *belle*), *celebrities*, a *complaint* ('ailment'), a *congregation*, a political *convention*, *curios* (for 'curiosities'), a *draw* ('ravine'), *engine* (see Foley [439], p. 49), the Chicago *exposition*, a *favor* (given at a party), a *growth* (on a tree), colloquial *help* ('servants'), *manners*, a *medium* (see Ficke [445]), *novelties*, *penitentiary*, a *plantation*, a *safety* (bicycle), a window *shade*, a *stamp*, a *weight*. In modern slang there is frequent use of abstract nouns in this manner, as in a *fright* ('a frightful person'), a *natural* ('one who excels in something because of unusual native ability'), a *terror* ('a terrifying or very disagreeable person').

Attention has already been called to the practice of using abstract nouns as titles and in forms of address applied to persons of exalted or honorable status, such as *His Grace*, *His Holiness*, *Your Honor*, *Your Majesty*, *Excellency*.

Some English adjectives, instead of shifting from the concrete to the abstract like those named in the previous section, have gone in the opposite direction. *Buxom* originally meant 'obedient', 'yielding'; *dizzy* was 'foolish'; *homely* meant 'homelike', 'simple', and is still used at times with a meaning approaching its earlier significance; *large* once meant 'liberal', as in the noun *largess*; and *uncouth* was earlier 'unknown'. But gradually these words have moved from the realm of spiritual to that of physical ideas.

When an adjective is substantivized and accepted as a noun, it frequently becomes more concrete, as in the case of *bitters*, a *cold*, *goods*, *slacks*, *sweets*, and *wrongs*. Such nouns are most likely to be concrete when they can be pluralized.

116. *Figurative Gender*

When the loss of most of the inflectional endings of nouns and adjectives left the English language free from the necessity of indicating carefully the grammatical gender of every noun used, the way was clear for the use of a natural gender based upon sex distinction rather than upon a seemingly arbitrary choice of inflectional endings. Grammatical gender remains in English inflection, as has been shown in Section 87, only in a few pairs of words, such as *father* and *mother*, or in endings like *-ess*, as in *duchess*, or in compounds like *he-goat*. But owing to the retention of gender inflectional forms in the personal pronouns (*he, she, it*, etc.), it is still possible to distinguish the gender of nouns of the so-called common gender, such as *teacher* and *person*, and to go even farther and in a fanciful manner assign gender to nouns ordinarily considered neuter. This figurative or rhetorical assignment of gender, usually known as personification, has long been common in poetry and also in the colloquial usage of most speakers of English who have relations of affectionate familiarity with boats, locomotives, automobiles, flags, guns, tools, airplanes, musical instruments, and the like. Svartengren has found in American usage, especially, a very marked tendency to personify as feminine many "concrete things made or worked upon by man".[448] So one is likely to say of an automobile, "*She*'s running perfectly."

In certain contexts it has long been customary to treat as feminine persons certain abstract ideas such as *Justice, Liberty, Nature, Philosophy, Pity*, the *Soul*, and *Wisdom*. The names of the seasons, such as *Autumn*, and of the arts and sciences, such as *Sculpture* and *Mathematics*, are usually treated as feminine. But *Cruelty, Fear, Murder*, and *War* are generally masculine.

There are also generally accepted conventions as to the figurative genders of certain concrete nouns pertaining to nature, and also collective nouns of a social character. The masculine gender is assigned commonly to rivers, oceans, mountains, winds, time, and the sun; but cities, states, nations, churches, universities, and colleges are more likely to be regarded as feminine. The moon and the earth are today feminine; in the Anglo-Saxon period the moon was masculine, and the sun feminine, just as in Modern German.

Undoubtedly there enters into this practice of assigning gender to inanimate things a strong personal element of affection or fear, of respect or awe or dread. But it is not unlikely that to some extent the practice of the Greeks and Romans in respect to their mythologies has had its influence upon English usage, as in the case of *war*, of which the god in Roman mythology was the masculine Mars.

117. *The Weakening of Meanings*

In an earlier edition of the Century Dictionary the verb *weaken* is conveniently defined as "to lessen or reduce the strength, power, ability, influence, or quality of " something, more especially of the body or of the mind. One of the most striking results of the tendency to generalize the meanings of English words, to spread them out so that they will cover more ideas, has been a dilution, or thinning out, of these meanings. This is true of those general-utility words named in Section 113, such as *business* and *proposition*, for instance; for a man may conduct a *business* which keeps nobody *busy*, and in the colloquial usage of today a *proposition* may not have been *proposed* by anybody. The weakening of good, expressive words like *keen* and *grand* in order that they may be utilized as "counter words" has been remarked already; it is one of the regrettable aspects of slang. This weakening of meaning has also been very aptly named fading (see Greenough and Kittredge [432], p. 235) and can frequently be charged also to that tendency to exaggerate which the rhetoricians have named hyperbole. Indeed, it is often difficult to determine whether the weakening of a meaning has come about through generalization in response to the need of a more general term or has resulted from too much exaggeration in the expression of a very ordinary idea. In the case of the verbs that have become linking verbs and have taken the place of older verbs meaning 'become', as in '*fall* sick', '*run* dry', '*stand* ready', and '*turn* cold', the normal meaning of the verb has almost faded out; in the auxiliary use of certain verbs, as in '*dare* say', '*let's* go, '*will* come', the meaning is greatly reduced; and in the idiomatic uses of others the weakening of the usual meanings is obvious, as in 'I'm *going* to sit here a while', 'It *got* to be a nuisance', 'How did he *come* by so much money?'

In the following list most of the words have been reduced because of too frequent exaggeration:

afraid I can't come
astonish (once 'stun')
an *atrocious* mistake
awfully kind
the village *bastile*
considerable loss
a *corking* story
a *cute* child
die laughing
a *divine* cake
enchanting view

fear I haven't any
a *heavenly* day
mighty nice of you
mortify (once 'make dead')
a *putrid* time
a *ripping* play
a *stunning* gown
terribly small
tickled to death
a *vamp* (from *vampire*)
very little

118. *The Substitution of Meanings*

As a result of a series of changes in meaning (such as specialization, generalization, etc.), certain words have acquired meanings quite different from their original meanings. Such gradual substitution can generally be accounted for if the history of the word is known. Examples are given below, with both the earlier and the later meanings:

belfry: a watchtower; later, a bell tower.
candidate: clothed in white; an aspirant for office etc.
carbuncle: a little coal; then, a gem; now, a sort of boil.
cardinal: hinged; then, principal, chief; later, a church dignitary; often, red.
carnival: a meatless time; now, generally, a festival.
caste: pure; now, a hereditary class.
chapel: a short cloak; a church or room for worship.

THE SUBSTITUTION OF MEANINGS

clock: a bell; now, a timepiece.
commencement: beginning; often, finish of a college course.
concordance: a gospel harmony; now, an alphabetical index of words or subjects in a book.
coroner: officer appointed by the crown; investigator of unexplained deaths.
defend: often, prohibit; now, generally, protect.
dial: daily; face of a timepiece etc.
dicker: a set of ten; now, to barter.
dilapidate: throw stones apart; now, bring into partial ruin.
diplomat: bearer of a diploma; hence, a governmental representative.
express: squeezed out; often, a fast train or bus.
family: servants; now, members of the household, often exclusive of the servants.
gazetteer: a journalist; a geographical dictionary.
gossamer: goose summer; gauzy fabric.
journey: a day's doings; now, a trip (often of many days).
junket: a basket woven of rushes; a festive excursion.
knight: a youth; now, a man who has been dubbed knight and granted the title *Sir*.
leech: a physician; later, a bloodsucking worm.
mass: originally a Latin participle meaning 'dismissed'; now, a church service.
miniature: painted in red; now, often, small, on a small scale.
omelet: a thin plate; now, a dish prepared with eggs.
party: a part or division; often, a body of persons, or (colloquial) a person, or a social gathering.
pedigree: foot of a crane; now, a record of ancestry.
petticoat: a small coat; later, a woman's skirt.
pen: a feather; a writing instrument.
quick: alive; now, generally, active or rapid.
rostrum: a beak (especially of a ship); a platform.
rubric: red; a red manuscript heading; then, a heading.
second (unit of time): a second, or further, subdivision of time; now, one sixtieth of a minute.
side: wide; hence, the wide surface.
tide: time; now, usually, periodic ocean movement.

The results of these substitutions in meaning are sometimes very interesting. McKnight has commented upon the paradoxical character of certain expressions (*English Words and their Background* [435], p. 209); he cites *green* blackberries, which are red, a typewritten *manuscript*, and a weekly *journal*. He might have added that *squares* are sometimes triangular in Boston and circular elsewhere.

In the case of doublets there are some strange relationships to be found as a result of semasiological substitution; *grotesque* is cognate with *grotto*; *dike* and *ditch* were once the same word; *plum* and *prune* were the same; *noon* was the *ninth* hour of the day; and *poison*, like *potion*, was once a mere drink.

Sometimes meanings go far astray in the course of a few generations. Indeed, in the growth of slang, substitutions are made in a relatively short time, as in the college slang expressions *bone* ('study hard'), *crib* ('plagiarize, cheat'), *pipe* ('easy course'), *pony* ('a translation'), and *snap* ('something easy').

119. *The Pejorative Tendency*

Various English words have gradually become depreciatory in their meanings; that is to say, they have deteriorated, or, as other philologists have expressed the idea, they have become degraded or degenerate, so that they are generally regarded as terms of disparagement. This pejorative, or depreciatory, tendency in English words is closely allied to social changes and tendencies, and the shades of disparaging meaning that a word may acquire are not always easily appreciated. Even when a pejorative suffix like *-aster* in *poetaster* is used, or the belittling *-ling* in *hireling* and *weakling*, or *-ster*, as in *dabster* and *punster*, its depreciatory influence is not always felt. A perfectly good word of one generation may become a term of disparagement in the next. But in general there are three groups of words which may be considered here, namely, those that have been gradually degraded in meaning, those others — mostly slang or colloquial — which are coined or adapted from time to time as derogatory or disparaging terms, and those, finally, which are taboo chiefly because they refer to unpleasant or intimately personal matters.

In the following list only earlier values are given:

boor: peasant
brat: child
busybody: busy person
cad: cadet
churlish: of or pertaining to a countryman
conceit: conception
counterfeit: imitate
courtesan: courtier
crafty: skillful
daft: neat, dexterous
degraded: reduced in rank
designing: planning
doom: judgment
dunce: a Duns Scotus man
fiend: enemy
gossip: sponsor in baptism
hoard: a treasure
hussy: housewife
hypocrite: actor
idiot: private person
impertinent: not pertinent
insane: not healthy
knave: boy (German *Knabe*)
lewd: ignorant
lust: pleasure, desire
naughty: worthless
officious: serviceable
outlandish: foreign
paramour: by love
pedant: schoolmaster
prejudice: fore-judgment
profane: secular
prude: modest
saloon: hall
sanctimonious: holy
seduce: lead away
silly: happy, blessed
smug: trim, neat
swindler: totterer
villain: serf
vulgar: of the common people
wanton: not trained, untaught
wench: child
wily: clever, cunning
wrangle: argue
wretch: outcast, exile

Other words that have shown a pejorative tendency are *blooming* (a British euphemism for *bloody*), *childish* ('puerile', 'immature'), *criticism* ('unfavorable criticism'), *dole* ('governmental charity'), *dumb* ('stupid'), *fast* ('dissolute'), *fellow* ('a man of no account'), *fiddler* ('a mediocre violinist'), *peculiar* ('queer'), *pious* ('hypocritical'), *plausible* ('specious'), *puritanical* ('overstrict religiously'), *simple* ('foolish', 'stupid'), *suggestive* ('indecent'), etc.

There has always been a bounteous crop of slang or colloquial derogatory words, colorless synonyms for the most part. To those already mentioned (p. 417) might be added many others from various periods of the language, such as *buncombe* or *bunk, claptrap, piffle, riffraff, rubbish, soft soap, taffy, twaddle,* a *washout.*

Verbal taboos, as already noted (p. 431), are a varied and changing lot, since speakers differ greatly as to their personal likes and dislikes. But there is a body of words that are very generally avoided by people of refinement and good taste because they refer to unpleasant or intimately personal matters. For some of them euphemistic substitutes are sought, and others are simply avoided altogether in public speech. The British avoidance of *bloody* has been commented upon; until recently *damn* and *hell* were not allowed to intrude into good usage · *die* is avoided very often; *stink*, *stench*, and *vomit* are disliked by many people, except in certain uses, such as that of *vomit* with reference to volcanic eruptions; *snout* is taboo to some; and so on. Any student of the English language could add to this list other words that he would not use because of their unpleasant meanings — words that are taboo in polite society.

There are, of course, numerous words that have been abused and misused until they are avoided by many careful speakers and writers of English. But the deterioration has not gone so far, yet, that the words have become seriously pejorative in character. They are avoided, usually, because of their badly overworked state rather than because of unpleasant meanings or connotations (see page 429).

120. *The Ameliorative Tendency*

There are other words, however, that have undergone a gradual elevation in their meanings, often because they are associated with the more aristocratic things in life. This has been true particularly of words relating to social classes, such as *alderman* ('elder man'), *butler* ('bottle server'), *duke* ('leader'), *earl* ('freeman'), *knight* (a 'youth'), *lady* ('loaf-kneader'), *lord* ('loaf guardian'), *marshal* ('horse servant'), *mayor* ('superior'), *steward* ('sty ward'); it can also be observed in certain other nouns like *cavalier* ('horseman'), *diplomat* ('holder of a diploma'), *minister* ('one who serves'), *pastor* ('shepherd'), *sergeant* ('servant'), *statesman* (a 'man

Sec. 120] THE AMELIORATIVE TENDENCY 565

of the state'). *Brow* has become a more poetical term than it was when it pertained to the eyebrow, merely; *fame* was once 'rumor', and *pluck* was originally 'viscera' or 'vitals' and has undergone the same process of amelioration that *guts* is undergoing today.

Some of the best of our adjectives had very ordinary meanings in earlier times: *chivalrous* came from a noun meaning 'horse' and took on additional meaning as it was applied to knights; although *civil* still means 'pertaining to the state', it is often used with the derived meaning 'polite', just as *polite* and *polished* have themselves been promoted from the earlier, more concrete idea of 'polish'; *courtly* and *courteous* have generally retained the better ideas associated with the court and have lost the less desirable connotations; *gentle* and *genteel* have become much more idealistic since they ceased to mean merely 'of the *gens* or tribe', although, in the case of *genteel*, a pejorative reaction has set in; both *precious* and *costly* have come to mean much more than merely 'of great price or cost'; *urbane* is more than just 'citified', 'characteristic of a city dweller'; and *manly, womanly,* and *boyish* refer, today, to the most pleasing qualities of man, woman, and boy. The overenthusiastic usage of modern colloquial speech has given an appreciative quality to various other adjectives, such as *grand, great, keen,* in much the same way that an effusive German adopts *kolossal* or *wunderbar* as his favorite expression of appreciation.

Corresponding to the slang or colloquial derogatory terms already discussed, there has always been an equally bounteous crop of eulogistic words, colorless words of approbation. Some have already been listed above and elsewhere (p. 417), and many others could be found all down through English literature and colloquial usage, such as *bully, crackajack, dandy, fetching, glorious, humdinger, lallapaloosa, magnificent, peerless, thrilling.*

Of course this amelioration of words is, like the deteriorating process already discussed, dependent largely on social conditions and attitudes, and, as Withington has shown in his brief discussion of "rehabilitated words", it is always active. In his notes for a chapter on regeneration of meaning [455] he has mentioned, in addition to certain words discussed above, *cunning* (formerly 'knowing'), *debate* (once 'physical strife'), *dote* ('be stupid'), *enthralled* ('enslaved'), *fond* ('foolish'), *fun* (once a low, cant word), *innocent* ('ignorant'), *nice* ('foolish'), *shrewd* ('cursed'), *sturdy* ('cruel', 'stern'), and *Yankee* (a word of contempt). While hyperbole tends to weaken words, as we have shown, it "often helps to make words less disagreeable", as in the case of '*beastly* weather', '*horribly* slow', 'a *rotten* time', '*terribly* lazy', '*vile* music'.

121. *Popularization of Learned Words*

One of the most striking tendencies during the past few decades has been the popularizing of learned words. The increased interest in gardening has familiarized many people with the scientific names of plants, such as *delphinium* (the larkspur), *dianthus* (the pink), *dicentra* (Dutchman's breeches), *euphorbia* (spurge), *gladiolus, heliotrope, pentstemon,* and *phlox*. Indeed, the true "garden fan" of today often scorns to employ the popular names of flowers because of their very careless application in the less scientific past, and so the good old-fashioned *marigold* has become a *calendula*, the *foxglove* masquerades as *digitalis*, and the Kansas *sunflower* is likely to turn up as the Californian's *helianthus*.

The widespread use of the automobile and radio has, as everyone realizes, popularized many technical words, such as *aërial, amplifier, carburetor, compression, condenser, differential, ethyl, microphone* (slang *mike*), *rheostat, static,* and *transmission*. Common popular terms have also been given specialized meanings and have then been dropped back into the stream of popular usage, notably a *clutch, to ground,* a *hookup, knock,* and *tubes*.

More recently the psychologist has been educating the general public, and such technical terms as a *complex, introvert* and *extrovert, moron,* and *psychoneurosis* are being bandied about, with a fair degree of understanding of their meanings.

POPULARIZATION OF LEARNED WORDS

In the realm of medicine and surgery, real and pseudo, popular interest in the ailments of mankind has for centuries tended to popularize the technical terminology of the moment. In the medieval period of English the theory of the four elements, or temperaments, caught the popular imagination, and, along with the *horoscope,* people talked learnedly of *choleric, melancholic, phlegmatic,* and *sanguine* temperaments. A little later it was of the *humors* that Englishmen complained. Today we hear constantly of *appendicitis, arthritis, chiropractors, diagnosis, germs* (*bugs* in slang), *infection, influenza* (or *flu*), *neurotics, osteopaths, scalpels* (though patients often *go under the knife*), *stethoscope, thermometer, tonsillitis, tuberculosis* (formerly *consumption*), *X rays*; and various ailments (and their remedies) are becoming popular as the ingenuity of the advertiser finds more and more menaces to the health of mankind.

Many more examples might be given of the popular use of learned words, such as those pertaining to theology, philosophy, and mathematics; the tremendous influx of the more learned words and phrases of Latin, French, and Greek has already been enlarged upon in Sections 70-71 and 74. Moreover, in Greenough and Kittredge's chapter on "Learned Words Become Popular" (*Words and their Ways in English Speech* [432], p. 29) many familiar terms are cited which the average speaker would not suspect of having once been learned or highly technical, such as *disaster* and *quality.*

It is interesting to observe the effects of the present-day adoption of learned words by the common man. In many instances his careless and uncomprehending use of technical terms has certainly tended to lessen their exactness and efficiency. Examples of this may be found in the use of the psychological *moron,* the medical *influenza,* the mathematical *proportion,* and the rhetorical *proposition.* On the other hand, correct use of the technical language of specialists has undoubtedly become more widespread within a very few years. Indeed, "orismological sesquipedalianism", as it has been aptly called, has been much employed of late as a form of smoke-screen writing intended to assist advertisers in convincing the common man of the superior merits of articles advertised. He is overwhelmed with learned words.

The task of the lexicographer has been so much increased by this popular interest in learned and technical terms that every general editor of a comprehensive dictionary finds it necessary nowadays to employ a large body of technical experts whenever he sets to work to compile or revise his dictionary. While Noah Webster felt competent a century ago to handle this part of his dictionary work by submitting "the several articles" on the arts and sciences to two learned men at Yale, consulting occasionally a few "other gentlemen distinguished for scientific attainments", today the list of experts collaborating in the editing of the twentieth-century editions of the same dictionary is a formidable one. In the Second Edition of the New International Dictionary (1934) one hundred and forty-seven special editors are named as helpers in the work of compilation. In "a partial list of departments edited by specialists" for the New Standard Dictionary more than forty names are given, and in the list of collaborators for the Century Dictionary Supplement of 1909 seventy-eight editorial contributors are named, who helped to enlarge the dictionary to the extent of upward of one hundred and twenty thousand words and phrases, including "not a few words which had appeared in special glossaries and technical dictionaries". If, back in 1656, the lexicographer Thomas Blount found himself "gravelled" by the many strange words that he encountered in his reading, it is not surprising that after nearly three centuries of steady accumulation of highly learned and technical words the English lexicographer should find it necessary to call in many specialists to assist, as Blount would say, in "interpreting all such hard words, whether Hebrew, Greek, Latin, Italian, Spanish, French, Teutonick, Belgick, British or Saxon, as are now used in our refined English Tongue".

This tendency to use learned words is, on the whole, a hopeful sign insofar as it indicates a popular desire to acquire more highly specialized knowledge and to learn the special terms necessary to express that knowledge.

122. Extinction of Words and Meanings

Since the use of words and of meanings is largely a matter of habit, — habit of the individual and also habit of great bodies of English speakers, — it is possible to measure the coming and going of these linguistic habits only very roughly and inexactly. Language has been defined as a vehicle for conveying thoughts and emotions from one person to another individual, or from one person to numerous others, and the gradual disuse of a word or of a meaning of a word is to be ascribed to the same causes that remove automobiles from service and relegate them to the junk yard or the dealer in antiques: sometimes they are crowded out by the new models that are put on the linguistic market; sometimes they are of that ephemeral and transitory slang which is seldom durable and lasting; sometimes they have become worn out because of abuse and misuse. The unabridged dictionary gives space to many of these old models, turned in for newer ones, and also lists the outworn ones. But the dictionary does not always indicate which words are slowly going out of use and seldom heard in conversation or rarely found on the printed page. Individual speakers, and also great bodies of speakers, differ so much in respect to the words they use that no lexicographer could hope to estimate or appraise to the satisfaction of all the vitality of each word that he lists; for one word will prove strong and vigorous, another will show defective or useless parts, and another will, when examined, prove completely dead. We have already discussed the archaic and obsolete element in English (Sec. 13); in this present discussion, therefore, it is the dying words and meanings with which we are concerned, and the reasons for their approaching extinction.

Apparently the great increase in the number of words in the English vocabulary is leading to the loss of some of the more highly specialized words. By the process of conversion (see Secs. 58 and 67) one word form is serving in the place of several: to have the *blues* is to be *melancholy*; a *bid* is often used colloquially instead of an *invitation*; *pay* is a verb, an adjective, and a noun equal to *payment*. Conversion of a proper name by the process of commonization allows one word to take the place of several; so a *Shylock* makes it unnecessary to say "a revengeful, merciless Jewish moneylender", and by utilizing the term *pasteurize* one avoids explaining the process each time the idea occurs. Likewise by the use of verb-adverb combinations (see Sec. 53, p. 297) many special verbs are avoided; one can use *lay out* and thereby obviate the need for *arrange* (grounds), *exert* (oneself), *exhibit, expend, extend, map out, plan in detail, prepare for burial*, and the like. Moreover, through the thinning out of many synonyms numerous words or word meanings are being dropped; *suffer* is no longer commonly used with the meaning 'to permit', but is now somewhat bookish in this sense; Krapp says in his *Comprehensive Guide to Good English* that "the word *blow* in the sense *come into bloom* is archaic and poetic"; and one rarely hears in colloquial English such words as *abide, chide, damsel, delve, firmament, raiment, sojourn,* and *twain*. From any list of synonyms it is possible to select several that are seldom used today; and if the words in any dictionary be inspected, many of them will be found listed with archaic or obsolete meanings included (see page 41).

Where pairs of synonyms come into competition, usually one is less commonly used than the other; so *congratulate* is more often heard than *felicitate, face* is preferred to *visage, strike* is superseding *smite, cry* is preferred to *weep* in colloquial usage, *wain* has yielded to its doublet *wagon*. The use of *nice* as a term of approval has lately tended to crowd out the meanings 'fastidious' and 'minutely accurate'. In the case of slang, in a given community there is seldom more than one word in general use at a time for approval and one for disapproval; *crackajack* and *punk*, for example, ceased to function as soon as another pair became popular. The mortality rate for slang words is very high.

Other words seem to lose favor because some element of confusion enters into their use. The clash between *cleave* 'adhere' and *cleave* 'cut' threatens to do away with both; *to hale*, meaning 'to haul', is no longer popular; *to muse* may have been discouraged by *the Muses*; *seldom* and *whilom* are survivors of the once-common use of an adverbial dative plural in Anglo-Saxon, now no longer used; *wont* is too nearly like *won't* and is yielding to *accustomed*. Bridges has insisted that the confusion arising from the use of homophones is driving many of them out of use; he has listed in his "table of homophones that may seem to be presently falling out of use" such words as *barren, bate, bier, cession, cite, clime, fain, gambol, isle, meed*, and *mien*.[352] Undoubtedly this possibility of confusion does exert some influence in causing people to select other words which are less likely to be confused.

And, finally, as we have noted in an earlier study of archaic English (Sec. 13), words are being constantly dropped from common use because the things that they name are left behind or else renamed; it is seldom that one hears *hoop skirt, to joust* (spelled also *just*), *kerchief, livery stable, postboy*, and *tin shop*, and new names are supplanting *butcher shop, drug store, graveyard*, and *undertaker*.

123. *Isolated Survivals*

A few linguistic fossils remain in use in Current English, largely because they are embedded in stereotyped phrases which people like to use because they rime or alliterate or have developed very special meanings. Sometimes they have been retained because lovers of Shakespeare and the Authorized Version of the Bible have become fond of them. Occasionally a word has been preserved in English dialect and is known only as a dialectal survival.

Riming phrases are 'go *pell-mell*', '*to* and *fro*', *willy-nilly*. Words not commonly used occur in such alliterative phrases as 'in fine *fettle*', 'neither *kith* nor *kin*', 'leave in the *lurch*', 'with might and *main*', 'a pig in a *poke*', 'rumors are *rife*', *shilly-shally*, 'all *spick* and *span*' (see Weekley [438], p. 148), treasure-*trove*, 'wax and *wane*', 'for *weal* or woe', 'widow's *weeds*', 'go to *wrack* and ruin'. Other conventional phrases that have aided in preserving old words and meanings are 'a *bower* of roses', 'in high *dudgeon*', 'give up the *ghost*' ('spirit'), '*hue* and cry', 'without *let* or hindrance', 'just as *lief*', 'at *loggerheads*', '*metes* and bounds', 'in common *parlance*', the '*quick* and the dead', '*stem* the tide', 'make the *welkin* ring', and 'in days of *yore*'.

There are some other old words that have maintained a fairly isolated existence in English, even though they have not always been embedded in phrases; examples are 'gates *ajar*', 'pay something *to boot*', '*brook* no opposition', *chilblains*, 'to *heel in* plants', Scottish *ken*, *lukewarm*, 'a *moot* court', '*rue* it', 'for the *sake* of', 'an old *saw*' ('saying'), *scion* (of an old family), 'go *scot*-free', 'bar *sinister*', '*warp* a boat into its berth', *werewolf*, *whilom*, *to wit* (legal), '*wreak* vengeance'.

Some old occupational words have survived chiefly in family names. Examples are *Baxter* ('baker'), *Chandler* ('candle-maker'), *Fletcher* ('arrow-maker'), *Wainwright* ('wagon-maker'), *Webster* ('weaver').

Among the amalgamated compounds listed in Section 64 will be found traces of some other old words, such as *-sip* (= *sib*) in *gossip*, *-band* in *husband*, *-shal* in *marshal*, *-tril* (= *thrill*) in *nostril*, *sti-* in *stirrup*.

124. *Ambiguous Words and Phrases*

When people become doubtful or uncertain as to the meaning of a word because it can be understood in two or more distinct and different senses, then its ambiguity becomes a hindrance to the effective expression of thought, rather than a help, and users of the language begin to worry about the proper use of the word. A foreigner has been quoted as saying that he was often perplexed by the great number of meanings which many English words possess (see page 106); many persons using English as their mother tongue have the same trouble in learning all the fine shades of meaning which a word is capable of expressing. But this is the price which English-speaking people must pay for the tremendous growth which

Sec. 124]   AMBIGUOUS WORDS AND PHRASES   573

their language has experienced in the last few centuries; for it has produced many groups of synonyms, the members of which are all slightly different and yet all partake of one central idea (see Sec. 83), and it has so developed many single words that numerous meanings radiate from them (see Sec. 112). Whether it is harder to remember all the synonymous words that center about a single idea or to know the various special meanings that center in a single word does not concern us just now. The earnest student of English is constantly seeking to increase his understanding of both.

But there are various ambiguous words which have developed two meanings so distinct that they stand like signposts at the crossroads with arms pointing in two different directions. Even though the experienced traveler of linguistic highways is not seriously confused by these ambiguous words, some of them, nonetheless, have provoked frequent and sometimes heated discussions.

The processes of generalization and specialization have produced a certain amount of confusion in the case of words commonly used as proper names: *Anglo-Saxon* is used in this book, for example, as a name for the earliest period of the English language, and it is also being used today, as Malone has insisted [460], as a general term for English and Americans together; *Gothic* is used by the philologist as a name for the language of the Goths, and has been used in England as descriptive of a form of eighteenth-century novel; *Catholic* is commonly used in connection with the Roman Catholic Church, but as a common adjective it still means 'general'; *Latin* is the language of the Romans, but is frequently applied to all the Romanic nations of later times; *Old English* has been widely advocated as a name for the language used by the early Anglo-Saxons, but *old English* often reaches back no farther than the sixteenth century; a *Mason* is a member of a certain secret society, but a *mason* is a worker with stone, brick, or the like.

An *artichoke* is sometimes an edible flower, at other times an edible root, distinctively called *Jerusalem artichoke*; a *turtle* is a bird, and it is also a hard-shelled reptile; a *bibliog-*

raphy is a list of titles of books, articles, etc., but *bibliography* is the history and description of books and manuscripts [461]; a *legend* for the student of medieval religious literature means 'the life of a saint', but in more general modern usage it is a 'tradition'; an *undertaker* is one who undertakes something, and more specifically he is a 'mortician'; when a speaker mentions 'the *age* of Chaucer' (Sec. 35), he might refer to Chaucer's period or to his years; and a *grist* is 'grain to be ground' or 'the meal that is produced by the grinding'.

Certain adjectives likewise display a troublesome ambiguity at times. *Curious* can be applied to a person displaying curiosity, but it means 'strange' or 'rare' when applied to a thing; *fast* is both 'firmly fixed' and 'swiftly moving'; *hateful* is, according to the dictionary, 'full of hate' and also 'odious'; *hulled* has recently forced an investigation by the staff of the Bureau of Plant Industry of the United States Department of Agriculture because it can mean either 'deprived of hulls', as in *hulled barley*, or 'having hulls', as in *black-hulled*. The hyphen in the compound helps to indicate the meaning when the word is written; but the distinction is not so clear when the word is spoken.[462] The adjective *healthy* has been often abused in colloquial usage because not only has it been applied to people and animals enjoying health, but it has been substituted for *healthful*, which means 'health-giving'.

Certain nouns of a verbal nature are ambiguous because they can be so used in a sentence that the following noun can indicate either the recipient or the performer of the action implied: in 'the man *in charge of* the posse' the man may be either the head of the posse or intrusted to it; 'it was the *conviction* of the lawyer' may mean 'the opinion of' or 'the convicting of' the lawyer; the '*conclusion* of the assembly' may be its ending or its decision.

Many verbs are ambiguous unless they are explained or defined by their context: *dispatch* means 'send as a messenger' or 'put to death'; to *dress* a person is to put on more covering, but to *dress* poultry is chiefly to remove their covering; *help* means 'assist' and negatively 'avoid'; to *trim* a hat is

Sec. 124]   AMBIGUOUS WORDS AND PHRASES   575

to put on ornamentation, but to *trim* a budget has come to mean removing the trimmings; a newspaper humorist has called attention to the ambiguous newspaper caption "Diving into River, Car *Turns Turtle*"; *wear* sometimes means 'wear well', with no implication of attrition, and sometimes it indicates impairment because of wear. Such verbs as *feel, look, show, smell, taste*, all have this ambiguous quality. It is most wise to continue to insist that *learn* shall be restricted to the meaning 'acquire information' and not used as a substitute for *teach*; the father who wanted the teacher to *learn* his child might well have meant either of two quite different things.

The ambiguity of many verb-adverb combinations has already been illustrated (Sec. 53, p. 302), and the danger of confusion in their use has been indicated. When a doctor *gives up* a patient, anxious friends like to know whether he despairs of her life or transfers her case to a better physician; one can do a friend a favor if he *holds* him *up* on a slippery street, but a great wrong if he uses a gun on a dark night; the man who *fought with* the Turks may have fought against them or in their behalf; one can *play out* the game to the end or *play out* before the game is ended. Such colloquial combinations have too many different meanings to be desirable for careful and exact writing, although speakers manage them fairly well in ordinary conversation.

There are various words in very common use today about which speakers are confused because those who may be supposed to know most about them cannot agree as to just what they mean. Especially ambiguous are *culture, education, genius, humanism*, a *lyric* poem, *originality, poetry, romanticism*[463], and the more recently coined *technocracy*. Probably no lexicographer can hope to give a permanent and clear-cut and satisfying definition of any one of these words, because they are of too broad a scope to be crowded into the pigeonholes of any dictionary, however large it may be.

In the preparation of this book, ambiguity of meaning has been frequently encountered in the selection of terms and definitions, and an attempt has been made at times to indicate the reason for selecting one meaning of a philological term and rejecting another. In concluding this survey of the English language of the present day, a summary of some of those decisions may prove helpful, and, as a partial review of the classifications that have been made, chapter by chapter and section by section, it may clarify further the method of study that has been followed. Fortunately not all the terms of English philology are ambiguous; but a few have required a thoughtful and careful definition and limitation.

Philology and *philologist* have generally been used as pertaining to the science of linguistics, although their broader Latin meaning, 'love (or lover) of learning or literature', has often lurked in the background, since this whole study of language is an attempt to explain language in the light of the culture that it expresses (see page 8). *Grammar* has sometimes been used in its broader sense as 'the entire scientific study of language', and not as 'the science which treats of the classes of words, their inflection, their syntactical usage, etc.' (see pages 8, 118). The use of *composition* as a grammatical term for the compounding of words has been distinguished from the rhetorical use as it pertains to the putting together of sentences into the larger units of prose and poetry (see pages 9, 335). The twofold use of *etymology*, as 'that branch of philology which treats of the derivation of words' and as 'the history of a word', has been recognized (see page 11).

The varied meanings of *slang*, *dialect*, and *jargon* have been sifted and meanings selected as far as possible which could be clearly comprehended; *slang* has been explained, although it has not been very closely defined (see page 28), *dialect* has been limited to the speech of social classes and certain localities (see page 51), and *jargon* has been confined to a 'crude form of speech arising from the confused and haphazard mixture of two or more existing languages'. The ambiguous term *American* has been regularly applied to citizens of the United States, even though its broader application has been recognized (see page 279).

Conversion is a very general term; in this book it has been restricted to mean 'a shift from one part of speech to another, or within a part of speech'. Likewise *cognate* has been limited in its use so as to exclude related forms one of which is derived from the other by the usual derivative processes (see page 399). *Doublets* have been defined as 'those pairs of related words that function alike as the same part of speech' (see page 402). The term *homonym* has been accepted as a term broad enough to cover both words spoken alike and words spelled alike, even though some of the earlier philologists have been content to use the word in narrower senses (see page 407).

An effort has been made to keep separate the use of *gender* as applied to grammatical categories in earlier times and as it has come to mean 'distinction of sex' in later English usage. The term *case* has been defined in such a way as to allow of the inclusion of both inflectional forms and syntactical uses. And the process of *conjugation* of a verb has been recognized as distinct from the 'schematic arrangement' known as *a conjugation*. The restriction of grammatical *phrases*, as a practical matter, to the three types is an arbitrary but convenient definition of another ambiguous word (see page 488); and while the term has been used in a broader sense generally in this book, the practice of many grammarians in adhering to the narrower scope of the word can be justified on practical grounds.

And, finally, as an excellent illustration of the practical value of making certain arbitrary definitions of terms for the use of linguistic students, the philosophical uses of *concrete* and *abstract* have been ignored and their usual grammatical meanings extended somewhat so that they could be applied to words naming the tangible and physical and definite, on the one hand, and, on the other, to words naming things intangible and more vague (see page 555).

125. *Idiomatic English*

But of all the ambiguous words employed in this book, none is likely to call for more careful definition than the term *idiom*. An idiom, or idiomatic phrase, has already been defined for the purposes of this book as a phrase that has developed a meaning which cannot be readily analyzed into the several distinct ideas which would ordinarily be expressed by the words composing the phrase (see page 13). It transcends, therefore, the ordinary syntactical constructions and must be studied as a grammatical unit, or entity, in itself. On the other hand, *the idiom of English* is a very broad term and includes all the peculiarities and idiosyncrasies of our native tongue — its idioms, its peculiar syntactical constructions, and other conventional practices of an unusual character. To understand thoroughly the idiom of the English language is to know the language most intimately, as only a speaker born to the tongue or a foreigner far advanced in its study can hope to know it.

Idioms. By their very nature idioms are often hard to classify. Somewhat adjectival in their function are such phrases as *all in*, 'exhausted', *all up*, 'at an end', *down and out*, 'defeated', 'overcome', *hard up*, 'impoverished', 'it's *up to you*', 'incumbent upon', 'dependent upon', *well off*, 'affluent'. There are many adverbial idioms, such as *all in all, at any rate, by and large, by hook or crook, every now and then, far and wide, in cahoots, just as soon*, '*kind of* queer', *of course, off and on, right away*, '*sooner* go with you', *the sooner the better*.

Many idiomatic phrases are built around verbs, as in *is to be* ('will be'), *beat all hollow, beg the question, curry favor, fight shy of, get rid of, had better* and *had rather*, '*have been to* Rome', *have to go* ('must go'), *pay on the nail, run riot, sit tight*. Especially rich in idiomatic usages are the verb-adverb combinations like *bring to* ('resuscitate'), *call off* ('revoke'), *come by* ('acquire'), *get on* ('succeed'), '*hold out* for higher pay', *light out* ('depart'), *pull through* ('survive').

Figurative phrases, such as *go against the grain, call his bluff, a skeleton in the closet*, and mere conventional phrases like *safe and sound, come and go, hither and yon*, do not come under the head of idioms, if our original definition be adhered to. They are a part of "the idiom of English", as we shall see; but because they are easily analyzable into their component elements, they are not idioms.

IDIOMATIC ENGLISH

The Idiom of English. Although it is a difficult undertaking to attempt to explain in detail just what is meant by the idiom, or genius, of the English language, a fairly comprehensive definition can be gained just by summarizing the general and outstanding peculiarities of usage and meaning that have been studied in the foregoing chapters. For the idiom of any language is made up of the habits and usages peculiar to that language or not generally found in other languages.*

Certainly it is worthy of note that

a. The use of active verbs as passives, as in 'The cloth *washes* well', is a noticeable feature of English usage (p. 296).

b. Verb-adverb combinations have assumed so important a place in Modern English colloquial speech that the foreigner finds them often very confusing (p. 297).

c. The English practice of conversion, likewise of growing importance in colloquial speech, must be reckoned with by the student of our idiom (pp. 316, 357).

d. The so-called retained object is a peculiarly English construction, and it is not easy for a foreigner to determine which verbs can be used with it (p. 478).

e. The use of the expletives *it* and *there* is different from the practice of many other languages (p. 502).

f. The postponement of prepositions to the end of relative clauses, as in 'the man you were speaking *of*', has developed in English until it must be considered an essential feature of English idiom (pp. 507, 538).

g. Elliptical clauses, such as '*When fully grown*, it weighed a ton', are represented to some extent in other languages; but the ellipsis in this construction, as well as in some others, can fairly be considered a phase of English idiom (p. 511).

h. The more colloquial irrational constructions of Modern English, such as 'the *richest of any* university', must be included by the student of English idiom, whether he approves or not (p. 513).

i. One of the most complicated phases of English idiomatic speech is to be seen in the manifold and various uses of English phrasal verbs. Those little niceties of meaning resulting from the use of *shall* and *will*, of *may* and *can*, of *could* and *would* and *should*, challenge even the speaker born to the idiom (p. 522).

---

* It would, of course, be rash to assert that the usages here listed as idiomatic are never found outside of English; but most of them are probably exceptional enough to lend a distinctive character to the English language.

j. The uses of gerundial constructions have become so perplexing that both foreigners and native users of English have been endeavoring lately to determine their proper and peculiar place in the idiom of today (p. 531).

k. And, finally, of the syntactical problems of the individual who would familiarize himself thoroughly with the usages of Current English, the selection of just the right preposition to use after a verb, noun, or adjective, as in *consist of, confidence in,* and *devoid of,* often proves most troublesome (p. 536).

l. Of course the idiomatic phrases discussed earlier in this section must be reckoned an important part of English idiom.

m. Various phrases and single words figurative in their use, like *fill the bill, high and dry, let sleeping dogs lie, pull together, rest on one's oars,* and *sidetrack,* while they have not met our definition of idiomatic phrases, do, nevertheless, constitute a very important part of that English idiom with which the learner is sure to have contacts.

n. So, likewise, the many conventional or stereotyped phrases, like *as cross as two sticks, go to wrack and ruin, one and all, sink or swim, sooner or later,* must be counted among the idiomatic features of English.

o. Various amalgamated phrases, such as *aboard, a-going, alive, o'clock,* challenge the learner of English idiom because they must often be used in peculiar and restricted ways.

Idiom is like the comfortable and homely atmosphere of an old dwelling; it comes to a language only after long and loving use. It is not always rational or logical, and consequently it often violates the principles of accepted grammatical practice. But after it becomes established, it remains in spite of its irrational and unusual character. In characterizing the English language and comparing it in a general way with other languages (Sec. 28), we have commented upon the simplicity of its grammar, its cosmopolitan vocabulary, its antiquated spelling, and the richness and colorfulness that have characterized it from earliest times; but it was not possible to add so early in this study of the language these various peculiarities of its idiom which have been examined and appraised later in the book. For idiom cannot be measured by syllables or counted in words or tested for grammatical accuracy; it is too varied and intangible for such tests.

CHAPTER XIV

IMPROVEMENT OF THE ENGLISH LANGUAGE

FOR the last four centuries Englishmen have been striving to improve the English language. This endeavor has taken various forms, but outstanding among them have been the plans for controlling English usage through an academy of some sort, the effort to improve the methods of studying and teaching the language, the schemes for simplifying the very troublesome spelling, and, more recently, the plans for utilizing English in the formulation of artificial supplementary languages which could be used internationally. Since these matters all have a bearing on the future development and use of the English language, it is worth while to consider them seriously, both in the light of earlier developments as they have been indicated in the foregoing chapters and also in their possible relations to the future growth of English.

126. *Movement for an Academy*

After Caxton had faced the question of how the English vocabulary should be improved, through most of the sixteenth century critics like Ascham and Nash argued about the best methods of embellishing and improving the English language (see page 331), and finally the idea took shape that there should be an authoritative body of scholars and writers who should pass upon questions of linguistic usage as well as on questions of literary style. The French Academy had been successfully launched, with royal recognition in the year 1635, and many Englishmen felt that they should have a similar body of scholars and critics to act as a court of final appeal in linguistic controversies. The introduction of many foreign words troubled some critics, while others were concerned chiefly with the need of a reform of English spelling; but all of them felt that some *authority* should be found, either an individual or a group, who could be depended upon to settle controversial matters. Various persons suggested and urged the foundation of an academy, including such influential writers as Gabriel Harvey, John Dryden, and Jonathan Swift.

By the beginning of the eighteenth century, interest in grammar had increased to such an extent that it too was included in the purposes for which the academy should be established. When Samuel Johnson undertook to compile his great Dictionary, he did so with the hope that it would be "a dictionary by which the pronunciation of our language may be fixed, and its attainment facilitated; by which its purity may be preserved, its use ascertained, and its duration lengthened". But by the time his work was completed, he had come to realize much more fully the changing and unstable character of a language such as his own and the hopelessness of undertaking to "fix" any living tongue. Nevertheless Johnson was strongly influential in establishing and regularizing the forms and usages of English, and this has been recognized even while his shortcomings have been criticized. Likewise, in America, Lindley Murray and Noah Webster exerted a very great influence in the regularizing of grammatical practice, as well as in the fixing of the vocabulary, especially in the early decades of the nineteenth century.

However, the need of an academy was still felt by certain persons interested in the improvement of English, and continues to be felt even in the present day. As late as 1930 an article appeared in the *Quarterly Review* of London, advocating the establishment of such an academy. After a discussion of some of the less desirable features of present-day English, such as the spelling, misuses of certain words, and syntactical bugbears like the split infinitive, the author concluded by expressing an opinion that the language does need an academy of letters.[477]

When the late poet laureate of England, Robert Bridges,

in collaboration with Henry Bradley and other eminent British scholars and writers, founded the Society for Pure English, it was with the understanding that no real academy was intended, as conceived of by earlier advocates; but it was proposed "that a few men of letters, supported by the scientific alliance of the best linguistic authorities, should form a group or free association, and agree upon a modest and practical scheme for informing popular taste on sound principles, for guiding educational authorities, and for introducing into practice certain slight modifications and advantageous changes".[478]

This society began publication in 1919, and when, in 1922, certain leading American philologists proposed to interested scholars of England the organization of a permanent international body of scholars and men of letters representing the principal English-speaking peoples, "to maintain the traditions and foster the development of our common tongue", a cordial reply came from the men active in the Society for Pure English, with a warning, however, against "the establishment of an authoritative academy, tending to divorce the literary from the spoken language"

In America the National Council of Teachers of English has been even more inclined to avoid dogmatic pronouncements on English usage, and has made its *English Journal* available for a great variety of papers on the use and teaching of the English language. Indeed, its publication of Leonard's *Current English Usage* [401] as the first of a series of monographs has even led some careless readers of the book to assume that the society is officially encouraging various questionable locutions, just because the answers to a general questionnaire have indicated a certain degree of tolerance on the part of those questioned.

As a matter of fact, the arbitrary insistence of the older grammarians and purists on certain forms and usages in English speech has driven some modern students and teachers to such an extreme in their aversion to narrow and unreasonable and very positive grammatical doctrine that they are inclined to ignore authority almost altogether and accept popular usage as the determining factor. But the very fact that many able philologists, and various organizations like the Society for Pure English and the promoters of "Better English Week", have so unanimously agreed upon the need for concerted effort looking toward the maintenance of the integrity of the English language indicates that the majority of thoughtful students of English feel that some sort of scholarly supervision and guidance is desirable for users of the language. After all, academy or no academy, it is a fact that standard literary English actually has been consciously developed and somewhat jealously guarded for more than three centuries, has been taught in schools and standardized in dictionaries and grammars, and has been watched over by printers and writers; and while the popular colloquial usages have undergone many changes, standard literary practice has been more and more carefully defined.

For four centuries critics have been proposing various radical schemes for the phonetic spelling of English, for the "purification" of the language through the dropping of borrowed terms, and for the dropping of most of its formal and syntactical grammar. But the more conservative and clear-sighted students of the language have recognized that the great stream of English thinking and its linguistic expression will go steadily on, not greatly affected by the earnest endeavors of individuals and groups of people to change it and improve it.

Insistence on "better English" rather than on "pure English" has been advocated by most thoughtful philologists and teachers of the art of expression, in recent years. It has been urged throughout this book because it is an ideal which can always be present in the study of a living tongue like English, whereas the fixity implied in "pure English" can be attained only in a dead language, such as classical Latin or Greek. Moreover, the ideal of better English challenges a speaker to study all through his life the expression of his thinking, in order that he may constantly improve both the thinking and the language used to express it.

And, finally, while the movement for an academy has always recognized the wisdom of selecting for membership scholars who would know the history of the English language, with its trends and changes and good points and bad, its linguistic successes and its failures, today a much broader scholarship is demanded than ever before, in those who are chosen to advise in matters of English usage. One is no longer content to base his decision as to the best use of a doubtful locution merely on the opinion or prejudices of a certain authoritative lexicographer or grammarian, or even of some special body of scholars or academy; rather one wants to know the reasons for their decisions.

127. *Grammatical Methods and Nomenclature*

Not only has there been a prolonged endeavor to improve the English language itself, but of late there has been a growing desire to improve also the study and teaching of the language. As we have pointed out earlier in this book, the study of our language has been confined until quite recently to a consideration of the more restricted field of grammar (which has usually comprised the classification, inflection, and syntax of words), to practice in spelling correctly, and, rarely, to etymological studies. Until the Report of the British Joint Committee on Grammatical Terminology was published in 1911 [480], there had never been a concerted effort to improve and clarify the terminology of English grammar; and even today the methodology and terminology of English philology are largely a matter of individual choice and caprice. The many-sidedness of the English language, as a subject for study, has kept the philologists so busy evolving different methods of presentation, and finding new terms to use with them, that it is not easy to sift their methods and select the best, or to choose terms that will be acceptable to and understood by the greatest number. Some such attempts at selection have been called to the attention of the student, in the preceding chapters, and reasons set forth, also. Before any attempt is made to review in detail the more important among the methods of presentation that have been selected and employed, certain fundamental principles underlying this presentation should be emphasized:

a. Any sound presentation of the facts of English speech must recognize the ever-changing nature of language.

b. It is impossible to present the subject of language clearly and definitely unless careful definitions of terms be made and somewhat arbitrary classifications be agreed upon for the sake of convenience.

c. A certain amount of repetition is inevitable, if various points of view be chosen, because, in order that the many-sided character of English may be brought out, it is often necessary to display a locution in several different ways.

d. After terms have been defined as well as possible and classifications agreed upon as fully as may be done, it is important to recognize that there are many hybrid or confused constructions which the grammarians should be content to accept as such, not only because of the difficulty of classifying them exactly, but also because they are used by people as a sort of linguistic evasion of the responsibility of clear-cut expression, at times when speakers choose to make general and even vague statements and do not wish to stop under the circumstances to make exact and careful statements.

e. It is important to utilize a method and terminology that is adapted to the age of the student, and also one that can be applied as far as possible to other languages than English. It has seemed advisable, for example, in teaching verb forms to younger children, to employ the terms *regular* and *irregular*; in this book, however, the terms *weak* and *strong* have been used for the more advanced study of the English verb. And it is necessary to have certain terms for Latin or French or other foreign grammar which English may not need. But if the method be kept simple and the terms well defined, such adaptations may be easily made.

A broad and widely comprehensive method of treatment might well be named first of all. It is generally agreed that a well-rounded study of the English language must take cognizance of its pronunciation and spelling, its functional classifications, its derivational methods, the inflection and syntactical uses of its words, and its semasiological processes. But any study of English that progresses from phase to phase in the order just given will make increasingly clear the impossibility of separating the study of meanings from the other phases of study. Consequently the other phases of language study — the study of inflection, syntax, etc. — inevitably lead up to a climax in a final survey of changes of meaning (see Sec. 4).

If one thinks of the various units of speech as ranging from sounds and letters through words, phrases, clauses, and sentences to the larger, rhetorical paragraph, stanza, etc., he will find some confusion but will generally be able to clarify his thinking about them if he applies the test of use and does not depend too much on form. This is true especially of the units of intelligible speech discussed in Section 5.

Two important methods of approach to the study of our language sometimes necessitate quite different procedures but usually arrive at about the same end; the scientific study examines and appraises somewhat more leisurely all locutions, good, bad, and indifferent, while the artistic study seeks to arrive as promptly as possible at the best usages. The best contemporary thought on this subject leads, as we have found in the attitude of philologists and writers alike toward an academy, to the opinion that the science of linguistics and the art of expression should go together. The scientist can help by setting up standards; but the artist must make use of them, unless he is willing to fall back on authority, a very weak and unsatisfactory procedure (see Sec. 8).

In various other cases of conflicting methods, a choice must be made: Shall sounds be represented by the scientific or the natural alphabet (see Sec. 21)? Shall verbs be classed according as they express action, state, or being, or according to their aspects (see Sec. 53)? Shall word etymologies be taken up one by one, or shall they be studied according to processes and tendencies (see page 330)? Shall syntactical constructions be considered twice, in order to present them first as elements in the sentence, and secondly as they pertain to the various parts of speech (see page 469)?

It is surprising to find so much variation still in the definitions of certain philological terms: *conversion* means to some scholars merely a shift from one part of speech to another, but it may also be applied to changes within each class, as in this book (Sec. 58, p. 317); *composition* has often been restricted to compounds made from separate words, but it is also broadened in scope so as to include words formed by the use of suffixes and prefixes (Sec. 61); *homonym* has been limited in application to words spelled alike, or it has been extended to take in words pronounced alike also (Sec. 82); *case* has been defined as form or as use or as both (Sec. 87, p. 445); and *gender* has been regarded as grammatical form and also as sex distinction (Sec. 116); even *tense* is somewhat ambiguous in that it may be applied strictly to the three "times", or it may be extended to include certain expressions of completion (see page 453). And there are other ambiguous terms (see Sec. 124).

But if difference of opinion has resulted in confusion as to how a term should be used, it has also led in some instances to the very unfortunate accumulation of a great variety of names for the same thing. "In the very desire for betterment," says the Report of the American Joint Committee on Grammatical Nomenclature [480], "we have reached a multiplicity of terms, even for grammatical relations about the nature of which there is no real difference of opinion, as, for example, those seen in the italicized words in 'John is *good*', 'This is *John*', 'I admire *John*', 'We made John *president*.' For the first of these, there are nine different names in twenty-five of the English grammars in use in the United States today, for the second ten, for the third seven, and for the fourth eighteen." Such confusion as this and a marked tendency to invent new terms for use in new grammar books lead to the conviction that to agree upon almost any term that is generally comprehended is better than to allow such a state of chaos to continue.

Possibly one of the most important of the more recent contributions to the study of English grammar has been the insistence that not all categories are clear-cut and well defined, but that there are forms and usages that may be termed hybrids, or fusions. Words cannot always be converted so completely that there does not remain at times an element of confusion (see Sec. 58); certain etymologies are obscure because popular etymologizing has so thoroughly confused different words and meanings that scholarly research may never succeed in throwing light on earlier forms and uses (see Sec. 69); syntactical constructions are sometimes irrational, but they are none the less convenient, because they are shortcuts which often serve their purpose better than more elaborate and more pedantic constructions (see Sec. 102). Functional, derivational, and syntactical fusions must be reckoned with in the study of Current English.

Many cynical and disparaging charges of pedantic narrowness and dogmatic insistence on forms and uses have been brought against the grammarians; but those scholars of the present day who know something of the history of the English language are generally so far from pedantry and dogmatism in their attitude toward contemporary usage that they are sometimes in danger of not emphasizing enough those features of the English language which should be emphasized and cherished and preserved in the general effort to maintain the integrity of the language.

128. *Spelling Reform*

For four hundred years thoughtful students have been longing for a phonetic spelling of English, a system in which each sound has its own peculiar spelling, in which each letter represents just one sound. But during that period our spelling has been growing worse, if possible, in the accumulation of duplications, owing to the fact that, while the system of Middle English sound representation has been largely retained, from time to time other methods of spelling certain sounds have been tried out, which have given such additional spellings as *ie* in *chief*, and foreign words have been introduced with a great number of exotic spellings, such as *ue* in *dialogue*. Today, as a result of this experimentation and this foreign corruption, the eight long vowel sounds in common use are represented by at least sixty-six different spellings, and the other vowel and consonant sounds by an equally great variety of spellings (see Sec. 47). Or, if we look at this situation from the standpoint of letters, there is scarcely a letter in the English alphabet that does not represent from two to eight different sounds.

The radical reformer would go so far as to modernize the spelling by substituting the International Phonetic Alphabet, spelling *fail*, for example, with *e*, as *fel*, and *ship* with ʃ, as ʃ*ip*. But the more conservative reformers would be content to use the letters of the present system, as *a* for the vowel sound in *fate* and *sh* for the first consonant sound in *ship*, simply agreeing that each spelling be limited so as to indicate just one sound. They would not attempt to change the medieval set of sound representations now in general use, but they would agree upon certain outstanding spellings among them and endeavor to make the others conform to these. They would, for instance, retain the *a* in *fate*, but change the *ai* of *fail*, the *ei* of *sleigh*, the *ea* of *break*, the *ao* of *gaol*, the *au* of *gauge*, etc., making this whole group of spellings conform to a single type of spelling, if possible; they would, likewise, retain the *sh* in *ship*, but change the spellings of *schist*, *sugar*, *pshaw*, *chef*, *ocean*, *nation*, etc., so that they would also conform. They would attack some of the more exotic spellings, such as the *ph* in *philosophy*, the *æ* in *diæresis*, the *ch* in *character*, the *gu* in *guard*, and the *tte* in *cigarette*, spelling these words as *filosofy*, *dieresis*, *caracter*, *gard*, and *cigaret*. They would endeavor, as far as possible, to make it easier for a child or a foreigner to pronounce every word correctly just by looking at the spelling, and to spell every word correctly just by following such simple rules of spelling as these: the sound [ē] is spelled *a* in English, the sound [f] is spelled *f*, the sound [k] is spelled *c* before back vowels, the sound [g] is spelled *g* before back vowels. This would not be perfect phonetic spelling, be it noted, because the *c* would still represent different sounds in *caracter* and *city*, and the *g* in *gard* and *gin*; but such improvement, they hope, would pave the way for a later agreement on still more phonetic spellings, eliminating the *c* altogether ultimately, and substituting *j* for *g* in all words like *gin*. They would attack the worst cases of inconsistency at first and, later, hope to improve still further.

Some reformers are inclined to stress the waste that results from the use of so many digraphs or trigraphs in English spelling, such as the *sh* in *ship*, the *dg* in *edge*, the *tch* in *catch*, the *ph* in *philosophy*, the *ss* in *pass*, the *ll* in *fell*, the *th* in *then*, and the *nn* in *dinner*. But they find some serious difficulties in replacing these with single letters because the English alphabet lacks characters for *sh, dg, tch,* and *th* and it would be necessary to invent new ones which would be strange, and objectionable to many persons now using the English language. Moreover, they would find it necessary to adopt some special method of distinguishing vowel length in words like *diner* and *dinner*, if they were to simplify the double *n*. Consequently many spelling-reformers are inclined to retain some of the spelling digraphs, merely making their use more uniform and consistent.

Of course the widespread use of silent *e* in English spelling shocks the feelings of many thrifty souls among the would-be reformers of our spelling, and they lop it off wherever it can be removed without seriously impairing the effectiveness of the spelling of a word. Inasmuch as the final *e* has been gradually sloughed off in many words since the reformers went to work in the sixteenth century, it is not hard to continue the process in such words as *definite, determine, favorite, juvenile,* and *promise,* and more especially *cigarette, gazelle,* and *programme*. But in *active, carve,* and *delve,* while the *e* is equally useless, the reformer is likely to encounter more opposition to the dropping of it because the writer of English is not accustomed to a final *v*. Moreover, the *e* cannot well be dropped from words like *college, owe,* and *terrace* until the spelling of the sounds immediately preceding it shall have been provided for in some manner, for *colleg, ow, and terrac* would not be feasible spellings. More than the mere dropping of a final silent *e* is required in such words. So in words like *browse, cheese, freeze, ooze,* and *please,* the final *e* could be dropped; but it would be necessary to accustom writers of English to a somewhat unusual final *z* in *freez* and *ooz,* and in simplified *brows, chees,* and *pleas* the *z* sound of the final *s* would still cause difficulty, as it already does in many other English words. And, finally, in words like *hope, ride, spite, tune,* the silent *e* cannot be spared until some other plan is adopted for indicating that the preceding vowel is not short. Hence the elimination of a final silent *e*, while it would reduce the number of seemingly useless letters by a considerable percentage, would cause some serious complications which the reformer is not yet ready to face, unless he be a very radical and ambitious reformer.

The many silent *e's* in suffixes, particularly in *-ed, -er,* and *-es,* have been the cause of much concern to spelling reformers and have been attacked in some respects, although it has been found necessary to retain some of them for one reason or another. In some cases of the pluralization of nouns by the addition of *-s* or *-es,* as in *cities* and *rates,* the *e* is required to make clear the pronunciation of the preceding sounds; but the hopelessly inconsistent practice of adding *-es* to some *o*-ending nouns, as in *negroes,* but merely *-s* to others, as in *pianos,* fairly clamors for some sort of spelling reform to bring about uniformity of practice, inasmuch as there are probably few spellers who could spell correctly the plurals of the entire list, if some sixty or eighty of these nouns were named.

As to the dropping of the silent *e* from past-tense endings of weak verbs usually spelled now with *-ed,* there is some difference of opinion. At present the practice is to add *-ed* (or *d* when the word ends in *e*) to form the past tense and past participle of all weak verbs, except those irregular groups listed in Section 90, such as *bend, bet, burn, catch, lose,* and *meet*. In the case of verb stems ending in *-d* or *-t,* such as *bond* and *flit,* the *e* of the suffix is pronounced (*bonded, flitted*); but in all the others it is silent (*robbed, locked,* etc). Some poets of the past have omitted this silent *e* but have inserted an apostrophe in its place, as in *cabl'd, serv'd, wrong'd.* But more recently reformers have endeavored to drop this silent *e* of the past-tense forms, as in *cald, carrid, followd, receivd, robd*; and in addition they would use final *-t* when the ending is so pronounced, as in *askt, effervest, helpt, kist, notist.* This change is in the direction of greater confusion rather than greater uniformity in the group of several thousand weak verbs, since it necessitates the setting up of numerous subrules and exceptions. The method of procedure in forming the past tense and past participle of weak verbs would be about as follows:

1. Add -d to verbs ending in voiced consonants, usually, as in *bagd, humd, longd*.
2. Add -t to verbs ending in voiceless consonants, usually, as in *archt, dropt, fixt*.
3. Simplify double final consonants before adding -d or -t, as in *fild, mist*.
4. Add -ed or -d to verbs ending in -d and -de or -t and -te, as in *bonded, boded, parted, pasted*, because the e must be pronounced.
5. Add -d when the final consonant plus e of the verb is preceded by a long-vowel monograph, as in *agonized, paled, robed, wired*.
6. Add -d after ge [= dʒ], as in *changed, obliged, raged*.
7. Add -d after ce [= s], as in *danced, faced, reduced*; or else go a step farther and spell the ce as s, as in *danst, notist*.
8. Perhaps the -ed should be used in *carried, pitied*, etc., to show that the sound of the i (from y) is not the same in these words as that of i in *rapid* and *tepid*.
9. Perhaps the -ed should be used in such past-tense forms as *chilled, crowed, deafened, grinned, milled, willed*, and similar cases where the dropping of the silent e would lead to serious confusion with other words like *child, defend*, etc.

The elimination of various silent consonants is also made much of in the reforming of present-day English spelling. Silent *gh* of words like *night, ought, taught, thorough*, and *though* presents in each instance a slightly different problem; *debt* and *doubt* are generally simplified to *det* and *dout*; the *l* is sometimes dropped from *could* and *should* and *would*; the *k* of *knee* and *know*, the *g* of *gnaw*, and the *p* of *receipt* are usually dropped in reformed spelling; and various other silent letters are done away with. There is no uniform rule of simplification possible in the case of silent consonants because they differ so widely.

Those reformers who are not yet ready to go as far as a complete phonetic system of spelling have attacked spellings here and there which seem unnecessarily troublesome; they are content, for the present, with making these special groups conform to other more common groups, thereby eliminating duplication. So they would get rid of the *ei* spelling which parallels the *ie* spelling, changing *receive* to *recieve*, for example, to conform to words like *chief* and *thief*; they would change *succeed* to *succede*, to conform to *precede* and *recede* and the rest of the verbs derived from the Latin *cedo*; and they would make final *-re* conform to the *-er* group, changing *ogre* to *oger*. They would be satisfied, for the time being, to reduce the existing confusion by making spellings of groups of similar words conform more nearly than they do at present.

The almost hopeless confusion now existing in the spelling of unaccented vowels, as in *carriage, copious, lettuce, money, pity, tortoise*, has discouraged reformers from attempting improvement in this part of the spelling field until the accented vowels shall have been improved somewhat. If the syllables *-ance* and *-ence* of *abundance* and *evidence*, *-y* and *-ey* of *cranky* and *donkey*, *-le*, *-el*, *-il*, and *-ol* of *able, level, evil*, and *vitriol*, could be made more uniform, much uncertainty would be done away with.

And, finally, and perhaps with most promise of immediate success in reform, those numerous individual duplications in English spelling which cause so much discussion and perplexity are usually made the first object of attack. In the second circular, issued by the Simplified Spelling Board in March, 1907, a list of three hundred words spelled in two or more ways was made the basis of a new reform movement. In this list appeared such pairs as *accouter — accoutre, adz — adze, bark — barque, chapt — chapped, clamor — clamour, cue — queue, draft — draught, ether — æther, fulfil — fulfill, glycerin — glycerine, mold — mould, plow — plough, prolog — prologue, sulfur — sulphur*, the first spelling of each pair being recommended as the simpler and better form.

Since the organization of the American Spelling Reform Association in 1876, interest in the subject, both in America and in Great Britain, has been fairly steady and continuous. In 1883 the American Philological Association and the Philological Society of London agreed on a set of twenty-four rules for the simplification of English spelling, and a list of some thirty-three hundred words was issued. With varying degrees of interest and success, spelling-reformers have been utilizing these rules and this word list since that time (see The Century Dictionary and Cyclopedia [21], Vol. VIII, Supplement). In 1906 a Simplified Spelling Board was created in America, and it began a program of gradual education of the spelling public. It seized first upon twelve words approved some years earlier by the National Educational Association, namely, *catalog, decalog, demagog, pedagog, prolog, program, tho, altho, thoro, thorofare, thru,* and *thruout.* Then in 1907 it promulgated its list of three hundred words, as noted above, with some attempt at a set of rules. The second list, published in 1908, was classified more carefully. Third and fourth lists followed soon, and in 1919 these four lists were revised and arranged alphabetically in a *Handbook of Simplified Spelling* [485], with a set of rules to govern simplifications. In the meantime an increased activity among British reformers led to the organization in 1908 of the Simplified Spelling Society, with a membership composed of most of the leading English philologists.

In March, 1925, the first number appeared of a quarterly called *Spelling,* published jointly by the Simplified Spelling Society, the Simplified Spelling Board, and the Spelling Reform Association. In its initial editorial the "three distinct possible and appropriate lines of progress" which are favored by the three groups were set forth as follows:

One important group sees no immediate prospect of securing popular support for the necessarily drastic changes involvd in *any* simple and consistent sceme of spelling, and therefore believs that maximum progress is to be achievd by recommending with the weight of competent authority a moderate number of wel chosen simplifications, not so numerous as to transform the general appearance of the printed page, and to seek the widest possible adoption of this first step, both for its intrinsic merits and as a demonstration that rational simplification of English spelling by conscious and deliberate effort is possible and desirable. To this group the present program of the Simplified Spelling Board wil make the strongest appeal.

Another group sees no immediate prospect of introducing into the alfabet new letters to represent those sounds for which the present 26 letters do not and can not provide simple and consistent representation, but does see clearly the immense advantage of a complete and logically consistent sceme so simple that it can be presented on a postcard and learnd in an hour, of immediate and important educational value as a teaching device in the elementary schools. This group will find much the best solution yet offerd to the problem of a uniform, complete, and consistent spelling of English with no new letters or diacritics in the spelling sceme workt out by the Simplified Spelling Society.

A third group questions the wisdom or practicality of expending the immense amount of energy required to effect *any* substantial change in existing spelling conditions on any admittedly partial or temporary objectiv, and prefers therefore, in spite of the immense obstacles in the way of any immediate general adoption, to deal with the only wholly simple, satisfactory, and ultimate solution — complete fonetic spelling, using such new letters as a minimum precision one-sign one-sound alfabet may require. This group wil find expression in the Spelling Reform Association.

Since the rules promulgated by the Simplified Spelling Board seem to be generally accepted by all of these groups, at least as a preliminary, temporary step toward a more thoroughgoing reform of English spelling, they should be examined in the light of the general principles and methods already discussed. To facilitate such an examination the list printed in Part 3 of the board's *Handbook of Simplified Spelling* [485] (pp. 6–10) has been somewhat arbitrarily rearranged, and the rules numbered consecutively, as follows:

Modification toward phonetic spellings

1. æ, œ, initial or medial. SPEL e. EXAMPLES: *ciclopedia, esthetic,*[*] *fenix, maneuver, medieval, subpena.* BUT: *alumnae, striae,* etc.
2. **ise** final pronounst as if speld **ize.** SPEL **ize.** EXAMPLES: *advertize, advize, apologize, rize, surprize, wize,* etc.

---

[*] In these lists of illustrations as they are printed in the *Handbook*, words such as *esthetic* are not italicized but are printed in roman "if given as preferd or alternativ spellings by one or more of the leading American dictionaries (Century, Standard, Webster's)." For it should be noted that the board has in many instances merely attempted to standardize simpler spellings which are already quite generally employed by writers and recommended by dictionaries. But inasmuch as there is still much diversity in practice, in reprinting the lists here no effort has been made to distinguish new from current simplifications. The student must therefore consult the dictionaries. Throughout this book (*Current English*) such words have been spelled according to the editorial policy of the publishers.

3. **ou** before **l**, pronounst like **o** in *bold*. Drop silent **u**, except in *soul*.
   Examples: *bolder, colter, mold, molt, sholder.*
4. **y** between consonants. Spel **i**. Examples: *analisis, fisic, gipsy, paralize, rime, silvan, sithe, tipe.*

Other respellings not covered by these rules are recommended as follows: *burlesk, buro* (for 'bureau'), *frend, grotesk, mark* (for 'marque'), *maskerade, picturesk, siv, slight* (for 'sleight'), *tuch, yoman, yu, yung, yungster, yunker.*

Simplification of digraphs

5. **ch** pronounst like **c** in *car*. Drop silent **h**, except before **e, i, y**.
   Examples: *caracter, clorid(e), corus, cronic, eco, epoc, mecanic, monarc, scolar, scool, stomac, tecnical.*
6. **Double consonant** before e final silent. Drop last two letters.
   Examples: *bagatel, bizar, cigaret, creton, gazet, giraf, gram, program, quadril, quartet, vaudevil,* etc.
7. **Double consonant** final. Reduce double to single; but in **-ll** only after a short vowel, and in **-ss** only in monosillables. Retain *gross, hiss, off, puss*. Examples: *ad, bil, bluf, buz, clas, dol, dul, eg, glas, les, los, mes, mis, pas, pres, shal, tel, wil.* But not: *al* (for 'all'), *needles* (for 'needless'), *rol* (for 'roll'), etc.
8. **ea** pronounst as in *head* or as in *heart*. Drop the silent letter.
   Examples: *bred, brekfast, hed, helth, hevy, insted, lether, plesure, wether; hart, harty, harth.*
9. **gh** pronounst **f**. Spel **f**; drop the silent letter of the preceding digraf. Examples: *cof, draft, enuf, laf, ruf, tuf.*
10. **ph** pronounst **f**. Spel **f**. Examples: *alfabet, emfasis, fantasy, fantom, fonograf, fotograf, sulfur, telefone, telegraf.*
11. **rh** initial. Drop silent **h**. Examples: *retoric, reumatism, rime, rithm, rubarb,* etc.
12. **sc** initial pronounst as if speld **s**. Drop silent **c**. Examples: *senery, sented, septer, sience, simitar, sissors.* But: *scatter, sconce, scooner,* etc.

Elimination of silent e

13. **e** final silent. In the following cases drop **e**:
    a. After a consonant preceded by a short vowel strest.
    Examples: *bad* (for 'bade'), *giv, hav, liv,* etc.
    b. In *ar*(e), *gon*(e), and in *wer*(e) when not pronounst to rime with *there*.

c. In the unstrest final short sillables **ide, ile, ine, ise, ite, ive,** pronounst as if speld **id, il, in, is, it, iv.** EXAMPLES: *activ, bromid, comparativ, definit, determin, engin, genuin, practis, promis, textil,* etc.

d. After **lv** and **rv.** EXAMPLES: *involv, twelv, valv; carv, curv, deserv, serv,* etc.

e. After **v** or **z** when preceded by a digraf representing a long vowel or a difthong. EXAMPLES: *achiev, believ, freez, gauz, leav, reciev, sneez,* etc.

f. In **oe** final pronounst **o.** EXAMPLES *fo, ho, ro, to, wo.* RETAIN **e** in inflections **-oed, -oes,** as *hoed* (not *hod*), *foes* (not *fos*).

14. **ed** final pronounst **d.** When the change wil not suggest a wrong pronunciation, drop silent **e,** reducing a preceding double to a single consonant. EXAMPLES: *anserd, carrid, delayd, doubld, examind, fild, pleasd, preferd, robd, signd, sneezd, traveld, worrid,* etc. BUT NOT: *bribd* (for 'bribed'), *cand* (for 'caned'), *changd* (for 'changed'), *fild* (for 'filed'), *usd* (for 'used'), etc.

15. **ed** final pronounst **t.** When the change wil not suggest a wrong pronunciation, spel **t,** reducing a preceding double to a single consonant, and changing **ced, sced,** final, to **st.** EXAMPLES: *askt, fixt, helpt, wisht; addrest, kist, past, shipt; acquiest, advanst, commenst, effervest, notist,* etc. BUT NOT: *bakt* (for 'baked'), *deduct* or *dedust* (for 'deduced'), *fact* or *fast* (for 'faced'), *hopt* (for 'hoped'), etc.

A more detailed discussion of problems involved in the simplification of such verbs appears on page 592.

Elimination of other silent letters

16. **bt** pronounst **t.** DROP silent **b.** EXAMPLES: *det, dettor, dout, indetted, redout.* RETAIN **b,** when pronounst, in *subtil(e).*
17. **gh** pronounst like **g** in *gas.* DROP silent **h.** EXAMPLES: *agast, gastly, gerkin, gost, goul.*
18. **gm** final. DROP silent **g.** EXAMPLES: *apothem, diafram, flem, paradim.*
19. **gue** after a consonant, a short vowel, or a digraf representing a long vowel or a difthong. DROP silent **ue.** EXAMPLES: *catalog, dialog, harang, leag, sinagog, tung* (with change of vowel also).
20. **mb** final after a short vowel. DROP silent **b.** EXAMPLES: *bom, crum, dum, lam, lim, thum.* BUT NOT: *com* (for 'comb'), *tom* (for 'tomb'), etc.

21. **ough** final. Spel **o, u, ock,** or **up** when pronounst as if so speld.
   EXAMPLES: *altho, -boro, boro, do, donut, furlo, tho, thoro; thru; hock; hiccup.*
22. **u** silent before a vowel medial. DROP **u**. EXAMPLES: *bild, condit, garantee, gard, ges, gide, gild.*

Other eliminations of silent letters which do not come under any one of these rules are recommended as follows: *anser, campain, cask* (for 'casque'), *catar, delite, diarea, foren, hemorage, hemoroid, iland, ile, ilet, morgage, sorgum, sovren, spritely, tisic, tisis.*

Reduction in the number of spellings used for sounds

23. **ceed** final. SPEL **cede**. EXAMPLES: *excede, procede, succede.*
24. **ei** pronounst like **ie** in *brief*. SPEL **ie**. EXAMPLES: *conciet, deciev, iether, inviegle, reciev, wierd.*
25. **re** final after consonant except **c**. SPEL **er**. EXAMPLES: *center, fiber, meter, theater.* BUT NOT: *lucer* (for 'lucre'), *mediocer* (for 'mediocre'), etc.

Elimination of troublesome spellings of unaccented vowels

26. **ey** final unstrest, pronounst like short final **y**. DROP silent **e**.
   EXAMPLES: *barly, chimny, donky, journy, mony, pully, trolly, vally, whisky.*
27. **our** final, with **ou** pronounst as a short (obscure) vowel. DROP **u**.
   EXAMPLES: *color, favor, honor, labor, Savior.*

Under this head would be included, also, *counterfit, forfit.*

It will have been observed that various examples given in the foregoing lists are already approved as duplicate or variant forms (sometimes even as preferred forms) by many people; in listing such spellings and then adding others, the reformer is throwing his influence on the side of the simpler and better forms and at the same time strengthening his case for reform by taking advantage of trends already observable in present-day English spellings. Such spellings as *bromid, catalog, center, cigaret, color, draft, medieval, meter, past* (verb), *plow, program, rime,* and *sulfur* are familiar to very many people; some of them are listed by dictionaries as preferred spellings, as already observed (see footnote on page 596).

It will also be observed that the "But not's" in the foregoing rules are fairly numerous and show that these reforms fall far short of being complete and final. In some instances they are admittedly makeshifts, temporary expedients which aim at more satisfactory final changes in English spelling. Perhaps the most noticeable of these exceptions pertain to the indication of vowel length in English; and until the users of the English language agree upon some one method of showing that a vowel is long or short, there can be little hope of a satisfactory reform of English spelling. At present there are, as we have already observed (Sec. 47, Notes 1–5), five outstanding methods of showing vowel length; until English spellers can agree upon some one of these to the exclusion of the others, there can be little hope of a fundamental and satisfying improvement of English spelling, because so many of the other improvements that have been suggested conflict with these spellings for vowel length that few changes can be carried through completely and uniformly.

As long as doubled consonants are generally presumed to indicate a preceding short vowel, as in *dinner*, such simplifications as *speling* will be felt as violations of this fundamental principle of English spelling. Hence, to avoid the presumption of shortness in the vowel, it is necessary to avoid writing two consonants together; and so, in applying rule 14, *bribed* and *filed* must not be written *bribd* and *fild*, and in using rule 15, *baked* and *hoped* cannot be spelled as *bakt* and *hopt*.

The very general use of a final silent *e* after a single consonant to indicate that a preceding vowel is long is so well recognized that no violation of it is offered anywhere in the rules above: in rule 13 no words like *bide* or *hale* are included, but, on the other hand, the *e* is dropped from *bade*, *give*, *have*, and *live*, just because they do violate this general principle of English spelling; in rule 19 *rogue* and *vague* are retained because removal of the *ue* would incur danger of a shortening of the preceding vowels; in rule 23 the *e* is preferred in the case of *excede*, *procede*, and *succede*; and when the silent letters in *delight* and *sprightly* are eliminated, *delite* and *spritely* are recommended as better spellings. And not only do the reformers of spelling seem to prefer this method of indicating vowel length, but, as has been shown (see page 232), there is a fairly strong popular tendency to resort to it in such spellings as *flite, nite, rite.*

Gemination, or doubling, of the vowel, as in *need* and *food*, though it has been tried out by English spellers more than once during the long period of English linguistic history, never has been very popular, and is not seriously considered today by spelling-reformers as a desirable method of showing vowel length.

Likewise the use of other digraphs, as in *chief, goal, main, neat,* and *vein,* is not looked upon with favor by most reformers, because there are too many different digraphs used for the same sound, because digraphs do not always indicate long vowels, and because the use of digraphs for long vowels is neither economical nor phonetic. And yet, just because no one method of indicating vowel length has been agreed upon by the reformers of English spelling, in rule 24 the *ei* of words like *deceive* is merely changed to the slightly more popular *ie*. No serious effort has been made yet by the Simplified Spelling Board to rid the language of the many digraph spellings for long vowels.

Even the elimination of the silent-consonant method of indicating vowel length, which has developed accidentally and haphazardly in such words as *fight, night, calm, palm, comb, tomb,* and *talk,* has not been urged much by those who are attempting a gradual and progressive simplification. There is, obviously, not much use in changing such spellings until some agreement shall have been reached as to the most desirable method of showing vowel length.

In view of what has just been said regarding the need of some fundamental method of indicating vowel length and the failure so far of spelling-reformers to face the problem, — except, of course, for those extremists who offer complete phonetic writing with a scientific phonetic alphabet, — it is interesting to note that the Swedish scholar Zachrisson has faced the question, and in his new system of reformed English spelling, which he has named "Anglic", has advised the use of a diacritical *e* after each long vowel, as in *beed* (for 'bead'), *fiel* (for 'file'), *goel* (for 'goal'), *mael* (for 'mail'), *ues* (for 'use').[486] But because this adds a new, sixth, method to those already employed in the spelling of English, one that is even more unusual than any one of the other five, there is some doubt as to whether it will prove acceptable to the generality of English and American spellers.

Since Anglic differs so markedly from the tentative and somewhat diffident recommendations of the other spelling-reform groups in that it is, as its author has insisted, "the oenly Simplified Speling of English which is wurkt out and agreed upon in evry deetael and konsequently kan be imeediitly uezd for aul praktikal purpuses", it offers an interesting contrast to the efforts of those other reformers who are affiliated with the three groups in England and the United States.

Conclusions

The simplification of English spelling through the selection of certain spellings for certain sounds and the consequent elimination of duplications and overlappings, through the dropping of digraphs, of silent letters, and especially of silent *e*, and through the avoidance of much uncertainty by giving preference to one spelling where more than one is now found for the same word — these are all simplifications greatly to be desired.

But since the English language is being read or spoken by so large a portion of the world's population at the present time, and since the spelling of it has been so largely standardized by printers, stenographers, authors, teachers, and lexicographers that the radical changing of the system would prove an extremely expensive matter, it seems likely that the only hope of reform lies in a gradual introduction of such changes as at the moment are feasible.

The spelling of English is, as Henry Bradley has insisted [229], not merely a matter of indicating the proper pronunciation of words. Because written words stand for ideas, in silent reading most older readers are able to gain the ideas directly from the printed page without taking the intermediate step of pronouncing the words. For this reason any generally accepted spelling becomes important and cannot be lightly tampered with. Even such conventions of spelling as the generally approved word endings and the avoidance of certain uses of some letters become important when regarded as a part of the business of silent reading. It seems, then, that the reformer might do well to refrain from violating the more general conventions until he has remedied the more troublesome inconsistencies.

Changes in spelling are constantly being attempted by commercial and other agencies, and to some extent reforms are instituted by popular initiative. These can be guided somewhat if they are given attention by philologists.

If it becomes necessary for the reformer to choose between shortening a word or lengthening it in the interest of greater uniformity in a group of words, it is more important to work for uniformity. If the choice were to lie, for example, between adding *-s* or *-es* to vowel-ending words like *solo* or *negro*, it is more important to spell all such words alike, one way or the other, than it is to eliminate one letter. More loss of time results from the uncertainty that forces people to reach for the dictionary to decide doubtful spellings than from the writing of additional letters.

129. *Artificial Languages*

As the world becomes more closely knit together by improvements in communication and transportation, increasingly numerous international gatherings of statesmen, scientists, scholars, fraternal organizations, and conferences of all sorts emphasize a steadily growing need of some international language which can be learned by all nationalities and employed by all on a common basis of friendship and equality. The idea of an international tongue is by no means a new one; for some three hundred years men have played with it and made experiments in creating artificial languages. Indeed, it is said that over two hundred different linguistic systems have been devised during that period.

But it is mainly during the past half-century that there has been a serious and widespread effort to put the matter on a satisfactory foundation through consideration of the purpose and scope of such a language, the elements that should enter into its makeup, and the linguistic features that are most desirable for it. Before an examination be made of some of the more outstanding systems offered during this period of fifty years, these various considerations should be understood, in order that it may be clear why the adherents of international languages have varied so much in their attitudes and opinions on the subject.

During the Middle Ages the international language of all scholarly men and women was Latin, and with ability to speak that tongue one could travel over the civilized world without difficulty. Then came a later period in which diplomatic affairs were discussed in French, and until the time of the World War French was the common tongue of statesmen, diplomats, scholars, and educated travelers in general. But within a relatively brief time, as we have already observed (Sec. 27), the English language has spread so greatly that today it is more nearly an international tongue than any other that can be named.

And yet, even though the use of English has increased so greatly during the last few decades, those who have looked at this matter from a truly international point of view have been more and more strongly of the opinion that a supplementary or auxiliary language is needed which would not supersede national tongues but would provide a common medium for all nations. They argue that national jealousies and rivalries would make it hard to agree on any existing tongue. It is true, as explained already, that the English language does contain a great many words borrowed from other languages; nevertheless it is a national tongue expressing primarily a national culture, and it would be a pity to substitute it or any other national tongue for the various languages of the earth, thereby sacrificing the cultures, and the tongues expressing those cultures, which contribute so variously to the intellectual and spiritual wealth of the earth.

It is, then, on the need of an auxiliary international language that most internationalists agree today. But on the nature of this language they have disagreed so widely during the past half-century that it would be impossible to do more here than list the various languages that have been advocated or launched. Some linguists would make a brand-new language, utilizing the most widely known words in the various contemporary tongues; they have accordingly offered Volapük, Esperanto, Idiom Neutral, Ido, Novial, and so on. Others would resurrect the older Latin, freeing it, however, from its elaborate inflectional system; they have promoted Lingua, Novilatin, Interlingua, otherwise known as Latino sine Flexione, and so on. Others, observing the cosmopolitan character of English and the great extent of its Latin borrowings, have searched out the most commonly used words of English, words generally found also in other present-day languages, and have endeavored to compile an irreducible-minimum list which could be utilized as a basis for international speech; the chief example of this kind of international tongue is Ogden's Basic English, with its recommended list of eight hundred and fifty words. And, finally, others, notably Zachrisson, the Swedish scholar, having observed the rapid spread of English, are inclined to take what seems to them the line of least resistance and use the English language as a whole, merely cleansing it of its objectionable system of spelling.

Since Ogden's Basic English is a mere reduction of the English vocabulary to the barest essentials, and since Zachrisson's Anglic is a similar reduction of the unsystematic spelling of English to a simpler uniform system, these can hardly be considered artificial languages and can therefore be dismissed from consideration here, particularly since they have both been discussed more appropriately in an earlier study of the spread of the English language (Sec. 27).

But even though English be excluded from consideration, and even though the linguistic internationalists do agree pretty well as to the word stock most useful for the making of an artificial language of this kind, still they have moved very slowly and reluctantly toward any sort of agreement as to the general form most desirable for such a language. For the grammatical simplicity of English has not always appealed to creators of artificial language. Shall the noun be given several case endings? Shall grammatical gender force the speaker to use gender forms of the articles? Shall verb, noun, adjective, and adverb all be made from the same stem with only minor changes in endings? Shall the language be fundamentally an inflectional or a syntactical language? On the whole, the tendency seems to be toward the creation of very simple grammar. Consideration of a few of these artificial languages will help to illustrate some of these problems.

In 1880 a German, J. M. Schleyer, brought out his Volapük. He had taken his words from European languages, largely from English, and had so changed them by the use of numerous prefixes and suffixes, and otherwise, that many of them are hardly recognizable. His nouns had four case endings; masculine and feminine endings were added to nouns as needed; verbs had various inflectional endings; and the German sounds represented by the letters ä, ö, ü, increased the difficulty of Volapük for people not accustomed to such sounds.[493]

So in 1887 a Polish oculist, Louis L. Zamenhof, introduced his plan of an artificial language under the title "Lingvo Internacia de la Doktoro Esperanto", the word *Esperanto* meaning 'someone hoping'. While this language did not really get under way until about the beginning of the twentieth century, it has won many adherents in various countries and has had a large measure of success.

The sounds of Esperanto have been kept relatively simple: five vowels, *a, e, i, o, u,* which are neither long nor short; six diphthongs; consonants as in English, except for about nine, such as $c = ts$ as in *bits,* $j = y$ as in *yes,* etc. The words have been selected from various languages, but have been subjected to a uniform procedure by the use of certain original prefixes and suffixes. Nouns, for example, end in -*o,* as *patro* ('father'), adjectives in -*a,* as *patra* ('paternal'), infinitives in -*i,* as *ami* ('to love'), and adverbs in -*e,* as *patre* ('paternally'). So the Latin *san-* (in *sanus* etc.) becomes *sana* ('healthy'), *mal-sana* ('ill'), *sanigi* ('to heal'), *sanigejo* ('hospital'), *sanigisto* ('doctor'), etc.

While most noun inflection has been avoided, the accusative case is retained, and the adjective must agree with the noun in case and number, as in the singular nominative, *bona patro* ('good father'), accusative, *bonan patron*, plural nominative, *bonaj patroj* ('good fathers'), accusative, *bonajn patrojn*. The verb is conjugated to show tense, with the present ending in *-as*, as in *mi vivas* ('I live'), the past in *-is*, as in *li vivis* ('he lived'), the future in *-os*, etc. Various phrasal verbs are made with *esti* ('to be'), as in *li estas foririnta* ('he has gone away').

Certain other prefixes and suffixes have been borrowed and adapted, or created, in order to produce special effects: *dis-* signifies dissemination, as in *dismeti* ('to put apart'); *mal-* gives a negative effect, as in *malbona* ('bad, not good'); *-an* is used for an inhabitant, member, etc., as in *urbano* ('town dweller'); *-in* is a feminine suffix, as in *patrino* ('mother'); *-ist* denotes profession or agency, as in *bonfaristo* ('benefactor'); etc.[494]

The lineal descendant of the earlier Volapük, and a strong rival of Esperanto for some time, was the language called Idiom Neutral, promulgated in 1902 by the Akademi International de Lingu Universal. By this time the advocates of an artificial language had realized that the vocabulary should be selected from those words which are known to the greatest number of languages. So the members of the Akademi made a systematic examination of the vocabularies of English, French, German, Spanish, Italian, Russian, and Latin, and while Idiom Neutral has not proved widely acceptable, the influence of this more scientific method of choosing the vocabulary has been felt by all makers of later artificial languages.

Already the marked disagreement among the linguistic internationalists had given rise to the formation of a Delegation for the Adoption of an Auxiliary International Language, and about 1907 this delegation appointed a committee with authority to discuss the chief linguistic projects and select the best one. The result was the choice of a modified form of Esperanto, which became known as Ido. This proved a strong rival of the older Esperanto, and, with its monthly magazine

Progreso, it has cut into the ranks of the Esperantists very seriously. Ido eliminates the accusative form of the noun and does away with the need of making the adjective agree in form with the noun, two points much criticized in Esperanto. On the whole, it has moved in the direction of greater grammatical simplicity, as well as of a more familiar vocabulary.[495]

In the meantime, those who favored the use of Latin as a basis for an international auxiliary language were at work, and under the leadership of the Italian scholar Giuseppe Peano, Interlingua, or Latino sine Flexione, was launched about 1903. Grammar is reduced to a minimum in this system, the suffix -*s* is used to indicate plurality, and the vocabulary is selected, to quote their own statement, as follows [496]:

> Interlingua es lingua universale que omne persona in modo facile scribe et intellige sine usu de speciale studio. Libro in Interlingua es diffuso supra plure regione de Europa, America, Africa, Australia, et Asia ubi cultura occidentale es noto. Interlingua adopta omne vocabulo que existe simile in Anglo, Germano, Franco, Russo, et Graeco. Et adopta omne vocabulo anglo-latino cum forma de thema (radice).

Anyone who knows Latin reasonably well should not have much difficulty in translating this passage of Interlingua text. But the almost complete lack of grammatical apparatus in this language is objected to by those who have been working at some form of Esperanto or Ido.

However, while students of international languages were endeavoring to make their offerings seem more natural to the public through a more careful selection of familiar words, there was dissatisfaction with the very artificial suffixes that had been evolved. So in 1922 Edgar de Wahl offered what he called Occidental, in which he frankly appealed to the Western world in his choice of words and also endeavored to use suffixes already in common use in the existing modern languages.

And, finally, and most recently, one of the greatest of the philologists interested in artificial languages, Otto Jespersen, of Copenhagen, proposed in 1928 his own new international language under the name "Novial".[497] Among the novel features of the new tongue are, he states, "the perfect agreement in flexion between substantives and pronouns, the use of the ground-form of verbs even in the perfect and passive, the elimination of *c* and *z*, and the e/a/o-words". The language is a well-planned one. It is an easy one to learn, because the grammar is very simple, and the choice of words is made as scientifically as could be hoped for.

But after this high point in scientific creative efficiency has been reached in the production of artificial languages, there are still many persons who question the value of the accomplishment and doubt the likelihood that any such language will prove permanent and satisfactory. T. C. Macaulay has remarked: [491]

When you give a man a grammar and a vocabulary, do you give him a language? Evidently, if the whole of language were comprised in grammar and vocabulary, the answer would be Yes. But language contains a third and equally important element, namely Idiom. Idiom may be described as the whole body of linguistic habit or convention belonging to each tongue. It is the result of the constant striving of man through countless generations to interpret with accuracy every aspect of his thoughts.

And it is on this matter of *idiom* that students of international language disagree. Some believe that an artificial auxiliary language can be devised which will be so simple and easy to acquire and so perfectly running a vehicle that all men will ultimately accept it as a mechanical device for international communication and transportation of ideas — a device like the radio and telephone, it is true, in its mechanical nature, but a useful one, nonetheless. But other students of language feel equally certain that no such mechanical language can live and persist, and so they propose to use one already widely known and employed, more especially English. They argue that the very ease of acquiring such auxiliary languages as those most recently devised, instead of being an argument in their favor, is rather a serious criticism of their value, since, they say, no language that is worth while can be learned overnight, as it were. Indeed, some philologists think that a simple artificial language, if it were able to survive the first few decades of its artificiality and become generally used, would so rapidly develop idiomatic features and other complexities of its own, accumulating so many and such fine distinctions in meaning, that like any other language it would soon be too complex to be learned quickly and mechanically. If such were the case, it might then become merely a matter of choice between learning an artificial auxiliary language, with no real cultural background, and devoting the same amount of time to learning some language already long established and already enriched by an old national culture.

However, even though the gradual increase of idiomatic characteristics should increase the difficulty of acquiring such an artificial language, the very lack of local or national idiomatic coloring might make it more generally acceptable to a great variety of nations. If so, then it might not make so much difference whether the language were compiled from a scientific choice of different linguistic stocks, like Idiom Neutral, or from the generally used Latin vocabulary, like Interlingua, or from an irreducible minimum of English words, like Basic English. Even the last-named form cannot be expected to carry with it much of the English idiom and would presumably be no more a rival of standard English than it would be of any other old national language.

130. *The Future of English*

The life of language is dependent upon so changeable and uncertain an element, namely, man's thinking, and so much can happen to it in the course of a few generations, that it would be rash to attempt to foretell the future of a language in any definite detail. At the same time, if the student has observed the various changes and trends in English discussed in the preceding chapters, he will find himself tempted to speculate concerning the probable future of the language. Hence the following observations have been assembled, not in the way of prophecy, but rather as a final summing up of this entire survey of the English language of today and as a basis for more intelligent speculation and conjecture.

The pronunciation of English words is likely to offer the first challenge to the linguistic prophet because the great variation in present-day English pronunciation obtrudes itself upon the consciousness of the observer most often, perhaps, of all the phases of Current English usage. The numerous variables listed in Chapter VI suggest possibilities of improvement and of more uniform practice to anyone who feels the need of standardization in English. But it should be obvious by this time that pronunciation is least likely to be permanently standardized because it is, of all the phases of language, least stable and least permanent. Nevertheless there are active today various agencies working to establish a more uniform pronunciation of the language. The greater intermingling of the speakers of the language, the increasing use of the telephone, the spread of the talking movies, and the sudden, almost universal use of the radio have brought into prominence the variableness of English pronunciation as never before. The results are already beginning to appear in the activities of the B.B.C. (British Broadcasting Corporation) [216], in the efforts of American broadcasting companies to train their announcers to speak the language more uniformly, in the closer coöperation of those who are training public speakers, and especially in the efforts of actors to secure greater uniformity in their pronunciation for stage and screen. The dictionaries are, of course, a great aid in this matter, and the work of English teachers in the public schools undoubtedly makes for closer attention to the problems of pronunciation, everywhere. So it would seem likely that dialectal and slovenly pronunciation of the English language will diminish rather than increase as the years go by. But it would be rash to assume that even these numerous agencies will altogether counteract the tendency of many careless or ignorant speakers to upset uniformity and continuity in pronunciation from generation to generation. Those elements that induce change (see Sec. 6) are always present in the life of a people and are bound to make some changes in English pronunciation, as any student of phonetics will agree.

The spelling of the language is in need of serious reforming, and it is hardly conceivable that so important a linguistic group as the speakers of English will go ahead in other cultural matters and not feel more and more keenly the need of improvement of the spelling of English. We shall probably never experience again so sudden and striking an influence on spelling as the introduction of printing proved to be, at the end of the fifteenth century; but a gradual improvement of conditions that have gradually developed in English spelling may well be expected. Whether this will come more rapidly from the strong efforts of groups of spelling-reformers or from the gradual and slow-moving innovations of a more natural sort, only the future can show. Spelling reforms seem to wax and wane from period to period; but the very fact that the attention of users of English is frequently called to the need of improvement can hardly fail to have some permanent effect.

Certain marked tendencies in the use of words and phrases have been discussed and stressed frequently in the foregoing discussions of Current English, and it is important to weigh them in endeavoring to forecast the future of the language. The gradual substitution of the verb-adverb combination, like *grow over*, for the older compound, like *overgrow*, has resulted in the avoidance of many special verbs, and it may ultimately drive out of general use a fairly large number of these older, longer, more highly specialized words, thereby reducing somewhat the used vocabulary of English. The growing practice of converting a word from one part of speech to another, as in the use of the verb *try* as a noun, is likewise resulting in the avoidance of many words like *attempt, endeavor, experiment, trial*. At present its most unfortunate use in "headline English" is causing much concern to lovers of good English. In a recent issue of a widely read city paper, for example, the following headings appeared on the front page alone: "*Air Tragedy* Victims"; "*Arms* Problem Up for Discussion"; "China Halts *Japan* Drive on Peiping"; "Clubman Snatched from *Train* Death"; "*Dynamite* Carrier Falls 50 Feet"; "Girl, *Crissy* Flyer Die in *Plane* Crash"; "*Girl Eye Removal* Decision Today"; "McAdoo Sets Pace for *Resort* Outing";

"*Race* Driver Pinned under Flaming Car"; "Roosevelt Near *Money* Compact with MacDonald"; "Heavy Losses by Nipponese in *Wall* Battle Reported". In each of these headings the italicized word or group is a modifier of the following noun. The prominence given day by day to such pidgin-English constructions can hardly fail to influence the speech and writing of unthinking readers of the daily papers, and have its permanent effect upon the grammar and vocabulary of the English language, unless a serious endeavor is made to counteract it.

While the increasing uses of the verb-adverb combination and of conversion mark, possibly, the most influential trends in Current English syntactical usage, developments of various other constructions are helping to change the pattern of English grammar and may lead to still other important changes in grammatical practice, although the more radical innovations may be discouraged by a growing appreciation of the close relation of sentence construction to the proper expression of thinking, and the need for greater exactness and clearness in expressing thought may have a helpful deterring influence. The grammatical pattern of a language is so essentially characteristic of it that such pattern is not so likely to undergo radical and rapid change as some other, less fundamental characteristic feature of the language. The substitution of syntactical usage for inflectional form has, as we have observed, been going on for centuries in English speech; and yet many of the rules of syntax that were observed in Anglo-Saxon are still valid in twentieth-century English, and even where the older construction based upon inflectional form has yielded in large measure to syntactical use, as in the case of genitive and dative constructions, the older usage is often reflected in a twofold practice in Modern English, as in '*man's* aspirations' or 'the aspirations *of man*'.

The variations and multiplications of meanings of words cannot, of course, be anticipated with any degree of certainty. The psychological causes of semasiological change are too uncertain and varying to allow of much prophesying; slang uses of older words, technical applications of general terms like *complex*, revival of archaic words or obsolete words, modification of meanings, as in the case of *pastor* and *parson* — these and many other kinds of semasiological change can take place almost overnight.

Some of the outstanding causes of change in the English language of the past are not likely to be effective in the future to the extent of producing equally marked changes in the language, if one may venture a guess at this point. The inflectional system of English, for example, was greatly reduced during that time of neglect when the Normans took the lead in British cultural affairs; but no such neglect of the language seems likely to permit in similar fashion a reduction of the vocabulary and the unloading of a great accumulation of English words comparable to that older unloading of the elaborate system of Anglo-Saxon inflection. Greater change might conceivably take place in American English if great numbers of foreigners were allowed to penetrate the United States for a prolonged period of years. But the policy of restricted immigration has made such change unlikely and has increased the effectiveness of the Americanization of foreigners.

And if there is not likely to be introduced among the English-speaking peoples a foreign influence which might permit of or cause deterioration or marked change in any phase of English linguistic practice, likewise the great causes of improvement in the language are not likely to be active again in such spectacular fashion as in the past. It would require some time for the culture of any other great nation of the world to so far outstrip the English of the present that it could make the great contribution to English culture and thought and language that was made by Greece, by Rome, and by France, in especial. When English life and thought were struggling up from barbarism, the Englishman welcomed any contribution to his intellectual and physical welfare; and in their periods of influence the Greek and Latin, the French, Italian, and Spanish, and other nations were able to contribute greatly to English cultural needs. Today the influence is working in the opposite direction, and the increase of English words in other tongues is becoming more noticeable (see Sec. 27).

Moreover, the exploration and colonization of the world is

too nearly completed to permit of the introduction again into English of as great a number of commercial and other words as came to England during the sixteenth, seventeenth, and eighteenth centuries, especially.

If, in this connection, the question arises of further increase in the use of the English language over the world, it may be regarded as equally certain that no such opportunities for the great spread of English will arise again as came during the period of the growth of the British Empire, during the development of the United States, or even as a result of the granting of protectoral powers to Great Britain after the World War. If English is to penetrate other nations further, the penetration is likely to be in two quite different ways: (1) It may spread in the form of an auxiliary international language, possibly as Anglic, possibly in more artificial fashion as Basic English; but certainly it will, in one way and another, inevitably exert some influence on other languages, just as any outstanding national culture is bound to do. (2) The growing study of English in other lands will be as sure to influence other languages to some extent as English has been itself affected in the past through the study of foreign tongues by Englishmen.

The future relations of British English and American English have already been conjecturally discussed (see page 164), and the opinion ventured that "it does not seem likely that British and American English will become more unlike than they are at present, since the causes that have induced differentiation in the past have been slowly yielding to other causes that favor unification". Because of this belief, the further opinion was offered that any rivalry that may have developed over the world between the two great branches of the English language may disappear ultimately, since the chances of their unification seem at the present time fully as good as the chances of differentiation.

In any effort at prognostication concerning the future of the English language, one must not overlook or discount the great stabilizing influence of the many people who strive for the standardizing of English speech. Not only is there a concerted movement to settle arguments over varying pronunciations, and movements to reform the spelling of English, but from the very beginning of the modern period of English there has been an almost never-ceasing demand for an academy to "fix" the language, and English scholars, while generally deprecating some of the connotations of "fix", have steadfastly replied to such a demand by encouraging various organizations intended "to maintain the traditions and foster the development of our common tongue" (see Sec. 126). No such fixing of English is likely to occur again as that which took place when printing was introduced into England, and schools and teaching could hardly produce any more conventionalizing effects in the next three centuries than the last three have witnessed; but the stabilizing and standardizing influence of the great modern dictionaries, the efforts of teachers to agree on questions of usage, the publication of the researches of philological scholars, the use of stylebooks by editors and printers — the cumulative influence of these stabilizing forces is amazingly and almost incalculably great.

There remains to be considered one more important question concerning the future development of the English language, one that pertains to the relation of standard literary English to the colloquial speech. Students of language have been much concerned over what has seemed to them an unfortunate divergence of standard literary usage and colloquial usage, but they have regarded such divergence from quite different points of view. Some have been concerned because of a seeming tendency of grammarians and lexicographers to standardize and establish words and usages, not realizing, apparently, that, after all, the grammarian and the lexicographer merely record what they think the generality of users of good English prefer; others have been equally concerned because of the constant defiance of well-established laws of procedure by those who promote the colloquial and the slangy in English, not realizing, seemingly, that spoken and written language are two somewhat different things. The former recognize the difference between standard literary English and colloquial English, but blame the grammarian and lexicographer for maintaining it; the latter do not recognize the necessity of such difference and so decry the very element in language which insures vitality and growth. De Sélincourt has remarked, in his discussion *The Future of English* [498]: "Obviously there must be standardization up to a point if people are to stick together, and we must be prepared to swallow it in considerable doses now that English is the language of two hemispheres. But the essential is that the point should be a point of agreement."

Any forecast of the future of English will be more dependable if it is based upon several considerations that have been fundamental in the present attempt at an appreciation of Current English:

Language is not an organism that contains within itself the possibilities of growth, like some plant, but it is merely the collection of habits by which a people express their thinking; and so it can be no less rich and varied, and no more efficient, than is the thinking of that people. Such continuity as the language possesses can be credited, therefore, to those historically minded people — of whom the world is surprisingly full — who respect the speech habits of older generations of English speakers enough to try to preserve them intact or relatively so. It is mainly for the use of these historically minded students of English life and thought and English speech that the dictionaries record so many of the older words and meanings. Historians know that the richness and expressiveness of a language such as English is cumulative, and not merely the throwing together of enough to express the thinking that needs expression at any one time.

Hence a selection of fundamental words such as Basic English offers must either fall far short of expressing the varied culture of a great people of the twentieth century or else must rapidly become modified and adapted to the needs of such varied expression. Certainly as an international language it would have to serve the purposes of a great people if it met the needs of representatives of various nations, with the variety of national cultures that might contribute to international intercourse. It could hardly be expected that speakers educated in the broad cultures of such modern nations as the French, the Germans, the Scandinavians, the Orientals, and others participating in international conferences would be content to limit themselves to such ideas as might be expressed by a restricted vocabulary, even with a flexible grammatical apparatus. And for the native speakers of English the adoption of such a restricted-vocabulary auxiliary tongue would mean that they would have to be very careful not to overstep the boundaries of the restricted vocabulary while addressing natives of other lands, — or else the natives of other lands would be compelled to learn the meanings of many words not included in the limited vocabulary. To use a limited English vocabulary and an unlimited one contemporaneously would involve each English speaker in a more careful, a more conscious discrimination and self-restraint than he now needs in moving from one speech level to another in present-day English.

Educated speakers and writers of Current English are likely to use more words more discriminatingly as time passes rather than fewer, and the gap between a carefully limited English vocabulary and an adequately representative one would become constantly harder to bridge. It is the tendency of educated and thoughtful speakers and writers to have more ideas and to think more clearly, and consequently to express their thinking more richly and variedly and effectively.

And, last of all, language cannot be "fixed" to any great extent; for if English life and thought continue to change and become more varied, the English language will likewise change and increase and become more rich and varied. Consequently a forecast of the future of the English language must be, for the most part, a forecast of the future of English life and thought.

BIBLIOGRAPHY

This bibliography consists largely of titles of books and magazine articles which have been indicated by the numbers scattered through the foregoing text. But an attempt has also been made to provide a general guide to all the material needed for a more intensive study of Current English as a whole, by including numerous books of a general nature; these have been marked with daggers. However, space does not permit of an exhaustive bibliography; many other interesting studies can be found listed in the bibliographical guides (Nos. 1–3).

GENERAL WORKS

Bibliographical Guides

1. † KENNEDY, ARTHUR G. Bibliography of Writings on the English Language from the Beginning of Printing to the End of 1922. Cambridge, Harvard Univ. Press; New Haven, Yale Univ. Press. 1927. xvi + 517 pp.
2. † Annual Bibliography of English Language and Literature. Edited for the Modern Humanities Research Assn. Cambridge, Eng., Bowes & Bowes. 1921 (for 1920) – date.
3. † KENNEDY, ARTHUR G., et al. Brief notices. In each issue of *American Speech*, in the "Bibliographical Department". 1925 – date. See No. 31, below.

Study and Teaching of the English Language

4. COOK, ALBERT S. The Higher Study of English. Boston, Houghton Mifflin Co. 1906. 145 pp.
5. CLAPP, JOHN M., ed. The Place of English in American Life. Report of an Investigation by a Committee of the National Council of Teachers of English. Chicago. 1926. 48 pp.
6. † FRIES, CHAS. C. The Teaching of the English Language. N. Y., Nelson & Sons. 1927. 187 pp.
7. PEDERSEN, HOLGER. Linguistic Science in the Nineteenth Century. Transl. by John W. Spargo. Cambridge, Harvard Univ. Press. 1931. x + 360 pp.

Grammar and Diction

8. † EARLE, JOHN. The Philology of the English Tongue. 5th ed. Oxford, Clarendon Press. 1892. xvi + 744 pp.
9. † SWEET, HENRY. A New English Grammar, Logical and Historical. Oxford, Clarendon Press. 1892–1898. 2 vols.

10. † EMERSON, OLIVER F. History of the English Language. N. Y., Macmillan. 1902. xiii + 415 pp.
11. † KRAPP, GEO. P. Modern English. Its Growth and Present Use. N. Y., Scribner's. 1909. xi + 357 pp.
12. MATTHEWS, BRANDER. Parts of Speech. Essays on English. N. Y., Scribner's. 1916. 350 pp.
13. † JESPERSEN, OTTO. Language: Its Nature, Development and Origin. London, Allen & Unwin. 1922. 448 pp.
14. MATTHEWS, BRANDER. Essays on English. N. Y., Scribner's. 1922. viii + 284 pp.
15. † THOMA, WILHELMINA. Language in the Making. A Word Study. N. Y., Harcourt, Brace & Co. 1922. xv + 207 pp.
16. † FOWLER, H. W. Dictionary of Modern English Usage. Oxford, Clarendon Press. 1926. viii + 742 pp.
17. † KRAPP, GEO. P. Comprehensive Guide to Good English. Chicago, Rand McNally & Co. 1927. xxxviii + 688 pp.
18. † KRAPP, GEO. P. The Knowledge of English. N. Y., Holt & Co. 1927. x + 572 pp.
19. † KRUISINGA, E. Handbook of Present-Day English. 5th ed. Groningen, Noordhoff. 1931. 4 vols.

See also Nos. 43, 140, 230, 337, 396, 399.

Dictionaries

20. † MURRAY, J. A. H., *et al.* A New English Dictionary on Historical Principles. Oxford, Clarendon Press. 1884–1928. 10 vols. Reprinted as the Oxford English Dictionary, in 12 vols. + supplementary vol. 1933.
21. † Century Dictionary and Cyclopedia. N. Y., Century Co. 1911. 12 vols. A revised and enlarged edition.
22. † LEWIS, WM. D., CANBY, H. S., and BROWN, T. K. The Winston Simplified Dictionary. Advanced edition. Phila., John C. Winston Co. 1926. xx + 1260 pp.
23. † FOWLER, H. W. Concise Oxford Dictionary of Current English. New ed. Oxford, Clarendon Press. 1929. xv + 1444 pp. 3d ed. 1934.
24. † EMERY, H. G., and BREWSTER, K. G. The New Century Dictionary. N. Y., Century Co. 1930. 2 vols.
25. † FUNK, ISAAC K., *et al.* New Standard Dictionary of the English Language. N. Y., Funk & Wagnalls Co. 1929. xxxviii + 2811 pp.
26. † WEBSTER, NOAH. New International Dictionary of the English Language. Springfield, Mass., G. & C. Merriam Co. 1929. cxx + 2620 + 188 pp. — Also: Second Edition, thoroughly revised and greatly enlarged. 1934.
27. † VIZETELLY, FRANK H. Practical Standard Dictionary of the English Language. N. Y., Funk & Wagnalls Co. 1925. xvi + 1309 pp.
28. † WEBSTER, NOAH. Collegiate Dictionary. 4th ed. Springfield, Mass., G. & C. Merriam Co. 1931. xl + 1222 pp.
29. † WYLD, HENRY C. Universal Dictionary of the English Language. London, Routledge. 1932. xx + 1431 pp.

BIBLIOGRAPHY

30. † LITTLE, WM., FOWLER, H. W., and COULSON, J. The Shorter Oxford English Dictionary on Historical Principles. Revised and edited by C. T. Onions. Oxford, Clarendon Press. 1933. 2 vols.

Periodicals

31. † *American Speech*. A Quarterly of Linguistic Usage. N. Y., Columbia Univ. Press. 1925–date.
32. † *Dialect Notes*. Publications of the American Dialect Society. Ed. by the Secretary. 1890–date.
33. † *English Journal*. Official Organ of the National Council of Teachers of English. Chicago. 1912–date. Monthly.
34. † *English Studies*. A Journal of English Letters and Philology. Amsterdam. 1919–date. Bimonthly.

CHAPTER I. PHILOSOPHICAL INTRODUCTION

35. † JESPERSEN, OTTO. The Philosophy of Grammar. London, Allen & Unwin. 1924. 359 pp.
36. † JESPERSEN, OTTO. Mankind, Nation and Individual from a Linguistic Point of View. Oslo, H. Aschehoug & Co.; Cambridge, Harvard Univ. Press. 1925. 221 pp.
37. † BLOOMFIELD, LEONARD. Language. N. Y., Holt & Co. 1923. ix + 564 pp.

Sec. 2. *Physiology versus Psychology of Speech*

38. MANDELL, SIBYL. "The Relations of Language to Thought". *Quarterly Jour. of Speech*, 17:522–531. 1931.

Sec. 8. Linguistic Standards

39. KRAPP, GEO. P. "The Test of English". *Amer. Mercury*, 1:94–98. 1924.
40. JAMES, A. LLOYD. "Standards in Speech". *Amer. Speech*, 8(2):3–14. April, 1933.

CHAPTER II. STANDARD ENGLISH AND ITS VARIANTS

41. MCKNIGHT, GEO. H. "Standard English". In his English Words, Chap. I. 1923. See No. 298, below.
42. SMITH, LOGAN P. "Popular Speech and Standard English". In his Words and Idioms, pp. 135–166. 1925. See No. 470, below.
43. SCOTT, FRED N. "The Standard of American Speech". In his Standard of American Speech and Other Papers, pp. 1–15. Boston, Allyn & Bacon. 1926.
44. BLOOMFIELD, LEONARD. "Literate and Illiterate Speech". *Amer. Speech*, 2:432–439. 1927.
45. KRAPP, GEO. P. The Knowledge of English, especially Chapters VI–VIII and XIII–XIV. 1927. See No. 18, above.
46. CHAPMAN, R. W. "Oxford" English. Soc. for Pure English Tract 37:539–563. 1932.

Sec. 9. Pure English?

47. MATTHEWS, BRANDER. "What Is Pure English?" *Harper's Mag.*, 130:550–553. 1915. — Repr. in his Essays on English, pp. 31–57. 1922. See No. 14, above.

Sec. 11. Slang

48. † BARRÈRE, ALBERT, and LELAND, CHAS. G. Dictionary of Slang, Jargon, and Cant, Embracing English, American, and Anglo-Indian Slang, Pidgin English, Gipsies' Jargon, etc. 2d ed. London, Bell. 1897. 2 vols.
49. † WARE, J. R. Passing English of the Victorian Era: A Dictionary of Heterodox English, Slang and Phrase. N.Y., Dutton & Co. 1909. viii + 271 pp.
50. † SMITH, CHAS. A. New Words Self-Defined. N.Y., Doubleday, Page & Co. 1919. viii + 215 pp.
51. McKNIGHT, G. H. "Slang". In his English Words, Chap. IV. 1923. See No. 298, below.
52. PAUL, H. G. "Slang — The Language Jester". In his Better Everyday English, pp. 121–134. Chicago, Lyons & Carnahan. 1924.
53. REEVES, H. F., *et al.* "What Is Slang? A Survey of Opinion". *Amer. Speech*, 1:216–220, 368. 1926.
54. † FARMER, JOHN S., and HENLEY, W. E. Dictionary of Slang and Colloquial English. N.Y., Dutton & Co. 1929. viii + 533 pp.
55. † PARTRIDGE, ERIC. Slang, Today and Yesterday. London, Routledge. 1933. x + 476 pp.
56. GORE, WILLARD C. Student Slang. Contributions to Rhetorical Theory II. Ed. by F. N. Scott. 1895. 28 pp.
57. WESEEN, M. H. "College Slang and Campus Cant". In his Dict. of Engl. Grammar, pp. 123–128. 1928. See No. 337, below.
58. Various authors. College Slang. *Dialect Notes*, 2:1–70. 1900; 4:231–238, 436. 1915, 1917; 5:60–73. 1919; 5:139–148. 1922. — Also: *Amer. Speech*, 3:131–133. 1927; 2:275–279. 1927; 3:218–221. 1928; 5:238–239, 305. 1930; 6:129–130, 203–206. 1930; 7:327–328. 1932.
59. LEE, GRETCHEN. "In Sporting Parlance". *Amer. Speech*, 1:369–370. 1926. — Also: *Literary Digest*, 109 (3):40–41. April 18, 1931.
60. BEATH, PAUL R. "Aviation Lingo". *Amer. Speech*, 5:289–290. 1930.
61. FRASER, EDWARD, and GIBBONS, JOHN. Soldier and Sailor Words and Phrases. N.Y., Dutton & Co. 1925. vii + 372 pp. — McCARTNEY, EUGENE S. "Additions" [to the foregoing volume]. In Papers of the Michigan Acad. of Sciences, Arts and Letters, 10:273–337. 1929. — KEELEY, MARY P. "A. E. F. English". *Amer. Speech*, 5:372–386. 1930. — BROPHY, JOHN, and PARTRIDGE, ERIC. Songs and Slang of the British Soldier, 1914–1918. 3d ed. London, Scholartis Press. 1931. vii + 383 pp.

For other studies of slang see also Nos. 204, 274, 327, 359, 361–363.

Sec. 12. Grotesque English

62. POUND, LOUISE. "Intentional Mispronunciations in the Central West". *Dialect Notes*, 5:133–138. 1922.
63. ZAD, Y., et al. "Mrs. Malaprop in Somerset". *Word-Lore*, 2:11, 226. 1927.
64. Anon. "'Spoonerisms' Not All Spooner". *Word Study*, 5(2):3–4. December, 1929.
65. TOROSYAN, H. T. "English from a Foreigner's Point of View". *Bookman*, 28:52–54. 1908.
66. REED, MARGARET. "Intentional Mispronunciations". *Amer. Speech*, 7:192–199. 1932.

Sec. 13. Archaic English versus Neologisms

67. † HALLIWELL, JAMES O. Dictionary of Archaic and Provincial Words etc. 7th ed. London, Routledge. 1924. xxxvi + 960 pp.
68. ARMSTRONG, SPENCER. "Let's Look It Up in the Dictionary". *Saturday Evening Post*, 198 (36):16–17, 55, 58. March 6, 1926. — Repr. as a pamphlet, with the title How Words Get Into the Dictionary. N.Y., Funk & Wagnalls Co. 1933. 31 pp.
69. WITHINGTON, ROBT. "Some Neologisms from Recent Magazines". *Amer. Speech*, 6:277–289. 1931.
70. DIKE, EDWIN B. "Obsolete Words". *Philological Quart.*, 12:207–219. 1933. — See also *Englische Studien*, 68:339–350. 1934.

Sec. 14. Newspaper English

71. WHITE, RICH. G. "Newspaper English". In his Words and Their Uses, pp. 28–43. 3d ed. Boston, Houghton Mifflin Co. 1880.
72. HILL, ADAMS S. "English in Newspapers and Novels". *Scribner's Mag.*, 2:371–377. 1887.
73. LOWES, JOHN L. "Headline English". New York *Nation*, 96:179. 1913.
74. WILLIAMS, TALCOTT. "Newspaper English". *North American Rev.*, 212:631–640. 1920.
75. HICKLIN, MAURICE. "Scribes Seek Snappy Synonyms". *Amer. Speech*, 6:110–122. 1930. — See also 2:34–38. 1927; 4:306. 1929; 5:173–175, 490–498. 1929–1930.

Sec. 15. Children's English

76. JESPERSEN, OTTO. "The Child". In his Language, pp. 100–188. 1922. See No. 13, above.
77. CHAMBERLAIN, ALEX. F. "Preterite Forms etc. in the Language of English-Speaking Children". *Modern Language Notes*, 21:42–44. 1906.
78. WHIPPLE, GUY M. "A Three Year Old Boy with a Vocabulary of 1771 Words". *American Mag.*, 73:121–122. 1911.
79. NICE, MARGARET M. "Length of Sentences as a Criterion of a Child's Progress in Speech". *Jour. of Educational Psychology*, 16:370–379. 1925.

Sec. 16. Dialects of English

80. WHITNEY, WM. D. "Local and Class Variations of Language: Dialects". In his Life and Growth of Language, pp. 153–178. N.Y., Appleton & Co. 1875; repr. 1899.
81. † WRIGHT, JOSEPH. The English Dialect Dictionary. London, Frowde. 1898–1905. 6 vols.
82. † WRIGHT, JOSEPH. The English Dialect Grammar. London, Frowde. 1905. xxiii + 696 pp.
83. WRIGHT, ELIZABETH. "The Varieties of English Speech". Quarterly Rev., 207:86–109. 1907.

Sec. 16, a. Local Dialects

84. HOW, CAPPY. "The Vorriner". Word-Lore, 2:16–17. 1927.
85. JOYCE, P. W. English as We Speak It in Ireland. 2d ed. London, Longmans, Green & Co. 1910. x + 356 pp.
86. CHAMBERLAIN, A. F. "Dialect Research in Canada". Dialect Notes, 1:43–56. 1890.
87. MORRIS, EDWARD E. Austral English. A Dictionary of Australasian Words, Phrases and Usages. London, Macmillan. 1898. xxiv + 525 pp.

Sec. 16, b. Foreign-English Dialects

88. BECKMAN, ROBT. "Notes on Swedish-American". Amer. Speech, 3:448–450, 464–465. 1928.
89. HOLTER, T. E. "Twenty Idioms Illustrating the Influence of Swedish on English". Amer. Speech, 6:216–217. 1931.
90. † BENTLEY, HAROLD W. Dictionary of Spanish Terms in English. With Special Reference to the American Southwest. N.Y., Columbia Univ. Press. 1932. xii + 245 pp.
91. MENNER, ROBT. J. "Popular Phonetics". Amer. Speech, 4:410–416. 1929.
92. BENARDETE, DOLORES. "Immigrant Speech — Austrian-Jewish Style". Amer. Speech, 5:1–15. 1929.
93. YULE, H., and BURNELL, A. C. Hobson-Jobson, Being a Glossary of Anglo-Indian Colloquial Words and Phrases etc. 2d ed. by W. Crooke. London, Murray. 1903. xlviii + 1021 pp. — Also: GOFFIN, R. C. Some Notes on Indian English. Soc. for Pure English Tract, 41:20–32. 1932.

Sec. 16, c. Social Dialects

94. GREENOUGH, J. B., and KITTREDGE, G. L. "Technical or Class Dialects". In Words and Their Ways, pp. 42–54. 1901. See No. 292, below.
95. SLOSSON, E. E., et al. "Words from the Arts and Sciences". In March's Thesaurus Dictionary, Appendix, pp. 96–190. 1925. See No. 355, below.
96. MORTON, WM. C. The Language of Anatomy. Soc. for Pure English Tract 9:1–19. 1922.
97. HORNBERGER, THEO. "The Automobile and American English". Amer. Speech, 5:271–278. 1930.

98. AMES, JOSEPH S., et al. Nomenclature for Aeronautics. Compiled by the National Advisory Committee for Aeronautics. Report No. 240. Washington. 1926. 77 pp. Revision publ. as Report No. 474. 1933.
99. DAVIDSON, LEVETTE J. "Sugar Beet Language". Amer. Speech, 6:10-15. 1930.
100. COMPTON, NELLIE J. "Library Language". Amer. Speech, 2:93-95. 1926.
101. ADAMS, R. F., et al. "Cowboy Speech". Amer. Speech, 3:168-169. 1927; 5:52-76. 1929.
102. BERNSTEIN, H. B. "Fire Insurance Terminology". Amer. Speech, 1:523-528. 1926.
103. LUDLAW, J. M. "Jottings in Legal Terminology". Trans. of the Philological Soc. for 1854, pp. 113-119.
104. MARSHALL, WM. W. "The Language of the Law". Antiquarian Mag., 11:244-250. 1887.
105. OPPENHEIMER, R. "Legal Lingo". Amer. Speech, 2:142-144. 1926.
106. FISHBEIN, M. "The Misuse of Medical Terms". Amer. Speech, 1:23-25. 1925.
107. MOORE, HELEN L. "The Lingo of the Mining Camp". Amer. Speech, 2:86-88. 1926. — Also: 4:368-374. 1929; 5:144-147. 1929.
108. RAMSAYE, T., et al. "Movie Jargon". Amer. Speech, 1:358-362. 1926; 3:364-368. 1928. — WILSTACH, F. J., in New York Times, March 11, 1928, p. 6. — ROOT, W., in Bookman, 68:622-624. 1929. — KNOX, E. V., in Living Age, 338:187-189. 1930.
109. ANSTED, A. Dictionary of Sea Terms. London, J. Brown. 1920. 324 pp. — BRADFORD, G. Glossary of Sea Terms. N.Y., Yachting, Inc. 1927. 294 pp. — WASSON, GEO. S., in Amer. Speech, 4:377-384. 1929.
110. NORTON, CHAS. L. Political Americanisms. London, Longmans, Green & Co. 1890. viii + 135 pp. — WIMBERLY, L. C., et al., in Amer. Speech, 2:135-139. 1926; 5:408-413. 1930.

Sec. 16, d. *"Little Languages"*

111. MUSSER, BENJ. "The Catholic Language". Amer. Ecclesiastical Rev., 75:573-583. 1926.
112. TIBBALS, KATE W. "The Speech of Plain Friends". Amer. Speech, 1:193-209. 1926. — Also: 8:2-14. 1933.
113. FULLER, N., et al. "Crook Argot". Amer. Speech, 3:254-255. 1928; 6:391-393. 1931; 7:99-118. 1931. — KLEIN, N., et al. "Hobo Lingo". Amer. Speech, 1:650-653. 1926; 2:385-392, 506. 1927; 4:337-346. 1929. — HOLBROOK, S. H., in Amer. Mercury, 7:62-65. 1926. — GIVENS, C. G., in Saturday Evening Post, 201 (41):48, 50, 54. 1929. — IRWIN, GODFREY. American Tramp and Underworld Slang. London, Scholartis Press. 1931. 264 pp.
114. HENCH, A. L. "From the Vocabulary of Automobile Thieves". Amer. Speech, 5:236-237. 1930.
115. Anon. "Language of the Speakeasy". Amer. Speech, 6:158-159. 1930.
116. YENNE, H., et al. "Prison Lingo". Amer. Speech, 2:280-282. 1927; 6:436-442. 1931.

117. KRAPP, GEO. P. "The English of the Negro". *Amer. Mercury*, 2:190–195. 1924.
118. GONZALES, A. E. The Black Border; Gullah Stories of the Carolina Coast. Columbia, S. C., The State Co. 1922. 348 pp. — SMITH, REED. Gullah. Bulletin of the Univ. of South Carolina, No. 190. 1926. 45 pp.

17. Jargons

119. BOAS, F. "Chinook Songs". *Jour. of Amer. Folk-Lore*, 1:220–226. 1888.
120. NICOLL, E. C. "The Chinook Language or Jargon". *Popular Science Monthly*, 35:257–261. 1889.
121. EELLS, MYRON. "The Chinook Jargon". *Amer. Anthropologist*, 7:300–312. 1894.
122. SHAW, GEO. C. The Chinook Jargon and How to Use It. A Complete and Exhaustive Lexicon of the Oldest Trade Language of the American Continent. Seattle, Rainier Publ. Co. 1909. xvi + 65 pp.
123. LEECHMAN, D., *et al.* "The Chinook Jargon". *Amer. Speech*, 1:531–534. 1926; 2:377–384. 1927; 3:182–185. 1928.
124. CHURCHILL, WM. Beach-la-Mar; The Jargon of Trade Speech of the Western Pacific. Publ. of the Carnegie Institution of Washington, No. 154. 1911. 53 pp.
125. HAYES, A. A., Jr. "Pidgin English". *Scribner's Mo.*, 15:372–377. 1878.
126. LELAND, CHAS. G. Pidgin English Sing-Song, or Songs and Stories in the China-English Dialect. 2d ed. London, Trübner. 1887. viii + 139 pp. — See also *Amer. Speech*, 5:148–151. 1929; 8:15–19. 1933.
127. JESPERSEN, OTTO. "Pidgin and Its Congeners". In his Language, pp. 216–236. 1922. See No. 13, above.

CHAPTER III. PHONETICS

128. † SWEET, HENRY. Primer of Phonetics. 3d ed. London, Frowde. 1906. 128 pp.
129. † JONES, DANIEL. Outline of English Phonetics. 3d ed. rewritten. N.Y., Dutton & Co. 1932. x + 326 pp. — See also No. 209, below.
130. † SOAMES, LAURA. Introduction to English, French and German Phonetics. 3d ed. revised by W. Viëtor. London, Macmillan. 1913. 300 pp.
131. † BARROWS, SARAH T., and CORDTS, ANNA D. The Teacher's Book of Phonetics. Boston, Ginn & Co. 1926. xi + 199 pp.
132. † WARD, IDA C. The Phonetics of English. N.Y., Appleton & Co. 1929. xi + 176 pp.

Sec. 21. A Phonetic Alphabet

133. JESPERSEN, OTTO, and PEDERSEN, HOLGER. Phonetic Transcription and Transliteration. Oxford, Clarendon Press. 1926. 32 pp.
134. KENYON, JOHN S. "The International Phonetic Alphabet". *Amer. Speech*, 4:324–327. 1929.

CHAPTER IV. THE RELATIONS OF ENGLISH TO OTHER LANGUAGES

135. KRAPP, GEO. P. "The Relationships of English". In his Knowledge of English, pp. 388–417. 1927. See No. 18, above.

Sec. 24. Cognate Languages

136. GILES, PETER. "Indo-European Languages". Encyclopædia Britannica, 11th ed., 14:495–500. 1910.
137. EMERTON, EPHRAIM. Introduction to the Study of the Middle Ages (375–814). Boston, Ginn & Co. 1898. xviii + 268 pp.
138. PEDERSEN, H. Linguistic Science in the Nineteenth Century. 1931. See No. 7, above.

Sec. 25. English Borrowings

139. KENNEDY, ARTHUR G. "Hothouse Words versus Slang". *Amer. Speech*, 2:417–424. 1927.
140. VIZETELLY, F. H. "The Foreign Element in English". In his Essentials of English, pp. 159–173. N.Y., Funk & Wagnalls Co. 1915.
141. BARNES, WM. An Outline of English Speech-Craft. London, Kegan Paul. 1878. viii + 92 pp.
142. Anon. "Book-Speech and Folk-Speech". *Library*, 3:294–300. 1891.
143. LOUNSBURY, T. R. "The French Element in English". *Harper's Mag.*, 116:698–704. 1908.
144. GRINSTEAD, W. J. "On the Sources of the English Vocabulary". *Teachers College Record*, 26:32–46. 1924.
145. ULLMAN, B. L. "Our Latin-English Language". *Classical Jour.*, 18:82–90. 1922.

Sec. 26. Foreigners' English

146. [LIEFDE, JAN DE.] "A Dutchman's Difficulties with the English Language". *Good Words*, 4:867–873. 1863. — Repr. in *Living Age*, 80:73–80.
147. Anon. "How the Portuguese Learn English." *Living Age*, 100:618–620. 1869.
148. Anon. "Portuguese English". *Saturday Rev.* (London), 35:248–249. 1873.
149. BLOCH, LOUIS. "The Ability of European Immigrants to Speak English". *Jour. of Amer. Statistical Assn.*, 17:402–416. 1920.
150. STONE, E. K., and COFFIN, E. W. "English Eccentricities in a Chinese School". *Pacific Monthly*, 24:61–63. 1910.
151. BLAND, J. O. P. "'English as She Is Wrote' in the Far East". *English Rev.*, 48:711–719. 1929.
152. ZACHRISSON, R. E. "Anglic and Speling Reform". *Anglic*, 1:5. 1930.

Sec. 27. The Spread of English

153. MATTHEWS, BRANDER. "Foreign Words in English Speech". *Harper's Mag.*, 107:476. 1903.
154. SCHINZ, ALBERT. "Will English Be the International Language?" *North American Rev.*, 189:760–770. 1909.
155. GUÉRARD, ALBERT L. "English as an International Language". *Popular Science Monthly*, 79:337–345. 1911.
156. VIZETELLY, FRANK H. "The Coming World Language etc." *Dial*, 59:312–313. 1915.
157. PORTERFIELD, ALLEN W. "English, a World Language". *Bookman*, 57:111–113. 1923.
158. KARPF, FRITZ. "English as the First Foreign Language". *English Studies*, 7:65–74. 1925.
159. SMITH, LOGAN P. "The English Element in Foreign Languages". In his Words and Idioms, pp. 28–65. 1925. See No. 470, below.
160. Anon. "Language of Diplomacy". *Living Age*, 337:99. 1929.
161. DOMINGUEZ, C. VILLALOBOS. "The Language of the Future". *Living Age*, 337:105–110. 1929. Transl. from the Buenos Aires literary monthly *Nosotros*.
162. Anon. "French-English". *Cornhill Mag.* (n. s.), 14:279–286. 1890.
163. BARBIER, PAUL. English Influence on the French Vocabulary. Soc. for Pure English Tracts 7 and 13. 1921–1923.
164. HOFRICHTER, RUTH. "English Loan-Words in German Periodicals". *Amer. Speech*, 3:34. 1927. — Also MCCLINTOCK, T., in *Amer. Speech*, 8 (4):42–47. 1933.
165. RE, EMILIO. "The Teaching of English in Italy". *Modern Language Teaching*, 15:1–4. 1919.
166. ICHIKAWA, SANKI. "English Studies in Japan". *English Studies*, 8:105–107. 1926.
167. ICHIKAWA, SANKI. "English Influence on Japanese". *Studies in English Literature*, 8(2):165–208. Tokyo. 1928. — Also: "Pronunciation of English Loan-Words in Japanese". In A Grammatical Miscellany Offered to Otto Jespersen, pp. 177–190. 1930. — Also: "English Influence on Japanese". In Essays by Divers Hands, publ. by the Royal Soc. of Literature, Vol. 9, pp. 125–148. 1930.
168. O'TOOLE, R. F. "Sports Slang in Latin America". *Amer. Mercury*, 21:336–338. 1930.
169. MCKINISTRY, H. E. "The American Language in Mexico". *Amer. Mercury*, 19:336–338. 1930.
170. YULE, EMMA S. "The English Language in the Philippines". *Amer. Speech*, 1:111–120. 1925. — See also 3:14–20. 1927; 4:276–285. 1929.
171. JACOBSON, ELI B. "The American Language Fights for Recognition in Moscow". *Amer. Mercury*, 22:79–83. 1931.
172. EKWALL, EILERT. "English Studies in Sweden". *English Studies*, 6:92–94. 1924
173. READ, WM. A. Louisiana-French. Louisiana State Univ. Series, University Studies, No. 5. 1931. xxiv + 253 pp.

BIBLIOGRAPHY

174. VAUGHAN, H. H. "Italian and Its Dialects as Spoken in the United States". *Amer. Speech*, 1:431–435. 1926; 2:13–18. 1926.
175. FLOM, GEO. T. "English Loanwords in American Norwegian". *Amer. Speech*, 1:541–558. 1926.
176. OGDEN, C. K. "Basic English". *Saturday Rev. of Literature*, 5:1193. 1929. — Also: Basic English. General Introduction, with Rules and Grammar. 3d ed. London, Kegan Paul *et al.* 1932. 95 pp.
177. ZACHRISSON, R. E. Anglic. A New Agreed Simplified English Spelling. Final revised ed. Uppsala, Sweden, Anglic Fund A.-B. 1930. 40 pp. — See also No. 486, below.

Sec. 28. Characteristics of English

178. MEREDITH, E. A. "National Language and National Character". *Princeton Rev.* for July, 1884, pp. 36–55.
179. FERNALD, JAS. C. "The Simplicity of English". *Harper's Mag.*, 119:618–623. 1909.
180. GRAVES, ROBT. "Impenetrability or The Proper Habit of English". *Fortnightly Rev.*, 126:781–792; 127:59–73. 1926–1927. — Also publ. as Hogarth Essays, Ser. II, iii. London, Hogarth Press. 1926.
181. KIRKCONNELL, WATSON. "Linguistic Laconicism". *Amer. Jour. of Philology*, 48:34–37. 1927. — See also 49:57–73, 283–285, 378–383. 1928.
182. JESPERSEN, OTTO. "Monosyllabism in English". *Proc. of British Academy*, 14:341–368. London. 1928.
183. TRNKA, B. "Analysis and Synthesis in English". *English Studies*, 10:138–144. 1928.
184. WAITE, CHAS. B. Homophonic Vocabulary Containing More Than 2000 Words Having a Like Sound and Like Signification in Ten Languages etc. Chicago, Waite & Co. 1904. 162 pp.

CHAPTER V. HISTORICAL BACKGROUNDS OF ENGLISH

185. † JEUDWINE, J. W. The First Twelve Centuries of British Story. London, Longmans, Green & Co. 1912. lix + 436 pp.
186. † CHAMBERS, R. W. England before the Norman Conquest. London, Longmans, Green & Co. 1926. xxvi + 334 pp.

Sec. 30. The British Celts

187. FÖRSTER, MAX. "Keltisches Wortgut im Englischen". In Festgabe für Felix Liebermann, pp. 119–142. Halle. 1921.

Sec. 31. The Romans in Britain

188. † HAVERFIELD, F. J. The Roman Occupation of Britain. Revised by Geo. Macdonald. Oxford, Clarendon Press. 1924. 304 pp.
189. HAVERFIELD, F. J., and MACDONALD, GEO. "Roman Britain". Encyclopædia Britannica, 14th ed., 4:158–165. 1929.

Sec. 32. Anglo-Saxon England

190. † ALLEN, GRANT. Early Britain. Anglo-Saxon Britain. London, Soc. for Promoting Christian Knowledge. 1904. vii + 237 pp.

Sec. 33. The Scandinavians in England

191. † COLLINGWOOD, W. G. Early Britain. Scandinavian Britain. London, Soc. for Promoting Christian Knowledge. 1908. 272 pp.
192. EKWALL, EILERT. "How Long Did the Scandinavian Language Survive in England?" In A Grammatical Miscellany Offered to Otto Jespersen, pp. 17–30. Copenhagen. 1930.

Sec. 34. The Anglo-Normans

193. † HUNT, WM. Early Britain. Norman Britain. London, Soc. for Promoting Christian Knowledge. 1884. xi + 276 pp.
194. † VISING, JOHAN. Anglo-Norman Language and Literature. London, Oxford University Press. 1923. 111 pp.

Sec. 35. The Age of Chaucer

195. † BATESON, MARY. Mediæval England, 1066–1350. N. Y., Putnam's. 1904. xxvii + 448 pp.

Sec. 36. The English Renaissance

196. TAYLOR, HENRY O. Thought and Expression in the Sixteenth Century, Vol. II, pp. 3–263. N. Y., Macmillan. 1920.

Sec. 39. The British Empire Today

197. "British Empire". In the Encyclopædia Britannica, 14th ed., 4:174–200. 1929.

Sec. 40. American Speech

198. † THORNTON, R. H. An American Glossary. Being an Attempt to Illustrate Certain Americanisms upon Historical Principles. Phila., Lippincott. 1912. 2 vols. Publication of Vol. III begun in Dialect Notes, 6 (Pt. iii) etc. 1931.
199. † CAIRNS, WM. B. British Criticisms of American Writings, 1783–1833. Univ. of Wisconsin Studies in Lang. and Lit., Nos. 1 and 14. 1918, 1922.
200. † TUCKER, GILBERT M. American English. N.Y., Knopf. 1921. 375 pp.
201. † MENCKEN, H. L. The American Language. 3d ed. N.Y., Knopf. 1923. ix + 489 pp.
202. † KRAPP, GEO. P. The English Language in America. N. Y., Century Co., for the Mod. Lang. Assn. of America. 1925. 2 vols.
203. Anon. "Automobile Nomenclature". Amer. Speech, 1:686. 1926.
204. SCOTT, FRED. N. "American Slang". Soc. for Pure English Tract 24:118–127. 1926.

205. Anon. "American Slang in London". *Amer. Speech*, 3:167. 1927.
206. CRAIGIE, WM. A. "The Study of American English". Soc. for Pure English Tract 27:199–216. 1927.
207. KURATH, HANS. "American Pronunciation". Soc. for Pure English Tract 30:279–297. 1928.
208. MASSEY, B. W. A. "Divergence of American from English". *Amer. Speech*, 6:1–9. 1930.

CHAPTER VI. PRONUNCIATION OF ENGLISH

209. † JONES, DANIEL. The Pronunciation of English. I. "Phonetics". II. "Phonetic Transcription". 2d ed. Cambridge, Univ. Press. 1919. xviii + 153 pp. — Also: English Pronouncing Dictionary. Rev. ed. London, Dent. 1924. xxviii + 426 pp. — See also No. 129, above.
210. † KRAPP, GEO. P. The Pronunciation of Standard English in America. N. Y., Oxford Univ. Press. 1919. xii + 235 pp.
211. † UTTER, ROBT. P. Every-Day Pronunciation. N.Y., Harper. 1918. 253 pp.
212. † KENYON, JOHN S. American Pronunciation. Ann Arbor, Geo. Wahr. 1924. vii + 200 pp.
213. † KRAPP, GEO. P. The English Language in America, Vol. II. 1925. See No. 202 above.
214. † PALMER, H. E., MARTIN, J. V., and BLANDFORD, F. G. Dictionary of English Pronunciation, with American Variants. N. Y., Appleton & Co, 1926. xlix + 435 pp.
215. KURATH, HANS. "American Pronunciation". 1928. See No. 207, above.
216. BRIDGES, ROBT., ed. "The B. B. C.'s Recommendations for Pronouncing Doubtful Words". Soc. for Pure English Tract 31:335–411. 1929.
217. † LARSEN, T., and WALKER, F. C. Pronunciation. A Practical Guide to American Standards. London, Oxford Univ. Press. 1930. viii + 198 pp.
218. † RIPMAN, WALTER. The Sounds of Spoken English. N.Y., Dutton & Co. 1930. vi + 152 + 232 pp.
219. POUND, LOUISE. "On the Pronunciation of 'Either' and 'Neither'." *Amer. Speech*, 7:371–376. 1932.
220. See also Dictionaries, Nos. 20–30, above.

Sec. 45. *Accentuation in English*

221. LINDELÖF, U. "Bemerkungen über einige Fälle von schwankender Aussprache eines vortonigen *i* im Englischen". *Neuphilologische Mitteilungen*, 32:47–53. 1931.
222. BRADLEY, C. B. "The Accentuation of the *Research*-Group of Words". Univ. of California Publ. in Modern Philology, 11:1–19. 1922.
223. HANEY, JOHN L. "Our Agile American Accents". *Amer. Speech*, 1:378–382. 1926. — See also JESPERSEN, OTTO. Modern English Grammar, 1:173. Heidelberg, C. Winter. 1909.

Sec. 46. Rhythm and Pitch

224. † SAINTSBURY, GEO. History of English Prose Rhythm. London, Macmillan. 1912. xiv + 489 pp.
225. ELTON, OLIVER. "English Prose Numbers". English Assn. Essays and Studies, 4:29–54. 1913. — Also: 5:7–51. 1914.
226. SCOTT, FRED N. "The Order of Words in Certain Rhythm-Groups". Mod. Lang. Notes, 28:237–239. 1913. — Repr. in his Standard of American Speech, pp. 191–198. Boston, Allyn & Bacon. 1926.

CHAPTER VII. ENGLISH SPELLING

227. † LOUNSBURY, THOS. R. English Spelling and Spelling Reform. N.Y., Harper. 1909. xiii + 357 pp.
228. † CRAIGIE, WM. A. English Spelling: Its Rules and Reasons. N.Y., Crofts & Co. 1927. viii + 115 pp.
229. BRADLEY, HENRY. "Spoken and Written English". In his Collected Papers, pp. 168–193. Oxford, Clarendon Press. 1928.

Sec. 47. Summaries of English Spellings

230. RAMSEY, SAMUEL. The English Language and English Grammar. N.Y., Putnam's. 1892. iv + 571 pp.
231. HAMILTON, FREDERICK W. Division of Words. Publ. by the Education Committee of the United Typothetae of America. 1918. 27 pp.

Sec. 48. General Comments on English Spelling

232. Rimes without Reason. By One Who Has Been Stung by a Spelling Bee. N.Y., Lake Placid Club, Forest Press. n.d. 16 pp.

CHAPTER VIII. THE CLASSIFICATION OF WORDS

233. STRONG, H. A., LOGEMAN, W. S., and WHEELER, B. I. "The Division of the Parts of Speech". In their Introduction to the Study of the History of Language, pp. 343–364. N.Y., Longmans, Green & Co. 1891.
234. SWEET, HENRY. "Parts of Speech". In his New English Grammar, Vol. I, pp. 35–153. 1892. See No. 9, above.

Sec. 50, A. Common Nouns

235. Anon. "Nouns of Multitude". Word-Lore, 3:60, 132. 1928.
236. Anon. "A Matching Test". Word Study, 6(3):2. 1931.

Sec. 50, B. Proper Nouns (Names)

237. † BARDSLEY, CHAS. W. Curiosities of Puritan Nomenclature. London, Chatto & Windus. 1880. xii + 252 pp.
238. † YONGE, CHARLOTTE M. History of Christian Names. New ed. London, Macmillan. 1884. cxliii + 476 pp.

239. † BARDSLEY, CHAS. W. Dictionary of English and Welsh Surnames. London, Frowde. 1901. xvi + 837 pp.
240. † BARBER, H. British Family Names. 2d ed. London, E. Stock. 1903. xii + 286 pp.
241. † HARRISON, HENRY. Surnames of the United Kingdom. London, Eaton Press; Morland Press. 1907–1915. 2 vols.
242. † TAYLOR, ISAAC. Words and Places. Repr. in Everyman's Library. London, Dent. 1911. 448 pp.
243. † JOHNSTON, JAMES B. Place Names of England and Wales. N.Y., Dutton & Co. 1916. vii + 532 pp.
244. † WEEKLEY, ERNEST. The Romance of Names. 3d ed. London, Murray. 1922. 263 pp.
245. MCKNIGHT, GEO. H. "Place-Names", "Personal Names". In his English Words, pp. 358–392. 1923. See No. 298, below.
246. BARKER, H. F. "Our Leading Surnames". *Amer. Speech*, 1:470–477. 1926. — Also: 1:596–607. 1926.
247. † WEEKLEY, ERNEST. Surnames. N.Y., Dutton & Co. 1927. xxii + 364 pp.
248. † BOWMAN, WM. D. The Story of Surnames. N.Y., Knopf. 1931. 287 pp.
249. † EWEN, C. L. History of British Surnames. London, Routledge. 1931. 528 pp.
250. † HOLT, ALFRED H. Wild Names I Have Met. Revised and enlarged edition. Williamstown, Mass., publ. by author. 1933. 32 pp.
251. FEIPEL, LOUIS, *et al.* "American Place-Names". *Amer. Speech*, 1:78–91, 395, 625. 1925–1926.
252. MOTT, GERTRUDE. A Handbook for Californiacs. San Francisco, Harr Wagner Publ. Co. 1926. xii + 104 pp.
253. HECK, H. J. "State Border Place-Names". *Amer. Speech*, 3:186–190. 1928.
254. SAGE, EVAN T. "Classical Place-Names in America". *Amer. Speech*, 4:261–271. 1929.
255. MEREDITH, MAMIE. "Picturesque Town Names in America". *Amer. Speech*, 6:429–432. 1931.
256. WESEEN, M. H. "Citizens of the States". In his Dictionary of English Grammar, p. 111. 1928. See No. 337, below. — See also *Amer. Speech*, 7:389. 1932.
257. "Names of dogs". *Notes and Queries*, (Ser. 7) 6:144–145. 1888; (Ser. 10) 2:101–103, 150–151, 232–234, 469–471. 1905.
258. "The Names of Men-of-War". *Saturday Rev.* (London), 45:426–427, 521–523. 1878.
259. POUND, LOUISE. "Word-Coinage and Modern Trade-Names". *Dialect Notes*, 4:29–41. 1913.
260. POUND, LOUISE. "The Kraze for 'K'". *Amer. Speech*, 1:43–44. 1925. — Also: 1:443–446.
261. HANSON, CHAS. L., *et al.* "The Title 'Professor'". *Amer. Speech*, 3:27, 256–257. 1927.

262. † FREY, ALBERT R. Sobriquets and Nicknames. Boston, Houghton Mifflin Co. 1895. 482 pp.
263. "Nicknames of the States". *Current Literature*, 24:41. 1898. — Also: WESEEN, M. H., Dictionary of English Grammar, p. 417. 1928. See No. 337, below.
264. "National nicknames". *Notes and Queries* (Ser. 9), 4:28, 90, 212–214, 238, 296, 401. 1899.
265. SUNDÉN, KARL. Contributions to the Study of Elliptical Words in Modern English. Uppsala, Almqvist & Wiksell. 1904. 233 pp.
266. "Parliamentary nicknames". *Notes and Queries* (Ser. 12), 12:188, 234, 317, 376, 497. 1923.
267. ADAMS, A. A., *et al.* "Nicknames of Inhabitants of Localities". *Word-Lore*, 3:57, 90. 1928.

Sec. 51. Pronouns

268. "You All" and "We All". *Amer. Speech*, 2:133, 343–345, 476, 496; 4:54–55, 103, 154, 328, 347–351; 5:173; 6:304–305. 1926–1931. — Also: *Amer. Mercury*, 29:116, 248–249, 377. 1933.

Sec. 53. Verbs

269. KENNEDY, ARTHUR G. The Modern English Verb-Adverb Combination. Stanford Studies in Lang. and Lit., No. 1. Stanford Univ. Press. 1920. 51 pp.
270. MALONE, KEMP. "Finite Verb Categories". In the Manly Studies in Lang. and Lit., pp. 374–382. Chicago. 1923.
271. LAMBERT, MILDRED E. "Prepositions and Adverbs as Solidary Modifiers". *Amer. Speech*, 4:228–243. 1929.
272. CURME, GEO. O. "Characteristic Features of Aspect in English". *Jour. of Engl. and Germ. Philology*, 31:251–255. 1932. — See also Chapter XIX of his Syntax. 1931. See No. 399, below.

Sec. 54. Adverbs

273. SWAEN, A. E. H. "Entirely, wholly, largely, frankly". *Archiv für das Studium der neueren Sprachen und Literaturen*, 134:48–58. 1916.
274. POUND, LOUISE. "Popular Variants of 'Yes'". *Amer. Speech*, 2:132. 1926.
275. RICE, WALLACE. "Go Slow — Proceed Slowly". *Amer. Speech*, 2:489–491. 1927.

Sec. 56. Conjunctions

276. OWEN, EDWARD T. "Meaning and Function of Thought-Connectives". Trans. of the Wisconsin Acad. of Sciences, Arts and Letters, 12:1–48. 1898.
277. † FERNALD, J. C. Connectives of English Speech. N.Y., Funk & Wagnalls Co. 1904. xi + 324 pp.

Sec. 57. Interjections

278. † SHARMAN, JULIAN. A Cursory History of Swearing. London, Nimmo & Bain. 1884. vii + 199 pp.
279. CARRUTH, WM. H. "Language Used to Domestic Animals". *Dialect Notes*, 1:263–268. 1893.
280. BOLTON, H. C. "The Language Used in Talking to Domestic Animals". *Amer. Anthropologist*, 10:65–90, 97–113. 1897. — See also: *Amer. Speech*, 7:454–455. 1932.
281. SWAEN, A. E. H. "Figures of Imprecation". *Englische Studien*, 24:16–71, 195–239. 1897.
282. HILLS, E. C. "Exclamations in American English". *Dialect Notes*, 5:253–284. 1924.
283. SCOTT, FRED N. "The Colloquial Nasals". In his Standard of American Speech, pp. 272–278. 1926. See No. 43, above.
284. † GRAVES, ROBT. Lars Porsena, or The Future of Swearing and Improper Language. N.Y., Dutton & Co. 1927. 77 pp.

Sec. 58. Conversion and Confusion of the Parts of Speech

285. KENNEDY, ARTHUR G. "The Substantivation of Adjectives in Chaucer". Univ. of Nebraska Studies, 5:251–269. 1905.
286. OWEN, EDWARD T. "Hybrid Parts of Speech". Trans. of the Wisconsin Acad. of Sciences, Arts and Letters, 16:108–252. 1908.
287. BERGENER, CARL. A Contribution to the Study of the Conversion of Adjectives into Nouns in English. Lund, Gleerupska Univ.-Bokhandeln. 1928. xvi + 222 pp.
288. KRUISINGA, E. "Conversion". In his Handbook, Pt. II, Vol. 3, pp. 96–161. 1931. See No. 19, above.

CHAPTER IX. THE DERIVATION OF WORDS

289. † SKEAT, WALTER W. Principles of English Etymology. First series, 2d ed. 1892. Second series. 1891. Oxford, Clarendon Press. 2 vols.
290. † JOHNSON, CHAS. F. English Words: An Elementary Study of Derivations. N.Y., Harper. 1892. 255 pp.
291. BRÉAL, MICHEL. "On the Canons of Etymological Investigation". Trans. of Amer. Philological Assn., 24:17–28. 1893.
292. † GREENOUGH, JAS. B., and KITTREDGE, GEO. L. Words and Their Ways in English Speech. N.Y., Macmillan. 1901. x + 431 pp.
293. SKEAT, WALTER W. Notes on English Etymology. Oxford, Clarendon Press. 1901. xxii + 479 pp.
294. † SKEAT, WALTER W. Etymological Dictionary of the English Language. 4th ed. Oxford, Clarendon Press. 1910. xliv + 780 pp. — Also: A Concise Etymological Dictionary. Oxford, Clarendon Press. 1911. xv + 664 pp.
295. † WEEKLEY, ERNEST. The Romance of Words. London, Murray. 1912. ix + 210 pp.

296. † UTTER, ROBT. P. Every-Day Words and Their Uses. A Guide to Correct Diction. N. Y., Harper. 1916. vii + 277 pp.
297. † WEEKLEY, ERNEST. Etymological Dictionary of Modern English. N.Y., Dutton & Co. 1921. xx pp. + 1660 columns. — Also: A Concise Etymological Dictionary. London, Murray. 1924. xx + 983 pp.
298. † MCKNIGHT, GEO. H. English Words and Their Background. N.Y., Appleton & Co. 1923. x + 449 pp.

I. CREATION AND ADAPTATION OF WORDS

299. † WEEKLEY, ERNEST. Words Ancient and Modern. London, Murray. 1926. viii + 163 pp.
300. † WEEKLEY, ERNEST. More Words Ancient and Modern. London, Murray. 1927. viii + 192 pp.
301. † WEEKLEY, ERNEST. Words and Names. N.Y., Dutton & Co. 1932. 200 pp.
302. † Anon. Picturesque Word Origins. Springfield, Mass., G. & C. Merriam Co. 1933. 134 pp.

Sec. 60. *Original Creation*

303. WHEATLEY, H. B. "Dictionary of Reduplicated Words in the English Language". Appended to Trans. of the Philological Soc. for 1865. London. 104 pp. — See also WOOD, F. A., in *Modern Philology*, 9:157–194. 1911.
304. SKEAT, W. W. "Report on 'Ghost-Words' or Words Which Have No Real Existence." Trans. of Philological Soc. for 1885–1887, pp. 350–374. — See also Trans. for 1903–1906, pp. 180–201. 1906.
305. STRONG, LOGEMAN, and WHEELER. "Original Creation". In their Introduction to the Study of the History of Language, pp. 157–169. 1891. See No. 233, above.
306. † MEAD, LEON. Word-Coinage. Being an Inquiry into Recent Neologisms. N.Y., Crowell. 1902. xi + 281 pp.
307. MATTHEWS, BRANDER. "The Art of Making New Words". *Unpopular Rev.*, 9:58–69. 1918.
308. KINNICK, CLAUDE. "Some First Words". *Word Study*, 7 (3):1–3; (4):3. 1932.

Sec. 61. *Word Composition: Suffixes and Prefixes*

309. POUND, LOUISE. "Vogue Affixes in Present-Day Word-Coinage". *Dialect Notes*, 5:1–14. 1918.
310. BURNHAM, JOSEPHINE M. "Three Hard-Worked Suffixes". *Amer. Speech*, 2:244–246. 1927.
311. MEREDITH, MAMIE. "'Doctresses', 'Authoresses', and Others". *Amer. Speech*, 5:476–481. 1930.
312. BARRY, PHILLIPS, *et al.* "Cafeteria". *Amer. Speech*, 3:35–37, 344, 477. 1927–1928.

BIBLIOGRAPHY

Sec. 63. Word Composition: Distinct Words

313. UHRSTRÖM, W. Pickpocket, Turnkey, Wraprascal, and Similar Formations in English. Stockholm, M. Bervall. 1918. 80 pp.

Sec. 65. Blends

314. BERGSTRÖM, G. A. On Blendings of Synonyms or Cognate Expressions in English. Univ. of Lund Ph.D. dissertation. 1906. xvi + 211 pp.
315. POUND, LOUISE. Blends. Their Relation to English Word-Formation. Anglistische Forschungen, No. 42. Heidelberg. 1914. 58 pp.
316. WITHINGTON, ROBT. "Some New 'Portmanteau' Words". *Philological Quart.*, 9:158–164. 1930. — See also *Amer. Speech*, 7:200–203. 1932.

Sec. 66. Clipped Words and Back Formations

317. WITTMAN, ELISABETH. "Clipped Words: A Study of Back-Formation and Curtailment in Present-Day English". *Dialect Notes*, 4:115–145. 1914.
318. SCHULTZ, WM. E. "College Abbreviations". *Amer. Speech*, 5:240–244. 1930.

Sec. 67. Conversion, or Functional Change

319. REINIUS, JOSEF. On Transferred Appellations of Human Beings, Chiefly in English and German. Göteborg, Wald. Zachrissons Boktryckeri. 1903. xv + 306 pp.
320. EFVERGREN, CARL. Names of Places in a Transferred Sense in English. Lund, Gleerup. 1909. xii + 123 pp.
321. SALMON, LUCY M. "Place-Names and Personal Names as Records of History". *Amer. Speech*, 2:228–232. 1927.
322. CARY, D. M. "Words from Surnames". *Word-Lore*, 3:103–105, 155. 1928.
323. JESPERSEN, OTTO. Veiled Language. Soc. for Pure English Tract 33:420–429. 1929.

Sec. 69. Confused Etymologies

324. † PALMER, A. SMYTHE. Folk-Etymology. A Dictionary of Verbal Corruptions or Words Perverted in Form or Meaning by False Derivation or Mistaken Analogy. London, Bell. 1882. xxviii + 664 pp.
325. MCKNIGHT, GEO. H. "Some Compound Etymologies". *Jour. of Engl. and Germ. Philology*, 12:110–117. 1913.
326. READ, ALLEN W., *et al.* "The Word *Blizzard*". *Amer. Speech*, 3:191–217, 489–490; 5:176, 232–235. 1928, 1930.
327. FISCHER, W. "American Slang *Guy* 'Fellow, Chap, Person'". *Anglia*. 54:443–449. 1931.

II. BORROWING OF WORDS

328. MATTHEWS, BRANDER. "On the Naturalization of Foreign Words". In his Parts of Speech, pp. 165–183. 1916. See No. 12, above.

Sec. 70. Latin Borrowings

329. † JOHNSON, EDWIN L. Latin Words of Common English. Boston, Heath & Co. 1931. viii + 327 pp.

Sec. 72. Celtic Borrowings

330. FÖRSTER, MAX. "Keltisches Wortgut im Englischen". 1921. See No. 187, above.

Sec. 74. Greek Borrowings

331. † SMOCK, JOHN C. The Greek Element in English Words. Ed. by Percy W. Long. N.Y., Macmillan. 1931. xiv + 356 pp.

Sec. 76. Borrowings from Other Romanic Languages

332. † BENTLEY, H. W. Dictionary of Spanish Terms in English. 1932. See No. 90, above. — See also *Amer. Speech*, 8(3):7–10. October, 1933.

Sec. 77. Miscellaneous Borrowings

333. TAYLOR, WALT. "Arabic Words in English". Soc. for Pure English Tract 38:567–599. 1933. — SKEAT, W. W. [Mexican Words, Brazilian, Peruvian, West Indian]. In his Notes on English Etymology, pp. 331–352. 1901. See No. 293, above.

Sec. 78. Hybrid Words and Phrases

334. NICHOLSON, GEO. A. English Words with Native Roots and with Greek, Latin or Romanic Suffixes. Linguistic Studies in Germanic, No. 3. Chicago. 1916. 55 pp.
335. JOHNSON, EDWIN L. "Hybrids". In his Latin Words of Common English, pp. 256–262. 1931. See No. 329, above.

CHAPTER X. THE MODERN ENGLISH VOCABULARY

336. LINDSAY, EDWIN Y. Etymological Study of the Ten Thousand Words in Thorndike's *Teacher's Word Book*. Indiana Univ. Studies, Vol. XII, No. 65. 1925. 115 pp.
337. † WESEEN, M. H. Crowell's Dictionary of English Grammar and Handbook of American Usage. N.Y., Crowell. 1928. x + 703 pp.
338. † WESEEN, M. H. Words Confused and Misused. N.Y., Crowell. 1932. vi + 310 pp.
339. † MAWSON, C. O. SYLVESTER. The Dictionary Companion. Garden City, N.Y., Doubleday, Doran & Co. 1932. xii + 479 pp.
340. VIZETELLY, FRANK H. How to Use English. A Guide to Correct Speech and Writing. N.Y., Funk & Wagnalls Co. 1933. x + 658 pp.

See also Dictionaries, Nos. 20–30, above, and The Derivation of Words, Nos. 289–302, above.

BIBLIOGRAPHY

Sec. 79. Size and Nature of the Vocabulary

341. TRENCH, R. C. On Some Deficiencies of Our English Dictionaries. London, Parker. 1857. 60 pp. — Rev. ed. in Trans. of the Philological Soc. for 1857, Pt. II. 80 pp.
342. WHEATLEY, H. B. "Chronological Notices of the Dictionaries of the English Language". Trans. of the Philological Soc. for 1865, pp. 218–293.
343. MURRAY, JAMES A. H. The Evolution of English Lexicography. Oxford, Clarendon Press. 1900. 51 pp.
344. STEGER, STEWART A. American Dictionaries. Univ. of Virginia Ph.D. dissertation. 1913. 147 pp.
345. VIZETELLY, FRANK H. Development of the Dictionary of the English Language. N. Y., Funk & Wagnalls Co. 1915. 44 pp.
346. For brief discussions of the New English Dictionary see *Bookman*, 67:141–144. 1928. — *Quarterly Rev.*, 250:238–243. 1928. — *London Mercury*, 18:178–185. 1928. — *Amer. Speech*, 4:22–27. 1928. — *The Periodical*, 13, No. 143. April, 1928. — *English Jour.* (college ed.), 18:396–403. 1929.
347. RAMSAY, ROBT. L. "Taking the Census of English Words". *Amer. Speech*, 8:36–41. 1933.

Sec. 80. Cognate Words in English

348. SKEAT, W. W. "List of Indogermanic Roots". In his Etymological Dictionary, pp. 751–761. 1910. See No. 294, above.

Sec. 81. Doublets and Triplets

349. ALLEN, E. A. "English Doublets". *Publ. of Mod. Lang. Assn. of America*, 23:184–239. 1908.
350. STEADMAN, J. M., Jr. "Phonetic Differentiation in English". *Studies in Philology*, 28:551–568. 1931.

Sec. 82. Homonyms

351. SKEAT, W. W. "List of Homonyms". In his Etymological Dictionary, pp. 737–748. 1910. See No. 294, above.
352. BRIDGES, ROBT. "On English Homophones". Soc. for Pure English Tract 2:3–48; and 4:32–33. 1919–1920.

Sec. 83. Synonyms and Antonyms

353. PIOZZI, HESTER LYNCH. British Synonymy; or, An Attempt at Regulating the Choice of Words in Familiar Conversation. Dublin, pr. by Wm. Potter. 1794. xx + 516 pp.
354. † FLEMMING, LOUIS A. Putnam's Word Book. N.Y., Putnam's. 1916. viii + 709 pp.

355. † MARCH, FRANCIS A. and FRANCIS A., Jr. Thesaurus Dictionary. A Treasure House of Words and Knowledge. 4th ed. Phila., Historical Publ. Co. 1925. 1190 + 251 pp.
356. † ROGET, PETER M. Thesaurus of English Words and Phrases. Enlarged by John Lewis Roget. New revised and enlarged ed. by Samuel R. Roget. N.Y., Longmans, Green & Co. 1933. xlii + 705 pp. — See also Mawson's edition of Roget. 1911; revised, 1932.
357. † CRABB, GEO. English Synonyms Explained. 11th ed. N.Y., Crowell. 1927. 801 pp.
358. † FERNALD, JAS. C. English Synonyms, Antonyms and Prepositions. 33d ed. N.Y., Funk & Wagnalls Co. 1929. xv + 729 pp.
359. PRENNER, MANUEL, *et al.* "Slang Synonyms for 'Drunk'". *Amer. Speech*, 4:102–103, 440–441; 5:231. 1928–1930. — Also: *New Republic*, 50:71–72. 1927.
360. GILL, M. A. "Words That Can Be Used in Place of the Word 'Said'". In his Underworld Slang, pp. 25–28. Kansas City, Mo., South Side Printing Co. 1929.
361. HAYDEN, MARIE G. "Terms of Disparagement". *Dialect Notes*, 4:194–223. 1915. — Also: WARNOCK, ELSIE. "Terms of Disparagement". *Dialect Notes*, 5:60–73. 1919.
362. POUND, LOUISE, *et al.* "'Blah' and Its Synonyms". *Amer. Speech*, 4:329–330. 1929. — Also: CURTISS, PHILIP. "Psychology of Tripe". *Harper's Mag.*, 159:385–388. 1929.
363. WARNOCK, ELSIE. "Terms of Approbation and Eulogy in American Dialect Speech". *Dialect Notes*, 4:13–25. 1913.

Sec. 84. *Individual Vocabularies*

364. HOLDEN, E. S. "On the Number of Words Used in Speaking and Writing". Bulletin of Philosophical Soc. of Washington, No. 2, Appendix, pp. 16–21. 1880.
365. BROWN, R. W., *et al.* "Size of the Working Vocabulary." New York *Nation*, 93:11, 262–263. 1911.
366. VIZETELLY, FRANK H. Essentials of English Speech, pp. 214–219. N.Y., Funk & Wagnalls Co. 1915.
367. TERMAN, LEWIS M. The Measurement of Intelligence. Boston, Houghton Mifflin Co. 1916. See pages 224–231, 281–286, etc.
368. GERLACH, FRED M. Vocabulary Studies. Colorado College Studies in Education and Psychology. 1917. 123 pp.
369. NICE, MARGARET M. "On the Size of Vocabularies". *Amer. Speech*, 2:1–7. 1926.
370. ROBINSON, HENRY M. "What's the Good Word? And How Many Good Ones Do You Know?" *American Mag.*, 111 (3):36–37, 154–156. March, 1931.
371. FINDLEY, WARREN G. Specialization of Verbal Facility at the College Entrance Level. A Comparative Study of Scientific and Literary Vocabularies. Columbia Univ., Teachers College Contributions to Education, No. 567. 1933. v + 76 pp.

Sec. 85. Relative Frequency of Words

372. † ELDRIDGE, R. C. Six Thousand Common English Words. Their Comparative Frequency. Niagara Falls, N.Y., 1911. 64 pp.
373. † THORNDIKE, EDWARD L. The Teacher's Word Book. N. Y., publ. by Teachers College, Columbia Univ. 1921. vi + 123 pp. — Also: New ed. with 20,000 words. 1932.
374. † HORN, ERNEST. Basic Writing Vocabulary. 10,000 Words Most Commonly Used in Writing. Univ. of Iowa Monographs in Education, First Ser., No. 4. 1926. 225 pp.
375. ZIPF, GEO. K. "Relative Frequency as a Determinant of Phonetic Change". Harvard Studies in Classical Philology, 40:1–95. 1929.
376. † FRENCH, N. R., *et al*. The Words and Sounds of Telephone Conversations. Bell Telephone System Technical Publications, Monograph B–491. N. Y., June, 1930. 35 pp.
377. † HALLIWELL, JAMES O. Dictionary of Archaic and Provincial Words etc. 1924. See No. 67, above.
378. SCOTT, FRED N. "Verbal Taboos". *School Rev.*, 20:361–378. 1912. Repr. in his Standard of American Speech, pp. 165–190. 1925. See No. 43, above.
379. FAUCETT, LAURENCE, and MAKI, ITSU. A Study of English Word-Values. Statistically Determined from the Latest Extensive Word-Counts. Oxford, Univ. Press. 1932. 282 pp.

CHAPTER XI. INFLECTION

380. † MORRIS, RICHARD. Historical Outlines of English Accidence. Rev. ed. by L. Kellner and H. Bradley. London, Macmillan. 1925. xiii + 463 pp.

Sec. 86. The Breaking Down of English Inflection

381. FERNALD, J. C. "The Simplicity of English". 1909. See No. 179, above.
382. KRAPP, G. P. "English as a 'Grammarless Tongue'". In his Modern English, pp. 59–62. 1909. See No. 11, above.
383. TRNKA, B. "Analysis and Synthesis". *English Studies*, 10:138–144. 1928.

Sec. 87. Declension of Nouns

384. SWEET, H. "Number". In his New English Grammar, Vol. II, pp. 44–48. 1898. See No. 9, above.
385. MELLEN, IDA M. "'Fish' or 'Fishes'". *Amer. Speech*, 2:246. 1927.
386. POUND, LOUISE. "The Pluralization of Latin Loan-Words in Present-Day American Speech". *Classical Jour.*, 15:163–168. 1919. — See also *Amer. Speech*, 3:26–27, 490. 1927–1928.
387. BALL, CARLETON R. "English or Latin Plurals for Anglicized Latin Nouns?" *Amer. Speech*, 3:291–325. 1928.
388. MAWSON, C. O. S. "Plurals". In his Dictionary Companion, pp. 35–53. 1932. See No. 339, above.

389. WESEEN, M. H. "Plurals without Singulars". In his Dictionary of English Grammar, pp. 475–476. 1928. See No. 337, above.
390. VICKERS, WALLACE J. The Concept of Case in English Grammar. Stanford Ph.D. dissertation (unpublished). 1925.
391. CALLAWAY, MORGAN, Jr. "The Number of Cases in Modern English". *Publ. of Mod. Lang. Assn. of America*, 42:238–254. 1927.
392. BAKER, HOWARD G. "Case in Some Early and Later English Grammars". Papers of the Michigan Acad. of Sciences, Arts and Letters, 14:525–535. 1931.

Sec. 90. Conjugation of Verbs

393. FOWLER, H. W., *et al*. "*Broadcast(ed)*: A Compromise". Soc. for Pure English Tract 19:32–36. 1925. — See also *Amer. Speech*, 3:30, 164. 1927.

CHAPTER XII. SYNTAX

394. †SMITH, C. ALPHONSO. Studies in English Syntax. Boston, Ginn & Co. 1906. 92 pp.
395. †SHEFFIELD, ALFRED D. Grammar and Thinking. A Study of the Working Conceptions in Syntax. N.Y., Putnam's. 1912. x + 193 pp.
396. †POUTSMA, H. Grammar of Late Modern English. Pt. I. 2d ed. 2 vols. 1928. Pt. II. 3 vols. 1914–1926. Groningen, Noordhoff.
397. THORNDIKE, E. L., *et al*. "An Inventory of English Constructions with Measure of Their Importance". *Teachers College Record*, 28:580–610. 1927.
398. HARRAP, HENRY. "The Most Common Grammatical Errors". *English Jour.* (college ed.), 19:440–444. 1930.
399. †CURME, GEO. O. Syntax. Vol. III of A Grammar of the English Language. Boston, Heath & Co. 1931. xv + 616 pp.
400. †KRUISINGA, E. "English Accidence and Syntax". In his Handbook of Present-Day English, Pt. II, 3 vols. 1932. See No. 19, above.
401. †LEONARD, STERLING A. Current English Usage. English Monographs, No. 1. Chicago, publ. for the National Council of Teachers of English. 1932. xxii + 232 pp.
402. †SEWARD, SAMUEL S., Jr. Handbook of English Writing. Boston, Ginn & Co. 1932. xvi + 429 pp.

Sec. 92. The Sentence in General

403. Anon. "Conversations in Scottish, Employing Vowels Only". *Academy*, 54:150, 256. 1898.
404. MCGOVERN, J. B. "Lengthy Sentences in English and French". *Notes and Queries* (Ser. 12), 6:309–310. 1920. — Also: *Saturday Rev.* (London), 142:613, 644, 677. 1926. — THORPE, C. D., in *Saturday Rev. of Literature*, 8:523, 573. 1932.
405. GILL, ROBT. S. "Speech Tunes and the Alphabet". *Amer. Speech*, 1:40–42. 1925. — Also: 1:315–316; 2:63–64; 4:98–99. 1926–1928.
406. SCUDDER, HAROLD H. "Sentence Length". *English Jour.*, 12:617–620. 1923.

Sec. 94. The Predicate

407. POOLEY, ROBT. C. "*Myself* as a Simple Personal Pronoun". *Amer. Speech*, 7:368–370. 1932.

Sec. 99. Concord

408. STOELKE, HANS. Die Inkongruenz zwischen Subjekt und Prädikat im Englischen und in den verwandten Sprachen. Anglistische Forschungen, No. 49. Heidelberg. 1916. xix + 101 pp.
409. Anon. Burlington Blues: "Is" or "Are"? Chicago, issued by the Traffic Dept. of the Chicago, Burlington & Quincy R. R. Co. 1926. 32 pp.

Sec. 100. Word Order

410. SMITH, C. A. "The Position of Words'. In his Studies in English Syntax, pp. 61–92. 1906. See No. 394, above.
411. FOWLER, H. W. "On Grammatical Inversions". Soc. for Pure English Tract 10:9–25. 1922.
412. LOUNSBURY, THOS. R. "'To' and the Infinitive". *Harper's Mag.*, 108:728–734. 1904.
413. FOWLER, H. W. "The Split Infinitive". Modern English Usage, pp. 558–561. 1926. See No. 16, above. — Also: "The Position of Adverbs". Soc. for Pure English Tract 15:7–15. 1923.
414. CURME, GEO. O. "The Split Infinitive". *Amer. Speech*, 2:341–342. 1927.
415. FOWLER, H. W. "Preposition at End". Soc. for Pure English Tract 14:18–21. 1923.

Sec. 104. The Pronoun

416. KENYON, J. S. "On 'Who' and 'Whom'". *Amer. Speech*, 5:253–255. 1930.
417. MENNER, ROBT. J. "Troublesome Relatives". *Amer. Speech*, 6:341–346. 1931.

Sec. 105. The Adjective

418. FEIPEL, LOUIS, *et al.* "'A' and 'An' before 'H' and Certain Vowels". *Amer. Speech*, 4:442–454; 5:82–85. 1929.
419. POUTSMA, H. "Observations on Expedients to Express Intensity and Emphasis". In the Curme Volume of Linguistic Studies, pp. 120–133. Language Monographs, No. VII. 1930.

Sec. 106. The Verb

420. ROYSTER, J. F., and STEADMAN, J. M. "The 'Going-to' Future". Manly Anniversary Studies, pp. 394–403. 1923.
421. LAMBERT, MILDRED E. "Modes of Predication" etc. *Amer. Speech*, 4:28–39, 137–144. 1928.

422. GOEDSCHE, C. R. "The Terminate Aspect of the Expanded Form". *Jour. of Engl. and Germ. Philology*, 31:469–477. 1932.
423. FRIES, CHAS. C. "The Periphrastic Future with *Shall* and *Will* in Modern English". *Publ. of Mod. Lang. Assn. of America*, 40:963–1024. 1925.

Sec. 107. The Verbals

424. KRUISINGA, E. "The Verbal *-ing* in Living English". *English Studies*, 12:24–31, 58–66, 110. 1930. — See also: JESPERSEN and FOWLER, Soc. for Pure English Tract 25:147–172. 1926; 26:192–196. 1927. — Also: *Amer. Speech*, 8(2): 63–66. 1933.
425. LINDELÖF, U. "The Subject of the Gerund in Present-Day English". *Neuphilologische Mitteilungen*, 34:1–10. 1933.

Sec. 109. The Preposition

426. FOWLER, H. W. "Preposition at End". 1923. See No. 415, above.
427. † VIZETELLY, FRANK H. Prepositions, How to Use Them. N.Y., Funk & Wagnalls Co. 1924. 44 pp.
428. WESEEN, M. H. "Prepositional Phrases and Idioms". In his Dictionary of English Grammar, pp. 492–514. 1928. See No. 337, above.

Sec. 110. The Conjunction

429. †FERNALD, J. C. Connectives of English Speech. The Correct Usage of Prepositions, Conjunctions, Relative Pronouns and Adverbs Explained and Illustrated. N.Y., Funk & Wagnalls Co. 1904. xi + 324 pp.
430. †VIZETELLY, FRANK H. Conjunctions; Their Use and Abuse. N.Y., Funk & Wagnalls Co. 1924. 33 pp.

CHAPTER XIII. SEMASIOLOGICAL CHANGE

431. †BRÉAL, MICHEL. Semantics. Studies in the Science of Meaning. Transl. by Mrs. Henry Cust. N.Y., Holt & Co. 1900. lxvi + 341 pp.
432. †GREENOUGH and KITTREDGE. Words and Their Ways in English Speech. 1901. See No. 292, above.
433. BRADLEY, H. "Changes of Meaning". In The Making of English, pp. 160–214. N.Y., Macmillan. 1904.
434. †WEEKLEY, E. The Romance of Words. 1912. See No. 295, above.
435. †MCKNIGHT, G. H. English Words and Their Background. 1923. See No. 298, above.
436. †BARFIELD, OWEN. History in English Words. N.Y., Doran. 1925. xii + 223 pp. — 2d ed. 1933.
437. †WEEKLEY, E. Words Ancient and Modern. 1926. See No. 299, above.
438. †WEEKLEY, E. More Words Ancient and Modern. 1927. See No. 300, above.
439. †FOLEY, LOUIS. Beneath the Crust of Words. Columbus, Ohio State Univ. Press. 1928. v + 158 pp.
440. POUND, LOUISE. "American Indefinite Names". *Amer. Speech*, 6:257–259. 1931.

441. †WEEKLEY, E. Words and Names. 1932. See No. 301, above.
442. †Anon. Picturesque Word Origins. 1933. See No. 302, above.
443. FUNK, W. J., et al. "Ten Most Beautiful Words". *Literary Digest*, 115, January 7, 1933. p. 17.

Sec. 112. Specialization in Meaning

444. MATHEWS, ALBERT, et al. "The Term 'Campus' in American Colleges". Trans. of Colonial Soc. of Mass., 3:431–437. 1897. — Also: *Notes and Queries* (Ser. 9), 1:384–385. 1898. — New York *Nation*, 66:285, 403–404. 1898.
445. FICKE, H. S. "A Note on the Word 'Medium'". *Philological Quart.*, 7:400–401. 1928.
446. MORSE, MARIAN L. "The Verb 'Operate'". *Amer. Speech*, 5:287–289. 1930.
447. JOSEPH, H. W. B. "On the Word 'Person'". Soc. for Pure English Tract 33:430–435. 1929.

Sec. 116. Figurative Gender

448. SVARTENGREN, T. H. "The Feminine Gender for Inanimate Things in Anglo-American". *Amer. Speech*, 3:83–113. 1927. — Also: Enlarged in *Dialect Notes*, 6:7–56. 1928.

Sec. 119. The Pejorative Tendency

449. TUCKER, GILBERT M. "Degraded Words". In Our Common Speech, pp. 32–77. N.Y., Dodd, Mead & Co. 1895.
450. SCOTT, F. N. "Verbal Taboos". 1912. See No. 378, above.
451. HAYDEN, MARIE G. "Terms of Disparagement". 1915. See No. 361, above. — Also: WARNOCK, ELSIE. "Terms of Disparagement". See No. 361, above.
452. POUND, L., et al. "'Blah' and Its Synonyms". 1929. See No. 362, above.
453. SCHREUDER, HINDRIK. Pejorative Sense Development in English. Univ. of Amsterdam Ph.D. dissertation. Groningen, Noordhoff. 1929. 196 pp.

Sec. 120. The Ameliorative Tendency

454. WARNOCK, ELSIE. "Terms of Approbation". 1913. See No. 363, above.
455. WITHINGTON, ROBT. "Rehabilitated Words". *Amer. Speech*, 5:212–218, 280–281. 1930.

Sec. 122. Extinction of Words and Meanings

456. HEMKEN, EMIL. Das Aussterben alter Substantiva im Verlaufe der englischen Sprachgeschichte. Univ. of Kiel Ph.D. dissertation. 1906. 63 pp.
457. OBERDÖRFFER, W. Das Aussterben altenglischer Adjektive und ihr Ersatz im Verlaufe der englischen Sprachgeschichte. Univ. of Kiel Ph.D. dissertation. 1908. 55 pp.

458. OFFE, JOHANNES. Das Aussterben alter Verba und ihr Ersatz im Verlaufe der englischen Sprachgeschichte. Univ. of Kiel Ph.D. dissertation. 1908. 79 pp.
459. TEICHERT, FRIEDRICH. Ueber das Aussterben alter Wörter im Verlaufe der englischen Sprachgeschichte. Univ. of Kiel Ph.D. dissertation. 1912. 77 pp.

Sec. 124. Ambiguous Words and Phrases

460. MALONE, KEMP, et al. "American and Anglo-Saxon". *Amer. Speech*, 1:371–377; 2:147; 3:80; 4:271; etc. 1926–1930.
461. SPINGARN, J. E., et al. "Bibliography". London *Times Literary Supplement*, 1928:44, 62, 80, 96, 112, 131, 150, 221.
462. KELLERMAN, K. F. "'Hulled' and 'Dehulled'". *Amer. Speech*, 4:186–187. 1929.
463. SMITH, L. P. "Four Romantic Words". In his Words and Idioms, pp. 66–134. Boston, Houghton Mifflin Co. 1925.

Sec. 125. Idiomatic English

464. † DIXON, JAMES M. English Idioms. London, Nelson. 1891. 384 pp. New ed. 1912. 288 pp.
465. † KLEISER, GRENVILLE. Fifteen Thousand Useful Phrases. 5th ed. N.Y., Funk & Wagnalls Co. 1919. 453 pp.
466. † HYAMSON, ALBERT M. Dictionary of English Phrases, Phraseological Allusions, Catchwords, etc. N.Y., Dutton & Co. 1922. xvi + 365 pp.
467. † BREWER, E. COBHAM. Dictionary of Phrase and Fable. New ed. Phila., Lippincott Co. 1923. 1158 pp.
468. † VIZETELLY, FRANK H., and DE BEKKER, L. J. Idioms and Idiomatic Phrases. N.Y., Funk & Wagnalls Co. 1923. 512 pp.
469. † HARGRAVE, BASIL. Origins and Meanings of Popular Phrases and Names Which Came into Use during the Great War. Phila., Lippincott Co. 1925. vi + 376 pp.
470. SMITH, L. P. "English Idioms". In his Words and Idioms, pp. 167–292. Boston, Houghton Mifflin Co. 1925. First publ. in shorter form in Soc. for Pure English Tract 12. 1923. 4th ed. 1933
471. † HAYES, R. J. Comparative Idiom: An Introduction to the Study of Modern Languages. Dublin, Hodges, Figgis & Co. 1927. vii + 108 pp.
472. † KIRKPATRICK, JOHN. Handbook of Idiomatic English. 3d ed. Heidelberg, C. Winter. 1927. viii + 317 pp.

CHAPTER XIV. IMPROVEMENT OF THE ENGLISH LANGUAGE

473. MACKAY, CHAS. "The Ascertainment of English". *Nineteenth Century*, 27:131–144. 1890. — Repr. in *Living Age*, 184:451–459. 1890.
474. † MOORE, J. L. Tudor-Stuart Views on the Growth, Status and Destiny of the English Language. Studien zur Englischen Philologie, No. 41. Halle, Niemeyer. 1910. xii + 179 pp.

475. † LEONARD, STERLING A. The Doctrine of Correctness in English Usage, 1700–1800. Univ. of Wisconsin Studies in Lang. and Lit., No. 25. 1929. 361 pp.

Sec. 126. Movement for an Academy

476. † FLASDIECK, HERMANN M. Der Gedanke einer englischen Sprachakademie. Jenaer Germanistische Forschungen, No. 11. Jena. 1928. ix + 246 pp.
477. WELLARD, J. H. "English and the Need of an Academy". *Quarterly Rev.*, 255:76–93. 1930.
478. Society for Pure English Tract No. 1. 1919.
479. MALONE, KEMP. "The International Council for English". *Amer. Speech*, 3:261–275. 1928.

Sec. 127. Grammatical Methods and Nomenclature

480. † Report of the Joint Committee on Grammatical Nomenclature. Appointed by the Nat. Educ. Assn., Mod. Lang. Assn. of America, and Amer. Philol. Assn. Chicago. 1914. viii + 65 pp. New ed. 1923. The report of the British committee appeared in 1911.

Sec. 128. Spelling Reform

481. MARCH, FRANCIS A. The Spelling Reform. Bureau of Education. Circular of Information No. 8, 1893. Washington, D.C. 86 pp.
482. † Circulars of the Simplified Spelling Board. N.Y. 1906–1913. Nos. 1–26.
483. † LOUNSBURY, T. R. English Spelling and Spelling Reform. 1909. See No. 227, above.
484. † VIZETELLY, FRANK H. Dictionary of Simplified Spelling. Compiled from Funk & Wagnalls' New Standard Dictionary. N.Y., Funk & Wagnalls Co. 1915. xv + 151 pp.
485. † Handbook of Simplified Spelling. Pts. 1–3. Simplified Spelling Bulletin, Vol. 8, Nos. 1–3. 1919–1920. 32 + 40 + 48 pp.
486. † ZACHRISSON, R. E. Anglic. A New Agreed Simplified English Spelling. Final revised ed. Uppsala, Anglic Fund A.-B. 1930. 40 pp. — See also Anglic. Eduekaeshonal Revue. Edited bimonthly by Helge Kökeritz. Uppsala, Sweden. 1930–1933.
487. ZACHRISSON, R. E. "Four Hundred Years of English Spelling Reform". *Studia Neophilologica*, 4:1–69. 1931.

Sec. 129. Artificial Languages

488. † GUÉRARD, ALBERT L. A Short History of the International Language Movement. London, Unwin. 1922. 268 pp.
489. COLLITZ, HERMANN. "World Languages". *Language*, 2:1–13. 1926.
490. † PANKHURST, SYLVIA. Delphos: The Future of International Language. London, Kegan Paul. 1927. 95 pp.
491. MACAULAY, T. C. "Interlanguage". SMITH, J. A. "Artificial Languages". Soc. for Pure English Tract 34:453–477. 1930.

492. † OGDEN, C. K. Debabelization. With a Survey of Contemporary Opinion on the Problem of a Universal Language. London, Kegan Paul. 1931. 171 pp.
493. † SPRAGUE, CHAS. E. Handbook of Volapük. 5th ed. N.Y., Chas. E. Sprague. 1888. viii + 119 pp.
494. † CLARK, W. J. International Language, Past, Present and Future. With Specimens of Esperanto and Grammar. London, Dent & Co. 1907. vii + 205 pp.
495. † BEAUFRONT, L. DE. Ido: Complete Manual of the Auxiliary Language, Grammar, Grammatical Exercises, etc. London, Pitman. 1919. 208 pp.
496. † Key to and Primer of Interlingua. London, Kegan Paul. 1931. 168 pp.
497. † JESPERSEN, OTTO. An International Language. London, Allen & Unwin. 1928. 196 pp. (Introduces Novial.)

Sec. 130. *The Future of English*

498. † DE SÉLINCOURT, BASIL. Pomona, or The Future of English. London, Kegan Paul. 1926. 94 pp.
499. KRAPP, G. P. "The Future of English". In his Knowledge of English, pp. 531–533. 1927. See No. 18, above.
500. WEEKLEY, ERNEST. "English as She Will Be Spoke." *Atlantic Monthly*, 149:551–560. 1932.

LIST OF WORDS FOR FURTHER STUDY

In studying each of the words listed, proceed as follows:

1. Give the spelling that you prefer or find recommended by the best authorities.
2. Give the best present-day pronunciation, if possible, and list variant pronunciations if you know of any, using the phonetic alphabet in representing the sounds.
3. Classify the word according to its general function in speech.
4. Tell the derivation of the word.
5. List any interesting cognate words in English; do not bother with mere derivative forms.
6. Discuss briefly the inflection of the word, if there is any.
7. Mention any peculiarities or problems of syntactical usage that may seem worthy of notice.
8. Note recent semasiological tendencies or changes.
9. Comment briefly upon the speech value or effectiveness of the word, rating it as standard literary, dialectal, etc.

Some questionable word forms and spellings have been included in the following list in order that the student may be compelled to make decisions regarding certain controversial matters. Slang words in the list will not always be found in the general dictionaries or readily explained. When a word form stands for several different words (for example, *fast*) or for several parts of speech (for example, *mean*), it will be necessary either to select just one for study or else to make a very extensive study so as to include all meanings and uses.

abdomen	adept	alas	ambition
abecedarian	admiral	alderman	amenities
abracadabra	advertisement	alert	amicable
abridge	affectation	algebra	amok
acclimated	Afrikaans	alibi	amphitheater
acid	aged	alligator	anemone
acoustics	ago	alloy	angle
acre	agonize	allude	Anglo-Saxon
adamant	aigrette	alma mater	Anzac
addict	alarum	amanuensis	apotheosis

LIST OF WORDS FOR FURTHER STUDY

apropos
arduous
Arkansas
aroint
artichoke
assassin
asthma
athletics
Atwood
audience

authority
auto
automaton
avenue
awry
bachelor
bacon
bairn
bait
bankrupt

battalion
bawlout
bayou
bead
Beauchamp
beauty
bedlam
beef
belfry
bench

benedict
bestial
bias
bicycle
bid
biography
biscuit
bishop
blackguard
blatant

bleach
blend

blizzard
blotto
bluecoat
bluff (verb)
board
body
bona fide
book

boot
bootlegger
booze
boughten
bowwow
box
brat
brazen
breviary
brick

bridegroom
brimstone
bring
broadcast
brother-in-law
brougham
Browning
bucket
buckwheat
bulldoze

bum
bunko
burgle (verb)
bus
butler
butter
buxom
by-law
cab
cabal

cabbage
cactus
caducibranchiate

cafeteria
cahoots
calaboose
calculate
calibre
California
call down

Cambridge
cameleopard
camouflage
campus
can (verb)
canal
candidate
canker
cannibal
canvass

caoutchouc
capital
carbuncle
cardinal
cargo
carnival
carouse
cartridge
cat
cattle

Cavalleria Rusticana
cavalry
cello
Celt
cerebrum
chaise longue
chalice
chamber
Chapman
Charley horse

Chauvinism
cheque
cherry
cherub

Chester
Cholmondeley
choose
Christmas
chukker
cinema

circus
citizen
cleave
clerk
click
clock
cloths
clutter
cobweb
cocaine

cockalorum
Cockney
cocktail
coffee
cold frame
coleslaw
combatant
comedy
commandant
committee

commode
compendium
compensate
complex
composition
concerning
conduit
congregation
coniferous
constable

contrary
contumely
conversion
coöperate
corbie

LIST OF WORDS FOR FURTHER STUDY

corn	Decameron	dunce	fiery
coroner	decapitate	durst	fifth
correspondent	decorous	each	
coterie	deer		finance
could		eat	fire (*verb*)
	delight	eaves	fish
couple	depot	ecstasy	Fitzpatrick
coupon	Derby	editio princeps	flannel
courageous	derring-do	effendi	flapper
courteous	despatch	egoist	flivver
cousin	desuetude	egregious	folio
cow	dial	Eiffel	fortuitous
coworker	dialectics	either	foursome
Cowper	dicker	elevator	
cranberry	dictionary		fowl
crawfish		elite	foxy
	die	Elizabethan	friendlily
crêpe	disk	engine	fro
crick	dismal	enhance	frugal
criticise	distributive	enough	futile
crocodile	dive (*verb*)	ensemble	gadabout
crocus	divvy up	enthusiasm	gadget
cross	docile	envelope	gainsay
crown	doctrine	err	gallant
cryptogram	dogie	esoteric	
cuckold	Don Quixote		gambol
cud		Esperanto	gangster
	dope	etc.	gantlet
culinary	doubt	ether	gaol
culture	dour	eventually	garage
cupboard	drab	Excalibur	garlic
cupidity	dragon	ex cathedra	gazetteer
curmudgeon	draught	fain	genius
cute	drawing-room	fairy	genteel
cynosure	dray	Faneuil	geyser
czar	drench	fast	
dandelion	dress		ghost
dastardly		fathom	gladiolus
	drought	fatuous	glaze
data	drunkard	fear	glooming
dazzle	ductile	feeze	golf
deaf	due	fête	goober
death	dukedom	fetid	goodly
debacle	dumb	fetlock	goose
debunk	dumb-bell	fiasco	gooseberry
			gossamer

LIST OF WORDS FOR FURTHER STUDY

gossip
Gower
graft
grammar
granular
grass
gratis
grewsome
gross
growler

guess (*verb*)
guest
gumption
gusto
guy
halidom
handkerchief
hang
hangar
hanker

Hants
harass
havoc
haywire
healthful
hearth
heir
hell
herculean
heroine

hex
hick
hike
himself
hippodrome
hiss
hoax
hobo
hocus-pocus
homeopathy

hominy
honor
hoodoo
hornbook
Hosea
hospital
hostile
hot
hotchpotch
huckster

hulled
humane
Humanism
humble
humbug
humdinger
humdrum
humour
hunch
hurtle

husband
hussy
hydraulic
hygiene
id est
idiom
idyl
ignoramus
impious
imply

incunabula
indeed
indefatigable
indict
indiscrete
indisputable
inexplicable
infamous
infer
influenza

ingénue
innards

inoculate
inquiry
instead
internecine
intrigue
introvert
invalid
irrefutable

irresponsible
isolation
its
Ivanhoe
Jack
January
jaunty
jazz
Jenny
jeopardy

jitney
jockey
Jones
jot
journal
Juarez
jug
juggle
jugular
juvenile

katydid
keen
kickshaw
kid (*verb*)
killdeer
kimono
kindergarten
kingfish
kitchen
knave

knickers
knight-errant
know
kodak

kowtow
lackadaisical
La Jolla
La Junta
lambrequin
language

lathe
lead (*noun*)
leal
leech
length
leniency
leopard
lexicographer
lief
lieutenant

liner
lining
listless
literature
livery
livid
look
lord
lorry
lotto

louse
lucifer
lucubration
luggage
lukewarm
luncheon
lyric
macadamize
macaroni
Macaulay

machination
machine
mackintosh
Manchukuo
manikin

LIST OF WORDS FOR FURTHER STUDY

March	mortify	omelette	phantom
marionette	mouse	omnium gatherum	phenomenon
marquee	mow	on	
marquis	Mrs.		philology
marshal		one	phlox
	mugwump	only	phonetics
martinet	mulatto	oodles	pianist
masculine	mumps	ooze	pickerel
mass	muscle in	opera	pickpocket
mathematics	musicale	orange	picnic (*verb*)
maudlin	namby-pamby	O'Reilly	picturesque
Maupassant	naphtha	organ	pie
Mauser	necromancer	originality	pingpong
me	ne'er	orthopedic	
meal	negro		pious
mean (*adj.*)		ought	place-name
	neither	outlaw	plaid
meat	nephew	outrage	plat
medicinal	news	ox	plaza
medieval	New York	Pall Mall	pleasure
melancholy	niche	panic	plethoric
memorandum	nickel	pansy	plight
mercantile	nickelodeon	paper	plum
meringue	nickname	paradox	plus
methinks	niggard	paraffin	
mezzotint	night		poesie
microphone		park (*verb*)	poison
	nightingale	parley	poor
mile	nimbus	parlous	poorly (*adj.*)
mill	nincompoop	parson	potwalloper
Milne	nomenclature	party	pox
minster	nonagenarian	passer-by	precedence
misadventure	none	passion	premier
mischievous	nonetheless	patio	preterit
moat	noon	patriot	pretty
mob	normalcy	patron	
monologist	Norwich		primarily
monologue		pea	primates
	nostril	peculiar	Princeton
monster	numskull	pecuniary	prismatic
Monterey	obsolescent	pen	process
moon	octopus	pencil	progress
moron	Oklahoma	people	prolog
mortgage	old	perfect	proven
mortician	Omaha	pesky	prythee
			puissance

LIST OF WORDS FOR FURTHER STUDY

- pumpkin
- pun
- purple
- pusillanimous
- putt
- put up
- quail
- Quaker
- quandary
- questionnaire

- queue
- quintuplet
- quiz
- ransack
- ransom
- rarebit
- rarefy
- raspberry
- raven
- Reading

- realtor
- reckoning
- rectify
- red
- referable
- religion
- remain
- renaissance
- renege
- research

- reveille
- Rhode Island
- rhythm
- riches
- ricksha
- right-o
- rigmarole
- rime
- rival
- road

- roadateria
- roadster

- Roble
- robot
- role
- romance
- rotisserie
- roustabout
- route
- rubbers

- rubric
- run
- sabotage
- Sacramento
- sacrilegious
- sad
- sagaciate
- salary
- salient
- saline

- salve
- sanguine
- satire
- Saturday
- sauce
- savant
- savvy
- schedule
- scientist
- scissors

- score
- Scottish
- scram
- sedan
- seem
- seethe
- sensibility
- sergeant
- shade
- shamrock

- shanty
- shavings
- sheep
- shindig

- shingle
- shock (*noun*)
- shoot
- shorn
- shorts
- show

- Shrovetide
- shuck (*verb*)
- sick
- sieve
- simon-pure
- simp
- singsong
- sirloin
- ski
- skid

- slanguage
- slaughter
- sleazy
- sleek
- sleigh
- slicker
- sloyd
- slump
- snappy
- snazzy

- soggy
- solo
- soot
- sorry
- sought
- sound
- sourdough
- soused
- sovereign
- sox

- spake
- spaniel
- spanner
- speak-easy
- speech
- speechify

- speed cop
- speedometer
- spider
- spiel

- splice
- spoof
- spoonful
- squash
- squire
- stadium
- staff
- stagger
- stampede
- standard (*adj.*)

- Stanford
- starve
- state
- status
- steppe
- stethoscope
- stirrup
- stooge
- stopgap
- stupid

- style
- subsidation
- suds
- sulfur
- sultana
- sultry
- superheterodyne
- supersede
- surly
- surround

- swagger
- swank
- swap
- swoon
- sympathy
- symposium
- syrup
- talent

LIST OF WORDS FOR FURTHER STUDY

Tamalpais	travel	victuals	whiz
tatterdemalion	travelogue	vignette	who
	treacle	villain	whoop
tattoo	tricky	Virginia	
tawdry	tripartite	virile	wight
tax	tryout	virtu	willy-nilly
technical	turbine		window
tell	turtle	viscount	wiseacre
temblor	twain	visor	wizard
tempo		vitascope	wombat
term	tycoon	vixen	wont
theatre	tyke	viz.	Worcester
they	typhoid	vocation	work
	tyre	vulcanize	workaday
thrive	unctuous	vulgar	
through	unspeakable	Vulgate	
Thursday	urbane	wain	worry
thusly	used to		wot
tidy	utilities		Wrens
tintinnabulation	vacuum	waitress	wringer
tip		walkathon	wrong
toad		wall	Yankee
tobacco	vagabond	walnut	yard
today	vagary	wampum	yellow
	vamp (*verb*)	warden	Yiddish
toffee	van	wary	yodel
tomato	vandal	washout	
toss	vase	wassail	Yosemite
totem	vaudeville	Watkins	you
touchy	vaunt		zany
tough	veal	wealthiest	zed
town	versatile	Webster	zero
Trafalgar		wedding	Zimmermann
tram	vertebra	welt	zone
tranquillity	very	wharf	zoology
	via	wheat	zymotic
trash	vicious	whereabouts	Zyzzogeton

CONCISE INDEX TO QUESTIONS OF GOOD USAGE

[Numbers refer to pages. For discussions of attitudes and policies in the use of English see pages 3, 16, 17, 20, 27, 183, 508, 512, 514, 543, 584, 602.]

Abbreviations, 254
Above as adjective, 325
Accentuation, variable, 86, 157, 223, 225
Active-passive verbs, 296
Ad for *advertisement*, 355
Adjectives, after *feel, smell*, etc., 476
  as adverbs, 306, 321, 324, 483
  comparison of, 449
  compounded, with hyphen, 253, 349
  ending in *-ly*, 490
Adverbial genitive, 305, 516
Adverbs, as adjectives, 306, 321, 325
  before prepositions, 505
  colloquial intensives, 306, 321
  comparison of, 449
  position of, 504
Agreement, of discordant subjects joined by *or*, 497
  of pronoun and antecedent, 498
  of singular verb with expletive *it*, 496
  of subject and verb, 495
  of tenses, 499
  of verb with collective nouns, 443, 495
  with expletive *there*, 496
  with indefinite subjects, 497
Ain't, 256
All of, 491
All the farther, 513
Almost or *most*, 327
Ambiguity of reference, 499
Ambiguous expressions, 572–577
Americanisms. See Subject Index *s.v. American speech*
An before *h*, 198
And as an illative, 312
Antecedent, agreement of pronoun with, 498
  reference to indefinite, 291, 473
Any for *any other*, 513

Anyway as an illative, 321
Appositives after introducing words, 482
Archaic words. See Subject Index *s.v. Archaisms*
Are after *none*, 497
Aren't I, 256
As or *so* in negative comparisons, 541
As for *that* or *who*, 289
As well or *better than*, 514
Athletics is or *are*, 495
Auxiliaries, discordant use of, 513
Awful, 29, 428, 552
Awfully, 306, 560
Awkward constructions, 490

Back of as preposition, 309, 511
Be and *were*, subjunctive, 521, 522
Between or *among*, 539
Blowed, 457
Briticisms. See Subject Index *s.v. British English*
Bursted, 462
Bus, 28
But, after negatives, 513, 534
  as an illative, 312
  as preposition, 539
  as relative pronoun, 289
By, for *with* or *at*, 539

Can or *may*, 524
Capitalization, 256
Case, after *but*, 539
  after infinitive *be*, 479
  after *is*, 476, 516
  after *than*, 327
  of subject of gerund, 319, 514, 530, 531
  of subject of infinitive, 479
Choice of words. See *Diction*
Clause, restrictive, 493
Clipped words, 354

658 CONCISE INDEX TO QUESTIONS OF GOOD USAGE

Collective nouns, agreement with, 443, 495
Colloquialisms. See Subject Index s.v. *Colloquial speech*
Colon, use of, 472, 483
Come quick, 306
Comma, use of, 472, 482, 494
Committee is or *are*, 495
Compare to or *with*, 536
Comparison of adjectives, 449
Comparison of adverbs, 449
Compound for simple pronoun, 474, 477
Compounds, pluralization of, 444
Considerable as indefinite adjective, 294
Consonant, doubling of final, 238, 248
Contractions of words, 26, 256
Contrasting sentences, 472
Could not help but, 513
Couldn't scarcely, 534
Counter words. See Subject Index s.v. *Counter words*
Cupfuls, 337, 444
Cups for *cupfuls*, 354
Cute, 552, 560

Dangling participle, 487
Dash, use of, 482, 483
Data, number of, 441, 442
Dear as adverb, 306
Demonstratives with *kind*, *sort*, 499
Detached conjunctions, 312
Diction, questions of. See Subject Index s.v. *Diction*
Different(ly) than, 513
Different to or *from*, 538
Division of words, 253-254
Don't for *doesn't*, 498
Don't, shan't, mustn't, 26, 256
Don't doubt but, 534
Double negatives, 534
Doubling of final consonants, 238, 248
Dove or *dived*, 455
Drive slow, 306
Drug for *dragged*, 458
Due to as a preposition, 309, 325

-e final, dropping or retention of, 243-245
Each, every, with singular verb, 497, 498
Ei or *ie*, 233
Either . . . or, with verb, 497
Ellipsis, use of, 508
Elliptical phrases, 511
Else, possessive, 449

Emphasis by word order, 500-501
Enthuse, 355
-er or *-or*, 236
Essential clause. See *Restrictive clause*
Et as past of *eat*, 432
Euphemisms, 431, 548
Evenings for *in the evening*, 516
Everyone with plurals, 497, 498
Exaggerated speech, 306, 559, 566
Except as conjunction, 322, 542
Expletives, *it, there*, with verbs, 496
-ey or *-y*, final, 251, 599

-f, -fe, plural of nouns in, 203, 218, 240
Final consonant, doubling of, 238, 248
Final *-e*, dropped or retained, 243-245
Final *-o* in noun plurals, 245
Final *-y* changed to *i*, 235, 251
Fine as adverb, 306
Folks, 270
For you and I, 518
Friendlily, 490
From whence, 535, 539
-ful, plural of nouns in, 444

Gender after indefinite pronoun, 498
Genitive, double, 491
Gent for *gentleman*, 355
Gerund, use of, after verbs, 530
  with genitival subject, 319, 514, 531
  with genitival object, 533
Go as noun, 318
Go places, 324
Good as adverb, 306
Got or *gotten*, 458
Got to for *must*, 526
Government is or *are*, 495
Grammatical traps, 496, 497, 499, 513, 542
Growed, 16, 457

Had better or *rather*, 578
Had (or *hadn't*) *ought*, 525
Hadn't only, 534
Hanged or *hung*, 359
Have got to, 526
Have to for *must*, 526
He don't, 498
Headline English, 42-44, 612
Healthy for *healthful*, 574
Help but, 513, 534
His or *her* after indefinites, 498
Hisn, hern, theirn, etc., 447, **517**
Hisself, theirselves, 289, 448
Home or *at home*, 511
Hybrid constructions, 513-514
Hyphenation at end of lines, 253
Hyphenation in compounds, 252, **349**

CONCISE INDEX TO QUESTIONS OF GOOD USAGE 659

Identical with, 537
Idioms. See Subject Index *s.v. Idiomatic phrases*
Ie or *ei*, 233
-ie or *-y*. See *-y* or *-ie*
If with object clause, 493
I'll, you'll, he'll, etc., 256, 522
Illatives, position of, 505
Illogical comparisons, 513
Illy, 305
In back of, 309
In regards to, 4
Indefinite subject, 473
Indicative mood for subjunctive, 521–522, 527
Infinitive, split, 506
Intensive pronouns, 474
Introductory adverbs, 311, 505
Irrational constructions, 512
-ise or *-ize*, 205
It as grammatical subject, 289, 474, 496, 516
It's me, 476, 516
Its or *It's*, 447 (footnote)
I've, we're, you're, etc., 26, 256

John, he, 486
Journalistic writing, 2

Kind, with *this* or *these*, 499
Kind of as adverb, 306
Knowed, 457

Learn for *teach*, 575
Leave for *let*, 100
Let's or *let us*, 528
Letters, plural of, 445
Like as conjunction, 322, 542
Likely as adverb, 307
Linking verbs followed by adjectives, 476
-ly incorrectly affixed, 305

Me after *is*, 476, 516
Most for *almost*, 327
Mr. and *Mrs.* not spelled out, 258
Muchly, 305
Myself for *I* or *me*, 474, 477

Namely, use of, 307, 482
Negatives, double, 534
Neither with plural verb, 497
Nice. See Word Index
Noble as adverb, 306
None with plural verb, 497
Nonrestrictive clauses, 493
Noun as conjunction, 311

Number, of collective nouns, 443–444, 495
of *kind, sort*, 499
of pronoun after indefinites, 498
Numerals, hyphen in compound, 252

-o, plural of nouns ending in, 245
Obsolete words, 38, 569
Off for *from*, 539
Off of, 539
Omission of verb, 510
On for *at*, 100
On the account of, 325
One, pluralization of, 448
One as subject, 473, 498
One . . . he, his, etc., 498 (footnote)
Oneself as reflexive, 291
Only, position of, 505
Or-constructions, verb with, 497
-or or *-our*, 236, 599
Order of words. See Subject Index *s.v. Word order*
Ought, 525
Overly, 305
Overworked words and phrases, 429

Parenthetical expressions, 487
Participles, dangling, 487
Past tense, variant forms, 454–462
Phone for *telephone*, 355
Phrasal substitutes for adjectives and adverbs, 490
Phrases, order of, 505
Pleonasm, 486
Plurals, double plurals of nouns, 442
like singulars, 270, 439
of compound nouns, 444
of foreign nouns, 440
of names, 444
of nouns in *-f, -fe*, 203, 240
of nouns in *-o*, 245
of nouns in *-y*, 235, 245, 251
of titles, 444
without singulars, 443
Possessive case with gerunds, 319, 514, 531
Postponed prepositions, 507, 538
Precede and *proceed*, 260, 599
Preposition at end of sentence, 507, 538
Prepositions, choice of, 536–537
Pronoun, agreement with antecedent, 498
Pronoun, case after *than, as*, 327
Proven, 458
Providing as conjunction, 310

Rather after *had*, 578
Read where, 512
Real good, 306
Redundancy, of adjectives, 416
  of prepositions, 539
  of subject, 486
Reference of pronouns, 499
Reflexive for simple pronouns, 474, 477
Regards to, 4, 325
Relative pronouns, agreement with antecedent, 498
  omitted, 511
  who or *whom*, 507, 517
  whose as neuter, 499
Restrictive clauses, 493
Rhetorical question, 470
Right as adverb, 306
Rode and *ridden*, 455

Same, uses of, 290
Says for *say*, 498
Semicolon, use of, 499
Sequence of tenses, 499
Shall and *will*, 522
Shouldn't ought, 525
Simple pronoun as reflexive, 517
Simply, expressing degree, 321
Sing, past tense, 456
Singularless nouns, 443
Slang. See Subject Index *s.v. Slang*
Slow or *slowly*, 306
So . . . as or *as . . . as*, 541
Someone else's, 449
Sort, with *these*, 499
Sort of, adverbial, 306
Spelling. See *Doubling*; *Final*; *Plurals*
  -er or *-or*, 236
  ie or *ei*, 233
  -ie changed to *-y* before *ing*, 244
  f or *ph*, 239, 597
  -or or *-our*, 236, 599
  -re or *-er*, 236, 599
  -t or *-ed* in past tense, 239, 593, 598
  x or *ct*, *cks*, *ks*, 241
  -y changed to *i* before suffixes, 235, 245, 251
  -y retained before suffixes, 235, 245, 251
Split infinitive, 506
Spoonfuls or *spoons full*, 337, 444
Style. See Subject Index *s.v. Stylistic matters*
Subjunctive, use of, 521, 522, 525, 526, 527, 529
Superlative, absolute, 520
Superlative degree, use of, 513

Sure as adverb, 307, 432
Swang or *swung*, 456
Syllabication, 87, 252–254
Synonyms. See Subject Index *s.v. Synonyms*

Tenses, sequence of, 499
Terribly, 306
Than as conjunction, 327
Than whom, 327
That and *which*, omitted, 511
That or *which*, 493
That there, 326
Their after *everyone*, 498
They, you, as indefinite subject, 291
Through for *throughout*, 539
Thusly, 305
Titles, use of, 283–285
Too modifying participles, 534
Traveler or *traveller*, 239
Trite expressions, 429, 552, 559
Try and for *try to*, 513

Up combined with verbs, 302
Up to, idiomatic, 309

Verb, agreement with subject, 495–498
  inflectional forms, 451–463
  simple and phrasal, 520–529
  used as noun, 318, 612
Verb-adverb combinations, 302
Very, modifying participles, 534

Want to, obligation or command, 525
Was for *were*, 498
Ways or *way*, 513
Well, adjective or adverb, 321
Were as subjunctive, 522
Whence with *from*, 535
Where . . . at, 508, 539
Whether or *if*, 493
Whether without *or*, 513
Who or *whom*, 507, 517
Whoever or *whomever*, 518
Whose as neuter, 499
With regards to, 325
Without for *unless*, 322, 542
Word order. See Subject Index *s.v. Word order*

-y or *-ey*, final, 251, 599
-y or *-ie*, 235, 245, 251
You for indefinite *one*, 473
You all, 289
You was, 498
Your or *you're*, 447 (footnote)

WORD INDEX

[Numbers refer to pages.]

a, 198, 293, 406, 427, 504
a historical work, 199
a little ways, 513
a person, 498
Aaron, 232
A. B. (Bachelor of Arts), 255, 284
abacot, 333
abash, 372
abate, 414
abated, 243
abatement, 414
abattoir, 431
abbess, 437
abbreviate, 203, 404
abbreviation, 254
A B C's, 548
abear, 344
abed, 351
Abercrombie, 125
Aberdeen, 275, 375
Aberford, 275
abet, 399, 405
abhorrence of, 537
abide, 186, 454, 570
abide by, 482
abject, 224, 556
ablaze, 477, 503
able, 115, 200, 228, 449, 594
ablutions, 430
aboard, 305, 308, 351, 477, 504, 580
abolish, 341
abound in, with, 536
about, 85, 187, 227, 298, 305, 306, 307, 308, 321, 426, 427, 538
above, 75, 76, 82, 308, 325
abrasion, 207
abridge, 404, 414
abridgment, 244, 414
abroad, 179, 325, 342, 351, 477, 491, 504

abrupt, 342
abscess, 345
abscission, 207
absence, 223
absent, 86, 223
absentee, 248, 338
absinthe (absinth), 250
absolve, 242, 250
absorb, 218
Absorbine, 282
absorption, 218
abstract, 224, 342, 577
abundance, 372, 374, 594
abuse, 190, 206, 408
abyss, 378
acacia, 400
accede, 202, 240, 345
accede to, 536
accelerate, 202
accentuate, 369
accept, 4, 342
acceptance, 338
acceptancy, 338
access, 345
accessary, 345
accessibility, 345
accessible, 345
accession, 345, 414
accessory, 340, 345
accident, 338
acclamation, 339
accommodate to, with, 536
accompaniment, 251
accomplish, 202
accord in, with, 536
according to, 309
accordingly, 307, 311, 535
account, 115, 426
account for, 482
accouter (accoutre), 182, 594
accretion, 414
accrual, 414, 416

accrue, 182, 231, 414
accrued, 243
accruement, 416
accumulate, 414
accumulation, 414
accuracy, 339
accurate, 339
accustomed, 571
ace, 18, 173
ache, 173, 202
achievement, 340
acid, 115, 206, 341, 400
acknowledge, 250, 416
acknowledgment, 244
acme, 400
aconite, 400
acorn, 37, 399
acoustic, 183, 197
acoustics, 339, 379, 443
acquiesce, 203, 303, 416
acquiesce in, 536
acquire, 203, 240
acquit, 83, 203, 214
acre, 37, 174, 202, 242, 268, 399, 440, 549
acreage, 243, 338
acrid, 400
acrobat, 400
Acropolis, 400
across, 298, 305, 308
acrost, 54, 220
act, 115, 201, 203, 416, 426
acted, 118, 434
action, 202, 215, 269, 339, 371
active, 591, 598
actor, 202
actorine, 437
actress, 339, 437
actual, 341
actuate, 371
acuminate, 189
acute, 189, 190, 235, 360, 400, 405, 407

661

WORD INDEX

A. D. (Anno Domini), 255
ad, 355
adagio, 201
Adam, 174, 235
adamant, 404
Adams, 278
adaptation, 115
add, 83, 200, 249, 426, 597
add to, 414
add up, 302
added, 417
addendum, 441
adder, 200, 236, 361
adder's-tongue, 348
addicted to, 537
addition, 208
addle, 242
address, 223
adds, 218
adds up, 296
adduce, 401
adept, 224
adept in, 537
adequate, 203, 371
adieu, 316
adipose, 341
adjective, 100, 120, 250, 266
adjoin, 401
adjourn, 246
adjutrix, 437
administrator, 438
administratrix, 437, 438
admiral, 383
admiration, 224
admire, 224
admission, 221, 416
Admission Day, 282
admit, 221
admit into, of, to, 482, 536
admittance, 242, 416
admonition, 339
ado, 399, 405
adobe, 381
a-doing, 54
adoption, 339
adown, 53
adrift, 305, 351, 504
adult, 224
advance, 6, 168, 414
advancement, 244
advantage, 168
advantageous, 201
adventure, 340, 362, 405

adverb, 255, 266
advertise, 205, 223, 596
advertisement, 22, 223, 225, 255
advice, 206, 442
advices, 442
advise, 205, 206, 401, 596
advocate, 203, 342, 362
adz (adze), 170, 201, 205, 215, 594
ægis, 175, 231, 233
aërial, 566
Aëro-Eight, 282
aëroplane, 39
æsthetic (esthetic), 233, 234, 596
afear, 364
afeard, 53
affair, 552
affectation, 418
affection, 418
affidavit, 369
affix, 342
afire, 351, 477
afloat, 325
afoot, 351
afore, 53
afraid, 363, 409, 427, 477, 560
African, 279, 339
African golf, 363
aft, 4, 203, 216, 305
after, 52, 201, 308, 310, 311, 322, 325, 542
afterglow, 347
aftermost, 450
afternoon, 4, 426
afterward, 305
again, 196, 305
against, 54, 196, 220
age, 201, 426, 574
aged, 201, 243, 319, 402, 416
agency, 338
agendum, 441
aggrandize, 414
aggrandizement, 414
aggravate, 414
aggravation, 414
aggregate, 342
aghast, 168, 477, 598
agile, 187, 201
agleam, 477
aglow, 292, 351, 477
agnostic, 400
agnosticism, 400

a-going, 580
agree, 531
agree in, on, to, with, 536
agreed, 417
agriculture, 202, 347, 399
ague, 173, 400
aguish, 407
ah, 209, 233, 246, 312, 334
Ah (I), 197
Ahab, 209
ahoy, 188
aid and abet, 415
aides-de-camp, 444
aigrette, 250, 339
ails, 205, 296
aim, 162
aim at, 482
ain't, 16, 256, 432, 534
ain't I, 498
air, 54, 170, 171, 409, 426, 442
air pocket, 58
airplane, 38
airs, 442
airship, 264
aisle, 186, 234, 247, 258
Aix-les-Bains, 35
ajar, 351
akimbo, 351
akin, 477, 491
Aksarben, 282
alarm, 192, 380
alarm clock, 387
alas, 38, 313, 334, 372
albacore, 383
albatross, 249, 367, 381, 383
albeit, 431
Albuquerque, 277
Alcatraz, 249
alchemy, 383
alcohol, 383
alchoholiday, 351
alcove, 383
alderman, 564
ale, 81
Alemite, 282, 340
alert, 380
alfalfa, 383
Alfred, 271
Alfred the Great, 286, 503
algebra, 383
alibi, 170, 248, 369

WORD INDEX

aliens, 318
alight, 186, 292, 460
alike, 305, 503
alimony, 170, 340
alive, 292, 325, 351, 477, 491, 580
alkali, 248, 383
all, 210, 291, 306, 427
all in, 292, 578
all in all, 578
all right, 307
All Saints' Day, 282
all the farther, 513
all up, 292, 578
all wet, 32
all-American, 347
allege, 201
alleged, 244
Alleghany, 277
allegory, 170
alleluia, 382
Allentown, 276
alley, 170
alligator, 170, 381
allotted, 238
allow, 416, 426
alloy, 223
all-powerful, 349
allude, 342, 556
alluvial, 183
ally, 223
Alma, 272
alma mater, 371, 400
almanac, 210
Almighty, 318
almond, 168, 210, 220
almost, 210, 239, 306, 327
alms, 168, 378, 410, 443
aloe, 181, 195, 234
aloetic, 195
aloft, 179, 305, 351, 376, 491, 504
alone, 254, 350, 503
along, 504
alongside, 305
aloof, 182
alpaca, 381, 384
Alps, 210
already, 239
also, 406
alter, 201
alteration, 430
alternate, 223
Althorpe, 276
although (altho), 310, 534, 540, 595, 599

although ... nevertheless, 541
although ... still, 541
although ... yet, 541
altogether, 306
alum, 170
aluminium, 158
alumna, 371, 437, 440
alumnæ, 176, 371, 440, 596
alumni, 371, 440
alumnus, 371, 437, 440
always, 239, 305, 347
A.M. (ante meridiem), 255
am, 427, 463
amanuensis, 441
amateur, 102
amazon, 358, 378, 554
ambassador, 375
amber, 200
ambition, 342, 555
ameliorate, 213
amen, 313, 316, 382
amenable, 176
amend, 405
amended, 417
amends, 443
American, 279, 319, 576
Amerind, 278
amiable, 404, 416, 422
amicable, 404, 416, 422
amid, 308
amidst, 54
amiss, 477
ammonia, 384
amœba, 233
among, 539
amorous, 174
amortize, 400
ampere, 211, 358
amphitheater, 343
ample, 211, 219
amplification, 414
amplifier, 566
amplify, 219, 414
amuck, 385
amuse, 205
amused at, 482
an, 198, 199, 249, 293, 405, 427
an' (and), 52, 54
an apple, 198
an expert, 198
an historical work, 198
an hour, 361
anæmic, 80

anagram, 343
analogue, 221
analogy, 221
analogy to, with, 537
analyse (analyze), 22, 205
analysis, 441
anarchy, 343
anathema, 399
anatomy, 235
ancestor, 345
ancestral, 345
ancestress, 345
ancestry, 345
anchor, 202, 212, 369
anchovy, 201, 381
ancient, 208
ancients, 318
and, 85, 211, 216, 228, 310, 312, 426, 427
Anderson, 274
anear, 53
anecdotage, 351
anecdote, 170
anent, 41, 308, 429, 431
anesthetic, 369
angel, 211, 378
anger, 212, 216, 217, 219, 376, 555
angina, 176
angle, 115, 202, 212, 242
Anglo-Saxon, 279, 573
angrily, 219
angry, 202
anguish, 79, 202, 212, 214, 216
animal, 235, 339, 426, 436
animule, 35, 351
animus, 371
ankle, 212, 216, 242
anklet, 339
Ann, 249
Anna, 274
annals, 443
Annamarie, 272
Anne, 211
anneal, 175
annex, 342
Annie, 251, 337
announce, 225
annual, 417
annular, 213
annunciation, 225
anoint, 188, 372
anon, 41, 305

another, 291, 293, 497, 498
another one, 497
answer, 168, 214, 247, 426, 599
answer the last summons, 548
ant, 115
antarctic, 343
ante up, 162
antebellum, 342
antecede, 345
antecedent, 345
antecessor, 345
antelope, 439
anterior, 450
anthracite, 340
anthropoid, 189
anthropology, 346
anticipation, 430
anticlimax, 414
antics, 404
antidote, 343
antipodes, 400, 443
antiques, 404
antithesis, 378, 441
antlered, 243
antonym, 245
anvil, 211, 216
anxiety, 205, 216
anxious, 212, 216, 237, 530
any, 172, 178, 211, 291, 294, 427, 513
anybody, 291, 448, 498
anyhow, 305, 307, 311
anyone, 291, 448, 498
anything, 291, 427
anyway, 311, 321
Anzac, 352
apace, 351
apart from, 309
ape, 115, 173
apern (apron), 220
apex, 441
apices, 441
apostle, 219, 247
apostolic, 219
apostrophe, 80, 176, 235, 248, 261, 343
apothecary, 399
apothegm, 246
Appalachians, 277
appall, 556
apparatus, 174, 440
appeal, 58, 405
appear, 476

appears, 296
appendices, 441
appendicitis, 176, 567
appendix, 441
applaud, 342
apple tree, 348
apple-polishing, 28
applesauce, 417, 556
apposite, 250
apprehend, 556
apprehensive for, of, 537
apricot, 171, 367, 382
April, 281
apron, 200, 361
apropos, 247, 373, 374
apt, 201, 416, 530
aptitude, 404
aquarium, 268, 339
Aquitania, 280
ar (our), 197
arabesque, 383
Arabian, 213
Arapahoe, 250
arbithraather, 52
arbitrament, 430
arbor, 200, 340
arborescent, 341
arbutus, 225
arc, 404
arcade, 380
arch, 404
archaic, 38, 198, 430
archangel, 253
archery, 338
archvillain, 343
Arco, 282, 352
are, 210, 427, 597
aren't I, 256, 498
aresouns, 333
Argentine, 176
argosy, 384
argue, 250
argument, 244, 340
aria, 174, 381
arid, 173
Arion, 210
arise, 342, 454
arithmetic, 255
ark, 369
arm, 210, 409
armada, 174, 381, 404
armadillo, 381
armful, 337
armfuls, 444
armistice, 339
arms, 410, 443

army, 167, 267, 270, 339, 404
aroint, 188, 333
around, 298, 305, 308, 504
arrange, 570
arrangement, 241
arrogant, 342
arthritis, 567
artichoke, 383, 573
article, 338
artillery, 443
artisan, 205, 339, 418
artist (artiste), 19, 340, 418
A.S. (Anglo-Saxon), 255
a's (he is), 52
as, 37, 83, 205, 249, 289, 290, 305, 307, 310, 311, 323, 350, 406, 427, 482, 534
as . . . as, 310, 541
as cross as two sticks, 580
as far as, 309, 310, 311, 322, 540, 542
as few as, 310
as for, 309
as if, 310, 494, 540
as little as, 310
as long as, 310
as much as, 310, 540
as regards, 4, 309
as soon as, 310, 487
as though, 310
as well as, 310, 491
as well or better than, 514
asafetida (asafœtida), 15, 172, 234, 387
ascend, 414
ascension, 208, 237
ascent, 414
ascertain, 170
aseptic, 343
ash, 208
ashamed, 503, 530
ashen, 208, 340
ashes, 443
ashore, 351
Asia, 173, 207
Asiatic, 279, 319
ask, 168, 206, 216, 221, 531
asked, 417, 598
askew, 325, 4⁻⁻
asleep, 503
asparagus, 4, 362

WORD INDEX

aspirin, 207
ass, 382
assassin, 358
assemble, 416
assented, 417
asserted, 417
assess, 400
assiduous, 400
assist, 342
assistant, 268
assize, 186, 400
assuage, 207, 214, 237, 258
assume, 182
assured, 417
assuredly, 307
aster, 201, 207
asterisk, 339, 379
astern, 351
asteroid, 379
asthma, 205, 237, 247, 259
astonish, 560
astray, 305, 325, 405, 504
astride, 306
at, 83, 87, 121, 170, 201, 298, 308, 427, 429
at any rate, 311, 578
at daggerlogs, 36
at daggers drawn, 36
at length, 13
at loggerheads, 36, 572
at sixes and sevens, 13
at the bottom of, 309
at the same time, 311
Atchison, 201
Athenian, 279, 294
Athens, 277
athirst, 503
athletics, 192, 443, 495
atlas, 249, 257, 358, 378
atoll, 385
atom, 174
atrocious, 201, 560
attaboy, 28
attach, 241
attack, 375
attainder, 268
attempt, 612
attend, 401
attendance, 250
attendant, 161
attention, 342
attenuate, 414
attic, 249
attitude, 340, 380, 404
attitude toward, 537

Attlebury, 274
attorney-general, 503
attorneys-general, 444
attribute complement, 476
au revoir, 19, 316, 373
auctioneer, 338
audience, 4, 557
auditorium, 340
auf Wiedersehen, 316
auger, 179
aught, 179
augment, 414
augmentation, 414
August, 281
Augusta, 437
Augustus, 272, 437
auk, 377
Auld Reekie, 286
aunt, 168, 231, 438, (cap.) 285
auntie, 268, 337
aunts, 211
aural, 179
auriferous, 347
Australian, 279
Autel, 352
authentic, 417
author, 204
authoress, 437, 438
authorities, 557
authorize, 205
auto, 355
autobus, 352
autocrat, 346
automaton, 441
automobile, 373
autumn, 179, 192, 211, 219, 235, 247, 269, (cap.) 558
autumnal, 211, 219
avarice, 250
avast, 350, 379
aventure, 362
average, 342
averse from, to, 537
aversion, 548
aviary, 339
aviation, 338
aviator, 174, 338, 340
aviatrix, 340, 437
avid, 232
avigator, 352
avocat, 362
avocation, 203
avoid, 188, 531
aw, 312

awake, 115
aware, 477
away, 83, 477
awe, 242, 251
awful, 29, 244, 249, 292, 340, 428, 552
awfully, 306, 321, 534, 560
awfully slow, 534
awkward, 340, 387
awl, 179
awn, 400
awry, 351, 477
ax, 37, 202, 221, 240, 251, 258, 362
axe, 251, 259
axis, 441
Axtell, 277
aye, 121, 173, 186, 231, 251, 307
azure, 83, 207, 237, 383

baa, 168, 248
baa-baa, 335
babble, 341
babbling, 322
babe, 173
babel, 358
baby, 46, 229, 334, 337
bacchanalian, 358
bachelor, 201, 241, 438, 550
Bachelor of Arts, 284
back, 170, 202, 248, 298, 305, 326, 511
back formation, 355
back of, 309
back out, 300
back-fire, 298
backgammon, 347
back-track, 162
backward, 214, 305, 340
backwards, 342
bacon, 174, 372
bad, 115, 170, 234, 257, 449, 450
bad and good, 14
badder, 47
baddest, 47
bade, 462, 597, 600
badge, 170
badger, 201, 240
Badger State, 286
badly, 306
badly soused, 33
baffie, 203
bag, 162, 170, 202, 426

WORD INDEX

bag and baggage, 228, 415
baggage, 160, 338
baggage-smasher, 33
bah, 209, 233, 312
bailiff, 249, 372
bairn, 344
bait, 377, 399, 406, 459
baked, 598, 600
baker, 268
balcony, 161, 170, 380
bald, 178, 193
baleful, 244
balk, 178, 202
ball, 178, 426
balloon, 339
ballot, 380
bally, 162
balm, 168, 404
balsam, 378, 404
baluster, 367, 406
bamboo, 385, 396
bamboozle, 30
Bamfield, 211
banana, 381, 384, 396
band, 170, 405, 409
bandanna, 383, 397
bandeau, 441
bandeaux, 441
bandit, 441
banditti, 441
bandy about, 40
bane (been), 56
Banff, 211
bang, 334
bang-up, 32, 301, 348
banish, 211
banister, 406
banjo, 160, 404
banjos, 245
bank, 376, 403
bankruptcy, 247
banned, 243, 409
banner, 372
bannock, 375
banns, 211, 249
banquet, 212, 216, 245
banshee, 53, 375
bantam, 211, 385
banter, 87
banyan, 213, 381
banzai, 385
Baptist, 280
bar, 220, 548
bar (bear), 169, 192
bar sinister, 572

barb, 403
barbarous, 378
barbecue, 381, 384
Bar-B-Q, 255
barber, 372
barberia, 339
bard, 375
bare, 171, 409, 412, 456
barely, 306
bareness, 253
bark, 167, 409, 594
bark up, 547
barks, 210
barm, 344
barn, 249, 350, 553
baron, 372
baroness, 437
Barr, 249
barren, 238, 571
barrier, 213
barring, 308
barrow, 344, 399
Barry, 173, 410
barter, 167, 300
base, 404
bases, 441
basic, 173
basilisk, 339
basin, 174
basis, 378, 404, 441
bask, 376, 377
basket, 426
basque, 374
bas-relief, 374
bass, 206, 409
basses, 243
basswood, 160
bastile, 560
bat, 170
batch, 215
bate, 571
bath, 168, 173, 204, 218, 232
bathe, 173, 204, 216, 218, 232, 242, 244
Bathite, 282
baths, 204, 218
Baton Rouge, 276
batten, 201, 236
batter and bemaul, 416
battered-up, 301
battery, 170, 268, 319
battle, 372
battle royal, 503
battle-axes, 444
batty, 556
bauer, 188

bawd, 405
bawl, 299, 300
bawl out, 300
bawlout, 28
Baxter, 337, 572
Bay State, 286
bayou, 161, 186, 234
bays, 245
bazaar, 383
B.B.C. (British Broadcasting Corporation), 255
B.C. (Before Christ), 255
be, 19, 52, 67, 295, 296, 321, 326, 409, 426, 427, 464, 476, 480, 497, 510, 521, 523
be (by), 52
beach, 175, 201, 250
Beach-Thompson, 349
bead, 200, 557
beadle, 200, 337
beaker, 404
beam, 175
beamed, 238
bean, 175
beanery, 338
bear, 90, 171, 210, 231, 344, 399, 409, 412, 436, 456
bearable, 344
bearably, 344
bearance, 344
beard, 175, 403
bearer, 344
bearing, 344
bearings, 344
beast, 172, 175, 232
beastly, 566
beat, 175, 201, 249, 426, 457
beat all hollow, 578
beat it, 162, 313
beaten, 458
beatific, 341
beau, 180, 231, 438, 441, 550
Beau Brummel, 287
Beaulieu, 276
beautiful, 85, 292, 387
beautify, 341
beauty, 189, 234, 557
beaux, 205, 247, 259, 441
beaux arts, 374
Beaver Crossing, 276
because, 306, 310, 312, 472, 487, 494, 534, 540

WORD INDEX

because of, 309
bêche-de-mer, 65
Becket, 202
become, 295, 476
bed, 84, 172
bedding, 557
bedimmed, 238
bedlam, 358, 382, 554
bee, 175, 231, 409, 438
bee line, 162
beef, 102, 372, 418, 442, 550
beefsteak, 111
beeg (big), 195
been, 176, 177, 211, 234
been eat'm, 66
beet, 57, 175, 369
beetle, 201, 399
beet-puller, 58
beeves, 442
before, 308, 310, 311, 322, 494, 534, 542
before long, 535
beg, 202
beg the question, 578
beggar, 268, 337, 356
begin, 455
begonia, 358
behavior, 213
behemoth, 209
behind, 209, 308, 309
behold, 313, 457
behooves, 296
belfry, 363, 379, 560
Belgian, 279
believe, 175, 262, 598
believing, 319, 465
belittle, 297, 342, 414
bell, 172, 248, 363
belle, 210, 242, 251, 262, 438, 557
belles, 318
belles lettres, 374
bellows, 210, 443
bells, 210
belong, 67
belongings, 443
beloved, 243
below, 305, 308, 504
Ben Lomond, 275, 279
Ben Nevis, 275
bench, 201, 211, 216, 241, 250, 376, 403
bend, 172, 406, 461, 592
beneath, 175, 450
Benedictines, 280, 294
benefactor, 343

benefactress, 437
beneficent, 292
beneficiary, 58
benign, 202
bent, 115, 211
benzine, 339
bequeath, 204
Berberis darwini, 370
bereave, 203, 460, 550
bereft, 203
Berkeley, 167
Berlin, 277
Bermuda (Bermudez), 356
berries, 246
berry, 173, 410
berserker, 377
berth, 184, 204, 344
Bertha, 271
Berwick, 275
beseech, 175, 460
beside, 253, 308
besides, 311
besiege, 241, 400
Bess, 287
best, 175, 207, 232, 264
bestial, 172
bet, 171, 172, 234, 257, 399, 405, 462, 592
bête noire, 373
Beth, 287
Bethlehem, 172
Betsy, 287
better, 264, 306, 321, 409, 414, 427
betterment, 414
Betty, 285, 287
between, 201, 214, 308, 539
betwixt, 430
Beulah, 277
bevel, 172
bevy, 172, 270
bewilder, 177, 210
beyond, 308
be-youtiful, 35
bias, 198
bias(s)ed, 239
Bible, 378
bibliography, 573, 574
bicycle, 379
bid, 177, 232, 234, 257, 364, 409, 456, 459, 462, 569
bid for, 297
bidden, 458
bidding, 238

bide, 84, 232, 242, 454, biding, 200 [600
bids, 201, 205
bier, 344, 399, 571
bifteck (beefsteak), 111
big, 195, 202
Big Ben Clocks, 282
bigamist, 340, 379
bight, 399
bijou, 207
bike, 355
bile (boil), 52, 186, 196
bilge, 210
bilk, 202
Bill, 287
billet-doux, 373, 374
billiards, 443
Billie, 287
Billings, 273, 337
billion, 440
billy goat, 437
bin, 125, 211, 375
bind, 193, 364, 406, 455, 456
bindery, 338
Bingen, 212
Bingham, 209
biography, 190, 222
biology, 186, 198
biped, 400
biplane, 343
birch, 201, 250
bird, 73, 184, 185, 189
birth, 184, 338, 344, 399
biscuits, 161
biscuit-shooter, 30
bishop, 208, 268, 369, 378, (cap.) 285
bison, 186, 439
bit, 57, 87, 177, 411
bite, 200, 236, 377, 399, 406, 454
bits, 201
bitter, 115, 177, 399
bitters, 557
bivouac, 249
black, 236, 427, 451, (cap.) 287
Black and Tans, 319
Black Prince, 287
blackball, 298, 556
blackbird, 348
blackbouler (blackball), 111
blackguard, 88, 202, 218, 246, 350
blacks, 318

blacksmith, 347
blah, 417
blame, 174, 404
blanked, 45
blare, 353
blarney, 53
blaspheme, 404
blast, 365
bleed, 460
blench, 406
blend, 406, 461
bless, 171, 172, 426, 461
bless us, 313
blessed (blest), 192, 201, 217, 243, 465
blew, 182, 457
blighter, 162
blimp, 28
blind, 406, 427
blink, 406
bliss, 177
blissful, 177
blithe, 177, 186, 238
blizzard, 149, 160, 177, 205, 364
block, 169, 234, 258, 546
blood, 185, 234, 258
bloody, 161, 431, 564
bloom, 399
blooming, 431, 563
blossom, 399
blotto, 417
blouse, 188
blow, 4, 47, 200, 215, 217, 248, 298, 353, 399, 457, 570
blow hot and cold, 13
blow in, 298, 302
blow out, 29, 301, 348, 416
blow up, 298, 301
blowed, 4, 47, 457
blowsy, 188
blubber, 353
blue, 183
bluebeard, 358
bluecoat, 548
blues, 444, 569
bluestocking, 548
bluff, 18, 160, 162, 597
Blumenthal, 399
blurb, 353
blurt, 353
boar, 438
board, 180, 193, 549
boast, 181, 232
boatswain, 218, 350

bobolink, 334
bobwhite, 334
Boche, 286
body, 169
body politic, 503
Boer, 380
Boethius, 88
bog, 202, 375
Bohemian, 294
boid (bird), 189, 197
boil, 186
boiled, 32, 547
boisterous, 189
bold, 83, 180
bolder, 410
boloney, 417
Bolshevism, 384
bolster, 207
bolt, 180, 201, 216
Bolton-Smith, 349
bomb, 169, 180, 194, 598
bon mot, 374
bona fide, 371
bonanza, 381
bonded, 243, 592
bone, 426, 562
bone up, 28
bonehead, 33, 348, 547
bonnet, 161
bonus, 371
boo, 312
boob, 182
booberine, 437
booby, 182
boohoo, 335
book, 119, 183, 234, 258
booking office, 161
booklet, 268, 339
bookseller, 348
boom, 182, 334, 379
boomerang, 152, 385
boon, 182
boor, 182, 184, 379, 563
boost, 182, 353
booterie (bootery), 338
bootleg, 356, 553
bootlegger, 356
boots, 161
booze, 44
Bopp, 200
borax, 383
Bordeaux, 276, 373
border, 210
bore, 344
born, 179, 405
borne, 179, 405
borough, 399, 599

borrow, 109
borrowing, 102
bosh, 417
bosky, 405
bosom, 182, 183, 205, 235
boss, 180, (cap.) 285
bossie, 47
Boston, 180, 234, 258, 277
Bostonian, 280, 319
bot (but), 57
botanize, 341
both, 179, 180, 291, 294
both . . . and, 310, 540
bother, 204, 242
botheration, 339
bothersome, 242
bottle, 548
bottom, 426
bough, 187, 246
bought, 179, 239
boughten, 340
boulingrin (bowling green), 111
Boult, 233
boun, 364
bounce, 188, 194
bound, 188, 364, 376, 409
bounden, 431
bourgeois, 384, 399
bourn, 180
bout, 399
bovine, 547
bow, 180, 187, 399, 426
Bowditch, 188
bowdlerize, 359
bowels, 443
bower, 234
bower of roses, 572
bowl, 180, 188, 200, 231, 233
bowlder, 410
bowls, 439
Bowser, 280
bowwow, 335
Bowyer, 338
box, 79, 83, 202, 215, 553
boy, 75, 82, 186, 188, 213, 234, 438, 554
boycott, 359
boyish, 340, 565
brace, 270, 440
braces, 440
brae, 376, 403

WORD INDEX

braggadocio, 358
braggart, 338
brags, 205
brains, 555
braise, 410
braised, 205
brake, 399
Brakeblok, 282
brand-new, 220
brandy, 379, 397
brass, 556
brat, 125, 375, 563
bravado, 381
brave, 404
bravo, 313, 380, 404
brays, 410
brazen, 340, 556
breach, 399
bread, 172, 234, 548, 597
breadth, 201, 204, 269, 338, 357
breadths, 357
break, 43, 172, 174, 194, 231, 298, 399, 429, 456, 590
break in, 416
breakfast, 172, 194, 348, 597
breast, 233
breath, 172, 204, 234, 260
breathe, 204, 244, 295
breeches (britches), 175, 176, 178, 442, 443
breed, 406, 460
breeze, 242
brethren, 439, 442
brew, 214
brewer, 214
bribed, 600
bric-a-brac, 335
brick, 399
brick up, 300
brickbat, 387
brick-red, 306
bridal, 350
bride, 438
bride elect, 503
bridegroom, 437, 438
bridges, 195
brief, 267
brigade, 338
brigand, 380
bright, 324
brightly, 306
brilliancy, 338
bring, 90, 177, 212, 298, 426, 460

bring in, 301
bring out, 297
bring round, 298, 485
bring to, 578
bringing-up, 348
Bristol, 277
British, 279, 294
Britton, 273
broad, 179, 231
broadcast, 349, 462
broaden, 414
broad-shouldered, 349
broadside, 348
Brobdingnagian, 333
brochure, 208, 374
brock, 375
brogue, 245, 375
broil, 188
broiler, 268
broken, 465
broken down, 301, 302
broken up, 298, 302
bromid, 245, 598, 599
bronchial, 212
broncho, 381
Broncs, 280
Bronx, 212, 216
bronze, 205, 242, 397
brooch, 180
brood, 406
brook, 184
brook no opposition, 572
broth, 179
brother, 204, 235, 399, 403, 438, 442, (cap.) 285
Brother Jonathan, 286
brothers, 442
brothers-in-law, 444
brougham, 182, 358
Broun, 234
brow, 75, 376, 403, 565
brown, 188, 200, 215, 292, (cap.) 274
Browning, 273, 337
browse, 188, 591
bruise, 182, 205, 231
brunch, 353
brung, 458
brusque, 184
brutal, 182
bruvver (brother), 46
buccaneer, 268, 384
Bucephalus, 280
buck, 438
bucket, 431
Buckeye State, 286

Bud, 287
Buddhism, 339
budge, 375
budget, 241
buffalo, 381, 397, 439
buffaloes, 245
buffalo-wallow, 39
buffer, 161
buffet, 247
buffeting, 238
bug, 4, 161, 202
bughouse, 60
bugs, 567
build, 177, 232, 234, 461, 599
builded, 41
builder, 337
bulb, 378
bulbul, 335
bulge, 210, 216
bulk, 185
bull, 32, 184, 438
bulldoze, 547
bullet, 184
bulletin, 380
bullion, 210
bullock, 249, 268, 337
bull's-eye, 348
bully, 565
bumbersoll, 35, 351
bumper, 161
bumpkin, 337
bunch, 270
buncombe (bunkum), 28, 320, 563
bundle, 185, 211
bungaloafer, 351
bungalow, 383
bunk, 563
bunker, 268
Bunyan, 213
buoy, 188, 234
buoyant, 189
burble, 332
burden, 185, 234, 258, 344, 399
burden with, 536
burdenless, 344
burdensome, 344
burdensomeness, 344
bureau, 189, 441, 597
burg, 210, 216, 399
burgess, 399
burglar, 210, 356, 399
burgle, 356
burgomaster, 399
burial, 213, 217, 356, 443

WORD INDEX

burn, 210, 300, 461, 592
burn off, 300
burnt, 201
burr, 184, 210, 231, 258
burrough, 185
bursar, 210, 339
burst, 73, 184, 462
bursted, 462
bury, 234, 258
bus, 28, 185, 249, 355, 406
bush, 184, 193, 234, 249, 258
bushel, 338
bushy, 405
business, 66, 251, 552, 559
busk, 376, 377
buskin, 39
busses, 243
bust, 73
busting, 28
busy, 177, 205, 234, 237, 258
busybodies, 444
busybody, 348, 563
but, 185, 289, 310, 312, 321, 426, 534, 539, 542
butcher, 184, 372, 379, 553
butcher shop, 15, 571
butler, 338, 553, 564
butt, 249
butte, 160
butter, 126, 369
button, 185
buxom, 557
buy, 186, 234, 417, 460
buy in, 302
buy up, 302
buzz, 185, 205, 248, 334, 597
buzz along, 162
buzzard, 547
buzzed, 205, 216, 217, 242
buzzes, 243
by, 85, 87, 186, 298, 305, 308, 321, 504, 539
by and by, 305
by and large, 578
by dint of, 309, 360
by gad, 314
by golly, 314
by gum, 314
by hook or crook, 578
by Jove, 314

by means of, 309
by my matins cheese, 315
by now, 535
by reason of, 308
by tens, 305
by the arms of Robin Hood, 315
by the foot of Pharaoh, 315
by the great horn spoon, 315
by this air, 315
by tonight, 323
bye, 200
bye (boy), 186
byplay, 342

C. (centigrade), 255
cab, 28, 170, 355, 406
cabal, 41
cabbage, 400
cabbage head, 387
cabin, 41, 235
cabinet, 41
cable, 174
cablegram, 352, 387
cabriole, 41
cabriolet, 406
cacao, 384
cactus, 100, 371, 378, 440
cad, 28, 355, 406, 549, 563
caddy, 111, 170, 385
cadence, 380, 407
cadenza, 380, 407
cadet, 355, 373, 406, 549
Caerleon, 125, 275, 375
café, 248, 374, 403
cafeteria, 18, 198, 225, 339
cage, 241, 244
caged, 244
cahoots, 578
cairn, 375
cairngorm, 375
caitiff, 404
cakewalk, 160
Cal, 287
calaboose, 161, 381
calculate, 295
calendula, 566
Calexico, 278
calf, 247, 372, 397, 418
Calgary, 210
calibre (caliber), 158, 383, 406

Calif. (California), 255
Californian, 279
Californiana, 339
Calipatria, 353
caliper, 406
Calistoga, 353
calix, 369, 404
calk, 179
call, 87, 178, 298, 376, 426, 427, 479
call down, 298, 416
call his bluff, 578
call off, 301, 578
call out, 301
calling-down, 348
calliope, 358, 378
callithumpian, 387
calm, 210, 220, 237, 247, 601
Calneva, 353
calumet, 39
Calvada, 353
calvary, 221
Cambridge, 275
camel, 369, 382, 397
cameo, 381
camera, 404
camm (calm), 35
camouflage, 207, 373, 394
camp, 211, 216, 405, 547
campanile, 381
camphor, 383
campus, 160, 235, 405, 550
can, 90, 295, 400, 412, 426, 427, 453, 463, 521, 525, 529, 530, 579
Canaanite, 340
Canadian, 279
canal, 405
cancer, 360, 404
candelabrum, 441
candidate, 560
candle, 369
candy, 161, 383, 397
cane, 211
canine, 341
canker, 360, 404
canned, 31, 32
cannibal, 384
cannonade, 338
canoe, 182, 384
canoeist, 243
cant, 400, 404

WORD INDEX 671

can't, 16, 168, 256, 427, 534
cantaloupe, 181, 234
cantata, 400, 401
canter, 28, 406
Canterbury, 275, 356, 399, 406
canto, 380, 400, 401
cantonment, 158
canvas, 249
canvass, 249
canyon (cañon), 160, 211, 213, 381
caoutchouc, 188, 259, 384
caow, 197
cap, 170
capable, 242
capable of, 537, 538
capacity for, 538
cape, 400
Cape Cod turkey, 363
capital, 400, 404, 407, 553
capitulate, 400
capitulated, 542
caprice, 175, 373
Capricorn, 370
caps, 354
capsule, 235
captain, 170, 235, 549, (cap.) 285
captive, 404
car, 80, 157, 167, 239, 427, 550
caravan, 355, 383, 406
carbuncle, 560
carburetor, 58, 566
carcass, 249
card, 210, 216, 405
card (coward), 197
cardiac, 202, 341, 370
Cardiff, 275
cardinal, 560
Cardinals, 280
care, 80, 171, 196, 426, 531
cargo, 167, 381, 404
carl, 40
Carlyle, 275
Carmel-by-the-Sea, 252, 491
Carmelites, 280
carmine, 404
carnal, 369
carnicería, 339
carnival, 560

Caroline, 437
caromed, 238
carouse, 188
carp, 200
carpenter, 210, 372, 375, 554
carriage, 196, 210, 235, 594
carry, 171, 173, 375, 431
carry out, 298
carryall, 347, 348
cars, 210
cart wheel, 548
Carthage, 277
cartoon, 339
Cartwright, 347
carve, 210, 216, 250, 591
cascade, 338
case, 577, 588
cash, 83, 208
cash register, 349
casket, 431
cassava, 384
cassock, 232
cast, 207, 376, 409, 462
castaway, 444
caste, 381, 409, 560
castle, 137, 372, 373, 404
cast-off, 301
casual, 207, 237
casualties, 548
cat, 121, 202
cataclysm, 253
catalogue (catalog), 100, 245, 343, 595, 598, 599
catarrh, 210, 237, 246, 599
catbird, 348
catch, 83, 170, 201, 405, 460, 591, 592
catch on, 301, 556
category, 378
cathedral, 343, 401, 404
Catherine, 378
catholic, 204, 257, (cap.) 280, 573
Catholics, 257
cattle, 242, 270, 359, 405, 407, 443, 550
caucus, 160, 384
caught, 179
cauliflower, 179
caulk, 410
cause, 179, 231, 372
cavalcade, 338
cavalier, 564

cavalry, 405, 443, 549
cave-in, 348
cavil, 171, 203
cayenne, 384
cease, 119, 242, 345, 369
ceaseless, 345
ceaselessly, 345
cede, 345
ceiling, 206, 233
celebrities, 557
celerity, 339
cell, 400
cellar, 400
cellophane, 400
cellular, 400
celluloid, 283, 359, 400
cellulose, 400
Celt (Kelt), 206
cemetery, 431
censure, 208
centenary, 157
center (centre), 219, 221, 236, 250, 374, 599
centigrade, 255
centipede, 400
central, 219
centrifugal, 224, 399
cereal, 175, 178, 198
cerise, 356
certain, 167, 294
certainly, 26, 307, 535
cess, 345
cessation, 345
cession, 345, 571
chafed, 218, 243
chagrin, 178, 207, 373
chair, 81, 171, 372, 401, 404, 418
chaise, 356, 401
chaise longue (chaise lounge), 4
chalice, 404, 550
chalk, 178, 369
chamber, 372, 404, 553
chamois, 247, 373, 397
champagne, 202, 358
championess, 339, 437
chance, 407
Chandler, 273, 572
change, 194, 195
changeable, 244
channel, 405
Channing, 273
chant, 400, 404, 550
chanticleer, 400
chaos, 202

WORD INDEX

chap, 28
chap(arajo)s, 443
chaparral, 381
chapel, 560
chaperon, 373
chaplain, 372
chapt (chapped), 594
chapter, 372, 400, 404
character, 202, 258, 378, 590, 597
characteristic, 37, 190
characteristic of, 537
characters, 44
charge, 375, 404, 553
chariot, 213, 375
charity, 173, 210
Charlevoix, 276
Charlotte, 207, 437
chart, 405
chary, 174
Chas. (Charles), 255, 437
chase, 201, 206, 215, 240, 369, 372, 405, 550
chasm, 79, 83, 171, 174, 191, 196, 202, 227, 235, 236, 250, 379
chassis, 58
chasten, 247
chastise, 205, 223
chastisement, 223, 244
château, 181, 373, 374, 404
Chatham, 220
chattel, 359, 372, 405, 407
chatter, 232
Chaucerian, 280, 294, 341
Chautauqua, 277
cheat, 359, 405
check (cheque), 119, 159, 202, 238, 260, 383
checker, 405
checkers, 383
checks, 206
chee-ild, 35
cheer, 555
cheerfulest, 451
cheese, 126, 205, 242, 369, 591
chef, 207, 237, 374, 400, 404, 590
chem, 354
chemist, 161
chequer, 202
cherise, 356

Cherokee, 277
cherry, 356, 443
cherub, 382, 441, 442
cherubim, 441, 442
chess, 383
chest, 126, 175, 369, 405
Chester, 126, 275
chesterfield, 358
chestnut, 201, 206, 237
chevalier, 207
chew, 182
chewink, 334
Cheyenne, 207, 277
Chicago, 207, 277
Chicagoan, 280
Chicagorilla, 353
chicken, 337
chicken-hearted, 547
chide, 457, 570
chief, 175, 231, 233, 257, 400, 404, 589, 601, (cap.) 285
chief cockalorum, 34
chieftain, 400, 549
chiffon, 207
chilblain, 87, 239
chilblains, 572
child, 177, 186, 201, 220, 225, 412, 439
childer, 96, 439, 442
childern (children), 220
childish, 563
children, 177, 210, 225, 439
chili, 56, 384
chill, 80, 83
chilled, 243, 412
chimney, 88, 599
chimpanzee, 384
chin chin, 67, 335
china, 358, 385
chinchilla, 381
Chinee, 278, 356, 362
Chinese, 279, 319, 338
chinook wind, 160
chinquapin, 384
chintz, 383
chip, 217
chirk up, 300
chiropodist, 400
chiropractor, 340, 379, 567
chitchat, 335
chivalrous, 565
chivalry, 207, 405
chix, 241
chlorine, 178, 339

chocolate, 381
Choctaw, 179
choice, 189
choir, 121, 186, 203, 234, 240, 259
chokingly, 306
choleric, 567
cholla, 56
choo choo, 48, 335
choose, 455, 479
chop chop, 67, 335
chop suey, 385
chorine, 437
chortle, 332
chorus, 378, 597
Choteau County, 276
chow chow, 67, 187, 335, 385
chowder, 188
Christ, 186, 314, 375, 378
christen, 358
Christendom, 337
Christian, 294
Christmas, 282, 350
chukker, 237, 259
chum, 201
chump, 353
church, 268, 369, 377, 378, 405
churlish, 563
chute, 182, 207
cider, 382, 397
cigar, 381
cigarette (cigaret), 590, 591, 597, 599
cinch, 206, 211
cinema, 161
cinematograph, 379
cinnamon, 382
cipher, 203, 237, 383, 404
circle, 268, 319
circulation, 58
circumscribe, 343
circumspect, 347
circumstances, 552
circus, 249
cisalpine, 343
cist, 206, 405
cite, 571
cities, 235, 246, 439, 446, 592
citizen, 553
citizenry, 268, 339
city, 80, 177, 191, 194, 206, 213, 232, 235, 237. 258, 372, 446, 447

WORD INDEX 673

civics, 443
civil, 249, 341, 565
civilize (civilise), 159, 259
claim, 174, 372
clam, 170
clamor (clamour), 174, 232, 340, 594
clan, 375
clane (clean), 174
clank, 334
clapboard, 219, 350
claptrap, 335, 563
claret, 235
Claribel, 272
clarinet, 173
Clark, 87
clasp, 168, 200, 207, 216
class, 168, 597
classics, 339
claw, 179, 248
Clay, 278
claymore, 375
clean, 174, 196, 296, 321
cleanse, 234
clean-up, 301
clear, 324
cleave, 203, 364, 409, 455, 459, 570
cleever (clever), 35
clef, 172, 249
cleft, 203
Clegg, 249
Clem, 287
clematis, 225
Clementine, 437
clench, 405
clergy, 270, 443
clerk, 167, 192, 202, 378, 553
clever, 172
click, 334
climate, 235
climb, 177, 186
clime, 571
clinch, 405
cling, 455
clip, 177
clique, 175, 176, 178
cloak, 547
clock, 215, 239, 561
clocks, 96
clockwise, 342
clomb, 459
Clorox, 282

close, 180, 205
close up, 300
closing-out, 301, 348
clost, 220
cloth, 179, 204, 442
clothe, 204, 244, 460
clothes, 179, 205, 405, 442
cloths, 405, 442
cloudy, 419
clove, 410
cloven, 458
clover, 181, 228, 232
clown, 188
cloy, 188
Clubb, 249
clubs, 200
cluster, 270
clutch, 58, 566
Co. (Company), 255
coach, 180
coagulate, 369
coal, 180, 202, 236, 258, 397
coal oil, 15, 160
coalesce, 341
coarctation, 414
coarse, 181
coat of arms, 349
coat of mail, 444
coatlike, 340
cob, 83
cobalt, 380
Cobb, 200
cobble, 341
cobra, 381
cock, 438
cock sparrow, 437
cockatoo, 149, 385
Cockney, 286, 366
cocksure, 349
cocoa, 384
C.O.D. (collect on delivery), 255
cod, 439
codex, 441
codices, 441
codify, 341
Cœur d'Alene, 276
coexist, 343
coffee, 169, 176, 235, 262, 383, 397, 403
coffin, 431
cog, 83
cognac, 213
cognate, 91, 400, 576
cognizance, 400

cognoscente, 381
cohesion, 175
cohort, 181, 401
coif, 189
coil, 188, 234
coin, 188
coincide, 198
coke, 180
Colchester, 126
cold, 83, 239, 362, 427, 557
cold feet, 31
cold shoulder, 357, 548
cold storage, 88
cole, 405
coleslaw (coldslaw), 161, 362
collapse, 250
collar, 169
collateral, 75, 76
collect, 86, 222, 269, 343, 402, 408
collecting, 269
collection, 269
collective, 242
colleen, 53, 375
college, 169, 241, 591
collegiate, 241
collier, 213
collimate, 333
colloquial speech, 26
cologne, 358
colonel, 121, 210, 259, (cap.) 285
colonnade, 380
color (colour), 159, 235, 599
Colorado, 381
colored people, 550
colt, 180
columbarium, 339, 548
colyum (column), 213
comb, 180, 211, 601
combine, 223
come, 39, 83, 114, 232, 298, 299, 422, 426, 427, 456, 464, 560
come about, 416
come and go, 578
come by, 578
come off, 302
comeback, 44
comedian, 437
comedienne, 437
comedy, 378
comfort, 211, 216
comical, 355

WORD INDEX

coming (comming, comin'), 4, 157, 210, 232, 262, 422
coming-out, 301
Concord stage, 39
command, 168
commandant, 225
commencement, 561
committee, 248, 270, 495
common gender, 436
commons, 318
communal, 225
communism, 384
communities, 44
comp, 354
compact, 224, 319
companion, 213, 400
company, 427
compare to, with, 536
compass, 249
compel, 251
compelled, 238
compensate for, 6
compile, 6
complaint, 557
complete, 6, 175, 232, 343, 426, 451
completely, 306, 451
completest, 451
complex, 43, 224, 566, 613
complexion, 203
complication, 222
composition, 9, 10, 576, 587
comprehend, 302, 404
compress, 223
compression, 566
comprise, 205, 404
comptroller, 211, 219, 237, 247, 260
compulsion, 210, 216
compunction, 555
compute, 404
comrade, 232, 381
conceal, 400, 417
concede, 345
conceit, 206, 404, 563, 599
conceive, 233
concept, 404
concern, 552
concerned about, in, with, 482, 537
concerning, 308, 325
concession, 345
concessionaire, 345
concessive, 345
conclusion, 574
concoct, 6
Concord stage, 39
concordance, 561
concrete, 35, 224, 577
condemn, 211, 219
condemnation, 211, 219
condense, 242
condenser, 566
condition, 552
condor, 384
conducive, 243
conducive to, 537
conduct, 401
conduit, 80, 105, 235, 401, 599
confectaurant, 352
confer, 184, 211, 216, 217
conference, 238, 262
confess, 416
confession, 238
confide in, to, 482, 536
confidence in, 537, 580
conformance, 416
conformity, 416
congenial, 77
congenital, 37
Congoleum, 282
congratulate, 417, 570
congregation, 212, 557
congress, 160
conifer, 347
conjugal, 401
conjugate, 401
conjugation, 577
conjunction, 266, 401
connect, 343
Connecticut, 246
connection (connexion), 203, 241
connive at, with, 536
connoisseur, 102
conquered, 45
conquest, 203
conscience, 208
consequently, 306, 307
Conservative, 280
consider, 479
considerable, 294, 560
considering, 308
consist, 401
consist in, of, 295, 482, 536, 580
constant, 401
constitute, 6
consulate, 339
consumption, 550, 567
contemplate, 97, 223
contemplation, 227
content, 224
contents, 224, 443
contest, 223, 228
continental, 370
contingent upon, 309
continue, 303
contract, 58, 86, 223
contradict, 343
contrary to, 325
contrast, 426
contrast with, 536
control, 251
controller (comptroller), 219, 260
convention, 557
conversion, 317, 576, 587
convert into, from, to, 536
convey, 405
convict, 223
conviction, 574
convoy, 405
cooden (could not), 52
cook, 184
cookie, 161
cooler (jail), 60
coolie, 149, 385
coon, 160, 384
coop, 182, 198
Cooper, 183
coöperate, 198
coöperative, 198, 252
coördinate, 88, 198, 371
cooties, 28
cop, 32
copious, 235, 594
copper, 32, 169, 358, 369, 397, 442, 548
coppers, 442
copyist, 251
coquette, 254
coracle, 375
cord, 180, 202
cords, 354
co-respondent, 252
cork, 179, 410
corker, 32
corking, 417, 560
corn, 37, 161, 399, 400, 403, 550
corner, 210
cornet, 400, 550

WORD INDEX

cornucopia, 400
Cornwall, 273
corolla, 369
corollary, 158
coronach, 375, 397
coroner, 169, 369, 561
corp, 356
corps, 105, 247, 407
corpse, 356, 407
corpus, 407
corral, 58, 381
correctest, 451
correspondence, 227
corridor, 380
corroborate, 302
corrupt, 343
corundum, 397
cosmetician, 339
cosmogony, 400
Cossack, 384
cost, 201, 232, 462
costly, 565
cost-plus, 253
cotillion, 213
cotton, 383, 396
cottonwood, 160
cotyledon, 378
cougar, 182
cough, 179, 231, 251, 259, 299, 300, 362, 597
cough up, 298, 300
could, 184, 200, 247, 362, 427, 454, 463, 521, 529, 579, 593
could (cold), 52
could not help but, 513
Council Bluffs, 277
count, 188, 194, 372, 404, 549
counteract, 342
counterfeit, 177, 234, 563, 599
countess, 339, 372, 437, 438
country (countree), 251, 372
county farm, 548
coupé, 182
couple, 200, 270
coupon, 190, 234
courage, 185, 201, 210, 234, 258
courageous, 241, 244
courier, 210
course, 181, 578
court, 401
courteous, 181, 565

courtesan, 181, 563
courtesy, 401
courtly, 565
courts-martial, 444, 503
cousin, 185, 411, 436, (cap.) 285
cove, 243
cover, 232
covering, 3
covey, 267, 270
cow, 187, 197, 439, 442
coward, 188, 194, 197, 214, 338
cowcatcher, 161
cower, 188
cowl, 188
co-worker, 252
Cowper, 183
cow-puncher, 58
coxcomb, 241
coxswain, 241, 350
coyote, 149, 180, 234, 384
cozen, 411
cozily, 251
crack up, 28
crackajack (cracker-jack), 32, 565, 570
cracked, 33
crackers, 161
craft, 168
crafty, 563
crag, 375
crake, 99
crane, 547
cranky, 262, 340, 594
cranny, 211
crap (crop), 54
crapehanger, 547
crash, 334
crass, 429
crater, 232
cravat, 384, 397
crave for, 536
craven, 174
craving for, 537
crawfish (crayfish), 362
crawl, 210, 233, 485
creak, 409
creaks, 206
cream, 175
creamery, 338
creamy, 340
create, 221, 459
creation, 221, 371
creative, 341
creature, 38, 176, 201, 221, 340

creed, 369, 548
creek, 175, 176, 178, 195, 405, 409
creep, 460
creeped, 47
crematorium, 340
crêpe de Chine, 374
crept, 465
crescent, 206
crew, 182, 248, 457
crews, 410
crib, 562
crick, 176, 405, 409
cried, 235
cries, 235
crimson, 383, 404
cripes, 314
crisis, 186, 441
crisp, 369
crisscross, 335
criteria, 441
criterion, 441
critic, 221, 249, 339, 355
critical, 341, 355
criticaster, 339
criticism, 221, 339, 563
criticize, 205, 341
critter, 176
crochet, 173, 208, 223
crock, 202, 215, 375
crocodile, 202, 547
Crœsus, 358
cromlech, 375
crooked, 243, 340, 556
croon, 334
crooner, 337
cross, 375, 405, 556
crosswise, 305
crotchet, 241
crow, 457, 547
crowd, 187, 270
crown, 239, 372, 546
Crozier, 207
cruces, 441
cruciferous, 399
cruel, 182, 214
Cruelty, 558
cruise, 410
crumb, 219, 598
crumble, 219, 414
crumble up, 301
crush, 208
crusher, 208
crutch, 185
crux, 185, 405, 441
cry, 235, 248, 570
crystallization, 58

cub, 185, 547
cubby, 185
cubic, 190
cuckoo, 182, 334
cud, 406
cue (queue), 594
cuff, 185, 248
cuisine, 203, 240
culio (curious), 67
cull, 185
culture, 120, 201, 240, 258, 429, 575
Culver, 210
cuneiform, 190
cunning, 566
cunningest, 451
cunningness, 337
cup, 185, 234, 258, 369
cupboard, 88, 200, 218, 350, 351, 553
cupful, 268, 337
cupfuls, 444
cupidity, 554
cups, 206, 354
cups full, 444
cur, 184
curb (kerb), 159, 259, 260
cured of, 482
curio, 355, 557
curious, 213, 574
curiouser, 451
currants, 320
current, 556
curriculum, 371, 441, 555
curry, 383
curry favor (curry fa-vel), 363, 578
curse, 73, 137, 184, 185, 196, 210, 216, 242
cursed, 243, 465
cursory, 184
curt, 400
curtail, 400
curtain, 401
curve, 242
cushion, 184
cuspidor, 431
cuss, 73, 185, 196
custom, 185
customs, 38
cut, 44, 74, 79, 202, 462, 542
cute, 239, 360, 405, 407, 552, 560
Cutex, 282
Cutler, 273

cut-out, 301
cutthroat, 348
cycle, 202, 206
czar, 204, 237, 259, 384, 437
czarina, 437

d' (do), 52
dabster, 562
dachshund, 380, 397
dactyl, 245
dad, 354, (cap.) 287
dada, 47
daddie (daddy), 47, 334
daffy, 340
daft, 405, 563
Dago, 245, 286
dahlia, 358, 369, 377, 396
dailies, 246
daily, 210, 417
Daimler, 211
dairy, 174
dais, 407
daisy, 350
Dakoming, 278, 353
Dakota, 277, 384
dale, 405
dam, 438
damask, 358, 382
dame, 372, 401
damn, 210, 237, 247, 314, 552, 564
damsel, 570
damson, 382
dance, 156, 170, 196, 401
dandelion, 350, 401
Danderine, 282, 339
dandy, 32, 565
Dane, 172, 225, 279
danger, 372, 401, 417
Daniel, 357
Danish, 132
Danvers, 211
D.A.R., 255
dare, 55, 295, 463, 521, 530, 560
dark horse, 59
darkling, 342
darky, 160
darling, 285, 337
darn, 184, 315
Darwinist, 340
data, 22, 171, 196, 371, 441, 442
datum, 371, 441
daub, 169
daughter, 179, 201, 438

daughterkin, 337
daunt, 401
David, 171, 203
Davis, 274
davit, 171
dawg, 170
dawn, 179, 231, 233
day, 174, 197, 311, 427
days, 410
daze, 173, 410
dazzle, 205, 237
deacon, 378, 404
deaconess, 437
dead, 319, 451
deadly, 490
dead-tired, 306
deaf, 173, 234
deal, 210, 405, 460
dean, 404
dear, 175, 177, 193, 306, 427
dear me, 313
deb, 172, 355
debate, 566
debit, 200, 407
debitus, 14, 361
débris, 247
debt, 14, 100, 236, 246, 259, 260, 361, 407, 593, 598
debunk, 343
débutante, 373
decalogue (decalog), 202, 245, 347, 401, 595
decapitate, 75, 76
decasyllabic, 401
decay, 414
decease, 345
deceased, 319
decedent, 345
deceit, 233
deceive, 80, 599, 601
December, 281, 401
decide, 6
decimal, 401
decision, 177
deck, 379, 403, 411
declaim, 170, 195
declamation, 195, 430
declamatory, 170
declension, 414
decline, 414
Decoration Day, 282
decorative, 158, 225
decrease, 414
decrement, 414
decretal, 59

deduce, 37
deduction, 414
deed, 175, 399, 416
deem, 175, 399
deemster, 399
deep, 175
deepen, 414
deep-rutted, 243
deer, 270, 372, 418, 439, 495, 550
deesh (dish), 57
defend, 561
defender and keeper, 415
defense, 405
defensive, 206
deficit, 223
definite, 341, 591, 598
deflate, 414
deflation, 414
deft, 405
degraded, 563
deign, 174, 211, 246
deity, 198
dekagram, 401
Dekes, 352
Delaborde, 273
Delatour, 273
delectable, 404
delegate, 339
delicate, 250, 341
delicatessen, 400
delight, 599, 600
delightful, 404
deliria, 414
delirium, 414
dell, 405
delphinium, 378, 566
deluded, 419
delusion, 183, 419
delve, 203, 570, 591
demagog, 595
demand, 170, 235
demented, 191
demesne, 247, 401, 404
Democrat, 280
demon, 175, 232
demonstrate, 225
den, 211
Denmark, 172, 225
density, 244
dent, 360
dental, 401
dentist, 401
Dentyne, 282
departure, 242
dependant, 338

dependent, 338
depose, 225
deposit, 404
deposition, 225
depository, 225
depot, 176, 247, 373, 374, 404
deprave, 170, 225
depravity, 170, 225
depreciate, 414
depreciation, 414
deprive of, 482
depth, 172
derangement, 36
derby, 358, (cap.) 167, 276, 376
derision, 207
derivative, 177
derive, 177
derogation, 414
derrick, 358
derring-do, 333
Des Moines, 276, 280, 373
Des Plaines, 276
Descartes, 273
Deschutes River, 276
descend, 414
descendant, 338, 357
descendent, 338
descent, 414
desert, 76, 223
desideratum, 371, 441
designing, 563
desirable, 243
desire, 531
desk, 407
desouled, 333
desperado, 245, 381
despicable, 225
despite, 308, 405
dessert, 205, 237
desuetude, 214, 430
detail, 223
details, 223
deteriorate, 295
determine, 591, 598
detour, 176
detract from, 536
Detroit, 189
deuce, 182, 206, 315
devastatingly, 306
development, 414
device, 206
devil, 172, 175, 194, 228, 235, 314, 369, 378, 552
devilish, 405

devise, 206
devoid of, 537, 580
devotee, 338, 374
dextrose, 352
dhow, 187
diabolical, 405
diæresis (dieresis), 590
diagnosis, 370, 379, 430, 567
diagram, 343, 378
diagram(m)ing, 239
dial, 548, 561
dialect, 50, 576
dialectal, 50
dial(l)ed, 239
dialogue (dialog), 242, 245, 589, 598
diameter, 347, 369
diamond, 210, 397, 404
dianthus, 566
diaphragm, 203, 210, 237, 379
diary, 221
dice, 206, 442
dicentra, 566
Dick, 287
dickens, 315
dicker, 561
dicks, 60
Dickybirds, 286
dicta, 441
dictaphone, 387
dictate, 401
dictator, 390
diction, 371, 401
dictionary, 158, 339, 401
dictum, 441
did, 296, 427
didn't, 427
die, 235, 248, 250, 376, 418, 431, 442, 560, 564
die a-laughing, 33
die away, 414
dies, 235, 442
differ from, in, on, with, 536, 538
difference, 537
difference between, in, 537
different, 427
different from, than, to, 162, 513, 537, 538
differential, 566
differing, 238
dig, 177, 457
dig in, 300
digest, 223

WORD INDEX

digitalis, 566
digression, 172
dike, 406, 562
dilapidate, 561
dilatation, 414
dilate, 414
dilemma, 343
dilettante, 381, 441
dilettanti, 441
diligence, 338, 374
dill, 200
diminish, 414
diminution, 414
diner, 232, 591
dingdong, 335
dinner, 211, 232, 237, 591
diphtheria, 204
diplomat, 561, 564
Dippaderry, 46
direct, 427
direction, 203, 222
directly, 305, 311
dirigible, 58, 178, 223, 341
dirt, 184, 376
dirt-cheap, 306, 349
dirty, 431
disability, 58
disagree, 416
disagree with, 482
disaster, 567
discalceate, 97
discard, 18, 553
discern, 205, 206, 237
discharge, 223
disciple, 330
discipline, 339
disclose, 200
discontinue, 119
discount, 414
discrimination, 430
discus, 249, 407
discuss, 249
discussion, 208
dish, 208, 369, 407
dishearten, 209
dishonest, 206
disintegrate, 429, 485
disk, 407
dislocate, 343
dismantle, 553
dismissal, 339
disorder, 206
disparity between, in, 537
dispatch, 574

display, 119
disport, 405
disputable, 223
dispute, 223
disquisition, 207
dissect, 239
dissyllabic, 343
distant, 401
distaste for, 537
distend, 414
distension, 414
distich, 378
distil, 251
ditch, 177, 406, 562
ditto, 401
ditty, 401
diurnal, 417
div (give), 46
divan, 383
dive, 455
dived, 455
diverge, 343
divers, 406
diverse, 406
diversity, 244
divine, 560
divorce, 181
Dixie, 286
dizzy, 177, 205, 557, (cap.) 287
do, 39, 52, 79, 80, 83, 182, 200, 231, 236, 248, 258, 295, 296, 298, 300, 321, 372, 393, 399, 426, 427, 463, 510, 521, 524, 530
do tell, 313
do up, 300, 393
doc, 355
docile, 181
dock, 379
doctor, 340, (cap.) 284, 285
Doctor of Philosophy, 284
doctorine, 437
doctress, 339, 437
doctrinal, 157
dodo, 381
doe, 180, 231, 250, 438
doe (go), 46
doer, 79
does, 185, 205, 234
doff, 350, 399
dog, 169, 179
dog house, 348
dog-cheap, 306

doge, 401, 404
doggie, 47, 48
doggy, 340
dogies, 58
dogmatic, 190
dogs, 4
doily, 358
doings, 443
doldrums, 353, 443
dole, 405, 563
doleful, 244
doll, 169
dollarature, 351
dolphin, 210
domain, 401, 404
dominate, 371, 401
domineer, 401
dominie, 401
Dominion Day, 282
domino, 401
don, 350, 399, 401
Doncaster, 275
done, 232
donkey, 87, 251, 594, 599
donor, 87
don't, 26, 37, 180, 256, 426, 427
doom, 563
doon, 53
door, 180
doors, 4
dope, 552
dopester, 337
Dorchester, 275
Dorena, 353
Dorking, 337
dormice, 439
dormitory, 340
Dorothea, 378
Dorsetshire, 275
dose, 206
Dosset (Dorset), 52
dotard, 253
dote, 566
doth, 185
Doty, 181
double, 226, 235, 262, 294
double-cross, 349
doublets, 577
doubt, 14, 100, 246, 259, 260, 361, 426, 593, 598
doubtless, 307, 535
douche, 182
dough, 548, 599
doughboys, 28

WORD INDEX

doughty, 188
dour, 188
douse, 188
dove, 410, 455
down, 125, 298, 305, 308, 321, 357, 375
down and out, 292, 578
down on, 308
down through, 308
downfall, 301
downpour, 342, 348
downward (downwards), 305
doze, 205
doze off, 298
dozen, 185, 235, 242, 270, 440
Dr. (Doctor), 255
drachm, 246
draft (draught), 594, 597, 599
drag, 377, 403, 459
dragged, 243
dragon, 407
dragoon, 407
drake, 369, 407, 438
drama, 168, 171, 248, 378
dramatic, 341
dramatical, 355
drame (dream), 174
draw, 47, 106, 377, 403, 546, 557
draw with, 297
drawed, 47
drawer, 179, 268
drawing, 557
dreadfully, 306
dream, 174, 364, 460
dreamt, 234
dreary, 175, 210, 556
dregs, 377, 443
drench, 199, 406
dress, 6, 461, 574
dress circle, 161
dress up, 300
dressing, 557
dressing-down, 301
dressmaker, 348
dribble, 341
Dri-Brite, 283
dried, 292
dried-up, 348
drier (dryer), 235
drift, 203, 337
drill, 200, 215, 403
drink, 199, 406, 455

drive, 453, 454
drives, 58
dromedary, 169, 346
drone, 438
drop off, 414
droshky, 384
drouth, 188, 269
drove, 270
drownd, 220
drowse, 550
drowsy, 188
drug, 458
drug store, 571
drugeteria, 339
druggist, 161
druid, 375
drum, 379, 397
drunk, 319, 431
drunkard, 268, 338
drunken, 458
dry, 235
dry up, 302
dryness, 235
dubitare, 14, 361
Dubuque, 276
ducal, 401
ducat, 380, 401
duchess, 401, 437, 558
duchy, 401
duck, 185, 409, 438
Duco, 282
duct, 401
dudine, 437
due, 84, 182, 407, 427
due to, 309, 325, 432
dug, 465
dug (dog), 57
dugout, 301, 319, 357
duke, 182, 202, 372, 401, 404, 549, 564, (cap.) 284
dull, 292, 597
dully, 306
duly, 244
duma, 384
dumb, 32, 211, 220, 556, 563, 598
Dumbarton, 125, 275
dumfound, 353
dun, 375
Dunbar, 275, 375
dunce, 242, 357, 554, 563
Dundee, 275
dune, 182
dungeon, 401
Dunkirk, 275

Dunn, 249
dunt (don't), 57
duodenum, 441
Duofold, 340
duplex, 294
duplicate, 427
durability, 416
duration, 416
during, 308
durst, 463
durstn't, 167, 530
dusky, 419
dust up, 298
Dutch, 250, 256, 279, 287
duty, 182
dwarf, 414
dwell, 201, 214, 217, 461
dwelt, 201, 239
dwindle, 201, 214, 414
dy (day), 174
dye, 200, 321
dying, 235
dynamo, 378
dynasty, 187
dyspepsia, 343

'e (he), 51
each, 241, 250, 291, 320, 427, 498
each one, 291, 497, 498
each other, 291
eager, 400, 530
ear, 400
earl, 210, 438, 564, (cap.) 284
earldom, 337
early, 185, 234, 305
earn, 184, 231
earnest, 382
earnings, 319
ear-splitting, 349
earth, 184
ease, 205
easier, 251
Easter, 206, 282
eastern, 341
easternmost, 450
easy, 306
eat, 79, 400, 403, 432, 456
eat up, 298
eatable, 341, 403
eave trough (eaves trough), 356
eaves, 356, 443, 550
ebb, 200, 249, 414

WORD INDEX

ebony, 382, 397
echo, 181, 202
echoes, 205, 245
eclipse, 344
econ, 173
economics, 173, 443
economize, 464
ecstasies, 246
ecstasy, 202, 240, 401
eczema, 58, 205
ed. (edition), 255
Edda, 377
edge, 201, 240, 400, 403, 591
edged out, 45
edible, 400, 403
Edinburgh, 275
editor, 236, 250, 356
editors in chief, 444
Edom, 175
education, 575
educator, 340
Edward, 271
Edward the Confessor, 286
ee (thee), 52
e'en (even), 256
eend (end), 54
e'er (ever), 256
eery, 175
effect, 343
effervesce, 341
effort, 172
e.g. (exempli gratia), 482
egg, 172, 202, 249, 376
egg on, 403
eggs, 83, 202, 215, 217
egoism, 339
egoist, 88, 173, 176
egret, 173, 250
Egyptian, 405
eh, 233
eight, 427
eisteddfod, 375
either, 83, 176, 187, 197, 204, 233, 237, 291, 293, 294, 427, 498, 599
either ... or, 310, 540
ejaculated, 430
eke out, 300
ekename, 285, 361
elaboration, 414
Elbe, 210, 216
elbow, 239
Elcar, 282

elder, 199, 450
elders, 267, 318, 357
eldest, 199, 450
Eldorado, 381
eldritch, 250
elect, 404, 479
election-day, 253
elective, 245, 341
electrical, 355
electrify, 341
electrocute, 352
electrolier, 352
elegiac, 225, 341
elephant, 369
elephant-like, 340
elevator, 111, 160
elf, 210, 216
élite, 404
Elizabethan, 22, 173, 280
elk, 210, 216, 439
Elliott, 213
ellipsis, 343, 441
elm (ellum), 35, 192, 197, 210
Elmonica, 353
eloquent, 341
else, 427, 449, 503
elves, 210
em (them), 52
embargo, 381
embellish, 372
embers, 443
embody, 342
embryo, 262
emerald, 397
Emmalou, 272
Empire Day, 282
Empire State, 286
employee, 176, 195, 248, 251, 268
emporium, 441
empress, 437
empty, 247, 449, 451
empty of, 537
emu, 248, 381
en (him), 52
enchanting, 560
enchantress, 437
encortif, 333
encyclopædia, 233
end, 175
endeavor, 612
endlong, 342
endow with, 536
endure, 184, 531
endwise, 342

energy, 343
engine, 187, 201, 550, 557, 598
England, 177, 193, 273
English, 127, 131, 212, 278, 279
enhance, 414
enjoy, 426
enlarge, 414
enlargement, 414
enough, 292, 427, 477, 503, 597
enow, 188
enrol (enroll), 249, 251, 342
enrolment (enrollment), 239
enter and come in, 415
enterprise, 373
enthralled, 566
enthuse, 356
enthusiasm, 182, 355, 378
entire, 427
entirely, 306
entrée, 404
entry, 404
envelope, 223
envious of, 537
environment, 430
epaulet, 245
ephemeral, 173, 344
Ephraim, 235
epic, 422
epical, 341, 355, 422
epicure, 358
epigram, 344
episcopal, 378
epistle, 219, 242
epistolary, 219
epitaph, 249
epitaphs, 36
epithet, 399
epoch, 344, 597
epoch-making, 349
equally, 306
equation, 207, 237
equator, 370
equipped, 238
era, 175
erase, 173, 206
ere, 310, 322, 409, 542
Eric the Red, 286
Erickson, 273
Erie, 277
Ernest, 437
Ernestine, 437

WORD INDEX

erotic, 294, 378
err, 184, 210, 231, 249, 257
errata, 168, 441
error, 426, 555
es (yes), 46
escheat, 359, 405
escutcheon, 39
esk (ask), 57, 173, 196
esophagus, 235, 379
especial, 207
especially, 307, 374, 405, 482
espionage, 35
esprit, 405
espy, 207, 405
Esq., 255, 283
Esquimaux (Eskimos), 205, 247, 384
esquire, 207, 374, 405
Essex, 275, 350
establish, 401
estate, 207, 359, 374, 401, 405, 407, 549
Esther, 201, 271
estop, 207, 405
et al. (et alii), 371
etc. (et cetera), 255, 371
etch, 400, 403
eternal, 324
Eternal City, 286
eternally, 451
Ethan, 172
ether (æther), 83, 159, 175, 204, 233, 237
ethics, 378, 443, 495
ethics is, are, 496
Ethiopian, 213
ethyl, 172, 566
etiquette, 245, 401, 404
etymology, 11, 255, 329, 576
eucalyptus, 400
eucharist, 189
eugenics, 346
eulogy, 344
euphorbia, 566
Eurasian, 278
Eureka, 189
Europe, 189
European, 279
Evan, 274
evangelic, 341
evangelist, 344
Evans, 172
evasion, 207, 237

eve, 81, 175, 231, 257
even, 172, 191, 196, 203, 427
evening, 238, 516
evenly, 342
evenness, 239
eventually, 305
ever, 172, 175, 305
Eversharp, 283, 347
every, 294, 324, 427
every now and then, 578
every once in a while, 13
everybody, 291, 347, 448, 498
everyone, 291, 448, 497, 498
everyone else's, 449
everything, 291
evidence, 262, 594
evil, 175, 249, 318, 450, 594
evoke, 343
ewe, 213, 237, 251, 438
ex, 172, 354
ex cathedra, 371
ex officio, 371
exacerbate, 414
exacerbation, 414
exact, 83, 202, 205, 215, 240, 258
exactly, 505
exaggerate, 414
exaggeration, 414
exalt, 224, 414
exaltation, 224
exam, 44, 354
examination, 85
example, 168, 405
exasperate, 414
Excalibur, 280
exceed, 345, 599
exceedingly, 306, 345
excel, 249, 251
excel in, 482
Excellency, 557
except, 4, 308, 322, 325, 539, 542
excepting, 308
excess, 345
excessive, 345
excessively, 345
exchange, 426
exchequer, 405
excise, 240, 391
exclaim, 236
exclamation, 236
excursion, 210

excuse, 426
excuse me, 313
executor, 338
executrix, 340, 437
exempt, 247
exercise, 202
exert, 79, 205, 570
exhaust, 209
exhibit, 209, 220, 570
exhort, 202, 209, 220, 224
exhortation, 224
exigency, 225
exist, 205, 295
exodus, 344
expand, 414
expatiate, 414
expect, 531
expectorate, 431
expedient, 175, 213
expedite, 400
expeditious, 208
expend, 570
expense, 426
experiment, 612
expert, 224
explode, 416
exploit, 189
export, 223
exposition, 557
express, 297, 426, 561
ex-secretary, 343
exsect, 240
extant, 202
extend, 401, 414, 570
extension, 414
extenuate, 414
exterior, 450
extinguish, 302, 416
extirpate, 223
extra, 427
extract, 223
extraordinary, 343
extras, 357
extravagant, 341
extravaganza, 381
extreme, 450
extremely, 306
extrovert, 566
exult, 224
exultation, 224, 227
ex-wife, 252
eye, 47, 186, 234, 426, 547
ez (as), 53

Fabian, 213
fable, 170, 225

fabulous, 170, 225
face, 206, 221, 244, 417, 426, 570
faced, 243, 244, 362
faces, 195
facial, 221, 244
facile, 399
facsimile, 248
fact, 203, 216, 221, 319, 399, 404, 426, 552
faction, 404
factual, 221
fade away, 33
fade-out, 58
Fahrenheit, 380
fail, 73, 84, 203, 590
fain, 571
fair, 73, 82, 171, 192, 210, 231, 233, 258, 427
fairest, 170, 171
fairy, 173
faith, 173, 372, (cap.) 272
fakir, 235, 383
falcon, 210, 247
falderal, 335
fall, 39, 73, 82, 203, 237, 258, 295, 298, 299, 406, 426, 457, 476, 560
fall away, 414
fall down, 301
fall off, 414
fall out, 416
falling out, 298
false, 178, 210, 216, 231, 250, 257, 372
falsehood, 387
falter, 178
fame, 565
familiar, 177, 213
family, 270, 495, 561
famish, 341
famous, 341
fan, 170
fancy, 240, 406
fandom, 337
fantasy, 240, 406
fantom, 240
far, 73, 82, 84, 87, 121, 167, 231, 247, 257, 305, 427, 450
far and wide, 578
fare, 121, 170, 171, 231, 257, 406
fare through, 301

farewell, 316
farmerette, 339
far-reaching, 253
farrier, 171
farseeing, 349
farther, 294, 305, 405, 410
farthing, 337
Fascist, 381, 441
fashion, 208, 404
fast, 106, 362, 408, 449, 546, 563, 574
fasten, 88, 201
faster, 449
fastest, 449
fat, 73, 74, 82, 170, 232, 427
fate, 173, 231, 232, 242, 257, 590
father, 3, 83, 90, 168, 191, 196, 197, 265, 400, 410, 438, 558, (cap.) 285
father-in-law, 349
fathom, 204, 549
fatigue, 175, 245
Fatty, 287
Fatty Williams, 285
fault, 179
favor (favour), 159, 259, 426, 557, 599
favor of, 537
favorite son, 59
fear, 43, 157, 177, 196, 560, (cap.) 558
fear for, 538
fear of, 538
feared, 175
fearful of, 537, 538
fearless, 324
feast, 373, 404
feat, 404, 439
feather, 172, 175
feather out, 300
feature, 552
February, 220, 255, 281
fed, 465
federal, 160
fee, 400
fee simple, 503
feeble, 404
feed, 400, 461
feel, 73, 74, 80, 82, 175, 249, 262, 426, 460, 575
feelings, 269
feesh (fish), 195
feet, 426, 439

feeze, 176, 409
feign, 174, 202
felicitate, 417, 570
feline, 242
fell, 73, 74, 82, 406, **459**, 575, 591
fell before, 45
fella, 66
fellow, 376, 426, 563
fellow citizens, 348
fellow-countrymen, 252
felon, 172, 175, 210, 554
felt, 239
feminine, 178, 187, 235, 242, 341
fence, 405
fender, 161
fennis, 66
ferry, 173, 406, 550
fertile (fertil), 157, 225, 245, 399
fetch, 400, 431
fetching, 565
fete, 121, 173, 231, 257, 374, 404
fetid, 172, 201
fetish, 173, 381
fetlock, 400
fetter, 400
feud, 75, 82, 182, 189, 190, 234, 400
fever, 172, 232
few, 189, 214, 234, 291, 294, 427
fewer, 79
fewest, 214
fez, 172, 384
fiancée, 373
fiasco, 245, 380, 404
fib, 548
fibula, 370
fickle, 242
fiddle, 337
fiddler, 563
Fido, 280
fie, 186, 312
fief, 400
field, 80, 175, 273
fiend, 172, 175, 193, 232, 319, 563
fierce, 29, 177, 210, 428, 554
fifteen, 218
fifth, 88, 204, 327
fifth-century, 253
fifths, 206
fiftieth, 340

WORD INDEX

fifty, 177, 194
fifty-four, 252
fight, 455, 601
fight shy of, 578
fight with, 575
figs, 202, 240
figure, 202
figure up, 302
fig-yure, 213
filch, 201
file, 157, 203
filed, 598, 600
filibuster, 59, 160, 262
filings, 319
fill, 177, 199, 210, 260, 426
fill the bill, 580
filling, 557
filly, 210
film, 192, 249
filter, 201
filth, 204, 269, 338
final, 186, 195, 243
finale, 381
finality, 195
finally, 239, 305, 451
finance, 223
find, 186, 455
findings, 319
fine, 27, 75, 186, 189, 306, 427, 428, 552
finger, 202, 212
fiord, 377
fir, 184, 231, 257
fire, 79, 186, 313
fireman, 161
firm, 105
firmament, 570
first, 184, 291, 294, 305, 427
first days, 59
first storey, 161
firstly, 305
fish, 90, 195, 362, 439, 442
fished, 208, 218
fishermen, 444
fishes, 440
fish-hatchery, 338
fishing-license, 252
fissure, 208, 399
fit, 74, 76, 82, 455
fitted, 238
Fitzgerald, 273
Fitzpatrick, 273, 374
five, 177, 194, 218
five by three cards, 14

fix, 177, 298
fixed, 201
fizz, 177, 334
flag, 377
flagellant, 202
flair, 102
flamingo, 381
flange, 174
flannel, 375
flannels, 548
flask, 82, 380, 404
flat, 376
flat tire, 30
flattery, 170
flat-topped, 243
flax, 418
flee, 460
fleece, 175
Flemish, 340
Fletcher, 273, 572
flibbertigibbet, 30
flied away, 47
flight, 337
flighty, 340
flimflam, 335
flimsy, 205
fling, 457
flipflop, 335
flirt, 111
flite, 232, 601
flitted, 243, 592
flivver, 57, 58, 203, 236, 238
flock, 270
floe, 377
floor, 180, 231, 258
flooring, 557
Flora, 399
floral, 399
Florence, 278
Florentine, 341
florid, 399, 404
Florida, 381
florin, 380
flounce, 188
flounder, 353, 377
flour, 188, 399, 406
flourish, 185, 210, 399
flow, 203, 215
flower, 399, 406
flowery, 404
flu, 58, 248, 355, 567
fluent, 341
fluke, 182
flume, 231, 258, 550
flurry, 353
flush, 353

Flushing, 208
flute, 397
fly, 295, 455
fly-by-night, 349
foal, 73, 82
foam, 403, 418
focus, 440
fodder, 400
foe, 180, 598
fœtus, 233
foible, 404
foil, 75, 82
foine (fine), 52, 187, 196
foist, 188
foliaceous, 341
folio, 181, 213, 248, 262
folk, 180, 195, 247, 270
folk etymology, 361
folk-lore, 252
follow, 169
follower, 213
folly, 74, 82, 169, 194
foment, 74, 82
fond, 566
font, 369, 405
food, 81, 182, 232, 400, 431, 601
fool, 73, 74, 75, 82, 169, 182, 194
foolish, 198, 340
foot, 184, 400, 440, 547, 549
foot up, 302
football, 253
footman, 439
foots, 47
for, 6, 179, 184, 193, 210, 298, 308, 321, 427, 478, 491, 542
for better or worse, 318
for crying out loud, 314
for example, 482
for instance, 482
for the sake of, 309, 572
for weal or woe, 571
for you and I, 518
forbear, 344
forbearance, 338, 344, 387
forbears, 431
forbid, 297
force, 442
forceps, 443
forcible, 105
Fordham, 275
foreclosure, 542
foregoing, 416

forehead, 169, 209, 220, 246
foreign, 169, 599
foreign to, 537
foremost, 294, 450
foreordination, 369
foresee, 342
forest, 169
foreword, 417
forfeit, 235, 599
forge, 201, 210, 216
forget-me-not, 348, 444, 491
forgive, 297, 342
forgive me, 313
forgo, 297
forlorn, 179
formality, 347
former, 294
formula, 440
forsake, 456
forsooth, 431
fort, 180, 181
forth, 204
forthcoming, 349
fortieth, 294
fortuitous, 183
fortune, 74, 82, 84, 217
forty, 269, 294, 400, 426
fossil, 341
foster, 400
foul, 75, 188, 234
foundation, 188, 190
foundry, 339
fount, 188, 405
fountaineer, 338
four, 180, 193, 291, 400
four by two, 14
fourteen, 400
fourth, 291, 340, 400
fourthly, 305
four-wheeled, 243
fowl, 188, 234, 550
fox, 199, 218, 337, 405
foxglove, 566
foxy, 547
foyer, 161, 373
frabjous, 332
fracas, 249
fraction, 399
fracture, 399
fragil (fragile), 245, 399, 404
fragment, 399
frail, 399, 404
frame, 203
framed, 60, 232

frame-up, 348
France, 170
Frances, 437
Francis, 274, 437
Franciscans, 280
Frank, 274, 406
Frankish, 279
Franklin, 278
frantic, 240
fraternal, 399
fraternity, 161, 399
fratricide, 399
fraud, 233
fraught with, 430, 537
frays, 410
Frazier (Fraser), 207
Fredonian, 279
free and easy, 228
freedom, 175, 269, 337
frees, 409, 410
freesia, 207, 369
freeze, 175, 205, 269, 409, 410, 455, 591, 598
freezing, 269
freight train, 161
French, 279, 406
French-Canadian, 349
frenzy, 211, 216, 240
fresco, 206, 381
fresh, 403
fret, 364, 400, 409
friar, 399, 403, 409
friction, 203
Friday, 273, 281
friend, 6, 172, 175, 194, 232, 234, 268, 319, 436, 597
friendlily, 490
friendly, 490
friendship, 269, 337
frier (fryer), 235, 268, 409
frieze, 175
fright, 29, 557
frigid, 241
frijole, 56
fringe, 241
Frisco, 355
frisk, 60
frisky, 403
fro, 40, 376, 403
frock, 553
frog, 169, 179
frolicsome, 340
from, 85, 308, 403, 427
from here, 323
from there, 535

from whence, 535, 539
front, 553
frost, 32, 180, **181**, 269
froth, 418
frothed, 216
frothy, 204
froward, 214
frown, 203, 215
frowsy, 234
froze, 180
fruice, 352
fry, 235
fryer, 409
fuchsia, 208, 237, 246, 371, 380, 396
fuel, 214
fugitive, 399
fugue, 399
fulfill (fulfil), 239, 251, 594
full, 74, 82, 83, 184, 199, 451
full-blown, 349
fulsome, 184
Fulton, 184
fun, 566
function, 212
fundamental, 369
fungus, 440
funnies, 337
funny, 251, 428
fur, 73, 82, 184
furniture, 250
furniture store, 348
further, 73, 75, 82, 405
furthermore, 307, **311**, 535
furthermost, 450
fury, 189
furze, 205, 210, 216
fuse, 189
fusible, 243
fusion, 339
fuss, 76, 82, 185
fustian, 384
futhorc, 352
futile, 187, 201
future, 190
futurity, 190
futyure (future), 201, 213

gab, 375
gadabout, 301
gadget, 552
gaffer, 53, 54
gage, 373, 405

gain, 379, 414
Gainaday, 283
gains, 205
gainsay, 52, 349, 431
gait, 376, 377, 403
gal. (gallon), 255
gala, 174
galantine, 39
gale, 174
gallant, 379, 406
galleon, 39
gallop, 379
gallop(p)ed, 239
gallows(es), 443
galore, 326, 375, 504
galumph, 332
gambol, 571
gamester, 268, 337
gammon, 66
gander, 438
Gandhiism, 339
gang, 270
gangster, 337
gantlet, 377
gaol, 121, 159, 174, 231, 403, 590
garage, 168, 207, 210, 223, 244, 373
garb, 210, 216
garden, 219, 379, 401
Gardner, 219
garlic, 350
garner, 399
garret, 173
garrison, 379
garth, 403
gas, 28, 44, 249, 332, 355
gasoline, 161, 176
gaspers, 162
gat, 31, 32
gate, 377, 403
gates ajar, 572
gather up, 301
gathering, 557
gauge, 121, 173, 231, 590
gauze, 358, 598
gavel, 262
Gawd, 170, 179
gay, 449   [591
gazelle, 210, 251, 259, 374,
gazette, 380, 597
gazetteer, 338, 561
gee, 314
gee whillikins, 314
gee whizz, 314
geese, 175, 242, 439
geisha, 173, 385

gelding, 240, 397
gem, 369
Gen. (General), 255
Gen. (Genesis), 255
gender, 577, 588
genealogy, 173
genera, 441
general, 200, 549, (cap.) 285
genesis, 400
genetic, 346
Geneva, 278
genius, 400, 442, 575
Genoese, 278, 294
genre, 373
gent, 355
genteel, 400, 406, 407, 565
gentile, 186, 400, 407
gentle, 372, 400, 406, 407, 556, 565
gentleman cow, 432
gentry, 270, 443
genuflexion, 241
genuine, 187, 417, 598
genus, 371, 400, 403, 441
geometry, 268
George, 210, 378
German, 279
german duck, 363
German-American, 349
germs, 567
gerrymander, 202, 352
get, 27, 115, 196, 240, 298, 299, 300, 376, 426, 427, 429, 456, 476, 546, 552
get ahead, 414
get down, 301
get off, 302
get on, 298, 416, 578
get over, 13, 297, 508
get rid of, 578
get up, 196
gether (gather), 173
geyser, 186, 187, 206, 234, 377
gherkin, 202, 598
ghost, 181, 202, 236, 246, 551, 598
ghoul, 182, 383, 598
giant, 186
giantess, 249, 437
gibberish, 202
giblets, 202, 443
Gibson, 377
giddap, 178, 316

gild, 199, 461
Giles, 200, 202
gill, 202
gilt-edged, 292
gimlet, 240
gimme (give me), 219
gin, 80, 83, 200, 590
ginger, 385
ginger ale, 387
gingham, 253, 385
Ginn, 202
ginned, 417
ginseng, 385
gipon, 39
giraffe, 251, 597
gird, 401, 461
girdle, 401, 403
girl, 184, 185, 189, 197, 438
girls, 47
girth, 401, 403
gist, 200, 215, 240, 258
git (get), 178
gite (light), 3, 46
gittin' (getting), 53, 54
give, 77, 83, 87, 94, 115, 177, 202, 232, 240, 298, 376, 426, 427, 456, 600
give in, 300, 301, 416
give up, 297, 575
give up the ghost, 572
glacier, 171
glad, 530, 556
gladden and delight, 415
gladiator, 52
gladiolus, 100, 225, 371, 440, 566
glads, 355
glamour, 174, 194
glare, 170, 171
glaring, 170, 171
glass, 173, 206, 362, 549, 597
glaucous, 249
glaze, 173, 206
glazier, 207, 237
gleams, 216
glee, 39
glen, 375
Glendale, 387
glimpse, 242
glisten, 247
glorious, 251, 565
glory, 179, 251, 339
gloss, 180

WORD INDEX

glove, 185, 234, 258
glow, 180, 202, 215
glue, 182, 250
glutinous, 36
glycerin (glycerine), 245, 594
gnat, 215
gnaw, 202, 211, 237, 246, 593
gnome, 211
gnu, 248, 384
go, 46, 79, 83, 87, 119, 202, 214, 219, 236, 240, 248, 258, 298, 299, 318, 426, 427, 453, 463, 476
go against the grain, 578
go for, 297
go off, 298, 416
go scot-free, 572
go the whole hog, 13
go to Halifax, 315
go to wrack and ruin, 580
go under, 297
go under the knife, 567
goal, 601
goatee, 268
God, 169, 179, 314
God Almighty, 503
goddess, 437
Godhead, 337
godlike, 292
godsib, 88
goes, 205, 218, 452
goil (girl), 189, 197
going, 237, 428, 560
goings-on, 348
goiter, 189
gold, 199, 318
gold brick, 547
gold-digger, 30, 547
golden, 292, 542
golden-haired, 349
golf, 210
golk, 333
gondola, 225
gong, 385
good, 183, 184, 264, 306, 313, 318, 427, 428, 442, 449
good afternoon, 316
good and bad, 14
good at, for, 537
good day, 316
good egg, 33
good evening, 316

good gosh, 313
good morning, 316
good night, 312, 316
Good Queen Bess, 287
good sport, 34
good-by (good-bye), 19, 26, 251, 316, 340, 350
good-bys, 444
gooder, 47
goodest, 47
goodly, 340
goodness, 268, 337
goodness gracious, 313
goods, 318, 357, 442, 557
goods train, 161
goofy, 28
Goold (Gould), 182
goose, 182, 362, 438
gooseberry, 218, 362
gopher, 382
gorilla, 384, 397
gory, 181
gosling, 205, 268
gospel, 350
gossamer, 350, 561
gossip, 18, 88, 350, 563, 572
got, 169, 526, 560
Goth, 279
Gothenburg, 277
Gothic, 169, 573
gotten, 458
gouge, 188
governess, 268, 437
government is, are, 495
governor, 340
grace, 206, 221, 244, 372, 442
gracefully, 306
graces, 442
gracious, 80, 208, 221, 244, 292
grade up, 300
gradient, 85
Grafonola, 282
Graham, 220, 246
grain, 399, 403
grammar, 8, 9, 10, 576
gramophone, 346
gramp, 354
granary, 211, 339, 399
grand, 428, 552, 559, 565
grandeur, 201, 235, 240
grandiose, 341
grandma, 48, 219
grandmother, 47
grands, 54, 55

grandson, 220
granny, 47, 337
Grant, 278
granular, 399
graph, 249, 253, 254, 264
graphic, 346
grass, 206, 218
grass-green, 306
grater, 410
gratis, 174, 371
gratitude, 340
grave, 170, 456, 556
gravel, 171
graven, 458
Graves, 273
graveyard, 431, 571
gravitate, 295
gravity, 170
gray, 248, 403, 422
gray hairs, 548
grayish, 340
graze, 206, 218
grazes, 452
greaser, 286
greasy, 206, 243
great, 174, 427, 552, 565
great big, 416
great guns, 313
great-aunt, 252
greatly, 306
greats, 54
greaves, 39
grebe, 175
green, 263, 548, 551, 562
Greenwich, 201, 214, 250, 275
Greenwood, 276, 277
grew, 457
grey, 22, 403, 422
grief, 372
grievance, 243
grievous, 243
grilling, 210
grilse, 242
grimace, 210
Grimalkin, 280
Grimsby, 276
grind, 412, 455
grinned, 412
grist, 574
grocer, 372, 554
grocery, 338
groceteria, 339
gross, 179, 180, 440, 597
grotesque, 181, 202, 341, 562, 597

WORD INDEX

grotesque English, 35
grotesqueries, 35
grotto, 562
ground, 566
Ground Gripper Shoes, 282
grounded in, upon, 537
group, 182, 231, 258, 270
grouse, 242, 270, 439
grovel, 169
grow, 47, 202, 215, 295, 414, 457
grow over, 612
growed, 16, 47, 457
growl, 334
grown-up, 301, 319
growth, 269, 414, 442, 557
Grub Street, 391
gruesome (grewsome), 259
gruffness, 239
guano, 381
guarantee, 373, 405, 599
guard, 167, 202, 236, 259, 268, 373, 379, 403, 590, 599
guard against, 536
guardian, 373, 405
guava, 202, 217, 240, 384
Guelph, 214
guerdon, 373
guerrilla, 381
guess, 100, 160, 426, 599
guessed, 412
guest, 100, 400, 412, 461
guide, 186, 373, 379, 401, 403, 599
Guido, 202
guild, 177, 599
guile, 373, 403
guilt, 177, 202
Guinevere (Gwinn, Guenevere), 83, 178, 202, 214
guise, 373, 401, 403
gull, 365, 409, 547
gunwale, 218, 350
guts, 565
gutta-percha, 385
guy, 57, 202, 320, 365, 409
Guy Fawkes, 365
guys, 245

Gwendolen, 202, 240
gym, 354
gymnasium, 441
gypsy, 384, 405, 597
gyrate, 200
gyroscope, 202
gyves, 200

ha, 312
habeas corpus, 58, 369
haberdashery, 338
habiliments, 97, 430
habit, 171
habits, 38
had better, 578
had rather, 13, 578
hades, 315
haggle, 202, 236
hail, 377, 400, 403
hain't, 54
hair, 170, 171
hairy, 173, 410
hale, 208, 237, 400, 403, 405, 430, 570, 600
hale and hearty, 415
half shot, 547
half-back, 347, 357
halibut, 400
halidom, 400
hall, 80, 116, 121, 178, 208, 400, 409
hallelujah, 209, 213, 237, 382
halloo, 316
hallowed, 213, 243
Halloween, 282, 400
Hallthwaite, 276
halo, 173, 245
halt, 178
halt and blind, 319
halter, 178
hamburger, 161, 358
hames, 210
hamlet, 211
Hamm, 249
hammer and tongs, 228
hammering, 211
hammock, 232, 249, 384
Hampton, 275
hand, 208, 547, 548, 549
handbook, 348, 349
handicraft, 337
handkerchief, 47, 246
handmades, 319
hand-me-downs, 349, 444
hands, 47

handsaw, 362
handsel, 246
handsome, 235, 242, 246, 450
hang, 212, 363, 457, 459
hang around, 295
hangar, 212
hanged, 359, 457
hangers-on, 301, 444
hangnail, 363
hanker after, 536
hanky, 47, 354
Hannah (Hanner), 220, 274
Hans, 274
Hants (Hampshire), 255
haound, 197
haow, 197
happen, 376, 416
happenstance, 352
happy, 170, 200, 236, 251, 325, 427, 449
har (hair), 169
harass, 223
harbinger, 211
hard, 167, 247, 306, 307, 427, 449, 530
Hard (Howard), 197
hard up, 292, 578
hard-boiled, 33, 547
harden, 341
hardly, 306, 534
hard-tack, 252
hardy, 379
hare, 171
harem, 383
harm, 210
harmonious, 430
harmony, 378
Harold Harefoot, 286
harp, 167, 397
Harriet, 213
Harry, 173, 410
harsh, 208, 216
hart, 78, 438
Hartford, 275
harum, 52
harum-scarum, 335
has, 249, 427
hash-slinger, 33
haste, 194
hat, 78, 121
hate, 80, 121, 295
Hate-Evil, 272
hateful, 574
hatred of, 537
hauberk, 39

WORD INDEX

haul, 233, 409
hautboy, 180, 231, 247
have, 86, 170, 203, 232, 295, 296, 321, 426, 427, 463, 521, 523, 597, 600
have and shall continue to, 513
have been to, 578
have got to, 526
have to, 218, 526
have to go, 578
haved showed, 4
haven't, 256
havoc, 364, 409
hawg, 170
Hawkeye State, 286
hawss (horse), 179, 196
hay, 213
Haymarket, 174
haymow, 187
haywire, 556
hazel, 174, 205
he, 11, 66, 85, 175, 288, 289, 328, 427, 447
he don't, 498
he himself, 515
head, 51, 400, 440, 442, 547, 548, 549, 597
headlong, 306, 342, 400
headquarters, 443
headstrong, 349
heal, 400
health, 234, 400, 597
healthful, 574
healthy, 574
heap, 175
hear, 247, 435, 460
heard, 83
hearken, 167
hearse, 184, 185
heart, 87, 167, 231, 548, 555, 597
heart-breaking, 349
hearth, 168
heat, 78
heat up, 297
heatedly, 306
heater, 175
heath, 172, 194, 204
heathen, 495
heather, 172, 194
heave, 242, 456
heaven, 79, 83, 172
heavenly, 560
heavy, 172, 203, 597
Hebron, 277

hectic, 429
hector, 320, 358
he'd, 256
hedge, 241
heebie jeebies, 335, 337, 444
heedless of, 537
heel in, 572
hegira, 383
he-goat, 437, 558
heifer, 172, 233, 234
heigh (hey), 312, 316
heigho, 312
height, 186, 234
heighten, 414
heir, 171, 209, 231
heir apparent, 503
heiress, 437
heirloom, 387
held, 43
held up, 33
Helen, 378
Helen Maria, 315
Helga, 202, 210
helianthus, 566
heliotrope, 347, 378, 566
he'll, 256
hell, 210, 314, 400, 564
hellion, 213
hello (hullo, halloo), 312, 316
hellophone, 352
helm, 400
helmet, 40, 400
help, 200, 210, 216, 312, 313, 513, 531, 557, 574
help meet, 333
helped, 200
helter-skelter, 335
hemisphere, 344
hemorrhage, 172, 210, 246, 599
hen, 400, 401, 438
hence, 306, 311
Henrietta, 437
Henry (Henery), 35, 437
her, 73, 105, 121, 184, 192, 293, 447
her intended, 319
herb, 209
herbaceous, 208
herculean, 358, 554
herd, 495
herdsman, 348
here, 305, 323, 427, 535
hereafter, 347
hereby, 535

heriot, 213
heritage, 372
hern, 293, 447, 517
hero, 175, 225
heroes, 245, 262
heroine, 225, 339, 437
heron, 379
hero-worship, 252
hers, 293, 447
herself, 289, 448
he's, 256
hesitancy, 338
heterogeneous, 344
hew, 182, 189, 208, 457
Hewlett, 209
hexameter, 378
hiatus, 88
hiccup (hiccough), 200, 202, 236, 259, 362, 599
hickory, 160, 384, 396
hidden, 177
hide, 177, 409, 417, 457
hideous, 217
hidjous (hideous), 217
hie, 235, 248
higgledy-piggledy, 335
high, 292, 321, 427
high and dry, 580
high jinx, 241
high-toned, 347
highway, 347
Hi-Heat Coal, 283
hill, 78, 268
hill and valley, 228
hillbilly, 359
hillock, 268, 337
hilly, 340
him, 11, 25, 66, 177, 427, 447
him's book, 47
himself, 25, 289, 448, 474, 477
hinder, 177
hindmost, 294, 450
hindrance, 338, 417
Hindu, 183
hinge, 547
hint at, 536
hippity-hop, 335
hireling, 337, 562
his, 205, 208, 289, 293, 426, 447, 504
His Grace, 557
His Holiness, 557
his showing, 514
hisn, 293, 447, 517

WORD INDEX

hisself, 289, 448
historical, 355
history (historie), 251, 339, 405
hit, 376, 454, 462
hit (it), 54
hitch, 250
hither, 305
hither and yon, 578
hitherto, 305
Hitlerites, 280
hit-runner, 44
hits, 206
hitting the hay, 31
Hittite, 279
hive, 243
hoard, 180, 563
hoarse, 250
hoary, 181
hoax, 28, 180
hobble, 200, 236
hobnob, 335
hobo, 180, 245
Hobson Jobson, 57
hock (hough), 202, 236, 259
hocus pocus, 335
hodgepodge, 335
hoe, 219, 598
hoedown, 348
hoeing, 219
hoes, 410
hog, 169, 179, 425, 547
hogshead, 549
hoist, 379
hoit (hurt), 189
hoity-toity, 189, 335
Hokies, 352
hokum, 417, 429
hold, 33, 83, 106, 208, 295, 298, 408, 457, 546
hold out, 578
hold up, 119, 297, 301, 326, 348, 578
hole, 78
holiday, 281, 350, 400
Hollander, 337
holler (hollo), 220
hollow, 169
hollyhock, 400
Holmes, 180
holster, 210
holy, 181, 262, 400
holy smoke, 313
homage, 374
home, 180, 198, 210, 323, 511

home-comings, 444
homeless, 340
homelike, 340
homely, 490, 557
homeopath, 347
homeopathy, 379
homer, 28, (cap.) 378
homestead, 347
homicide, 373
hominy, 384
homonym, 181, 245, 344, 577, 588
homophonous, 261
honest, 209, 246
Honest Abe, 287
honey, 185
honied, 191
honk, 334
honor (honour), 78, 159, 269, 442, 599
Honorable, 284
honorarium, 209
honorary, 169
honors, 442
hood, 161, 184
hoodoo, 182, 335, 384
hooey, 417
hoohoo, 312
hook, 162, 183, 184
hookup, 566
hoop, 183
hoop skirt, 40, 571
Hooper, 183
hoosegow, 60
Hoosier State, 286
hoot, 208
Hooverize, 341, 358
hope, 426, 531, 592, (cap.) 272
hoped, 600
hopeless, 340, 451
hop-head, 32, 60
hopped, 243
hoppergrass, 35
hops, 206
horehound, 362
horn, 400
hornet, 400
horoscope, 567
horrible, 242
horribly, 306, 534, 566
horrid, 169, 428, 556
horrors, 312, 313
hors d'œuvre, 374
horse, 11, 13, 179, 196, 268, 438, 440
Horseheads, 286

horse-radish, 11
horses, 11, 195, 205, 439
horsie, 47
hortatory, 341
horticulture, 401
hose, 410
hospitable, 225, 400
hospital, 169, 400, 407
host, 181, 400
hostel, 373, 400, 404, 407
hostess, 437
hostile, 187, 400
hostility, 400
hot, 80, 156, 169, 180
hot air, 417
hot dog, 315, 380
hotel, 374, 400, 404, 407
hound, 188, 362
hour, 188, 209
houri, 248, 383
Housatonic, 183
house, 82, 188, 205, 234, 258, 261, 268, 446, 447
house dog, 348
household, 209
houses, 243, 439, 446
Houston, 183
hovel, 169, 235, 242
how, 187, 214, 234, 248, 306, 310, 311, 534, 540
how are you, 316
how goes it, 316
how much, 306
Howard, 188, 197, 214
howdah, 209
howdy, 316
Howe, 187, 234
however, 307, 310, 311, 505, 535
howitzer, 384
howl, 188
hoyden, 189, 253
hubbub, 335
huckster, 337
hue, 182, 189
hue and cry, 572
huge, 209
Hugh, 182, 209
hulk, 185
hullabaloo, 34
hulled, 574
hum, 185, 210, 334
human, 209, 341, 406
humane, 406
humanism, 577

humanize (humanise), 159
humble, 209, 211, 363, 416
humble pie, 363
humbug, 417
humdinger, 30, 34, 565
humid, 189, 341
humiliate, 209
hummed, 211, 216
humming, 4, 262
hummock, 210, 337
humor, 148, 189, 209, 213, 217, 237, 555
humors, 567
humph, 312
hunch, 406
hunderd (hundred), 220
hundred, 185, 440
hundredfold, 294
hundredweight, 440
hung, 359, 457
hunger, 212, 269
hungry, 202
hunk, 406
hunky-dory, 340
Hupmobile, 352
hurdle, 268
hurdy-gurdy, 335
hurrah, 209
hurricane, 384
hurried, 191
hurries, 246
hurry, 73, 185
hurry up, 313
hurt, 105, 185, 189, 462
hurted, 462
husband, 205, 350, 376, 438, 572
hush, 185, 312
hush up, 302
hussy, 206, 350, 563
hydrangea, 170
hydraulic, 378
Hydrox, 282
hymn, 177, 211, 219
hymnal, 211, 219
hyperbole, 378
hypersensitive, 344
hypnosis, 340
hypocrite, 563
hypotenuse, 378, 401
hypothesis, 441

I, 46, 289, 422, 426, 427, 447
I declare, 313

I get you, 556
I says, 498
I thinks, 51
I want to know, 313
Ian, 274
ibis, 384
Ibsen, 548
ice cream, 160
icee, 67
Icelandic, 132
iciest, 251
icy, 243
idea, 186, 401
idear (idea), 220
identical, 294
identical with, 537
idiom, 177, 577
idiom of English, 578
idiot, 201, 217, 563
Idlewild, 281
idol, 186, 401
idyl (idyll), 186, 235, 249, 251, 259
i.e. (id est), 482
iern (iron), 220
if, 85, 177, 249, 310, 464, 493, 494, 540
if . . . then, 541
ignoramus, 174
ignore, 400
ikon, 384
il n'y a plus, 35
ile (oil), 52, 53, 196
ill, 161, 376, 450
I'll, 522
I'll be blamed, 315
I'll be blowed, 315
illegitimate, 343
ill-tempered, 387
illuminate, 343, 416
illumine, 416
illusions, 419
illustrate, 223
Illustrated, 319
illy, 305
I'm, 186
Imarket (Haymarket), 174
imbibe, 343
immediate, 217
immediately, 213, 307, 311
immejut (immediate), 201, 217
immure, 182
impede, 400
imperative, 464

impertinent, 563
impliable, 105
imply, 4
impossible, 343
impress, 223
improve, 414
improvement, 414
impugn, 211
in, 43, 85, 119, 249, 298, 305, 308, 321, 427, 429, 450, 504, 539
in accordance with, 309, 490
in addition to, 309
in back of, 309
in by, 308
in cahoots, 578
in case of, 309
in case that, 310
in charge of, 574
in common parlance, 572
in compliance with, 309
in consideration of, 309
in days of yore, 572
in fine fettle, 571
in front of, 309
in here, 535
in high, 318
in high dudgeon, 572
in lieu of, 309
in like manner, 311
in opposition to, 309
in order that, 310
in other words, 311, 482
in regards to, 4
in short, 311
in spite of, 309
in stir, 60
in terms of, 309
in the event that, 310, 491
in the stead of, 325
in view of, 325
inapt, 405
inasmuch as, 310, 491
inborn, 344
Inca, 384
incessancy, 345
incessant, 345
incessantly, 345
inch, 405
Inchcape, 275
Inchcolm, 275
inchoative, 198
incidental, 227
inclination for, to, 537
incline, 556

including, 308
incog, 355
incognito, 400
income, 301, 342
incomparable, 225
increase, 211, 216, 295, 414, 415
increment, 414
inculcate, 556
indeed, 307, 311, 326, 399
indenture (indentyure), 201
Independence Day, 282
index, 100, 401, 441, 442
Indian, 217
Indian summer, 160
Indians, 280
indicate, 401
indicative, 464
indict, 246, 401
indigo, 383
indisputable, 225
individual, 554
individually, 305
Indo-European, 349
induct, 297
inductile, 105
indulge in, 482
inelastic, 105
inept, 405
inertia, 371
inexplicable, 225
infallible, 343
infanta, 390
infantile, 187, 242
infantry, 443
infection, 58, 567
infer, 4
inference, 211
inferior, 450
infinite, 451
infirm, 319
inflate, 414
inflation, 414
inflect, 221
inflection (inflexion), 11, 203, 221, 241, 259
inflexible, 105
influence, 380, 404
influenza, 380, 404, 567
inhabit, 209
inhale, 209
initial, 177
Injun (Indian), 201
injure, 201
ink, 177

inn, 211, 249
innards (inwards), 219
innocent, 566
innocents, 318
inny (any), 178
inopposable, 105
inquest, 212
inquiry, 211, 223
ins, 357
insane, 563
inside, 309
insidious, 400
insignia, 442
insinuendo, 352
inspire, 343
inspirit, 430
instalment (installment), 239
instead, 325
instigate, 401
instill, 251
instinct, 224
institution, 227, 552
insular, 370
insulate, 404
insult, 223, 228
intake, 301
intelligentsia, 270, 384, 443
intended, 319
intense, 250
intensify, 414
intensity, 244
intercede, 345
intercedingly, 345
intercession, 345
intercessor, 345
intercessory, 345
interest in, 537
interior, 213, 450
interjection, 266
interloper, 386
International (Internationale), 384
interrupt, 416
interstate, 343
intervene, 175
interwoven, 386
intestate, 430
into, 308, 539
intoxicated, 431
intramural, 343
intrigue, 429
introduce, 343
introductory, 341
introvert, 347, 566
invalid, 224, 359

inveigle, 176, 599
invent, 6
Inverary, 275
inverecund, 333
Inverness, 275, 375
invitation, 569
invite, 121, 223
invoice, 189
Iowa City, 276
Iowans, 279
ipecac, 384
iris, 358
Irish, 279
Irish apricots, 363
irk, 202
irksome, 210
iron, 442
Iron Duke, 287
iron-gray, 349
ironing, 393, 557
irradiate, 343
irresponsible, 343
is, 47, 205, 249, 296, 427
is to be, 578
Isabel, 205
isinglass, 362, 379
island, 186, 247, 260, 361, 599
isle, 186, 362, 571, 599
isn't, 256
isolate, 22, 187, 197, 380, 404
Israelite, 279
issue, 189, 208, 237
isthmus, 247
it, 85, 266, 289, 290, 296, 326, 427, 447, 477, 496, 502, 579
it blows, 296
it hails, 296
it snows, 296
it thunders, 296
it was me, 516
Italian, 279
italic, 358
item, 186
Ithaca, 277
It'lldo, 281
its, 293, 447
it's, 256
it's me, 16, 476, 516
itself, 289, 448
Ivan. 274
I've, 26, 186, 256

jabberwocky, 332
jack, 382, (cap.) 287

WORD INDEX

Jack the Ripper, 503
jackasses, 286
Jackie, 287
jack-o'-lantern, 349
Jacob, 382
Jacobite, 280, 294
Jacques, 287
jade, 250
jaguar, 259
jail (gaol), 159, 201, 240, 403
James, 274
James's, 254
janizarie, 390
January, 281
Jap, 355
Japanese, 238, 279, 341
japanned, 238
jargon, 62, 576
jasmine, 383
jaunty, 407
javelin, 375
jay, 547
Jayhawker State, 286
jazz, 205
Jazzmusik, 111
jealous, 82, 201, 404
Jean, 274, 407
jeans, 176
jeer, 217
jeeze, 314
Jefferson, 278
Jehovah, 382
jehu, 320
jell, 172, 356
jellibees, 333
jelly, 356
Jennings, 274
jeopardy, 172
jeremiad, 358
Jerusalem, 314
Jerusalem artichoke, 573
Jerusalem the Golden, 503
Jesuit, 382
Jesus, 314
Jew, 182, 382
jewelry (jewellery), 268, 339
Jewess, 437
Jew's-harp, 363
jezebel, 358
jib, 379
jibe, 186, 200
jill, 80
Jim, 285

jiminy Christmas, 314
jimjams, 335, 444
jine (join), 186
jinks, 212, 241
jinricksha (jinrikisha), 385
jitney, 18
jitters, 444
jiu-jitsu (jujitsu), 385
Jo, 248
Joanna, 437
Joannes Duns Scotus, 357
Jock, 287
jockey, 359
John, 246, 255, 272, 274, 407, 437, 486
John Bull, 286
John o' Lincoln, 220
John Smith, 272
John Watkins, 273
Johnnie (Johnny), 251, 287, 337
Johnson, 273, 274
Johnsonese, 341
join, 186, 188, 401
join up, 300
joint, 188, 373
jointly, 305
joist, 188
jollity, 416
jollyup, 348
Jones, 274
Josephine, 339, 437
joss, 381, (cap.) 67
joss house, 387
jostle, 180, 201, 206
jot down, 300
journal, 562
journalese, 338, 341, 374
journey, 80, 251, 561, 599
joust, 39, 183, 571
jovial, 294, 357, 554
jowl, 188
joy, 188, 248
Jr., 255
jubilee, 382
Judd, 200
judge, 83, 185, 201, 215, 242, 250, 257, 372, 401, (cap.) 284
judged, 243
judges, 243
judgment (judgement), 58, 244, 254, 340
judicial, 369

Judith, 271
jug, 160
juggernaut, 383
jugular, 401
juice, 182, 551
Julesburg, 276
July, 281
jump, 44
jumping Jehoshaphat, 315
junction, 401
juncture, 401
June, 183, 281
jungle, 60
junior, 450, (cap.) 287
junk, 381
junket, 561
junta, 401
jury, 183, 184, 270, 372
just, 427, 450, 505
just as lief, 40, 572
just as soon, 578
justice, 242, 339, 372, (cap.) 558
justification, 430
juvenile, 157, 178, 187, 250, 341, 591
juxtaposition, 343

kag (keg), 57, 196
kah-kah, 64
kaikai, 66
kaiser, 437
kaiserin, 437
kale, 60, 405
kangaroo, 152, 385, 397
Kansas City, 280
Kantleek, 283
Kardex, 282
Katy Line, 352
Kazoo, 355
keen, 29, 32, 400, 428, 552, 554, 559, 565
keenly, 306
keep, 460
keep out, 300
keep up, 119
keeper, 236
keg, 172, 202, 377
ken, 400, 572
Ken-L-Ration (Kennel Ration), 255, 283
Kennesaw, 179
Kentucky, 277, 384
kerchief, 39, 400, 571
kernel, 210, 337, 399
kerosene, 160

WORD INDEX

ketch (catch), 173, 196
ketchup, 385, 397
kettle, 178, 369, 548
key, 80, 175, 231, 248, 547
Keystone State, 286
khaki, 168, 202, 236, 248
kibitzer, 57
kick, 33
kick-off, 18, 348
kid, 377
Kiddie-Kar, 282
Kildare, 275, 375
Kilkenny, 275
kill, 77, 83, 87, 202, 236, 406, 418, 461
killjoy, 348
kiln, 210, 237, 247
kilometer, 225
Kilpatrick, 275
kilt, 461
kimono, 385, 397
kin, 202, 400, 403
kind, 177, 186, 220, 400, 499
kind of, 306, 578
kindergarten, 102, 380
kindle, 177
kindlily, 490
kindly, 449, 490
kindred, 177, 270, 400, 443
kine, 439, 442
king, 438
Kingsthorpe, 276, 376
kink (king), 57
kinsman, 348
kirk, 377, 405
kirtle, 377, 400
kitchen, 126, 201, 240, 369
kitchenette, 339
kith, 400
kith and kin, 415
kitten, 337
kittle (kettle), 178
kitty, 47, 48, 337
kitty-cat, 335
Kleenex, 282
knack, 211
knapsack, 379
knave, 563
knee, 211, 215, 237, 246, 593
kneel, 460
knell, 551
knew, 183, 410, 457
knickerbocker, 358
knickers, 355, (cap.) 111

knickknack, 335
knife, 35, 186
knight, 561, 564
knight errant, 503, 555
Knight of Columbus, 280
knighthood, 337
knights errant, 100, 444
Knights Templars, 444
knit, 462
knock, 566
knock-out, 30, 348
knoll all, 4
Knott, 249
knout, 384
know, 47, 156, 180, 212, 214, 400, 409, 427, 457, 593
knowed, 47, 457
knowing, 79
knowingness, 337
knowledge, 400
known, 233
Know-Nothing, 280, 348
kodak, 77, 283, 332, 359
kohlrabi, 396
kopje, 380
Koran, 383
kosher, 382
kowtow, 385
kraal, 168, 232, 380
kraut, 187, 234
kumquat, 385

la, 312
lab, 354
label, 403
labor, 174, 209, 372, 599
laboratory, 157
laborious, 209
labyrinth, 204
lacked, 201
laconic, 358
lacquer, 202, 236, 374
lad, 376, 438
Ladd, 249
lade, 456
ladle, 337
lady, 174, 186, 197, 350, 372, 438, 564, (cap.) 283
Lafayette, 374
lain (rain), 67
laissez faire, 373
laith, 405
La Jolla, 56
La Junta, 56, 277
lallapaloosa, 30, 565

lamb, 210, 220, 237, 251, 598
lambkin, 268, 337
lamentable, 430
Lammas, 350
Lancaster, 126, 275
Lancs (Lancashire), 255
land, 94, 120, 210, 237
landlord, 437
landscape, 379
language, 7, 212, 338
languid, 202, 214
languish, 414
languor, 212
lantern, 211
lap, 547
lapel, 403
lapis lazuli, 171
lapped, 201
lapse, 170, 200, 206
large, 324, 449, 557
largess, 557
lariat, 381
larn (learn), 168, 192
Larsen, 273, 377
larva, 440
larynges, 441
larynx, 441
La Salle, 276, 373
lashed, 208
lass, 376, 438
last, 216, 294, 324, 427, 450
Lasuen, 207
latches, 243
late, 305, 306, 449
lately, 305
later, 87, 406, 550
latest, 294
lath, 170
lathe, 173, 204, 243
laths, 204
Latin, 573
latish, 340
latitude, 370
latter, 294, 406, 450, 550
laud, 179, 410
laugh, 170, 203, 237, 251, 259, 260, 597
laugh about, at, over, 482, 536, 537, 538
laughed, 201, 203
laughter, 168
launch, 179, 385
launderer, 393
laundress, 339, 431, 437
laundry, 393

WORD INDEX

Laura, 180, 234
Laurabel, 272
laurels, 548
Laurentian, 190
lava, 168
lave (leave), 52, 174
law, 121, 179, 214, 312, 376
law sakes, 314
lawdy, 314
lawn-mower, 349
lawr (law), 220
lawsy, 312
lawyer, 213, 268, 338
lax, 170
lay, 298, 299, 300, 346, 375, 406, 426, 429, 459
lay away, 302
lay by, 297, 508
lay out, 570
layman, 553
layout, 44
lazar, 358, 382
laze, 356
laziness, 251
lazy, 205, 356
lb. (*libra*, pound), 255
lead, 106, 409, 461, 546
lead off, 302
leaden, 238
leader, 238
leaf, 175, 203, 240
leaflet, 339
league, 175, 202, 598
leal, 210, 407, 550
lean, 460
lean-to, 357
leaped, 173, 238
learn, 184, 461, 575
learned, 408
learning-youth, 330
lease, 206
leased, 412
least, 175, 412, 461
leather, 172, 204
leatherette, 245, 339
leave, 100, 174, 176, 203, 460, 598
leave in the lurch, 571
leaven, 219, 234
leavening, 219
leaves, 203
leavings, 55)
lecture, 203, 216
led, 454
leech, 561
left, 203

leftovers, 301, 319, 348
leg, 376, 377
legal, 407, 550
legend, 173, 176, 574
legs, 431
Lehigh, 209
lei, 385
Leicester, 351
leisure, 173, 176, 207, 258
lemme (let me), 219
lemon, 232, 383
lemonade, 173, 338
lemon-yellow, 349
lend, 461
length, 204, 212
lengthwise, 306, 342
leniency, 213
lent, 239
Leo, 198, 384
Leonard, 172
Leonid, 379
leopard, 172, 234
less, 248, 306, 597
lessee, 268, 338
lessen, 409, 414
lessening, 414
lesser, 206
lesson, 409
lest, 54, 220, 310, 540
let, 295, 298, 364, 409, 427, 430, 462
let sleeping dogs lie, 580
lethal, 175
let's, 256, 528, 530, 560
letter, 427
letters patent, 100
lettuce, 235, 594
level, 172, 203, 594
level stress, 227
level(l)er, 239
lever, 172, 173, 238
leviathan, 382
levies, 191
Lewanna, 353
lewd, 563
lexicographer, 391
lexicon, 378
liable for, to, 530, 537
liar, 186, 235, 250, 337
libel, 338
Liberty, 257, 278, 558
library, 46, 220
libretto, 441
lice, 439
lichen, 186, 202

licked, 203
lidy (lady), 174, 186
lie, 186, 235, 244, 248, 295, 406, 456, 476
lied, 235
lief, 40, 572
lieu, 183, 231, 234
lieutenant, 157, (cap.) 285
life, 203, 218, 240
lift, 160
lifts, 452
ligature, 340
light, 3, 46, 83, 461
light out, 578
light up, 301
lighten, 219
lighter, 379
light-fingered, 431
lightning, 219
like, 186, 189, 308, 322, 432, 450, 482, 542
likely, 307, 416
likeness, 244
likewise, 306, 307, 311, 321
lilac, 383, 396
Lilliputian, 333
lily, 210, 272, 369, 396
limb, 177, 211, 246, 251, 598
limbs, 431
limequat, 352
limes, 211
limn, 247
limned, 211
Limpy, 287
Lincoln, 211, 237, 278, 351
linden, 177
line, 195
line up, 298
lineage, 195, 244
lineal, 244
linen, 418
lingo, 44, 62
lingua, 7
lingua franca, 63
linguist, 212
linoleum, 283, (cap.) 282
linotype, 349
lint, 177
lion, 369, 384, 397, 547
lioness, 437
lips, 80, 200, 215
liquid, 203

WORD INDEX

liquor, 202, 236, 374, 551
lisp, 207
listen, 88, 201, 206
listerine, 283, 359
lit, 417
literary, 158
lithe, 186
lithograph, 346
little, 177, 292, 306, 427, 449, 450
little shaver, 365
little tiny, 416
live, 203, 218, 232, 300, 597, 600
live down, 300
livelong, 430
lively, 340, 450
liver, 177, 409
livery stable, 571
lives, 203, 240, 243, 452
lizard, 205
Lizzie, 287
llama, 384
Lloyd, 188, 210, 235
lo, 180, 248, 312
load, 180, 231, 406
loaf, 180, 203, 218
loafer, 161
loan, 180
loan-words, 350
loath, 405, 477
loathe, 180, 261
loaves, 203, 218
lobby, 59, 160, 161, 404
local, 225
locate, 169
locative, 169, 225
loch, 375
lock up, 300
locked, 243, 592
locker, 232, 268
locks, 202, 215, 217, 240
locoed, 556
locution, 7
lode, 58, 180, 200, 406
lodge, 83, 404
lodgings, 557
lodgment, 244
log, 169, 179, 377
logic, 347, 355
logrolling, 59, 162
loike (like), 187
loiter, 189
London, 235, 275
Londoner, 280
lone, 83, 180

loneliness, 249
lonely, 244, 340, 450
lonesome, 340
long, 83, 179, 212, 449
long. (longitude), 255
long green, 548
Long Islander, 280
long shot, 59
long-drawn-out, 292, 301
longer, 259
long-legged, 243
long-lost, 349
look, 184, 298, 299, 300, 313, 476, 575
look out, 26, 297, 302, 313, 326
look up, 300, 301
lookers-on, 444
loom, 210
loopy, 162
loose, 376
looses, 37
loot, 383
loquat, 385
lor, 314
lord, 179, 180, 350, 410, 438, 564, (cap.) 283
lordling, 268
lore, 210
lorgnette, 211, 213, 245
lorry, 161
Los Angeles, 56
lose, 182, 205, 206, 460, 592
losed, 47
loss, 180, 206, 597
lost, 180, 181, 460
lot, 28, 156, 169, 180
Lothario, 320
lots, 80, 201, 215
loud, 187, 215, 306, 449
loudly, 306
Louisiana, 276
Louisville, 276
lounge, 188
lout, 187
love, 185, 232
love apple, 15
loved, 216
lover, 181, 185
low, 180, 321, 376
lower, 188, 414
Lowestoft, 276, 376
lowly, 416
loyal, 407, 550
Ltd. (Limited), 255

lud, 314
luggage, 160
Luke, 182
lukewarm, 572
lulu, 32
lunar, 183
lunatic, 82, 183, 210, 318, 556
lunch, 353
lunch time, 225
luncheon, 245
Lupus, 272
lurch, 405
lurid, 184, 429
lurk, 405
luscious, 208, 237
Lusitania, 183, 280
lust, 563
lustrous, 249
lute, 190, 397
Lutheran, 280
lutulent, 333
luxurious, 207, 258
luxury, 208, 258
lydite, 340
lye, 186, 234
lying, 244
lymph, 203
lynch, 359
lyric, 177, 575
lyrical, 341
lyricist, 177

macadam, 257, 358
macadamized, 388
macaroni, 380, 397, 406
macaroon, 406
machine, 80, 175, 208, 231, 257, 373
Mackay, 273
mackerel, 439
mackinaw, 397
mackintosh, 358, 375
Macmillan, 273
madam, 283, 285, 438, 441
madame, 404
made, 173
Madeira, 381
Mademoiselle, 283
madonna, 404
maelstrom, 121, 174, 231
magazine, 82, 176, 383
magic, 358, 383
magnesia, 358
magneto, 58
magnificent, 565

magnify, 414
magnolia, 369, 371
magnum opus, 371
mah-jongg, 385
mahogany, 384, 397
mahout, 149
maiden, 337
maidservants, 444
main, 121, 174, 231, 233, 258, 430, 601
maintain, 224, 236
maintenance, 224, 236
maize, 384
majesty, 201
major, 404, 450, 549, (cap.) 285
make, 173, 298, 299, 426, 427, 479
make love, 6
make no bones of, 13
make the welkin ring, 572
make up, 299, 346
makeshift, 348
make-up, 348
malapropism, 358
Malay, 173
male, 404
male cousin, 437
malign, 219
malignant, 219
Malkin, 280
mallet, 210, 237
mallow, 369
malpractice, 343
malt, 178
mamma, 47, 334
mammon, 382
mammoth, 384
mammy, 160
man, 4, 90, 170, 268, 288, 372, 438, 446, 447
man goeth, 41
mandarin, 383
mandate, 339
mandolin, 404
mane (mean), 174
man-eaters, 444
maneuver (manœuvre), 182, 231, 596
mange, 174
mango, 385
manhood, 269, 337
mania for, 537
manifold, 294
manikin, 337

Manitoba, 277
manlike, 340
manly, 565
manners, 557
man-of-war, 349
manor, 174
mans, 4, 47
manservant, 437
mantle, 372, 547
manuscript, 562
many, 172, 178, 210, 234, 254, 257, 291, 294, 320, 449, 450
manzanita, 381
map out, 570
mar, 167
march, 403, (cap.) 281
marconigram, 387
Mardi Gras, 282
mare, 438
Margaret, 378
marigold, 387, 396, 566
mark, 210, 216, 403
market, 43
marline, 379
marmalade, 102
marplot, 348
marquee, 356
Marquis, 284
marry, 173, 410
Marryat, 213
marshal, 210, 249, 350, 564, 572
Marshall, 249
martinet, 358
martyr, 167, 210, 378
martyrdom, 387
marvelous, 428
Marx, 210
Mary, 66, 170, 171, 174, 412
Marylanders, 279
masculine, 178, 187, 250, 404
maskee, 67
mason, 257, 372, 573, (cap.) 280, 573
Masonite, 282
mass, 369, 409, 548, 561
massacre, 105, 242
master, 168, 405, 438, (cap.) 283
Master of Arts, 284
mater, 403
maternal, 400
mathematics, 268, 443, (cap.) 558

matins, 59
matriculation, 542
matrimony, 340
matrix, 400
matron, 400
Matt. (Matthew), 255
matter, 552
Matthew, 271
mattock, 125
maudlin, 320, 382, 554
maverick, 359
mavourneen, 53, 375
Max, 170
maximum, 450
may, 83, 295, 453, 463, 521, 524, 529, 530, 579, (cap.) 281
Mayhen, 353
mayor, 404, 564
Mazola, 282
mazurka, 384
McAdam, 257
McDonald, 255
McDowell, 188
McFarland, 273
McGinnis, 273
McLean (McLain, McLane), 174, 274
McVeagh (McVey), 274
me, 47, 66, 422, 427, 432, 447, 477
me (my), 52
ME. (Middle English), 255
mead, 406
meadow, 406
mean, 96, 174, 210, 460
meander, 358
means, 443, 552
meant, 178, 239
measles, 443, 495
measure, 77, 80, 235, 300
measure out, 300
meat, 80, 551
meat and drink, 548
mechanic, 339, 597
meddle with, 482
media, 441
medico, 44
medieval (mediæval), 159, 198, 233, 258, 260, 596, 599
medium, 213, 441, 551, 557
medjum (medium), 201
meed, 571

WORD INDEX

meek, 175, 376
meek and lowly, 415
meerschaum, 208, 380
meet, 416, 460, 592
meetinghouse, 15, 59
megaphone, 347
melancholic, 567
melancholy, 569
Melican, 67
mellow, 449
melt, 455
melt away, 414
melted, 458
member, 172
memoir, 214
memoranda, 442
memorandum, 100, 371, 441
Memorial Day, 282
memory, 251
men, 171, 178, 288, 439, 446
menagerie, 338
mend, 403
Mennonite, 280
men-of-war, 444
menservants, 444
mental, 369
mention, 172
mercurial, 148, 358
mercury, 358
mercy, 372
meridian, 370
meringue, 245
meritorious, 173
merrier, 210
merry, 173, 410, 412
mesdames, 441
meseems, 41
mesh, 208
mesmerism, 380
mesmerize, 341, 358, 554
mesquite, 381
Messiah, 382
messieurs, 441
metal, 172, 406, 411, 412, 422
metaphor, 172
metastasis, 401
meter (metre), 80, 100, 172, 221, 236, 242, 259, 260, 599
metes, 430
metes and bounds, 415, 572
methinks, 296

method, 204
Methodist, 280
meticulous, 429
metrical, 172
metronome, 347
mettle, 406, 411, 412, 422
mews, 443
Mexicali, 278
Mexican, 279
mice, 439
Michaelmas, 282
Michigander, 353
Mick, 286
mickle, 405
microphone, 347, 566
Middleton, 275
Mid-Victorian, 294
mien, 571
might, 521, 529
might and main, 415
mighty, 560
mignonette, 213, 217, 245, 259, 374, 396
mikado, 385
mike, 354, 566
milage (mileage), 243, 338
Milanese, 280
mild, 412
mile, 186, 268, 368, 440, 549
militia, 270, 443
milk, 202
mill, 58, 369
milled, 412
millennium, 441
Miller, 272, 274
million, 177, 210, 213, 217, 269, 440
millwright, 347
mimic, 210
min (men), 52, 178
mind, 186, 189
mine, 293, 409, 447, 477
mine eyes, 447
mine host, 447
miniature, 177, 561
minimum, 450
minion, 213
minister, 564
minnesinger, 380
Minnesotans, 279
minnow, 443
minny (many), 178
minor, 450
minster, 369, 378, 404

mint, 210, 369
mint (meant), 178, 193
minute, 75, 76, 82, 224, 427
minutia, 440
minx, 212
miracle, 178, 330, 338, 372
mirage, 168, 207
Mirage Flats, 277
mirth, 416
misapprehension, 430
mischievous, 223, 225
miscreant, 342
miser, 551
miserably, 306
misery, 205
miss, 206, 260, 597, (cap.) 283
Miss Browns, 444
miss fire, 162
missal, 339
Misses Brown, 444
mission, 177
Mississippi, 277
Missouri, 205
Missouri meerschaum, 363
misspell, 239
mist, 461
mistake, 342
mistletoe, 206
mistress, 437, 438
miter (mitre), 177, 242
mither, 53
mitigate, 414
mitigation, 414
mixture, 202
mnemonic, 211, 237, 247
mob, 28, 270, 355
mobilization, 181
Mobiloil, 352
moccasin, 149, 384
mode, 405, 463
moderate, 242
Moderator, 284
modes and manners, 415
modiste, 340, 374
mogul, 383
moind (mind), 52, 187, 196
moist, 188
molasses, 161, 381, 397, 443
molest, 181
Mollie, 287

molt, 180
molten, 458, 465
mom, 354
moment, 311
momentum, 369
monarch, 346, 597
monastery, 404
Monday, 281
monetary, 75, 76, 169
money, 191, 211, 235, 251, 594, 599
money due, 503
money-making, 349
money's worth, 348
monk, 378, 438
monkey, 262
monograph, 347
monolith, 249, 346
monolog, 245
monoplane, 58
monsieur, 441
monsignor, 59
Montreal, 276, 280
moo moo, 48, 335
mood, 182, 405, 409
moody, 292
moon, 210, 211, 569
moor, 182, 210, 237
Moore (More), 184, 274
Moorish, 184
moos moos, 64
moose, 242, 384, 439
moot court, 572
moral, 179, 373
moratorium, 441
more, 19, 180, 427, 450
more cautious, 450
more cheerful, 450
more evenly, 450
more irritating, 450
more nearly, 451
more refreshing, 450
more talented, 450
moreover, 307, 311, 535, 542
Morgan Hill, 276
morn, 406
morning, 427
morocco, 358, 384
moron, 210, 566, 567
morris dance, 358
morrow, 169, 180, 406
mortal, 400
mortgage, 58, 247, 372, 400, 599
mortgagee, 251
mortician, 39, 339, 400

mortify, 400, 560
mortuary, 400
mosaic, 294
Mosher (Moser), 207, 237
Moslem, 383
mosquito, 175, 181, 245, 381, 397, 404
moss, 179, 180
most, 19, 327, 450
most all, 327
most beautiful, 327, 450
most clearly, 450
most everyone, 327
most finished, 327
most indefatigably, 450
most interesting, 450
most kind, 327, 450
most nearly, 451
most nearly complete, 451
most unkindest, 451
most well, 327
most wonderfully, 450
Motel, 352
moth, 179
mother, 74, 80, 257, 400, 403, 438, (cap.) 285, 287
mother bird, 437
Mother Hubbard, 15
motion, 269
motivate, 429
motor, 6, 84, 340, 459
motor coach, 6
motorcade, 338
motorcop, 32
motordrome, 346
motored, 25
motorist, 340
motorization, 181
motorize, 341
Motrola, 282
motto, 380
mould (mold), 22, 594, 597
mount, 188, 368
mourn, 181
mouse, 90, 120, 188
mouth, 188, 204, 261
mouthfuls, 444
mouths, 204
movable, 243
move, 182, 269
move up, 300
movie, 58, 161
movie star, 429

moviedom, 337
movies, 337
moving, 269
mow, 187, 457
Mr., 255, 258, 283, 405
Mr. Chairman, 284
Mrs., 205, 255, 258, 283
MSS. (manuscripts), 255
Mt. Shasta, 277
Mt. Tamalpais, 277
much, 241, 250, 291, 306, 405, 427, 449, 450
much-exercised, 253
muchly, 305
muckamuck, 64
muddle up, 300
muffed, 203
muffle, 242
mufti, 248
mugwump, 160, 280
mulatto, 381
mule, 75, 82, 189, 210, 234, 258, 259
multicolored, 343
multiplication, 414
multiply, 414
multitude, 267, 340
mummie, 47
mumps, 443
murder (murther), 313, 326, 400, 418, (cap.) 558
muscle, 206, 246
muse, 570
Muses, 571
music, 190, 221, 249, 268, 355, 397
musician, 208, 221
muskeg, 149
Muskegon, 277
musket, 404
muskrat, 362, 384
muslin, 358
must, 295, 453, 463, 521, 526, 530
mustache, 208, 223
mustache cup, 40
mustard, 338
mustn't, 26, 256
mutton, 372, 397, 418
muvver (mother), 46
muzhik, 384
muzzle, 185, 205
muzzle-loader, 39
my, 25, 75, 82, 248, 289, 293, 422, 427, 447, 477, 504

WORD INDEX

my liefest liege, 40
my prayers is, 54
myrmidon, 358
myrrh, 184, 210, 231, 258
myself, 25, 289, 320, 321, 347, 448, 474, 477
mystery, 364, 409
myth, 177, 204, 234, 258
mythology, 204

Nabisco, 282
nadder, 361
nadir, 383
Nægling, 280
nagged, 216
nail, 198
naïve, 198, 404
naked, 171, 243, 403
nalle, 333
namby-pamby, 335
name, 174, 267, 403, 479
namely, 307, 482
naow, 197
nap, 200
nape, 200
naphtha, 88, 203
napron, 361
narrate, 400
narration, 370
narrow, 171, 173, 449
narwhal, 377
nasts (nests), 57
nation, 170, 174, 237, 258, 370, 371, 590
national, 170, 171
native, 100, 404
natural, 557
naturally, 305
nature, 201, (cap.) 558
natury history, 4
natyure (nature), 201, 213
naught, 179
naughty, 179, 563
nausea, 208, 237
naval, 171, 341
nave, 203
navel, 171
navigator, 203
navvy, 203, 354
navy, 203, 211
nay, 307, 377, 403
neäme (name), 52
Neapolitan, 280
near, 175, 177, 450

nearly, 306, 505
neat, 601
neb, 172
Nebraska, 160, 277, 282
nebula, 440
nebulous, 172
necessary, 158, 225
necessity for, of, 537
N.E.D. (New English Dictionary), 255
need, 211, 237, 269, 295, 521, 530, 601
needle, 175
needn't, 530
ne'er, 41, 256
ne'er-do-well, 349
negligent of, 537
negress, 437
negro, 181, 248, 360, 381
negro spirituals, 318
negroes, 245, 439, 592
neighbor, 174, 200, 233, 350
neither, 176, 233, 291, 293, 497, 498
neither kith nor kin, 571
neither . . . nor, 310, 540
Neoplatonism, 344
nephew, 203, 236, 438
nestling, 268
neuralgia, 379
neuritis, 190, 235
neurosis, 340, 379
neurotics, 567
neutral, 183
never, 172, 191, 197, 220, 305, 326, 534
nevertheless, 307, 311, 505, 542
never-to-be-forgotten, 519
new, 11, 183, 197, 410
New Haven, 276
New Jerseyites, 279
New London, 276, 277
New Orleans, 276
New York, 226, 276
New Yorker, 280
newer, 11
newness, 11
news, 205, 218, 426, 443
newspaper, 218, 253, 348
next, 201, 294
nibs, 444

nice, 27, 29, 121, 195, 428, 552, 566, 570
nicely, 306
nicety, 195, 244
niche, 201, 241, 251
nickel, 397, 548
nickname, 285, 361
niece, 438
nifty, 292
niggard, 202, 366
nigger, 360
nigh, 450
nigh-guard, 366
night, 233, 269, 400, 426, 427, 593, 601
nightee, 67
nightingale, 350, 400
nightshade, 400
nil, 211, 249
nimrod, 358
nine, 403
nineteen, 340
ninety, 340
'nint (anoint), 54
ninth, 244, 562
Niobrara, 277
Nira, 352
nite, 232
nitrate, 339
niver, 51
nix, 307
nixy, 307
no, 67, 83, 87, 180, 197, 211, 248, 294, 307, 313, 377, 403, 409, 534
no one, 291, 498, 534
no sirree, 307
Noar (Noah), 220
nobility, 270, 443
noble, 181, 306, 400
nobles, 318
nobody, 291, 448, 498
nocturn, 400
nocturnal, 400
noes, 410
noise, 189, 242
nomenclature, 225
nominal, 210
nonbreakable, 386
nonce, 431
nonce word, 361
none, 232, 291, 342, 497, 534
none were, 497, 515
nonforfeiture, 58
nonnegotiable, 343

nonparticipating, 430
nonsense, 313
noodle, 182
nook, 249
noon, 211, 369, 403, 562
nor, 310
Norfolk, 275, 351
Norfolk capons, 363
Normans, 94
Norse, 376
north, 179, 305
northernmost, 450
Northmen, 94
Northumbria, 275
Northwestern, 341
Norwegian, 132
Norwich, 201, 210, 214, 219, 240, 247, 250, 275
nose, 410, 431
nostril, 350, 572
not, 67, 87, 156, 169, 180, 196, 232, 307, 534
not a whit, 40
not at all, 26
not merely ... but also, 540
not on your tintype, 315
not only ... but also, 310
not only ... but even, 540
notably, 307
notary, 339
notation, 370
notch, 250
note, 80, 180, 231, 232, 258
noted, 232
notes, 206
nothing, 37, 169, 204, 291, 534
notice, 339
noticeable, 243, 244
notion, 87, 181, 370
notwithstanding, 308
noun, 266, 267, 403
nourish, 210
nouveau riche, 373
novel, 169
novelties, 557
now, 82, 305, 323, 427
nowadays, 305
noxious, 203
nucleus, 440
nude, 403
nuggets, 58

nuisance, 183
numb, 251
number, 228, 426
numbs, 211
numskull, 548
nun, 369, 438
nuptials, 443
nurse, 185, 197
nusipepa, 66
nuss (nurse), 185
nut, 215
nutmeg, 387
N. Y. (New York), 255
nyctalopia, 400

o (of), 52, 54
oak, 202
oasis, 384, 441
oath, 180
oaths, 204
oats, 180, 391
obelisk, 390
obey, 174
object to, 536
objective, 203
obligatory, 225
oblique, 176
obscure, 343, 419
observatory, 340
obsolescent, 341
obsolete, 38, 430
obstacle, 401, 417
obstinate, 105, 371
occasion, 207, 232
Occident, 319
occiput, 400
occult, 400
occur, 343
occurrence, 238, 262
ocean, 181, 208, 237, 244, 259, 590
och (ach), 55
ocher (ochre), 202, 221
o'clock, 220, 580
octavos, 245
octet, 201
octoroon, 203
oculist, 340
odd, 249, 376
odd fellows, 257, (cap.) 257, 280
oddly, 342
odds, 201, 443
ode, 243
Odin, 181, 200
odious, 213
odjus (odious), 201

odor, 200, 431
o'er, 180, 256
œsophagus (esophagus), 235, 379
of, 6, 86, 203, 249, 258, 308, 406, 427
of late, 535
off, 83, 86, 179, 203, 231, 258, 298, 305, 308, 406
off and on, 578
off of, 539
offense, 262
offer, 203, 237, 343, 369, 426
offered, 239
office, 244
officer, 206, 338
official, 244
officious, 563
offset, 301, 342
offspring, 443
oft, 201, 203
often, 88, 105, 201, 247, 305, 412, 449
Ogden, 277
ogham, 202, 375
ogre, 202, 594
oh, 13, 156, 180, 209, 233, 312, 334
oh heck, 315
Ohio, 277
Ohiowa, 278, 351
oil, 188, 268
oil-bearing, 349
O'Keefe, 273
okeh (okay, O.K.), 44, 307
Oklahoma, 160, 277
Okoboji, 277, 384
old, 199, 210, 216, 220, 292, 449, 450
Old English, 573; old English, 573
Old Norse, 131, 132
oleomargarine, 202
Olga, 216
Olsen, 273, 377
Olympic, 294
Omaha, 179, 277
Omahog, 353
omelette (omelet), 242, 245, 561
omnibus, 406
omniscient, 208
on, 211, 249, 298, 305, 308, 321, 427

WORD INDEX

on account of, 309
on board, 351
on condition that, 310, 491
on fire, 351
on foot, 351
on location, 59
on shore, 351
on the contrary, 311
on the other hand, 311
on top of, 309
once, 121, 206, 211, 214, 216, 259, 305, 311
once word, 361
oncet, 220
one, 212, 214, 232, 237, 291, 294, 319, 405, 406, 426, 448, 473, 497, 498
one and all, 580
one another, 291
one by one, 305
Oneida, 277
ones, 448
one's, 293, 445, 448
oneself, 291
onion, 79, 83, 213, 237
onlooker, 342
only, 244, 505, 534
oodles, 200, 233, 444
ooze, 182, 205, 233, 591
opalescent, 341
Opaline, 282
open, 181, 200
openly, 306
opera, 248, 381
operate, 551
operates, 296
opossum, 160, 384
oppose, 343
or, 83, 85, 184, 193, 249, 310, 312, 328, 427, 482, 497
oracular, 36
oral, 179, 180
orange, 169, 383
orangeade, 338
orang-utan (orang-ou-tang), 385
oration, 404
orb, 44, 179
orbit, 201, 210
orchard, 201, 350, 387, 401
orchestra, 161
order, 426, 427, 546
ore, 180

Ore. (Oregon), 255
O'Reilly, 273
organ, 378, 397
organism, 378, 379
organization, 552
orie-eyed, 31
Orient, 319
originality, 575
oriole, 198
orison, 404
ornithology, 204
orphan, 203, 210, 412
orthographic, 253, 254
orthography, 10, 254
orthopedic, 179
osier, 181, 207
ossifer, 35
osteopaths, 567
ostrich, 169
other, 74, 185, 204, 288, 291, 427, 448
others, 288, 318, 448
other's, 293
otherwise, 342
Ottawa, 277
otter, 201, 232
ou (you), 46
ouch, 312
ought, 179, 295, 418, 453, 463, 521, 526, 593
ought to, 525
ould (old), 52
ounce, 188, 268, 369, 405
our, 188, 196, 197, 293, 447, 477, 504
ourn, 447
ours, 293, 447, 477
ourselves, 289, 448
oust, 188
out, 119, 187, 298, 302, 305, 325, 429, 450, 504
out of, 309
out with you, 13, 470
outcry, 348
outermost, 405
outlandish, 563
outlay, 348
outlet, 301
outlook, 342
out-of-the-way, 252
output, 301
outrage, 555
outrageous, 244
outreaching, 100
outrun, 297

outs, 357
outside, 309
Outsiders, 111
outstanding, 429
oval, 181, 191, 196, 203
Ovaltine, 282
oven, 181
over, 83, 119, 156, 181, 191, 227, 298, 305, 308, 321, 426, 427, 429
over with, 292
overalls, 551
overbear, 344
overbearing, 344
overbearingly, 344
overburden, 344
overburdensome, 344
overemphasis, 386
overfat, 349
overgrown, 349
overlay, 349
overly, 305
overrun by, with, 537
overtake, 297, 342
overthrow, 301
overwork, 297
owe, 180, 214, 231, 242, 251, 591
owing, 214, 243
owing to, 309, 325, 490
own up, 300, 301
ownership, 269, 337
ox, 372, 418, 446, 447
oxen, 96, 439, 446
Oxford, 275, 277
oxid, 245
oxidize, 341
oyster, 189, 235
ozone, 181

pabulum, 400
pace, 206
paced, 244
pacifist, 387
packed, 203
Paddy, 286
padre, 400
pagans, 318
pageant, 241
pagoda, 381
pail, 174, 431
pain, 442
paindemaine, 39
pains, 205, 442
pair, 406, 440
pajamas (pyjamas), 383

WORD INDEX

pal, 249
palace, 242
palaver, 381, 407
pale, 83, 174
Paley, 173
paling, 87, 557
pall, 551
palm, 168, 195, 220, 233, 247, 369, 601
palmate, 369
palmetto, 210
palsy, 178, 210, 216, 404
pampas, 384
pan out, 162
pander, 358
pandiculated, 97
pane, 200
panegyric, 190
panfray, 333
Panhellenic, 347
panic, 358, 378
panicky, 239
pans, 4, 47
pansy, 211
pantalets, 39
pantheon, 347
pantomime, 347
pantry, 400
pants, 443
papa, 334, 404
paper, 384, 404
paper and ink, 228
papoose, 384
papyrus, 384, 404
par, 210
parable, 407
parabola, 407
parade, 338
paradigm, 178
paradise, 378
paradox, 344
paraffin, 160
parallel, 451
paralysis, 404
paramount, 430
paramour, 563
parasite, 378
pardie, 314
pardner (partner), 218
pardon me, 313
parent, 170, 171
parenthesis, 441
parietal, 198
parley, 407
parody, 344
parole, 407
parrot, 173

parse, 206
parson, 167, 359, 405, 551, 554, 614
part, 157
part from, with, 536
partake, 342
partial, 210, 249
particular, 190
particularly, 307, 482
partly, 306
partridge, 439
party, 561
parvenu, 248
Paso Robles, 56, 277
pass, 83, 206, 238, 461, 591, 597
pass away, 431, 548
pass in one's checks, 548
passed (past), 201, 243, 599
passers-by, 444
passion, 208, 237
passive, 206, 237
Passover, 301, 348
past, 218, 243, 308, 427, 461, 599
paste, 173
pasteurize, 358, 570
pastime, 239, 350
pastor, 400, 418, 551, 564, 614
pastry, 373
pasture, 400
pasty, 404
Patapar, 352
patch, 241, 250
patent, 171, 201, 411
paternal, 400
paternoster, 400
path, 156, 196, 249
pathological, 204
pathology, 347
pathos, 204, 238
pathway, 214
patience, 269
patio, 381
patriarch, 378, 400
patrician, 400
patriot, 171, 174, 391, 400
patrol, 251
patrolled, 238
patron, 391, 400
patronage, 171
patroness, 437
patroon, 400
patty, 404, (cap.) 374

Paul, 179, 233, 437
Pauline, 437
pauper, 404
pause, 404
pavilion, 213
pawn, 400
Pawnee, 277
pay, 121, 174, 212, 231, 248, 569
pay dirt, 58, 162
pay on the nail, 578
pay something to boot, 572
pay up, 302
payee, 268
payment, 570
pea, 356, 362, 443
peace, 372
peach, 32, 484
peacharino, 34
peachy, 417, 484
pea-jacket, 387
peaked, 243
peal, 405
pear, 171, 369
pearl, 184
peärt, 52
peasant, 234
peasantry, 270, 339, 443
peck, 405
peculiar, 400, 563
pecuniary, 400
pedagog, 245, 595
pedal, 400
pedant, 563
pedestrian, 400
pedigree, 400, 561
peeg (pig), 195
peer, 406, 409
peerless, 565
peevish, 356
peignoir, 374
Peke, 355
pell-mell, 335, 571
pelt, 200, 236
pen, 461, 561
penalize, 173
pence, 442
pencil, 211
pending, 308
Pendleton, 275
penetrate, 211
penguin, 211, 212, 216
peninsula, 268, 344, 370
penitentiary, 557
pennies, 442
penny, 362, 442

WORD INDEX

pennyroyal, 362
Pennzoil, 283, 352
pens (pants), 57, 173
pensioner, 391
pentagonal, 378
pentstemon, 566
penurious, 183
peon, 381, 400
people, 80, 175, 231, 270, 426
pep, 172, 355, 556
pepper, 369, 383
per, 309
per se, 371
peradventure, 431
perch, 439
perchance, 431
perfect, 451
perfervid, 430
perfume, 223
perhaps, 209, 307
peril, 417
perimeter, 344
period, 178, 198
periodic, 355
Perkins, 337
permanent way, 161
permeate, 369
permit, 223, 343, 416
perquisit, 245
perscription (prescription), 220
Persia, 207
persiflage, 430
persimmon, 384
person, 38, 360, 405, 436, 552, 554, 558
personal, 185, 234, 257
personification, 190
perspire, 431
persuade, 207, 214
pertinacious, 105
perty, 221
perversity, 244
pese, 356, 362
petal, 369
Peter, 175, 253, 271, 378
peter out, 300
Peterborough, 275
Peterkin, 337
Peterson, 377
petrol, 161, 176
petticoat, 561
petunia, 384, 396
pew, 189, 200
pewee, 334
pewter, 189

phaëton, 198, 358
phalanx, 174
phantasms, 419
Pharisee, 382
phase, 409
pheasantry, 339
phenomenon, 100, 441
Phi Beta Kappa, 280
Philadelphian, 280, 339
philanthropy, 346
Philco, 283, 352
Philistine, 294, 358
philologist, 576
philology, 8, 222, 576
philosopher, 378
philosophical, 1
philosophize, 379
philosophy, 203, 262, 268, 347, 590, 591 (cap.) 558
phlegm, 210, 219, 224
phlegmatic, 219, 224, 567
phlox, 378, 566
phœbe, 334, 378
phœnix, 175, 233, 369, 596
phone, 253, 264, 355, 379
phonetics, 10, 203, 239, 443
phonograph, 148, 180, 181, 258, 347, 379, 597
phonography, 234
phonology, 10
phosphorus, 399
photo, 355
photograph, 347, 379, 597
phrase, 195, 410, 577
phraseology, 195, 244
phthisic, 121, 201, 247, 259
physic, 378, 597
physics, 203, 258, 260, 339, 443
physiognomy, 430
physique, 259
pianist, 223, 340
piano, 168, 211, 381, 397, 407
pianos, 245, 262, 439, 592
piazza, 380, 390, 407
pick, 405
pick out, 300
pickaninny, 66, 160

pickax, 37, 362
pickerel, 270, 439
picking and stealing, 415
pickle, 202
pickled, 31
picknickers (picnickers), 239
pickpocket, 348, 444
Pickwickian, 294
picnic, 249, 335
picturesque, 341, 597
pidgin, 66
pie, 235, 248
piecemeal, 306, 342, 387
pie-eyed, 417
piety, 550
piffle, 417, 563
pig, 195
pig in a poke, 571
pigeon, 201, 240, 241
Piggly Wiggly, 335
pigsney, 32
pike, 439
pile, 369
pilfering, 249
pilgrim, 380
pill, 29
pillage, 253
pillion, 375
pillow, 190
pilot, 161
pimento, 381
pin, 83
pinafore, 177, 211
pincers, 443
pine, 369
ping-pong, 335
pining, 232
pinnace, 250
pinning, 19, 232
Pint (Point), 54
pioneer, 400
pious, 563
pipe, 553, 562
pipe course, 28
pique, 202
pistol, 177
pitapat (pitypat), 335
pitch-dark, 306
pitched, 243
pitcher, 160, 404
pith, 177
pities, 246
pitiful, 251
pity, 79, 82, 177, 191, 201, 248, 550, 594, (cap.) 558

WORD INDEX

pivot, 80, 203
placate, 371
place, 200, 215, 407, 552
place-name, 252, 348, 350
placer, 58
plague, 245
plagued, 243, 465
plaid, 111, 170, 234, 258, 375
plain, 407
plainer, 410
plainness, 387
plaintiff, 372
plan, 407, 570
plane, 407
planer, 410
planet, 211
plank, 212
plant, 369
plantation, 557
plaster, 87, 170
plateau, 181, 441
platform, 160
platonic, 358, 378
plausible, 563
play out, 292, 301, 575
playful, 340
playlet, 339
playwright, 347
plaza, 407
pleas, 242
please, 242, 313, 591
pleasure, 172, 207, 597
pleb, 172
pliers, 443
plinth, 204
Pliny the Elder, 503
plough (plow), 22, 159, 187, 251, 259, 267, 594, 599
plover, 181
pluck, 565
plum, 210, 405, 412, 562
plumb, 412
plumcot, 352
plunge, 201, 211, 216
plus, 249
plutocrat, 378
P.M. (post meridiem), 255
pneumatic, 211, 215, 237, 247, 378, 379
pneumonia, 211
pocket, 379
pocketful, 337

podagra, 400
poet, 378
poetaster, 339, 562
poetic, 341
poetical, 341
poetry, 575
poets laureate, 444
pogrom, 384
poignant, 202, 211, 404
point, 188, 373
pointedly, 306
poise, 189
poison, 253, 404, 551, 562
poisonous, 341
Poker, 111
Polack, 384
polemical, 355
police, 175, 210, 443
policy, 169
polish, 300, 341
polish up, 300
polished, 565
polite, 565
politic, 221
political, 253
politician, 221
politics, 169, 253, 355, 443
Polk, 278
polka, 384, 397
polo, 383, 387
polygamy, 347
polyglot, 292, 347
Pom, 355
pomato, 352
Pomfret, 276
pommel, 338
pompelmoose, 99
ponch (punch), 57
pongee, 385
pontifical, 341
pony, 181, 562
poodle, 380
pooh, 233, 312
poor, 182, 183, 184, 318, 404, 510
poor and rich, 14
poorhouse, 225
poorly, 160
pop, 354
pope, 369, 404
pop-overs, 301
poppy, 369, 396
poppycock, 417
porch, 404
pore (poor), 184, 196

pork, 372
pork barrel, 59
porker, 268
porpoise, 235
porridge, 210
port, 126, 368
porter, 210
portico, 245, 380, 404
portion, 180, 210
Portugee, 278, 356, 362
Portuguese, 279, 356
pose, 404
possess, 400
possibly, 307, 535
possum, 547
postboy, 39, 571
posterior, 450
posthumous, 209, 246
postpone, 531
postwar, 343
potato, 181, 384, 396
potatoes, 245
potent, 180
potion, 404, 562
potlatch, 64, 250, 384
poudingue (pudding), 111
poultry, 180, 339, 443
pour, 180, 188, 231, 258
Powell, 273
power, 214, 372, 546
powwow, 384
pox, 241
pp. (pages), 255
practicable, 221
practical, 221
practice, 221
prairie, 149, 160, 373
prairie schooner, 15
Prairie State, 286
pram, 355
Pratt, 249
pray and beseech, 415
prayer, 171, 231
preached, 105
precede, 260, 262, 345
precedence, 223, 345
precedent, 345
preceding, 416
precession, 345
precessional, 345
precinct, 175
precious, 565
precipice, 254
precipitate, 429
predecease, 345
predecessor, 345

WORD INDEX

predicate attribute, 476
predicate nominative, 476
preëlection, 343
preëminence, 198
preëmpt, 198
preen, 405
preface, 417
prefer, 297
prejudice, 563
premise, 223
premium, 58
prep, 172
preparation, 194, 224
preparatory to, 537
prepare, 6, 194, 224
prepare for burial, 570
prepay, 176
preposition, 266
Pre-Raphaelite, 294
present, 223
Preserved, 272
president, 400
prespiration (perspiration), 221
Presque Isle, 276
pressure, 208
presume, 183
presuppose, 176
preterit, 245
preternatural, 343
pretext, 176
pretty, 177, 234, 253, 257, 428, 552
prewar, 386
prexy, 354
price, 427, (cap.) 273
priest, 175, 369, 378
priesthood, 269, 337
prig, 28
prima donna, 381
primacy, 339
primary, 341
primate, 319, 339, 357
prime, 369
primer, 178, 210
primrose, 362
prince, 549
prince regent, 503
princess, 437
print, 6
prior, 450
prior to, 537
prioress, 437
prism, 219
prismatic, 219
prison, 137, 372

privacy, 339
privateerin', 54
privates, 318, 357
prize, 205
pro and con, 371
probability, 86, 224
probable, 86, 224
probably, 244, 307
procedure, 345
proceed, 260, 262, 345, 599
proceedings, 345
proceeds, 443
process, 157, 181, 345
procession, 345
processional, 345
proclaim, 181, 195, 224
proclamation, 195, 224
produce, 223
productive, 253
prof, 354
profane, 563
Professor, 284
proficient in, 537
profiteer, 338
progenitor, 400
pro-German, 252, 343
programme (program), 242, 245, 250, 259, 260, 374, 591, 595, 597, 599
progress, 157, 181, 196, 223, 414
prohi, 44
project, 223
proletarian, 384
proliferant, 333
prolog (prologue), 245, 344, 594, 595
promenade, 174, 338
prominent clubman, 429
promise, 242, 250, 591, 598
prompt, 247
prone, 530
pronominal adjective, 320
pronoun, 180, 266
pronounce, 236
pronunciation, 236
proof, 183, 184
proof positive, 503
propædeutic, 235
proportion, 567
proposal, 205
proposition, 369, 552, 559, 567

props, 354
prosper, 414, 416
protest, 181, 223
Prothero, 274
protoplasm, 171
prototype, 344
prove, 182, 457, 476
proved, 457
proven, 340, 457, 458
provide, 224, 225
provided, 310
providence, 224, 225
providing, 310
provision, 225
provocation, 195, 224
provoke, 195, 224
prow, 200, 215
prowess, 97
prowl, 188
prude, 563
prune, 405, 409, 562
psalm, 168, 237, 247, 378
psalter, 206, 210
pseudo-scientific, 344
pshaw, 207, 237, 259, 312, 334, 590
psychic, 247
psychical, 378
psychoneurosis, 566
ptarmigan, 247
Ptolemy, 247
ptomaine, 201, 247
pueblos, 245
puerile, 235
puff, 203, 334
puffed, 203
puling, 190
pull, 184, 193, 298
pull through, 297, 300, 578
pull together, 580
pullet, 184
pullman, 358
pulpit, 548
pulverize, 295
Pulvex, 282
puma, 384
pumpkin, 211
punctual, 212
puncture, 216
pungent, 404
punk, 570
punster, 268, 562
puppet, 185
purchase, 417
pure, 22, 182, 189

WORD INDEX

pure English, 22
purism, 22
purist, 22
Puritan, 189, 209, 235, 294
puritanical, 209, 563
purlieu, 185
purloin, 188
purpose, 235
purr, 184, 249, 334
purse, 184
pursuant, 503
pursued, 243
pursuer, 243
pursuing, 243
push, 184
pusillanimity, 430
pussycat, 387
put, 184, 298, 299, 300, 426, 427, 429, 462
put off, 301
put on the spot, 548
put out, 301
put up, 508
put up with, 13
putrid, 560
putty, 185, 201
Pyrex, 282

quack-quack, 335
quad, 354
quadrant, 400
quadrille, 400
quadrillion, 97
quadroon, 400
quadruped, 400
quadruple, 294
quaffed, 216
quagga, 384
quail, 270, 439
Quaker City, 286
quakers, 257, (cap.) 257, 390
quality, 169, 339, 567
qualm, 168, 220
quandary, 157
quantity, 169
quarrel, 303
quarrel(l)ed, 239
quarry, 400
quart, 179
quarterly, 318
quartet, 245
quarto, 400
quartz, 179, 237, 380
quash, 44
quasi-scientific, 252

quay, 80, 121, 175, 231, 259
Quebec, 280
queen, 203, 214, 217, 240, 259, 438
queer, 79, 83, 177, 292
quell, 406, 551
query, 175
question, 172, 201, 240
queue, 189, 202, 234
quick, 203, 306, 561
quick and the dead, 572
quid, 406
quiescent, 341
quill, 210
quin (queen), 57
quinine, 187, 384
quire, 186
quit, 326, 462
quite, 306
quixotic, 294, 358, 554
quiz, 249, 332
quoits, 189
quondam, 214
quoth, 41, 463
quotient, 180

rabbi, 382
rabbit, 210
rabbitry, 339
rabid, 171
rabies, 171
raccoon, 384, 397
race, 244
race horse, 348
racial, 244, 386
racing, 267
racketeer, 338
radio, 18, 148, 174
Radiola, 282
radish, 170
radius, 369, 371, 404, 440
rafter, 170
raged, 243
ragged, 202
rags, 4
raid, 377, 403
railing, 557
raiment, 570
raise, 119, 205, 295, 376, 377, 403, 414, 546
ram, 438
rammed, 243
ran, 304
ranch, 211
rancho, 381

rand, 380
random, 379
range, 174
ranger, 254
ransack, 376
ransom, 373
rantipole, 99
rapid, 171, 228, 235
rapidly, 542
rapine, 171
rapped, 85
rare, 195
rarefy, 195
raspberry, 205, 218, 247
rat, 362
rate, 243
rates, 592
rather, 247, 578
ratio, 371
rational, 171
rationally, 342
rations, 171, 194
rattan, 385
rat-tat, 335
rattle, 201
rattling good, 417
ravel, 249
raven, 174, 364
ravenous, 364, 409
ravine, 175
raw, 410
ray, 404
raze, 205
razor, 205
razz, 238
razzed, 205
re, 58
reached, 105
reaction, 429
read, 175, 426, 461
Reading, 337
readjust, 88
reads, 296
ready, 530
real, 210, 306, 407
real good, 306
real-estate man, 39
realism, 339
reality, 190
really, 307, 535
realm, 172, 216
realtor, 39, 338, 340
ream, 210
reaped, 238
rear, 376, 377, 403, 406, 459
reason, 175

WORD INDEX

reason with, 536
reb, 172
rebirth, 344
reborn, 344
rebuke, 416
recede, 345
recedingly, 345
receipt, 247, 593
receive, 175, 176, 206, 231, 233, 236, 242, 262, 594, 598, 599
reception, 236
recess, 345
recession, 345
recessional, 345
recessive, 345
reckless, 340
reckon on, with, 536
reckon up, 302
recline, 295
recognize, 202, 400
recollect, 252
re-collect, 252
reconcile, 6
recondite, 225
reconnize (recognize), 219
reconnoitre, 242
recount, 176
Red, 287
Red River, 277
red tape, 548
red-headed, 243
redingote, 111
redness, 337
redoubt, 246
reduce, 414
reduction, 414
redundancy, 269
reef, 379, 459
reek, 202
reel, 375
re-establish, 252
reëvaluate, 198
re-examine, 252
referee, 195, 268
referendum, 441
referred, 238
refill, 343
reflexion, 241
reflux, 414
refract, 399
refreshment, 442
refuge, 399
refund, 223
refusal, 243, 339
refuse, 86, 206, 223, 228

regain, 176
regal, 407
regard, 405
regarding, 308
regards, 4, 325
régime, 207, 237, 258, 259, 374
region, 201, 240
regular, 341
regulate, 341, 371
rein in, 119
reindeer, 439
rejoice, 189
rejoinder, 401
relay, 223
relinquish, 212, 303
remain, 476
remain unbent, 119
remains, 443
remote, 450
renaissance, 120
rend, 461
rendezvous, 247
rendit, 333
renegade, 381
rennet, 172
renown, 188
rent, 372
replica, 381
report, 180
reprehend, 36
reptile, 157, 187
Repton, 275
Republican, 280
resave (receive), 52
research, 121, 223
resemblance between, to, 537
reservoir, 214, 220
reside, 225, 400
residence, 225, 400
residuary, 225
resign, 219, 224
resignation, 219, 224
resin, 405
resistance, 338
resources, 443
respect, 442
respecting, 308, 325
respective, 294
respectively, 305
respects, 442
respiratory, 225
responsible for, to, 537
rest on one's oars, 580
Resthaven, 281
result in, 295

résumé, 373
retail, 176
retrocession, 345
retrograde, 343
Reuben, 182, 231
Rev., 255
revel in, 536
revelant, 221
revelry, 339
revenue, 189, 250
reverberation, 227
reverence, 250
Reverend, 285
reverie, 235, 250, 251
revocable, 223
revoke, 223
reward, 405
Rex, 280
rheostat, 566
rhetoric, 210, 237, 246, 258, 379, 597
rheumatism, 58, 379, 597
rhizome, 210
rhomboid, 430
rhythm, 204, 210, 219, 378, 597
rhythmical, 219
rib, 177
ribald, 405
ribs, 200, 215
rice, 383
rich, 80, 83, 201, 241, 250
rich and poor, 14, 267, 319
rich heiress, 429
Richard the Lion-hearted, 287
richer, 436
riches, 379, 443
richest of any, 513, 579
Richmond, 276
rid, 462
riddle, 356, 443
ride, 82, 200, 250, 264, 265, 327, 328, 455, 592
ride the blind, 60
rided, 47
ridge, 80, 177, 217
ridged, 243
ridicule, 200
riffraff, 335, 563
rift, 203
rigger, 238
right, 221, 306, 321, 427, 601

WORD INDEX

right away, 13, 578
right off the bat, 13
right well, 306
righteous, 201, 221, 240
right-o, 162
rigid, 105, 241
rigmarole, 350
rigorous, 105
rile (roil), 186
rime, 597, 599
ring, 455
ringer, 212
ringlet, 268, 339
ringside, 347
rink (ring), 57
rinks, 212
riot, 198
ripe, 186, 234, 257
ripping, 32, 560
rise, 205, 206, 261, 406, 414, 455, 596
risk, 177, 202, 206
rite, 232
rites, 201
ritual, 210, 319
ritzy, 292, 340
rive, 203, 457
river, 79, 177, 203, 268
road, 179, 377, 403
road house, 225, 227
roadateria, 339
roadbed, 161
roadster, 58, 337
roam, 180
roamed, 211
roar, 334, 410
roast, 181
roast beef, 111
roaster, 268
rob, 119, 169, 200, 210, 232, 237, 379
Robb, 249
robbed, 216, 243, 592
robber, 238
robe, 180, 232
robin, 200
roc, 249
rock, 397
rocks, 548
rod, 32, 169, 440, 549
rode, 242
rodeo, 56, 58, 245, 258
roe, 438
roes, 410
rogue, 180, 202, 236, 600
roil, 186
role, 180, 373, 404

roll, 180, 404
Roman, 278, 279, 294
romance, 223
romanticism, 575
romanticists, 256
Rome, 277
ronning (running), 57
rood, 182
roof, 182, 183, 184, 195, 215
roofing, 557
room, 183
roomy, 340
roost, 182
rooster, 183
root, 182, 183, 184, 376
rope, 180
rosbif (roast beef), 111
rose, 180, 272, 362, 369, 410
roses, 205, 218
rosette, 245
rosin, 405
roster, 207
rostrum, 561
Rotarian, 256, 280, 341
rotatory, 157
rotten, 566
rotter, 162
rotund, 404
rouble, 384
rouge, 182, 207
rouged, 207, 216
rough-hewn, 349
rough-house, 252
roughs, 206
round, 220, 292, 298, 324, 404, 451, 549
round-up, 58, 253
rouse, 188
Rousseauist, 280, 294
roustabout, 188
rout, 187
route, 182, 183, 242
routine, 183
rove, 180
rover, 356, (cap.) 280
row, 187, 219
rowed, 4, 47
rowel, 188
rower, 219
rows, 205, 410
royal, 407
royalist, 340
rubber, 200
rubbers, 548
rubbish, 417, 563

rubric, 561
ruction, 203
rudder, 185
rude, 182, 183, 542
rue, 182, 572
ruffian, 213, 380
rug, 185
rugged, 192, 243
rule, 183, 190, 210
Rumanian, 279
ruminate, 556
rumors are rife, 571
run, 83, 185, 298, 299, 318, 326, 452, 455, 464, 476, 560
run down, 297, 508
run low, 414
run out, 297
run riot, 578
run up, 414
runabouts, 301
rung, 212
running, 4, 292, 337, 465
Runnymede, 277
runs, 304
rural, 184
rushed, 216, 243
rushes, 243
Russia, 208
rust, 185
rustle, 247
Rustum, 185
Ruth, 182

sabbath, 382
sable, 174, 384
saccharin (saccharine), 245, 341
sachet, 208
sack, 367, 384
sacrifice, 206, 237, 258
sad, 400, 556
saddle, 200
sad-eyed, 349
sadiron, 400
safe, 173
safe and sound, 415, 578
safety, 244, 339, 557
saga, 168, 377, 403
sago, 385
said, 172, 234, 417
sail, 268, 440, 548
sail in, 547
sailor, 338
saint, 372
St. John, 255
St. Louis, 276

WORD INDEX

salable, 173
sale, 206, 237
Salem, 174
sales, 205
salesman, 437
salient, 173
Salient Six, 282
Salisbury, 275
salmon, 168, 170, 210, 220, 439
salon, 404
saloon, 15, 339, 404, 563
salt, 178, 397, 442
Salt Creek, 277
saltcellar, 362, 387
saltpeter, 387
salts, 442
salutation, 316
salve, 247
Sam, 170
Sambo, 286
same, 290, 294, 427
same identical, 416
samovar, 384
sample, 170, 405
San Anselmo, 277
San Berdoo, 355
San Franciscan, 280
San Francisco, 277
San Jose, 56, 277
San Pablo, 277
San Rafael, 277
sanatorium, 340, 405
sanctimonious, 563
sand, 442, 556
sand pile, 48
sands, 442
sandwich, 214, 250, 358, (cap.) 275
Sandy, 286
sang, 116, 199, 454
sanguine, 211, 430, 567
sanitarium, 339, 405
Santa Ana, 227, 277
Santa Fe, 226, 248, 277, 280
Santa Rosa, 277
sapphire, 382, 383
sardine, 358
sargasso, 381
sartin, 52
sarvant, 52
sarved, 61
Saskatchewan, 277
Sat. (Saturday), 255
Satan, 382
satchel, 384

sated, 400
satiate, 208, 400
satiric, 177
satisfy, 400
satsuma, 385
Saturday, 281, 368
satyr, 171
saucy, 179
sauerkraut, 102, 188, 380, 397
sausage, 102
savannah, 384
savant, 44, 429
save, 173, 308, 431, 539
saving, 308
savings, 443
saviour (savior), 235, 260, 599
savvee, 66
savvy, 66
saw, 214, 403, 409, 468, 572
sawed-off, 348
sawing, 214
sawyer, 338, (cap.) 213
Saxon, 275
saxophone, 387, 397
say, 174, 218, 427, 460
says, 172, 234, 498
scabby, 403
scads, 286, 444
scald, 377
scale, 376
scalp lock, 39
scalpels, 567
scandal, 202, 206, 404
scandiculous, 352
Scandinavian, 132
scarcely, 306, 534
scarcity, 244
scare, 376
scarecrow, 348
scarlet, 383
scatter, 405
scaur, 400, 407
scenario, 59
scenic, 173, 206
schedule, 157, 208, 213. 242
scheme, 206
schism, 177, 206, 219, 237
schismatic, 219
schist, 207, 237
Schmid, 274
Schmitt, 274
scholastic, 59

school, 182, 202, 206, 369, 378
schoolhouse, 348
science, 206, 237, 246, 597
scientist, 386
scilicet, 307
scion, 572
scission, 207, 237
scissors, 205, 443, 551, 597
scoff, 238
scoff at, 482
scofflaw, 348
scoffs, 206
scone, 181
score, 400, 407, 440
Scotch, 279
Scots, 279
scrabble, 379
scrape, 376
scratchy, 340
screech, 403
scrouge, 182, 183
scrub, 406
scrumptious, 32, 417
scruple, 182
scuffle, 406
Sculpture, 558
scutcheon, 245
scythe, 204
sea, 175, 231, 248
seal, 206
Sealex, 282
seamstress, 173, 437
Search-the-Scriptures, 272
seas, 410
season, 175, 198, 253
seat, 401
secede, 260, 345
secesh, 345
seceshdom, 345
secession, 345
secessionism, 345
secessionist, 345
secessionizer, 345
second, 291, 294, 327, 426, 561
second days, 59
second story, 161
secondly, 305
secretary, 158, 220, 339
secure, 404
sedan, 58
sedate, 400
sedentary, 341, 400

WORD INDEX

sediment, 400
seduce, 343, 563
see, 87, 106, 248, 258, 427, 456, 546
see you later, 316
seed, 232
seeing, 212, 319, 465
seek, 460
seem, 295, 476
seems, 296
seen, 175
sees, 410
seesaw, 335
seethe, 455
seex (six), 57
seigneur, 407
seize, 233, 401, 410
seldom, 571
seldom-traveled, 349
select, 227
selection, 339
self-control, 252
selfsame, 294
self-starting, 347
self-sustaining, 252
sell, 460
sells, 296
semantics, 12
semaphore, 172
semasiology, 12
semifinals, 343
semivowel, 213
send, 427, 461
send-off, 301
seneschal, 379
senior, 407, 450
sensual, 208
sent, 178
separate, 404
separately, 305
September, 281
sepulchral, 430
seraglio, 441
seraph, 382, 441
seraphim, 441
serene, 450
serenely, 244
serf, 203
serge, 385
sergeant, 167, 235, 404, 549, 564, (cap.) 285
serial, 175, 213
seriatim, 371
serious, 175, 178
serjeant, 231
sermon, 168
serpent, 168

servant, 338, 404, 549
served, 243
service, 168, 210, 339
servile, 341
sessile, 400
session, 208, 400
set, 298, 299, 346, 401, 406, 459, 462
set about, 107
set off, 301
set up, 297
settle, 201, 300, 401
seven, 172, 175, 203, 326
seventy year, 54
sever, 172, 232, 404
several, 291
severally, 305
sew, 180, 231
Sewell, 214
sewer, 183, 231
sextet, 245
Sextus, 272
shaämed, 51
shabby, 403
shade, 405, 406, 550, 557
shadow, 406, 550
shaft, 58
shah, 383
shake, 456
Shakespeariana, 339
shale, 380
shall, 179, 295, 453, 463, 521, 522, 530, 579, 597
shally, 179
shame, 313
shamefaced, 362
shamefast, 362
shampoo, 383
shamrock, 53, 375, 396
shan't, 26, 256
shape, 207, 456
shard, 400
share, 400, 407
shark, 547
sharp, 210, 216
shatter, 405
shave, 456
shaved, 232
shavetails, 28
Shavians, 280
shaving, 268, 319, 357
shavings, 269, 319, 337, 357, 557
shawl, 397
shay, 356

she, 289, 365, 427, 447
shear, 400, 411, 456
shears, 400, 443
shed, 405, 462
she-dragon, 547
sheep, 372, 418, 439, 495
sheepshead, 348
sheer, 400, 411
sheer (share), 53
sheeting, 557
sheik, 176, 383
shelf-list, 58
shell, 207, 237
shellac, 249
shepherd, 209, 220, 418
sherbet, 383
Sheridan, 278
sheriff, 350
Sherman, 278
shew, 159, 180
shibboleth, 382, 390
shield, 175
shiest (shyest), 235
shillelagh, 53, 375
shilly-shally, 571
shine, 455
shined, 455
ship, 207, 404, 590, 591
ship ahoy, 316
shire, 210
shirt, 376, 397, 400, 403
shock, 207
shoe, 182, 231, 439, 460
shoeing, 243
shoes, 161
shone, 465
shook, 184
shoon, 439
shoot up, 414
shore, 400, 407
shore (sure), 184, 196
shorn, 181, 458
short, 181, 400
shortcomings, 444
shortcut, 348
shorten, 414
shorts, 318
Shorty, 287
Shotover, 276, 351
should, 6, 184, 234, 247, 258, 362, 418, 521, 525, 526, 529, 579, 593
shoulder, 200, 547, 597
shouldn't ought, 525
show, 83, 84, 180, 187, 457, 575, (cap.) 187

WORD INDEX

shower, 188
shrapnel, 358
shred, 462
shrewd, 566
shriek, 207, 403
shrift, 203, 218
shrill, 215
shrink, 414, 455
shrinkage, 338, 414
shrive, 186, 203, 218, 369, 455
shrub, 406
shuffle, 406
shunt, 161
shut, 298, 462
Shylock, 320, 358, 570
sib, 40, 572
sick, 65, 161, 376
sickem, 316
sicken, 295
sickness, 269
side, 206, 319, 561
side with, 300
sideburns, 35
sideling, 342
sidelong, 356
sidesaddle, 39
sidestep, 349
sideswipe, 347
sidetrack, 349, 547, 580
sidewalk, 347
siege, 175, 401
Sierra, 381
sieve, 177, 232, 233, 234
sigh, 186
sight, 269
sign, 211, 219, 300
sign away, 300
signal, 219, 261
signer, 261
signor, 213, 407
Silent Six, 282
silk, 369, 385, 397
silken, 210
Sillimanite, 282
silly, 563
silver, 216, 268, 442
silver screen, 59
simile, 97
simmering, 211
simonize, 341, 459
simony, 358, 383
simple, 563
simply, 321
simultaneous, 178
sin, 177
sin twisters, 35

since, 305, 308, 310, 311, 312, 322, 487, 534, 542
sincere, 211
sinecure, 187
sing, 78, 83, 199, 212, 237, 249, 406, 454, 455, 456
singe, 406
singeing, 241, 244, 259
singer, 212, 237, 259, 436
single, 294
single-handedly, 306
sing-sing, 335
singsong, 335
sinister, 556
sink, 295, 455
sink or swim, 580
sinner, 253
sint (sent), 178
Sioux, 259, 277
siphon, 203
sir, 283, 360, 407, 438
sire, 360, 372, 407, 438
sirloin, 362, 366
sirup (syrup), 178, 185, 234, 258, 383, 397
sis, 354
sister, 438, (cap.) 285
sister-in-law, 252
sisters-in-law, 444
sistren, 439
sit, 83, 400, 406, 456
sit tight, 578
situation, 552
six, 326
sixpence, 348
size, 186, 401
Sizzling Susan, 315
skald, 377
skedaddle, 30
skeleton in the closet, 578
skew-gee, 332
ski, 248, 377
skid, 376
skidoo, 30, 313
skiff, 404
skilful (skillful), 239
skill, 202, 206, 216, 376, 377
skin, 376, 377
Skinny, 287
skipper, 379
skirt, 31, 376, 397, 400, 403

skull, 206
skunk, 384
sky, 376
slack, 405
slacks, 557
slake, 405
slammed, 238
slams, 211
slander, 206, 404
slang, 26, 34, 170, 576
slangster, 337
slanguage, 352
slants, 211
slaughterhouse, 431
slaughtoist, 352
Slav, 249, 279
slave, 268, 358, 384
slaveholder, 39
slavery, 338
slay, 456
sleazy, 174
sled, 379, 403
sledge hammer, 387
sleek, 175, 176, 178, 405
sleep, 460
sleigh, 174, 209, 231, 377, 590
slept, 200, 216, 218
sleuth, 44
slick, 176, 405
slickery, 352
slide, 403, 455
Slim, 287
Slim Jones, 285
slime, 207
sling, 455, 456
slink, 455
slit, 462
slogan, 375
sloop, 207, 379
sloth, 181
slough, 188, 251, 375
slow, 214, 215, 306, 530
slow down, 302
slower, 214
slow-moving, 349
sloyd, 189, 377
sluggard, 338
slur, 184
slush fund, 59
slyly, 235
small, 207, 215, 422
smallest, 422
smallness, 337
smart, 411
smell, 431, 461, 476, 575
smelt, 461

WORD INDEX

smite, 455, 570
smith, 204, (cap.) 274
smoke, 207
smoking, 232
smug, 563
snail, 207, 215
snap, 334, 562
snares, 205
sneak, 207
snitch, 31
snob, 405
snoop, 207
snout, 431, 564
snowed, 4, 47
snub, 405
snuck, 458
so, 180, 206, 248, 290, 306, 510
so . . . as, 310, 541
so long, 316
so that, 310, 312, 494
soaked, 203
soap, 249
sobriquet, 247
soccer, 202
social, 208, 237
socialist, 268, 340
society matron, 429
socked, 28
socks (sox), 79, 83, 202
Socony, 282, 352
sod, 169
sodden, 458, 465
sofa, 383
soft, 179, 203
soft soap, 563
soften, 88, 201, 247
soh boss, 316
soil, 206, 210
soiled, 431
sojourn, 570
solan goose, 387
solder, 200, 247
soldier, 180, 201, 240
solemn, 219, 235, 242
solemncholy, 352
solemnity, 219
solo, 28
Solomon, 320
solstice, 401
somber, 211, 216
sombrero, 245, 381, 397
some, 291, 292, 320
some guy, 554
somebody, 291, 498, 554
somehow, 306
someone, 291, 498

someone else's, 293, 449
someone's else, 449
Somersetshire, 275
something, 291
sometime, 305, 325
somewhat, 306
son, 185, 268, 409, 438
song, 179
songsmith, 347
sonny, 229, (cap.) 287
sont (sent), 54
Soo Line, 355
soon, 183, 305, 449
sooner, 578
sooner or later, 580
soort, 51
soot, 182, 183, 184, 197, 401
soporific, 341
soprano, 381, 404
sorrel, 169, 237
sorrow, 169, 180
sorry, 169, 313, 530
sort, 181, 499
sort of, 306
sot (set), 54
soul, 180, 188, 206, 233, 558
sound, 77, 188, 220, 476
sour, 188
souse, 242
soused, 31, 33
south, 188
South Dakota, 226
southerly, 204
southernmost, 450
southwest, 305
sovereign, 404, 599
soviet, 384
sow, 187, 409, 438, 457
sox, 241
soy, 385
spa, 168, 248
space, 206, 244
spacious, 244
spade up, 300
spake, 41, 456
spalpeen, 53, 375
span, 170, 440, 455, 456
spangle, 170
spaniel, 358
spanner, 161
spans, 440
spare, 207, 216
sparrow, 171, 173
sparrowgrass, 4, 37, 362
Spartan, 294

spasm, 171, 174, 205, 209, 219, 224, 254, 378
spasmodic, 209, 219, 224
spat, 355, 462
spatula, 440
spavin, 171
speak, 456
special, 207
specialize, 239
specially, 374, 405
species, 356
specifically, 307
spectacle, 338, 347
spectators, 4
speech, 9, 10, 269
speechless, 249
speed, 320, 461, 485, 551
speed up, 300
speeding, 319
speedometer, 387
spell, 461
spelling, 10
spelling bee, 15
spelt, 201
spend, 369, 461
sperrit (spirit), 54
sphinx, 203
Spick, 286
spick and span, 571
spiffy, 292, 417
spile (spoil), 186
spill, 200, 461
spilt, 201, 239
spin, 455
spinach, 383
spinster, 211, 337, 438
spirit, 404
spit, 431, 462
spitch (speech), 57
spite, 405, 592
spitfire, 348
spittoon, 339, 431
splashed, 208
spleen, 555
splendid, 313
splice, 379
splint, 201
split, 462
spoil, 186, 461
spoilt, 461
Spokane, 170
spondulix, 30, 34
spoon, 183
spoonfuls, 337, 444
spoons, 354

WORD INDEX

spoor, 182
spore, 207, 430
sport, 111, 405
sporting (sportin'), 157
spouse, 188
sprawl, 200
spread, 414, 462
sprier (spryer), 235
sprightly, 600
spring, 455, 456
sprite, 404, 405
sprouts, 556
spuds, 28
spume, 403
spur, 44
sputum, 190
spy, 207, 405
squad, 169, 400
squadron, 400
squall, 179
squalor, 174
square, 400, 451, 562
squaw, 160, 384
squawl, 207
squeak, 207, 334
squiffy, 162
squire, 207, 216, 374, 405
squirearchy, 346
squirm, 210
squish, 353
St. (street), 255
stability, 219
stable, 219, 401
staccato, 381
stack, 403, 407
stack up, 162
stacks, 58
Stacomb, 352
stadium, 371, 441
staff, 168, 173, 442
stage, 355, 401
stagecoach, 39
stair, 171
stake, 401, 403, 407
stallion, 438
stalls, 161
stalwart, 214
stamen, 369, 401, 441, 442
stamina, 442
stamp, 557
stanch, 168
stanchion, 401
stand, 201, 216, 295, 401, 456, 476, 560
stand under, 297

stand up, 298, 300, 485
standard English, 23
stands, 295
stang, 455
stanza, 380, 401
star, 167
stare, 171
stark, 105
starter, 428
starve, 167, 376, 418, 551
state, 207, 359, 374, 401, 405, 407, 549, 552
States-General, 503
statesman, 564
static, 401, 566
station, 401
stationary, 171
statistician, 339
statistics, 443
statue, 189, 401
status, 171, 174, 401, 407
statute, 401
stave, 457
staves, 173, 442
stay, 401
steadfast, 347, 362
steak, 121, 174, 233, 401, 407
steal, 172, 207, 233, 269, 456
stealing, 269
stealth, 269
stealthy, 172
steelyards, 176
stein, 186
stem the tide, 572
stem-winder, 39
stench, 431, 564
stenography, 190
stentorian, 358
step, 172
step on it, 313
stepfathers, 444
Stephen, 378
steppe, 384
sterling, 185
stethoscope, 567
steward, 350, 564
stewed, 417
stick, 401, 406, 457, 546
stickleback, 401
stickt, 47
stiff, 546
stigma, 401
stigmatize, 401
stile, 411

stilettos, 245
still, 305, 307, 311
still-hunt, 252
stillness, 239
stimulus, 440
sting, 207, 401, 455
stink, 431, 455, 564
stirred, 243
stirrup, 350, 572
stitch, 401, 406
stitches, 428
Stixall Glue, 283
stock, 169, 401, 407
stockade, 401
stocking, 401
stoic, 358
stoicism, 206
stoker, 161, 401
stolen, 181
stomach, 47, 192, 597
stone, 435
stone-cold, 349
stone-dead, 306
Stonethwaite, 276
stool, 401, 418, 551
stop, 119, 207, 313, 326, 369, 405, 531
storage, 243
store, 161, 180, 267
store furniture, 348
storekeeper, 348
story (storey), 210, 405
stout, 187, 449
stove, 180
stow, 401
straddle, 353
straight, 174, 292, 306, 324
straight ticket, 59
straight-edged, 340
straight-life, 58
strain, 207
strait, 404
straits, 174
strap, 359, 405
strata, 171, 441, 442
Stratford, 275
Stratford-on-Avon, 252, 275
Stratton, 275
stratum, 405, 441
straw, 179
stray, 405
streaks, 44
Streatham, 275
street, 126, 368, 405
street car, 160

WORD INDEX

strength, 212, 267, 327
strengthen, 327, 414
stretch out, 302
strew, 457
strict, 404
stricture, 203
stride, 455
strike, 243, 455, 570
string, 458
striped, 243, 465
stripes, 44
strips, 44
strive, 458
stroke, 546
stroll, 207
strong, 105, 179, 346, 454
strong fella, 66
strongest, 212
strop, 359, 405
strophe, 176, 248
structure, 203
strut, 58
strychnine, 187
stubble, 185
stuck-up, 292, 401
student sing, 44
studio, 381, 404
studios, 245
study, 404
studying, 251
stuff, 27, 427, 552
stuffed, 465
stuffing, 337
stuffocate, 35, 352
stunning, 560
stupid, 341
sturdy, 379, 566
stwone (stone), 52
style, 186, 234, 258, 411
suave, 168, 214
sub, 356
sub rosa, 371
subcontract, 343
subdued, 45
subjective complement, 476
subjunctive, 464
subordinate, 292
subpœna, 80, 175, 231, 233, 246, 369, 596
subside, 414
subsidence, 414
substantive, 267
substitute, 356
substitute for, 537
subterfuge, 343

subtle (subtile), 201, 246, 259, 260, 598
subtract, 414
subtraction, 414
succeed, 236, 260, 343, 345, 429, 594, 599
success, 345
successful, 345
successfulness, 345
succession, 77, 80, 236, 345
successional, 345
successive, 345
successiveness, 345
successor, 345
succotash, 249
such, 185, 241, 250, 290, 291
such as, 482, 541
such ... that, 541
sucker, 547
sucrose, 58
suddenly, 306
suds, 443
sufel, 39
suffer, 343, 399, 570
suffice, 206
suffocate, 411
Suffolk, 275
sugar, 207, 237, 383, 397, 590
suggest, 343
suggestive, 563
suit, 183, 206, 234, 404
suitable, 183
suitatorium, 340
suite, 175, 404
sulphur (sulfur), 148, 594, 597, 599
sultan, 210, 437
sultana, 437
sum total, 100
sum up, 302
sumach, 207
summer, 94, 210, 237
summon, 343
summons, 443
sumptuous, 247, 341
sun, 409
sun room, 227
Sunday, 281
sunflower, 566
Sunflower State, 286
sung, 78, 199, 454
sunshine, 268
super, 354
super-elegant, 252

supererogation, 430
superfluity, 86
superfluous, 86, 225
superimposed, 429
superior, 213, 450
supersede, 400
supersensitive, 343
supple, 184, 197
support, 119, 343
supraliminal, 343
supreme, 450
sure, 183, 184, 193, 195, 207, 218, 258, 307, 404, 432, 530, 535
surely, 307, 535
surety, 195
surmount, 342
surname, 386
surprise, 205, 596
surrender, 343
surrey, 358
survey, 223
suspect, 223
suspicion, 339
Sussex, 275
sustain, 119, 343
sutthin', 54
swain, 377
swallow, 169
swan, 169, 179
swang, 455, 456
swank, 162
sware, 456
swarm, 179, 270
swarthy, 179, 204
swear, 207, 214, 456
sweat, 431, 462
Swede, 273, 279, 287
Swedeburg, 276, 277
Sweden, 214
Swedish Christmas turkey, 363
sweep, 460
sweepings, 319, 443, 557
sweets, 161, 557
swell, 207, 217, 417, 455
swellegant, 352
swerve, 203
swim, 455, 456
swindler, 563
swine, 214, 372, 439, 547
swing, 406, 455, 456
swinge, 406
switch, 161
swoll, 459
swollen, 207, 214, 458, 465

WORD INDEX

swoon, 207, 214
sword, 214, 247
sy (say), 174
sycamore, 177, 383, 396
syllabus, 333, 440
syllogism, 206, 344
sympathy, 344, 555
synagogue, 177
syncope, 262
syndic, 401
synonyme, 242
synopsis, 441
syntax, 11, 344
synthesis, 399, 441
system, 343, 401
systematize, 459

Tabby, 280
tabernacle, 404
table, 79, 83, 85, 170, 209, 219, 222, 227, 250
tableau, 234, 441
tableaux, 205, 247, 441
tablet, 209
tabloid, 283
taboo, 66, 182, 231, 385
tabular, 219
tactics, 443
taffeta, 383
taffy, 563
tail, 547
tailor, 174, 194, 268, 372
take, 174, 186, 298, 299, 346, 376, 426, 427, 457, 476, 546
take for a ride, 548
take in, 301
take out, 58
take over, 297, 482
take up, 301
talcum, 179
talk, 233, 247, 299, 300, 427, 601
talk up, 300
talkie, 59.
tall, 324, 449
taller, 116, 250
tallest, 116
Tam o' Shanter, 220, 491
tamales, 56
tamarack, 249
tambo, 66
tame, 401
Tammany, 384

tamper with, 536
tan, 46
tandem, 235
tangerine, 178
tango, 212
tank, 381
tantalize, 358, 378
tapioca, 384, 397
tapir, 384
tapped, 238
tariff, 203, 249
tarnal, 168, 192
tarp, 354
tartan, 375, 397
tartar, 167, (cap., Tatar) 383
task, 170, 221, 405
tassel, 206
taste, 207, 476, 575
tattler, 210
tattoo, 385
taught, 179, 199, 246, 454, 593
taunt, 179
tavern, 404
tawdry, 179, 233, 359
tax, 221, 405
taxi, 355
taxpayer, 253
Tay Pay, 287
Taylor, 272
tea, 149, 176, 248, 385, 397
teach, 199, 401, 460, 575
teachable, 387
teacher, 201, 267, 436, 558
teak, 149, 385, 397
team, 270, 279
teamster, 211, 216
tear, 409, 456
tea-room, 111
tease, 556
technique, 373
technocracy, 575
Teddy, 287
tedious, 217
tedjous (tedious), 201, 217
teem, 67
teeter, 175
teeter-totter, 335
teeth, 96, 175, 199, 204, 439
teetotaler, 35
telegram, 346
telegraph, 346, 379, 597

telephone, 148, 169, 172, 181, 203, 225, 347, 379, 459, 597
telephonic, 169, 225
telephoto, 347
telescope, 347
television, 387
tell, 427, 597
temblor, 404
temperament, 37
temple, 369
tempt, 247
ten, 340, 401
tenacious, 105, 401
tender, 401, 450
tenderfoot, 162
tendon, 401
Tennessee, 277
tenor, 211
tense, 401, 588
tent, 401
tenuous, 403
tepee, 175
tepid, 172, 191
terminal, 210
terrace, 591
terrible, 173
terribly, 306, 534, 560, 566
terrier, 213
terrific, 341
terrify, 341
terror, 269, 557
terse, 429
terseness, 244
tertium quid, 371
testatrix, 437
tête-à-tête, 373
tetrarch, 400
Texaco, 172, 283
Texan, 341
Texarkana, 278
textile, 225, 598
Thames, 172, 205
than, 310, 327, 406, 540
than whom, 327
thane, 204
thank, 204
thank you, 313
thanks, 26, 313, 443
thanks a lot, 313
Thanksgiving Day, 282
that, 204, 237, 289, 290, 293, 310, 320, 323, 427, 448, 468, 493, 494, 499, 504, 540
that is, 482

WORD INDEX

that is to say, 482
that which, 289
thatch, 403
thawed, 47
the, 3, 72, 73, 204, 293, 324, 325, 427, 504
the . . . the, 541
The Bull, 281
The Dalles, 276
the darker, the better, 520
the first, 290
the former, 290
The Fourth, 282
The Hub, 286
the latter, 290
the more, the merrier, 520
the second, 290
the sooner the better, 578
The Tabard, 281
The White Horse, 281
theater (theatre), 219, 223, 235, 242, 260, 599
theatrical, 219
theäze, 52
Thebes, 204
thee, 59, 447
their, 196, 293, 376, 447
theirn, 447
theirs, 293, 447
theirselves, 289, 448
them, 85, 204, 376, 426, 427, 447
theme, 399
themselves, 289, 320, 321, 448
then, 83, 104, 115, 121, 204, 305, 311, 323, 406, 591
then again, 311
thence, 305
Theodore, 378
theology, 204
theorist, 340
theory, 378
there, 171, 204, 231, 257, 266, 305, 323, 326, 328, 427, 502, 535, 579
therefore, 306, 311
thereof, 535
thermometer, 378, 567
thesaurus, 399
these, 77, 80, 288, 290, 448, 499

thesis, 378, 399, 441
thews, 38, 183
they, 121, 174, 204, 231, 289, 291, 376, 427, 447
they're, 256
thick, 204
thief, 326
thievish, 431
thimble, 219
thin, 77, 80, 83, 204, 237, 401, 403, 449
thin juice, 58
thin out, 414
thine, 293, 447
thing, 27, 427, 552
thing-names, 100
think, 204, 212, 295, 427, 460
thinks, 212
thin-lipped, 349
thinnest, 238
thinning-out, 301, 414
third, 291, 294, 327
third person plural, 503
thirdly, 305, 327
thirteen, 340
this, 177, 204, 249, 290, 293, 320, 427, 448, 499, 504
this once, 323
thither, 305
thole, 403
Thomas, 201, 258, 272
Thomas Black, 273
Thomas Weaver (Webster), 272
thon, 353
thorough (thoro), 185, 406, 593, 595, 599
thoroughfare (thorofare), 301, 595
thoroughly, 306, 307
those, 290, 448, 499
thou, 25, 38, 41, 187, 234, 248, 289, 447
thou seest, 41
though (tho), 180, 246, 251, 310, 593, 595, 599
though . . . nevertheless, 541
though . . . yet, 310
thought, 179, 204, 233, 239
thousand, 440
thrall, 376

thrash, 405
thrashes, 359
thread, 233
threat, 172, 234
three, 104, 269, 288, 291, 294, 326
three by five cards, 14
threefold, 294, 340
three-sided, 292
thresh, 405
threshes, 359
threw, 410, 457
thrice, 305
thrift, 203
thrifty, 218
thrill, 204, 215, 403, 556
thrilling, 565
thrive, 203, 218, 376, 457
throstle, 180
through (thru), 246, 298, 305, 308, 406, 410, 539, 595, 599
throughout (thruout), 308, 539, 595
throw, 4, 47, 197, 204, 429, 457
throw over, 297, 301
throwed, 4, 47, 457
thrown, 233
thrust, 462
thug, 149, 385
thumb, 219, 220, 598
thunder, 211
thunderation, 339
Thursday, 281
thus, 204, 249, 306
thusly, 305
thwack, 204, 214
thwart, 204, 214, 217
thy, 248, 293, 447
thyme, 186, 201, 236
thyroid, 204
thyself, 448
tick, 177
ticket, 401, 404
ticket office, 161
tickled to death, 560
ticktack, 335
tide, 94, 561
tidings, 443
tidy, 177, 186, 194, 232
tie, 234, 235, 248
tiffin, 203
tiger, 186, 369
tight, 547
tigress, 437

WORD INDEX

tike (take), 174, 186
tile, 369
till, 201, 308, 311, 376
timber, 177, 211
time, 186, 427
time immemorial, 503
times, 227
time-taking word, 101
timid, 177, 210
tin, 548
tin shop, 571
tincture, 212
tine, 401
tinge, 244
tingeing, 243, 244
tinner, 337
Tiny, 287
Tipperary, 46
tipple, 200
tipsy, 417
tirade, 174
tire (tyre), 159, 259, 260
tire of, 482
tireless, 340
'tis, 256
tissue, 208
titanic, 294
tithe, 401
title, 186, 219
title-entry, 58
titter, 177
titular, 219
to, 248, 298, 308, 406, 427, 478, 491, 510
to and fro, 40, 571
to fully comprehend, 506
to further improve, 506
to just miss, 506
to thus split, 506
to wit, 482, 572
tobacco, 149, 381, 384
toboggan, 384
today, 197, 252, 305, 427
toddy, 383, 397
to-do, 393, 399, 405
toilet, 189
token, 401
told, 180, 220
tolerable, 341
tolerate, 341, 403, 531
tolls, 205, 218
tomahawk, 149, 160
tomato, 149, 174, 196, 384
tomatoes, 245

tomb, 182, 601
tomcat, 437
tome, 201, 236, 258
tomiok, 66
tomorrow, 252, 323
tom-tom, 334, 335, 385
ton, 406, 440, 549
tone, 169, 401
tongs, 443
tongue, 245
tonguester, 337
tonic, 169
tonight, 252, 323
tonsillitis, 176, 567
too, 182, 258, 306, 406, 534
too bad, 26
too much, 306
too (much) disappointed, 534
took, 202
tooth, 182, 199, 401
tootle off, 162
top, 83
topaz, 249
topcoat, 225
topmost, 450
topography, 190, 191
topple, 341
toppled, 45
Topsy-like, 340
torn, 181
tornado, 381
tortoise, 594
Tory, 179, 280, 294, 375, 391
toss, 180, 196, 206
total, 181
totem, 384
touching, 308
touchy, 340
tough, 185, 234, 258, 597
toughen, 341
toughs, 319
tour, 188
touraco, 334
tournament, 185
tow, 187, 401, 403
toward, 180, 188, 194
towards, 308
towed, 47
towel, 188
tower, 214, 372
Towle, 188
town, 188, 234
township, 337

toy, 188, 245
traceable, 244
traced, 244
tracing, 243
trade-union, 111
traffic, 202
trafficking, 239
tragedy, 378
train, 211
tram, 160
tranquil, 212
transact, 206
transcendental, 227
transcontinental, 343
transfer, 206, 223
translate, 297, 399
translation, 235
transliteration, 227
transmission, 566
transport, 223
trapeze, 175
trappings, 443
trash, 552
travail, 406
travel, 249, 295, 406, 418
traveling, 3
traveller (traveler), 22, 239
travelogue, 352
treacle, 161
tread, 456
treason, 372
treasure, 207, 372, 399
treasure-trove, 571
treat of, with, 536
treelike, 340
trek, 149, 153, 380
trekking, 202, 236, 237
trembling, 320
tremendjous (tremendous), 217
tremor, 404
trepang, 385
très bien, 35
trial, 612
tribunal, 35
trillium, 198, 213
trilogy, 177
trim, 574, 575
trinity, 369
trinket, 212
trio, 88, 175
triple, 294
triple-plate, 298, 349
trireme, 39
tristate, 343
triumph, 203

WORD INDEX

triumphing over, 45
trodden, 458
Trojans, 280
troll, 377
tropic, 347
tropical, 370
trough, 203, 251
troupe, 242
trousers, 443
trousseau, 181, 223, 441
trousseaux, 205, 247, 441
trout, 439
trow, 188
Troy, 277, 278
truck, 161
truck horse, 348
true, 250
truly, 307
truncate, 371
truncheon, 245
trunkful, 337
trust in, to, with, 536
trustee, 268, 359
trusty, 359
truth, 257, 269
try, 201, 215, 318, 553, 612
try and, 513
trying, 235
tryoutee, 338
tsetse, 384
tub, 232
tuba, 397
tube, 183, 232, 566
tuberculosis, 340, 431, 567
tuck (took), 54
Tuesday, 183, 197, 281
tuft, 185
tug, 401, 403
tulip, 383
tum (come), 46
Tumble-Inn, 281
tummy, 47
tumor, 58
tumtum, 64
tun, 406
tune, 401, 592
tuner, 232
tungsten, 377, 397
tunnel, 211, 232
turban, 383
turkey, 358, 363, (cap.) 185
turkhen, 352
turmoil, 188

turn, 43, 184, 298, 299, 476, 560
turn up, 301
turncoat, 348
Turneresque, 341
turnout, 301
turpentine, 186
turps, 28
turquoise, 189
turtle, 397, 573, 575
turtledove, 387
tutorial, 183
twaddle, 563
twain, 201, 214, 217, 406, 440, 570
'twas, 256
tweezers, 443
twenty, 340
twenty mile, 54
twenty-six, 252
twice, 305, 327
twicet, 220
twig, 201
twilight, 201
Twin Cities, 286
twirl, 210
twirler, 28
twit, 214, 401
two, 182, 214, 247, 248, 291, 294, 406
two by four, 14
two by two, 305, 327
twofold, 227, 294, 327
two-thirds, 253, 269
two-year-olds, 319
type, 85
typewriter, 356
typography, 195, 222
tyranny, 178
tyrant, 201

ugh, 312
ugly, 376
uh-huh, 26, 307
ukase, 384
ukulele, 385
ulna, 210
ulterior, 450
ultimatum, 174
ultra-stylish, 252
ultra-violet, 343
umbrella, 380
unable, 530
unanimous, 451
unawares, 306
unbear, 344
unbearable, 344

unbearably, 344
unbelievin', 53
unbending, 105
unborn, 344
unburden, 344
unceasing, 345, 386
unceasingly, 345
uncle, 202, 438
Uncle Sam, 286
unconscious of, 537
uncontent, 31
uncouth, 182, 188, 400, 418, 557
unction, 212
unctuous, 556
under, 305, 308
undergo, 297
underneath, 305
understand, 297, 342, 401
undertake, 349
undertaker, 39, 571, 574
undertow, 348
undoubtedly, 307, 535
Uneeda Biscuits, 283
unfurl, 342
unfurnished, 211
unguent, 202
unh-unh, 26, 307
unicellular, 343
uniform, 347
union, 189, 211, 213, 233, 257, 371, (cap.) 278
Union City, 276
Uniontown, 276
unique, 189, 202, 374, 451
unitarian, 369, (cap.) 280
unite, 212, 213, 259
universal, 227
universe, 347
university, 168, 406
unknown, 418
unless, 310, 534
unmentionables, 432
unnamed, 239
unrelated, 386
untie, 227
until, 251, 305, 308, 311, 322, 542
until lately, 535
until now, 323
until then, 535
unto, 308
unyielding, 105

WORD INDEX

up, 83, 85, 119, 298, 300, 302, 305, 308, 309, 429, 450, 504
up against, 309
up to, 308, 309, 578
upbearer, 344
upend, 349
uphold, 297
upon, 308
uppity, 340
uproar, 227
ups and downs, 323
Upsala, 277
upset, 44, 297
upstairs, 305
up-to-date, 253
upturn, 301, 342
upward (upwards), 305, 342
urban, 406
urbane, 406, 556, 565
urn, 233
us, 74, 233, 447
usage, 206
use, 189
used, 295, 521, 598
used to, 218, 527
useful, 213, 237
useless, 244, 254
usher, 161, 208, 233
Usonian, 279
usual, 207
Utah, 179, 231
utopian, 292, 358, (cap.) 292
utter, 294
uttermost, 405
Uxbridge, 275

vacation, 190
vaccine, 178
vacuum, 369, 371
vag, 355
vagary, 174
vague, 173, 245, 600
vail, 203
valentine, 358
valet, 210, 247
valiant, 292
valkyrie, 377
valley, 251, 599
value, 189, 234
vamp, 560
vampire, 356, 560
van, 355, 383, 406
Van Buren, 273
Van Doren, 179

Van Dyck, 273
vandal, 554
vane, 218
vanilla, 381
vanish, 211
vanquish, 212
Vapex, 282
vapid, 171
vapor, 174, 232
variance with, 537
various, 294
varlet, 375
varmint (varmin), 168
varsity, 168, 406
vary, 173, 410
vase, 206
vaseline, 206, 282, 283, 359
vassal, 375
vast, 404
vat, 218
veal, 4, 203, 236, 262, 372, 418, 551
vehicle, 401
veil, 404
vein, 211, 233, 601
velar, 341
veld, 149, 153, 380
Venetian, 280
vengeance, 241, 244
venial, 213
Venice, 277
venison, 205, 372, 418
venture, 405
veracious, 341
verandah (veranda), 209, 246, 381
verb, 255, 266, 403
verb-adverb combination, 298
verbatim, 371
verbose, 206, 341
vermin, 270, 403, 443
Vermonters, 279
versatile, 157, 225, 245, 556
verse, 184
version, 210, 216
versus, 308
vertebra, 371, 440
vertex, 441
very, 173, 294, 306, 410, 427, 534, 560
very (greatly) disappointed, 534
vest, 175
Vesuvius, 213

vet, 172, 355
veto, 245, 369
via, 309
viaduct, 401
viaticum, 401
vibrate, 371
vicar, 339
vice, 221, 244
vice presidents, 444
vice-regent, 343
vicinage, 416
vicinity, 416
vicious, 208, 221, 244
victoria, 358
victory, 248, 339
Victrola, 282
victuals, 177, 246, 259, 431, 443
videlicet (viz.), 307, 482
vie, 235, 244, 248
Viennese, 280 [325
view, 189, 190, 203, 234,
view of, 537
vignette, 213
vigorous, 202
viking, 377
vile, 177, 203, 566
vilify, 177
villain, 563
vine, 404
vinegar, 400
vineyard, 349
violent, 105
Violet, 272
violin, 381
virile, 178
virtue, 310, 442
virtuoso, 441
visage, 417, 570
viscount, 247
vise, 186
visible, 401
vision, 177, 401
visor, 186, 205
visual, 207
vital, 177, 186
vitality, 190
vitals, 443
vitascope, 387
vitriol, 235, 594
vivid, 177
vixen, 199, 202, **218**, 337, 405, 437, 547
viz. (videlicet), 307, 482
vocal, 169, 194
vocative, 169, 194
vodka, 384

WORD INDEX

vogue, 245
voice, 189
void, 189
voile, 404
volcano, 181, 245
Völkerwanderung, 93, 127
volplane, 58
volt, 203, 358
vomit, 564
Von Arnim, 273
Von der Leyen, 273
voodoo, 182, 335, 384
vorpal, 332
vow, 187
vowel, 83, 249
voyage, 338, 401, 418, 551
vrom (from), 52
Vulcan, 357
vulcanize, 357
vulgar, 563
Vulgate, 369
vulnerable, 210
vur (for), 52
vying, 244

waäy, 52
waddle, 169
wade, 551
waft, 170
wag, 355, 401
wage, 244, 405
wages, 443
wagon, 38, 379, 401, 403, 570
wail, 214, 377, 410
wain, 38, 379, 401, 403, 570
Wainwright, 572
waist, 172, 174
waistcoat, 172, 225
wait, 119, 295, 427
waiter, 554
waitress, 249, 339, 437
waiver, 268
wake, 53, 406, 457, 459
walk, 179, 453, 553
Walkathon, 352
walked, 105, 116
walks, 116
wall, 126, 214, 237, 368
Walla Walla, 335
Wallsend, 275
walnut, 350
walrus, 350
Walsh, 407

Waltham, 275
Walter, 179, 273
wampum, 384
wane, 414
want, 427, 525
wanton, 169, 350, 563
wants, 211
war, 179, 193, 372, (cap.) 558
warble, 200
ward, 179, 379, 403
warden, 372, 405, 551
ware, 171
warm, 179, 192
Warm Springs, 277
warming pan, 15
warmth, 211, 216
warp, 179, 572
warped, 200
warrant, 179, 405
warrantee, 373
Warren, 393
Warrenite, 282, 340
warrior, 213
Warsaw, 179
wart, 179
Warwick, 275
wary, 174
was, 51, 169, 205, 249, 326, 427
wash, 220, 579
washed, 208
washerwoman, 431
washes, 296
washing, 393, 557
Washington, 278
washout, 563
wassail, 206
waste, 83, 404, 414
waste away, 295, 414
wastelbread, 39
Wat, 273
watch, 406
water, 179, 424
watered, 292
Waterloo, 277
waters, 442
Watkin, 273
watt, 358, 410
wave, 243
Waverly, 277
wax, 414, 431
wax and wane, 571
waxen, 40
way, 174, 513
ways and means, 415
we, 289, 427, 447

weaken, 295, 414
weakling, 202, 337, 562
weal, 172, 214, 430
wealth, 204, 269, 338
wealthy, 172, 319
weapon, 172
wear, 105, 171, 410, 414, 458, 575
Wearever, 283
weariness, 267
wearing-down, 301
weary, 175
weasel, 205
weave, 456
Weaver, 274
Webster, 274, 278, 337, 572
Wednesday, 220, 246, 281
weed, 40
weeding-knife, 58
weeds, 430
week, 427
weep, 570
Weeping Water, 277
weevil, 175
weigh, 121, 233, 401
weight, 174, 337, 557
weir, 175, 233
weird, 175, 177, 233, 599
welcome, 298, 316, 376
welfare, 239
well, 262, 306, 321
well off, 292, 578
we'll, 256
wellaway, 372
well-bred, 349
well-planned, 253
well-to-do, 393
welly (very), 67
Welsh, 208, 279, 407
Welsh rabbit (Welsh rarebit), 4, 363
Weltgeist, 102
wen (when), 209, 410
wench, 563
wend, 406, 461, (cap.) 279
went, 178, 214, 239, 249, 454, 461
Wentworth, 214
were, 214, 522, 597
were (where), 209
we're, 26, 256
werewolf, 572
Wessex, 275

WORD INDEX

Westclox, 241
westernmost, 450
wet, 172, 292, 462
wets and drys, 59
we've, 256
whack, 209
whale, 209, 410, 547
wharf, 210, 216
what, 169, 198, 209, 234, 257, 289, 290, 296, 310, 320, 323, 324, 410, 427, 540
whatever, 290, 293, 310, 347
whatsoever, 290, 347
wheat, 267, 268, 318
wheedle, 175
wheel, 548
wheelbarrow, 171
when, 79, 83, 209, 214, 217, 240, 305, 310, 311, 323, 324, 410, 472, 493, 534, 540
whence, 311, 534, 535, 539, 540
whenever, 305, 310
where, 105, 171, 209, 214, 305, 311, 323, 324, 410, 493, 534, 535, 540
where ... at, 508, 535, 539
where ... from, 539
where ... there, 541
whereabouts, 443
whereby, 310
wherefore, 306, 311, 323
wherein, 310
whereof, 311, 540
whereon, 535, 540
whereupon, 311
wherever, 305
wherewithal, 430
whether, 290, 310, 493, 513, 540
whether ... or, 310, 513, 541
which, 201, 241, 250, 289, 290, 293, 310, 311, 320, 323, 493, 494, 540
whichever, 290, 293, 310
whichsoever, 290
whiffletree, 406
Whig, 280, 391
while, 214, 310, 410, 534, 540

whilom, 177, 186, 431, 571, 572
whimper, 253
whippletree, 406
whippoorwill, 334
whisky, 375, 397, 599
whistle, 201, 247
whit, 40, 406
Whitby, 276
white, 292, 324
white plague, 431
White Sox, 280
whitewash, 298, 349
whitewashed, 45
whither, 204, 209, 311, 324, 534, 540
Whitsuntide, 282
whittle, 177, 209
whiz, 30, 205, 249
who, 182, 208, 214, 237, 247, 248, 265, 288, 289, 290, 310, 320, 323, 432, 448, 449, 472, 493, 507, 517, 540
who ... to, 517
who did you see, 16, 517
who else's, 449
whoever, 290, 310, 448, 518
whole, 208, 214, 247, 262, 377, 400, 405
whole day through, 538
whole world, 548
whole-hearted, 349
whole-heartedly, 306
wholly, 181, 244
whom, 327, 448, 517
whomever, 448, 518
whomsoever, 448
whoop, 208, 214, 247, 334
whopper, 548
whose, 205, 293, 448, 499
whose else, 449
whosever, 293, 448, 518
whosoever, 290
why, 209, 214, 306, 310, 311, 323, 324, 472, 534, 540
whys and wherefores, 323
wi' (with), 51
Wichita, 277
wide, 317
widen, 318, 341, 414
widgeon, 201

widow, 438
widower, 438
widow's weeds, 40, 571
width, 201, 204, 318
wienerwurst, 102, 380
wienies, 320, 337
wife, 203, 218, 438, 446, 447
wig, 355
wiggle, 341
wight, 38, 40, 406
wigwam, 160, 384
wild, 177, 232
wildebeest, 380
wilderness, 177
wile, 373, 403, 410
wilful (willful), 239
Wilhelmina, 437
Wilkins, 337
will, 238, 295, 296, 321, 427, 453, 463, 521, 522, 530, 560, 579, 597, (cap.) 287
will keep, 296
Will Long, 273
William, 213, 272, 437
William Atwell, 272
William Monday, 273
Williams, 273, 274
Williamson, 273
Willie, 46, 229, 287
willies, 444
willingness, 337
will-o'-the-wisp, 444, 491
willy-nilly, 571
Wilson, 274
wily, 563
win, 455
win out, 297
wince, 211
wind, 177, 188, 194, 406, 409, 455
windbag, 30
windbreak, 348
winder (window), 220
winding up, 107
windlass, 249
window, 177, 268, 350
window-blind, 357
window-shopping, 252
windshield-wiper, 348
Windsor, 220
Windy City, 286
wine, 211, 368, 397, 404
wing, 376
winged, 243

WORD INDEX

wint (went), 178, 193
winter, 94, 211, 214, 219
wintry, 219
wiping, 200
wisdom, 177, 205, 269, 337, (cap.) 558
wise, 177, 205, 401, 403, 596
wiseacre, 401
wish, 177, 208
wisht, 220
wistaria, 369
wit, 401, 403, 442, 551
witch, 438
witchcraft, 337
with, 177, 204, 298, 308, 426, 427, 429
with might and main, 571
with reference to, 309
with regard to, 309
withdraw, 297, 414
wither, 253
withhold, 297
within, 308, 504
without, 308, 322, 542
without let or hindrance, 572
withstand, 342, 349
witness, 401
wits, 442
witty, 177, 228
wives, 203, 205, 218, 439, 446
wizard, 401, 438
woful, 244
wolf, 184, 203, 234, 258, 547
woman, 182, 183, 350, 438
womanly, 490, 565
womb, 182
wombat, 385
women, 177, 234, 258, 259, 260, 439
won, 214
wonder, 185, 330
wonderful, 340
wonderfuller, 451
wonder-worker, 348
wont, 169, 530, 571
won't, 16, 180, 198, 256, 427, 534, 571
woo, 182, 214, 248
wood, 184, 234
wooden, 340
Woods, 273

woof-woof, 335
wool, 184
woozy, 548
wop, 60, (cap.) 286
Worcester, 207, 247, 259, 275
word, 94, 403
word-strain, 100
wore, 214
work, 6, 269, 298, 299, 300, 429, 436, 442, 460
work days, 6
work over, 297
work up, 300
worked, 11, 201, 236, 258, 406
worker, 11, 268
workman, 349
works, 296, 442
world, 192, 197, 350
world over, 538
worm, 184, 403, 547, 551
wormwood (wermod), 362
worried, 210, 598
worry, 73, 105, 185, 234
worse, 184, 185, 206, 231, 258, 306
worser, 37
worship(p)ed, 239
worst, 73
worsted, 247, 259, 358
wort, 376, 551
worth, 476, 503
worthy of, 537
wot, 41, 463
would, 6, 184, 247, 362, 427, 521, 526, 529, 579, 593
wound, 182, 183, 188
wow, 312, 334
wrack and ruin, 571
wrang, 455, 456
wrangle, 542, 563
wranglers, 58
wrath, 210, 247
wreak vengeance, 572
wreathe, 244
wreck, 172, 214
wren, 210, 214, 215, 237
wrench, 161, 214, 247
Wrens, 352
wrestle, 206
wretch, 553, 563
wriggle, 295
Wright, 272

wring, 214, 455
write, 455
write down, 302
write-up, 301
writhe, 186, 204
writhed, 243
wrong, 179, 212, 247, 306, 321, 376, 450, 556
wronged, 243
wrongs, 557
wroth, 179, 181, 210
wrought, 406
wurden, 52
wurrum, 52
wuss (worse), 185
wust (worst), 73
wuth (worth), 53
wy (why), 209
Wycliffites, 280
Wynot, 278
Wyomingites, 279
Wyuta, 278

X rays, 567
Xenophon, 204, 237, 258
Xerxes, 204
Xmas (Christmas), 255
Xtian (Christian), 255

yacht, 259, 379
yah, 56, 307
Yahoo, 333
Yale, 213
yaller (yellow), 220
yam, 384, 397
Yankee, 212, 286, 566
yard, 167, 379, 401, 403, 440, 549
yardage, 338
yarrow, 210
yawl, 213, 380
yclept, 41, 463
ye, 52, 289, 447
yeah, 313
year, 157
year 900, 504
yearling, 337
yearly, 417
yearn for, 482
Yeats (Yates), 174
yelk, 172
yellocution, 352
Yellowstone, 213
yeoman, 180, 350, 597
yeomanette, 339

WORD INDEX

yes, 249, 307, 313
yesterday, 174
yet, 83, 84, 305, 307, 311
yew, 189
yez, 52
Yiddish, 380
yield, 119
yir (your), 53
yoke, 401, 440
yolk, 210
yon, 53, 54, 290, 293, 320
yonder, 293, 305, 320
yoost, 56
yore, 213, 237
yore (your), 184
York, 275
you, 3, 25, 38, 46, 47, 182, 248, 289, 291, 426, 427, 447, 473, 597
you all, 289
you bet, 307
you don't say, 313
you was, 498

you'd, 256
you'll, 256
young and old, 319
young-uns, 54
your, 184, 210, 293, 427, 447, 477
Your Grace, 285
Your Highness, 285
Your Honor, 285, 557
Your Majesty, 285, 557
you're, 256, 447
you're welcome, 313
yourn, 447
yours, 293, 447, 477
yourself, 289, 448, 474
yourselves, 289, 448
youse, 52
youth, 188, 189, 213
you've, 26, 256
Ypres, 35
yucca, 384
Yule, 213

zay (say), 52, 204, 218
zeal, 172, 204

zealous, 172, 404
zealous in, for, 537
zebra, 381, 384
zee (zed), 160
zenith, 204, 383
zero, 83, 204, 210, 237, 383, 404
Zerolene, 282
zeros, 245
zigor, 4
zigzag, 335
zinc, 380
zip, 334
zither, 397
zodiac, 204
Zomerset (Somerset), 205
zone, 204
zoo, 198, 355
zoölogy, 88, 180, 181, 196, 198, 204
zoom, 28, 334
zore (sore), 205
zounds, 314
zure (sure), 52, 218

Addenda

Africa, 256
Baltimore, 256
barrel-organ, 252
bellow, 295
chaotic, 173
conundrum, 235
disease, 205

greater, 410
Hampshire, 256
hemoroid, 599
hoed, 47
Liberals, 256
lime, 210
morgue, 245

shop, 161
stammering, 211
Stella, 210
sump, 211
tabulate, 170
warum, 52
yea, 307

SUBJECT INDEX

[Numbers refer to pages unless other subdivisions are specifically indicated.]

Abbreviations of words, 254, 285, 286, 482
Ablaut. See *Gradation*
Absolute nominative, 486, 516, 531, 533
Absolute personal pronoun, 447; 293, 477, 517
Absolute phrase. See *Nominative absolute*
Absolute superlative, 520
Abstract to concrete, 556
Abstract nouns, 267, 269, 285, 319, 326, 337, 338, 555, 558, 577
Absurdities in spelling, 259
Academy, movement for, 581
Accent marks, 85
Accent shift, effects of, 76, 86, 224, 406
Accent-leveling, 222
Accentual word pairs, 223; 86
Accentuation, 85, 157, 221, 238, 406
Accusative case, 446, 484
Action, nouns of, 269
Active voice, 463, 523
Active-passive verbs, 296, 321, 579
Adaptation v. borrowing, 330
Addison, Joseph, 98
Addition of consonants, 220; 54
Address, direct, 486
Adjectival clauses, 493; 310, 474, 484, 540
Adjectival elements in nouns, 484
Adjectival modifiers. See *Modifiers, adjectival*
Adjectival participles, 243, 292, 320, 322, 458, 465, 484, 489, 503, 523, 531, 533
Adjectival phrases, 484, 490, 578
Adjectival pronouns. See *Pronominal adjectives*
Adjectives
 accentuation, 224
 definition, 266, 291
 classification, 292, 320, 321
 as adverbs, 306, 321, 324, 483
 derivation, 340, 348, 351

substantivation, 318; 267, 278, 510, 557
 comparison, 449, 492
 syntax, 519; 476, 484, 485, 499, 502
Adjunct objective. See *Predicate objective*
Adverbial accusative. See *Adverbial nouns*
Adverbial clauses, 494; 485, 511, 540
Adverbial dative, 571
Adverbial elements in verbs, 485
Adverbial genitive, 305, 516
Adverbial modifiers. See *Modifiers, adverbial*
Adverbial nouns, 323, 484, 516
Adverbial participles, 322, 485
Adverbial particles, 307
Adverbial phrases, 311, 485, 489, 490, 578
Adverbial prepositions. See *Prepositional adverbs*
Adverbs
 definition, 266, 305, 321
 classification, 305, 310, 321, 323, 325, 520
 as adjectives, 306, 321, 325, 450, 483
 derivation, 342; 305, 351, 371
 comparison, 449
 syntax, 534; 311, 323, 475, 477, 484, 504, 520
Ælfric, 130, 265, 267, 451
African loan-words, 384
Afrikaans, 153
Age of Chaucer, 140, 574
Agreement. See *Concord*
Albanian language, 92
Alcuin, 131
Alfred the Great, 129, 132
Alliteration, 44, 282, 334, 415, 571
Alphabet, phonetic, 80–85, and inside back cover
Alphabetic sentences, 471
Amalgamated compounds, 350, 572
Amalgamated phrases, 292, 305, 325, 351, 477, 503, 504, 580

725

SUBJECT INDEX

Ambiguous consonant-spellings, 80, 244, 261
Ambiguous words, 298, 302, 316, 572
Ameliorative change in meaning, 564
American Indian words, 276, 384
American Joint Committee on Grammatical Nomenclature, 588
American names, 276
American speech, 154, 168, 169, 181, 187, 190, 236, 240, 256, 283, etc.
American Spelling Reform Association, 594
Amerind. See *American Indian*
Analogy, 4, 14, 47, 447, 517
Analytic v. synthetic languages, 118, 119, 434
Ancren Riwle, 138
Angles, 93, 127
Anglic, 115, 601, 605
Anglo-foreign dialects, 111
Anglo-Normans, 135
Anglo-Saxon Chronicle, 125, 129, 132, 137
Anglo-Saxon element, 275, 337, 340, 341, 342, 344, 347, 399
Anglo-Saxon England, 126
Anglo-Saxon language, 95, 96, 129, 435
Anglo-Saxon period, 123
Animal calls, 315
Animal names, 280
Anomalous verbs, 454, 462
Antecedent of pronoun, 288, 289, 290, 498
Anticipation, 4
Anticipatory modifiers, 487, 533
Antonyms, 413
Apostrophe, use of, 254, 445, 446
Appositional genitive, 491
Appositive modifier, 519
Appositives, 473, 482, 491, 516, 517
Approbation, words of, 29, 32, 417, 565
Arabic loan-words, 383
Archaisms, 38; 15, 430, 447, 452, 456
Argot, 28, 59, 62
Armenian language, 92, 95
Articles, definite and indefinite, 198, 266, 293, 504
Artificial languages, 603; 113
Ascham, Roger, 331, 380, 581
Aspects of verbs, 303, 341, 479, 523, 527
Assertion, adverbs of, 306, 535
Assimilation, 88, 218
Attitudes and policies
for the use of English, 3, 16, 17, 20, 25, 27, 183, 508, 512, 514, 543, 584, 602
for the study and teaching of English, 6, 62, 70, 80, 119, 166, 199, 230, 261, 263, 265, 308, 327, 329, 418, 435, 445, 454, 465, 468, 469, 480, 512, 514, 543, 545, 552, 576, 585–589, 617. See also Preface, pp. v–ix
Attribute complement. See *Predicate nominative*
Attributive modifier, 519, 531, 533
Augmentatives, 339
Australian English, 55, 152
Australian loan-words, 152, 385
Authority, 581–585, 587
Authorship, genitive of, 491
Auxiliary language, 113, 603
Auxiliary verbs, 295; 256, 321, 453, 462, 521

Back formations, 354
Backgrounds of English, 122
Bacon, Francis, 148
Balto-Slavic languages, 92, 95
Barnes, William, 100
Basic English, 114, 605, 610, 617
B. E., Gentleman, 16
Beach-la-Mar jargon, 65, 118
Bede's *Ecclesiastical History*, 125, 127
Beowulf, 131
Bible, 20, 98, 117, 147, 271, 316, 333, 415, 452, 571
Biblical words, 271, 358, 382
Blends, 351; 35, 278, 282
Blount, Thomas, 147, 333, 390, 425, 568
Boer dialect, 153, 380
Boners, 36
Borrowings from English, 111
Borrowings in English, 22, 96, 102, 149, 330, 366, 395
Breath sound *h*, 78, 208
British Broadcasting Corporation, 611
British Celts, 124
British Empire today, 150; 108
British English, 156, 168, 169, 181, 186, 190, 196, 204, 212, 225, 229, 236, 256, 259, 260, etc.
British Joint Committee on Grammatical Terminology, 585
Bullokar, William, 147

Calls for animals, 315
Camden, William, 272
Canadian English, 55, 152
Cant, criminal, 16, 28, 59, 62
Capitalization, 256
Cardinal numerals, 291, 294, 326

SUBJECT INDEX

Carroll, Lewis, 332, 351
Case, 445
Catholic terms, 59
Causal clauses, 310, 494
Causative verbs, 406
Cause, adverbs of, 306
Causes, of linguistic change, 14, 29, 38, 43, 49, 50, 55, 87, 161, 192, 217, 330, 351, 354, 547, 549; of vowel change, 86, 87, 192
Cawdrey, Robert, 147
Caxton, William, 144, 331, 380, 581
Celtic languages, 93, 95, 375
Celtic loan-words, 53, 99, 125, 275, 374
Celtic place-names, 125, 275, 375
Celts in Britain, 124
Characteristics of English, 19, 115, 222, 227, 579
Chaucer, Geoffrey, 123, 140, 144, 146, 149, 314, 460
Chaucerian Age, 140
Children's English, 45; 3, 334, 354, 422
Chinese. See *Pidgin English*
Chinese loan-words, 385
Chinook jargon, 63, 112
Christian names, 271, 285, 437
Chronological names, 281; 255
Classification of words, 10, 263, 267, 316, 319, 327, 468, 483, 542
Clauses, 12, 310, 472, 476, 484, 485, 487, 492, 505, 511, 540
Clipped words, 354; 172, 406
Close *o*, 180
Closed syllable, 87, 231
Cockney dialect, 157, 174, 186, 197, 209, 220
Cognate languages, 91
Cognate object of verb, 477
Cognate words in English, 274, 398, 402
Collective nouns, 267, 270, 279, 319, 440, 443, 495, 499
Collective proper names, 278, 286
College slang, 28, 354
Colloquial speech, 15, 26, 256, 292, 306, 309, 313, 323, 325, 327, 339, 340, 355, 440, 444, 447, 450, 458, 470, 473, 476, 484, 493, 496, 498, 509, 511, 513, 516, 522, 523, 534, 547, 554, 616, *et passim*
Colon, use of, 472, 483
Colorfulness of English, 32, 121, 580
Combinations of consonants, 79, 83, 88, 193, 215, 240
Comma, use of, 472, 482, 494

Common case, 445, 479
Common gender, 436
Common nouns, 267
Commonization of names, 320; 257, 283, 294, 357, 378, 553
Comparative constructions, 310, 327, 510
Comparison, clauses of, 494
Comparison, conjunctions of, 310, 327
Comparison of adjectives, 449, 492
Comparison of adverbs, 449, 492
Complements of verbs, 480
Complete verbs, 475; 324, 480
Completion, verbs of, 523, 533
Complex sentences, 472, 474, 493, 499
Composition, defined, 9, 335, 576, 587
    of words, 335, 346, 348
Compound adjectives, 348-349; 253, 292, 340, 440
Compound etymology, 364
Compound interrogative pronouns, 290
Compound names, 275, 276, 349, 376
Compound nouns, 348; 252, 444, 484
Compound personal pronouns, 289, 320, 448, 474, 477. 517
Compound prepositions, 308
Compound relative adverbs, 310, 535, 540
Compound relative pronouns, 290, 448, 473, 493, 518
Compound sentence, 472
Compound subject, 474, 496
Compound verbs, 297, 349
Compound words, 225, 252, 292, 297, 308, 335, 346, 348, 350, 386, 444
Compounding elements, 346
Compounds, amalgamated, 350, 572
Compounds, tautological, 387
Concessive clauses, 310, 494
Concord, 443, 495
Concrete nouns, 267, 319, 555, 557, 577
Concrete to abstract, 555
Conditions, 310, 494, 502, 521, 522
Confused etymologies, 360, 459
Confusion, elements of, 4, 35, 293, 296, 316, 320, 322, 360, 408, 442, 480, 487, 512, 531, 539, 588
Conjectural phrasal verbs, 524
Conjugation of verbs. 451; 47, 239, 242
Conjunctions, 266, 309, 321, 494, 511, 540
Conjunctive adverbs. See *Illative conjunctions*
Conjunctive pronouns. See *Relative pronouns*

SUBJECT INDEX

Connectives. See *Conjunctions*
Conservatism in language, 18, 29, 31, 34, 162
Consonant change, 209, 214, 217–221, 406
Consonant combinations, 79, 83, 88, 193, 215, 240
Consonantal vowels. See *Vocalic consonants*
Consonants, 76, 83, 199, 215–221, 236, 406
Contamination, 4
Contingent propositions, 528
Continuant consonants, 77, 203, 215
Contraction of words, 26, 254, 447, 522
Controversial etymologies, 364
Conventional phrases, 14, 429, 571, 578, 580
Conventional spellings, 258
Conversion, 316; 119, 301, 307, 313, 357, 428, 480, 576, 579, 587, 612
Coördinate clauses, 472
Coördinating conjunctions, 310, 321, 540
Copula, 476
Copulative verbs. See *Linking verbs*
Correct English, 468. See also *Pure English*
Correlatives, 310, 520, 540
Counter words, 29, 102, 428, 552, 559
Creation, original, 332
  v. borrowing, 330
Creation and adaptation of words, 330
Creators of words, 332
Criminal cant, 16, 28, 59, 62
Customary action, verbs of, 304, 526

Dangling participle, 487
Danish language, 94, 95, 131
Danish place-names, 275, 376
Dash, use of, 482
Dative case, 6, 446, 478, 491, 502
Declarative sentence, 469, 501
Declension, of nouns, 436; 203, 240, 243, 245, 592
  of pronouns, 447
Defective verbs, 462, 526
Deferred. See *Postponed*
Deferred subject, 473, 474, 496, 502
Definitions of words. See *Words defined*
Degeneration of meaning, 562
Degraded words, 562
Degree, adverbs of, 306, 321, 534
  clauses of, 310, 494
Demonstratives, 288, 290, 293, 320, 448, 499

Dental consonants, 78, 200, 204, 211
Dependent clauses. See *Subordinate clauses*
Depreciatory suffixes, 337, 339, 562
Depreciatory words, 29, 417, 562
Derivation of words, 11, 329, 389, 576
Derivational suffixes, 335–346. See also *Suffixes*
Derivative words, 169, 170, 172, 177, 194, 209, 218, 219, 221, 224, 225, 236, 239, 243, 244, 251, 268, 337–347, etc.
Derogatory words. See *Depreciatory words*
Descriptive adjectives, 292, 519
Detached conjunctions, 312
Development of English, 3–5, 5–7, 14, 38, 118, 122–154, 192–199, 218–221, 227, 330, 389, 395–396, 423, 434, 515, 520, 542, 545, 556, 569, 584, 610–618
Diæresis, use of, 198, 252
Diagraming, 323
Dialectal pronunciations, 49–55, 168, 169, 173, 174, 176, 178, 179, 184, 185, 186, 189, 190, 201, 204, 217, 220, etc.
Dialects, 49, 111
Diction, questions of, 303, 415, 418, 474, 538
Dictionaries, history of English, 147, 155, 389, 425
  use of, 41, 81, 183, 252, 254, 262, 418, 424, 432, 458, 496, 538, 552
Dictionary-makers. See *Lexicographers*
Dictionary-making. See *Lexicography*
Dieresis. See *Diæresis*
Digraphs, 75, 233, 236, 241, 248, 249, 258, 260, 601
Digraphs, simplification of, 597
Diminutives, 268, 285, 286, 337, 339
Diphthongization, 174, 180, 183, 197
Diphthongs, 75, 82, 174, 180, 186–190, 234
Diplomatic tongues, 109, 604
Direct object. See *Object, direct*
Direct v. indirect questions, 493, 501, 524
Disparagement. See *Depreciatory*
Distributive adverbs, 305
Distributive numerals, 327; 305
Division of words, 253
Dogmatic grammarians, 543
Double adverbs, 324
Double genitive, 491
Double negative, 534

SUBJECT INDEX

Double object, 478
Double pluralization, 442
Double relative pronoun, 289, 324
Double suffixes, 338, 339, 345, 346
Doubled words. See *Reduplicated words*
Doublets and triplets, 402, 442, 549, 562
Doubling, of consonants, 232, 237–239, 248, 249, 600
 of vowels, 232, 248, 601
Dryden, John, 582
Duplications in spelling, 259, 594, 599
Durative aspect of verbs, 303, 479, 523
Dutch language, 94, 95
Dutch loan-words, 379, 403
Dyslogistic words. See *Depreciatory words*

East Germans. See *Gothic language*
Ecclesiastical words, 59, 284, 369, 378, 396, 552
Echoic words. See *Onomatopœic*
Economy in language, 508, 554
Ellipsis, 26, 508, 528. See *Omission*
Elliptical clauses, 511
Elliptical genitive, 510
Elliptical phrases, 511; 324, 486, 531
Elliptical sentences, 470, 508
Elliptical words. See *Clipped words*
Embedded clauses, 290, 493
Emphasis, positions of, 500, 520
Emphatic verb forms, 524
Empire, British, 150
English abroad, 104, 109
Ephemeral locutions, 32
Epithets, 285, 286, 503
Esperanto, 606
Etymology, 11, 329, 576
Eulogistic words, 29, 32, 417, 565
Euphemism, 431, 548
Euphony, 19, 33
Evasive constructions, 323, 487, 490, 497, 509, 513, 586
Evasive forms, 355, 412, 490
Evasive words, 554
Exaggeration, effects of, 306, 559
Exclamation, 312, 486
Exclamatory phrases, 313, 486
Exclamatory sentences, 469
Exclamatory words. See *Interjections*
Exhortation, verbs in, 528
Exotic spellings, 258, 590
Expansion of English, 298, 344, 545, 549, 555
Expansion of modifiers, 489, 490, 494, 503

Explanatory conjunctions. See *Introducing words*
Expletives, 326; 266, 289, 296, 473, 474, 496, 502, 516, 579
Explosive consonants, 77, 200, 215
Extinction of words, 569

Factitive object. See *Objective complement*
Factitive verbs, 479
Fading of meanings, 559
False homophones, 411
Family names. See *Surnames*
Feminine suffixes, 339, 437, 438
Figurative change, 302, 547, 558
Figurative gender, 558
Figurative usage, 121, 547, 578, 580
Fillers, 510
Final letters. See *Word endings*
Final unaccented syllables, 79, 191, 194, 196, 219, 235, 236, 242, 248, 250, 594, 599
Folk etymology, 37, 57, 356, 361
Foreign noun plurals, 440
Foreign-English dialects, 55
Foreigners' English, 37, 100, 102, 118, 325
Form v. use, 5, 12, 466
Formal (or literary) English, 15, 430, 473, 487, 507, 527, 528, 535, 570, etc.
Franks, 93, 379
Free compounding elements, 346
French loan-words, 372; 98, 138, 144, 245, 247, 276, 370, 403–405, 441
French prefixes, 342
French spellings, 236, 247, 259, 374
French suffixes, 338, 340, 341
Frequency of words, 425; 274
Frequentative verbs, 341
Fricatives. See *Continuant consonants*
Functional change. See *Conversion*
Functions of words, 10, 263
Fusion, 317, 322, 360, 588
Future of English, 164, 610
Future tense, 453, 522

Gaelic languages, 95
Gaimar, Geffrai, 137
Gemination. See *Doubling*
Gender, 436; 116, 498, 558, 577
Genealogy of English, 95
General functions of words, 10, 263
Generalization in meaning, 552, 559
Genitival adverb. See *Adverbial genitive*
Genitival object, 491, 533

SUBJECT INDEX

Genitival subject, 514; 319, 517, 530, 531
Genitive, double, 491
Genitive case, 6, 322, 435, 446, 484, 491, 517, 531, 533
Geoffrey of Monmouth, 137
Gerald de Barri, 137
German loan-words, 102, 380
German-American locutions, 55, 100, 539
Germanic features of English, 120, 139, 227, 458, 459
Germanic languages, 93, 95
Germanic loan-words, 379
Gerund
 definition, 464
 classification, 269, 319, 489
 inflection, 465
 v. infinitive, 479, 530
 syntax, 530; 319, 473, 478, 479, 484, 489, 506, 514, 516, 517, 518, 530, 531, 533
Gerundial phrases, 506, 514, 530, 531
Ghost words, 333
Gibbon, Edward, 98
Glide sounds, 79, 88, 198
Good English, 23
Gothic language, 93, 95, 573
Gower, John, 123, 143, 370
Gradation, 199, 454
Grammar defined, 8, 118, 465, 576
Grammarians, 7, 147, 435, 543, 583, 589, 616
Grammarless language, 118, 465
Grammatical gender. See *Gender*
Grammatical method. See *Method*
Grammatical traps. See *Traps*
Greek compounding elements, 346
Greek language, 92, 95
Greek loan-words, 98, 239, 370, 378, 441
Greek prefixes, 343
Greek suffixes, 339, 341, 379
Greeting, exclamations of, 316
Grimm, Jacob, 105
Grotesque English, 34
Growth of English. See *Development*
Gullah negro dialect, 61, 63
Gutturals. See *Velar consonants*

Harvey, Gabriel, 582
Hawaiian loan-words, 385
Headline English, 42-44; 2, 612
Hebrew loan-words, 382, 441
Hellenic language group, 92, 95
Helmont, Jan Baptista van, 332
Hiatus, 88, 198
Higden, Ralph, 142

High German speech, 94
Highland Scottish loan-words, 375
Hindu. See *Indian*
Historical backgrounds, 19, 122
Historical present tense, 521
Hobson-Jobson, 57
Homographs, 408, 411
Homonyms, 407, 577
Homophones, 408, 571
Hortatory. See *Exhortation*
Hothouse words, 97, 333, 430
Hume, David, 390
Hybrid constructions, 512; 324, 491, 511, 586, 589
Hybrid parts of speech, 322, 588
Hybrid words and phrases, 99, 385
Hyperbole, 559, 566
Hyphenation, 251

Iambic measure, 227, 302
Icelandic, 94, 131, 135, 377
Ideas v. thoughts, 12, 263, 467, 470
Identifying adjectives, 294
Identifying pronoun, 290
Identifying terms. See *Introducing words*
Idiomatic phrases, 13, 37, 107, 309, 482, 488, 510, 512, 515, 560, 578
Idiomatic verbs, 482, 521, 523, 525-527, 578
Idiom Neutral, 607, 610
Idiom of English, 577, 579, 609
Idioms. See *Idiomatic phrases*
Ido, 608
Illative conjunctions, 311; 307, 472, 487, 505, 535, 541
Imitation, 4, 46
Immigration, effects of, 55, 103
Imperative interjections, 313
Imperative mood, 464
Imperative sentences, 469
Impersonal pronouns, 289, 473, 477, 516, 517
Impersonal verbs, 296
Implied pronoun, 516
Imprecations, 313
Improvement of English, 100, 146, 330, 581, 614
Inchoative. See *Ingressive*
Incomplete verbs, 476
Indefinite adjectives, 293
Indefinite article, 198, 293, 504
Indefinite pronouns, 288, 291, 448, 473, 497, 498
Indefinite subject, 473; 291, 498, 516
Independent clauses. See *Principal clauses*

SUBJECT INDEX

Independent elements, 485
India, English in, 57, 151
Indian, American. See *American Indian*
Indian language group, 92, 95
Indian loan-words, 383, 385
Indicative mood, 464
Indifferentiation, vocalic, 197
Indirect discourse, 493, 529
Indirect object. See *Object, indirect*
Indirect questions, 290, 493, 501, 540
Individual vocabularies, 47, 420
Indo-European languages, 91, 95
Indo-Germanic. See *Indo-European*
Infinitive
  definition, 464, 489
  split, 506
  subject of, 479, 481, 516, 529
  syntax, 529; 295, 320, 473, 476, 478, 479, 484, 485, 489, 506, 514, 521, 522-528, 533
Infinitive phrases, 473, 476, 485, 489
Inflection, 11, 116, 264, 434, 558, 613
  loss of, 5, 116, 434, 558, 613
Influence, of consonant combinations, 193
  of *l*, 193
  of light syllables, 194
  of *r*, 192
Ingressive verbs, 303, 341
Intensive adjective, 294
Intensive adverbs, 306, 321
Intensive pronouns, 289, 320, 448 474, 477
Intentional mispronunciations, 35
Interjections, 266, 312, 326, 334, 486
Interlingua, 608, 610
International English, 113, 604, 615
International languages, 603
International Phonetic Alphabet, 81, 260, 590
International Phonetic Association, 81
Interrelation of sounds, 37
Interrogation, verbs in, 524
Interrogative adjectives, 293
Interrogative adverbs, 534; 493
Interrogative pronouns, 288, 290, 320, 324, 448, 493
Interrogative sentences, 469, 501, 524
Intoxication, words for, 31, 417, 547
Intransitive verbs, 480; 299
Introducing words, phrases, etc., 307, 482
Introductory adverbs. See *Illative conjunctions*
Inversion, 502, 520

Irish English, 52, 154, 174, 176, 178, 345, 439, 462
Irish language, 95, 125, 375
Irish loan-words, 375
Irrational constructions, 512, 579, 580
Irregular verbs, 454, 459
Isolated survivals, 40, 515, 571
Italian loan-words, 338, 380, 404, 441
Italic language group, 92, 95
Iterative aspect of verbs, 304, 526

Japanese loan-words, 385
Jargons, 62, 112, 118, 149
Johnson, Samuel, 147, 154, 390, 582
Journalistic writing, 2
Joyce, James, 333
Jutes, 93, 127

Labial consonants, 78, 200, 210, 214
Labialization, 79, 193, 217
Labiodental consonants, 78, 203
Laconicism of English, 117
Langland, William, 123
Language, and thinking, 2, 5, 13, 226, 292, 423, 424, 432, 544, 556, 584, 617
  defined, 7, 569, 617
  purposes of, 2, 423
Languages, related, 90
Latin compounding elements, 347
Latin language, 92, 95, 604
Latin loan-words, 98, 126, 171, 233, 275, 309, 345, 368, 430, 440, 450
Latin plural endings, 440
Latin prefixes, 342
Latin suffixes, 339, 341, 371
Latin v. English, 123, 136, 148, 370
Latino sine Flexione, 608
Layamon's *Brut*, 138
Learned words popularized, 148, 566
Lengthening consonant combinations, 193; 175, 177, 180, 182, 188, 232
Lengthening of vowels, 195
Leveling of accent, 222
Levels of speech, 15, 101
Lexicographers, 147, 365, 390, 568, 582, 616
Lexicography, 17, 34, 39, 81, 147, 365, 370, 393-394, 425, 538, 546, 551, 569, 575, 616
Limiting adjectives, 293, 519
Lingo, 16, 62
Lingua franca, 63
Linguist defined, 8
Linguistic change, causes of, 14
Linguistic standards, 17
Linking verbs, 476; 324, 479, 480, 559

SUBJECT INDEX

Liquid consonants, 78, 209, 215, 216
Literary dialect, 55, 61
Literary English. See *Formal English*
Little languages, 59
Loan-words, 22, 96, 102, 149, 330, 366, 395
Locative clauses, 494
Locution, defined, 7
Long vowels. See *Vowel length*
Longest sentences, 471
Loss, of inflection, 5, 116, 434, 558, 613
 of initial syllable, 405
 of words and meanings, 38, 569
Low German dialects, 94, 95
Lowell, James R., 53, 62
Lowering of vowels, 196

Makeshifts in spelling, 259
Malapropisms, 36
Malayan loan-words, 385
Manner, adverbs of, 305, 321
 clause of, 310, 321
Mapes, Walter, 137
Marie de France, 137
Meaning, changes in, 467, 544
Measure words, 440, 549
Mercians, 129
Metaphorical change, 547
Metathesis, 220, 406
Method, grammatical, 585; 263, 324, 327, 330, 435, 469, 545
Metonymy, 548
Middle English period, 123
Milton, John, 421
Minsheu, John, 366
Misleading spellings, 261
Mispronunciations, 35, 361
Modal adverbs, 307, 535
Mode. See *Mood*
Modern English period, 123
Modifiers, adjectival, 483; 292, 320, 322, 493, 499, 502, 516, 519, 530, 533, 540
 adverbial, 484; 323, 490, 494, 504, 516, 520, 530, 534, 540
Monosyllabism of English, 117, 300, 428
Months, names of, 281
Mood of verbs, 463, 521, 529
Morphology. See *Inflection*
Müller, Max, 420
Mulcaster, Richard, 147
Multiplication of meanings, 119, 359, 546, 549
Multiplicative numerals, 327; 294, 305
Murray, Lindley, 147, 155, 158, 304, 582
Mutation, 199, 439, 450, 459

Names, 256, 270, 294, 320, 353, 357, 382, 407, 437, 572, 573
Nasal consonants, 78, 210
Nasalization, 193
Nash, Thomas, 331, 581
National Council of Teachers of English, 583
Native elements in English, 97, 101, 120, 275, 300, 337, 340, 342, 344, 347, 399, 403, 405, 426, 458
Necessity, verbs expressing, 526
Negation, 306, 524, 534
Negative verb-forms, 524, 534
Negro dialect, 60, 187
Neologisms, 38
New England dialect, 53, 58, 79, 89, 164, 165, 190, 197, 220
New English Dictionary, 148, 391
Newspaper English, 41, 333, 429, 631
Nicknames, 285, 337
Nomenclature of grammar. See *Terminology*
Nominative absolute, 486, 516, 531, 533
Nominative case, 446, 472, 486, 516
Nonrestrictive clauses, 493
Nonsense words, 333
Norman loan-words, 137, 372, 395
Normans, 94, 124, 135
Norse. See *Scandinavian*
North Germans. See *Scandinavians*
Northern English, 151
Northumbrians, 129
Norwegians, 94, 131
Notional verbs, 296, 321, 463, 477
Noun clauses, 493; 310, 474, 478, 493
Nouns
 accentuation, 223
 definition, 266, 267
 classification, 267, 327
 derivation, 269, 271–283, 337, 348
 as conjunctions, 311
 adverbial, 323, 484, 516
 inflection, 436; 203, 205, 218, 240, 243, 245, 592
 syntax, 515; 484, 486
Novial, 608
Number, 438, 452, 495
Numerals, 266, 269, 288, 291, 294, 305, 326, 340, 504

Oaths and imprecations, 313
Object, direct, 477, 481, 502, 515, 517, 529, 530, 588
 indirect, 478, 481, 491, 502, 517
 of gerund, 491, 533

SUBJECT INDEX 733

of preposition, 481, 489, 516, 518, 535
    retained, 478, 579
Object clauses, 493
Objective, predicate, 479
Objective case, 445, 446, 517
Objective complement. See *Predicate objective*
Objective constructions, 477, 517
Objective genitive, 491, 533
Obligation, verbs expressing, 525
Obscure vowels, 190, 235
Obsolescence, 38; 15, 569
Occidental, 608
Old English. See *Anglo-Saxon*
Omission
    of consonants, 219
    of letters, 243, 245, 254, etc.
    of subject, 509, 516
    of verb, 510
    of modified noun, 510
    of connectives, 511
    of prepositions, 511, 531
    of participles, 486, 531
Onomatopœic words, 48, 64, 334
Onomatopoetic. See *Onomatopœic*
Open *o*, 178
Open syllables, 87, 231
Order of words. See *Word order*
Ordinal numerals, 291, 294, 305, 327, 340
Organs of speech, 70
Original creation, 332
Orismological sesquipedalianism, 567
Orm's *Ormulum*, 138
Orthography. See *Spelling*
Overlapping etymologies, 363, 409
Overworked words and phrases, 429

Pairs of words. See *Word pairs*
Palatal consonants, 78, 202, 212, 213
Palatalization, 217
Parenthetical expressions, 307, 487
Participial adjectives. See *Adjectival participles*
Participial phrases, 484, 485, 489
Participial prepositions, 308
Participles
    definition, 464
    classification, 292, 319
    inflection, 464
    syntax, 531, 533; 295, 319, 322, 484, 485, 486, 503, 514, 521, 523
Partitive genitive, 491, 497
Parts of speech, 10, 263, 265, 316, 327, 515, 542
Passive nouns, 268
Passive voice, 463; 296, 481, 523, 533

Past tense, 453; 201, 239, 242, 500, 521, 525, 526, 527, 529, 592
Patois, 62
Patronymics, 273
Pattern of English, 19, 25, 258, 474, 512, 514, 542, 613
Peano, Giuseppe, 608
Pejorative change in meaning, 562
Pennsylvania "Dutch" dialect, 55, 524
Perfect infinitive, 526, 533
Perfect participle, 533
Perfect tenses, 523, 524
Periods of English, 123
Periphrastic. See *Phrasal*
Permission, verbs of, 524
Persian language group, 92, 95
Persian loan-words, 99, 383
Person, defined, 447
    of verbs, 452, 497, 498
Personal names, 271; 256, 285, 353, 358, 373, 377, 378, 407, 437, 572
Personal pronouns, 288, 289, 447
Personification, 558
Philology, defined, 8, 576
Philosophy of language, 1
Phonetic alphabet, 80–85, and inside back cover
Phonetic spelling, 89, 260, 584, 589, 596
Phonetics, 10, 70
Phonology, defined, 10
Phrasal adjectives, 490, 519
Phrasal adverbs, 490
Phrasal comparison, 450, 492
Phrasal conjunctions, 490
Phrasal dative, 6, 478, 491, 502
Phrasal genitive, 6, 435, 491, 533
Phrasal idioms. See *Idiomatic phrases*
Phrasal indefinites, 291
Phrasal interjections, 313, 491
Phrasal parts of speech, 490
Phrasal prepositions, 308, 490
Phrasal verbals, 533
Phrasal verbs, 522; 118, 490, 492, 530, 531, 533, 579
Phrases, 488; 12, 13, 444, 482, 484, 486, 487, 505, 572, 577, 580
Phrases, idiomatic. See *Idiomatic phrases*
    stereotyped. See *Conventional phrases*
Physiology v. psychology of language, 3, 88, 196
Pickering, John, 279 (footnote)
Pidgin English, 66, 118, 613
Piozzi, Hester Lynch, 418

SUBJECT INDEX

Pitch, 229; 158
Place, adverbs of, 305
  clauses of, 310, 494
Place-names, 274; 125, 126, 135, 226, 255, 256, 286, 320, 350, 353, 355, 358, 375, 376, 381, 384
Pleonasm, 486; 66, 516. See also *Redundancy*
Pluralization, of compounds, 444
  of nouns, 438; 203, 205, 218, 240, 243, 245, 592
Policies. See *Attitudes*
Popular etymology. See *Folk etymology*
Popularization of learned words, 148, 566
Portmanteau words. See *Blends*
Portuguese loan-words, 381
Possession, genitive of, 491
Possessive case. See *Genitive case*
Possessives, 293, 322, 477, 504
Possibility, verbs expressing, 524
Postponed prepositions, 507, 538, 579
Postpositive modifiers, 503, 504, 519, 531, 533
Potential mood, 529
Power, verbs expressing, 525
Predicate adjective, 476, 477, 490, 520, 531
Predicate modifiers, 476, 520
Predicate nominative, 476, 516, 588
Predicate objective, 479, 588
Predicate of sentence, 475
Prefixes, 342; 253, 386
Prepositional adverbs, 119, 292, 297, 298, 305, 308, 321, 504, 508
Prepositional phrases, 119, 484, 485, 489
Prepositions
  definition, 266, 308, 321
  classification, 308
  derivation, 308
  postponed, 507, 538, 579
  syntax, 535; 505, 507, 542
Primary accent, 85, 222
Principal clauses, 472, 492
Principal parts of verb, 453
Progressive verbs, 303, 523, 531
Pronominal adjectives, 293, 320
Pronouns
  definition, 266, 288, 293, 322
  classification, 288, 320, 324
  declension, 447
  syntax, 516; 473, 474, 476, 477, 480, 498, 540
Pronunciation
  in general, 10, 166, 611

  of foreigners, 104
  American v. British, 156
Prop words, 319, 448
Proper adjectives, 294
Proper names. See *Names*
Proper names to common nouns. See *Commonization*
Proper nouns. See *Names*
Properties, grammatical, 435, 436, 451
Prosody, 8
Pseudocompound sentences, 472
Pseudoplurals, 443
Pseudosuffixes, 282
Psychology of language, 3, 68
Punctuation, 472, 482, 486, 494
Puns, 298, 411
Pure English, 22, 68, 100, 584
Purists, 22, 100, 331, 583
Puritan names, 272
Purpose, clause of, 310, 494
  infinitive of, 485, 494
Purposes of language, 2

Quaker speech, 59
Quality of vowels, 72, 166, 192, 196
Quantity of vowels. See *Vowel length*
Questions, 493, 501, 524

Radiation, 549
Radio, influence of, 165, 566, 611
Raising of vowels, 196; 175
Reciprocal pronouns, 291, 517
Reduction of consonantal vowels, 219
Redundancy, 416, 535, 539. See also *Pleonasm*
Redundant verb forms, 458, 462
Reduplicated words, 67, 334
Reference of pronouns, 499
Reflexive pronouns, 289, 291, 321, 448, 474, 477, 517
Reform, of English spelling. See *Spelling reform*
  of grammatical terminology, 585
Regeneration of words, 564
Regular verbs, 454
Relations of English, 90
Relative, omitted. See *Omission of connectives*
Relative adverbs, 310, 311, 323, 534
Relative clauses, 290, 320, 484, 493
Relative frequency of words, 425; 274
Relative pronouns, 288, 289, 310, 320, 323, 448, 473, 493, 499, 518, 540
Renaissance in England, 145, 369
Restrictive clauses, 493
Result, clauses of, 310, 494
Retained indirect object, 479

SUBJECT INDEX

Retained object, 478, 579
Revival of silent letters, 195, 219, 243, 247, 261
Rhetorical art, 9, 311, 418. See also *Stylistic matters*
Rhythm, 226; 158
Rhythmical word pairs, 228, 415
Romanic loan-words, 380; 98–99, 367, 372, 395
Romans in Britain, 125
Root infinitive, 464, 489, 521, 529
Russian. See *Slavic*

Sanskrit language, 92, 95
Sanskrit loan-words, 383
Saxons, 93, 127
Scandinavian language group, 93, 95, 131
Scandinavian loan-words, 99, 134, 376, 403
Scandinavian place-names, 135, 275, 376
Scandinavians in England, 131
Schleyer, J. M., 606
Scientific and scholarly growth, 147
Scottish dialect, 53, 141, 151, 170, 290
Scottish Gaelic. See *Highland Scottish*
Secondary accent, 85, 222
Semantics. See *Semasiology*
Semasiological change, 359, 544
Semasiology, 12, 265, 544
Semicolon, 472
Semivowels, 78, 212
Sentence equivalents, 12–13, 307, 470
Sentences
  definition, 12, 469
  of children, 48
  accentuation, 86, 500
  classification, 469, 472
  syntax, 468
  pseudocompound, 472
Sequence of tenses, 499, 529
Shakespeare, William, 20, 98, 154, 333, 421, 452, 571
Sheridan, Richard Brinsley, 36
Short circuits, syntactical, 506, 512
Shortcuts, orthographic, 254
  semasiological, 554
  syntactical, 288, 451, 484, 485, 487, 509, 513, 542
Shortening, of vowels, 195; 169, 170, 172, 177, 194, 224, 460
  of words, 254, 354; 51, 52, 54
Silent consonants, 201, 219, 233, 246, 593, 598, 601
Silent *e*, 241; 232, 250, 591, 597, 600

Simple conditions, 527
Simple sentences, 472
Simple verbs, 521
Simplification, of diphthongs, 197
  of double consonants, 239, 251
  of grammar, 119, 434, 465, 613
  of vowel digraphs, 236, 597
Simplified spelling. See *Spelling reform*
Simplified Spelling Board, 595, 596
Simplified Spelling Society, 595
Singularless nouns, 270, 443, 495
Singulars, misunderstood, 278, 356, 362, 443
Size, of English vocabulary, 389, 545
  of individual's vocabulary, 47, 420
Slang, 28; 16, 161, 355, 417, 547, 555, 556, 557, 563, 570, etc.
Slavic languages, 92, 95
Slavic loan-words, 99, 383
Slavonic. See *Slavic*
Smoke-screen writing, 567
Social dialects, 51, 57
Society for Pure English, 583, 584
Somerset dialect, 51, 204
Sounds of speech, 70, 166
South African dialect, 153
Southern dialect of United States, 60, 79, 89, 164, 165, 168, 190, 197, 220, 289
Southern English of England, 151, 410
Southern mountaineer dialect, 54
Spanish-American dialect, 56
Spanish loan-words, 277, 338, 381
Specialization in meaning, 549, 554
Speech defined, 9
Speech units, 12
Spelling, 10, 115, 121, 159, 230, 257
Spelling reform, 589; 138, 240, 412, 461, 584, 612
Spenser, Edmund, 333
Spirants. See *Continuant consonants*
Split infinitive, 506
Spoonerisms, 4, 36
Spread of English, 107, 615
Stabilizing influences, 20, 25, 100, 146, 164, 390, 543, 581, 616
Standard English, 22, 584, 602, 616
Standards of speech, 17, 23, 328
Stereotyped phrases. See *Conventional phrases*
Stop consonants. See *Explosive consonants*
Stress. See *Accentuation*
Stretch forms, 35
Strong adjectives, 116
Strong verbs, 454–459; 199

SUBJECT INDEX

Study of English, 109, 585. *See also Attitudes and Policies*
Stylistic matters, 20, 257, 413, 418, 429, 432, 473, 474, 483, 486, 494, 500, 502, 505, 506, 538, 541, 545, 554
Subject, of gerund, 319, 514, 516, 517, 530, 531
  of infinitive, 479, 481, 482, 516, 518, 529
  of sentence, 472, 501, 509
Subjunctive mood, 464, 521, 522, 525, 526, 527, 529
Subordinate clauses, 492; 288, 310, 320, 472, 473, 493, 499, 518, 540
Subordinating conjunctions, 310, 472, 487, 493, 540, 541
Substantival infinitives, 464, 473, 476, 489, 529
Substantivation, 318; 267, 278, 557
Substantive clauses. *See Noun clauses*
Substantives, 267, 473
Substitutes, for inflectional forms, 491; 5, 119, 434, 466, 613
  for nominative absolute, 487
  for nouns. *See Pronouns*
  for pronouns, 535; 310, 540
Substitution, of consonants, 221
  of meanings, 560
Suffixes, 335; 273, 275, 276, 374, 376, 379, 387, 437, 450, 562. *See also Word increase*
Suffixion. *See Word increase*
Superfluous prepositions, 539
Superlative absolute, 520
Superlative degree, 449; 327
Supine, 465 (footnote)
Suppletive adjectives, 450
Suppletive verbs, 462
Surnames, 272, 337, 572
Survivals, isolated, 571; 40, 515
Swedish-American dialect, 56
Swedish language, 94, 131
Swedish loan-words, 377
Swift, Jonathan, 333, 582
Syllabic consonants. *See Vocalic consonants*
Syllabication. *See Hyphenation*
Synecdoche, 548
Synonymous word pairs, 415–418; 301, 570
Synonyms, 31, 105, 120, 301, 413, 570
Syntax, 11, 467
Synthetic v. analytic languages, 118, 119, 434

Taboo words, 431, 562, 564
Tautological compounds, 387
Teaching of English, 109, 585
Temporal clauses. *See Time clauses*
Tennyson, Alfred, 51, 98
Tense, 453, 521, 522, 523
Tenses, sequence of, 499, 529
Terminology, 6, 476, 479, 575, 585, 587
Teutonic languages. *See Germanic languages*
Thought. *See Language*
Time, adverbs of, 305
Time clauses, 310, 494
Titles of respect, 283; 255, 557
Trade and conquests, 148
Trade names, 282, 340, 352, 359
Transition sounds. *See Glide sounds*
Transitive verbs, 477; 300, 406, 480, 481
Traps, grammatical, 496, 497, 499, 513, 542
Trevisa, John, 142
Triplets and doublets, 402
Tristram Shandy, 314
Trochaic measure, 227, 302
Twofold function of words, 10, 265

Umlaut. *See Mutation*
Unaccented vowels, 76, 80, 82, 190, 219, 235, 248, 594, 599
Uninflected noun plurals, 439, 495
Uninflected verb tenses, 462
Units of speech, 12
Unstressed. *See Unaccented*
Unvoicing of consonants, 218
Usage. *See Concise Index, p. 657*

Vandals, 93
Variable inflectional forms
  noun plurals, 439–444
  pronominal forms, 447
  adjective comparison, 449–451
  verb principal parts, 454–462
Variable pronunciations. *See Chapter VI, passim*
Variable spellings. *See Chapter VII, notes 8, 13, 16, 17, 18, 21, 25, 27, 31, 36–38*
Velar consonants, 78, 202, 212
Verb phrases. *See Phrasal verbs*
Verb-adverb combinations, 297; 6, 119, 416, 482, 490, 508, 536, 570, 575, 578, 579, 612
Verbal adjectives. *See Adjectival participles*
Verbal noun, 269, 319, 338, 489, 557, 574. *See also Gerund*

SUBJECT INDEX

Verbals, 464; 269, 292, 295, 319, 473, 484, 489, 514, 521, 529
Verbids. See *Verbals*
Verbs
  accentuation, 223
  definition, 266, 295
  classification, 295
  derivation, 341, 349, 406
  inflection, 451; 47, 201, 239, 242, 592
  complete or linking, 475; 324, 480
  syntax, 520; 118
Vocabularies, of individuals, 420; 47
  special, 58
Vocabulary, of Modern English, 389
  size and nature of, 389, 545
Vocabulary growth, 5, 144, 330, 389, 395, 423, 569
Vocalic consonants, 79, 83, 191, 196, 209, 219, 235, 236, 242, 250
Vocalization, 190, 191, 196
Vocative, 486, 516
Voice of verbs, 463, 523
Voiced consonants, 77, 200, etc.
Voiceless consonants, 77, 200, etc.
Voicing of consonants, 86, 218
Volapük, 606
Vowel change, 192; 51, 52, 53, 54, 57, 405
Vowel length, 72, 87, 166, 191, 194, 195
  methods of indicating, 84, 231–233, 592, 600–602
Vowel shortening, 195; 169, 170, 172, 177, 224, 460
Vowels, 72, 82, 167, 231, 405
  spelling of, 82, 231–236, 257, 589, etc.

Wace, 137
Wahl, Edgar de, 608
Weak adjectives, 116
Weak verbs, 242, 454, 459–462
Weakening, of meanings, 559
  of vowels, 76, 86, 224
Webster, Noah, 147, 155, 158, 304, 391, 568, 582
Welsh language, 95, 375
Welsh loan-words, 375
West Germanic languages, 93, 95

West Saxons, 129, 132
Western American dialect, 89, 164, 168, 170, 191
Wishes, verbs expressing, 528
Word composition, 335, 346, 348
Word division, 253
Word endings, 248, 597
Word increase, effects of
  vowel shortening, 169, 170, 172, 177, 194, 224, 460
  consonant change, 209, 214, 218, 219, 221
  accent shift, 224, 225
  spelling change, 235, 236, 238, 239, 240, 244, 251
  spelling variation, 243, 244, 245, 251
  revival of silent *e*, 195, 243
Word order, 500; 106, 119, 300, 326, 519, 541
Word pairs
  accentual, 223; 86
  consonantal, 203, 204, 206, 218
  rhythmical, with *and*, 228, 415
  adjective-participle, 243, 458, 465
  reduplicated words, 67, 334
  overlapping etymologies, 363, 409
  French and Anglo-Saxon, 372, 418
  doublets, 402, 442
  derivational, 297, 338, 416
  homonyms, 408
  synonymous, 301, 415, 416, 417, 570
  gender words, 438
  inflectional, 442, 449, 454–462
Word stress. See *Accentuation*
Word values, recognition of, 542
Words defined and distinguished, 6, 12, 316, 333, 334, 359, 363, 393, 403, 408, 422, 425, 542, 546, 551
Word-shortening. See *Shortening of words*
World English, 113, 604, 615
Wyclif, John, 123, 141, 143

Yankee dialect, 53
Yiddish loan-words, 57
Yiddish-American dialect, 56
Yorkshire dialect, 51

Zamenhof, Louis L., 606

ST. MARY'S COLLEGE OF MARYLAND LIBRARY
ST. MARY'S CITY, MARYLAND

32715